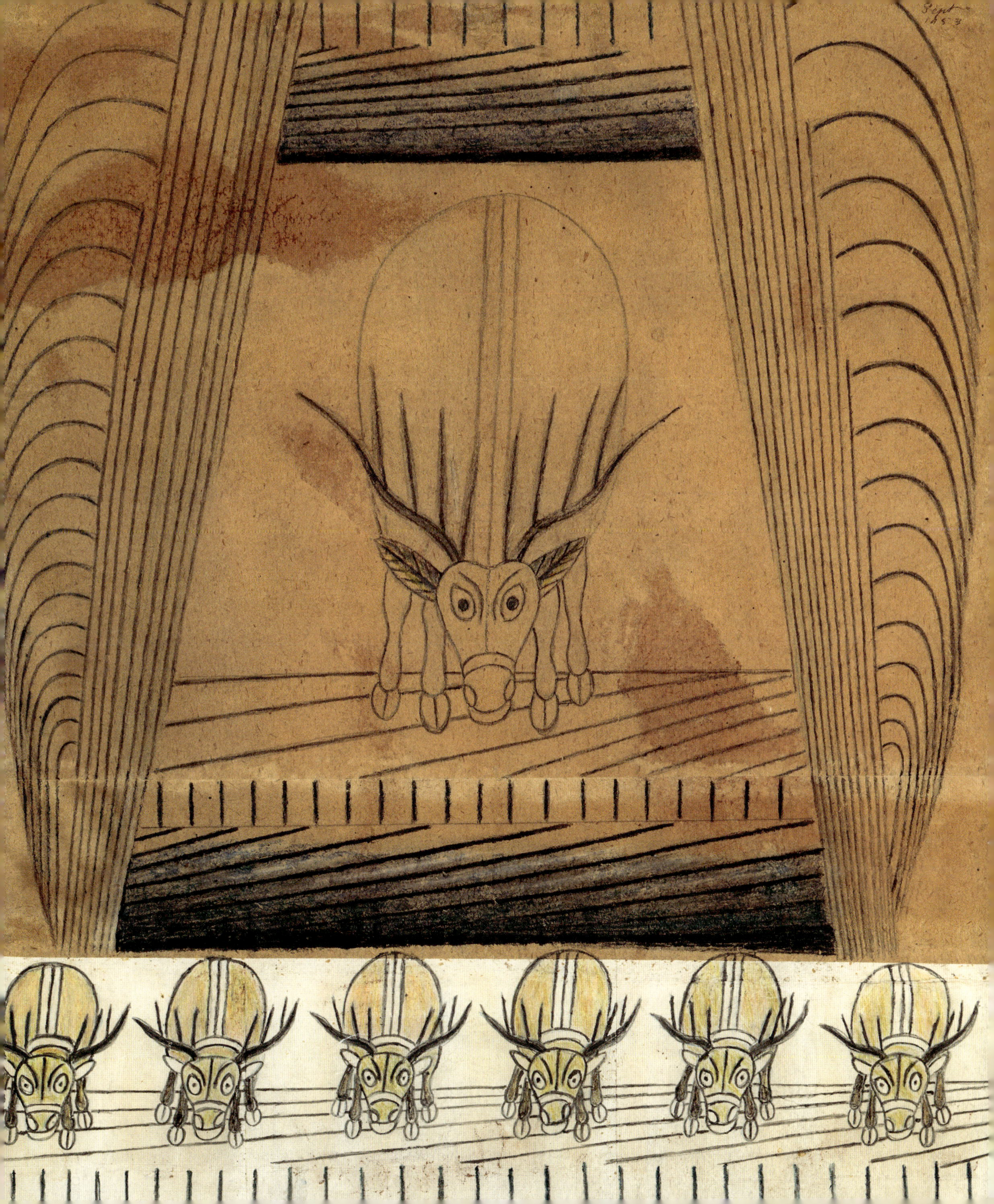
Sept

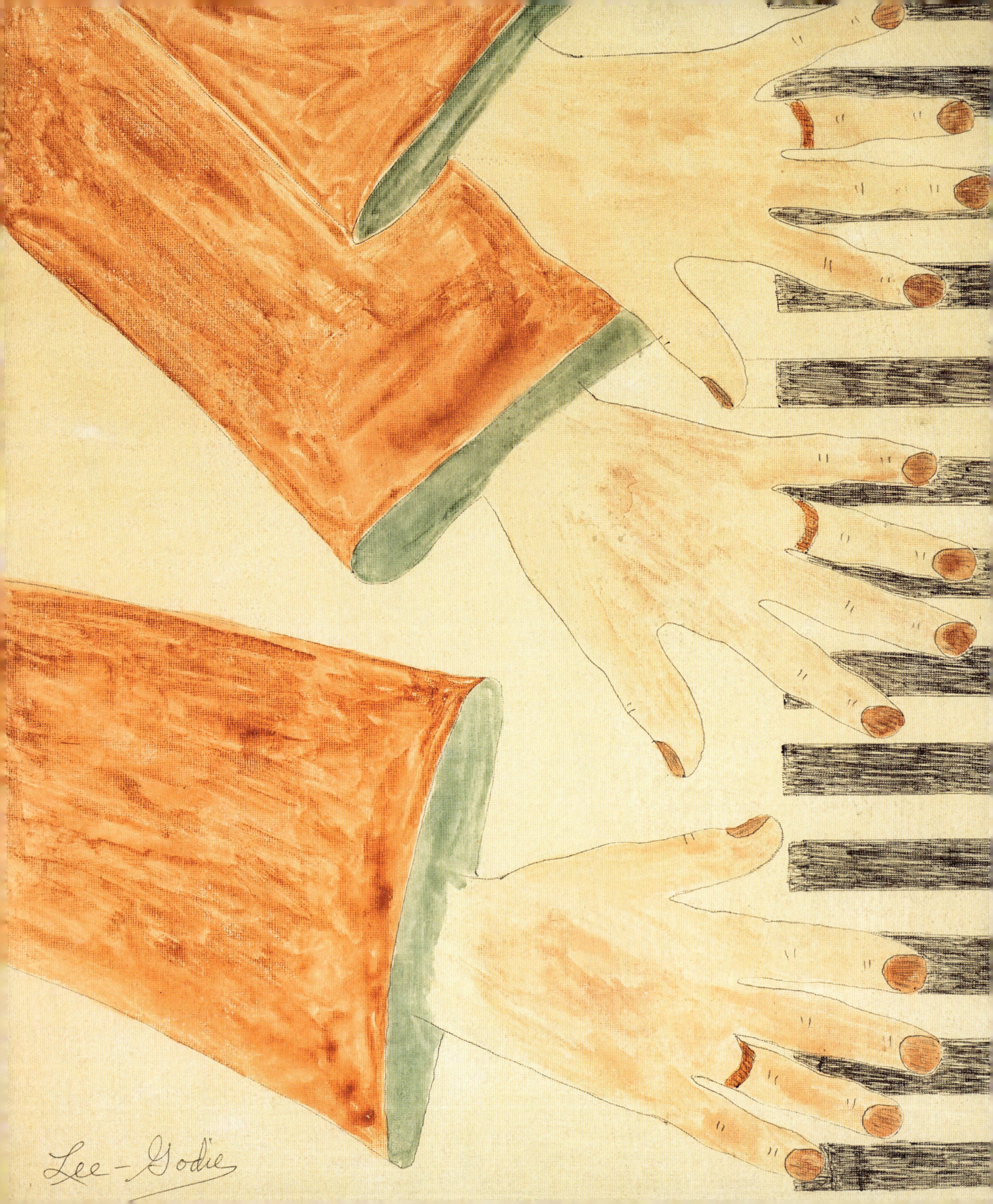
Lee-Godie

3/6/20

Dear Rachelle and Julian –
it took a FedEx package to bring us together after
failing to meet in Cambridge or Phila over 50+ years.
We hope you will be able to visit the gallery and the dance studio when we all return.
Best,
Victor

OUTSIDER & VERNACULAR ART

The Victor F. Keen Collection

Essays by

Frank Maresca | Edward M. Gómez | Lyle Rexer

Contributions by Alejandra Russi

Edited by Laura Lindgren

HIRMER

THE BETHANY MISSION GALLERY

PHILADELPHIA

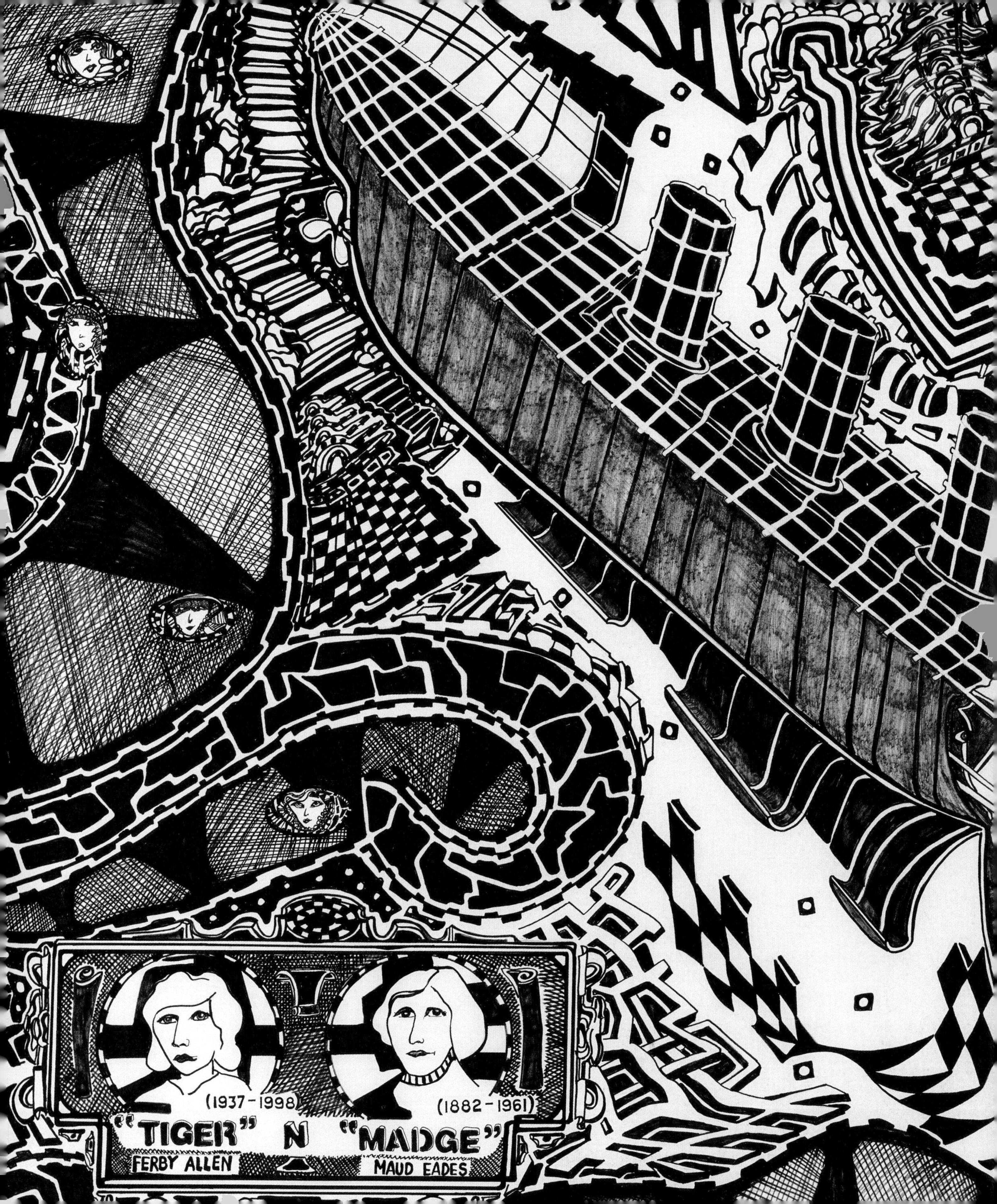
(1937-1998)
(1882-1961)
"TIGER" N "MADGE"
FERBY ALLEN
MAUD EADES

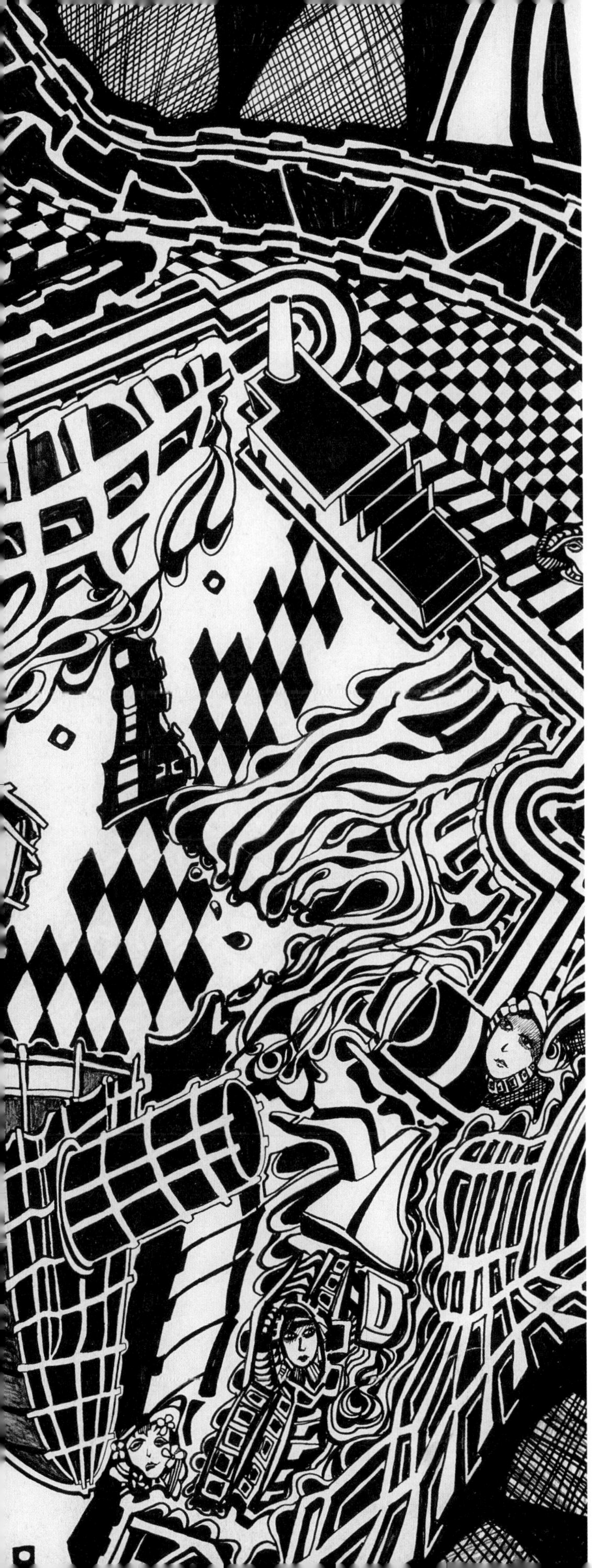

CONTENTS

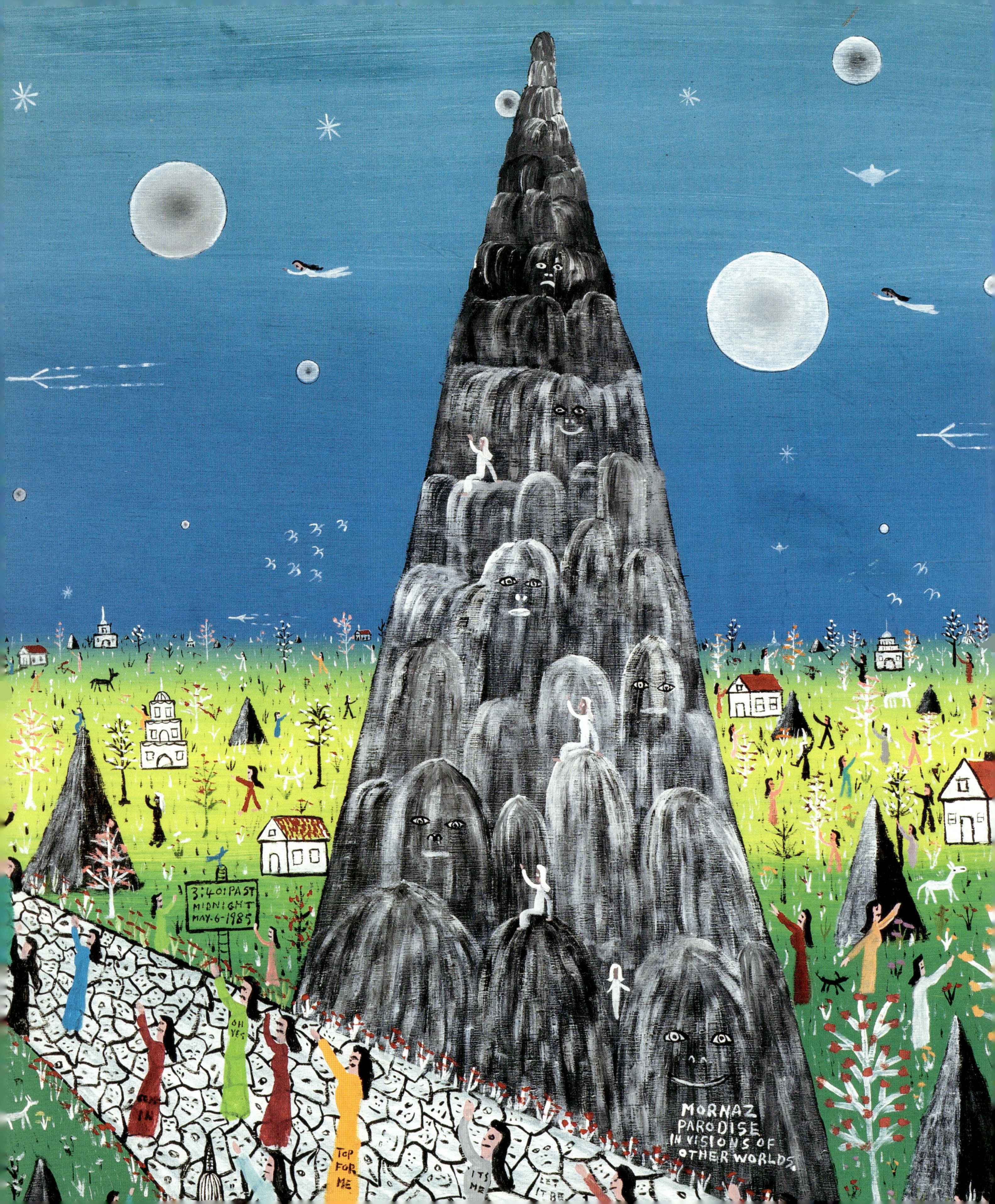
3:40 PAST
MIDNIGHT
MAY-6-1985
OH YES
TOP FOR ME
ITS ME
LET IT BE
MORNAZ
PARODISE
IN VISIONS OF
OTHER WORLDS.

PREFACE

Before Victor Keen and I met in January 2017, when he visited the Sangre de Cristo Arts and Conference Center in Pueblo, Colorado, we had had several conversations about his extensive and outstanding collection of outsider art.

Victor left his native Pueblo long before the Arts Center became a force in his hometown. Opened in 1972, the Center expanded in 1982, again in 2000, and now its 90,000+ square feet includes seven art galleries, numerous makers spaces, collection-care areas, a five-hundred-seat theater, a conference center, schools of dance and ballet, a children's museum, an outdoor sculpture garden, and a concert area on a five-acre site. The facility is owned by Pueblo County with additional operating support from the city of Pueblo. In 2018 the Center is on track to have hosted more than 130,000 visitors.

In Pueblo it is important for people to know where you attended high school. In our conversations I learned that Victor graduated from Central in 1959 and was awarded a full scholarship to attend Trinity College in Hartford, Connecticut. He was captain of Central's league championship basketball and track teams. His family has a long tradition with Central, as his father and his father's siblings all graduated from there. Upon graduation from Trinity, Victor attended Harvard Law School, and following graduation from Harvard and a two-year clerkship at the U.S. Tax Court in Washington, D.C., he embarked on a highly successful forty-year career as a tax and business lawyer at a major law firm in New York City and later a firm in Philadelphia.

When I was fortunate to visit Victor's Bethany Mission Gallery in Philadelphia with my spouse, Judy Lee, we experienced the magnitude of his collection firsthand. Our four-day stay in the gallery deepened our appreciation of outsider art. An entire roomful of work by James Castle and works by numerous other beacons in the pantheon of outsider artists—Bill Traylor, Howard Finster, Joseph Yoakum, and scores of others—are displayed throughout the gallery's two floors. While pursuing my MFA at the University of Chicago in the late 1970s I had occasions to meet Yoakum and another outstanding Chicago outsider artist, Lee Godie. There is a special kind of magic at the Bethany Mission Gallery, and we hope to bring a touch of this to the Sangre de Cristo Arts Center with this exhibition. The Pueblo presentation of the Victor Keen collection includes no fewer than thirty-eight artists represented by 127 of their creations.

When I first learned of the Keen collection and explored it online, I instantly felt a connection with the Arts Center's sizable collection of santos from the southwestern United States. Santeros, like outsider artists, use materials at hand (such as native pine and cottonwood) and create pigments from natural materials for their art. It seems fitting to bring such a collection to Pueblo, in keeping with the mission of the Arts Center that it "creates artistic learning experiences for everyone." This exhibition without doubt has something for everyone and is an outstanding opportunity to share with our visitors a collection that pushes the boundaries of art. We are very grateful to Victor and to his spouse, Jeanne Ruddy, for making possible every aspect of this exhibition. Pueblo is blessed to have such a philanthropic native son.

Jim Richerson, CEO
Sangre de Cristo Arts Center
Pueblo, Colorado

Howard Finster, *Visionary Landscape #4,494* (detail), 1985 (p. 105)

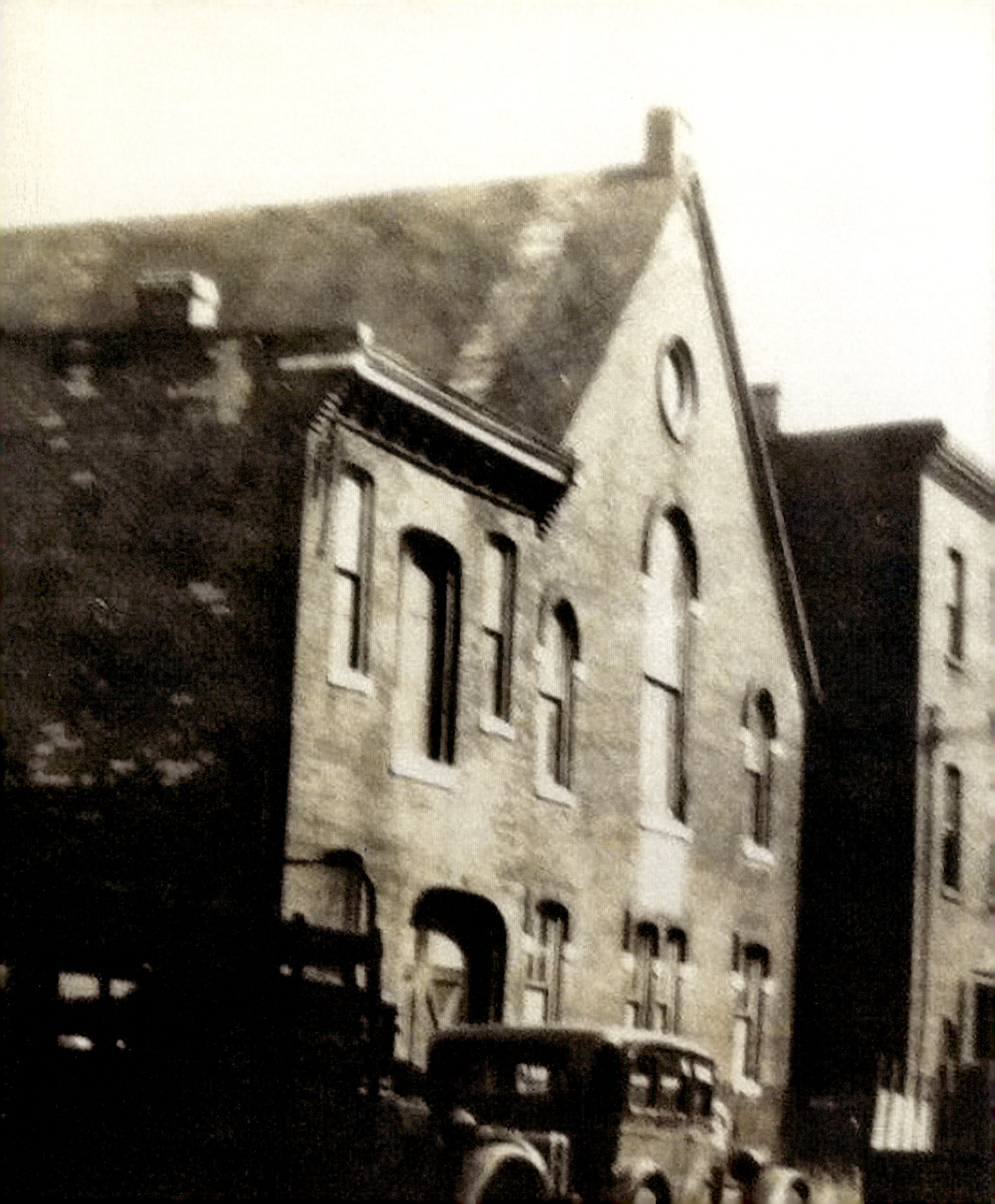

FOREWORD VICTOR F. KEEN

Visitors to my Bethany Mission Gallery in Philadelphia often ask what it was that attracted me to the world of outsider art, the primary focus of my collection. It's not an easy question to answer. Like other collectors, I have found the question challenging and have concluded that to a large extent the allure is visceral and not easily articulated, though I occasionally have pondered the "why" of my collection.

It's a question as complex as the much-debated question of how best to refer to the art itself. "Outsider," "self-taught," "naïve," "visionary," "untrained" are terms variously used and no one term seems entirely satisfactory to describe this category of art. In fact, I side with Roberta Smith, senior art critic of the *New York Times*, on the topic. After considering the limitations of "outsider," "self-taught," and a new entry, "outlier," she wrote, "At this point I think of the words of the little boy refusing to eat his vegetables in the famous *New Yorker* cartoon: 'I say it's spinach, and I say the hell with it.' Let's just call all of it art and proceed." (*NYT* May 24, 2018)

Still, for convenience, I refer to "outsider" art and "outsider" artists, as a shorthand with the understanding that others may favor other descriptives. Outsider art is not a "school" of art; what sets it apart is the circumstances and characteristics of the artist. The biographical narrative of every outsider artist is unique, but most share one or more of the following: no or only limited art training; living with mental or physical infirmities; poverty; educational deficit; being held back by racial discrimination. Most did not create their art for others, and many made no effort to share the work with anyone; some even affirmatively withheld it from the view of others.

Outsider artists who may have sought recognition generally were uninterested or unaware of the commercial art world and made no effort to benefit monetarily from their art. Many used "found" materials and tools to create their art, typically motivated by a passion, sometimes bordering on compulsion or obsession, and pretty much always free of financial motive.

Working and often living alone, with little or no interest in exposing their work to the outside world, many of the artists themselves had to be "found." Most outsider artists were not discovered in their lifetimes, and to the extent their work had monetary value it was initially truly nominal.

I have found these aspects of the outsider art world compelling, including the fascinating (though almost always terribly challenging and unfortunate) variations in the individual artists' personal circumstances. But personal challenges and disadvantages for the artists aside, the art must stand on its own.

It was well after I was finished with school (Pueblo Central High, Trinity College, Harvard Law) that I developed any real interest in art or in collecting. My first collecting interest, beginning around 1975, was Catalin radios (colorful plastic radios made in the '30s, '40s, and '50s). In the late '70s a college friend introduced me to Frank Maresca, then transitioning from a successful career as a fashion photographer to become co-owner of Ricco/Maresca Gallery in New York, which has become one of the most prestigious outsider art/folk art galleries in

The Bethany Mission, early twentieth century

the U.S. My awareness of outsider art grew in time from conversations with Frank.

In 1996 I joined a Philadelphia law firm whose chairman, Shelton Bonovitz, along with his wife, Jill, owned an extensive outsider art collection, much of which was hanging on the walls of the law firm. Being surrounded by outsider art day to day further reinforced my engagement with it. I began acquiring outsider art at art fairs in New York and from auction houses such as Slotin Folk Art, in Buford, Georgia, Material Culture in Philadelphia, and Christie's in New York. Frank has been a mentor in my collecting all along.

It is rare that the art of any one of the artists represented in the collection bears the slightest resemblance to the work of another artist in the collection (though the work of each artist is generally readily recognizable and distinctive). The art varies dramatically in theme, style, and subject matter (e.g., religious, representational, or abstract images, inclusion of text, and so on). The works also differ widely in the materials used. For example, James Castle painted on found paper, the inside of matchbooks or used envelopes, using soot and spit applied with a stick. Sam Doyle painted with house paint on found wooden boards and corrugated roofing material. Edward Deeds drew with crayons and pencil, almost exclusively on ledger paper from "State Hospital No. 3," a mental hospital in Nevada, Missouri, where he was a residential patient. Lee Godie created paintings using a variety of mediums, including watercolor, pencil, tempera, ballpoint pen, and crayon and on a number of surfaces, such as canvas, poster board, sheets of paper, and discarded window blinds.

Today, the work of these artists, and in fact the work of virtually all of the artists in the collection, are represented in major museums and major collections in the U.S. and internationally. But other than through some isolated loans of a few artworks to museums such as the Smithsonian American Art Museum, a branch of the Los Angeles Eli Broad Museum, and the Kohler Arts Center in Wisconsin, my collection has been housed in Philadelphia since the opening in 2012 of my gallery, Bethany Mission Gallery. The relatively long-term out-of-town exhibition at the Sangre de Cristo Arts Center in Pueblo, Colorado, is a first for the collection.

That this artwork should travel 2,000 miles to a town in Colorado not widely known as an art mecca may call for an explanation. Pueblo is my hometown, where I lived in the same house with my parents, two brothers, and a sister from my birth until I left for college in Connecticut years later. My siblings and I all graduated from Pueblo Central High (listed in the National Register of Historic Places), as did my father, who was also born in Pueblo. Although I have no family remaining in Pueblo, I have returned for all of my high school reunions and at other times to see old (and now they *are* old) friends and to visit familiar sites. When I left Pueblo in 1959 there were no museums or art centers of note there beyond those focusing on local history or local industry. Over the years when I returned from time to time to Pueblo, I became familiar with Pueblo's award-winning Sangre de Cristo Arts Center (the SDC), opened in 1972 and now featuring three gallery spaces that exhibit art by local, regional, and national artists as well as an auditorium that hosts local and national touring opera, dance, and theater.

A number of friends in Pueblo, most of them unfamiliar with outsider art, strongly suggested to me that the SDC would be an ideal venue for introducing this segment of the art world to Pueblo. On meeting Jim Richerson, the CEO of

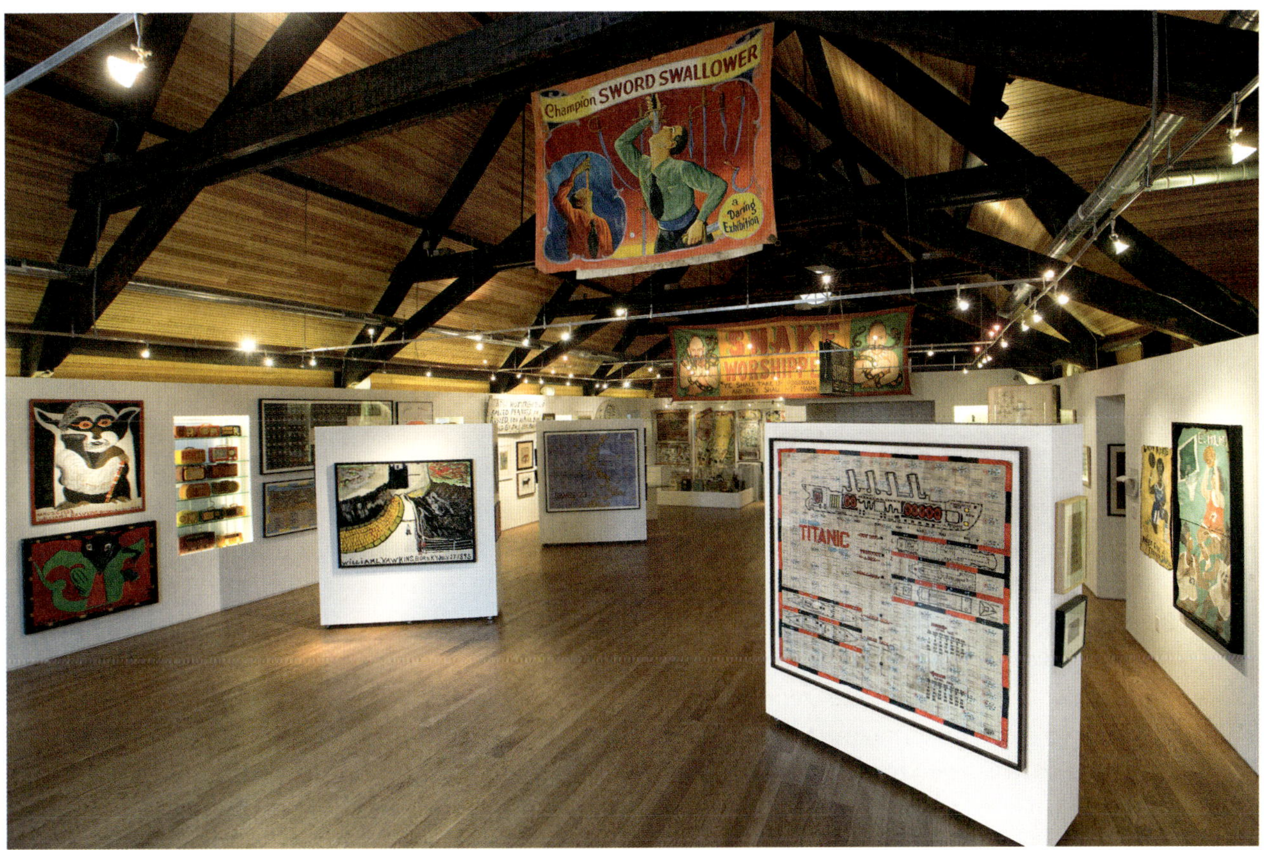

the SDC, and SDC's chief curator, Liz Szabo, it became clear that, while SDC had not previously shown outsider art in its galleries, there was interest in exploring the idea. Their interest grew into mutual enthusiasm and serious excitement when Jim and Liz visited Bethany Mission Gallery in Philadelphia.

While I have been assembling my collection of outsider art (and vintage radios and toys) for decades, it was not until 2012 that I opened the Bethany Mission Gallery, a story that warrants a bit of digression.

Before we married, Jeanne Ruddy, my wife and my partner in the collection, was a principal dancer with the Martha Graham Dance Company and subsequently a member of the dance faculty at the Juilliard School in New York City. In the early 1990s we relocated from New York to Philadelphia, and in 2000 Jeanne founded a contemporary dance company, Jeanne Ruddy Dance. We soon acquired a nineteenth-century building on Brandywine Street, originally a horse stable, and renovated it for Jeanne's dance company as well as to serve as a rehearsal and performance venue for others. We designated this space The Performance Garage.

When a two-story building adjacent to the Performance Garage became available, we acquired it, initially with a view to expansion of the Performance Garage. The building was owned and operated by a family counseling center, and we knew virtually nothing of the building's history aside from having seen at the top of the facade, carved in marble, a barely legible BETH . . . and a date of construction of 18-something. Before we knew anything more about the building, we had determined that expansion of the Performance Garage into that space was neither feasible nor necessary, and I began displaying a portion of the collection in the new building.

A few years later we stumbled upon a periodical published by the local Friends Historical Association, *Quaker History, African-Americans and Quakers*. Astonishingly, the pamphlet included a twenty-page footnoted article, "The Bethany Mission for Colored People"—*our building*! Here we learned that the Bethany Mission for Colored People had been founded by Philadelphia Quakers in the mid-1850s and that in 1869 they had built the Brandywine building. Bethany's core mission was to bring literacy to Philadelphia African Americans, primarily children and young adults of modest circumstances or worse, within the context of religious instruction and moral education. Bethany continued to operate in this endeavor until the 1930s, though with diminishing attendance due to the proliferation of African American churches in Philadelphia providing similar opportunities.

After a two-year renovation, we opened the space in 2012 as the Bethany Mission Gallery (BMG). A high percentage of the artists whose works are in the collection were African American and/or lived in poverty; what's more, many of the artists could neither read nor write. Thus, it is that by sheer accident or serendipity, the art and artists in the collection are in significant alignment with the character and goals of the original Bethany Mission.

While at present BMG does not have public hours and is not a tax exempt 501(c)(3) charitable organization, we are readily available to give gallery tours by appointment for groups large or small. In addition, we hold many activities and events at BMG without imposing any charge or rent.

For example, in the last few years, we have presented a lecture by the artist George Widener (one of the few living artists in the collection, and a friend, many of whose pieces are included in this exhibit). In addition, we've held a BMG gallery tour for the faculty and board of directors of the Pennsylvania School for the Deaf, which was signed for the benefit of the nonhearing participants, and screened the documentary film on the life and work of James Castle, a major artist also represented in the collection who could neither speak nor hear his entire life long. Finally, we've also hosted tours and fund-raising events for a number of national, state, and local political candidates; hosted events for Philadelphia charitable and cultural organizations; and made the gallery available for theatrical productions.

Knowledgeable visitors to BMG—collectors, art gallery dealers, and others affiliated with galleries or museums operating in the arena of outsider art—have often proclaimed the BMG space a unique and ideal setting for the collection. Over the years I have immensely enjoyed developing relationships and friendships with fellow collectors, enthusiasts, gallery owners, and museum personnel in the outsider art spaces throughout the country. When the time comes for me to relinquish my stewardship of the art, it is my hope that it can continue to reside in what I regard as its truly fitting home in the BMG.

ACKNOWLEDGMENTS

It takes a team of experts to bring together an exhibition and catalogue of this caliber, and I'm grateful for the work contributed by esteemed figures in the scholarship of outsider art who have written for this catalogue: Frank Maresca, Lyle Rexer, and Edward M. Gómez. A loyal friend of more years than we care to count, the ever sagacious Frank Maresca has been an outstanding mentor and key in the creation of this catalogue. My thanks go as well to Alejandra Russi at Ricco/Maresca for her invaluable contributions to the biographical texts. Thanks, too, to Donald Kennison for his careful proofreading. I'm especially grateful to Laura Lindgren not only for her expert editing, design, and production management of this exquisite catalogue, but for connecting us with Hirmer Verlag, the esteemed art book publisher of international renown, where Rainer Arnold oversaw the beautiful printing of this volume.

At home in Philadelphia, at the Bethany Mission Gallery Gabrielle Lavin Suzenski and Gary Smith have provided crucial assistance. In Pueblo I am thankful to Jim Richerson, SDC's CEO, and his spouse, Judy Lee. I add my appreciation to Jim's as well for the Arts Center's entire staff who brought the exhibition to life, and specifically Elizabeth Szabo, curator of visual arts, LuDel Walter, collections manager, Alyssa Parga, director of marketing and development, and Kathy Berg, office supervisor. I am thankful for a supportive board that encourages such efforts as bringing the Victor Keen collection to the Arts Center, especially board chair Wendy Rapp and past chair Dorothy O'Dowd. The Arts Center and its extensive programming would not be possible without the support of the Pueblo County Commissioners and the Pueblo City Council.

Finally, I am immeasurably grateful to my wife, Jeanne Ruddy, who was instrumental in the original design of the Bethany Mission Gallery. Jeanne has been my partner from the beginning not only in selecting the art for the gallery but in holding all of the delightful events it has been our privilege and joy to host in our gallery.

—VFK

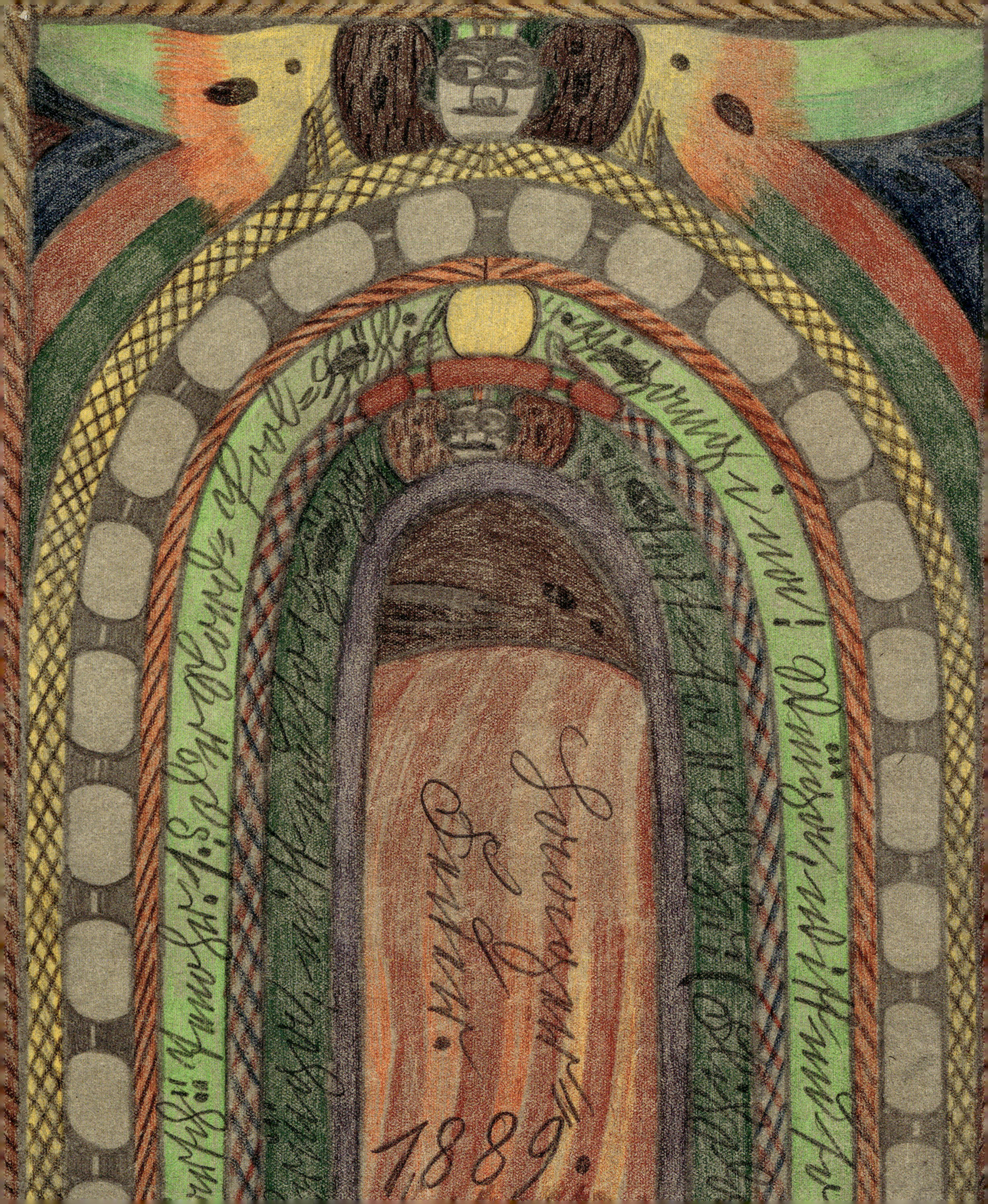
1889.

PEAS OR CARROTS FRANK MARESCA

When Ricco/Maresca Gallery was founded thirty or so years ago, most of the art that we showed—self-taught, outsider, and folk—fell under the catchall label *folk art*. Very little effort was made to categorize the three (very separate) fields. About twenty years ago, a number of people—who, like ourselves, were unhappy with the blanket term—started using the term *self-taught*. At pretty much the same time, the Outsider Art Fair came along, taking its name from Roger Cardinal's 1972 book *Outsider Art*. Cardinal's term was a loose English translation of *art brut*, a name conceived by the French modernist artist Jean Dubuffet to refer to art that was raw and uninfluenced, not driven by ego, and thus an antidote to the corruptive potential of mainstream culture in art.

Immediately popular, the outsider label became the winner in the contest for an all-inclusive definition. I suppose it is easy to understand why that happened and why it remains true to this day . . . Secretly or openly, everybody wants to be an "outsider." No one—in their heart—really wants to be normal; the romantic figure of the iconoclast is sexy and smart. I generally hate labels and believe that they are best suited to supermarket shelves rather than categorizations in art. It has always been my argument that the only criterion by which anything should be judged is quality. In my conversations with Roberta Smith and Jerry Saltz (senior art critics of the *New York Times* and *New York* magazine, respectively), we have all been in agreement that perhaps it should all just be called art; there is no difference between Henri Matisse, Gerhard Richter, Henry Darger, or Martín Ramírez. The works of each of these artists have the capability of being hung side by side and igniting compelling visual experiences and a riveting discussion. The only problem with all of that is . . . people just seem to need labels in their life. If that *is* to be the case, those labels should mean something—in other words, be accurate.

Self-taught, outsider, folk art: how do we differentiate between these three? Outsider art, as I define it, is essentially a politically correct version of Dubuffet's definition of art brut, which he also called the art of the insane. My explication of those terms would be art that has been produced by people working so far outside of society as we know it that they often need the company of caregivers. Such was the case with artists Martín Ramírez (a mental patient who produced his entire body of work within a California mental hospital), Adolf Wölfli (a farmworker and handyman who conjured a vast alternate universe in the confines of the Waldau Clinic in Switzerland), Ken Grimes (an American artist who has spent most of his life investigating extraterrestrial existence through his work while living at Fellowship Place in Connecticut), and Günther Schützenhöfer (a resident of the famed Gugging House of Artists in Vienna, whose arresting drawings in graphite transport us to the core of human creativity).

Self-taught art, by contrast, is simply art that is produced outside of the art historical

Adolf Wölfli, *Lagerfeuer* (detail), c. 1915–16 (p. 245)

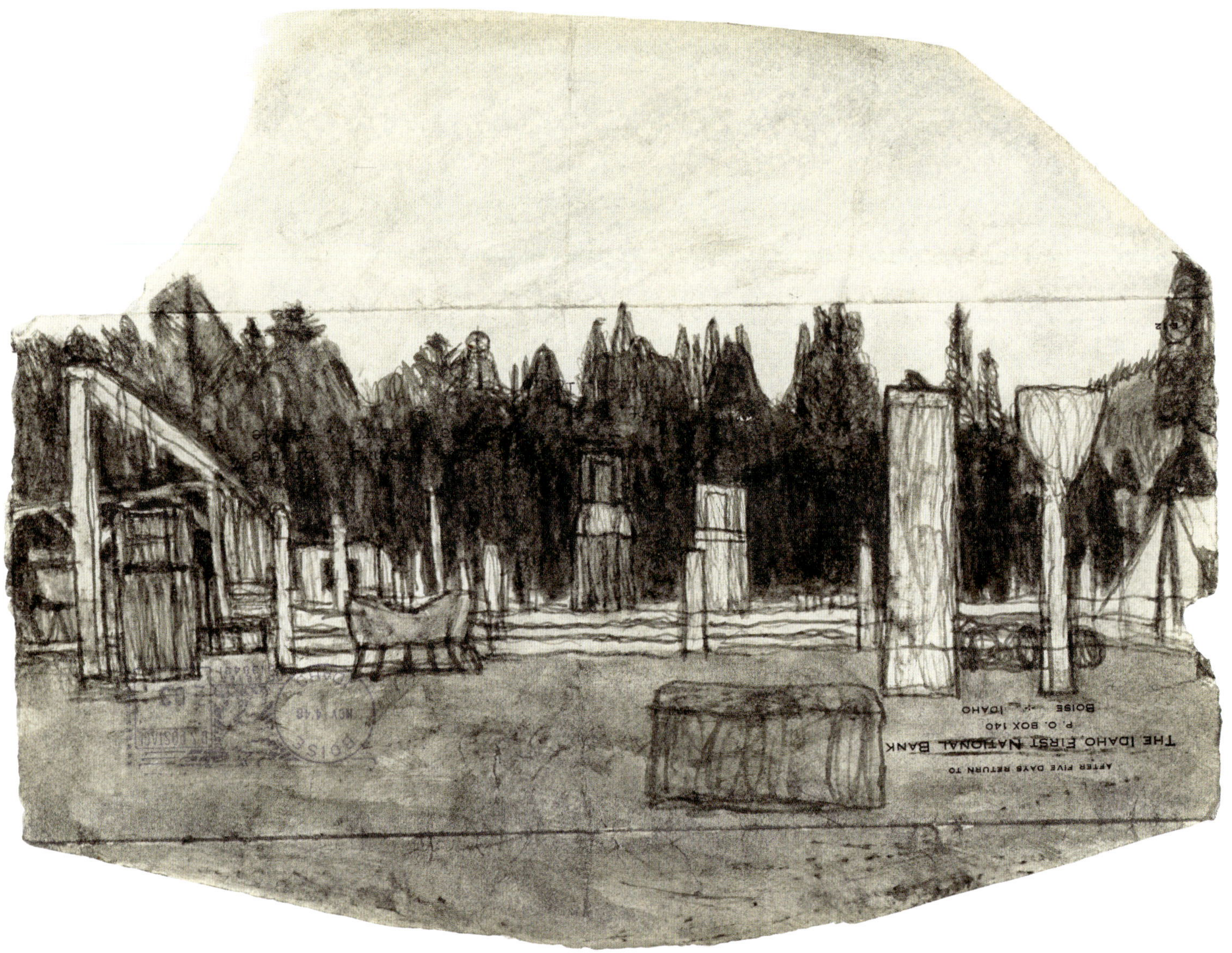

continuum, art that is not of the academy. Artists such as George Widener (a calendar savant capable of complex calculations based on dates and historical events) and the African American artists Thornton Dial, Bill Traylor, and William Hawkins (all with no formal education and who nonetheless produced world-class bodies of work) fit into this category. I often refer to self-taught art as a gift, something that an artist is born with and develops intuitively through nonacademic training. Self-taught art is very much related to folk art; the only significant difference is that folk art often comes out of a utilitarian tradition: skills passed from parent to child, master to apprentice. A few examples of folk art are quilt making, wood carving, pottery, and iron work.

A fourth category (or label, if you will) would be self-educated—designating those gifted people who have become their own teachers through books, travel, and research—learning everything that would be learned within the formal structure of a school, except that they did it, or they are doing it, on their own. I make very little distinction, if any, between self-educated artists and those with academic backgrounds. I am not saying that everyone needs the self-taught purity of Bill Traylor . . . Times have changed, degrees of influence and methods of communication have changed with them, but I do believe it is important to have contextual awareness when it comes to these easily misunderstood categories and oeuvres.

Artists working in isolation transport themselves through the limitless labyrinth of the brain. Isolation can take many forms, physical, geographical, and otherwise. The particular isolation of the artist James Castle, who was profoundly deaf and living in a rural area, contributed to the way in which he perceived and rendered the world. Henry Darger, who lived alone in a single room on Webster Avenue in Chicago and worked menial jobs at Catholic hospitals, created a world that, while it owes much to the popular culture of his time, was a pure voyage of the mind. As the concept of isolation continues to shift and lines are constantly blurred, I still believe there will always be gifted artists who are born with utterly unique minds. Some of them could legitimately be called outsiders and will always be out there to be discovered, perhaps for the first time at Bethany Mission Gallery or any of the soon-to-be museum venues. Victor Keen—a close and old friend—has taken up the art baton and run with it in a quest for excellence that has always been his trademark.

Frank Maresca is an American art dealer and co-founder of Ricco/Maresca Gallery in New York City. A longtime advocate of self-taught, folk, and outsider art, he has championed and showcased the work of artists creating on the margins of the art historical mainstream for more than thirty-five years. Through many gallery exhibitions, museum collaborations, key publications, and philanthropic work, Maresca—who is currently on the advisory boards of *The Brooklyn Rail*, Intuit in Chicago, *Raw Vision* magazine, and Fountain House Gallery—has sought to diminish the tradition of separating art into conventional categories of fine art and vernacular art.

OPPOSITE: James Castle, *Untitled (Landscape with farm buildings on envelope)*, n.d. Soot and saliva on found paper, 7¼ × 9½ in. (18.4 × 24.1 cm)

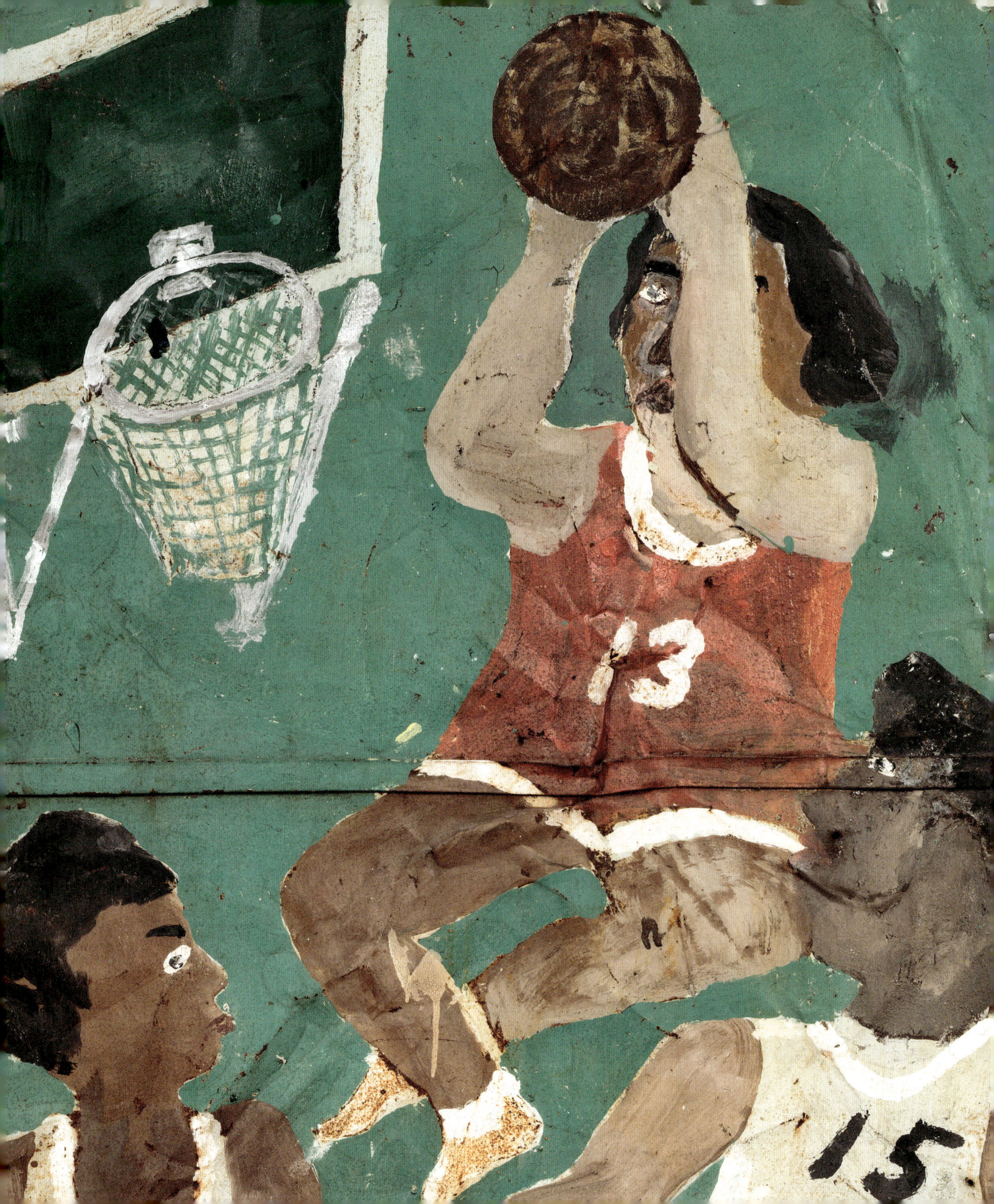
13
15

AN UNWITTING VISION & QUIRKY CHARM

EDWARD M. GÓMEZ

Some of the most ardent and active collectors—of art, antiques, or just about anything else—are made, not born.

Unlike their counterparts who seem to be instinctively compelled to search for, amass, and even hoard their temptation-teasing must-haves, these more low-key hunter-gatherers are likely to point out, when asked what drives their collecting impulses, that the paintings, weather vanes, rocking chairs, pocketknives, old master prints, bottle caps, Elvis Presley images, or old cars they pursue seem to find and captivate *them* as much as *they* seek out such inestimable treasures. For some collectors, seduction is a two-way affair.

Born and brought up in Colorado, where he shone as a high school athlete on the basketball court and the track field, Victor Keen is quick to admit that over the years, as he became a lawyer and enjoyed a successful career, art found him as much as he discovered art—its pleasures, mysteries, and can't-live-without-it allure. Today, he recalls that thanks to a sequence of events whose chronology has blurred, he stumbled into various early encounters with art, each of which drew him more deeply into a resonant personal dialogue with certain kinds of anonymous, everyday objects and with the creations of numerous recognized artists, too—and right into the arms of that enigmatic force: the collecting bug.

Stung—or smitten—Keen gave in and over time assembled what have come to be acknowledged as some of the more individualistic and unexpected holdings of their kinds in private hands in the United States today. In fact, over several decades he has put together a distinctive collection of collections, of which an assortment of works by outsider and other self-taught artists forms a large, notable part. The often compelling, hard-to-label kind of creativity all of his acquisitions evince is both the real subject of Keen's collection as a whole and, at the same time, the irresistible object of his pursuit.

"Even after many years, I'm still an amateur when it comes to collecting," Keen says matter-of-factly as he shows a visitor around his Bethany Mission Gallery, a renovated, nineteenth-century Quaker meetinghouse located just north of Philadelphia's downtown historic district, in which his treasures are now on display. Nevertheless, Keen's knowledge and understanding of art have been shaped as much by happenstance (stumbling upon desirable artworks or objects in galleries or at auctions) as they have by deliberation (the diligent research he does before acquiring an artist's work for the first time, often in consultation with his friend and mentor the New York art dealer Frank Maresca). Thus, perhaps unwittingly, over the years Keen has developed that rare attribute—a personal aesthetic sensibility—that distinguishes genuine collectors from mere acquirers who, notably in the contemporary-art field, seem to be able to do their shopping only when led by the hand by trend-chasing "art advisers."

It is thanks to that sensibility—call it a personal approach to looking at and appreciating art, and to making decisions about what to purchase and take home—that an unlikely gathering

Sam Doyle, *E. Holmes* (detail), c. 1978–81 (p. 87)

of remarkable finds has found shelter and a showcase in Keen's private gallery. Among them: in-depth holdings of works by such noteworthy outsider or self-taught artists as James Castle, Sam Doyle, Martín Ramírez, and George Widener, among others, and a smattering of contemporary photographers' images, alongside antique metal toys and piggy banks; salt and pepper shakers, cups, pitchers, and little shoes made of luminous milk glass; electric toasters; corporate employees' name badges from the early twentieth century; and art deco–era plastic radios.

Keen observes, "When it comes to explaining what the label 'outsider' means in relation to so-called mainstream culture, you can have some rather broad characteristics in mind. Something can be regarded as coming from or occupying a place outside the 'mainstream' in many different ways." Touched by what he calls the "naïveté" inherent in the creations of certain known artists and other, unknown artisans (the expressive simplicity of the line in a Lee Godie self-portrait, or the captivatingly odd image of a sword swallower downing *three* sabers in an old circus-sideshow banner), Keen suggests that, above all, it is the unaffected qualities of the artworks and objects that catch his eye that make for the kind of impact he is seeking. It's one that is unmistakable and unexpected—and that packs the same punch each time he examines such discoveries anew.

"I've learned a lot about art and artists from the discussions I've enjoyed with dealers and other specialists over the years, but coincidence has also played a part in my art-collecting experience," Keen explains. Several years ago, for instance, he caught a local television-news report about George Widener, a self-taught maker of unusual drawings who was then based in North Carolina and was described as an autistic savant. Keen was fascinated by his detailed depictions of cities or disaster-doomed ships like the *Titanic*, one of the artist's favorite subjects, and by the ways in which Widener filled his peculiar pictures with representations of complex mathematical calculations concerning natural or human-provoked disasters, birthdays, or other groups of related dates projected, with great precision, backward or forward in time.

Keen recalls, "When I heard Frank Maresca's name in the news report and saw that he had begun showing this artist's works at his gallery, I raced there to meet Widener and see for myself his amazing drawings. That first encounter led to my collecting George's work in depth and to a long-lasting, meaningful friendship with this artist, which has been as rewarding to me as the opportunity to live with and admire his art."

Similarly, with their bloodred and earthy tones and their strange air of the dreamlike and the visceral, the Argentine-born artist Marcos Bontempo's paintings on paper seized Keen's imagination, and he acquired nearly two dozen of them. A few years ago, he was introduced to Bontempo's *Se detiene ingrávida la vida* (*Life, Weightless, Stops*), a 160-page, large-format, one-of-a-kind artist's book made in 2010 that is filled with boldly outlined faces and animal forms evoking primordial forces and Jung's grand musings about humanity's collective unconscious.

"Instantly, I knew that I had to acquire this extraordinary work of art," Keen explains, adding, "Not only did it complement the Bontempo works I already owned, but it was also so powerful on its own that I knew it would become a centerpiece of my collection that I would return to again and again—and, indeed, I have."

Perusing his holdings, Keen stops to savor "the always fluid line" in a group of Thornton Dial's drawings; splashy paintings of faraway places made in house paint on board by William

Hawkins, a black American self-taught artist from Kentucky who spent most of his life in Ohio; "two big heads looking out over the populace" in a large, semiabstract painting on board by Purvis Young; an antique, painted-metal statuette showing a biblical Jonah in a rowboat coming face to face with a rather cute, not-so-menacing whale; and assorted "scarecrows" made with metal can lids, scraps of fabric, and other cast-off materials by the blind, Memphis-based artist Hawkins Bolden (who claimed that he could recognize colors by touch).

"Most of this work doesn't look like it was made by people who felt constrained," Keen notes, offering one of the most understated observations ever about the makers of what has become known, for its unpredictability as much as for its exuberance, as "outsider art." Throw in the toasters, radios, and little milk-glass *objets* in the form of Victorian women's shoes, an owl, or a pair of binoculars, along with the complex compositions incised into wooden slabs and painted with ink by Prince Twins Seven-Seven, a Nigerian artist inspired by Yoruban myths, that are also on view at Bethany Mission Gallery, and the quirky, unique character of Keen's collection—which is both its calling card and its charm—comes into sharp focus.

A "sensibility" is, admittedly, one of those contemporary artspeak notions from which many a critic, curator, or serious artist would prefer to flee rather than be forced to define, but precisely because his collection of collections has turned out to be so curiously diverse but emphatically—and refreshingly—*not* encyclopedic in scope or ambition, it calls attention to Keen's essential role as an unlikely art aficionado who became a passionate collector and gave it form.

Unlike some of his peers who feel compelled to "fill in" real or imagined "gaps" in their holdings and obligatorily acquire token, if not always the most emblematic, works by certain artists in an effort to create wall-filling, textbook-complete presentations, Keen has had the good sense to know when to stop acquiring a particular artist's productions or a certain kind of object and to take stock of and appreciate what he has brought together.

Today, his collection of collections has reached a certain substantive, critical mass; seen in the form of a well-curated selection of pieces from its various parts, from outsider art paintings and drawings to old toys and a good sampling of those sleek, century-old radios, humming with optimism about a future that long ago came and went, its dynamic character reveals itself in the unexpected formal, historical, and aesthetic dialogues that emerge between such disparate products of the human imagination. For visitors to Bethany Mission Gallery and viewers of this revealing exhibition and catalogue, an opportunity to savor such a diversity of creative expressions, while also sensing Keen's enthusiasm for them and the spirit of discovery that has long buoyed his collecting adventure, is one of this unusual survey's most satisfying rewards.

Edward M. Gómez is an art critic and historian, graphic designer, and curator. He is the senior editor of the outsider art magazine *Raw Vision* and a member of the advisory council of the Collection de l'Art Brut in Lausanne, Switzerland. He has written for the *New York Times*, *Art + Auction*, *ARTnews*, *Art in America*, *Hyperallergic*, and many other publications. He is the author or co-author of numerous publications, including *Genqui Numata* (Franklin Furnace Archive), *Dictionnaire de la civilisation japonaise* (Éditions Hazan), *Yes: Yoko Ono* (Abrams), and *The Art of Adolf Wölfli: St. Adolf-Giant-Creation* (American Folk Art Museum/Princeton University Press).

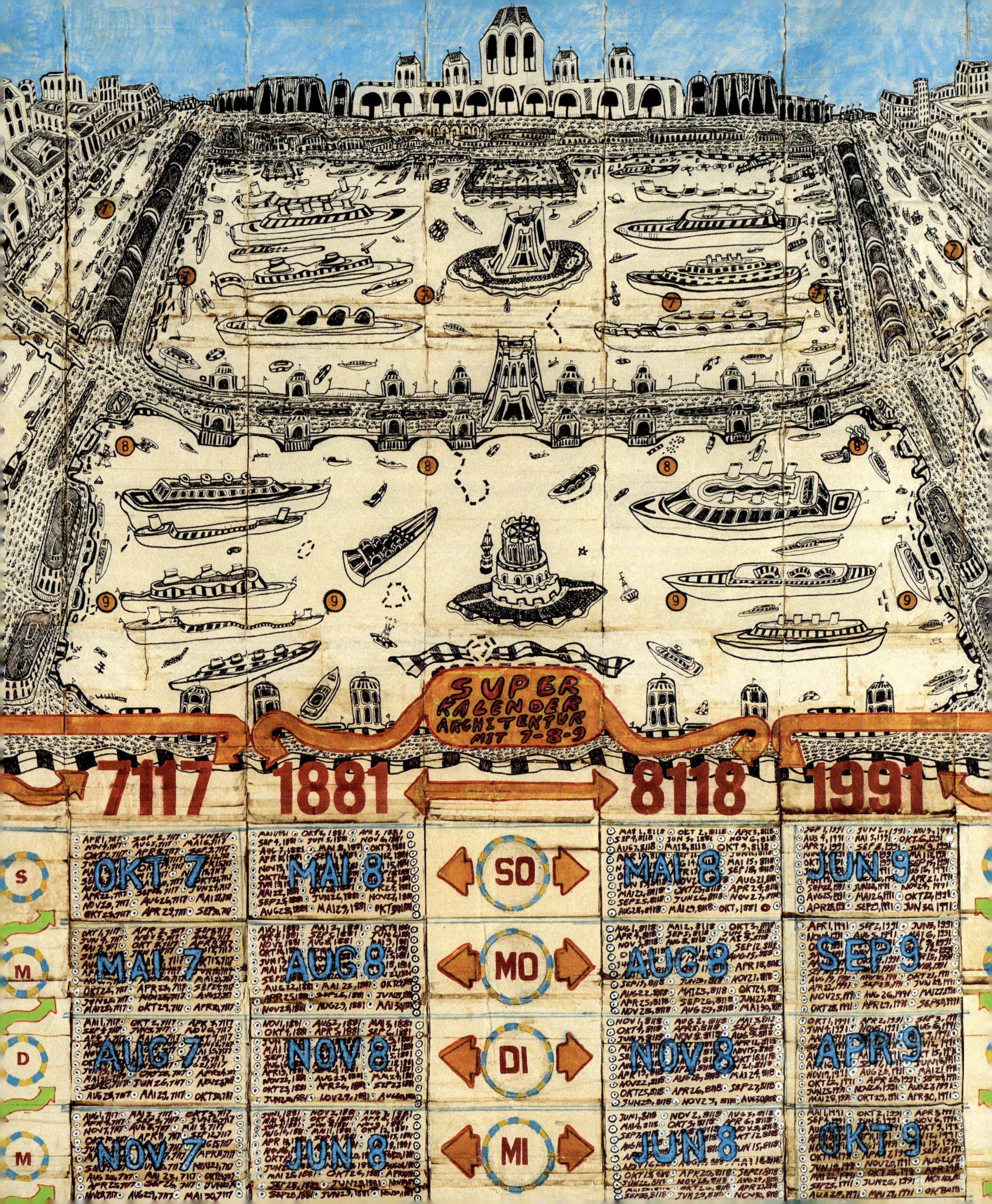
SUPER KALENDER ARCHITEKTUR MIT 7-8-9
7117
1881
8118
1991
S
M
D
M
OKT 7
MAI 8
SO
MAI 8
JUN 9
MAI 7
AUG 8
MO
AUG 8
SEP 9
AUG 7
NOV 8
DI
NOV 8
APR 9
NOV 7
JUN 8
MI
JUN 8
OKT 9

THE KEEN COLLECTION
Dances between Concept and Form

LYLE REXER

> The impossibility of penetrating the divine pattern of the universe cannot stop us from planning human patterns, even though we are conscious they are not definitive.
>
> —Jorge Luis Borges

As for creativity, it just comes naturally. Well, yes and no. Ask artists why the things they make look the way they do, ask where the choices come from, and the likely answer is silence, evasion, obfuscation, or a discussion of techniques. The translation of some concept, the germ of an intuition, into visual form eludes description. It is, after all, what the work is about, what the work *is*. For those of us who look, however, the pleasure and joy of art is experiencing how concept and form unite, and how the pressure of ideas and inspiration is channeled through techniques and strategies into something unprecedented, never before seen. Of course, we are latecomers to the actual process of creating, and we see it through a rearview mirror, with our thinking caps on. In the past and still today there are those who insist that whatever we say about art tends to kill whatever we see, that feeling and thinking cannot coexist, much less enrich each other.

When it comes to self-taught and outsider art, there is a special barrier to a full embrace by head and heart. In the face of this supposedly raw art, we are often exhorted with evangelical force to renounce analysis and lay aside what we carry of knowledge and experience—what the artist Jean Dubuffet called asphyxiating culture—in favor of genuine response. We are supposed to divest ourselves of reason like acolytes giving up their worn and worldly garments before entering a temple. This assumes that the work of self-taught, unsanctioned artists embodies no ideas, has no content, and must be admired for its authenticity, its singularity, its utter refusal to communicate. It is a message without a code, aesthetic form dancing alone in a purified darkness of unknowing.

Victor Keen's collection of art and design objects, and especially his collection of so-called outsider art, offers a very different invitation. It rewards everyone who thinks and looks at the same time. As if it were a brilliantly lit stage, the collection makes us intimate witnesses to the dance between concept and form.

Victor Keen has built his collection intuitively, and since he has many facets and interests, the collection cannot be reduced to a simple statement about taste or vision or strategy. A collection that embraces work by Clementine Hunter and Ken Grimes with equal enthusiasm (not to mention work by Richard Tuttle, long canonized by the art world) defies labels. Nevertheless, certain works and artists in this collection exhibit a strong sense of form connected intimately with a worldview, to such a degree that the choices these artists make in

George Widener, *Megalopolis 789* (detail), 2011 (p. 235)

their work seem not just right but inevitable. The very diversity of the collection has highlighted the distinct character of these artists' work, and I am compelled to explore this in more detail, to chart the steps of their dance.

This essay focuses on several artists whom I find most intriguing and in some key ways closely related. There is not room in its limited scope to explore other important themes, for example, why William Hawkins, represented in the Keen collection by some of his finest works, ought to be regarded as one of the great American painters of his generation, or how the work of Bill Traylor, the son of a slave, has come to be seen not as a species of benign folk cartoon but as a coded narrative of the post-Reconstruction South. The evidence is here at Bethany Mission, Keen's display gallery and performance space in Philadelphia, for anyone who pays a visit.

The better part of one room at the Bethany Mission is devoted to the work of James Castle. Over the decades, Castle's work has risen in critical esteem, attention, and value, and it is not an overstatement to say that Keen has gone all in on this work, with some thirty-eight pieces. By now Castle's story is well publicized—how he grew up in rural Idaho, deaf, unable to speak, read, or write, how he drew like a savant with ink made of saliva and charcoal. The subjects of these drawings are generally regarded to be based on the artist's memories of dwellings, rooms, and rural scenes in his life. This is fine as far as it goes, but a closer look at Keen's selection and at works outside the collection reveals a more complex set of tactics.

Castle made many drawings using letters in combination and filled notebooks with tiny pictorial inventories, possibly based on mail-order catalogues. It is clear that he was fascinated by the combinatory aspect of images and signs. Letters go together in different groups and these groups—words—also go together to make up phrases and sentences. By the same token, Castle's drawings of rural scenes and interiors, precise as they are, have a kind of interchangeability. Certain objects and elements and even scenes reappear. A redwood tree with a tunnel carved through it recurs like a totem. It is likely that he saw such a thing on a novelty postcard, and he places it in a variety of settings. The example from the Keen collection is a group of several drawings depicting corrals. Or perhaps only one "corral," for taken together they look less realistic and more like a theme and variations.

I go into some detail about Castle because his work embodies the paramount importance of a visual order. It is not shackled to a world strictly observed and remembered but is fabricated from elements of the observed. This is not to imply that Castle is some sort of conceptual artist, but his drawings are experimental in a way that has scarcely been considered. That is, they seem to treat drawings—and cardboard assemblages, which Keen's collection also contains—as things that can be arranged from elements. Not a kit of parts exactly but, if we look past their anecdotal realism, they often seem a little like that. These works were made with such jealous attention by the artist, I believe, because the visual order, the formal organization of visual reality, and his ability to control it were paramount to him, perhaps as a confirmation of a more general order or coherence, or at least its possibility.

The dominance of an intentional visual order is everywhere in the Keen collection and makes a case for the presence of modern design objects in that same collection. Keen's assortment of antique toasters and plastic radios were among the earliest expressions of his collecting impulse. They explore industrial typologies, that is, categories of man-made forms that are variations on a theme. They have a relationship to some of the paintings and drawings in the collection precisely because they repeat themselves, with a difference. The designs are tied to their function but, within that limit, the variations are almost endless.

Idiosyncratic drawings from Idaho and manufactured radios? Together they prompt the question: Why is it that artists use repeating forms? With trained contemporary artists—those, say, from the 1960s onward—the reasons are fairly obvious. They often involve some sort of philosophical or cultural agenda. Taking Andy Warhol as an example of the latter, the repetitions of imagery in many of his most famous paintings, from soup cans to electric chairs to Marilyn Monroe, suggest a preoccupation with the recurring appearance in popular media of certain brands and photographs, especially of celebrities. They carry an aura of heightened reality because of their widespread circulation. They become the stuff of dreams. In an important way, repetition (and duplication) of images is their subject.

The situation is different when we approach outsider artists like Castle or Martín Ramírez, who is also strongly represented in Keen's collection. By outsider, I mean at least that they stand outside art historical contexts and discussions of circulating cultural images and ideas. So what to do with repeating motifs or forms that don't seem to refer to anything or make a point about visual patterning? Critics have tended to treat their formal repetitions, especially with Ramírez, as a kind of obsessive decoration, an excess, a horror vacui. Ramírez, who spent a long period of his life in two California mental hospitals, repeatedly used vertical lines to create frames around the central figures of many drawings and curved lines to render train tunnels in other images. In one of his signature images in the Keen collection, a horseman is shown in a kind of niche, which is elaborated outward with repeated vertical lines. Ramírez drew this subject many times, each slightly different. Admittedly, the artist's reliance on a graphic technique does look compulsive, like a machine that reduces everything to a formula. But it also distinctly recalls the architectural motifs from pre-Columbian Mexico that Ramírez almost certainly would have experienced early in his native Jalisco. Even his central figures, especially his horsemen, resemble uncannily the style of Mesoamerican glyphs and murals. The more we look, the more ceremonial his drawings appear. Anything but casual and impulsive.

Impelled but not impulsive. Impelled toward significant form, to look the way they do and no other way. Of course, that seems like a tautology: what else could they look like? But the artists want us to understand why they are presenting the images the way they do. They seem to be saying: the only way you can appreciate what I am communicating is to engage its special appearance. This challenge occurs frequently in the works at Bethany Mission. Perhaps the clearest example is the paintings of Ken Grimes. Grimes has long been captivated by the concept of life existing in other parts of the universe—and by the possibility that aliens may have had and even still do exert an influence on the thoughts and actions of humans here on Earth, including himself. We can argue whether the notion of alien visitation and possession are expressions of mass hysteria and, as represented in popular culture, a form of kitsch. For Grimes they are the organizing principle of all his works, which are by far the most programmatic in the collection and make the most dramatic design statement. Grimes works with diagrammatic, cartoonlike imagery and text in two colors, either white over black or black on white. The several pieces in Keen's collection are heavily text based, containing an extended, highly personal argument for visitation. Dense, hand-lettered, and under tight control, the works resemble a report, and in the context of his more imagistic work they might be considered an ongoing communiqué, loaded with evidence and speculation. The important thing is not whether Grimes is right (or even whether he is sincere, authentic, paranoid) but that he has developed the perfect form for his communication, one based on his imagining of an "official" (and presumably suppressed) scientific document. No color, no "beauty," only information. This content across all Grimes's output is backed up by a host of other aesthetic decisions, from type size to the manipulation of telescope imagery. To paraphrase the media theorist Marshall McLuhan, Grimes's visual medium *is* the message.

George Widener provides a conceptual bookend for Grimes. Keen has one of the most extensive collections of Widener's work and knows the artist well. While Grimes may be in the grip of an idea that demands a single form, Widener is possessed of an awareness of pattern in events that requires a multitude of iterations. His aptitude for mathematical calculation is prodigious, and his drawings meticulously summarize that connection to pattern and number. One of the important works by Widener in the Keen collection is a colorful graphic presentation of a mathematical magic square, and it is worth quoting Widener for a deeper glimpse into his intentions.

> Magic squares, in the traditional mathematical sense, are grids of integers whereby all rows and columns add up to an identical sum. I extrapolated this concept and created the world's first "magic time square," where dates are fitted in alignment with the magic square integers—making the dates add up to an identical sum instead. The next challenge was to create dates that not only resulted in an identical overall sum, but that reflected a common theme. For example, I might fit natural disasters to the above magic square and find hurricanes that not only fit the integers but also occurred on Fridays. This idea has appeared in my past work in various ways: I created stacks, sequences, and progressions of dates using similarities and differences.

If Ramírez's work is allegoric and Grimes's darkly ecstatic (Aliens, yes! The sooner the better!), Widener's is hermetic. That is, his concepts have to be deciphered from the imagery and text, like some cabalistic speculation by ancient Jewish mystics. As the above indicates, the artist can provide some intricate explanations, but they are less important, perhaps, than an overall tendency to link disparate phenomena into a vast network: colors, forms, geometric figures, calendrical dates, and certain types of events, especially natural disasters. There is a great deal of play in Widener's drawings, but the play is always linked to pattern and pattern to a larger order that remains beyond the capacity for full disclosure in any single image. All works are merely glimpses of that overarching order.

Or maybe not. It could be that Widener doesn't believe that these manifestations of local order confirm or even imply any larger design. He is not the second coming of William Blake. He shows us these patterns as a kind of cosmic game, just as playful as James Castle's notebooks but more ambitious, demanding, perhaps deceptive. What is it, then, that we see in these drawings? Traces of an unrecognized reality-behind-reality or a labyrinth without a center, without a Minotaur, a myth, a story? One turning after another into a new corridor or a dead end that requires our retreat? Which raises the question, who is George Widener? An artist or the master of a game? And what is an artist? A creator ex nihilo, forging images in the furnace of the unconscious? More likely a recombiner, an arranger of memory and information, enlisting his own pain in the service of multiple imagined possibilities. In Widener's case, perhaps he is a croupier at a cosmic dice table who has seen every possible combination and knows one thing for certain: the next throw can never be predicted.

And what, for that matter, is a collection of art if not the expression of one person's willingness, renewed over and over, to experience at close hand the dance of concept and form, whether it leads to knowledge, enlightenment, or the sheer pleasure of visual exhaustion?

Lyle Rexer is a writer, critic, curator, and columnist for *Photograph* magazine. His publications include *The Edge of Vision: The Rise of Abstraction in Photography*, *Jonathan Lerman: The Drawings of an Artist with Autism*, *How to Look at Outsider Art*, and *Photography's Antiquarian Avant-Garde: The New Wave in Old Processes*; his articles and essays have appeared in *Raw Vision*, *Art in America*, *Aperture*, the *New York Times*, *Modern Painters*, *Parkett*, and *Tate Etc.*

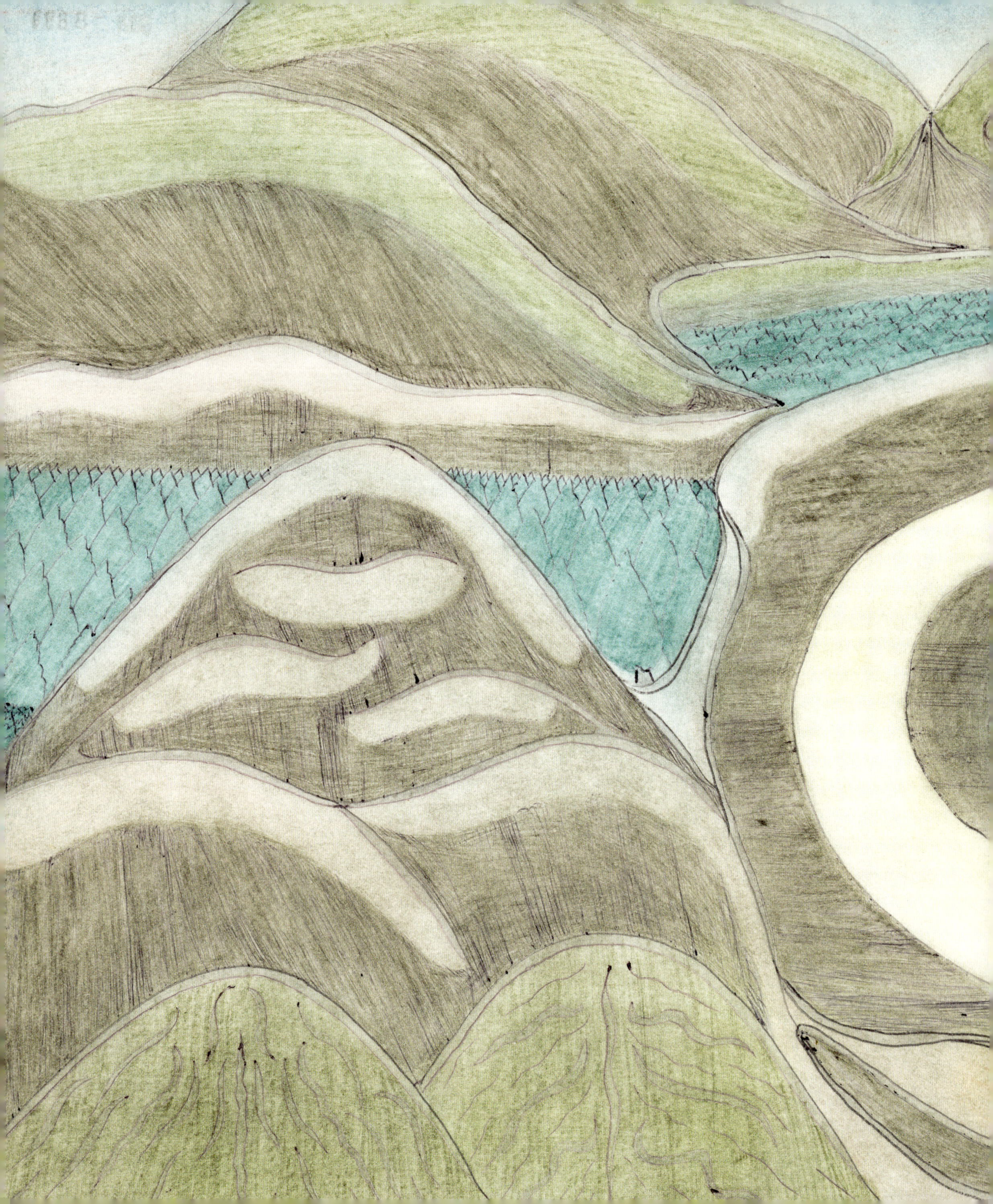

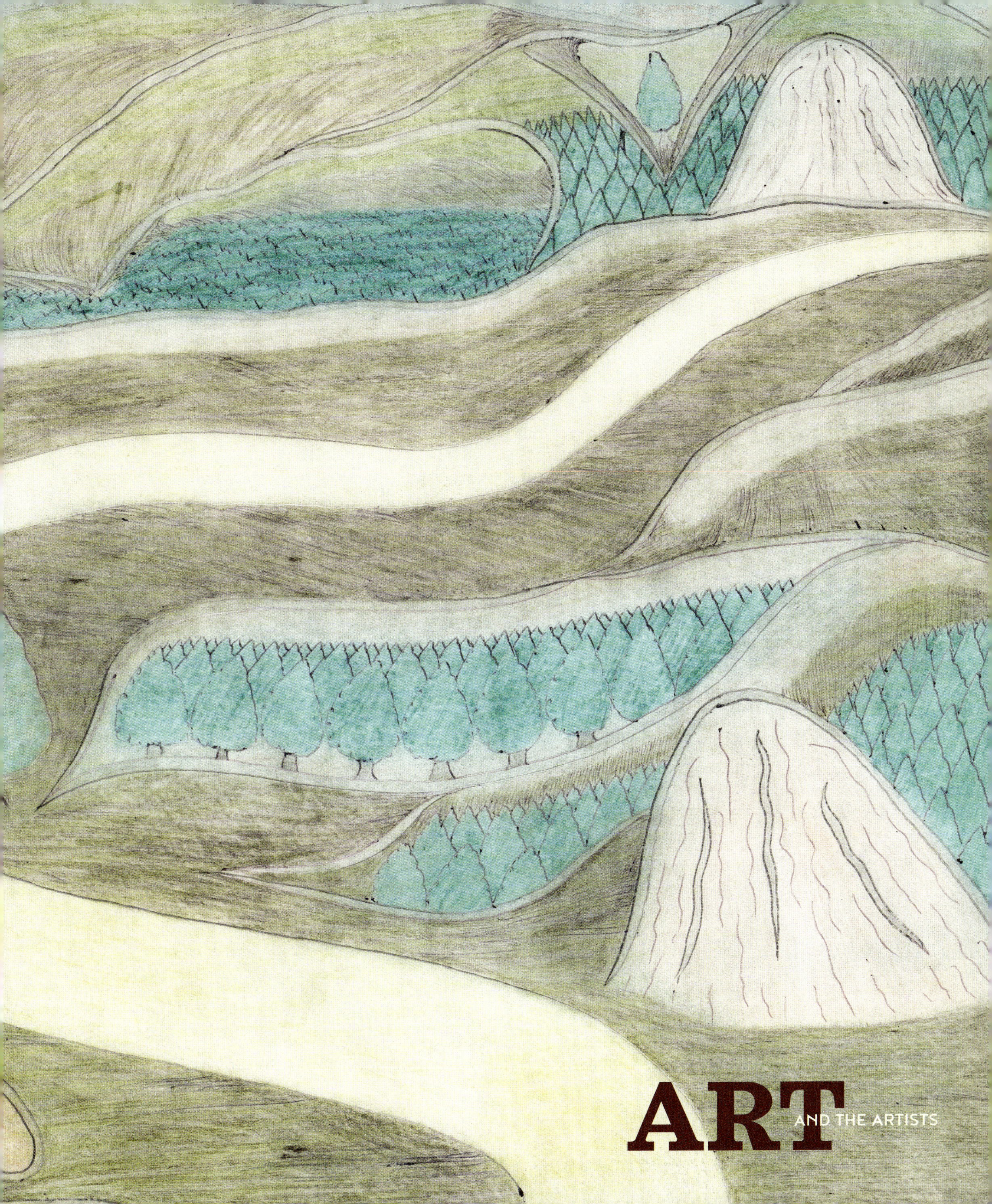
ART
AND THE ARTISTS

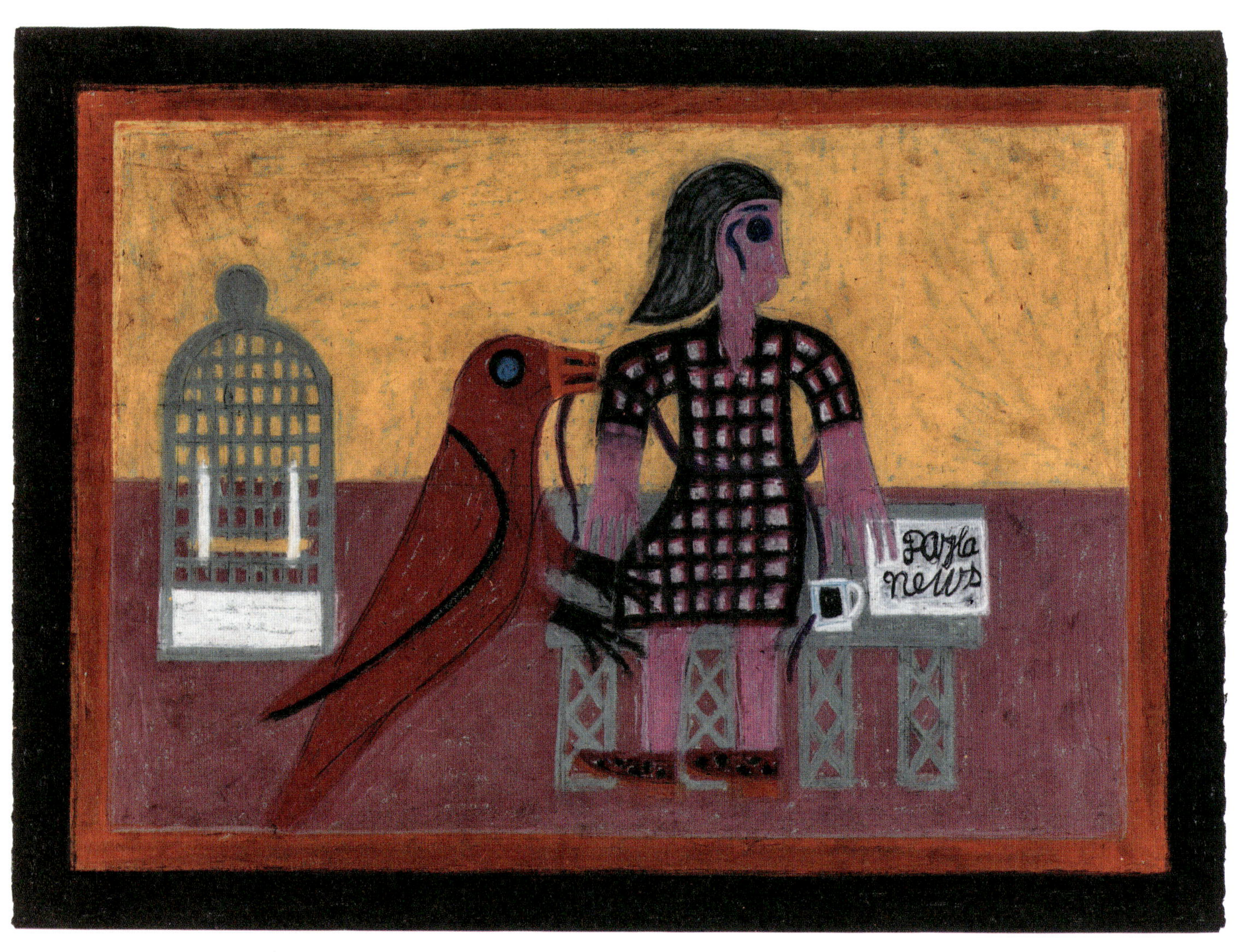
news

EDDIE ARNING

1898–1993

Eddie Arning grew up in a Lutheran community in Germania, a small rural town in Midland County, Texas. In his youth, he suffered from severe bouts of depression and anxiety and was later officially diagnosed with dementia praecox, more commonly known as schizophrenia. Arning spent the next three decades in several mental institutions. His development as an artist began late in life, when he was in his mid-sixties, when a hospital worker encouraged him to draw and provided the necessary materials. At first, he completed several coloring books; then he began depicting isolated forms—flowers, animals, musical instruments, and tools, among other autobiographical subjects—in wax crayon on paper. He soon began to take inspiration from printed media and pop culture imagery in ads, photographs, and magazine illustrations and started working with Cray-Pas oil pastels, which expanded his color range and imbued his shapes with a supple, weightless look.

Arning's mature works are sophisticated, compact arrangements where no part of the surface is left untouched and his bold grasp of color and composition are fully developed. Arning created flat pictorial spaces (exteriors and interiors) where stylized human figures appear within multiple frameworks. A heightened awareness of balance and rhythm suffuses even his simplest subject matter with mystery and magnetism—as the different shapes and pigments gracefully weave in and out of each other with the utmost economy.

Between 1964 and 1974 Arning created more than two thousand works that make up his oeuvre. After this decade of inexhaustible productivity, for refusing to abide by the rules, he was asked to leave the facility in which he resided. He moved in with his widowed sister, but the change permanently disrupted his creative momentum. When his sister could no longer care for him, he moved into a nursing home, where he died at age ninety-five. Since its debut, Arning's work has appeared in a number of exhibitions, including a yearlong solo show at the Abby Aldrich Rockefeller Folk Art Museum in Williamsburg, Virginia (1985)—one of the many institutions that own his work. His work is also in the permanent collections of the American Folk Art Museum (New York), the High Museum of Art (Atlanta), Intuit: The Center for Intuitive and Outsider Art (Chicago), the Milwaukee Art Museum, the Museum of Fine Arts (Boston), the Minneapolis Institute of Art, the Philadelphia Museum of Art, and the Smithsonian American Art Museum (Washington, D.C.).

Eddie Arning, *Untitled (Bird Cage)*, 1968–70. Crayon and Cray-Pas on paper, 19 × 25 in. (48.3 × 63.5 cm)

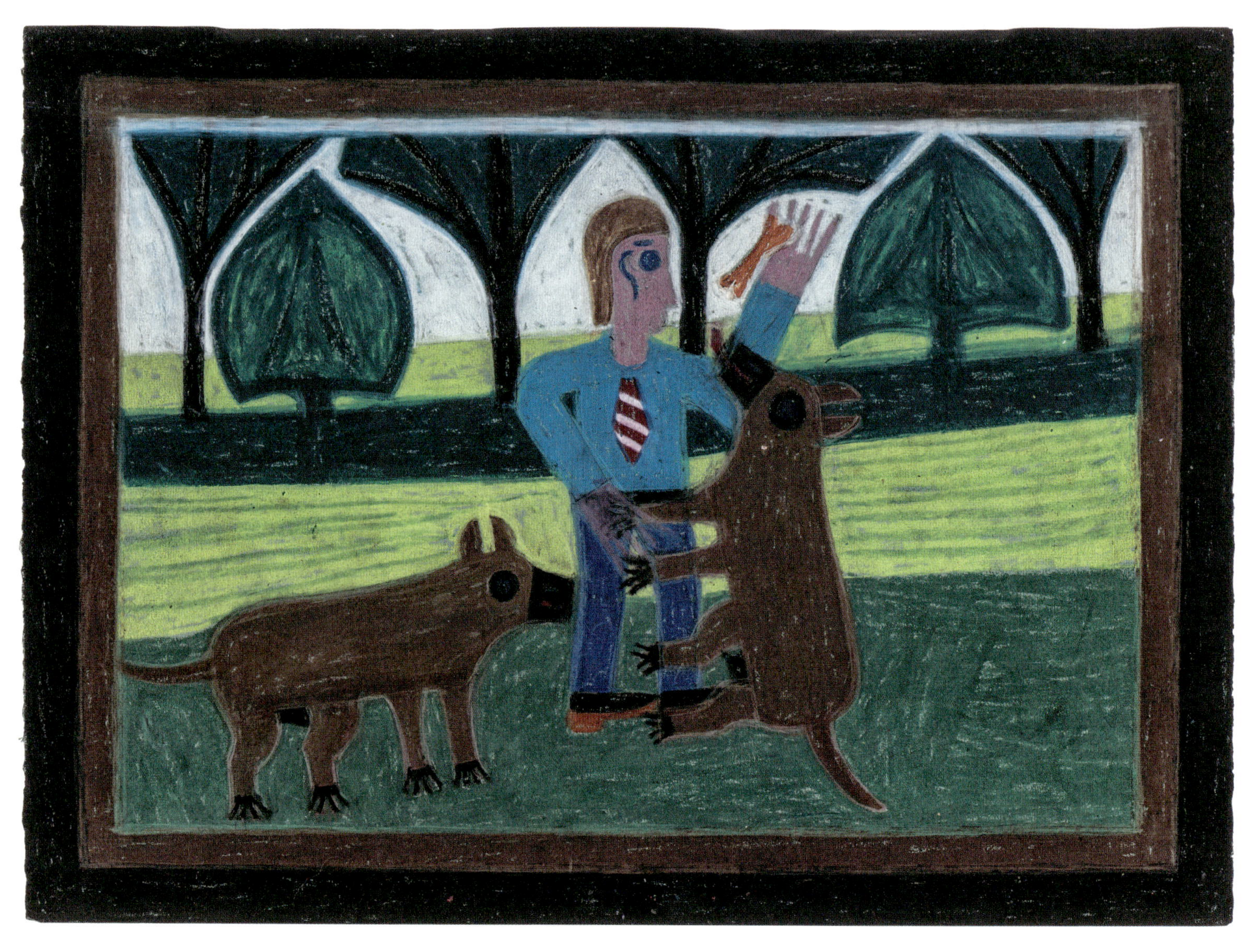

Eddie Arning, *Untitled (Man with Dogs)*, 1968–70. Crayon and Cray-Pas on paper, 19 × 25 in. (48.3 × 63.5 cm)

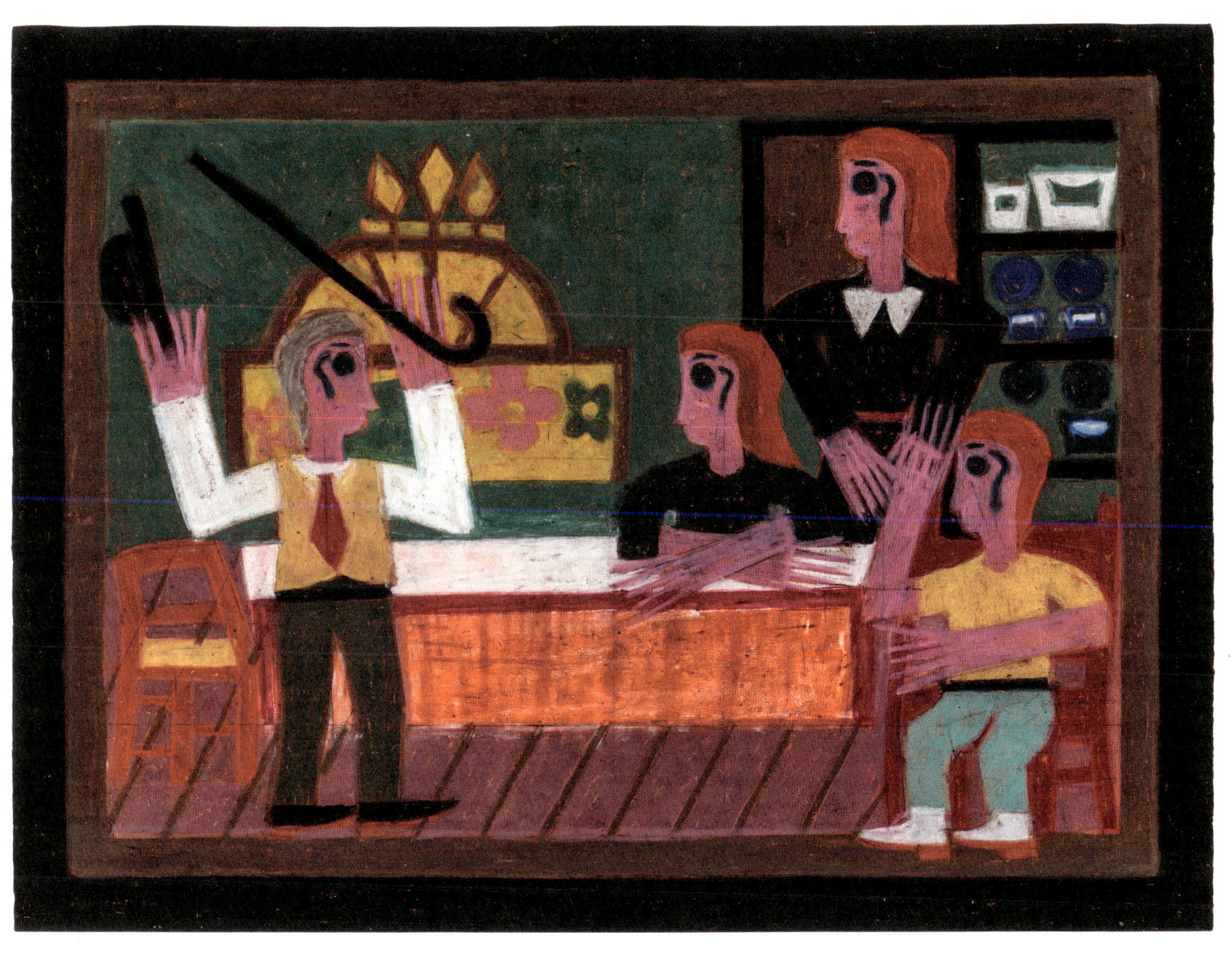

Eddie Arning, *Untitled (Dinner Table)*, 1968–70. Crayon and Cray-Pas on paper, 19 × 25 in. (48.3 × 63.5 cm)

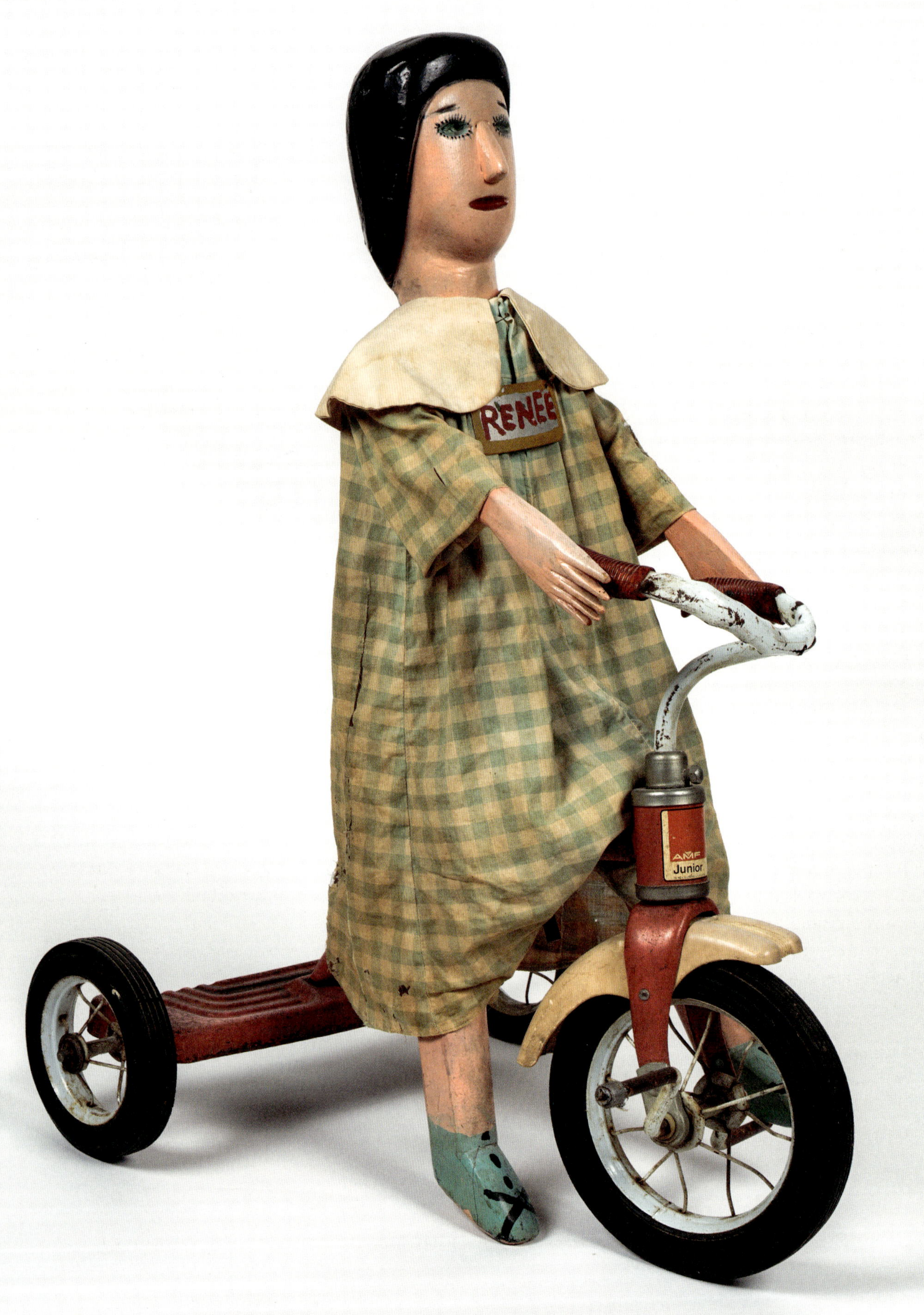
RENEE
AMF
Junior

CALVIN BLACK

1903–1972

From a young age Calvin Black had to take on the role of raising his siblings, and although he received very little schooling in his native state of Tennessee, he taught himself to read and write. While traveling for work in carnivals and circuses he met his wife, Ruby. Shortly after they married in 1953, they moved to a plot of land off of Ghost Town Road in the Mojave Desert, where initially they set up a rock shop that they eventually transformed into a now legendary art environment named Possum Trot. This make-believe town was inhabited by more than eighty near life-size dolls that Black carved and painted (in redwood and pine with enamel house paint) and Ruby dressed in costumes sewn from old clothing. The site was also home of the Bird Cage Theater, where Black's "Fantasy Doll Show" took place. In this spectacle, for a 25-cent admission charge, visitors could see the artist's muses brought to life through his ingenious automaton mechanization, accompanied by shrill, high-pitched recordings of Black performing dialogues and songs in his own voice. Black's dolls often represented the particular traits, names, and personalities of women he'd known. Visitors were encouraged to tip them individually, and Black used the tip money to buy that individual doll accessories and trinkets.

The story of the Blacks coming to own a piece of arid land and conjure this spirited milieu out of sheer imaginative will is the equivalent of a foundational myth in the field of self-taught art. For two decades, travelers passing through on Highway 15 would see welcoming whirligigs and handwritten signs: "Open," "Powered by mother nature," "Unique carved dolls," "Look but don't touch," "Doll Land," "gowns by Ruby," "Beautiful Dolls of the Dessert Waste Land." But Possum Trot village was like a mirage that appeared as swiftly as it vanished. When Black died in 1972, Ruby continued to care for her husband's creations, but after her own death in 1980 the site fell into decay and was finally disassembled. The couple had no children or known relatives, but thankfully Black's remarkable creation was preserved in a short documentary film, *Possum Trot* (1977), by Allie Light and Irving Saraf, and through the dolls themselves, who now are in various private and museum collections, including the American Folk Art Museum (New York), the Milwaukee Art Museum, the Newark Museum (New Jersey), the New Museum (New York), the Smithsonian American Art Museum (Washington, D.C.), and the Kohler Arts Center (Sheboygan, Wisconsin).

Calvin Black, *Renee (Possum Trot Figure)*, c. 1953–69. Carved and painted wood with fabric clothing, found tricycle, 32 × 24 × 18 in. (81.3 × 61 × 45.7 cm)

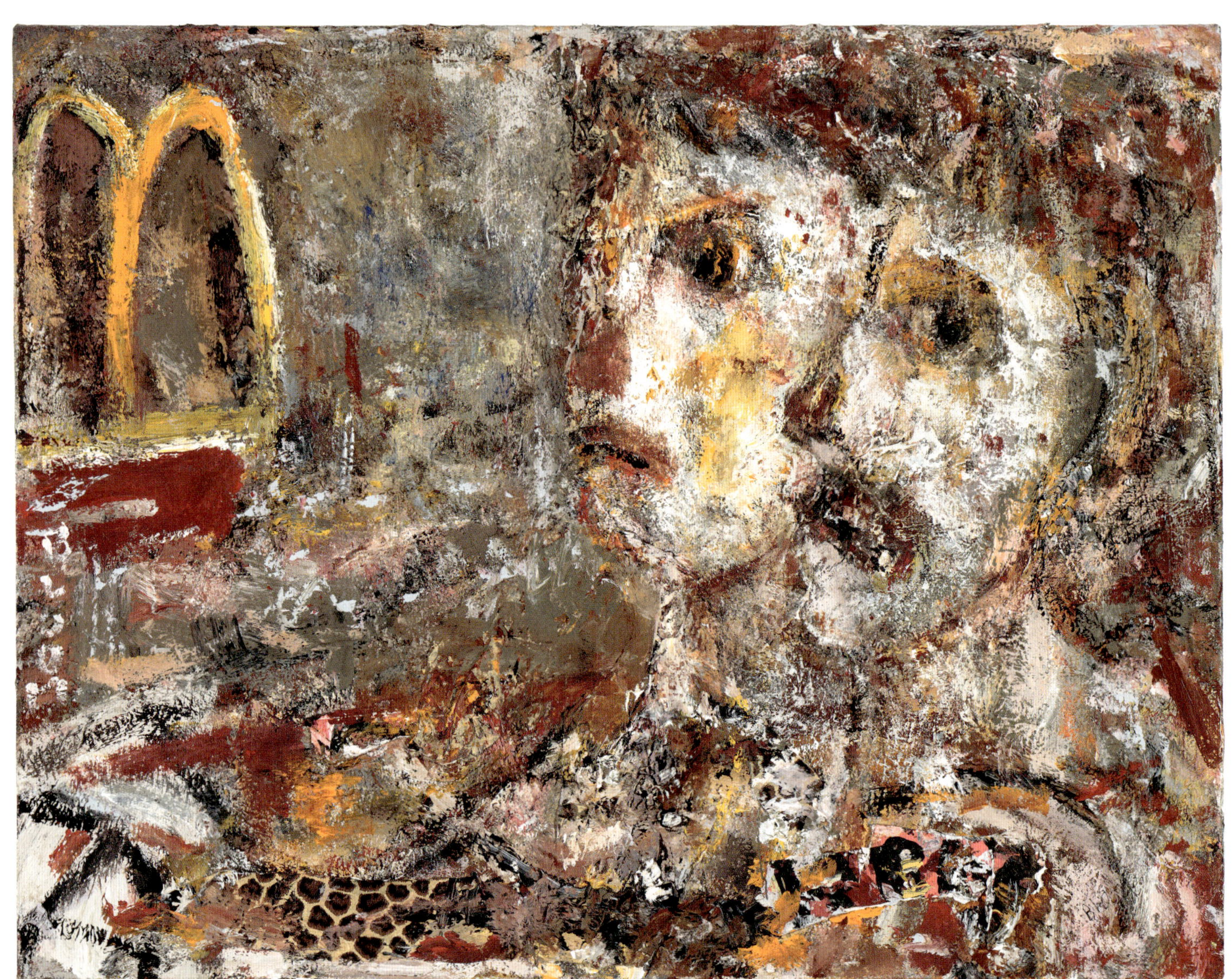

JIM BLOOM

b. 1968

Jim Bloom attended Temple University with the intention of studying film but dropped out after a year to pursue writing. Bloom is originally from Allentown, Pennsylvania, and his life has been fraught with obstacles and trauma; after leaving college, circumstances diverted him from his purpose. To get by he worked odd jobs but began using drugs and finally wound up living on the street. A near-fatal combination of psychiatric and recreational drugs resulted in his forcible hospitalization in 1994 and several months of neuroleptics—an experience that left him with a permanent feeling of alienation. In a 2002 car accident Bloom suffered a debilitating back injury that developed into dystonia, a neurological disorder that causes involuntary muscle contractions resulting in slow repetitive movements, painful cramps, or abnormal posture. Unable to sit for long periods of time and unsettled by the mental issues that resulted, Bloom began to express his pain and frustration through art, working in short bursts as his ailment allowed.

His earliest output was raw with anger and charged with wit and irony. Bloom paints with acrylics, house paint, watercolors, crayons, markers, pencils, pen, or charcoal on cardboard and found objects such as wood, newspaper, and paper plates. Building texture with cut paper and cardboard layers, he produces collage-like compositions that are often scrawled with words or open-ended captions hinting at a story line behind the scene depicted. His art helps him to get away from his tics and anxiety about fitting in, and to tackle the things in himself or in others that make him the most uncomfortable: inappropriate situations, personal or observed vulnerabilities, awkward or petty interactions between people, gossip, taboo, bad behavior, and sexual deviances. His recent large-scale paintings are a conjunction of expressive prowess and caricature at its best; they function like motion picture stills, full of suggestiveness and implicit information, all within the framework of Bloom's cunning and deeply dark sense of humor.

"His . . . method is unplanned, yet altogether intuitive, gutsy and urgent," as Ron Schira wrote in *Raw Vision*. "The work begs correlations and incurs influences from contemporary icons such as Jean-Michel Basquiat for his raw approach and use of text and then also to Red Grooms for cut-out forms and raised surfaces. In later works one may recognize similarities or affinities to the coloration and all-over style of an early Willem de Kooning because Bloom evenly distributes his sweeping line about the surface while placing colors in just the right spots . . . If the artworks have one overriding commonality, it would be to emphasize the frailty of his final product and how vulnerable both he and the public are to the unnecessary cruelties of people, no matter what facet of society they belong to."

Bloom was discovered by Robert Bullock of Coalition Ingenu, a nonprofit organization that promotes art by self-taught creative individuals with histories of homelessness and mental conditions. This association helped him secure gallery representation, and he currently works full-time as an artist.

Jim Bloom, *Golden Arches*, n.d. Mixed media on canvas, 24 × 30 in. (61 × 76.2 cm)

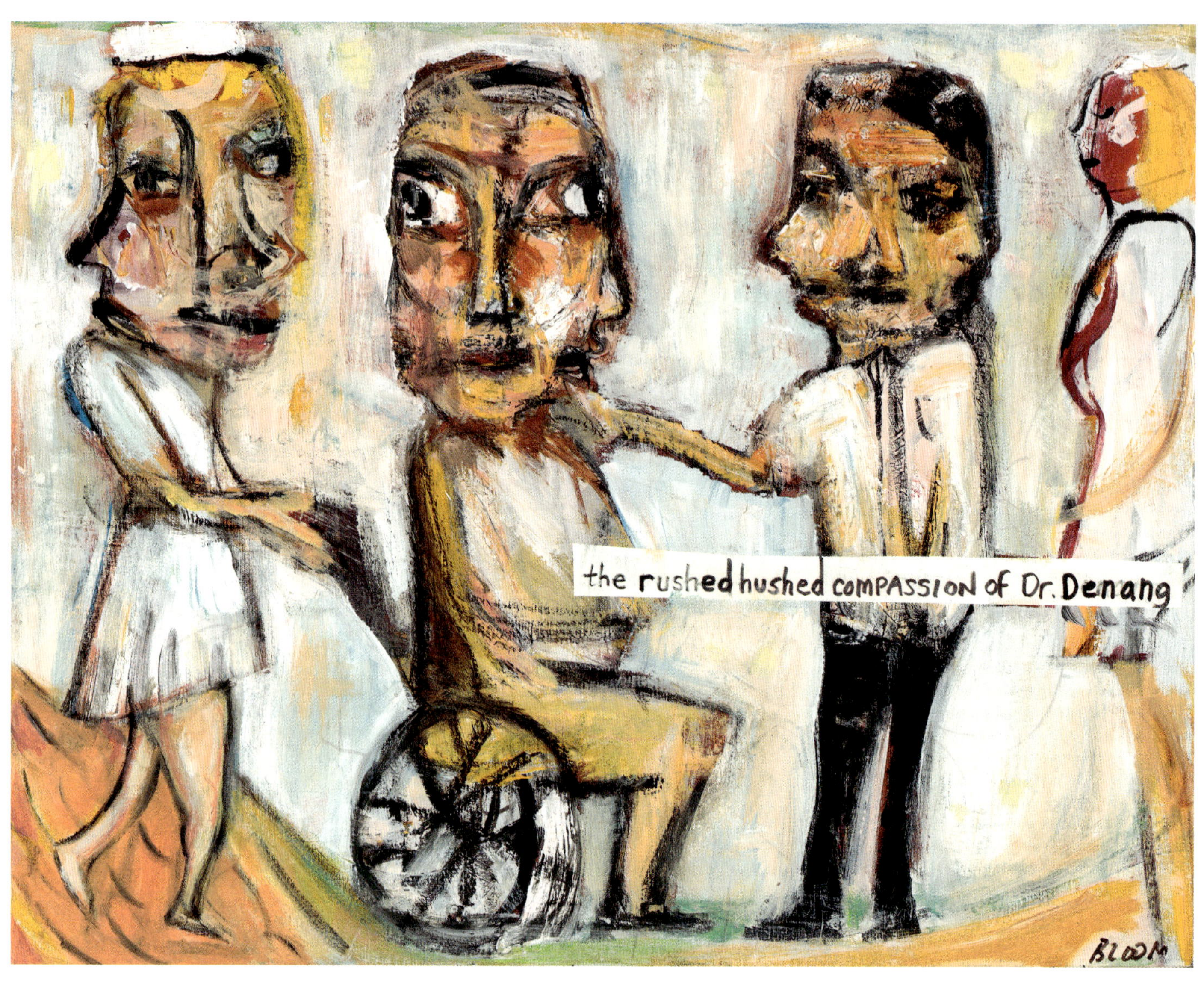

Jim Bloom, *The Rushed Hushed Compassion of Dr. Denang*, n.d. Mixed media on canvas, 24 × 30 in. (61 × 76.2 cm)

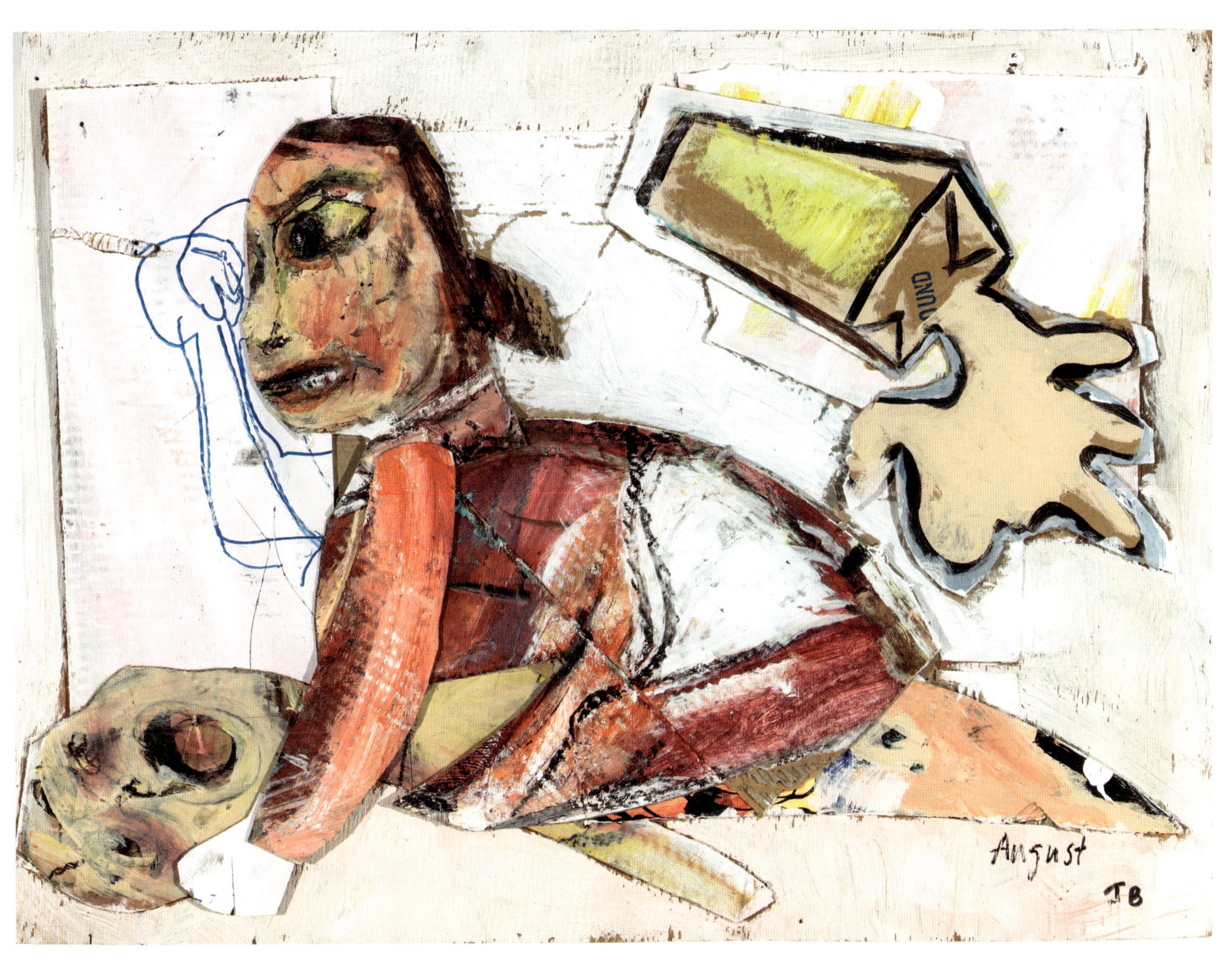

Jim Bloom, *Spilled Milk*, n.d. Mixed media collage on wood, 24 × 31 in. (61 × 78.7 cm)

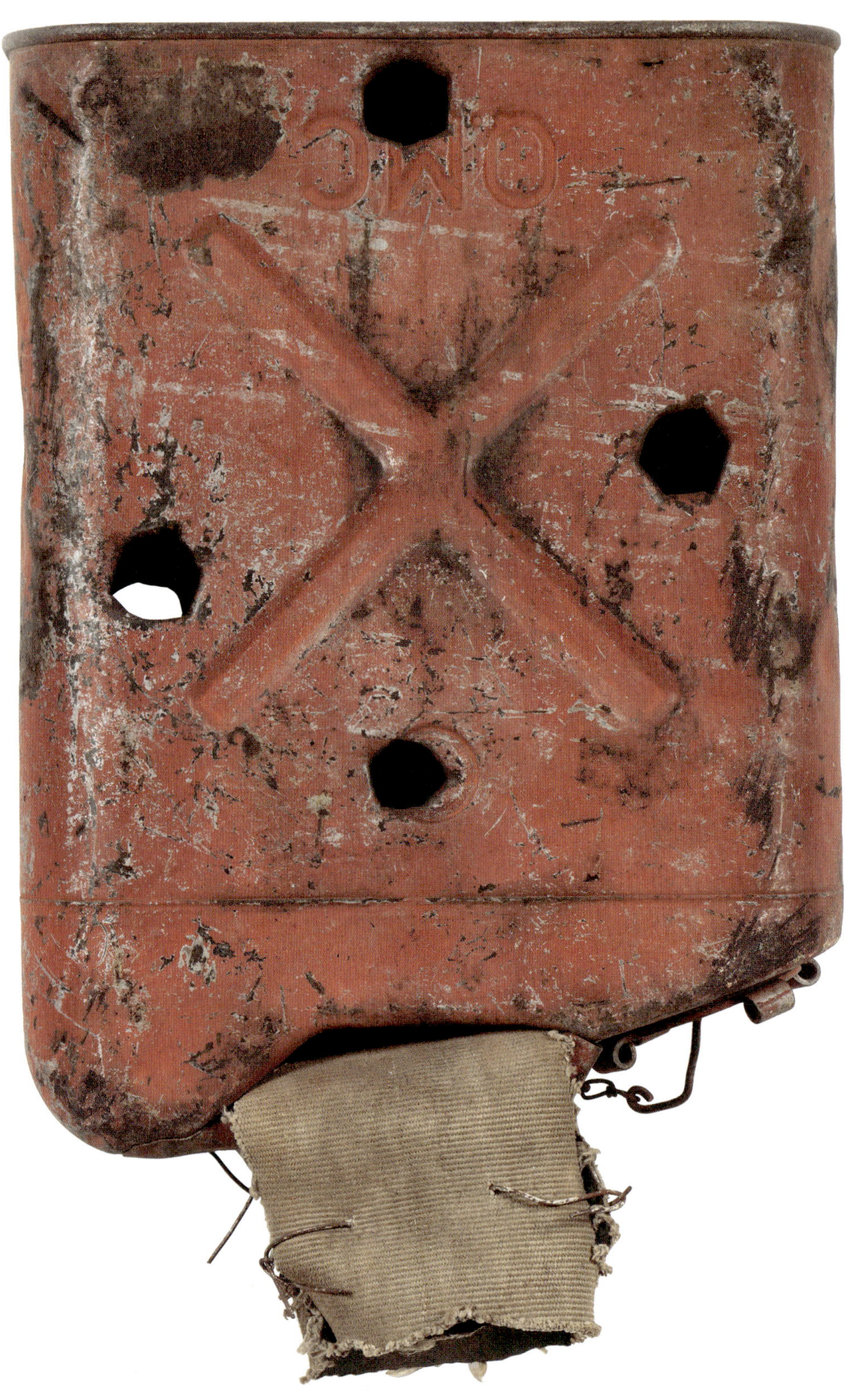

HAWKINS BOLDEN

1914–2005

At around age seven Hawkins Bolden became blind from an accidental blow to the head in a baseball game. Frail and epileptic, Bolden received no formal education. As he developed a heightened sense of touch that awakened his creativity, he started making from found materials all kinds of objects: kites, leg stilts, toys, homemade radios, and the inventive scarecrow sculptures for which he later became well known. Bolden and his identical twin, Monroe, were born in Bailey's Bottom (Memphis, Tennessee) to parents of Creole and African American descent who cared for Bolden until they died and his sister, Elizabeth, took over his care. Bolden lived most of his life in the same house and never married. Between 1965 and 1970 he started making scarecrows to frighten birds away from the vegetable garden he kept in his yard, a practice that led him to hoarding objects scavenged from streets and alleyways: metal lids, pots, pans, tin cans, buckets, license plates, hoses, trays, chairs, clothing, and metal and carpet scraps among them.

Using string and wire, Bolden created from these found objects assemblages and sculptures representing human forms and faces. He used handmade tools to drill holes in them for eyes or mouths and used various fabrics and materials for tongues, ears, and hair. Bolden's works offer an engaging fusion of industrial materials with a raw tribal sensibility, and while most tend toward the figurative, many are skillfully abstracted. "His 'studio' is unique among artists' studios," writes the art dealer, collector, and advocate of self-taught southern artists William Arnett. "Bolden collects his materials and tosses them into the dark, damp crawl space beneath his house. To retrieve them for use when he is inspired to create, he walks, stooped, on all fours, his right hand reaching—swinging—along the dirt floor, until he grasps the components that he requires. He then hammers, cuts, twists, attaches, and bends materials into his scarecrows."

In time, Bolden's finished pieces filled his backyard, creating an installation in progress that attracted the attention of many onlookers, including Arnett as well as Michael Galbreth, from the cooperative art duo "The Art Guys," who recalled in an interview for Intuitive Eye, "[A]t the time I was seeing Rauschenberg and I saw the same kind of gestures, the same use of materials, picking up the world and rearranging it . . . [Bolden] was engaging the world, figuring it out in a direct physical way. There is also the aspect of a frayed tether to Africa and African artistic traditions associated with protective totems. I recognized in Hawkins a direct link to that, his ancestral place."

Bolden has been part of numerous gallery and museum exhibitions, including *Passionate Visions of the American South* at the New Orleans Museum of Art (1993), *Souls Grown Deep: African American Vernacular Art of the South* at Emory University's Michael C. Carlos Museum in Atlanta (1996), and *Parallel Unknown* at Hirschl & Adler Modern in New York (2017). His work is in the collections of the Smithsonian American Art Museum (Washington D.C.), the Kohler Arts Center (Sheboygan, Wisconsin), the American Visionary Art Museum (Baltimore), the Ackland Art Museum (Chapel Hill, North Carolina), and the Souls Grown Deep Foundation (Atlanta).

Hawkins Bolden, *Scarecrow (Large Gas Can)*, c. 1980–85. Found object assemblage, 14 × 9 × 4 in. (35.6 × 22.9 × 10.2 cm)

Hawkins Bolden, *Scarecrow (Yellow Disc with Blue Ears and Tongue)*, c. 1980–84. Found object assemblage, 11 × 11 × 2 in. (27.9 × 27.9 × 5.1 cm)

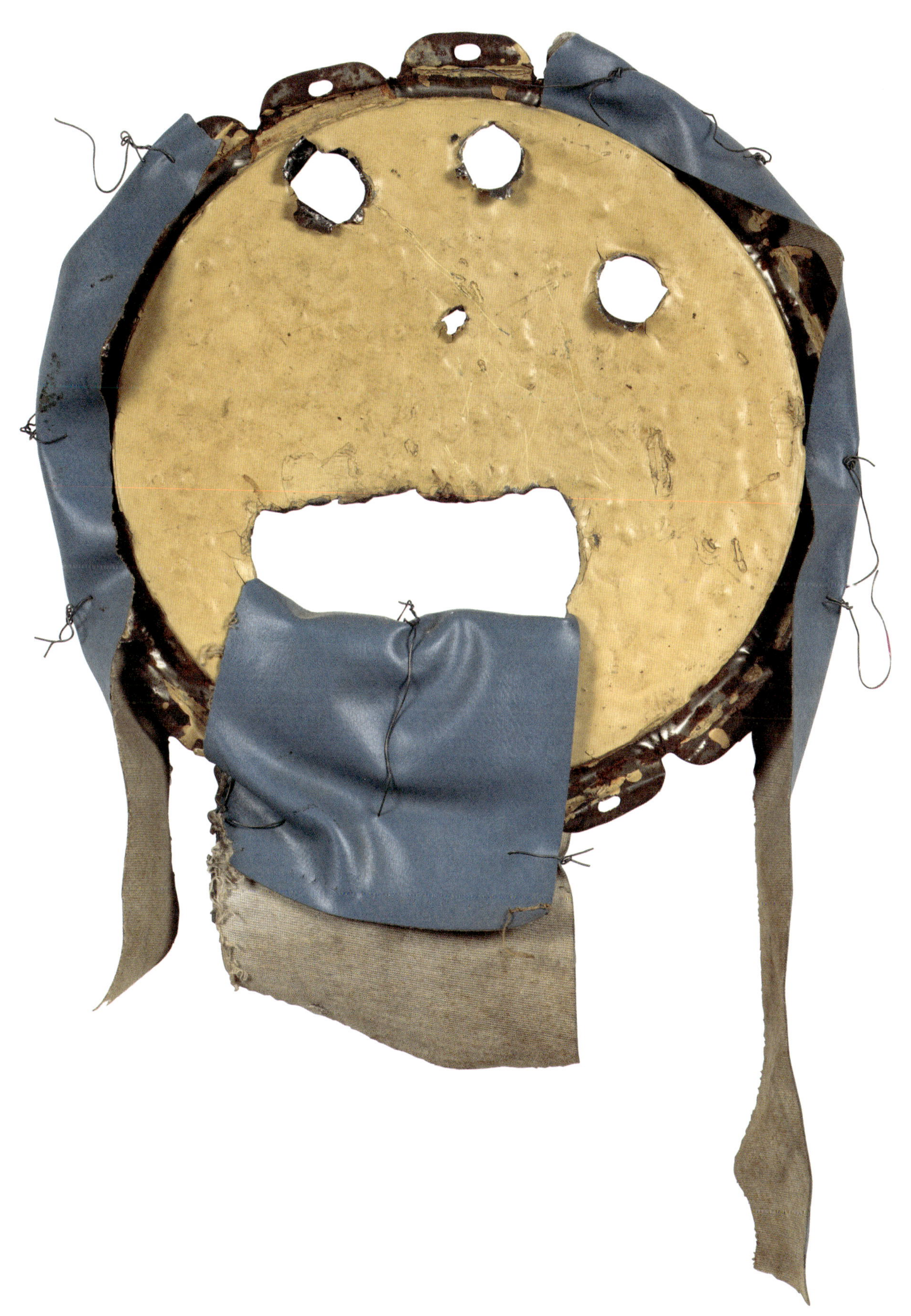

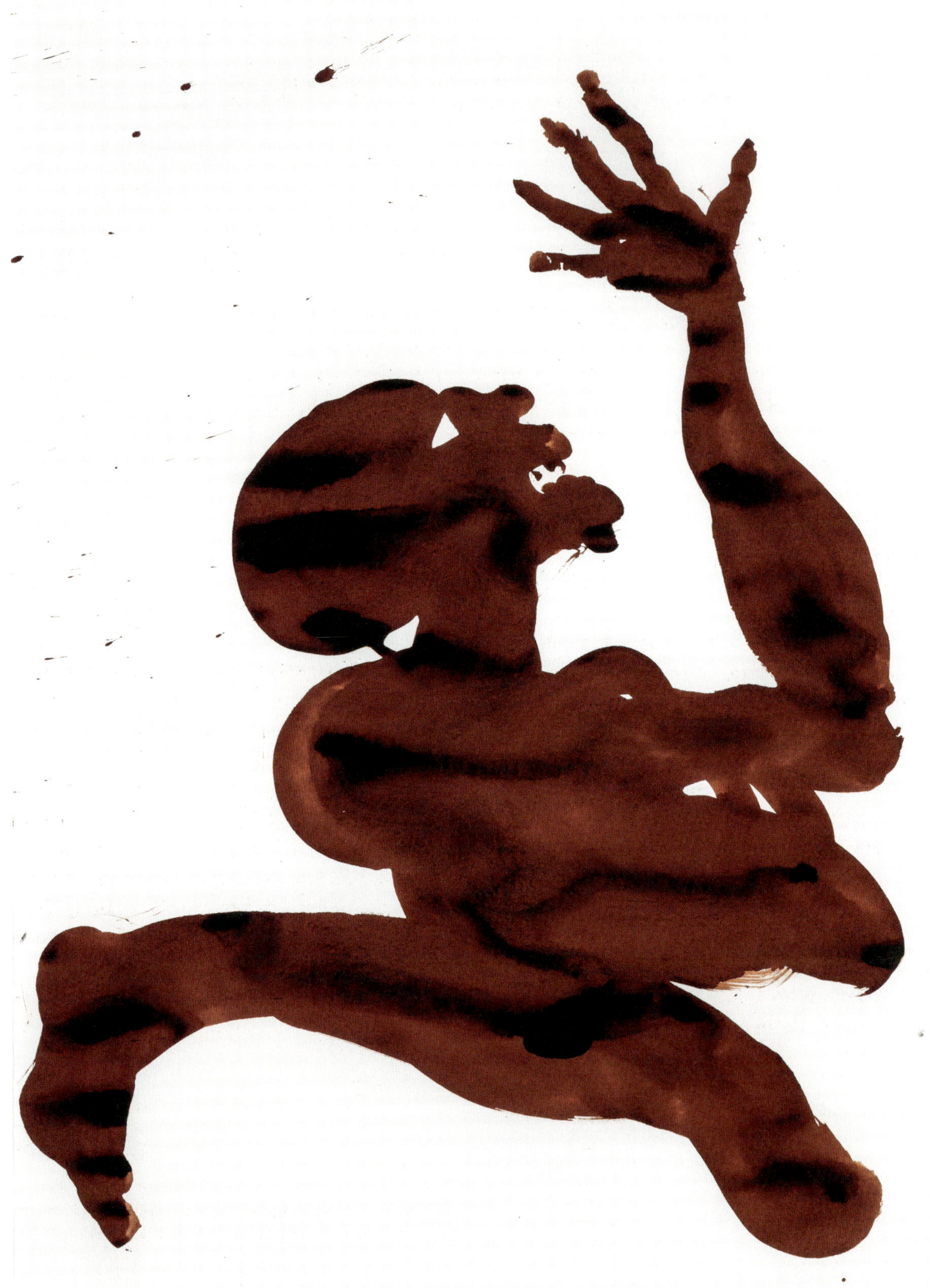

MARCOS BONTEMPO

b. 1969

In the mid-1970s, following the Argentine coup d'état that would drive the country into an era of neo-fascist military dictatorship, Marcos Bontempo migrated permanently with his family from his native Córdoba, Argentina, to Ronda, Spain. Bontempo's strict Catholic upbringing and profoundly rooted notions of guilt conceivably form the underpinnings of his psychotic episodes and his restless devotion to art. A kind of modern-day Romantic, he is so vitally connected with his work one might dare visualize his mind being composed not merely of neurotransmitters and electrical synapses but his very working materials: ink, acrylic paint, oxidized iron, and shimmering salt. His days and nights revolve around his studio, the nucleus that connects him to the world and to himself.

When nighttime obscures the striking Ronda backdrop, Bontempo brings to life the compelling iconography for which he is best known. With a supreme economy of means, he creates dynamic sites that host an array of humanoids, animals, hybrid and amorphous beings or their parts, and mythological beasts that invoke complex psychological moods. Bontempo has a sophisticated, virtually musical grasp of forms moving through negative space; his individual works can be seen as self-contained dimensions that are also part of a master symphony Dionysian at heart as his individuality morphs into the pathos and ecstasy of his visions.

Crouching, Bontempo paints on the floor and has always preferred paper over the stiffness of canvas, befitting the spontaneity and gestural swiftness of his process. His command of lyrical brushwork and color, at times bold and free flowing, at others, exacting, and his use of visual and tactile texture conjure figuration as seamlessly as they break it. Shapes and figures are poised in an expressive stillness, warping and stretching, falling and floating, skipping or swaying in distress, yet at the same time, it's all purely abstract matter. His larger works employ an expressionistic technique: unexpected negative spaces appear between vigorous strokes. His smaller works are populated by creatures that seem stencil cut from lacelike constellations or mineral formations enclosed by delicate flourishes and quiet bursts of color. Bontempo's preoccupation with shape and corporeality vis-à-vis the intangible and spiritual spheres of experience creates a hypnotic tension that carries throughout the entire opus. Bontempo's work is held in private and museum collections in the United States and Europe.

Text excerpted and adapted from Alejandra Russi, "Marcos Bontempo: Light and Dark," www.riccomaresca.com.

Marcos Bontempo, *Untitled (Man with raised hand)*, 2012. Ink and salt on paper, 39½ × 27½ in. (100.3 × 69.9 cm)

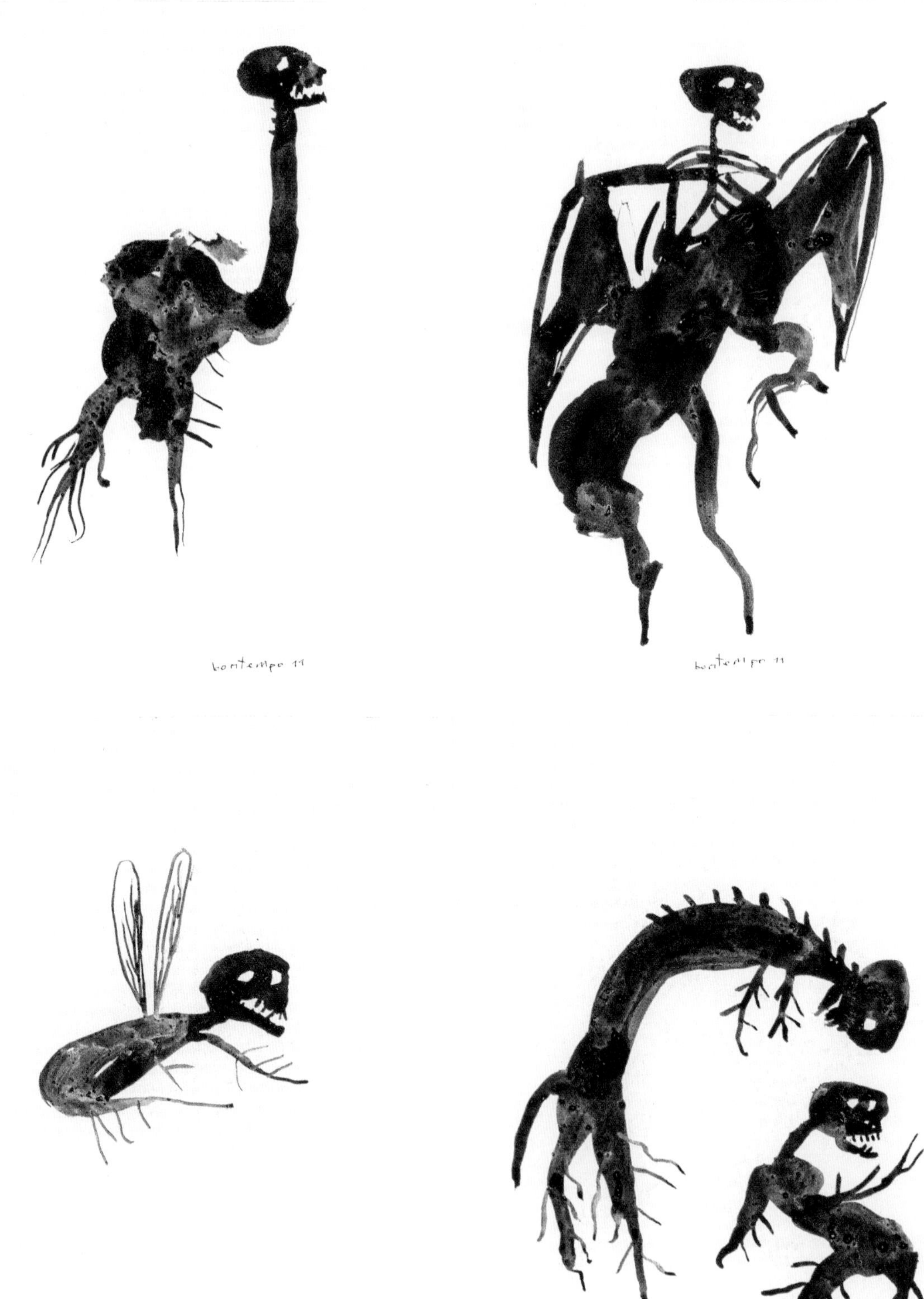

Marcos Bontempo, *Untitled #1–8*, 2011. Ink and salt on paper, 11½ × 8 in. (29.2 × 20.3 cm) each

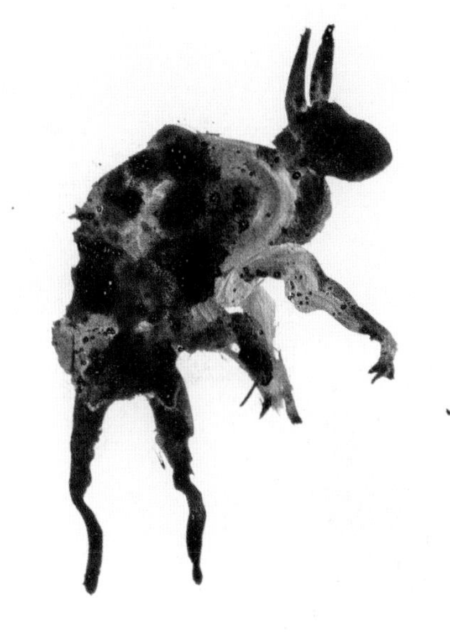
bontempo 11

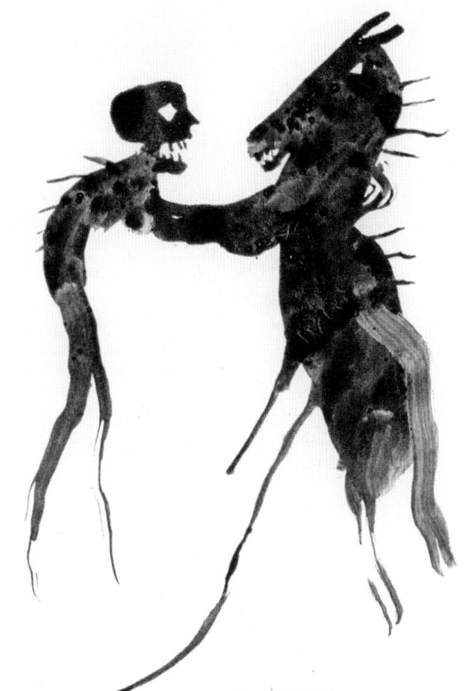
bontempo 11

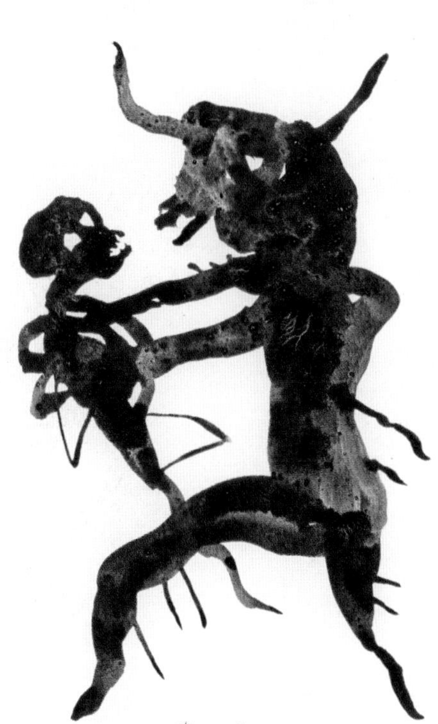
bontempo 11

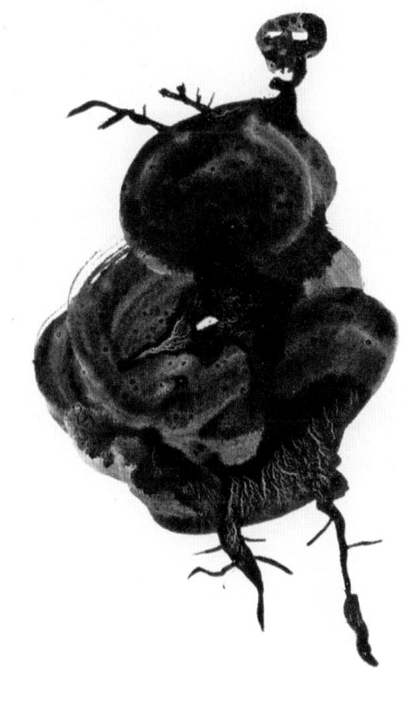
bontempo 11

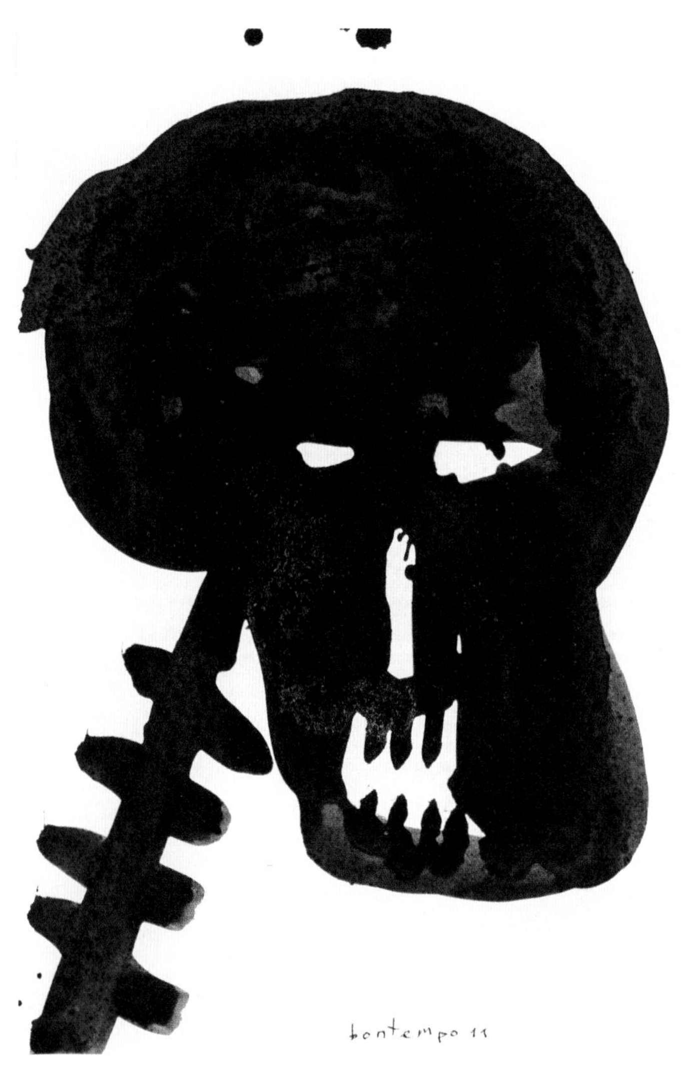

Marcos Bontempo, *Heads #1–12* (1 of 12), 2011. Ink and salt on paper, 11¾ × 8½ in. each (29.8 × 21.6 cm)

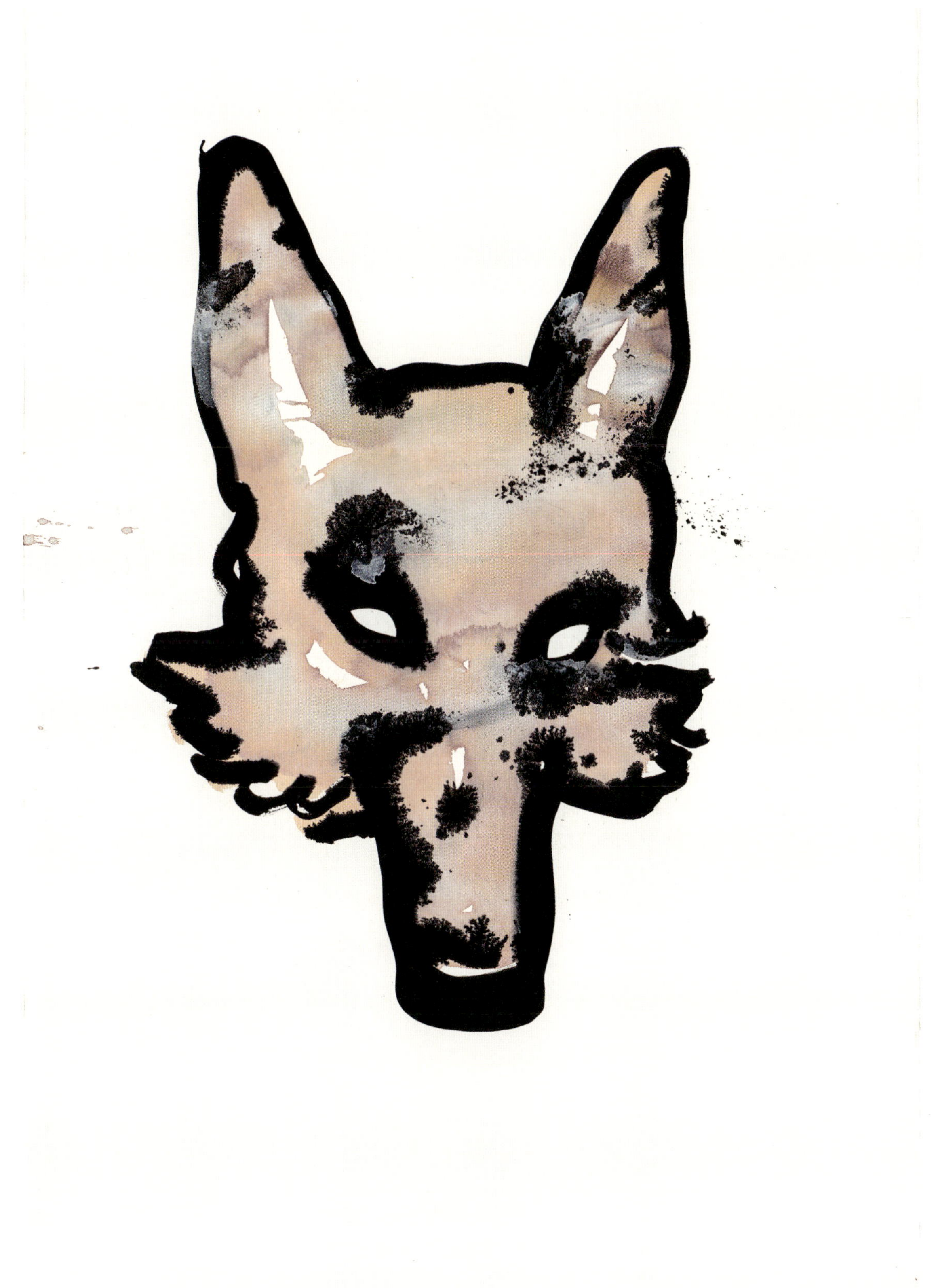

Marcos Bontempo, *Untitled (Fox)*, 2016. Ink and salt on paper, 48 × 32 in. (121.9 × 81.3 cm)

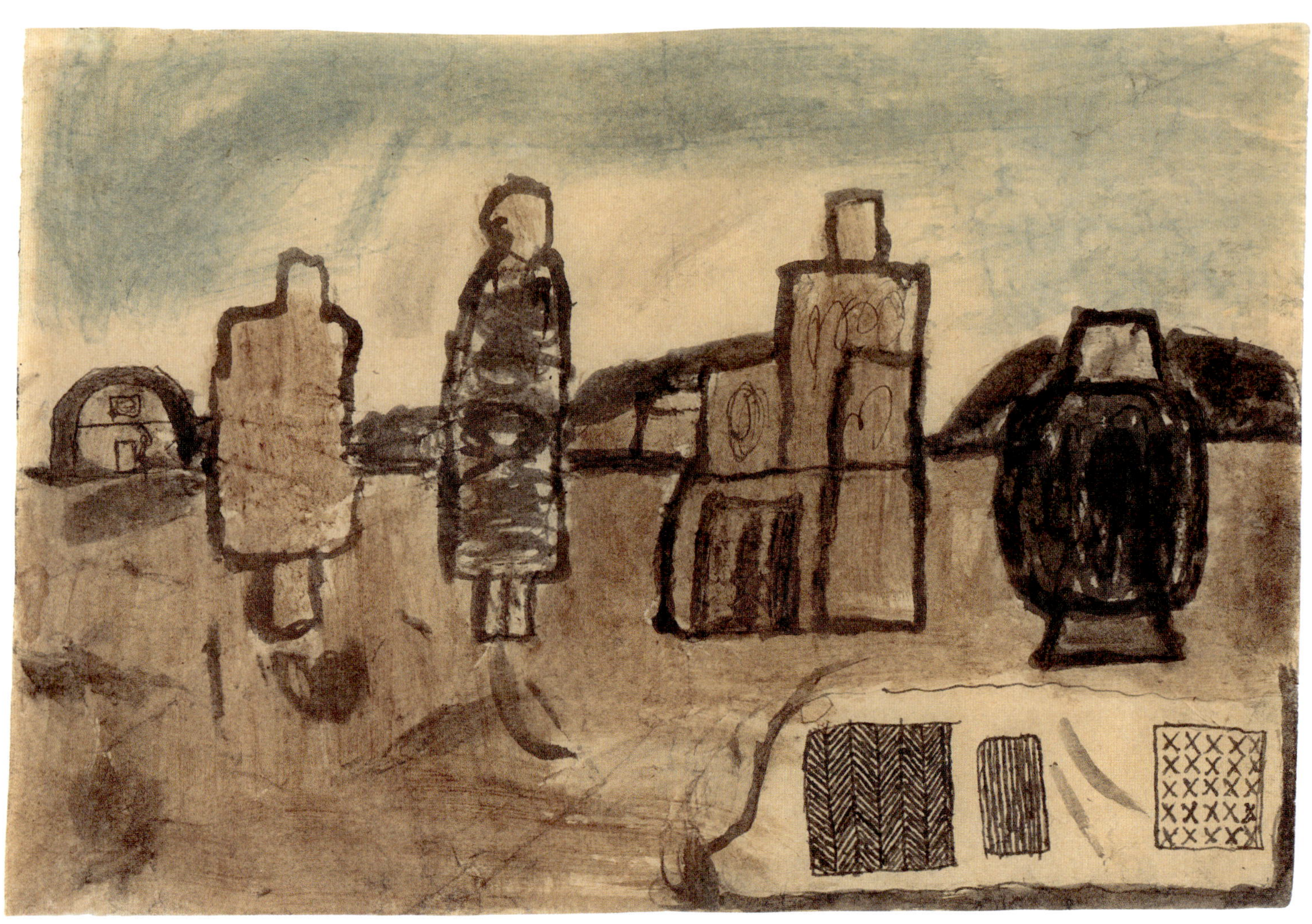

JAMES CASTLE

1899–1977

James Castle was born prematurely, and profoundly deaf, in the mountainous town of Garden Valley, Idaho. His mother was a midwife and his father a postmaster who ran the local post office and general store from the family's home. Perhaps owing to his disability, Castle, the fifth of seven children, did not attend school before the age of ten, but spent most of his time at home, drawing and crafting objects from a very young age. He attended the Idaho School for the Deaf and Blind in Gooding from 1910 to 1915, where he was taught an oral method of communication involving lip reading and voice training, though it is unclear to what extent he could read or write.

Castle devoted his long, secluded life to creating an immense opus that comprises drawings, paintings, assemblages, sculptural objects, text pieces, and artist's books. Although he knew little about the world beyond his narrowly circumscribed community and nothing about art history, today his work is regarded as parallel to vanguard art of the twentieth century. Castle worked entirely with found materials; his daily rummage of trash cans provided an abundant supply of discarded paper, printed media, and empty containers. He used soot that he gathered from a wood-burning stove and mixed with his own saliva as his main pigment, which he applied with matchsticks, fountain pen tips, and even apricot pits rather than brushes. He took endless inspiration from every corner of his quiet existence, sensitively rendering landscapes, buildings, interiors, animals, and people. A mix of impressionism, realism, and abstracted figuration marks his signature style of rendering with smudged atmospheric textures, architectural lines and patterns, and schematic totemic figures in imagery that is at once serene and imbued with a profound sense of mystery.

As an obsessive chronicler, Castle was captivated by the written word—surely for its graphic qualities, but likely also because its denotation remained inscrutable to him in a way that images were not. In illustrating seemingly every aspect of his immediate surroundings and reality, even those he could not fully grasp, Castle opened many windows into his mind and into his evolution as an artist. In her essay on Castle in the book *The Hidden Art*, Lynne Cooke described Castle's method: "From his memories and the trove of printed material he amassed, he created a recursive relationship between his real and imaginary worlds that not only sustained his work over decades, but became the basis for a sophisticated understanding of the concept of artistic identity and the practice of artmaking."

In the 1950s Castle's work was introduced to the art world through the efforts of his nephew Bob Beach. Castle's first solo museum exhibition was held in 1963 at the Boise Art Museum (which today has the largest collection of works by the artist in any museum) and his work has continued to be extensively exhibited. In 2008, the Philadelphia Museum of Art mounted *James Castle: A Retrospective*, which toured nationally. In 2011 the Museo Nacional Centro de Arte Reina Sofía in Madrid organized a major exhibition of Castle's work titled *Mostrar y almacenar* (Show

James Castle, *Untitled (Landscape with Building and Figures)*, n.d. Soot on found paper, 10⅞ × 15¾ in. (27.6 × 40 cm)

and Store). In 2013 his work was included in the Venice Biennale's centerpiece exhibition *The Encyclopedic Palace*, and in 2017 the Whitney Museum of American Art in New York included Castle in the exhibition *Where We Are*. Most recently, in 2018, his work was featured in *Outliers and American Vanguard Art*, a traveling exhibition organized by the National Gallery of Art in Washington, D.C. Castle's work is in the collections of the Museum of Modern Art in New York, the Whitney Museum of American Art, the New York Public Library, the American Folk Art Museum (New York), the Berkeley Art Museum, the Boise Art Museum, Intuit: The Center for Intuitive and Outsider Art, the Art Institute of Chicago, the High Museum of Art (Atlanta), the Philadelphia Museum of Art, the Tacoma Art Museum, and the Milwaukee Art Museum.

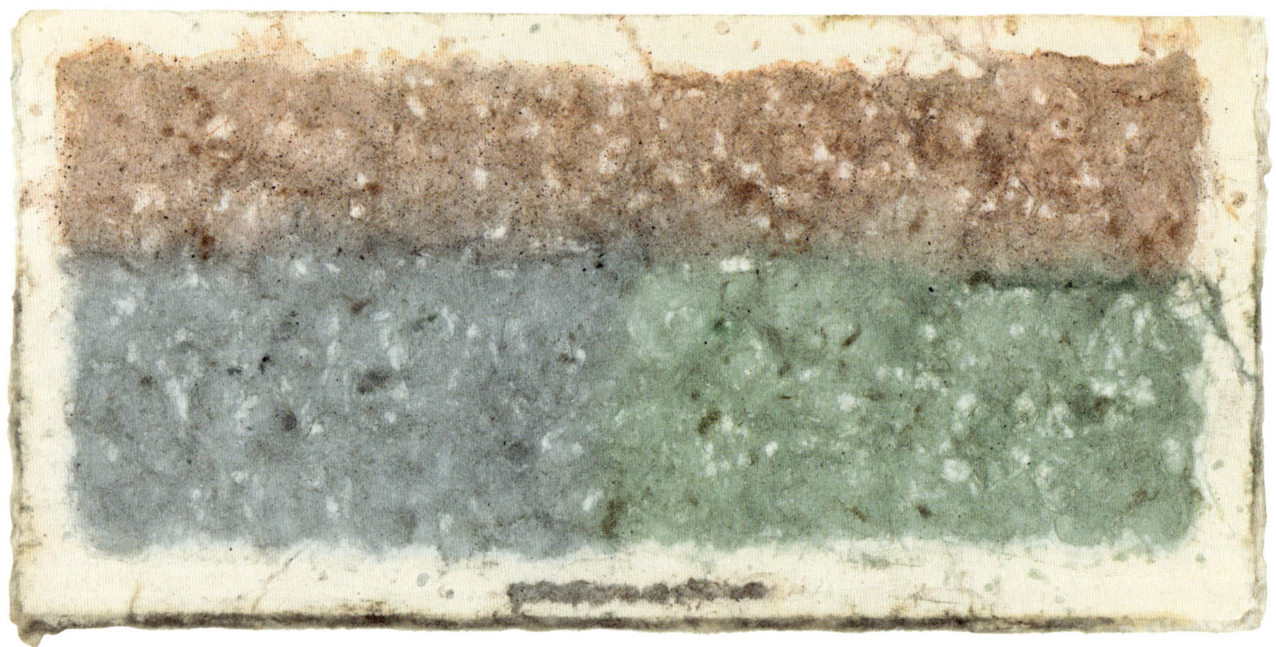

James Castle, *Untitled (Colored Abstraction)*, n.d. Found paper, colored pulp, 3⅞ × 6¾ in. (9.8 × 17.1 cm)

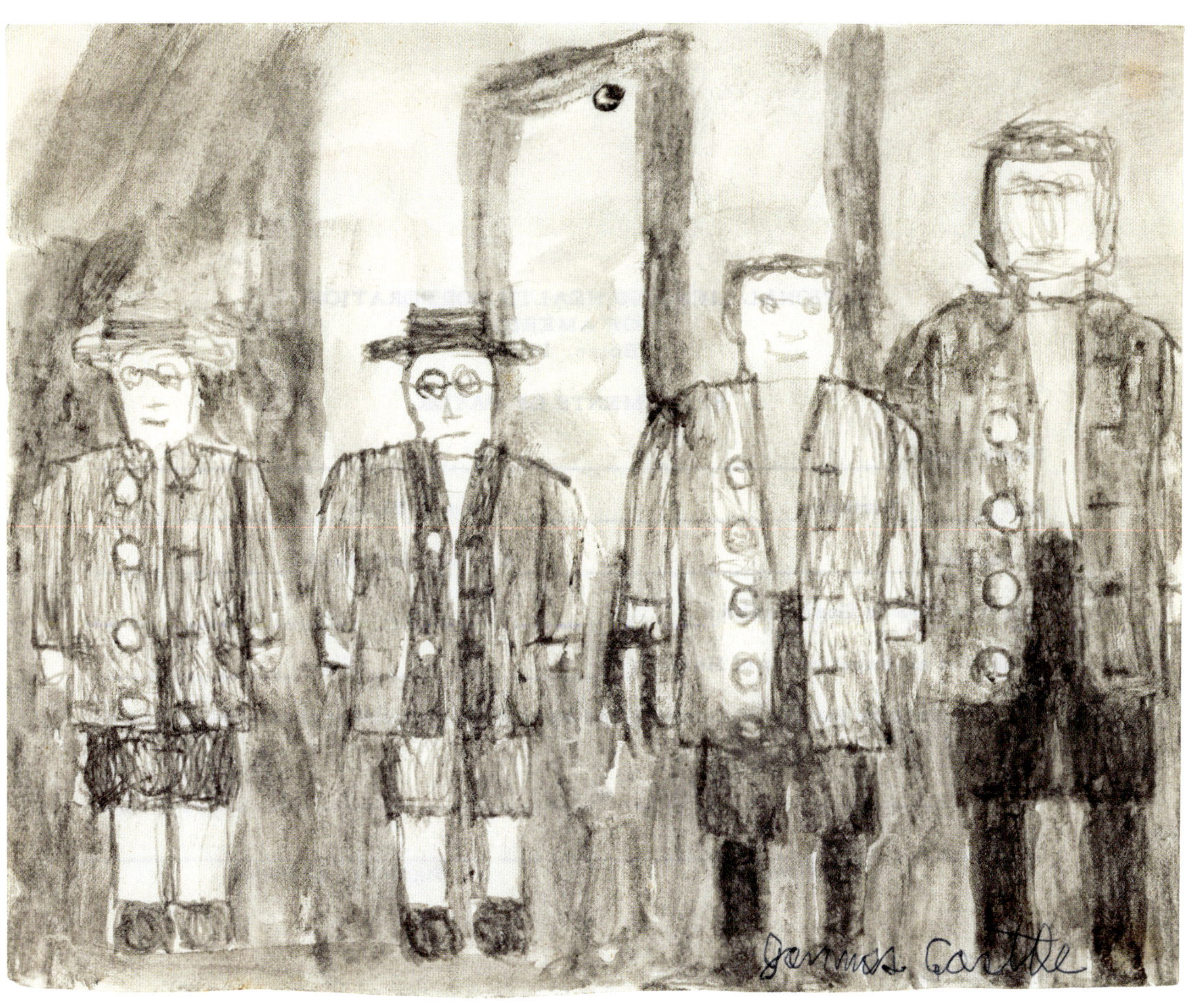

James Castle, *Castle Family*, n.d. Graphite and soot on paper, 7 × 8½ in. (17.8 × 21.6 cm)

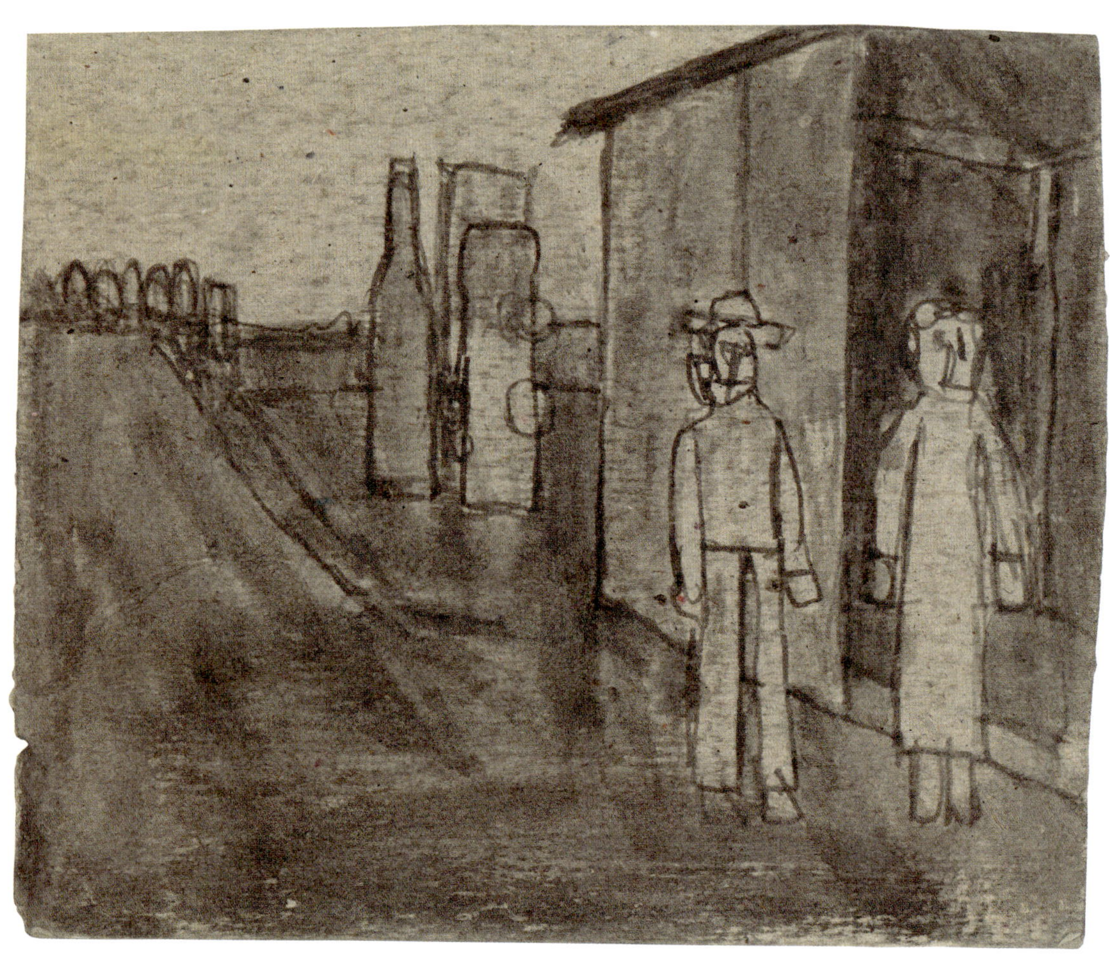

James Castle, *Untitled (Friends)*, n.d. Crayon on found paper, 8 × 10½ in. (20.3 × 26.7 cm)

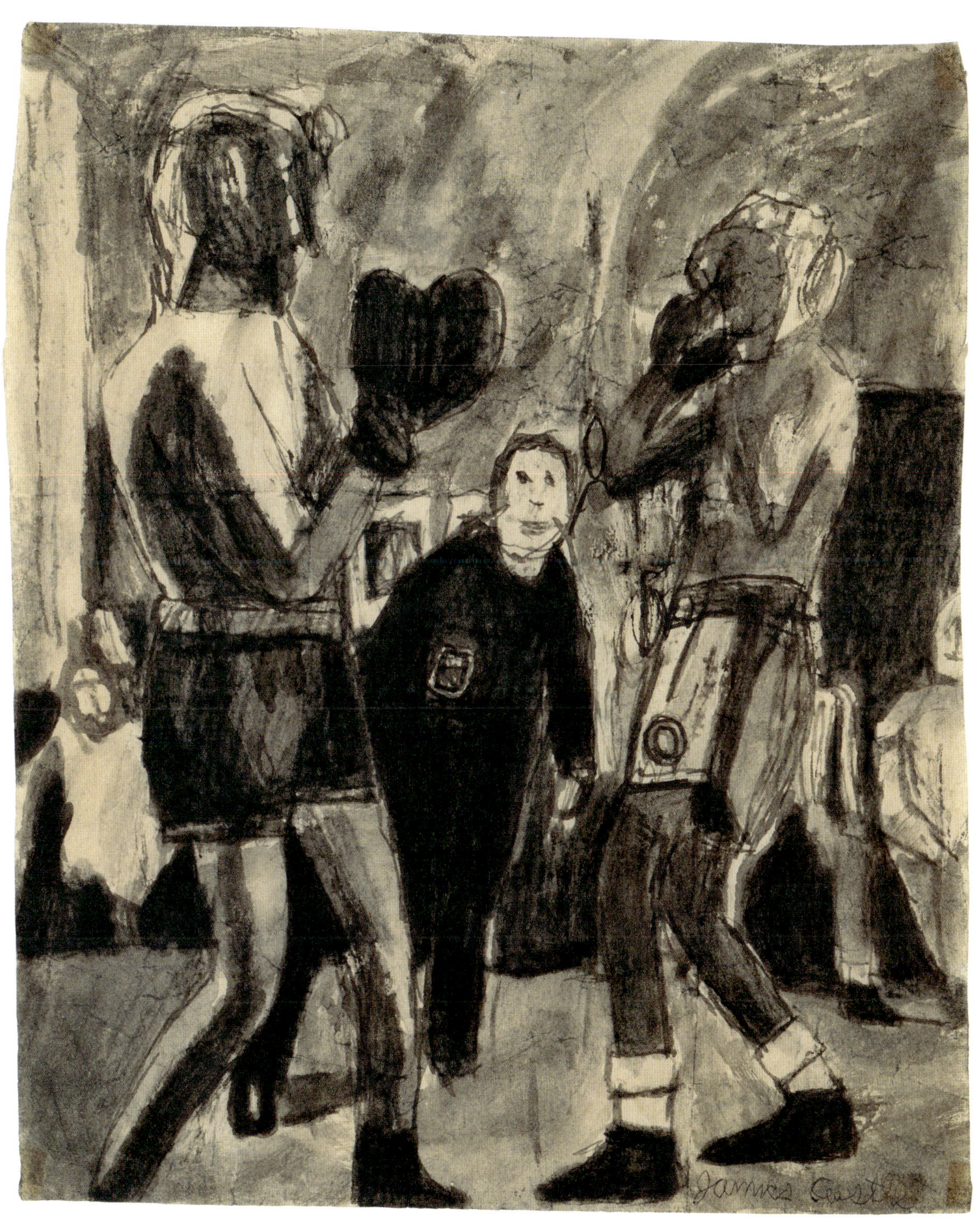

James Castle, *Untitled (Boxing Match)*, c. 1955–65. Soot and saliva on found paper, 13¼ × 10¾ in. (33.7 × 27.3 cm)

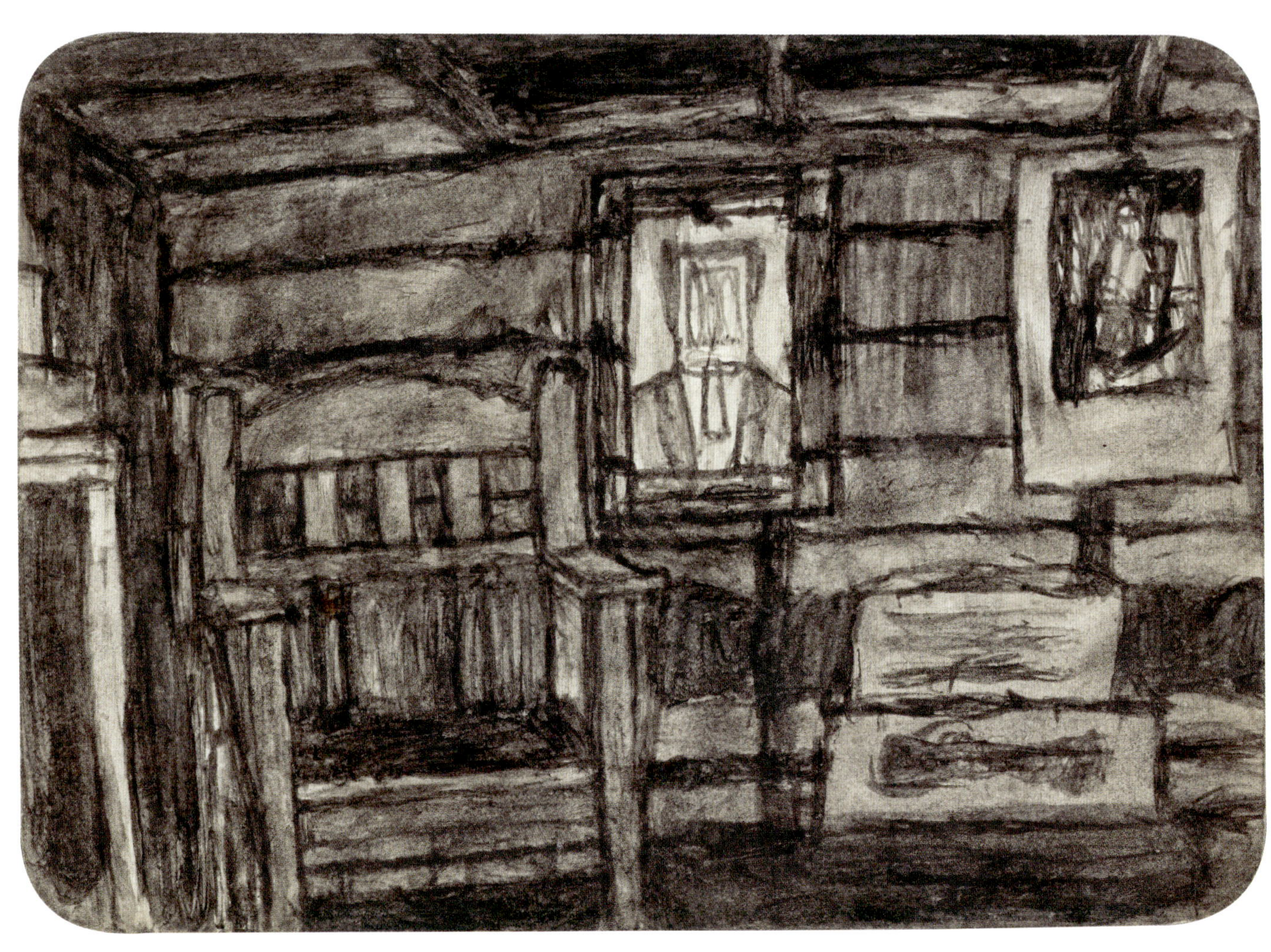

ABOVE AND OPPOSITE: James Castle, *Interior Views* (two-sided drawing), n.d. Soot and saliva on found paper, 6½ × 9 in. (16.5 × 22.9 cm)

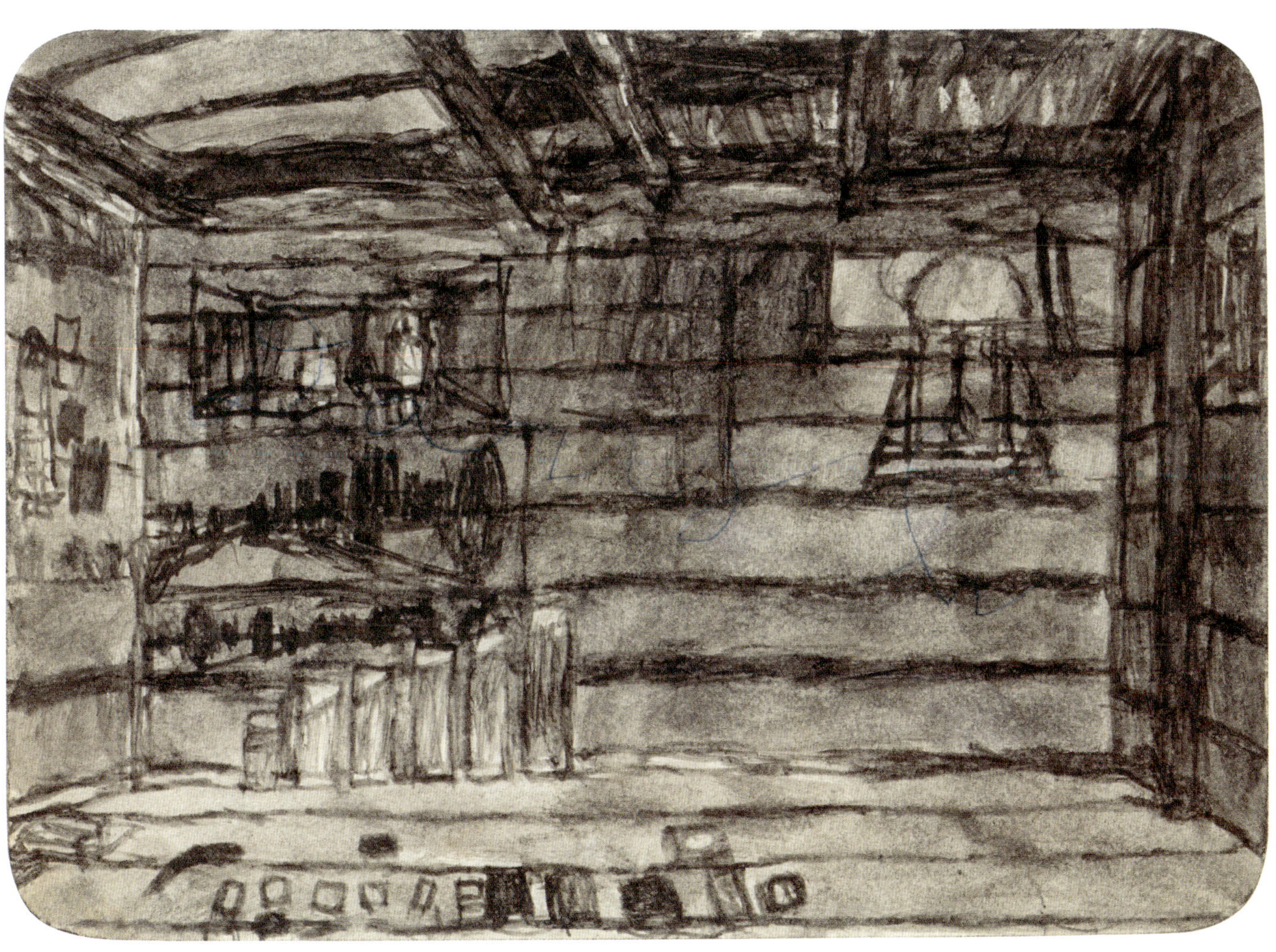

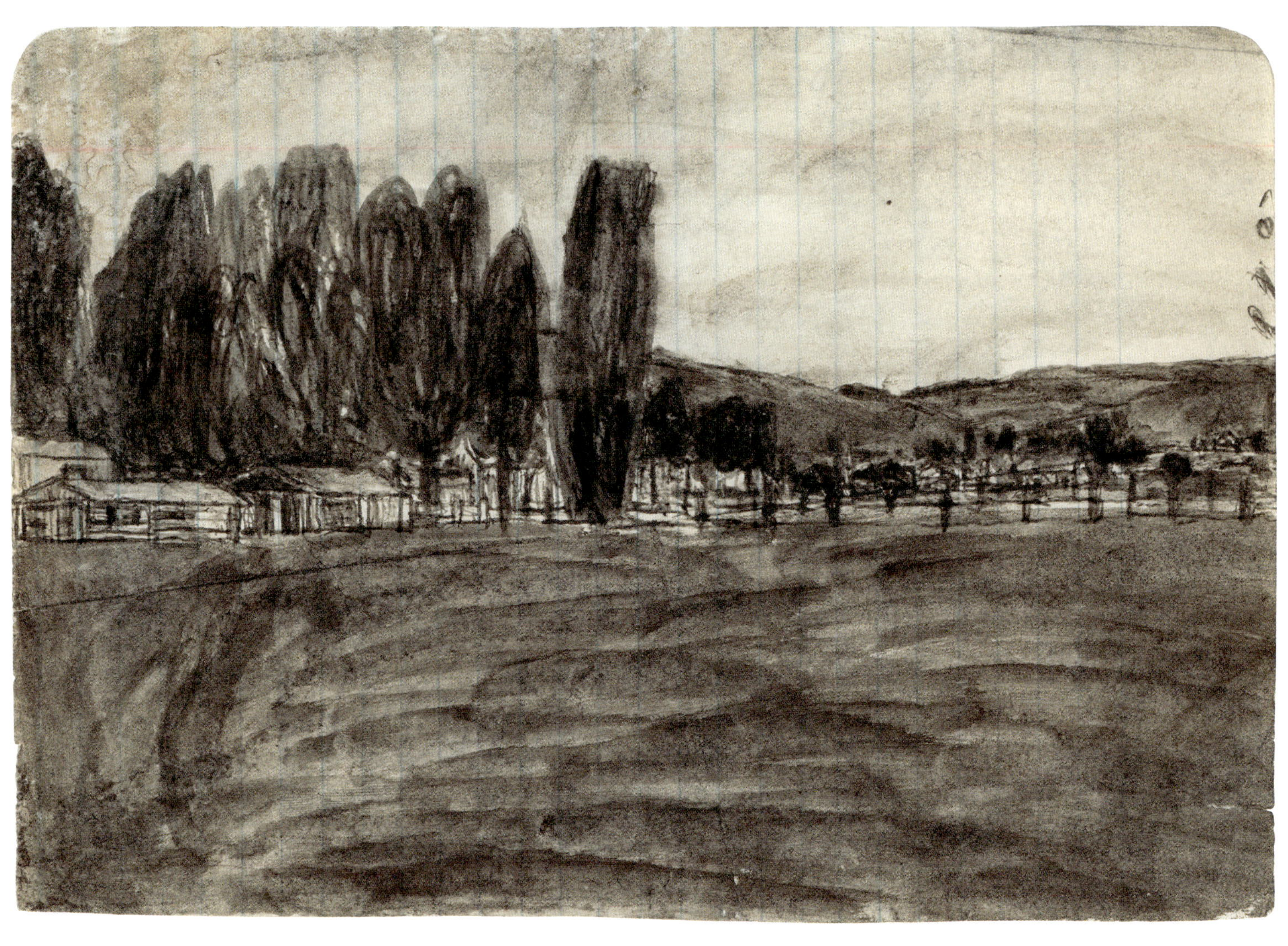

James Castle, *Untitled (Landscape Panorama)*, n.d. Soot and saliva on found paper, one of twelve drawings, 8½ × 11 in. (21.6 × 27.9 cm) each

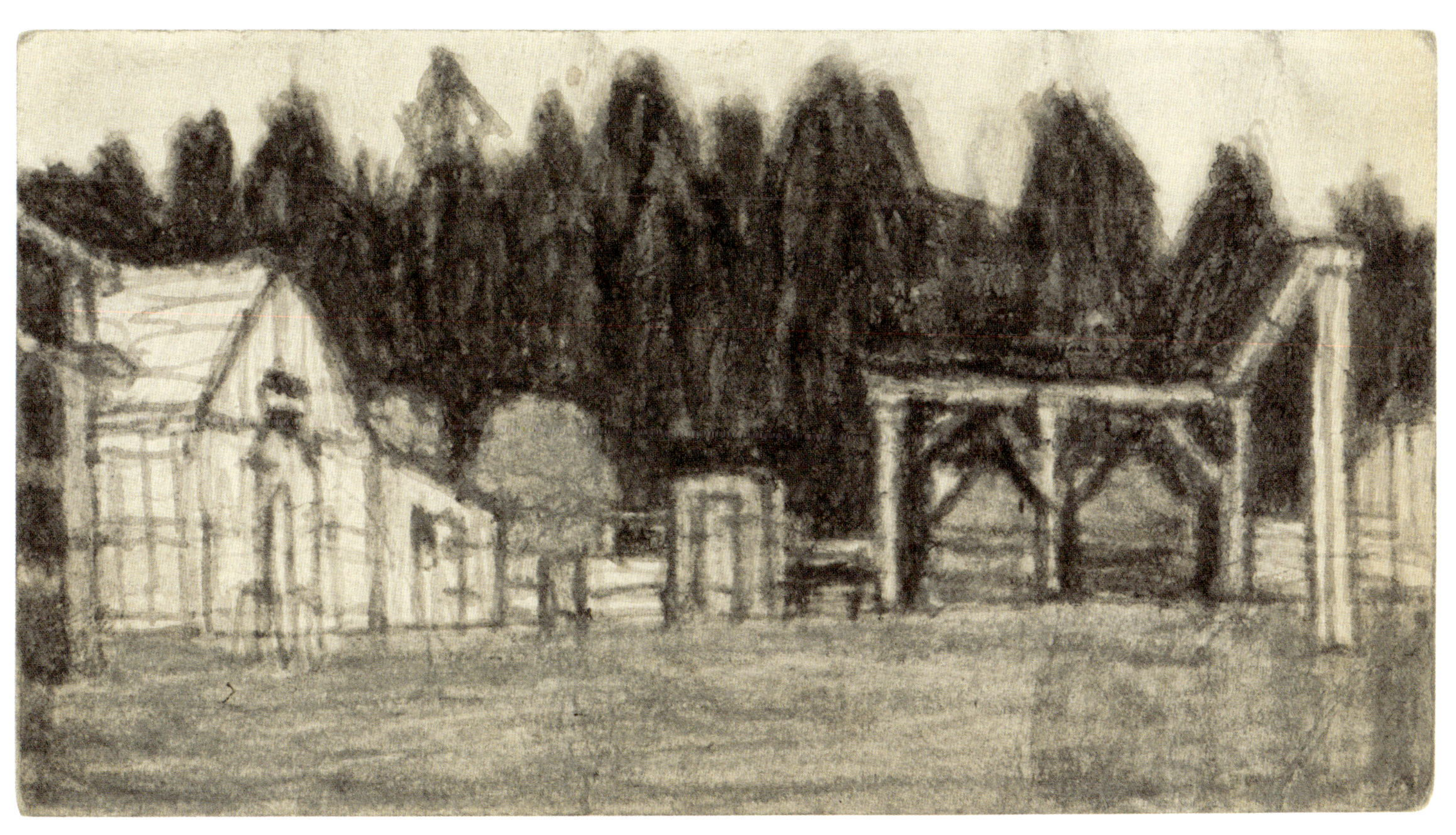

James Castle, *Untitled (Landscape Panorama)*, n.d. Soot and saliva on found paper, one of twelve drawings, 8½ × 11 in. (21.6 × 27.9 cm) each

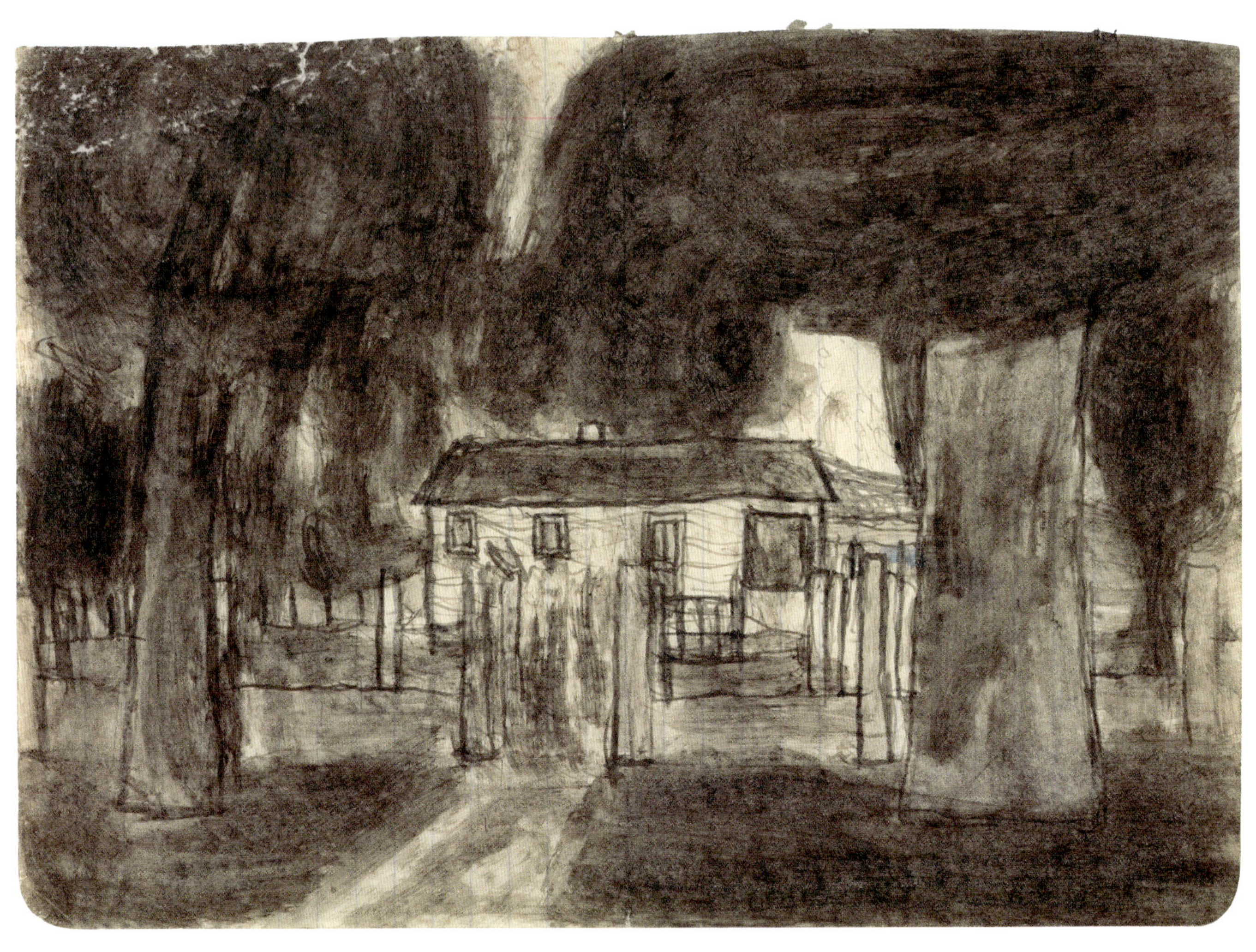

ABOVE AND OPPOSITE: James Castle, *Untitled (Barn Interior and Landscape)* (two-sided drawing), n.d. Soot and saliva on found paper, 6 × 6½ in. (15.2 × 16.5 cm)

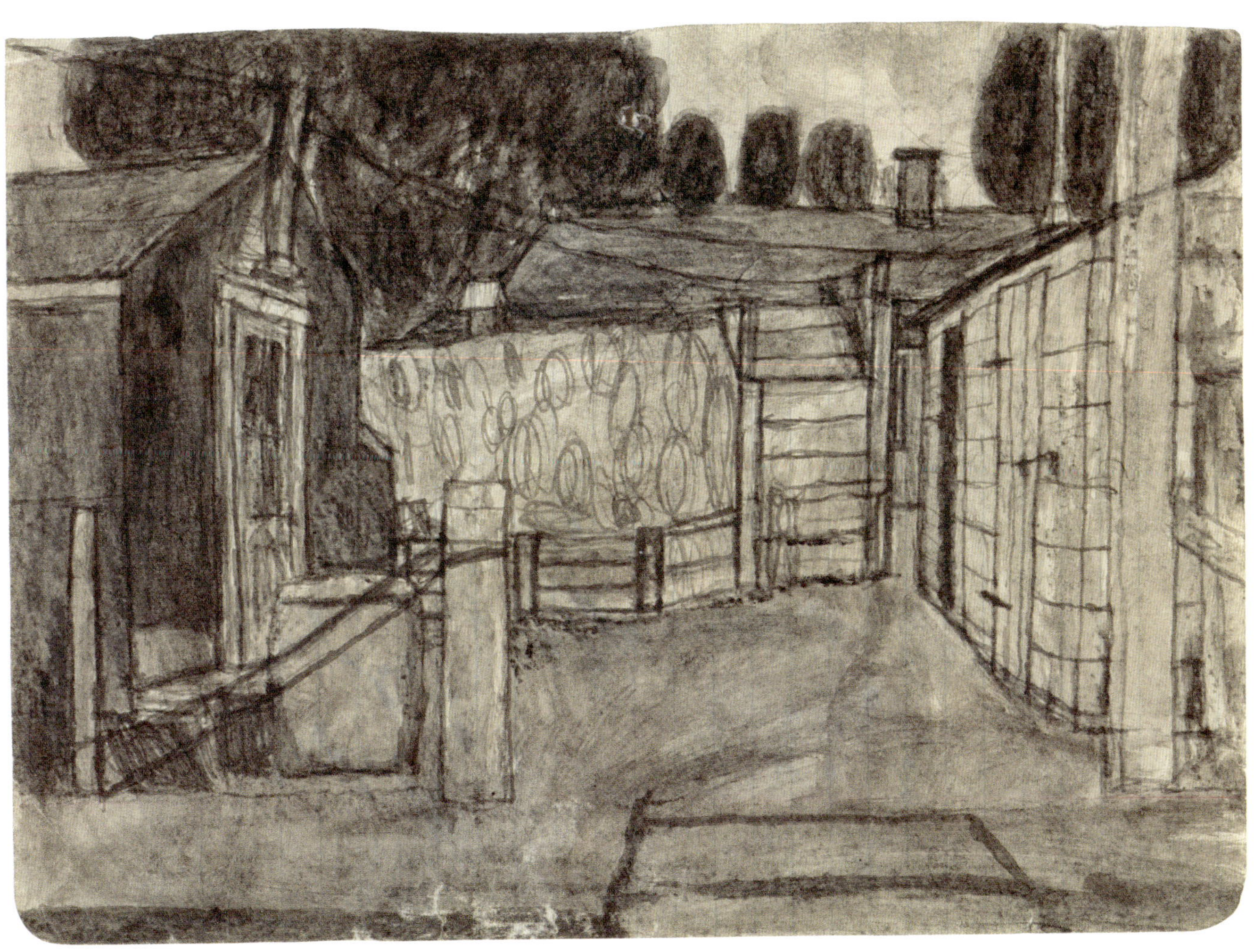

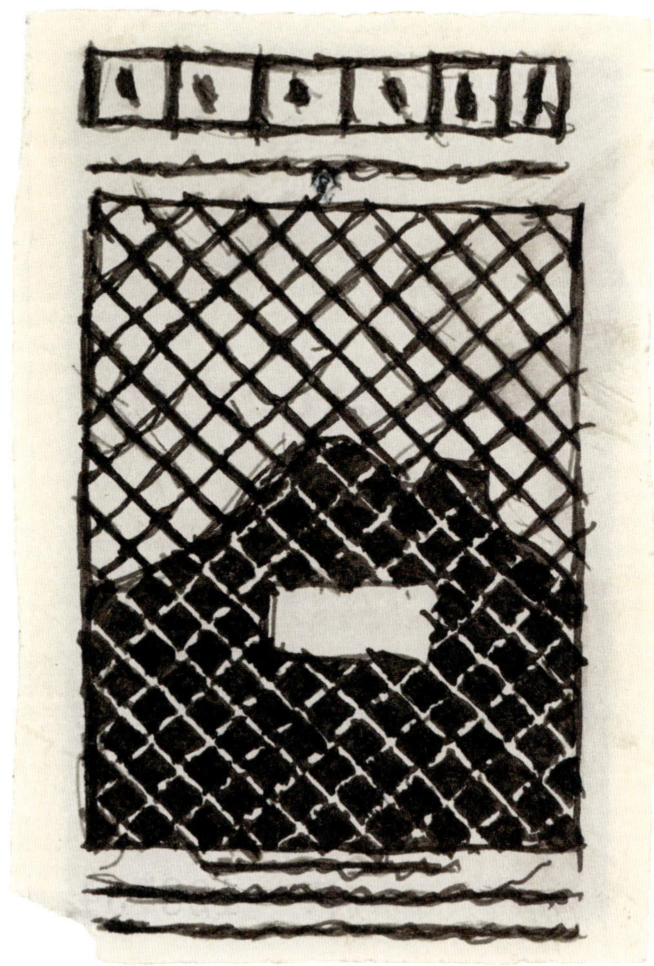

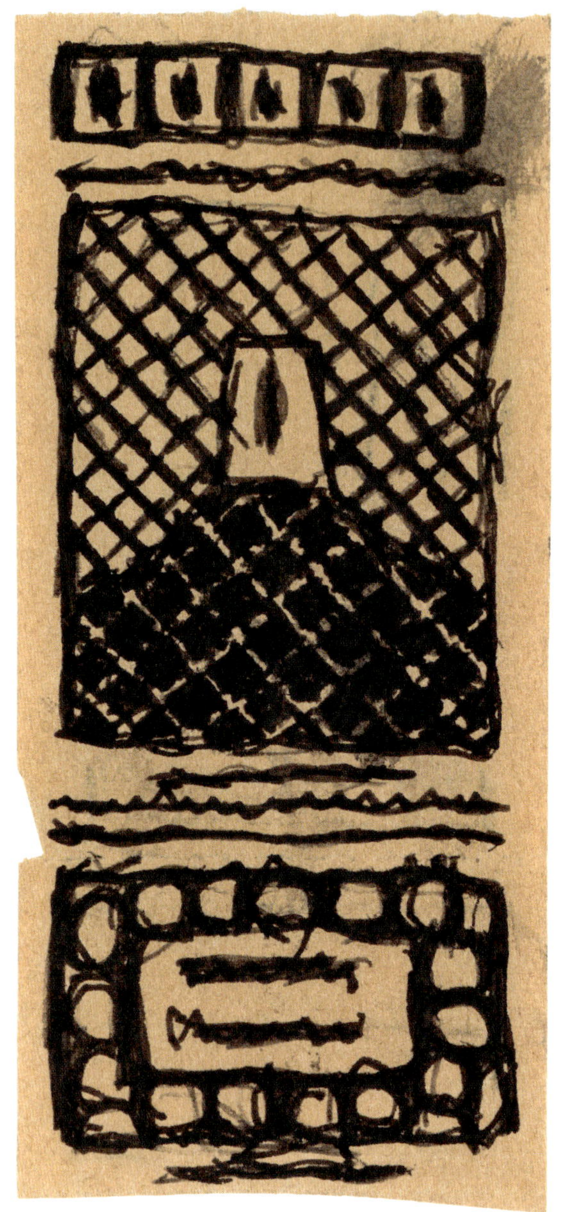

James Castle, *Untitled Patterned Landscape*, n.d. Soot and saliva on "Crusade for Freedom" card, 4½ × 3 in. (11.4 × 7.6 cm)

James Castle, *Untitled* (*Block Patterns*), n.d. Soot and saliva on Sears Roebuck receipt, 4⅞ × 2¼ in. (12.4 × 5.7 cm)

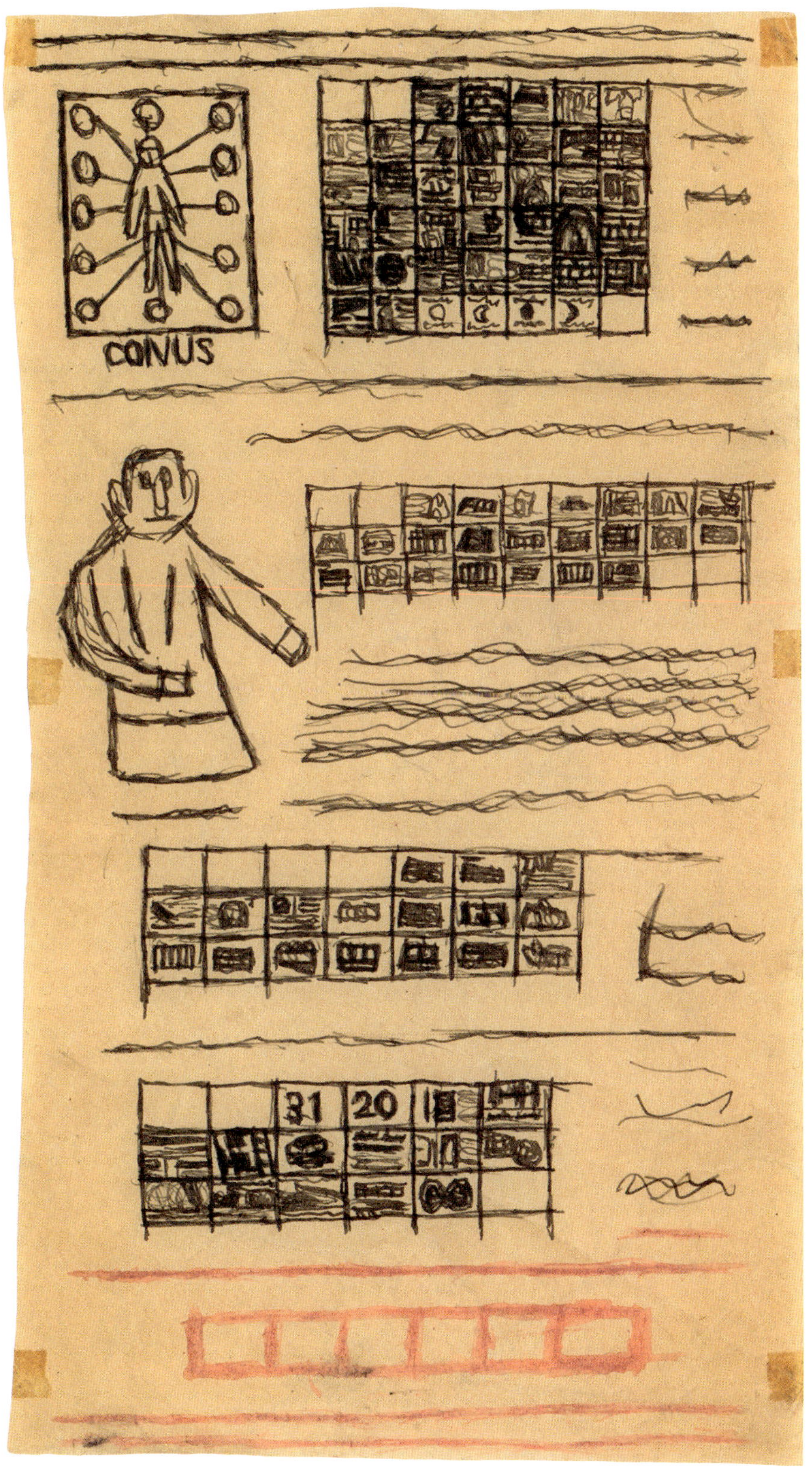

James Castle, *Untitled (Text and Symbols with Pink Bottom)*, n.d. Soot, saliva, and colored pencil on found paper, 15¼ × 8¼ in. (38.7 × 21 cm)

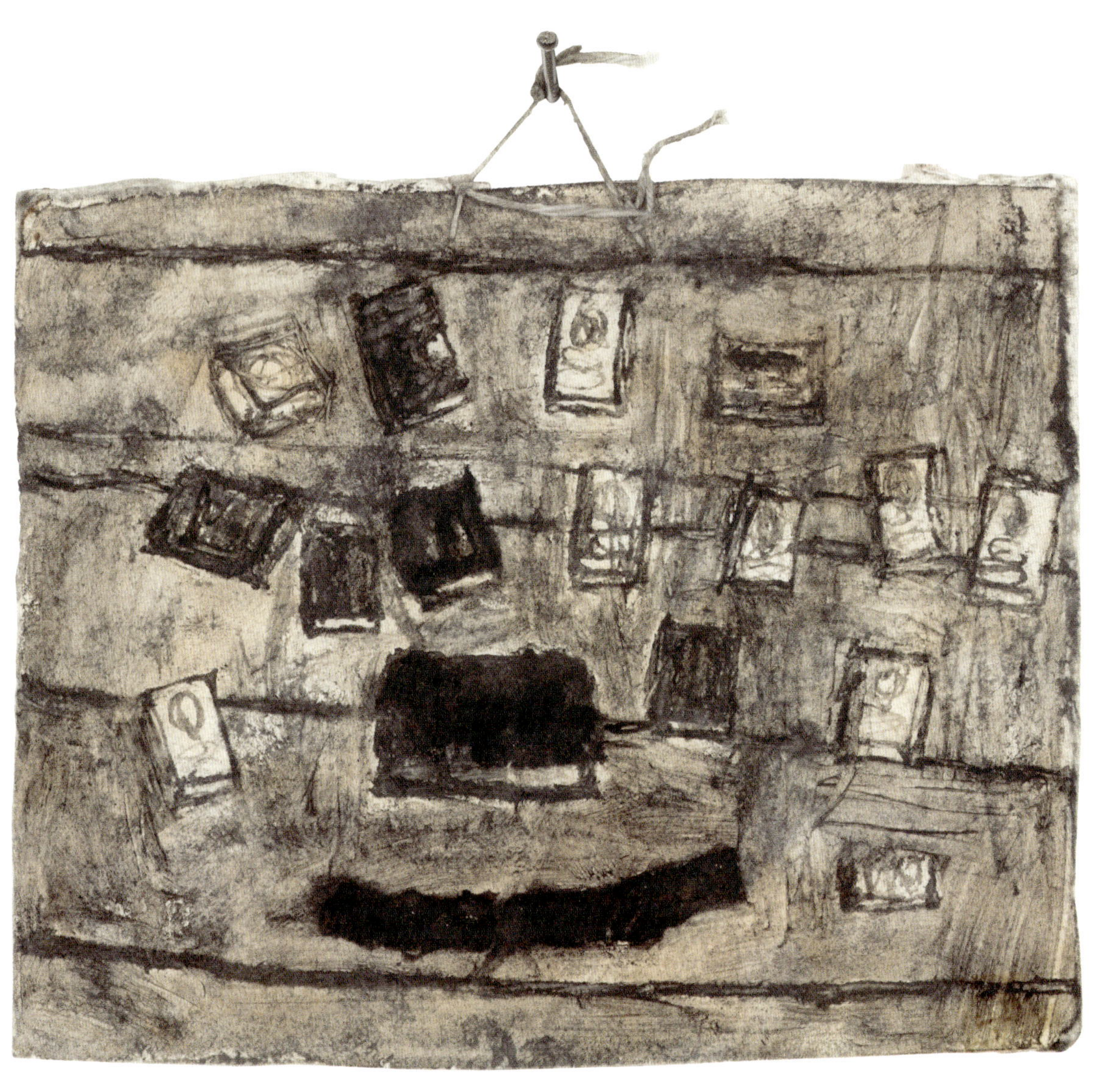

James Castle, *Untitled (Books Displayed Along a Wall)*, n.d. String, soot, and spit on flattened "Arden Ice Cream" carton, 4½ × 5½ in. (11.4 × 14 cm)

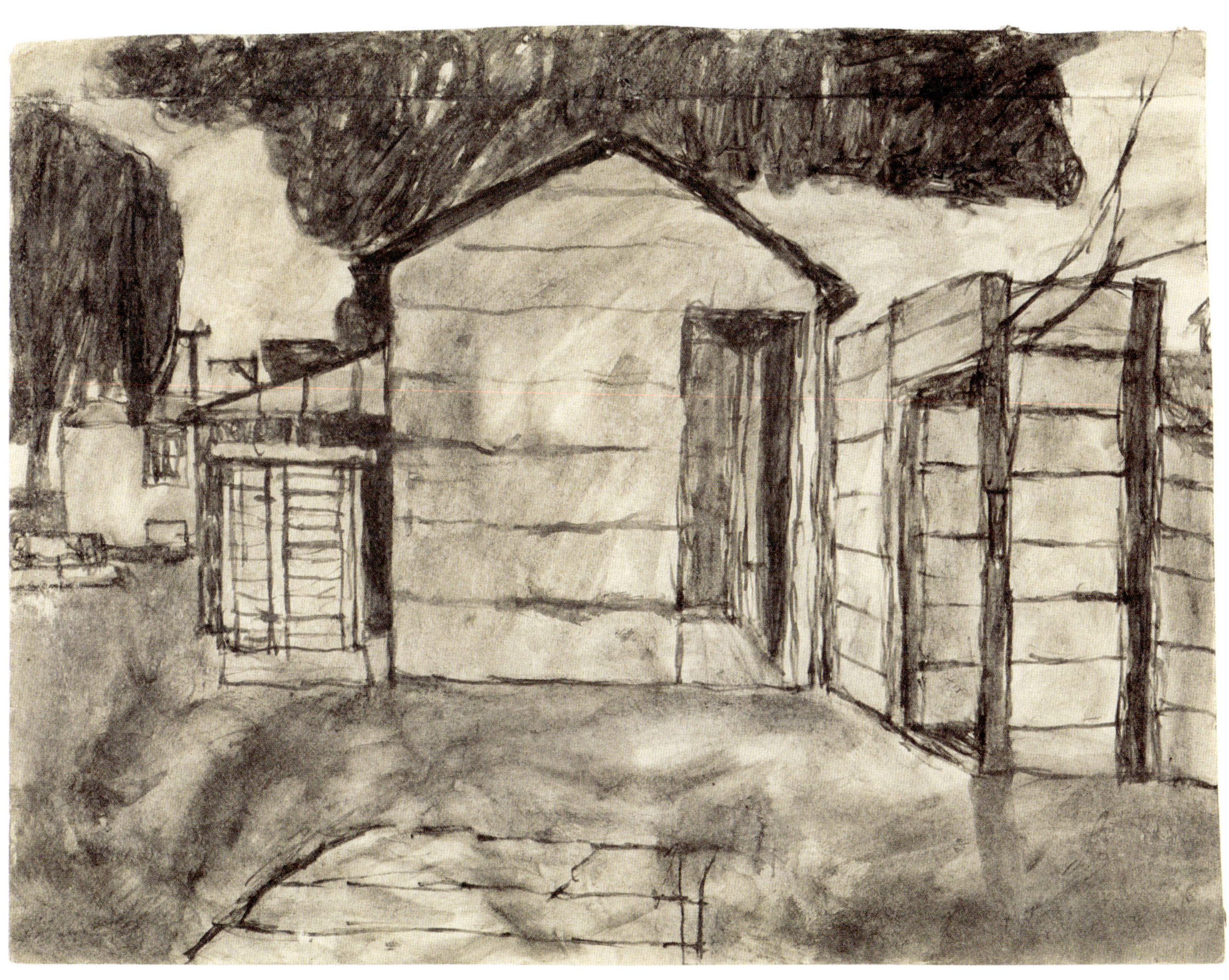

James Castle, *Untitled (Shed and Fence)*, n.d. Soot and saliva on found paper, 10 × 12¾ in. (25.4 × 32.4 cm)

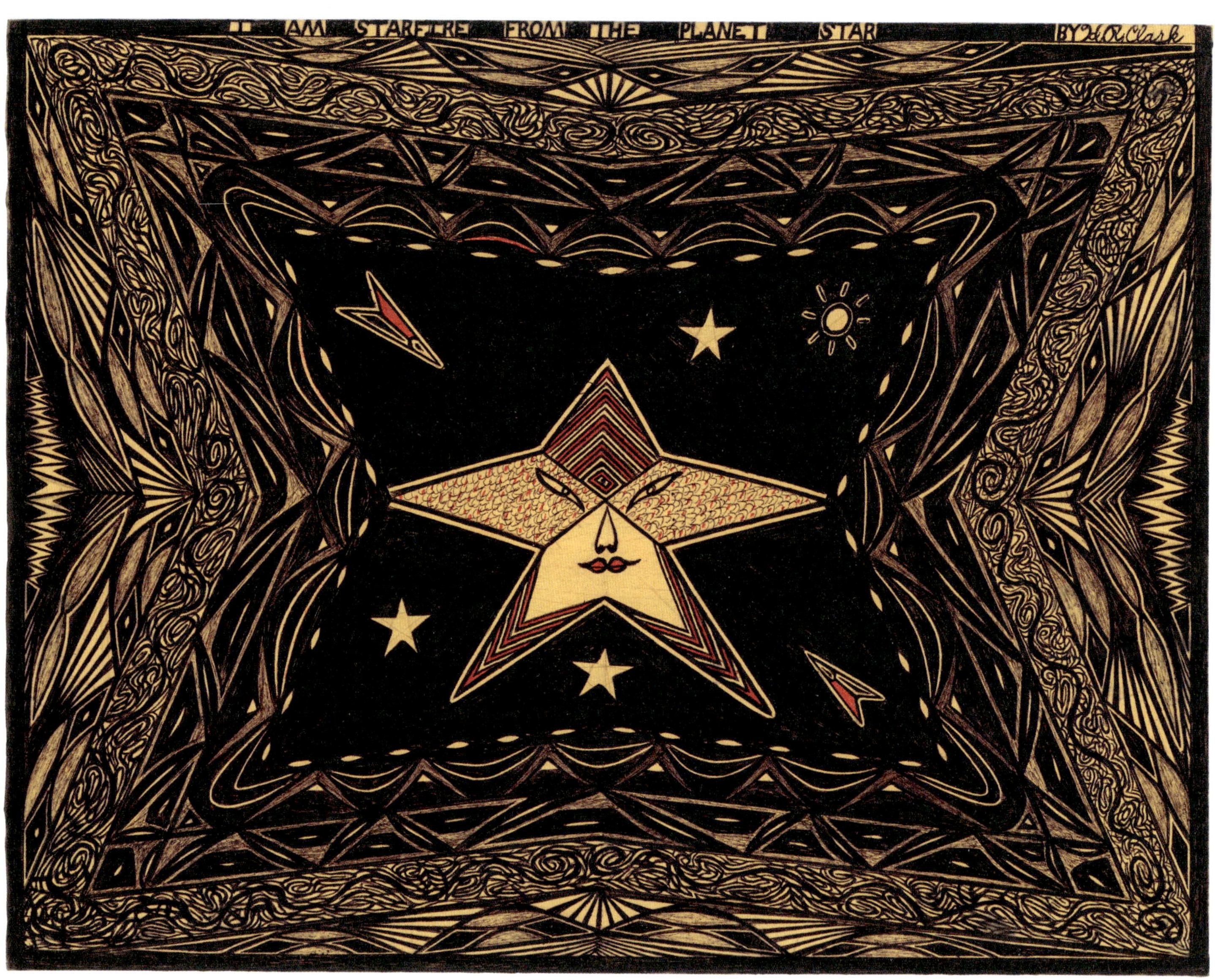
I AM STARFIRE FROM THE PLANET STAR
BY Clark

HENRY RAY CLARK

1936–2006

Born in Bartlett, Texas, Henry Ray Clark moved with his family to Houston after the Great Depression. At age fourteen Clark dropped out of school and soon entered a life of gambling, drug dealing, and pimping that earned him the nickname and alter ego "The Magnificent Pretty Boy." In 1977 a series of drug-dealing convictions led to his sentencing under the "three strikes" law (enacted to remove persistent offenders from the community) to serve twenty-five years in prison for attacking a man in a betting dispute and use of a lethal weapon. While serving time in Huntsville State Penitentiary, Clark began to draw. He was discovered by William Steen, a Houston artist and arts advocate, present when Clark won a juried prize in the 1989 Texas Department of Corrections Art Show—the same event at which Frank Jones (p. 141) had been unanimously awarded first prize the 1964 inaugural show.

Using pens and markers on manila envelopes, Clark typically portrays a single, central character (an extraterrestrial being, esoteric demigod, or allegorical figure); like an insect trapped in amber, the subject usually appears within a solid color field, which is peppered with a few emblems of interplanetary whim: a sun, small rocket ships, swooshes, twinkles, and stars. Beyond this nucleus, there's always a kaleidoscopic framework that occupies most of the composition. The artist bends line and color into an overall effect of controlled asymmetry, fluidly integrating organic shapes, shadings, or abstract scripts and flourishes that resemble numbers and notation. Clark's visual poetics imply an urgency to obliterate any vestige of untouched surface, a case of horror vacui somewhat reminiscent of Adolf Wölfli (p. 243). Clark's works are often so saturated with ink that they become furrowed with texture. A short declaration of name and provenance of the subject is often present, e.g., "I am starfire from the planet star." Clark's cast of characters has the aura of a magnified deck of fortune-telling cards, at times solemn and cryptic, at times witty. Evident in the declarations is the unfettered confidence of a man who despite being physically captive reasserted himself as the autocrat in the worlds of his own invention.

Clark was released from prison in 2001. He died in 2006 after trespassers broke into his home and shot him. His work has been included in numerous exhibitions, including *Living Folk* (Hirschl & Adler, 1990), *Passionate Visions of the American South* (New Orleans Museum of Art, 1993), *Spirited Journeys: Self-Taught Texas Artists of the Twentieth Century* (Archer M. Huntington Art Gallery, College of Fine Arts, the University of Texas at Austin, 1997), *Seeing Stars* (Menil Collection, Houston, 2012), and *Insiders* (Ricco/Maresca Gallery, New York, 2017). Clark's work can be found in the Milwaukee Art Museum and the Smithsonian American Art Museum (Washington, D.C.).

Text excerpted and adapted from Alejandra Russi, "Insiders: Henry Ray Clark and Frank Jones," www.riccomaresca.com.

Henry Ray Clark, *"I Am Starface,"* 1999. Marker and pen on manila folder, 11½ × 15¼ in. (29.2 × 38.7 cm)

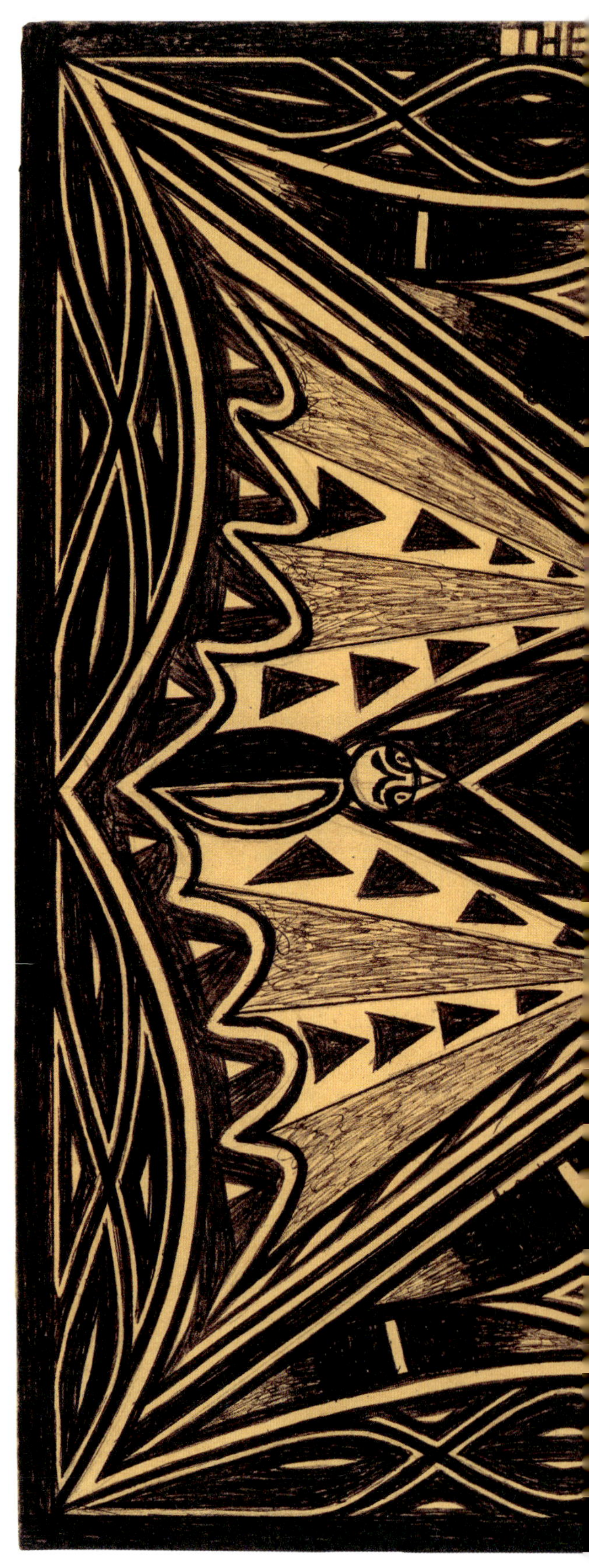

Henry Ray Clark, *Untitled*, 1999. Marker and pen on manila folder, 11½ × 15¼ in. (29.2 × 38.7 cm)

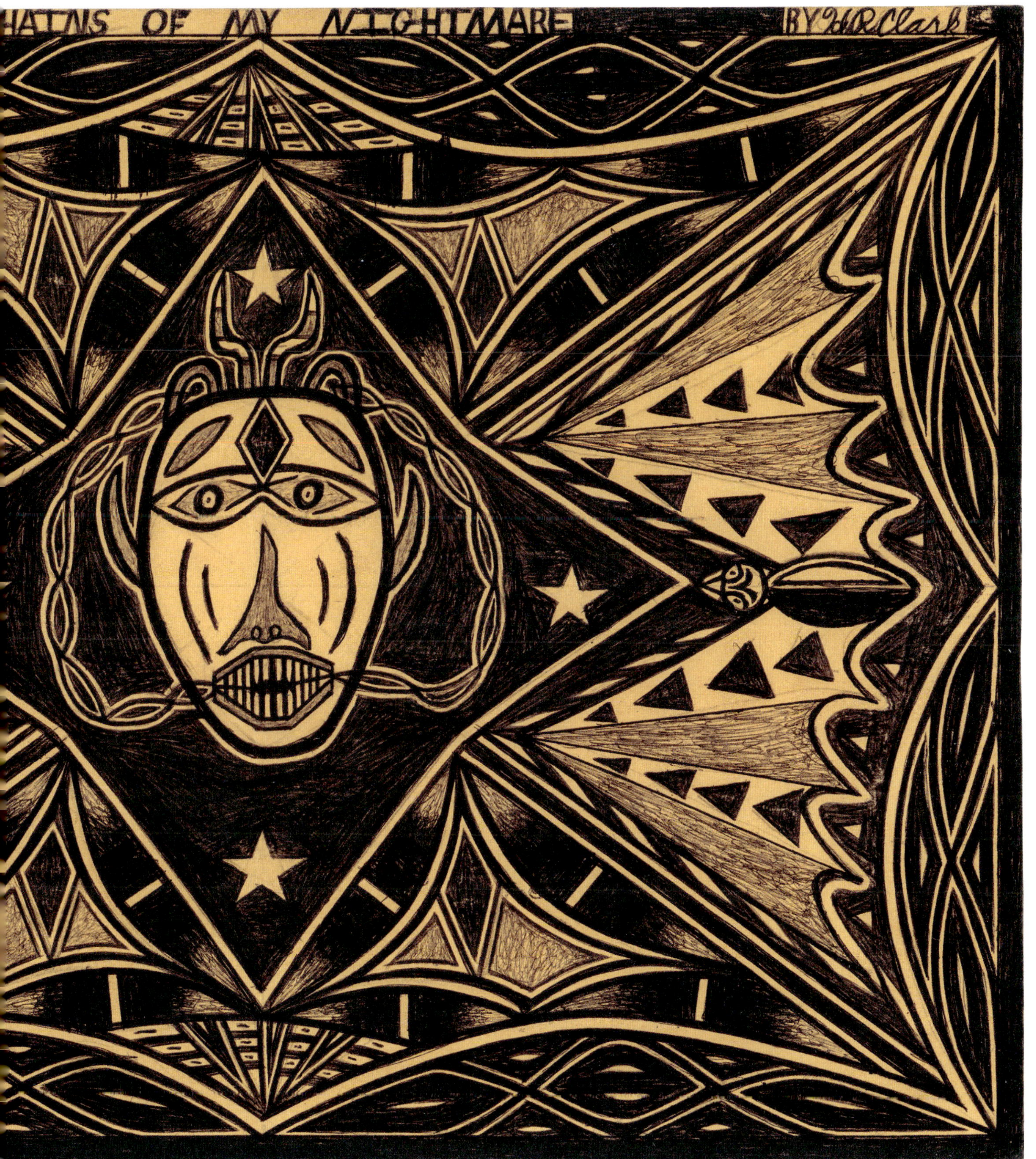
HAINS OF MY NIGHTMARE
BY HR Clark

BOARD OF PATIENTS MUST BE PAID IN ADVANCE.—At its First Session After Receiving This Account, the County Court Shall Allow and Pay It.—See Section 4873, Chapter 72, R. S. 1899.

116

STATE HOSPITAL NO. 3.

NEVADA, MO., ________________ 190__

________________________________ For ________________________________

Address ________________________________

TO J. R. WALTON, TREASURER, DR.

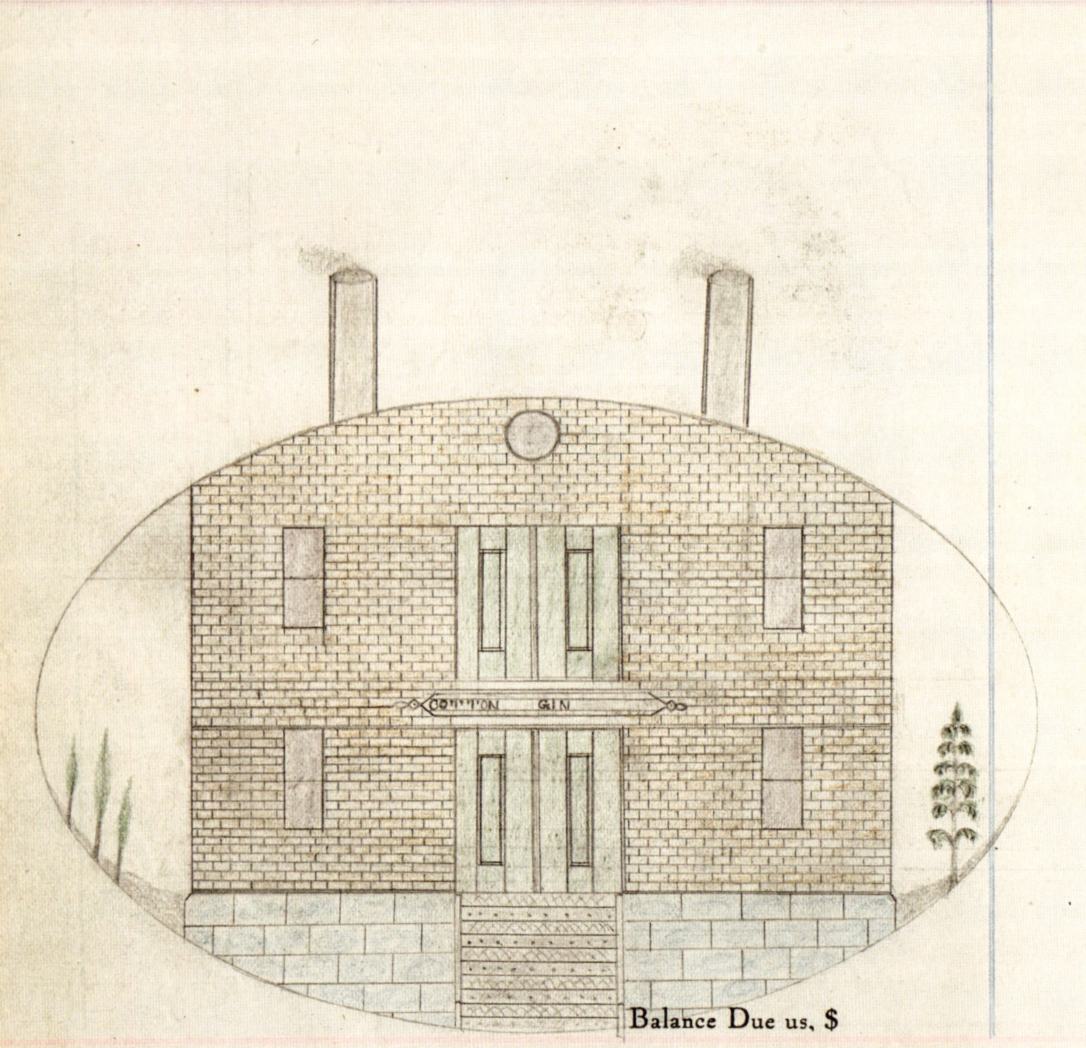

Balance Due us, $

In Testimony Whereof, I hereunto set my hand and affix my official seal, this .... day of .... 190.....

....
Superintendent.

Please Return This Statement When You Remit.

J. R. WALTON, Treasurer.

EDWARD DEEDS

1908–1987

In Springfield, Missouri, in 1970 a teenage boy found a hand-bound collection of 283 numbered drawings in a dumpster. Made with graphite and crayon on stationery from "State Hospital No. 3" in the town of Nevada, most were double sided; none were signed. In the delicately colored, serene world portrayed in the work, sorrow or turmoil seems unimaginable. Whimsical landscapes, animals, vintage cars, toylike steamboats and trains, precise architecture, clothing, Edwardian women, nineteenth-century beaux, and imaginary Civil War soldiers fill the pages.

For thirty-six years this discovery remained in the man's possession, unseen by others, until 2006, when he decided to sell it on eBay. A Kansas book dealer acquired and resold the work for $10,000 to an artist–art collector in St. Louis who in turn sold it to the New York art dealer Harris Diamant, who took it to the Outsider Art Fair and gave the still unknown artist the epithet "The Electric Pencil" after the inscription "ECTLECTRC" in drawing number 197. Soon "The Electric Pencil" was signed for representation by Hirschl & Adler Galleries. In 2011, in hopes of uncovering the identity of the artist, Diamant asked the *Springfield News-Leader* newspaper to print a selection of the illustrations, which Julie Deeds Phillips—Deeds's niece—happened to see.

James Edward Deeds Jr. (known as Edward), the oldest of five children, was born in Panama (while Deeds Sr. served military duty as paymaster aboard the U.S.S. *Marblehead*) and later moved with his family to McCracken, Missouri. Deeds was ill-treated by his father, who often beat him for unwillingness to do farmwork and eventually banished him to a cabin. When in a quarrel Deeds threatened his brother Clay with an ax (possibly as a joke), his father sent him, at age twenty-five, to the School for the Feeble Minded in Marshall, Missouri. From there he was transferred in 1936 to the Missouri State Hospital No. 3 and diagnosed with dementia praecox and schizophrenia (it seems likely he was autistic). He remained in residence for nearly four decades.

The State Hospital No. 3 was a nineteenth-century building erected under the Kirkbride Plan, intended to reform through institutionalization the ways in which the mentally ill were housed and treated. By the 1930s, the Kirkbride philosophy was contested and the asylum overcrowded, unhygienic, and understaffed. Patients were routinely given electroconvulsive therapy—ECT—letters that Deeds included in some artworks. By the mid-1960s, arthritis caused him to stop drawing, and he gave his album of drawings to his mother. He was transferred in 1973 to a nursing facility in Christian County, where fourteen years later he died. The Missouri State Hospital No. 3 closed in 1991 and was demolished in 1999. Misplaced by the family, Deeds's album wound up in an attic, and eventually in the trash, from which the teenage boy rescued it in 1970.

A catalogue raisonné was published in 2010, followed by *The Electric Pencil: Drawings from Inside State Hospital No. 3*. In 2013 the Collection de l'Art Brut in Lausanne, Switzerland, mounted a retrospective exhibition. Deeds's work is in the abcd Collection (Paris), the Treger Saint Silvestre Collection (São João da Madeira, Portugal), and numerous private collections.

James Edward Deeds, *Cotton Gin* (side 116 of two-sided drawing *Junetta/Cotton Gin 115/116*), c. 1936–66. Graphite and crayon on ledger paper, 9¼ × 8⅜ in. (23.5 × 21.3 cm)

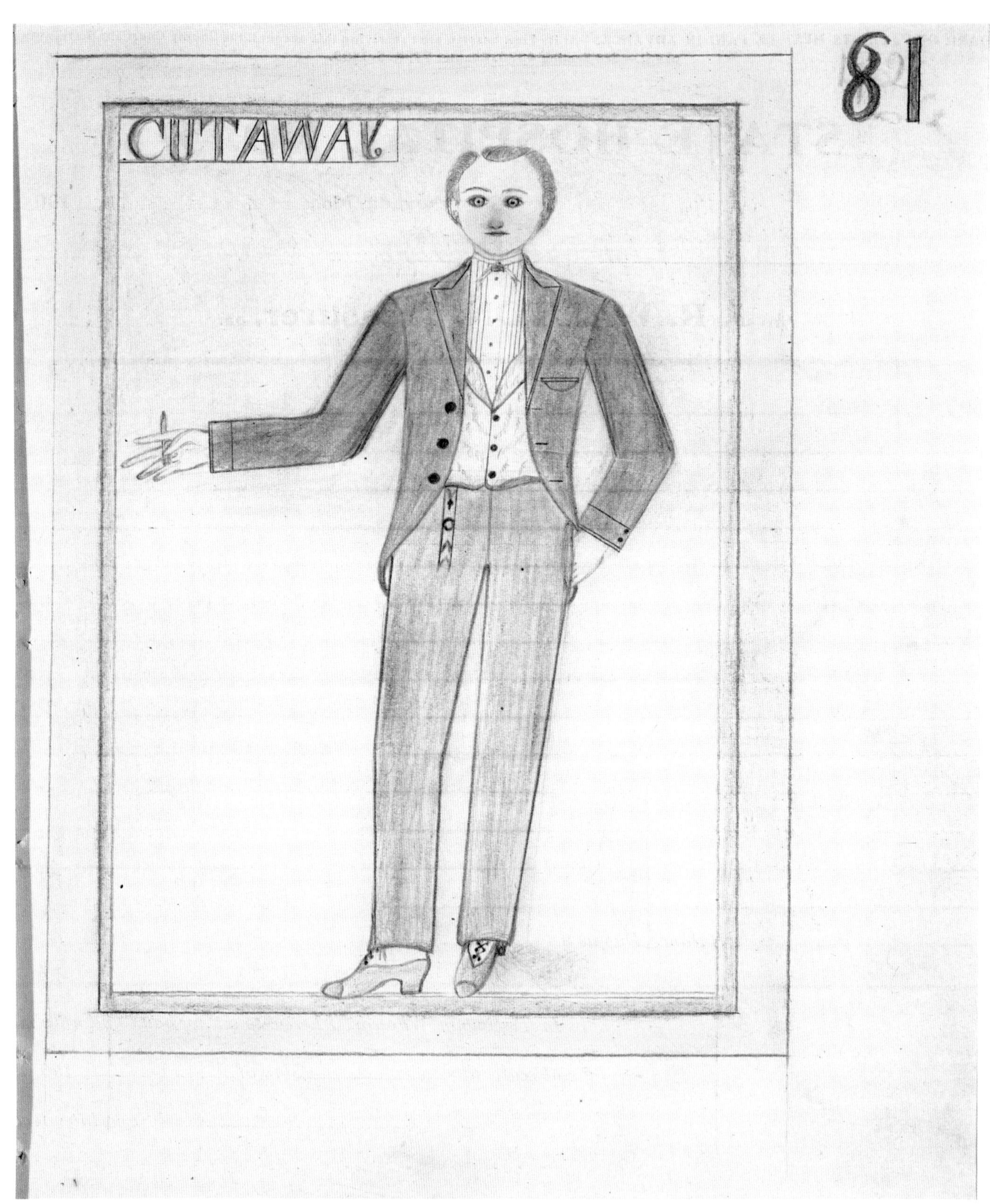

ABOVE AND OPPOSITE: James Edward Deeds, *Cutaway/Hats and Caps, 81/82* (two-sided drawing), c. 1936–66. Graphite and crayon on ledger paper, 9¼ × 8⅜ in. (23.5 × 21.3 cm)

BOARD OF PATIENTS MUST BE PAID IN ADVANCE.—At its First Session after receiving this account, the County Court shall allow and pay it.—See Section 4873, Chapter 72, R. S. 1899.

82

STATE HOSPITAL NO. 3.

Nevada, Mo., ... 190....

HATS AND CAPS

.... for ....

TO J. R. WALTON, Treasurer, DR.

SHIRT

LEDGER

DAY DATE

POST

Balance Due us $

In Testimony Whereof, I hereunto set my hand and affix my official seal, this .... day of .... 190....

.... *Superintendent.*

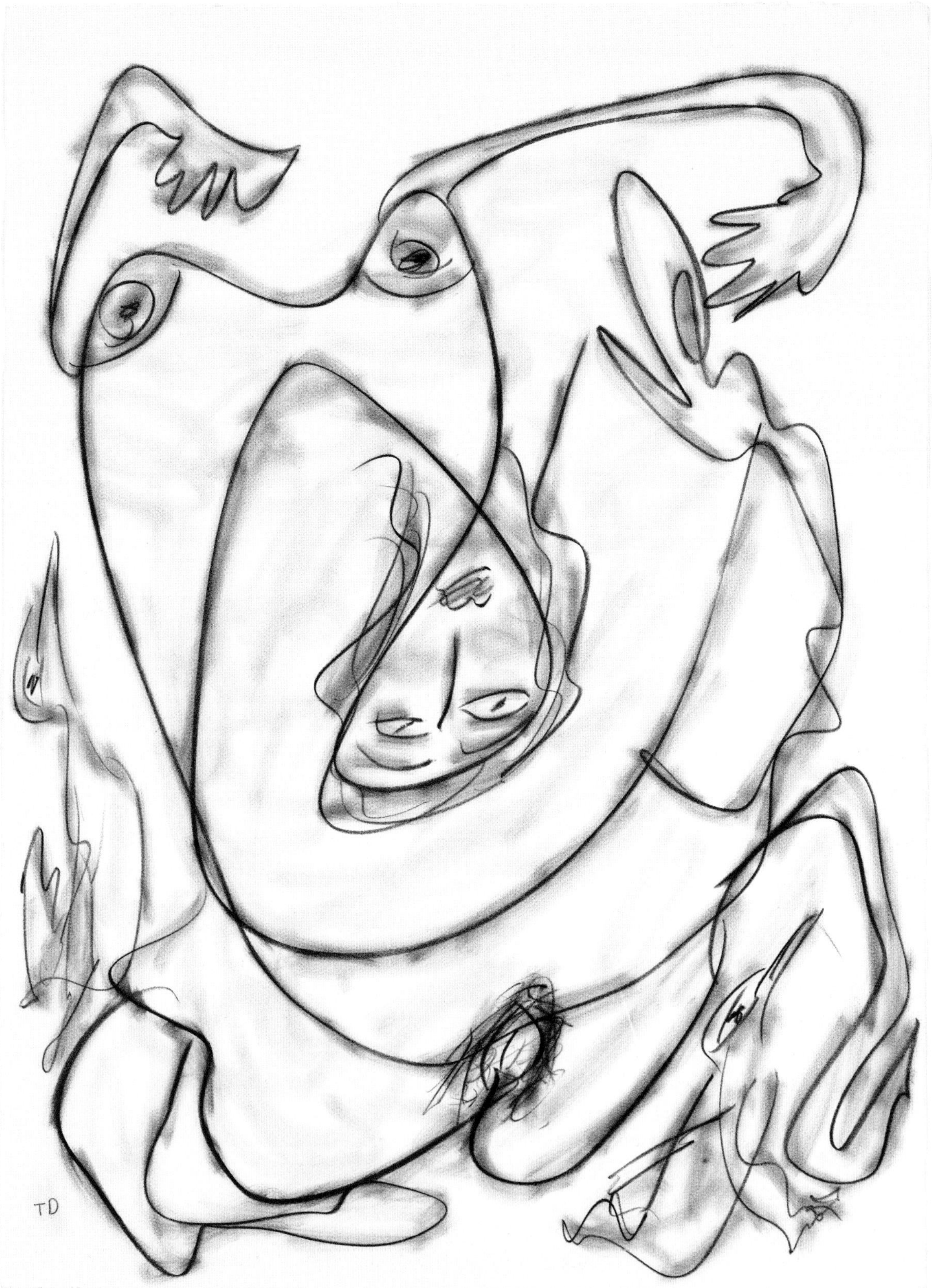
TD

THORNTON DIAL

1928–2016

Thornton Dial Sr. was born in Luther Elliot's plantation in Emelle, Alabama. Poverty stricken and deprived of toys, as children Dial and his siblings constructed their own playthings out of found objects—a habit that later influenced his sculptural work. From a very early age Dial was put to work picking cotton; he did not attend school enough to become fully literate. He later worked as a farmer and at all kinds of heavy labor (cement and iron pouring, bricklaying, pipe fitting, carpentry, house painting), as well as iron and steel metalwork for the Pullman Standard Company, where he was employed for close to thirty years. During this time, Dial got married and had four children, and after retiring at age fifty-five he devoted himself exclusively to art. In the decades that followed, Dial created a powerful oeuvre that recounts the brutal history of the African American experience, the shameful stain of the Jim Crow era, the nascent civil rights movement, and race and gender relations against a backdrop of conflict and democratic ideals.

Dial created paintings, assemblages, sculptures, and drawings. His three-dimensional work is notable for combining everyday objects and their different textures and volumes with his painter's sensibility for color. "I only want materials that have been used by people, the works of the United States, that have did people some good but once they got the service out of them they throwed them away," he has explained. "There's some kind of things I always liked to make stuff with. I'm talking about tin, steel, copper, and aluminum, and also old wood, carpet, rope, old clothes, sand, rocks, wire, screen, toys, tree limbs, and roots. You could say, 'If Dial see it, he know what to do with it.' " In his works on paper, which he began making after a critic wrote that he could not draw, Dial focuses mainly on the subject of women and erotic interactions between male and female figures. The fluid, expressive quality of these works, considered alongside the ornate flamboyance of his three-dimensional works, results in an interesting equilibrium. The winding lines, fragmented shapes, and lucid pigment smears in Dial's drawings demonstrate the instinctive drive behind his art practice at large—or, as he put it, the struggle to make something beautiful with one's own hands. Beauty for Dial is, however, tinged with darkness, trapped in the complexities of social history and never cleanly figurative or abstract.

Dial was discovered in the 1980s by William Arnett, a writer, curator, and art collector from Atlanta focused on self-taught and folk art by southern artists. Since then, Dial's work has been acquired by many museums, including the Metropolitan Museum of Art in New York, which in 2018 mounted the exhibition *History Refused to Die: Highlights from the Souls Grown Deep Foundation Gift*, titled after a work by Dial; the Whitney Museum of American Art (New York); the American Folk Art Museum (New York); the Smithsonian American Art Museum and the Hirshhorn Museum and Sculpture Garden (both in Washington, D.C.); the High Museum of Art (Atlanta); the Milwaukee Art Museum; the Philadelphia Museum of Art; the Museum of Fine Arts (Houston); the Indianapolis Museum; and the Birmingham Museum of Art (Alabama).

Thornton Dial, *Untitled*, c. 1995. Charcoal, graphite, and pastel on paper, 41 × 29½ in. (104.1 × 74.9 cm)

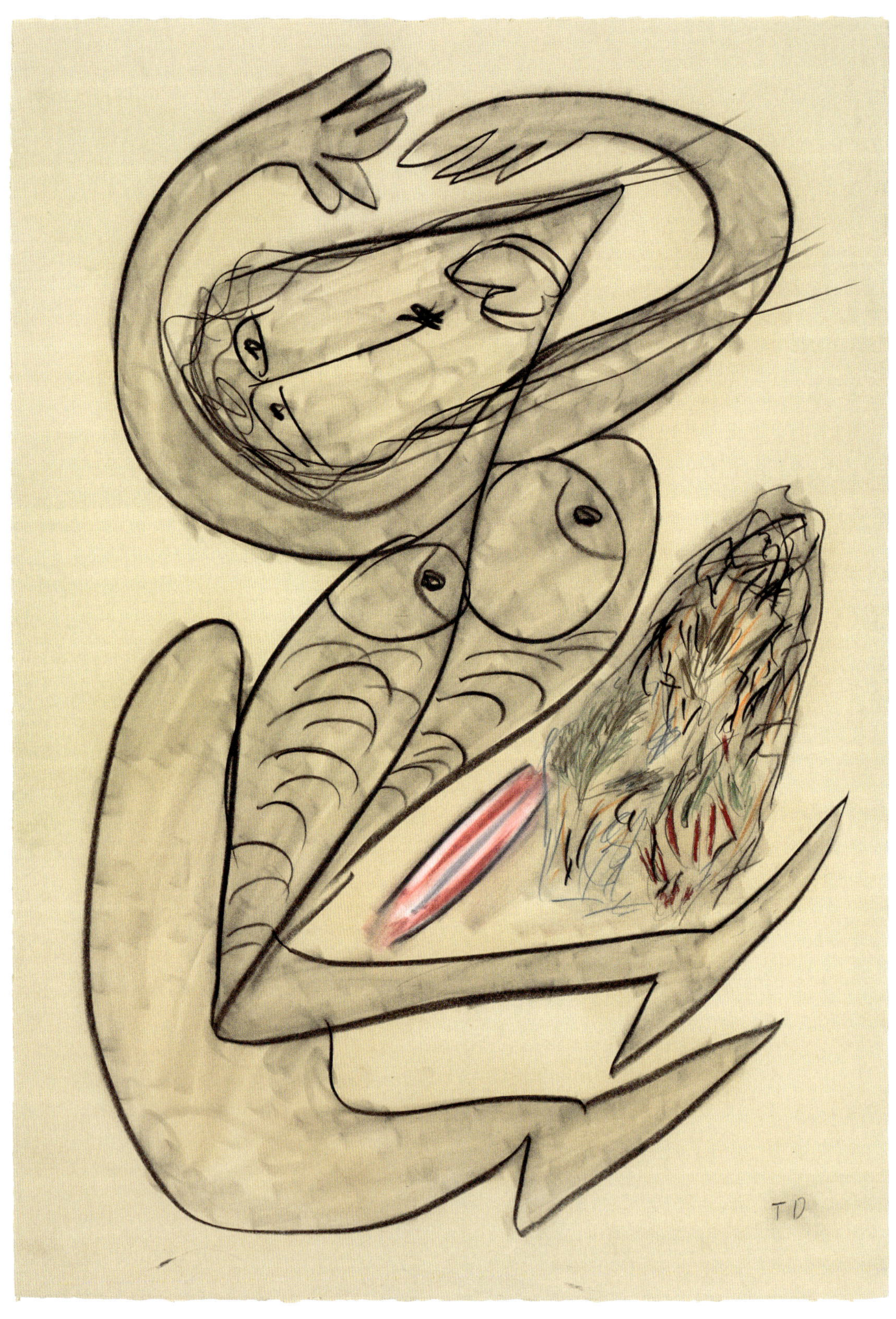

Thornton Dial, *Untitled*, c. 1995. Charcoal, graphite, and pastel on paper, 44¼ × 30¼ in. (112.4 × 76.8 cm)

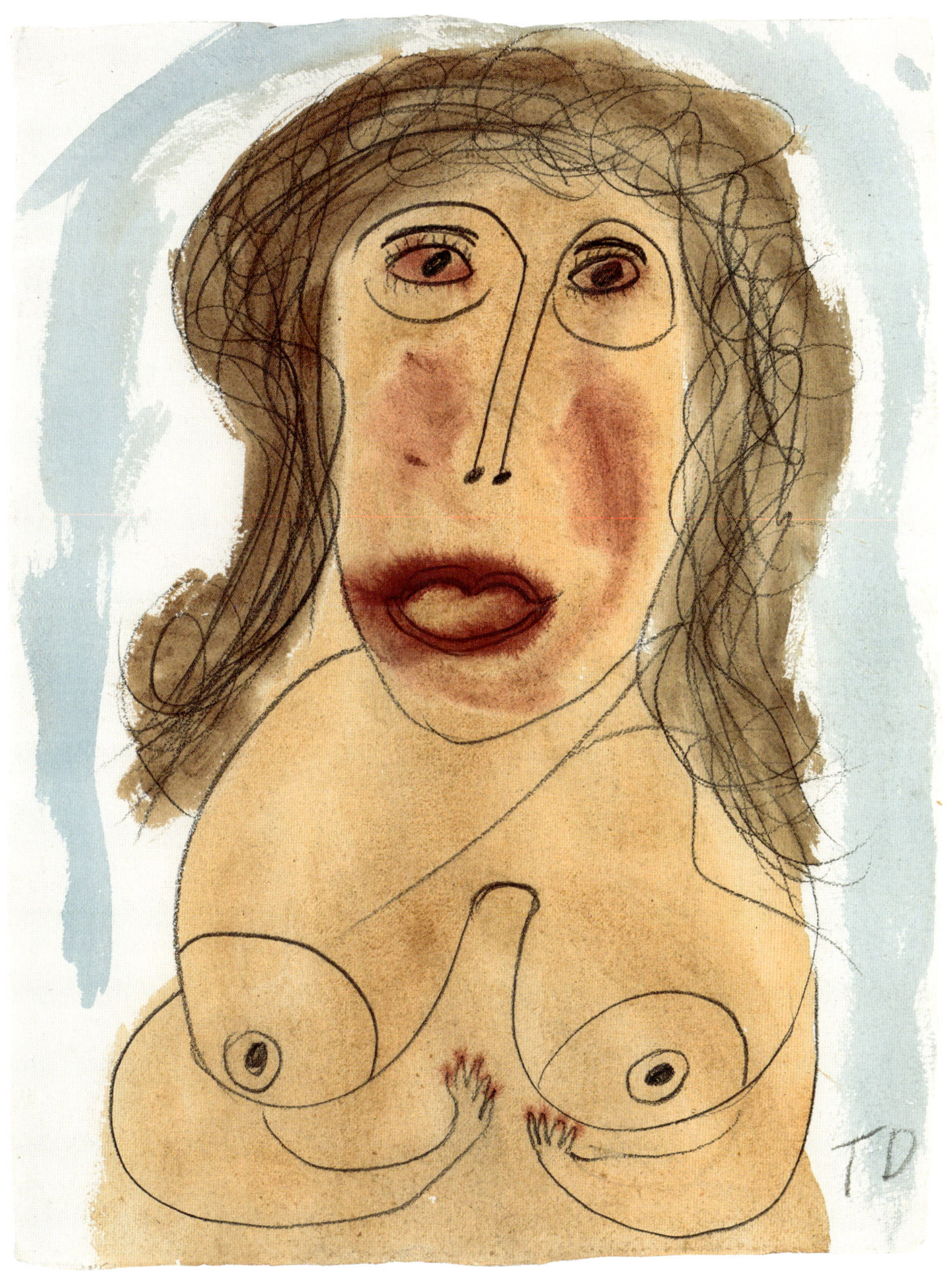

Thornton Dial, *Nude*, n.d. Watercolor and graphite on paper, 30 × 22 in. (76.2 × 55.9 cm)

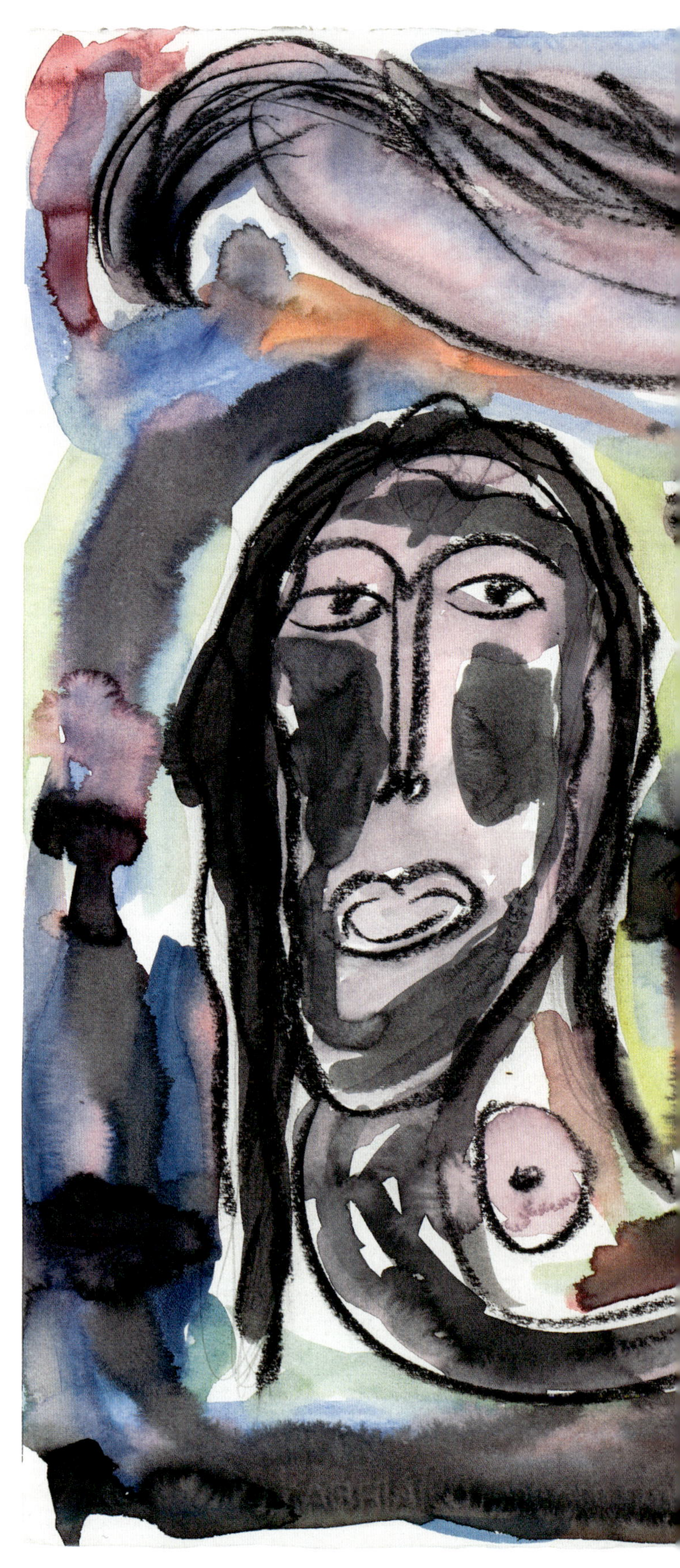

Thornton Dial, *Whole World Picture*, c. 1991.
Watercolor on paper, 22 × 30 in. (55.9 × 76.2 cm)

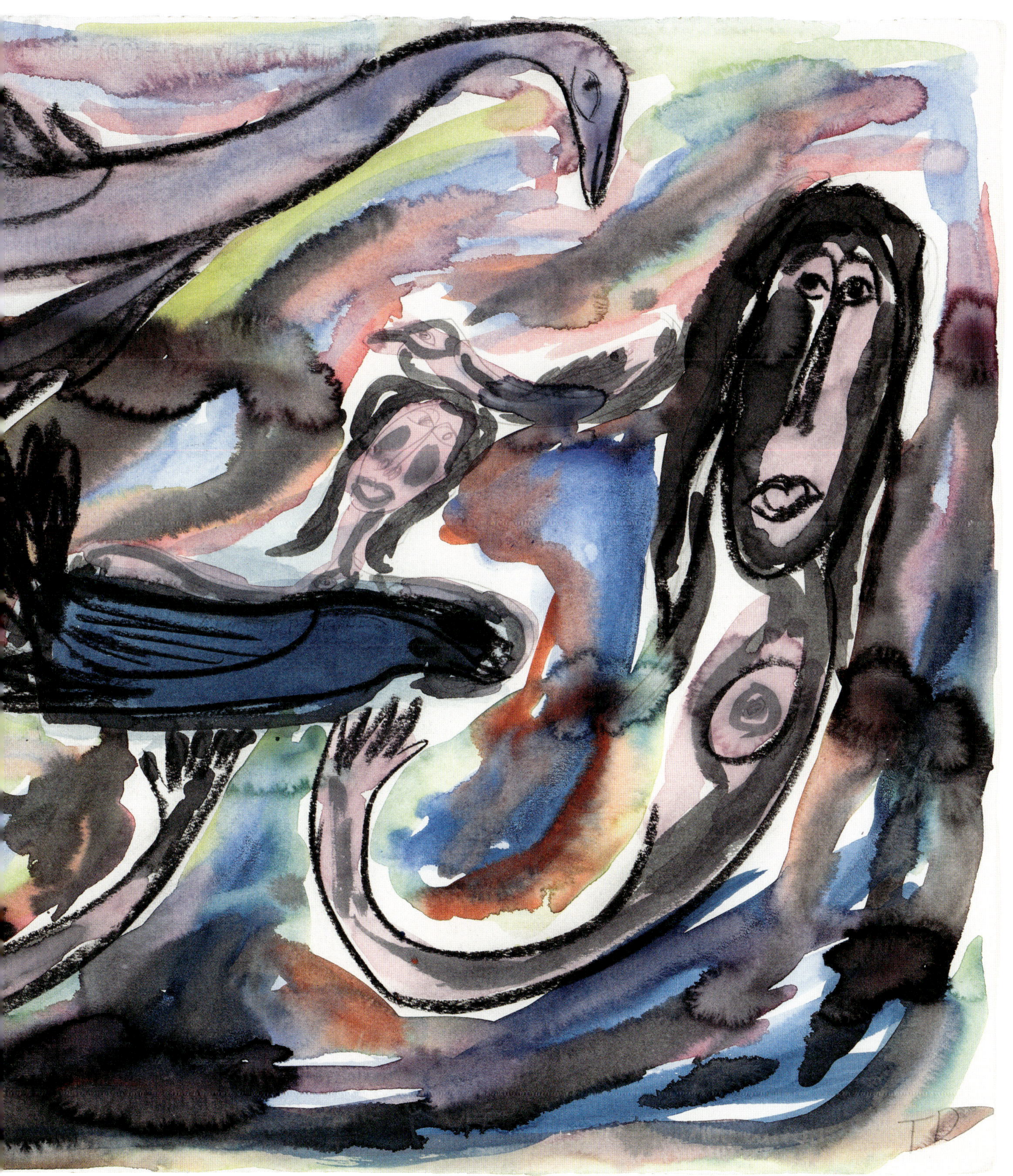

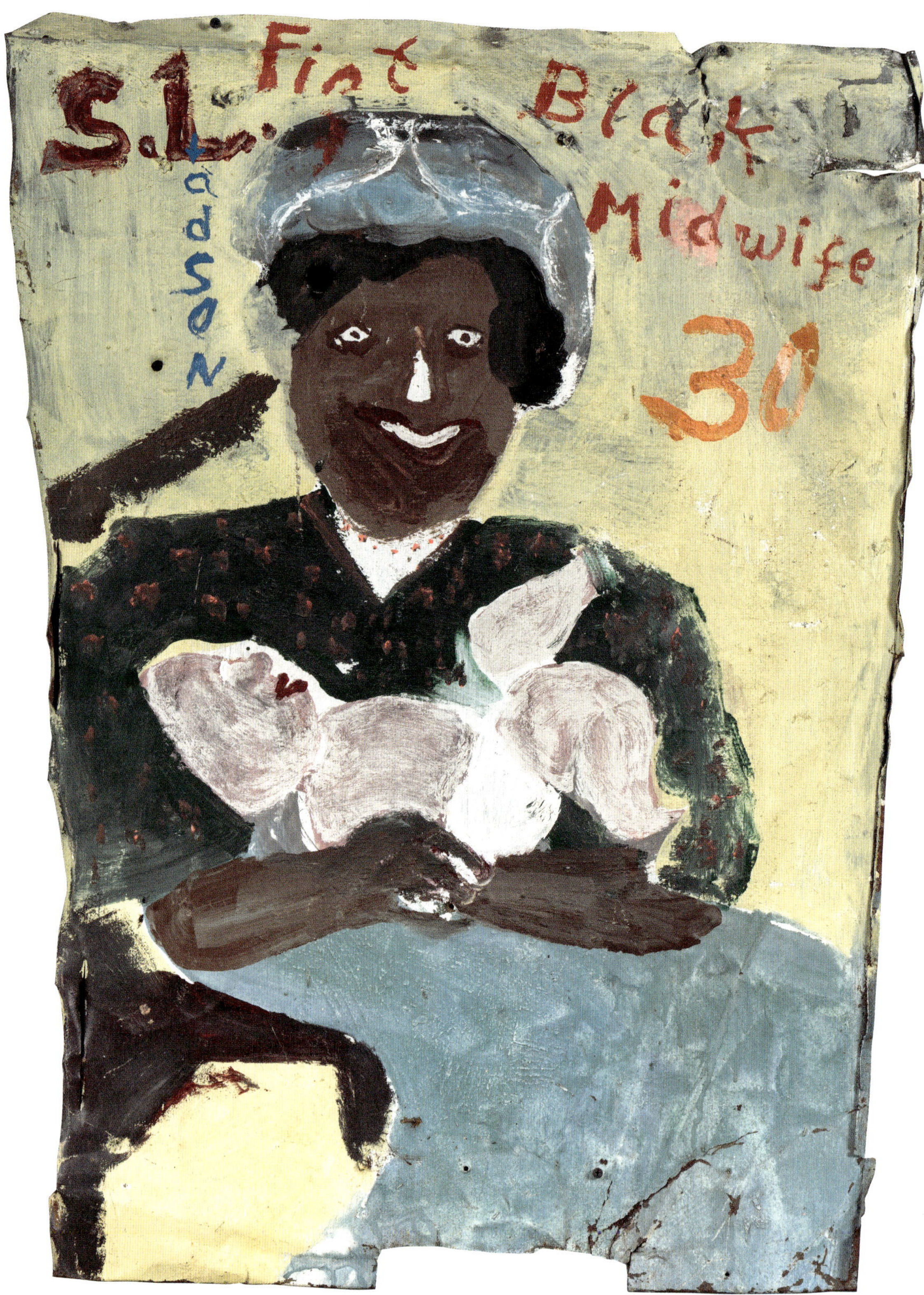
S.L.
tadsoN
Fist Blak
Midwife
30

SAM DOYLE

1906–1985

Sam Doyle was a native of the island of St. Helena, off the South Carolina coast. Discovered about 1520, St. Helena was occupied by the Spanish, French, and English until the American Revolution. During the years of the infamous transatlantic slave trade, many captured Africans were brought to the American islands, and in St. Helena, this population engendered the Gullah culture, which preserved African folk traditions. Doyle attended the Penn School, founded in 1862 to teach skills to newly liberated slaves, but family difficulties led to him dropping out after the ninth grade. Although his artistic talent was recognized from an early age, Doyle did not pursue further studies or full-time practice as an artist until his retirement in the 1960s. He held a variety of jobs, including store assistant, porter, and laundry worker on a Marine Corps base. He was married and had three children, but when the marriage ended his wife and children left him and eventually moved to New York.

It was about this time when Doyle focused all his energy on art and fully explored the pictorial lexicon that he had begun to develop in his spare time since 1944. He worked on plywood boards or pieces of ungalvanized roof tin with house paint (the materials most readily and cheaply available) and the outside of his house rapidly became a gallery for his work as well as a place for locals to learn about their shared history, reimagine their present, and connect to people from the mainland. In seeking to memorialize the accomplishments and idiosyncrasies of his fellow islanders and the African American community at large, Doyle became a visual historian and storyteller whose subjects ranged from legendary characters in the island's folklore (the frightening and playful "Old Hag" and "Jack-O-Lanton") to American icons (Martin Luther King Jr., Ray Charles, Jackie Robinson, and Joe Louis among them) to close acquaintances and notable members of the Gullah society.

Doyle's gestural technique in his portraits and narrative works captured the soul and vivacity of his subjects. His palette varied radically from one painting to the next, but his signature mode of representation—an expressive, abstracted, flattened figuration—remained recognizable across the board. Straightforward as it may seem, Doyle's work is always embedded with implicit or explicit commentary and several layers of meaning; in its mission to entertain, preserve, and educate, it remains one of the most valuable insights into the Gullah culture that has ever been produced. In 1982 Doyle's work was included by curator Jane Livingston in the pioneering exhibition *Black Folk Art in America 1930–1980* at the Corcoran Gallery of Art in Washington D.C. The exhibition provided Doyle's only trip away from home and brought him praise and recognition far beyond St. Helena. Today, Doyle's work is in private and museum collections around the world, including the American Folk Art Museum (New York), the Los Angeles County Museum of Art, the Milwaukee Art Museum, the High Museum of Art (Atlanta), the New Orleans Museum of Art, the Museum of Fine Arts (Houston), the Philadelphia Museum of Art, and the Smithsonian American Art Museum (Washington, D.C.).

Sam Doyle, *S. Ladson Firt Blak Midwife*, c. 1980. Paint on found metal, 38 × 24 in. (96.5 × 61 cm)

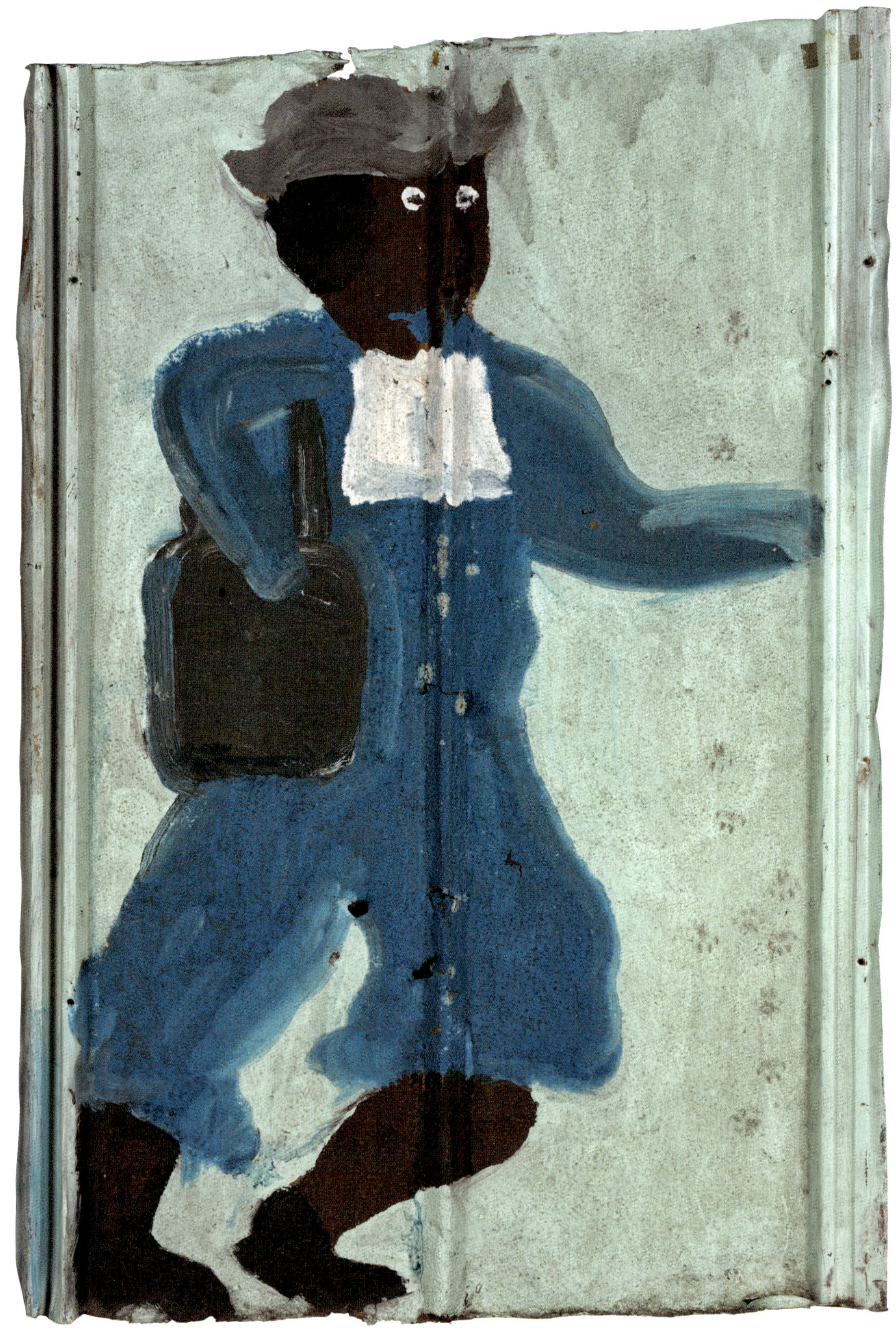

Sam Doyle, *Colonial Man*, c. 1978–81. Paint on found roofing tin, 42 × 29 in. (106.7 × 73.7 cm)

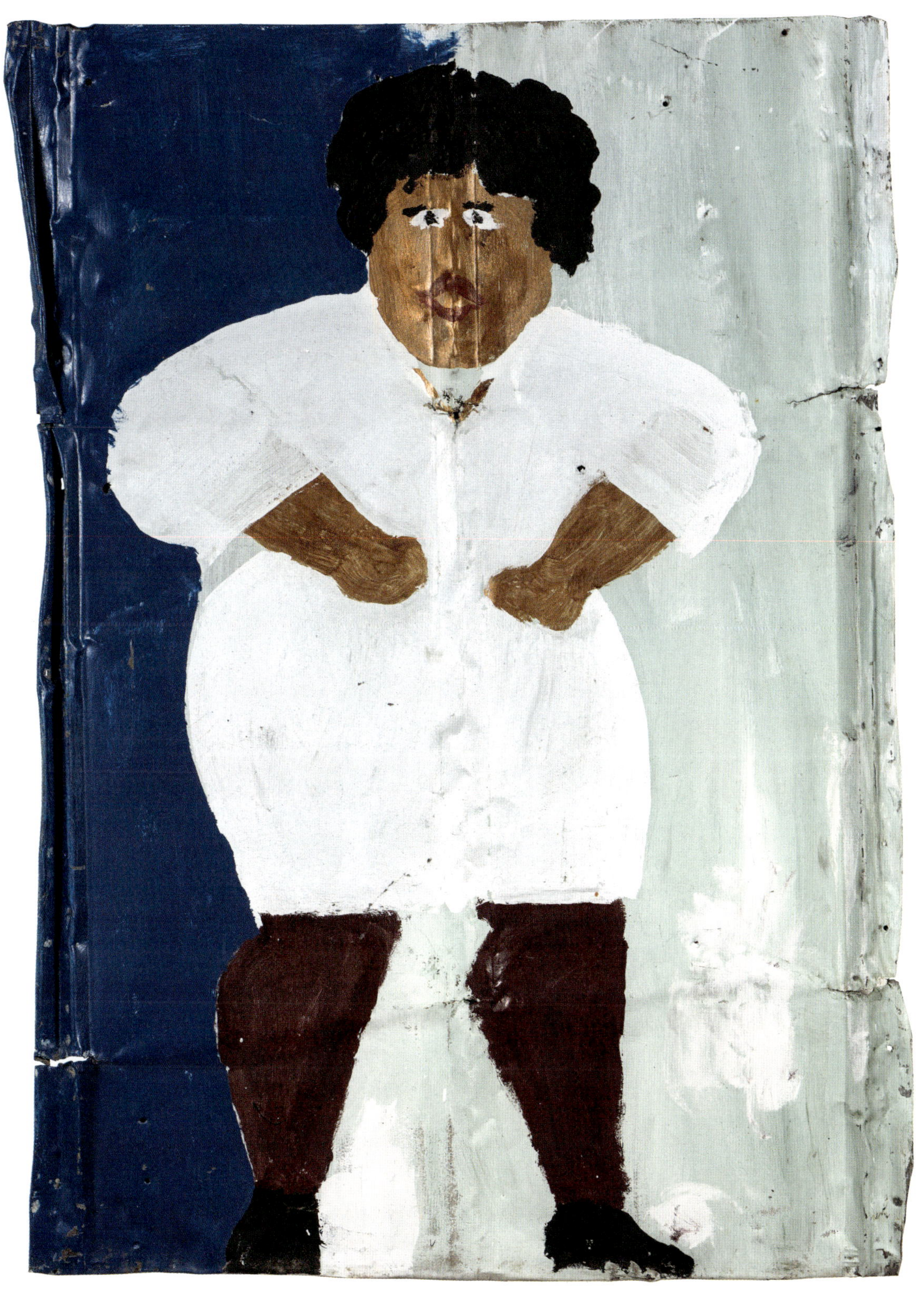

Sam Doyle, *Tough Lady*, c. 1980–84. Paint on found roofing tin, 38 × 26 in. (96.5 × 66 cm)

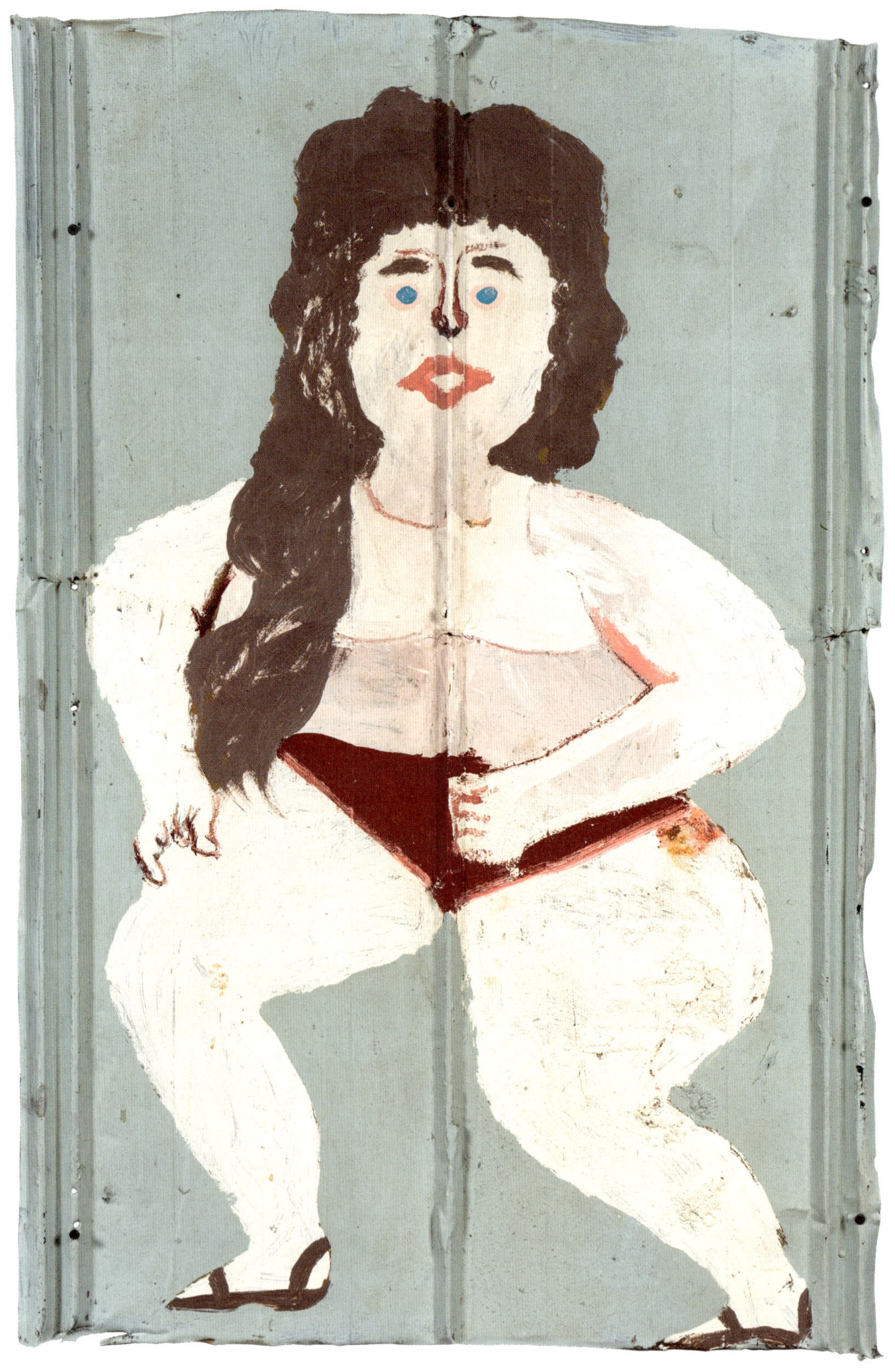

Sam Doyle, *Try Me*, c. 1983–84. Paint on found roofing tin, 41 × 26 in. (104.1 × 66 cm)

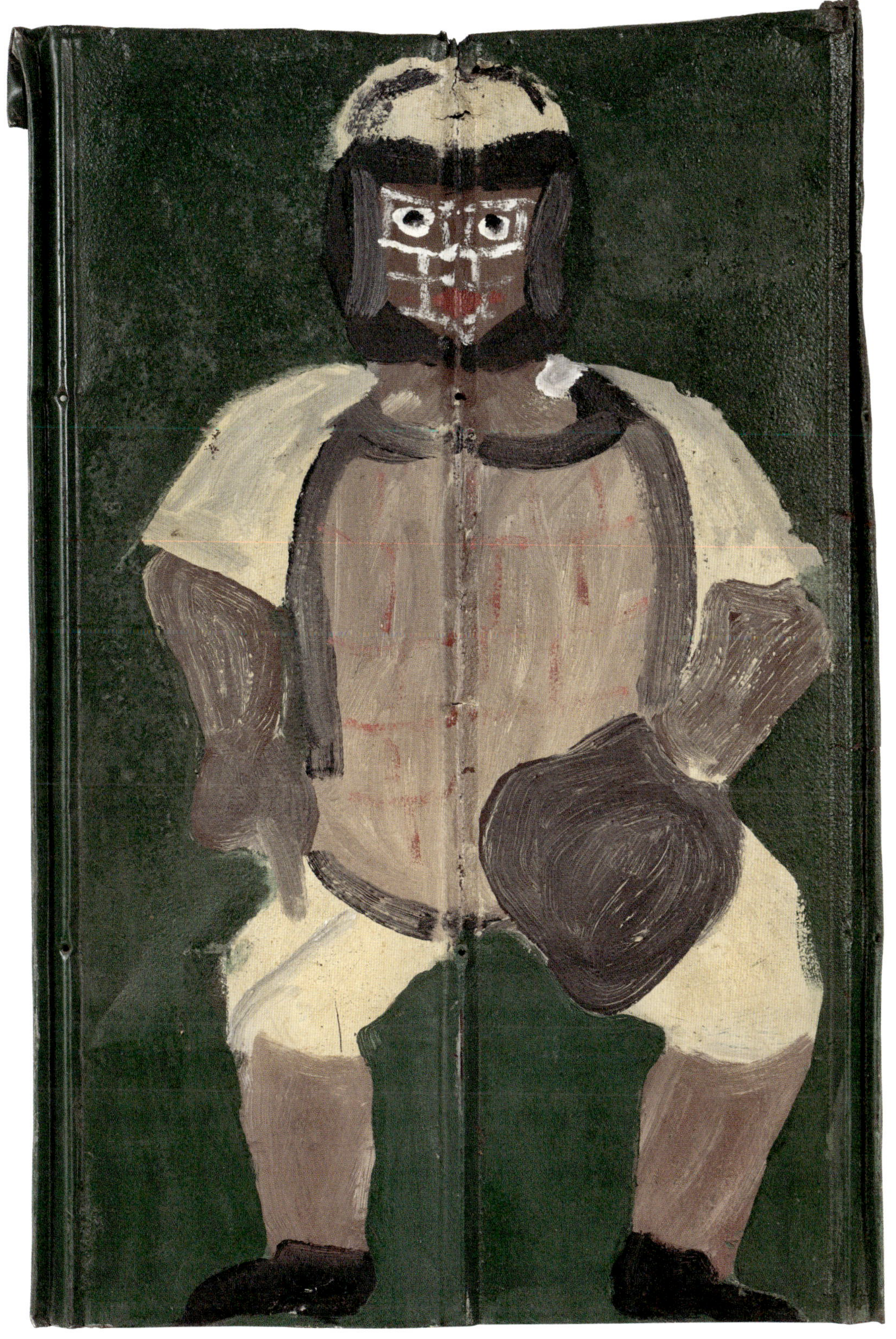

Sam Doyle, *Negro League Baseball Catcher*, n.d. Paint on found metal, 41 × 26 in. (104.1 × 66 cm)

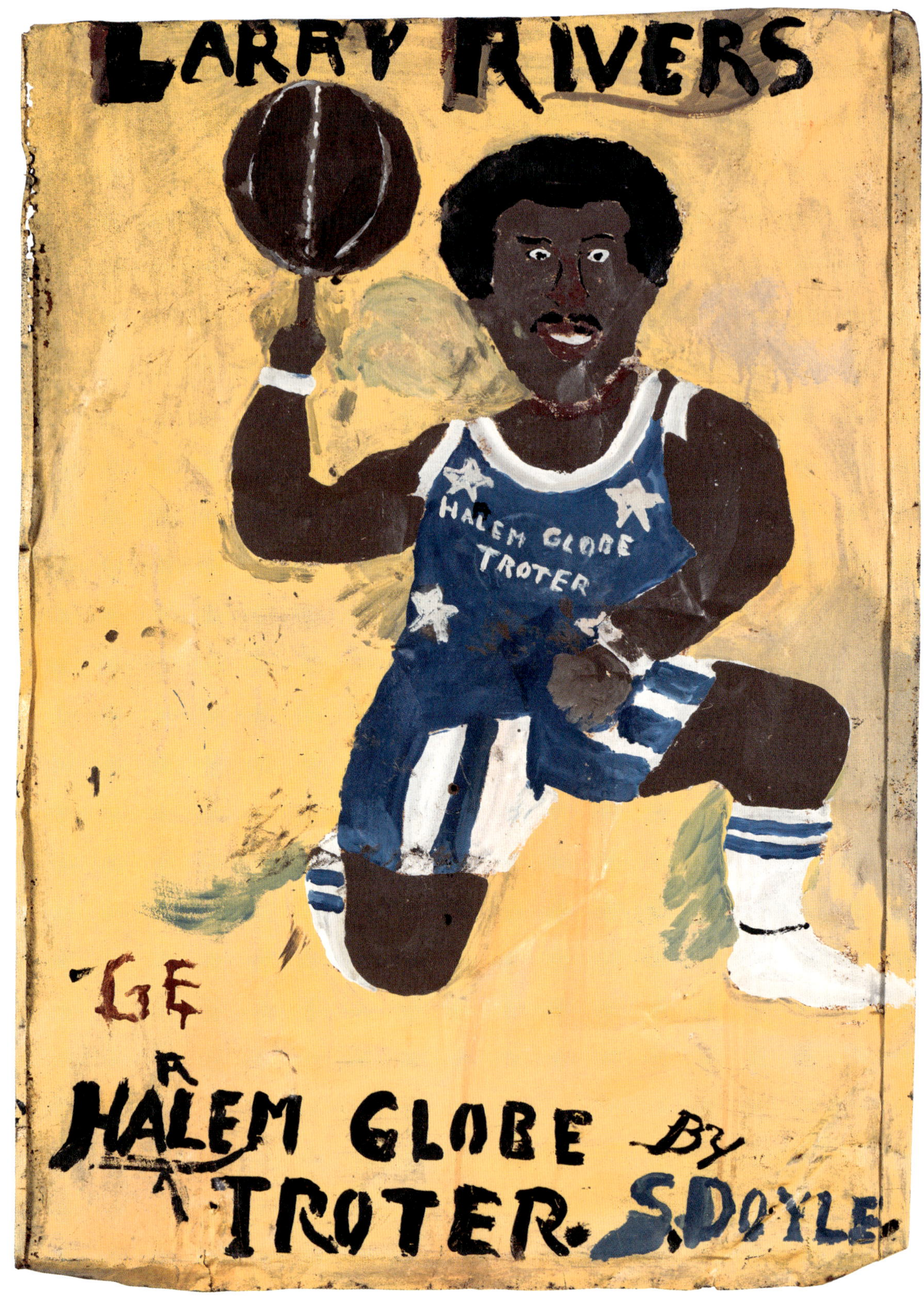

Sam Doyle, *Larry Rivers*, c. 1970–80. Paint on found metal, 41 × 28½ in. (104.1 × 72.4 cm)

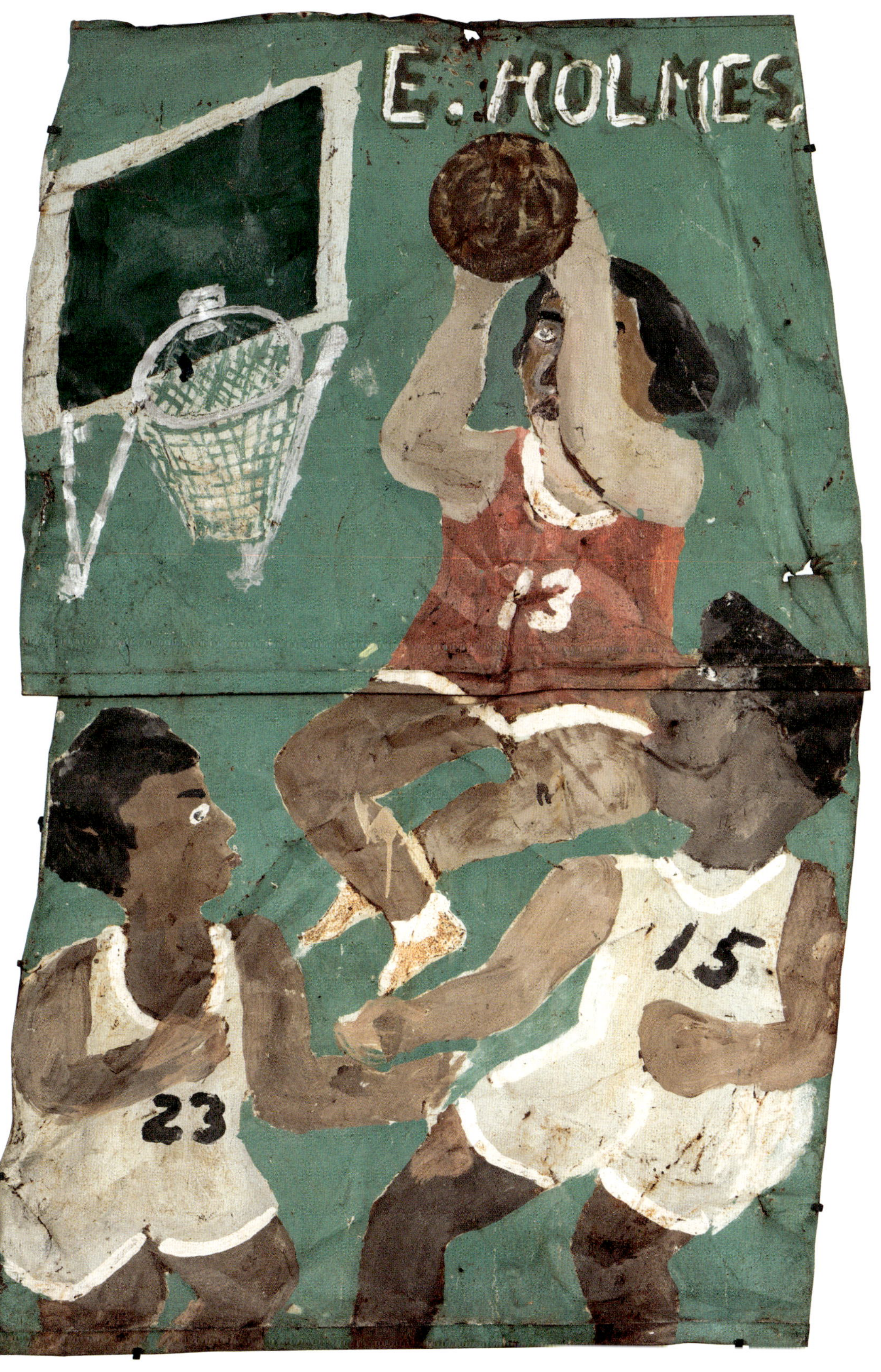

Sam Doyle, *E. Holmes*, c. 1978–81. Paint on found metal, 56½ × 36 in. (143.5 × 91.4 cm)

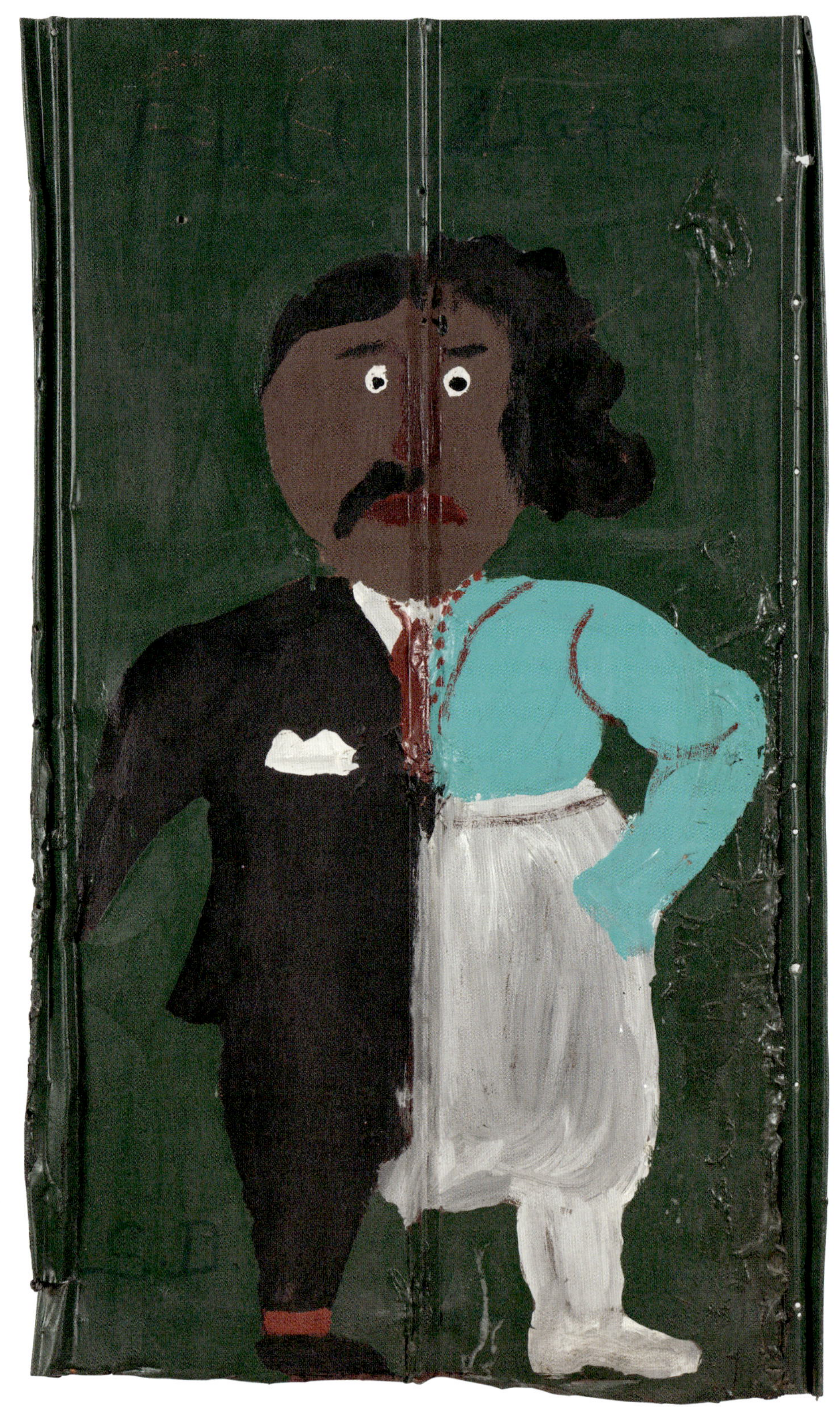

Sam Doyle, *She-He*, c. 1983–84. Paint on found roofing tin, 43 × 24 in. (109.2 × 61 cm)

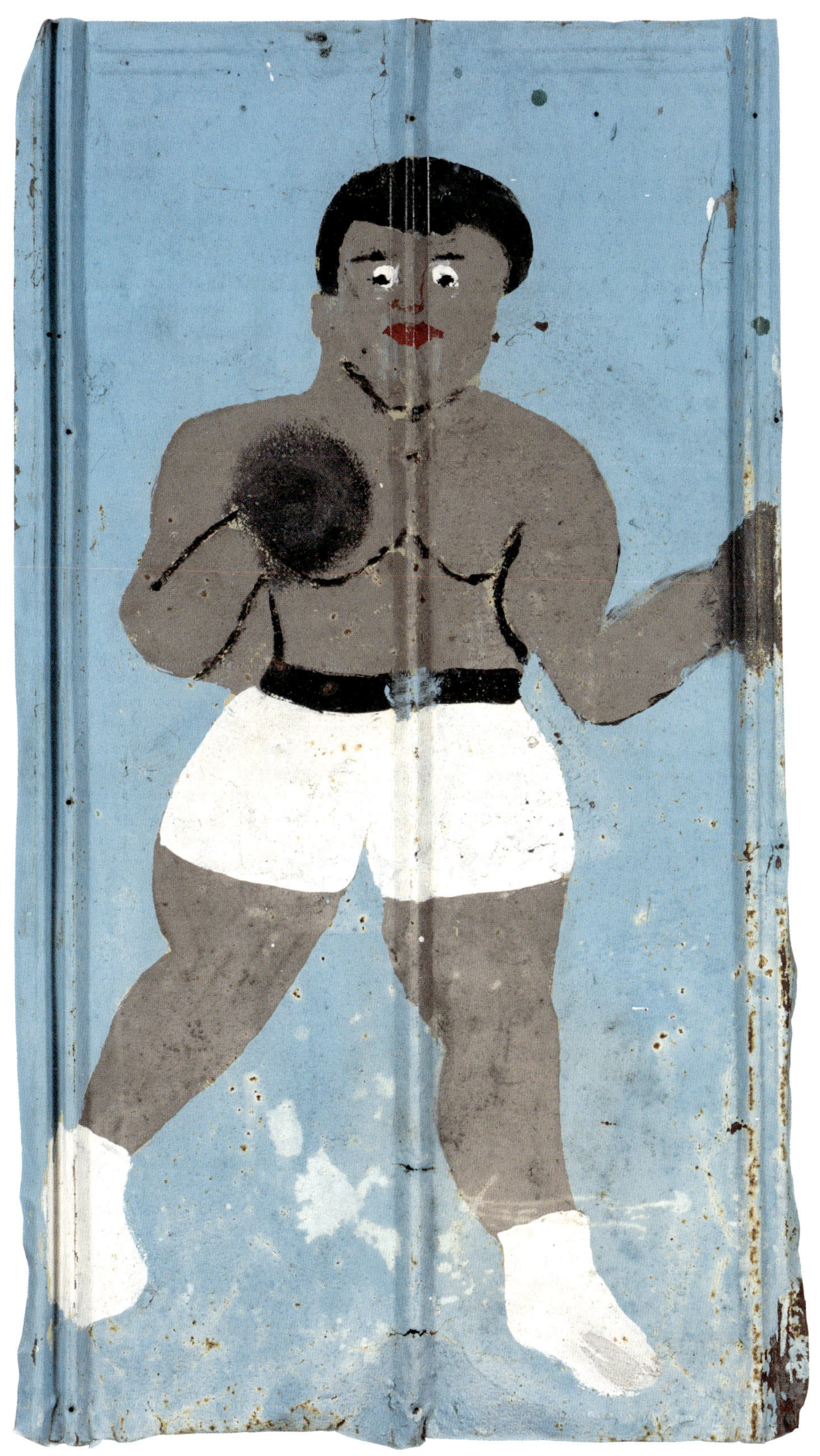

Sam Doyle, *Joe Louis*, n.d. Paint on found metal, 49 × 26 in. (124.5 × 66 cm)

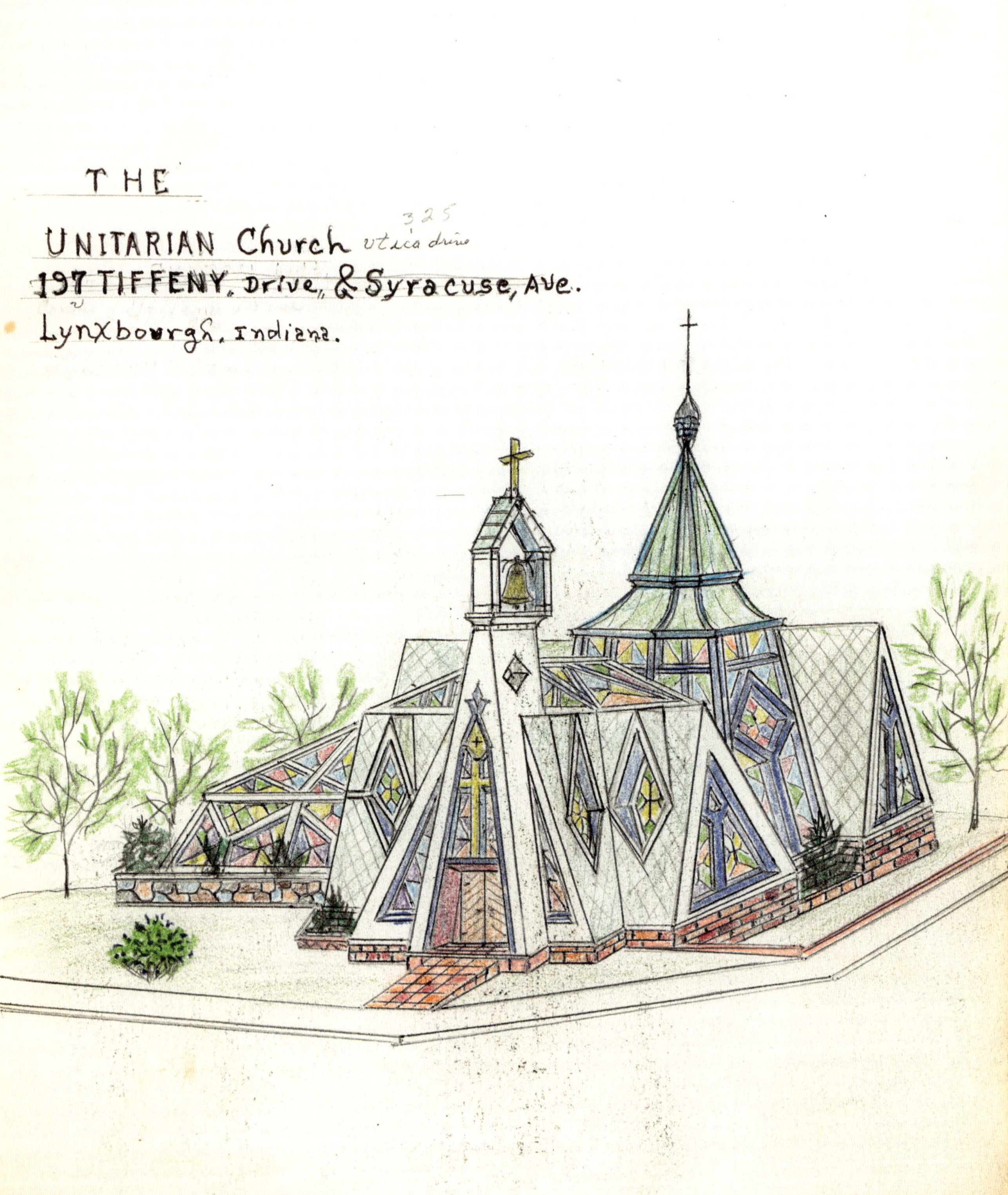
THE
UNITARIAN Church
325 Utica drive
197 TIFFENY. Drive, & Syracuse, Ave.
Lynxbourgh. Indiana.

JÀCQUES DE DÛ-GLASS

1931–1993

Siting it within the state of Indiana, in a series of finely drafted, meticulous, and imaginative drawings Jàcques de Dû-Glass created an imaginary town called Lynxbourgh, which he filled with architectural illustrations and landscapes that blur the line between reality and fiction. Dû-Glass was born James Donald Beatty to a single mother who gave him up for adoption. He was raised by the Douglass family on their farm in the outskirts of Warsaw, Indiana (in Kosciusko County), and did not receive a formal education. As a middle-aged man, after reportedly finding that "Douglass" had French origins, he changed his name to Dû-Glass, creating an alter ego befitting the self-taught artist demiurge, the creator of the parallel reality in his work.

Lynxbourgh is not, however, a site of fantastical events or otherworldly creatures, but resembles and incorporates the environment in which Dû-Glass lived: many buildings illustrated have real counterparts, and there are churches and temples, boulevards, lavish suburban homes with tidy gardens, libraries with American flags, fraternal lodges, homesteads, YMCAs, schools, and metropolitan features. Dû-Glass was particularly interested in the visual motif of architecture and in the history of specific buildings in Indiana, but through his subtle tinkering with reality and denotation, as Joseph Yoakum did with his sprawling, imaginary landscapes (p. 247), Dû-Glass found a way to reaffirm his agency and express his ideals. Lynxbourgh strikes the viewer as a Platonic notion, a highly developed place existing only in the mind's eye but made fully visible on paper.

In his lifetime, Dû-Glass saw only sporadic success, and his career as an artist was fruitless. He was discharged from many jobs and his insecurity about his sexuality caused his marriage to fail. As is the case of so many self-taught artists, Dû-Glass's work went on to receive posthumous recognition; exhibitions of his art have been held at Carl Hammer Gallery (Chicago), Lindsay Gallery (Columbus, Ohio), and the Outsider Art Fair (New York), and his work was included in the group exhibition *Farfetched: Mad Science, Fringe Architecture and Visionary Engineering*, curated by Tom Patterson and Roger Manley at the Gregg Museum of Art and Design in Raleigh, North Carolina, in 2013.

Jàcques de Dû-Glass, *The Unitarian Church, Lynxbourgh, Indiana*, c. 1992. Graphite, ink, and colored pencil on paper, 12 × 9 in. (30.5 × 22.9 cm)

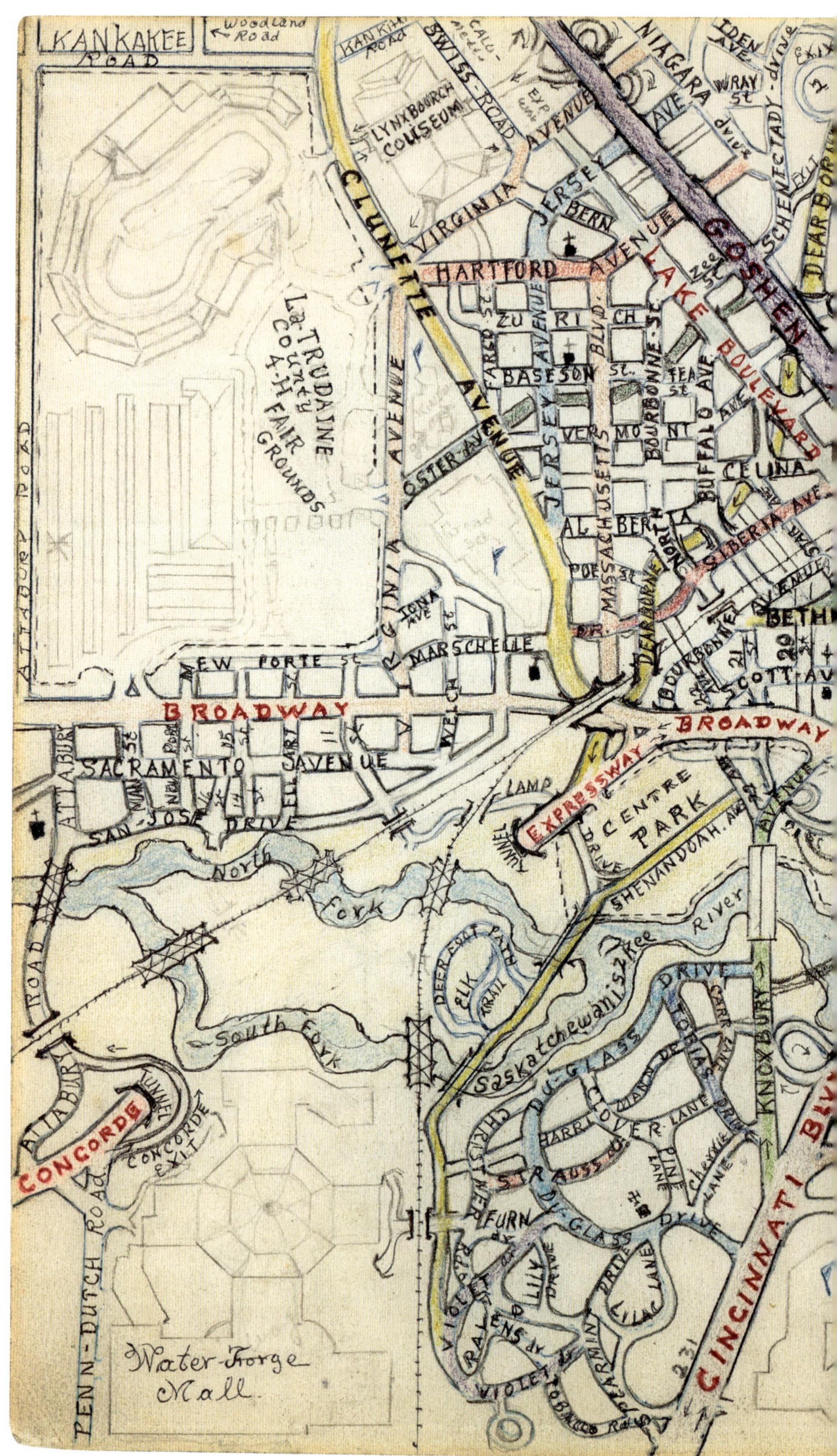

Jàcques de Dû-Glass, *Map of Lynxbourgh, Lynxbourgh, Indiana,* c. 1992. Graphite, ink, and colored pencil on paper, 12 × 18 in. (30.5 × 45.7 cm)

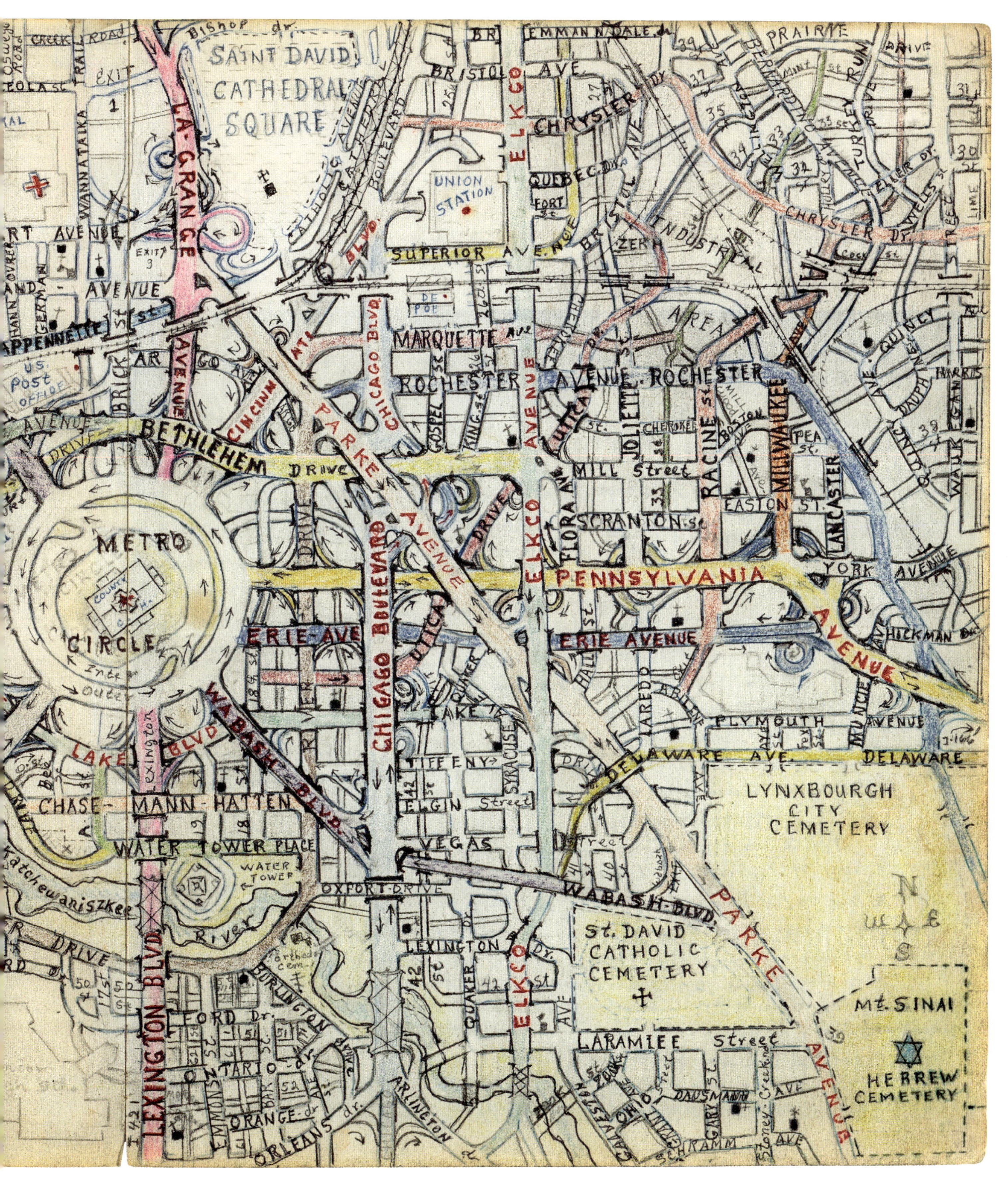

SAINT DAVID CATHEDRAL SQUARE
UNION STATION
SUPERIOR AVENUE
BRISTOL AVE
CHRYSLER DR.
QUEBEC DR.
ELKCO
LA-GRANGE AVENUE
CHICAGO BLVD.
MARQUETTE AVE
ROCHESTER AVENUE ROCHESTER
PARKE AVENUE
BETHLEHEM DRIVE
MILL STREET
SCRANTON ST.
EASTON ST.
RACINE ST.
MILWAUKEE
LANCASTER
METRO CIRCLE
COUNTY C.H.
PENNSYLVANIA AVENUE
ERIE AVE
ERIE AVENUE
CHICAGO BOULEVARD
UTICA
SYRACUSE
LAKE BLVD
WABASH BLVD.
LEXINGTON BLVD.
CHASE-MANN-HATTEN
WATER TOWER PLACE
WATER TOWER
OXFORD DRIVE
PLYMOUTH AVENUE
DELAWARE AVE.
DELAWARE
LYNXBOURGH CITY CEMETERY
ST. DAVID CATHOLIC CEMETERY
MT. SINAI HEBREW CEMETERY
LARAMIEE Street
LEXINGTON DR.
ONTARIO
ORLEANS DR.
ARLINGTON
BURLINGTON
DRIVE
US POST OFFICE
INDUSTRIAL AREA
YORK AVENUE
HICKMAN DR.
QUINCY
PRAIRIE
N
W E
S

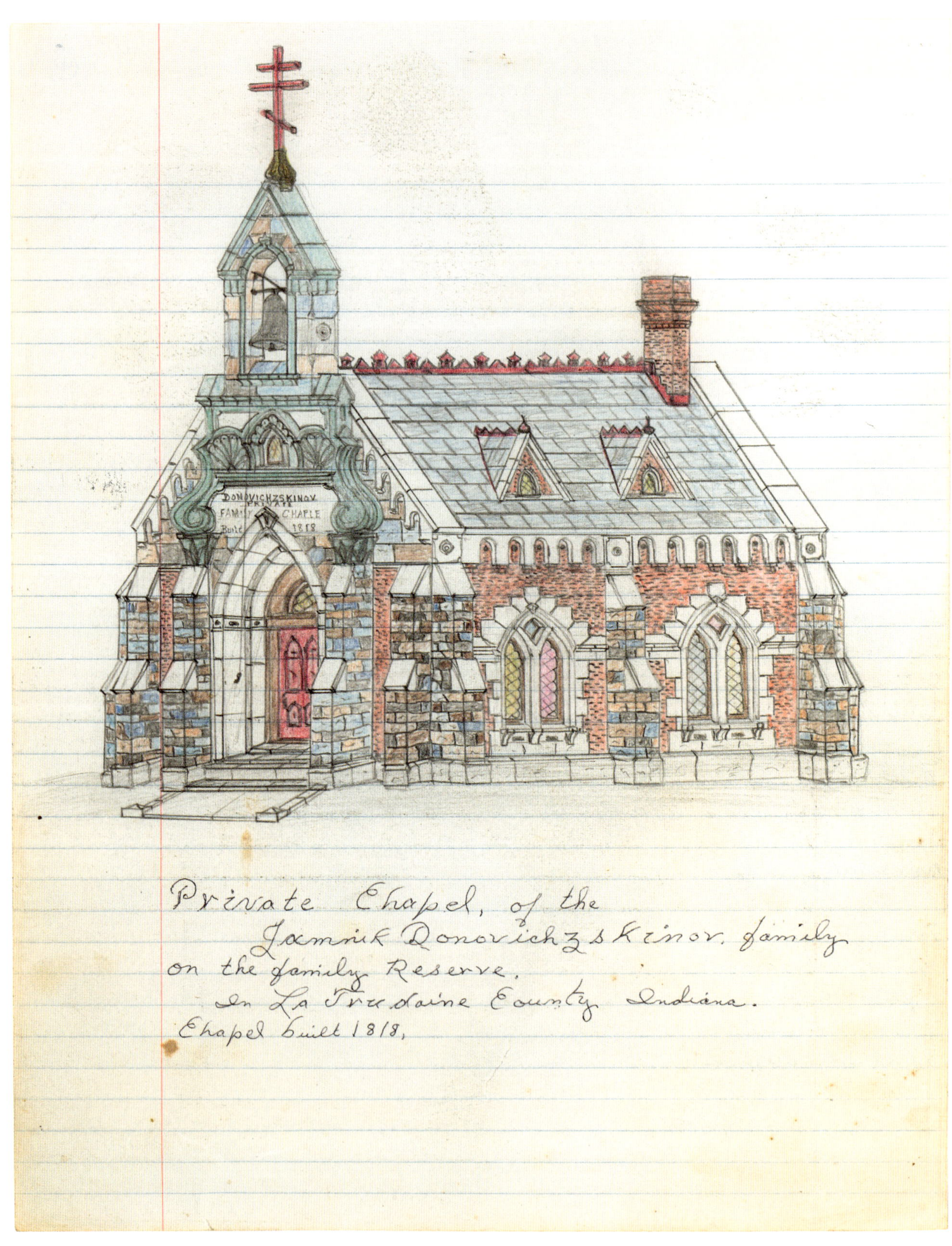

Jàcques de Dû-Glass, *Private Chapel of the Donovich Z. Skinor Family, Lynxbourgh, Indiana*, c. 1992.
Graphite and colored pencil on paper, 11 × 8½ in. (27.9 × 21.6 cm)

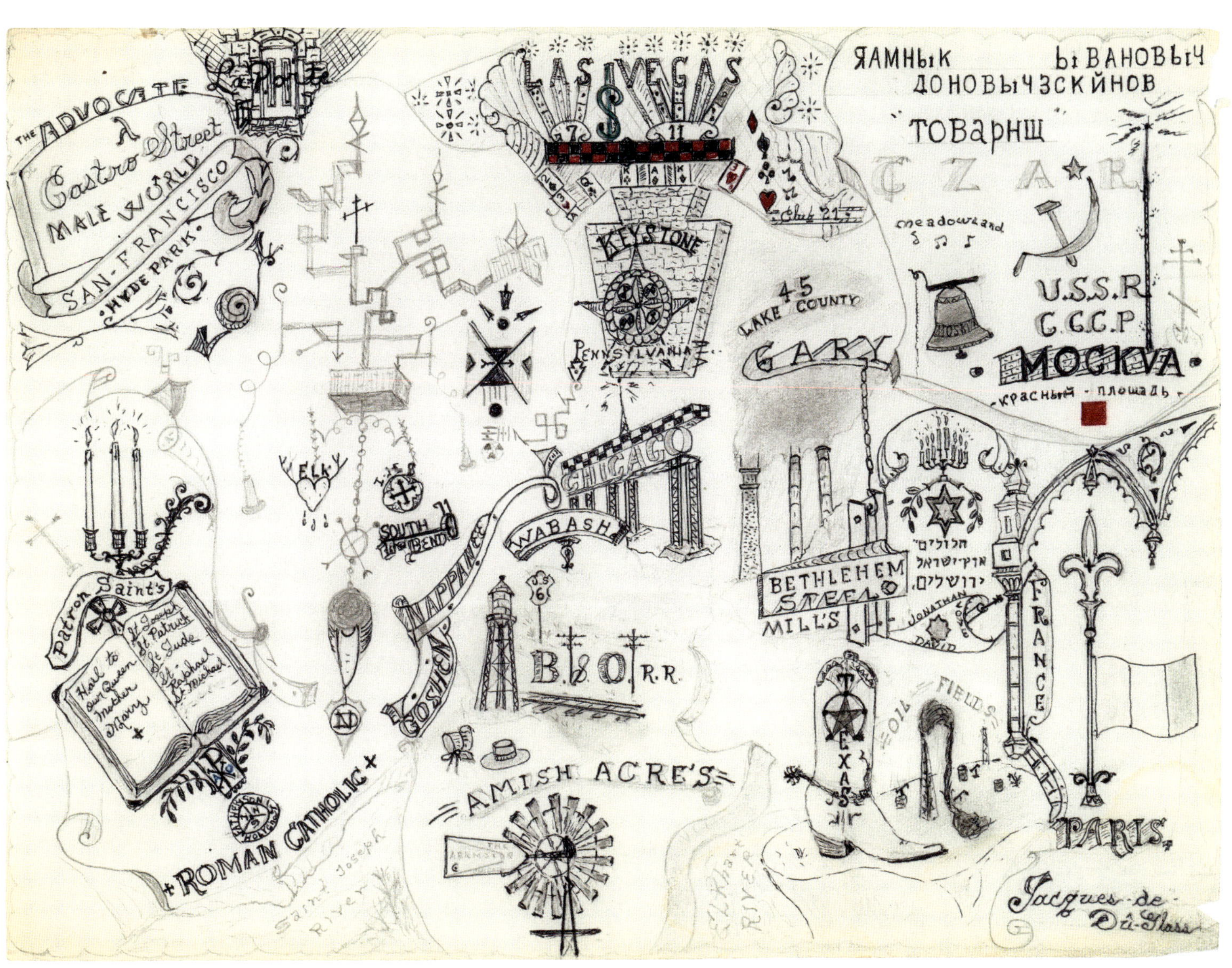

Jàcques de Dû-Glass, *Untitled (Studies)*, c. 1992. Graphite and ink on paper, 8½ × 11 in. (21.6 × 27.9 cm)

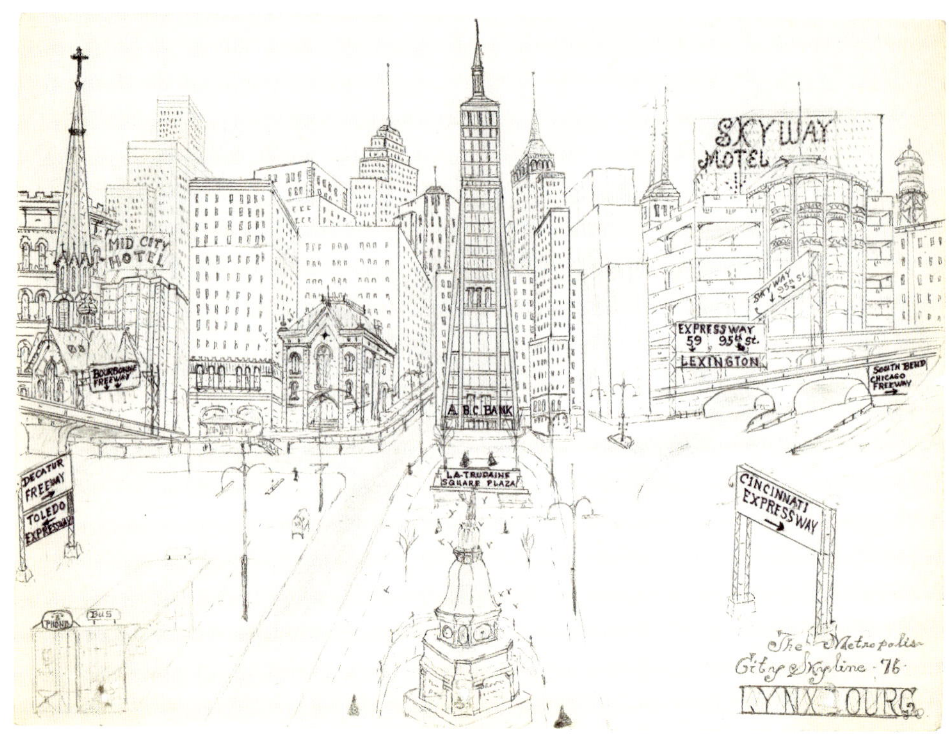

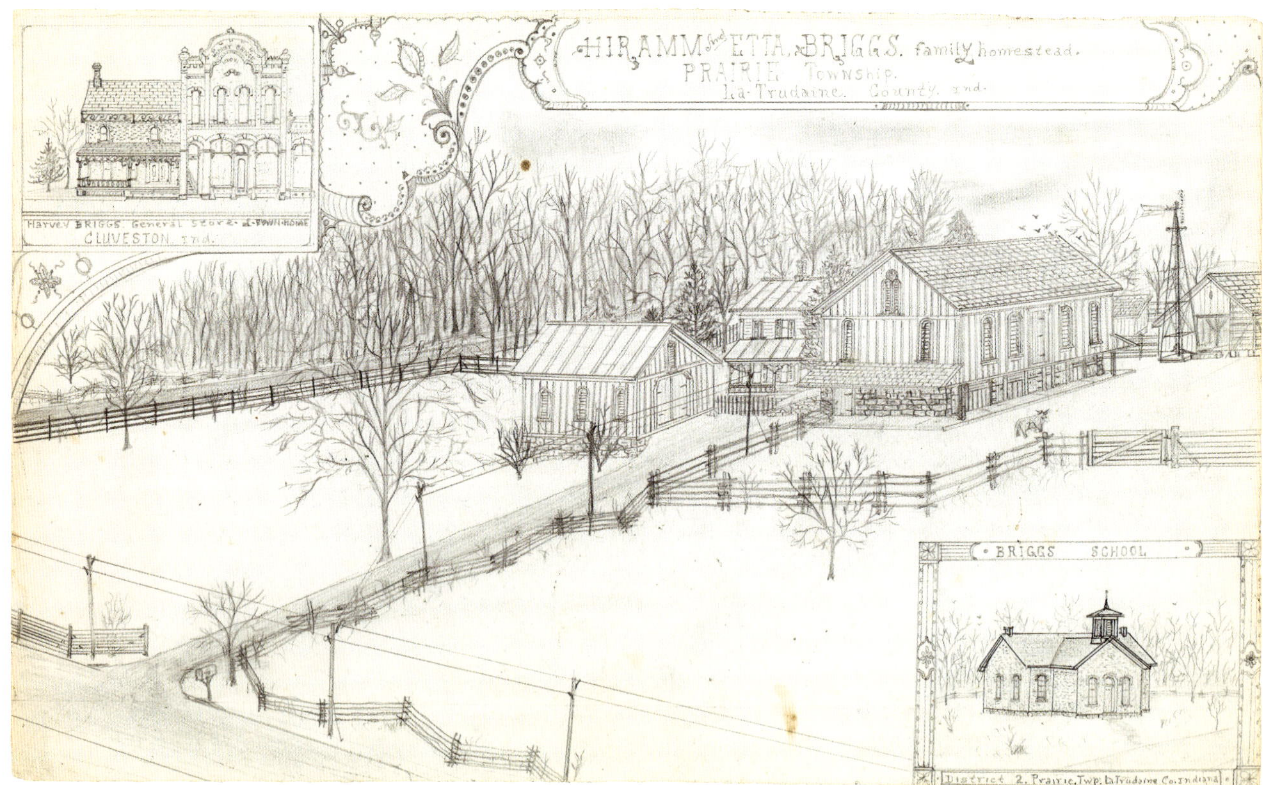

Jàcques de Dû-Glass, *The Metropolis City Skyline, Lynxbourgh, Indiana*, c. 1992. Graphite and ink on paper, 8½ × 11 in. (21.6 × 27.9 cm)

Jàcques de Dû-Glass, *Hiram & Etta Briggs Family Homestead, Lynxbourgh, Indiana*, c. 1992. Graphite on paper, 10½ × 17 in. (26.7 × 43.2 cm)

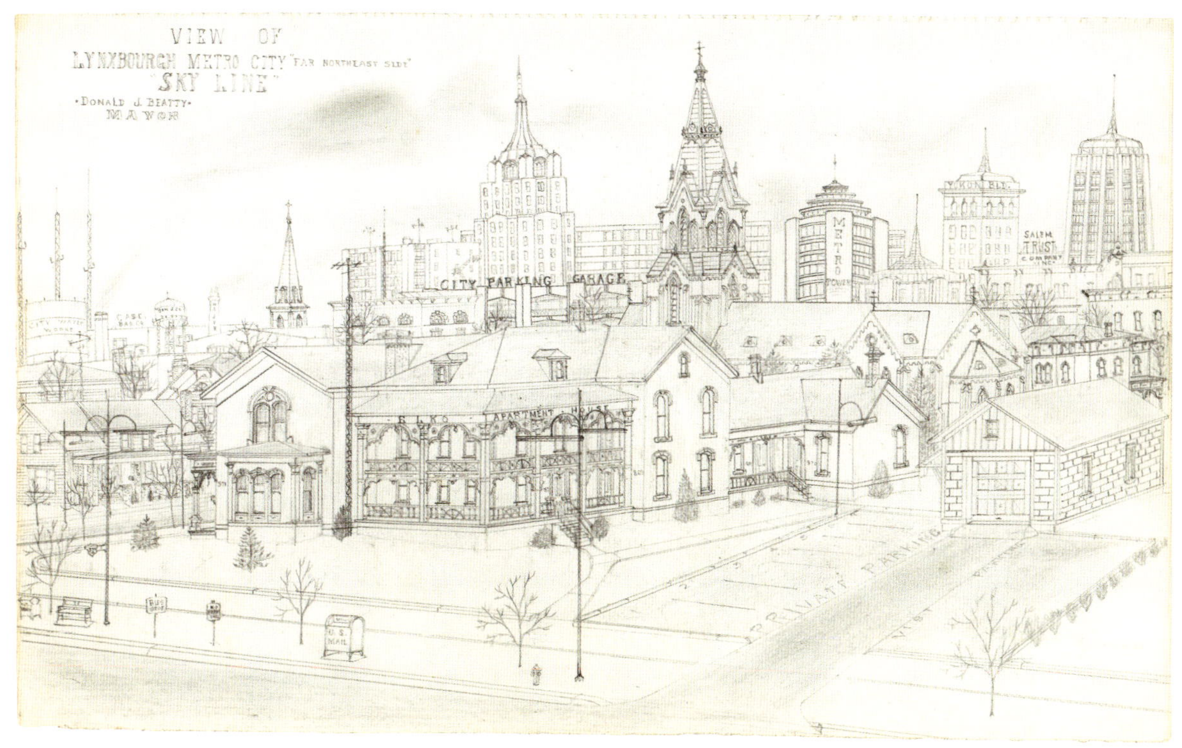

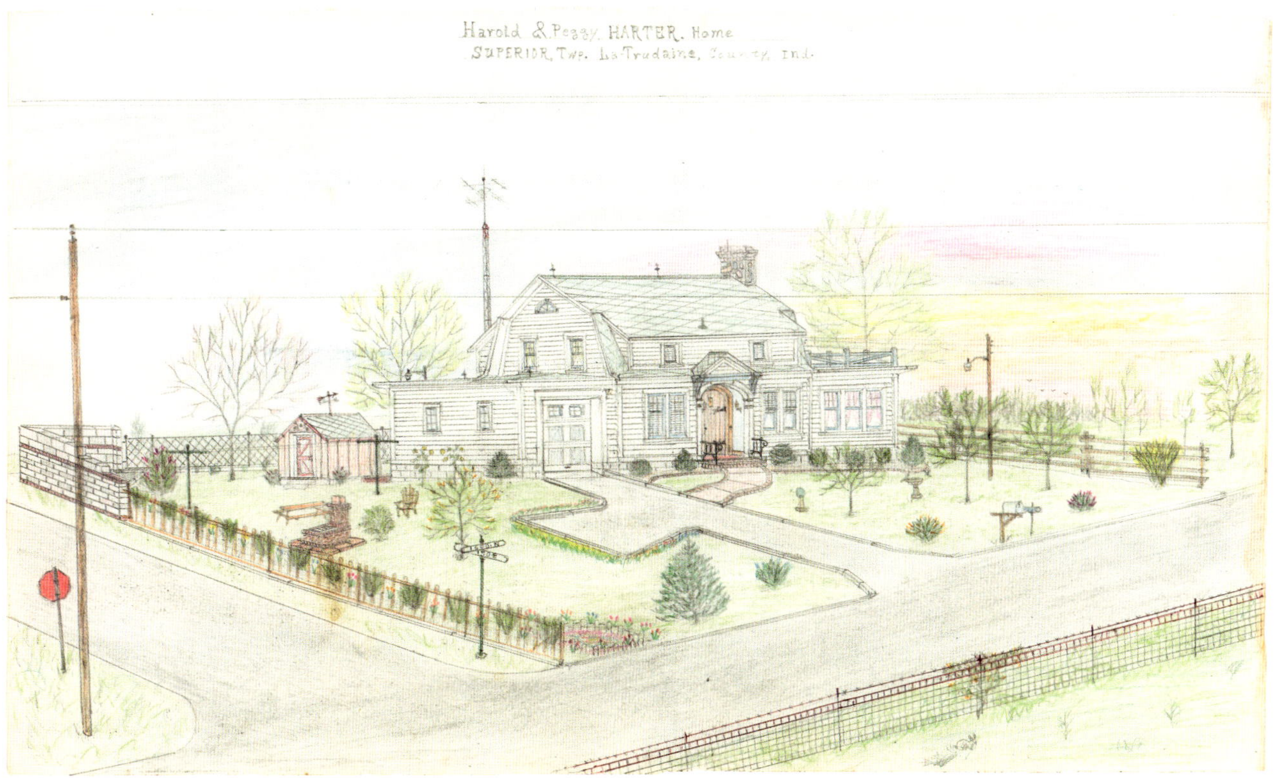

Jàcques de Dû-Glass, *View of the Lynxbourgh Metro City Sky Line, Lynxbourgh, Indiana*, c. 1992. Graphite and colored pencil on paper, 11 × 17½ in. (27.9 × 44.5 cm)

Jàcques de Dû-Glass, *Harold & Peggy Harter Home, Lynxbourgh, Indiana*, c. 1992. Graphite and colored pencil on paper, 10 × 17½ in. (25.4 × 44.5 cm)

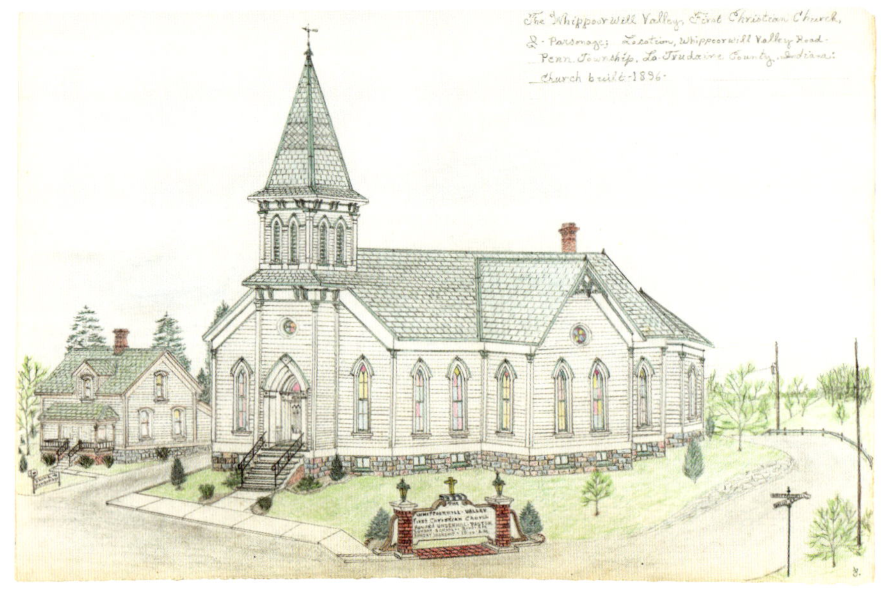

Jàcques de Dû-Glass, *Whipporwill Valley First Christian Church, Lynxbourgh, Indiana*, c. 1992. Graphite and colored pencil on paper, 12 × 17½ in. (30.5 × 44.5 cm)

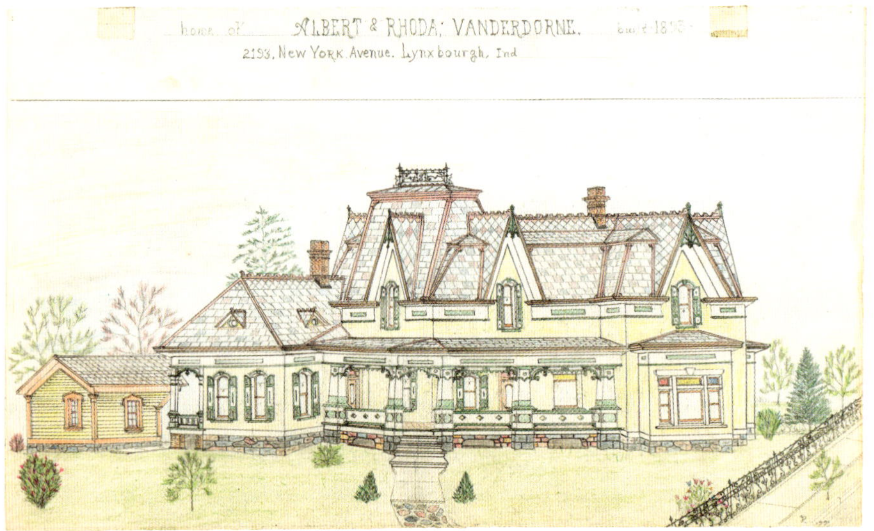

Jàcques de Dû-Glass, *Home of Albert & Rhoda Vanderdorne, Lynxbourgh, Indiana*, c. 1992. Graphite and colored pencil on paper, 10¾ × 17½ in. (27.3 × 44.5 cm)

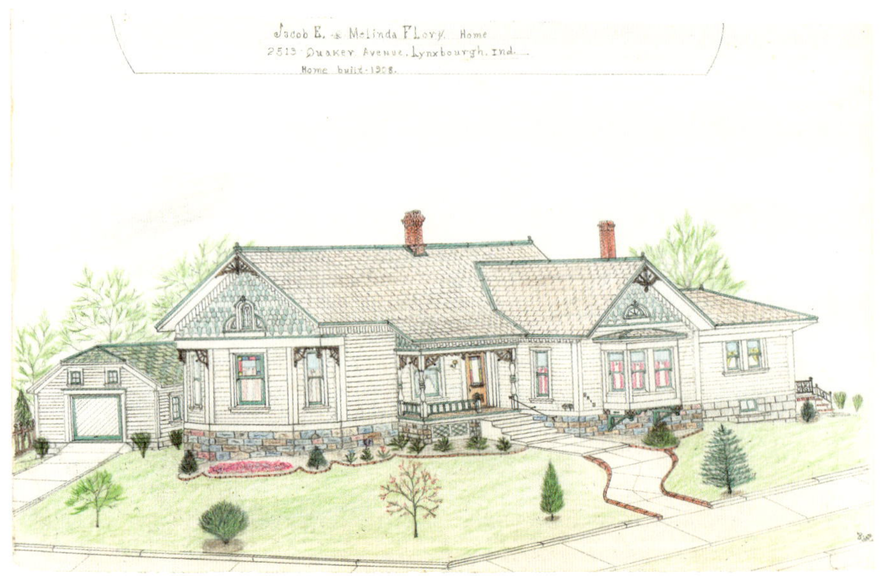

Jàcques de Dû-Glass *Jacob & Melinda Flory Home, Lynxbourgh, Indiana*, c. 1992. Graphite and colored pencil on paper, 11½ × 17¼ in. (29.2 × 43.8 cm)

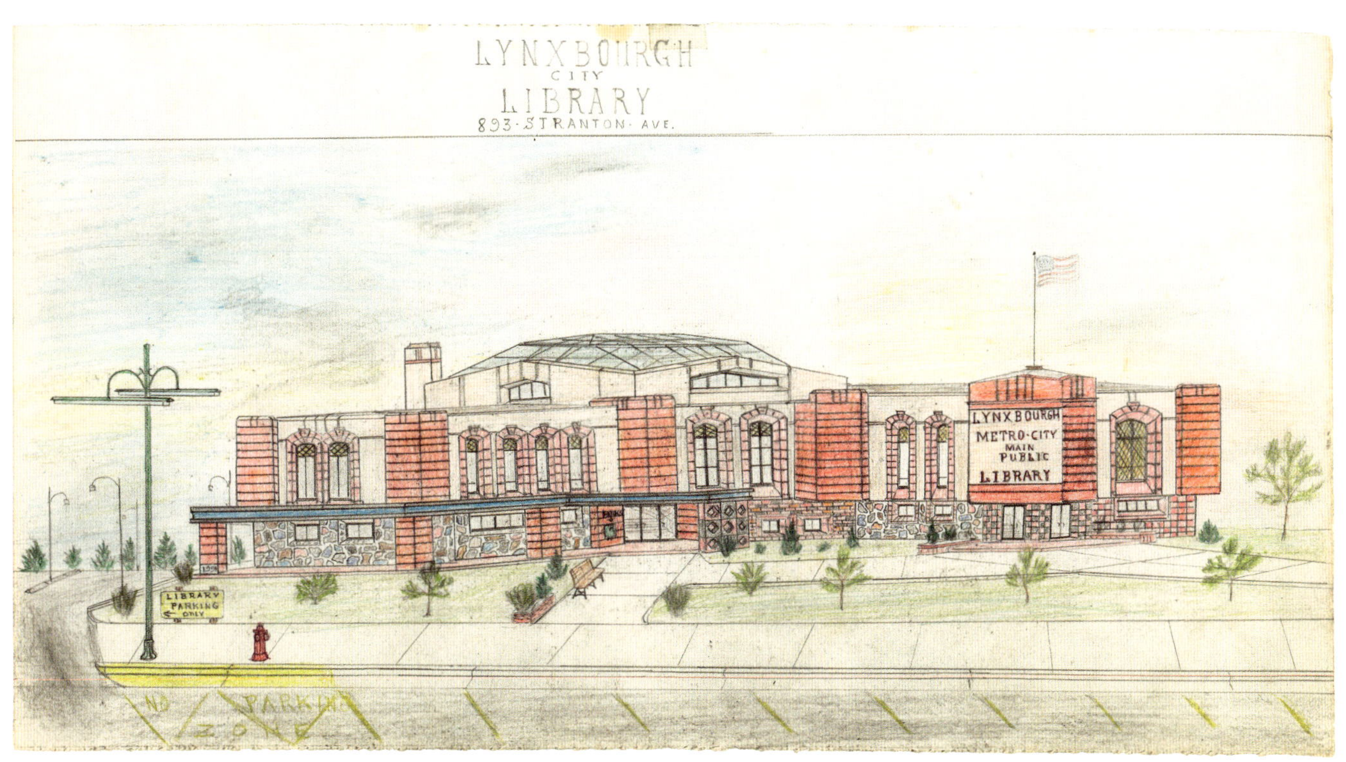

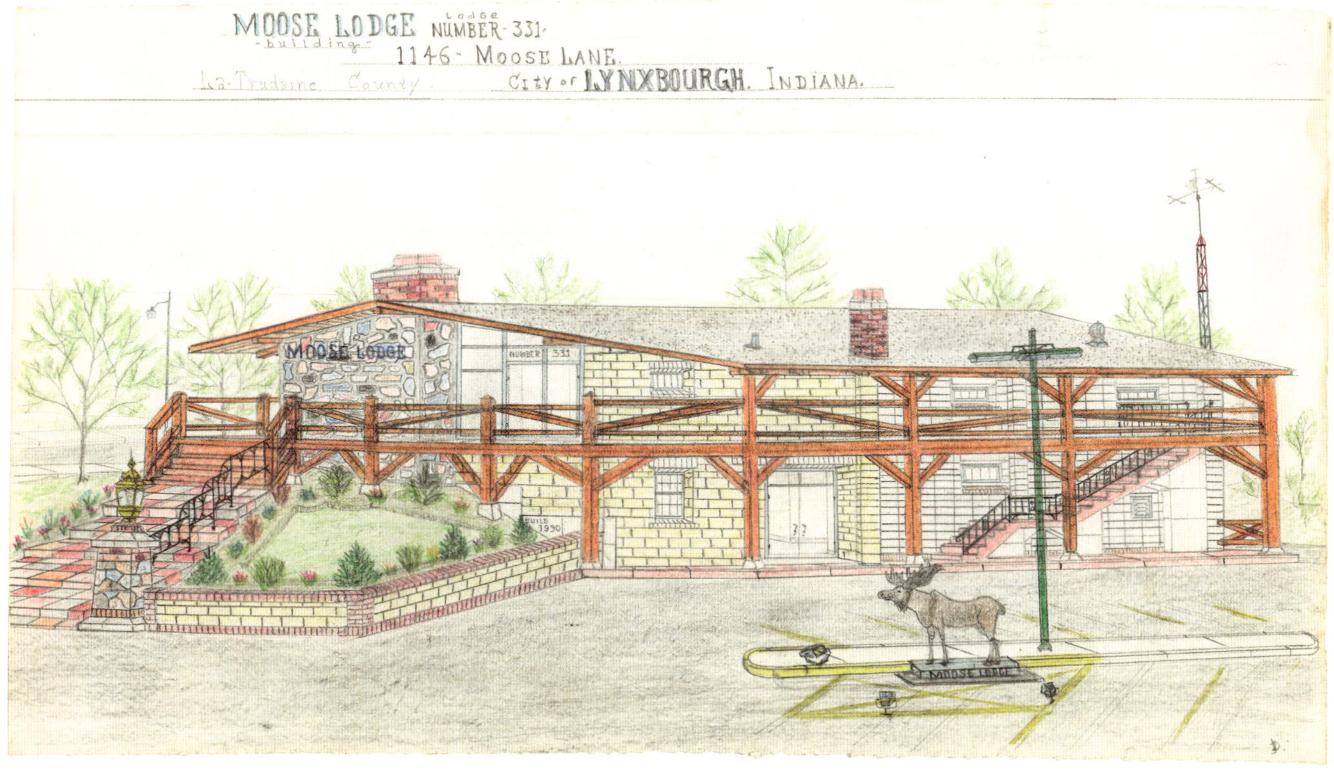

Jàcques de Dû-Glass, *Lynxbourgh City Library, Lynxbourgh, Indiana*, c. 1992. Graphite and colored pencil on paper, 9¾ × 17½ in. (24.8 × 44.5 cm)

Jàcques de Dû-Glass, *Moose Lodge, Lynxbourgh, Indiana*, c. 1992. Graphite and colored pencil on paper, 11 × 17½ in. (27.9 × 44.5 cm)

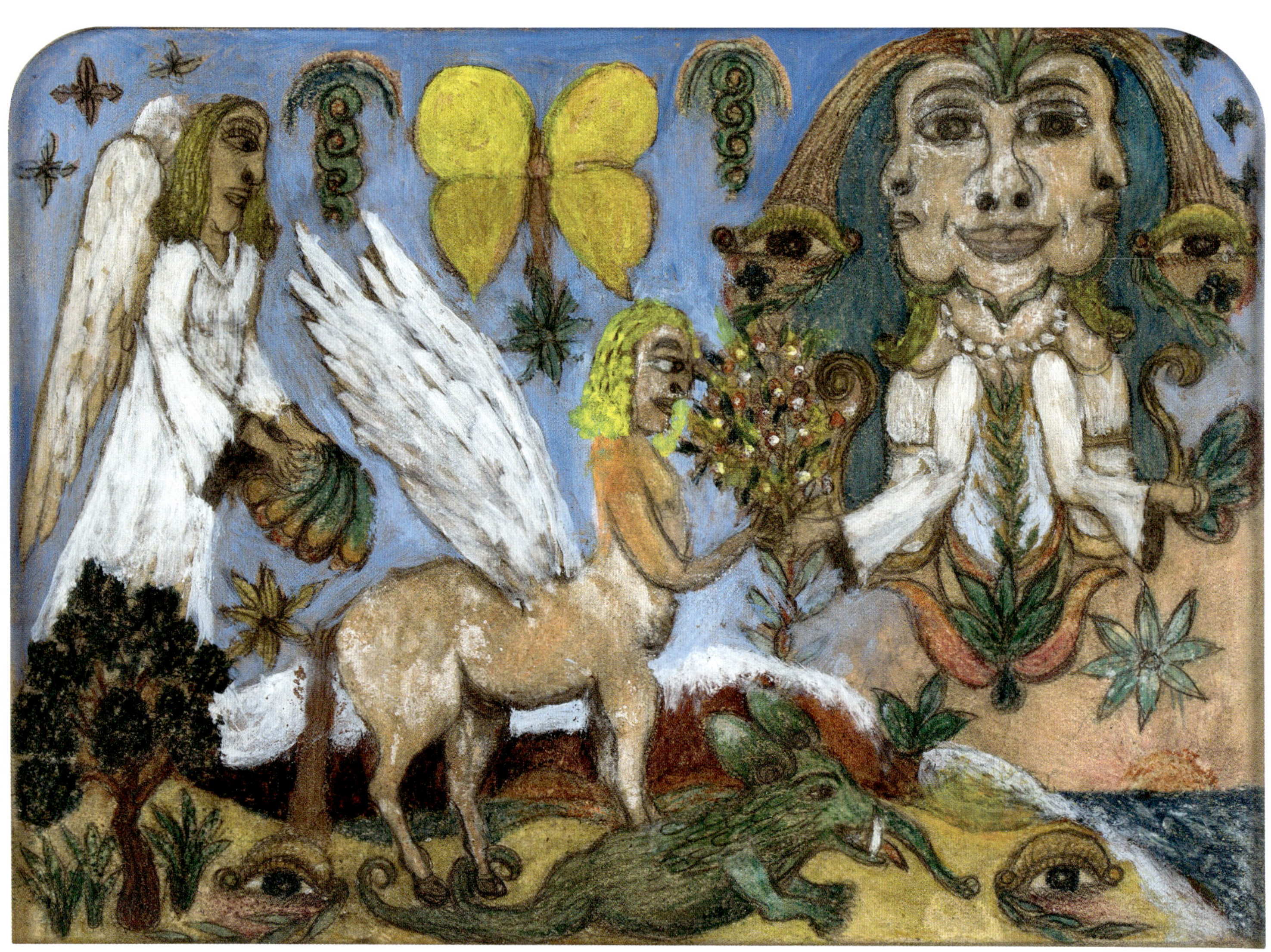

MINNIE EVANS

1892–1987

The work of Minnie Evans depicts visions and dreams of an intimate, deeply spiritual world that expands like a kaleidoscope. Evans's ancestors were slaves brought to the United States from Trinidad, and her mother was only thirteen years old when Minnie was born in a log cabin in Long Creek, Pender County, North Carolina. She attended school through the sixth grade, dropping out to sell oysters and clams. In 1908 Evans moved with her family to Wrightsville Beach, in New Hanover County, North Carolina, where she remained for most of her life. Employed as a domestic worker, she married, had three sons, and in the mid 1930s discovered art. In 1948 she took a job as a gatekeeper at Airline Gardens in the Pembroke estate, a post that she held for more than twenty-five years, her most prolific as an artist. Evans routinely created hundreds of drawings and sold them to visitors for a few dollars, but in 1961 she had her first exhibition at the Little Gallery in Wilmington, and soon met the photographer Nina Howell Starr, who became her main patron and promoter.

Evans began working with crayons and later incorporated graphite, ink, wax, oils, and collage into her work, a fusion of a rich visual imagination, biblical tradition, and island folklore. She claimed to have had visions since early childhood, and her religious faith inspired most of her creations. The persistent symbolism in Evans's paintings was something she herself could not explain; working intuitively, she produced lush, sprawling, dense compositions with a sense of rhythm and symmetry. Brightly colored sinuous botanical motifs and patterns enclose the faces of deities, animals, mythological creatures, and a winged God. Flowers, leaves, and butterflies intertwine with calm open eyes, smiling lips, and blooming halos. "The paintings and colored drawings of Minnie Evans are surrealistic without intellectualism or self-consciousness," as the art historian Regenia A. Perry has described them. "They are the works of a visionary who equated God with nature, color with His divine presence, and dreams and visions with reality . . . [H]er paintings shimmer with the complexity of Byzantine mosaics. And like Byzantine mosaics, Evans' works embody a common religious intent and express the omnipotence of God."

Evans retired from her job at Airline Gardens in 1974 and moved to an assisted living facility in 1981, where she continued to draw and paint until her death at age ninety-five. Evans's work is in the collections of the Cameron Art Museum (Wilmington, North Carolina), the Smithsonian American Art Museum (Washington, D.C.), the Museum of Modern Art (New York), the Whitney Museum of American Art (New York), the American Folk Art Museum (New York), and the Newark Museum (New Jersey).

Minnie Evans, *Angel with Centaur and Creatures*, 1978. Mixed media on paper, 9¼ × 12½ in. (23.5 × 31.8 cm)

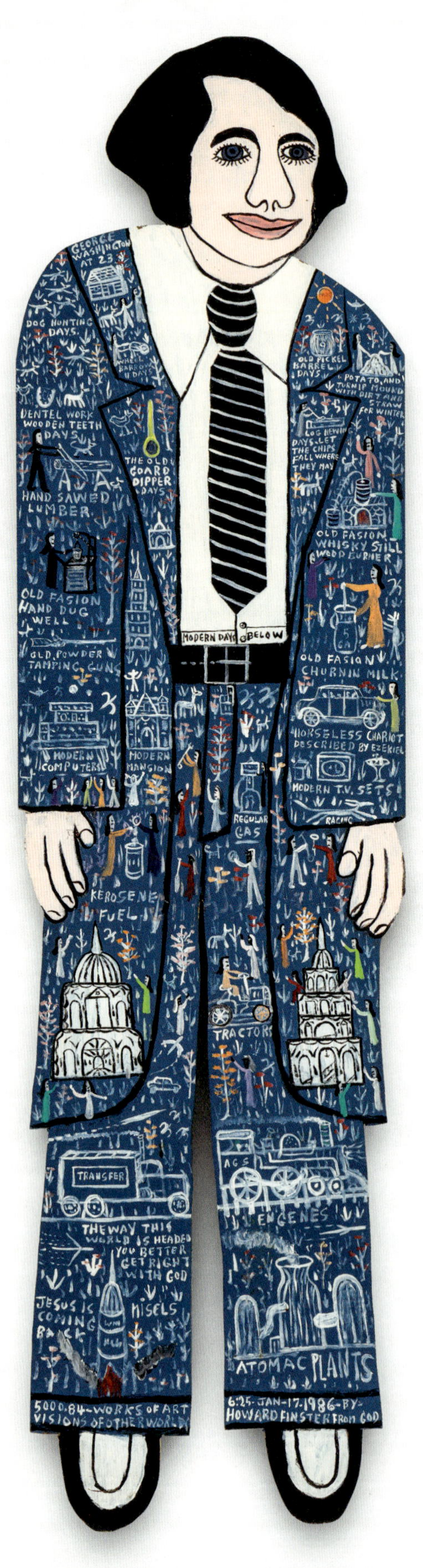
GEORGE WASHINGTON AT 23
DOG HUNTING DAYS.
WHEEL BARROW DAYS
OLD PICKEL BARREL DAYS
POTATO, AND TURNIP MOUND WITH DIRT AND STRAW FOR WINTER
DENTEL WORK WOODEN TEETH DAYS
THE OLD GOARD DIPPER DAYS
LOG HEWING DAYS, LET THE CHIPS FALL WHERE THEY MAY
HAND SAWED LUMBER.
OLD FASION WHISKY STILL WOOD BURNER
OLD FASION HAND DUG WELL
MODERN DAYS BELOW
OLD POWDER TAMPING GUNS
OLD FASION CHURNIN MILK
HORSELESS CHARIOT DESCRIBED BY EZEKIEL
MODERN COMPUTERS
MODERN MANSION
MODERN T.V. SETS
REGULAR GAS
RACING
KEROSENE FUEL
TRACTORS
TRANSFER
ENGENES
THE WAY THIS WORLD IS HEADED YOU BETTER GET RIGHT WITH GOD
JESUS IS COMING BACK
MISELS
ATOMAC PLANTS
5000.84-WORKS OF ART VISIONS OF OTHER WORLDS
6:25-JAN-17-1986-BY-HOWARD FINSTER FROM GOD

HOWARD FINSTER

1916–2001

Howard Finster was born in Valley Head, Alabama, one of thirteen children in the Finster family. He attended school through only the sixth grade, delivered his first sermon at age sixteen, and was eventually ordained at the Violet Hill Baptist Church and went on to lead many other small rural churches over the next forty years. In 1935 he and Pauline Freeman married, and they had four daughters and one son. To support his family, he worked at all kinds of side jobs, including carpentry, plumbing, bricklaying, and mechanical repairs—which Finster, famously charismatic, seemed to have taken in stride. The reverend's first creative expression was in the form of outdoor environments: first a garden museum in Trion, Georgia, which he began as early as 1945, and then what came to be known as the Paradise Garden, constructed on a two-acre plot of land that Finster acquired in the early 1960s in Pennville, Georgia. Paradise Garden was an immersive setting planted with an ornate flora of man-made artifacts and trinkets. When he decided to retire from preaching in 1965—having found that his spoken faith had lost impact in his congregation—Finster focused entirely on Paradise Garden. Then, one day in 1976, a vision that he repeatedly recalled came to him and gave a higher purpose to his work. As recounted in a 1984 interview with Liza Kirwin, Finster described how when he dipped his finger in white paint, he saw a human face on the ball of his finger, and "while I was lookin' at it a warm flash kind'a went all over me, all the way down, and it said, 'Paint sacred art.' And I said to it, I said, 'I cain't do that. I know professionals can, but not me.' And it comes to me again and it says, 'How do you know?' I said, 'How *do* I know that I cain't paint.' I tuck a dollar out of my wallet, and I pasted it on a piece of plyboard and went out in front of my shop, and I started drawing George Washington off that dollar bill."

From that moment on, Finster, a self-proclaimed "man of visions," worked tirelessly, joyfully, and with unyielding faith in his mission, producing more than 46,991 works of art in his remaining years. He created mixed-media sculptural objects and painted with enamel in a precise, graphic manner on all kinds of surfaces and objects, among them wooden boards cut geometrically or irregularly, filing cabinets, metal barrels, saw blades, shoes, and even telephones.

Finster's message was meant to be simple and forceful: God is love, humankind must follow His teachings, salvation comes to those who do . . . Finster's works are endless variations on these ideas, a compulsiveness that echoes the ritual reiteration of church sermons. Most of Finster's work is richly scripted with writings in which he relays the lessons of the Bible along with his thoughts and musings. Life and death, good and bad, heaven and hell were the strict dichotomies that concerned him. In this sense, Finster's iconography is always allegorical and didactic, yet it's also playful, owing as much to popular culture as it does to biblical references and emerging as a complex system of images and words interwoven with sacred and secular allusions. Finster created imaginary apocalyptic landscapes in which he tried to illustrate the currents of mankind moving between salvation

Howard Finster, *George Washington at 23, #5,084*, 1986. Enamel on board, 51½ × 13½ in. (130.8 × 34.3 cm)

and damnation; he portrayed the church as the center of the universe, but his lens was wide enough to include UFOs. He also created cutout wooden silhouettes of various icons, characters, and historical figures: Coca-Cola bottles, cats, and many variations of Uncle Sam, Hank Williams, Elvis Presley, self-portraits, angels, Jesus, and several presidents of the United States served for his intricate microcosms. *George Washington at 23 #5,084* (p. 102), for example, encompasses a visual and verbal landscape that describes the past and present of the American way of life. Finster was drawn to founders, leaders, and trailblazers because he counted himself among them.

Unlike most self-taught and outsider artists, Finster's art was widely celebrated during his lifetime. He had his first important solo show in 1979 at Phyllis Kind Gallery in Chicago, after which his work was shown at the Corcoran Gallery of Art, the New Museum, the Venice Biennale, and the U.S. Library of Congress. He appeared twice on *The Tonight Show Starring Johnny Carson*, painted album covers for the Talking Heads and R.E.M., and was commissioned to paint an eight-foot Coca-Cola bottle for the 1996 Olympic Games. Finster's work is in museums and collections worldwide, including the Whitney Museum of American Art (New York), the Smithsonian American Art Museum (Washington, D.C.), the High Museum of Art (Atlanta), the Philadelphia Museum of Art, the Milwaukee Art Museum, the American Folk Art Museum (New York), the Abby Aldrich Rockefeller Folk Art Museum (Williamsburg, Virginia), and the abcd Collection (Paris).

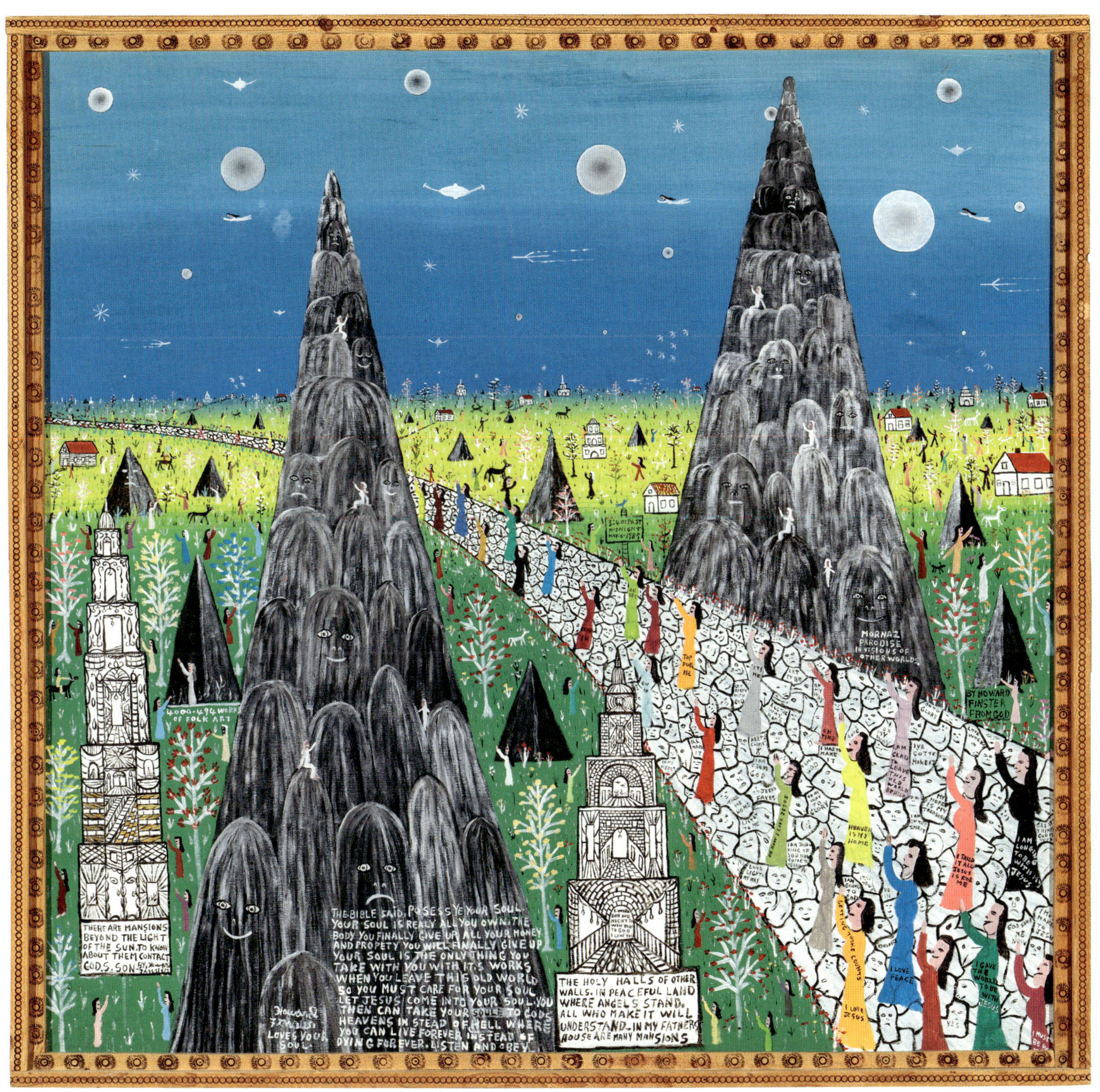

Howard Finster, *Visionary Landscape #4,494*, 1985. Paint on wood, 48 × 48 in. (121.9 × 121.9 cm)

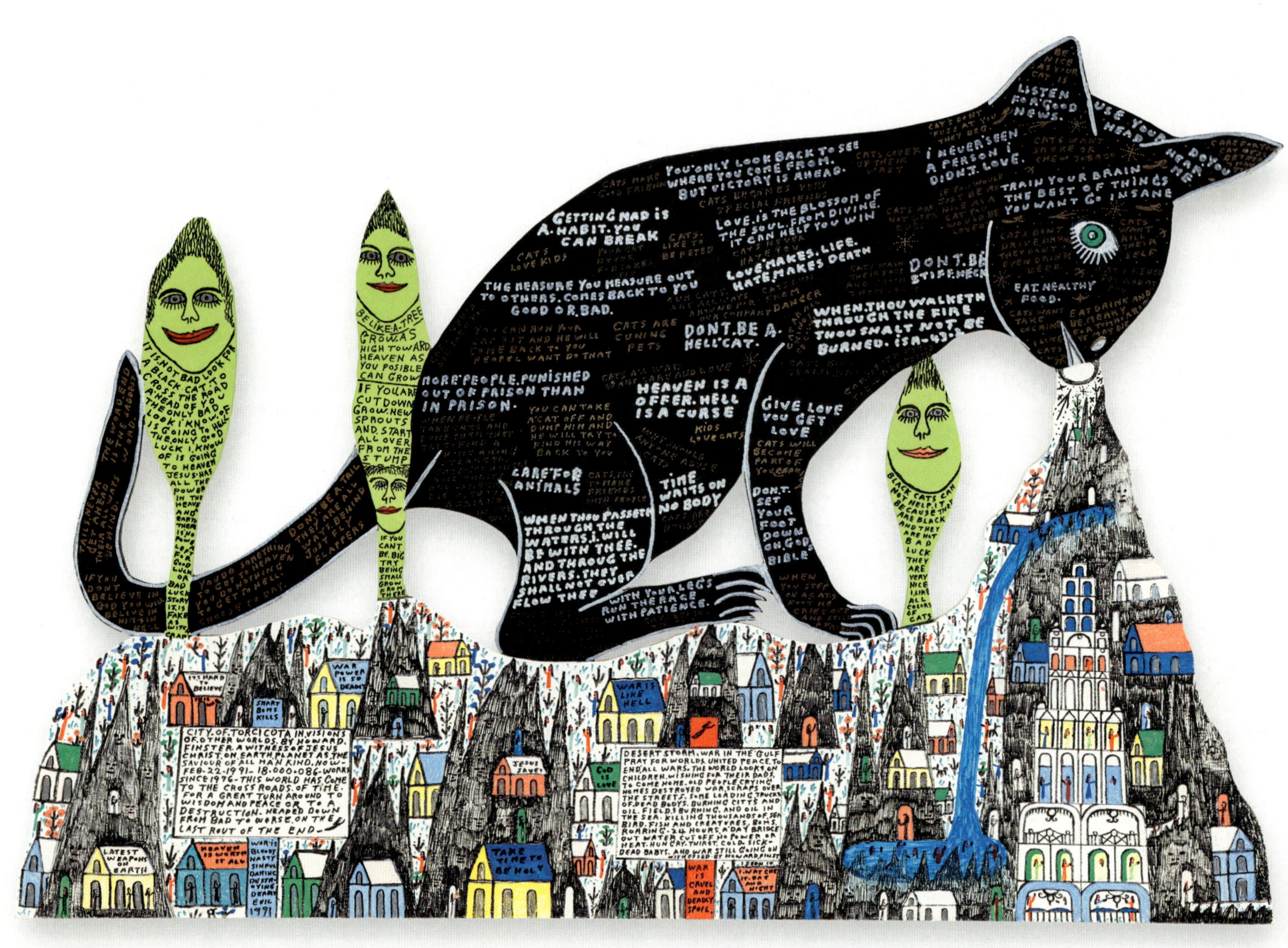

Howard Finster, *Black Cat of Desert Storm #18,086*, 1991. Paint and marker on board, 37 × 51 in. (94 × 129.5 cm)

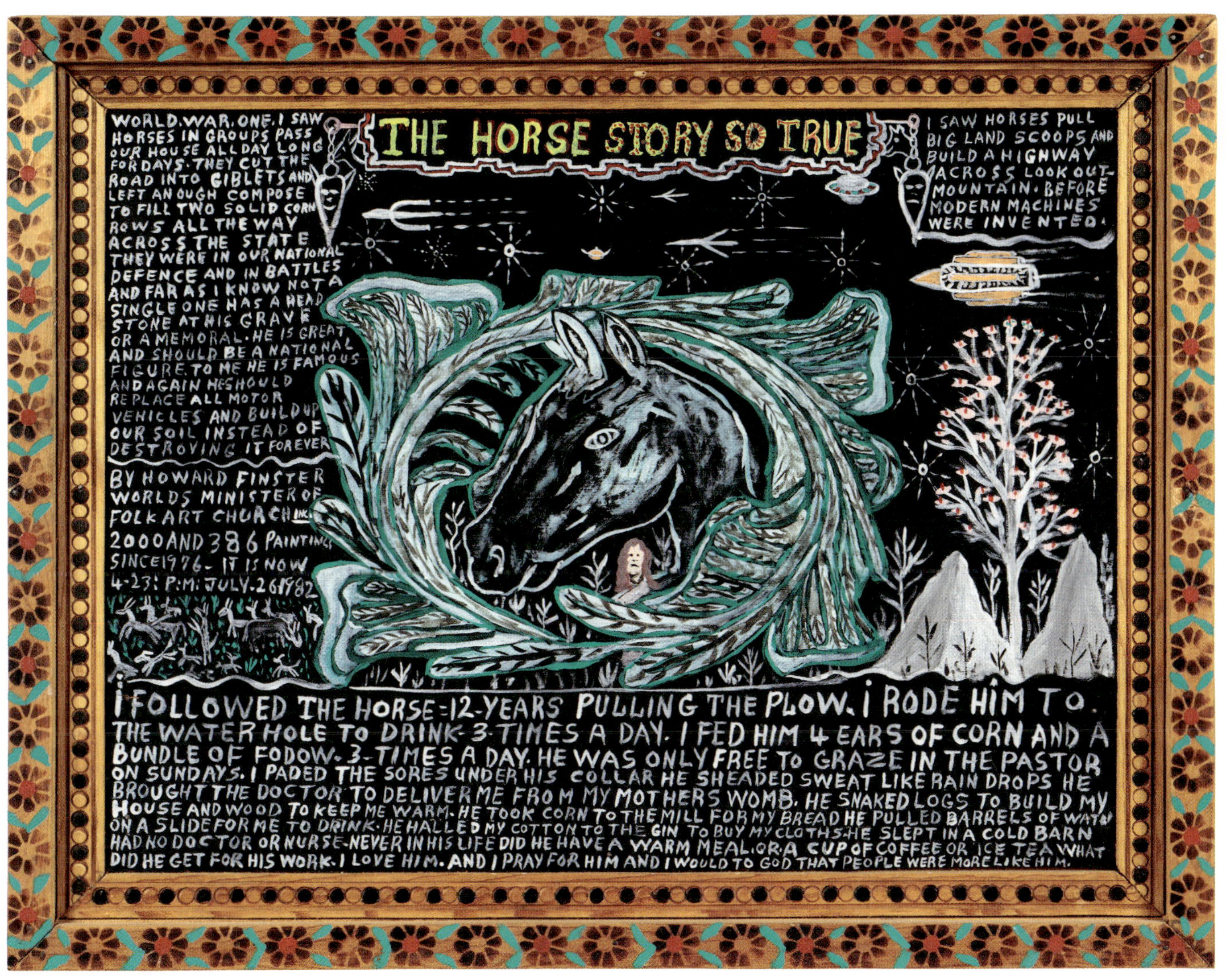

Howard Finster, *The Horse Story So True #2,386*, 1982. Enamel on wood, 15¼ × 19¼ in. (38.7 × 48.9 cm)

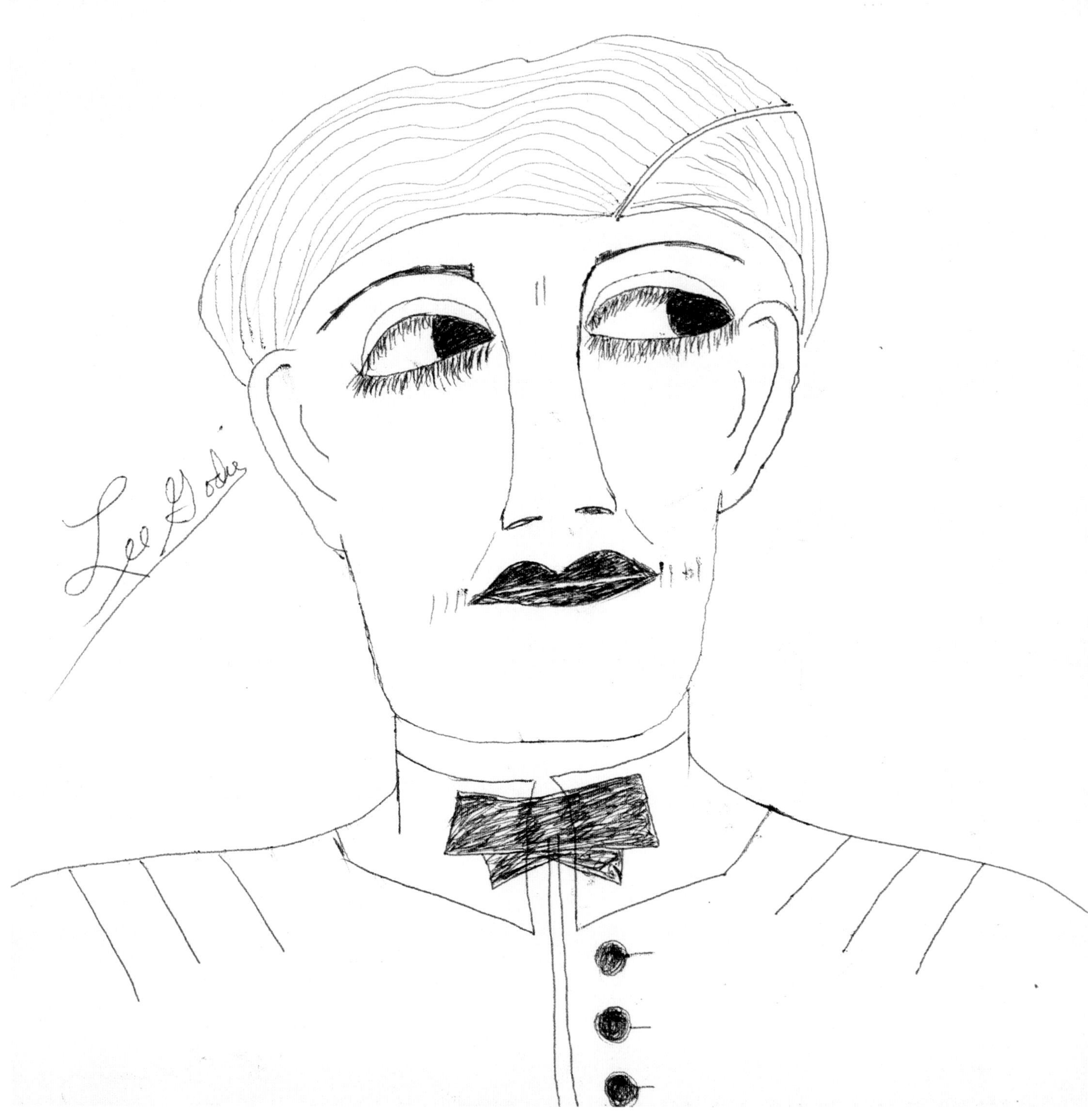
Lee Godie

LEE GODIE

1908–1994

One day in 1968 Lee Godie appeared on the steps of the Art Institute of Chicago with a bunch of artwork to sell. She was homeless by choice and referred to herself as a "French impressionist" and she remained a centerpiece in the city's cultural landscape until shortly before her death. Godie sold her drawings and paintings to passersby (but only if she liked them) for very little money and in time garnered the attention of the art world. She was wary of talking about her life before her self-fashioned debut as an artist, but what is known is that she was born Jamot Emily Godee and was married in the 1930s. She had three children, one of whom died in the early 1940s. Divorce followed, as well as the death of her eldest daughter, who contracted diphtheria. The two deaths apparently led her to believe that illness could be cured by faith rather than medicine. By the 1960s Godie lost her home and took to the streets, becoming a full-time performer, constantly disguised behind many alter egos. As Anna Saunders described her in a 2013 *Telegraph* article, "Colourful and unpredictable, she was as likely to appear wrapped in a toga and fur coat one day as in full safari regalia the next. To downtown workers she was a local character—a beloved part of the city's gritty, urban fabric. . . ."

Godie's subjects included half-bust portraits of imagined characters, especially big-eyed women with impossibly abundant eyelashes, stylishly outfitted in patterned or 1920s fashions that flow into the picture's background. She also portrayed passersby from her spot at the Art Institute, friends, famous people, herself, as well as still lifes, birds, and other animals. She used various traditional and found materials and invented a format called "pillow paintings": two drawings stitched together and stuffed with newspaper. Godie also made many photobooth self-portraits assuming different personas by painting her face, displaying props, and wearing singular attire. She also often altered the prints, scratching the surface and coloring them. These images are a window into the dichotomies of Godie's life on the street—the hardships and the aggressive fantasy, her undiagnosed mental state and her indefatigable shrewdness for survival.

Press coverage of Godie during the last years of her life caught the attention of her surviving daughter, Bonnie Blank, who found her mother and in 1991 was appointed her legal guardian (by then, Godie was suffering from dementia). That same year, Richard M. Daley, Chicago's mayor at the time, proclaimed September "Lee Godie Exhibition Month," urging residents of the city to pay homage to the artist. Godie had two solo exhibitions at the Carl Hammer Gallery (Chicago, 1991 and 1993), a retrospective at the Chicago Cultural Center in 1993, and her work was included in *Art in Chicago 1945–1995* at the Museum of Contemporary Art (Chicago) in 1996. More recently, Intuit: The Center for Intuitive and Outsider Art mounted the exhibition *Finding Beauty: The Art of Lee Godie* (2008). Godie's works are in the permanent collections of the Smithsonian American Art Museum (Washington, D.C.), the American Folk Art Museum (New York), the Museum of Contemporary Art and Intuit (Chicago), the Milwaukee Art Museum, and the Arkansas Art Center (Little Rock).

Lee Godie, *Man's Portrait*, n.d. Ink on paper, 16½ × 16 in. (41.9 × 40.6 cm)

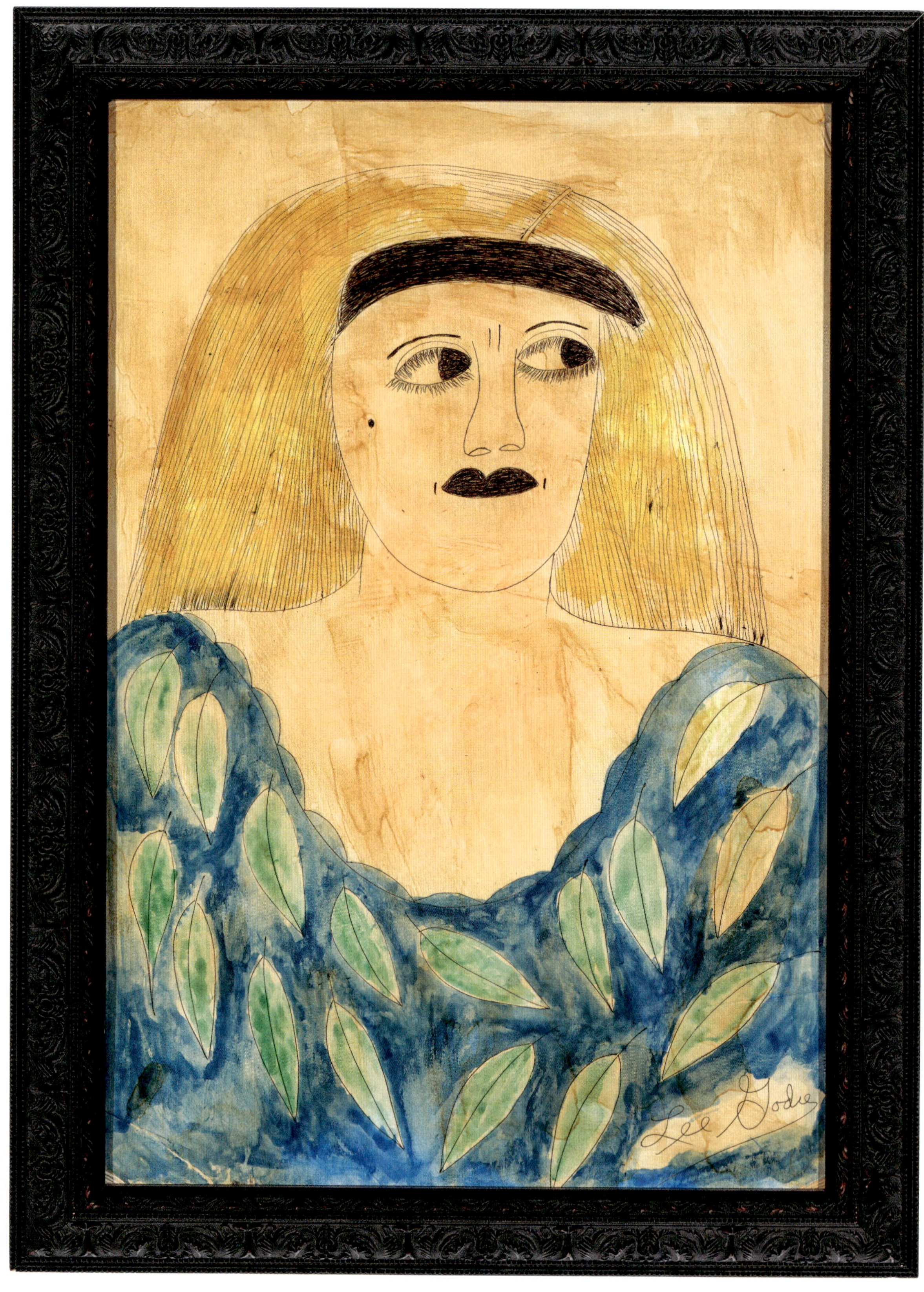

Lee Godie, *Untitled (Portrait of a Lady)*, n.d. Ink and enamel on paper, 29 × 19½ in. (73.7 × 49.5 cm)

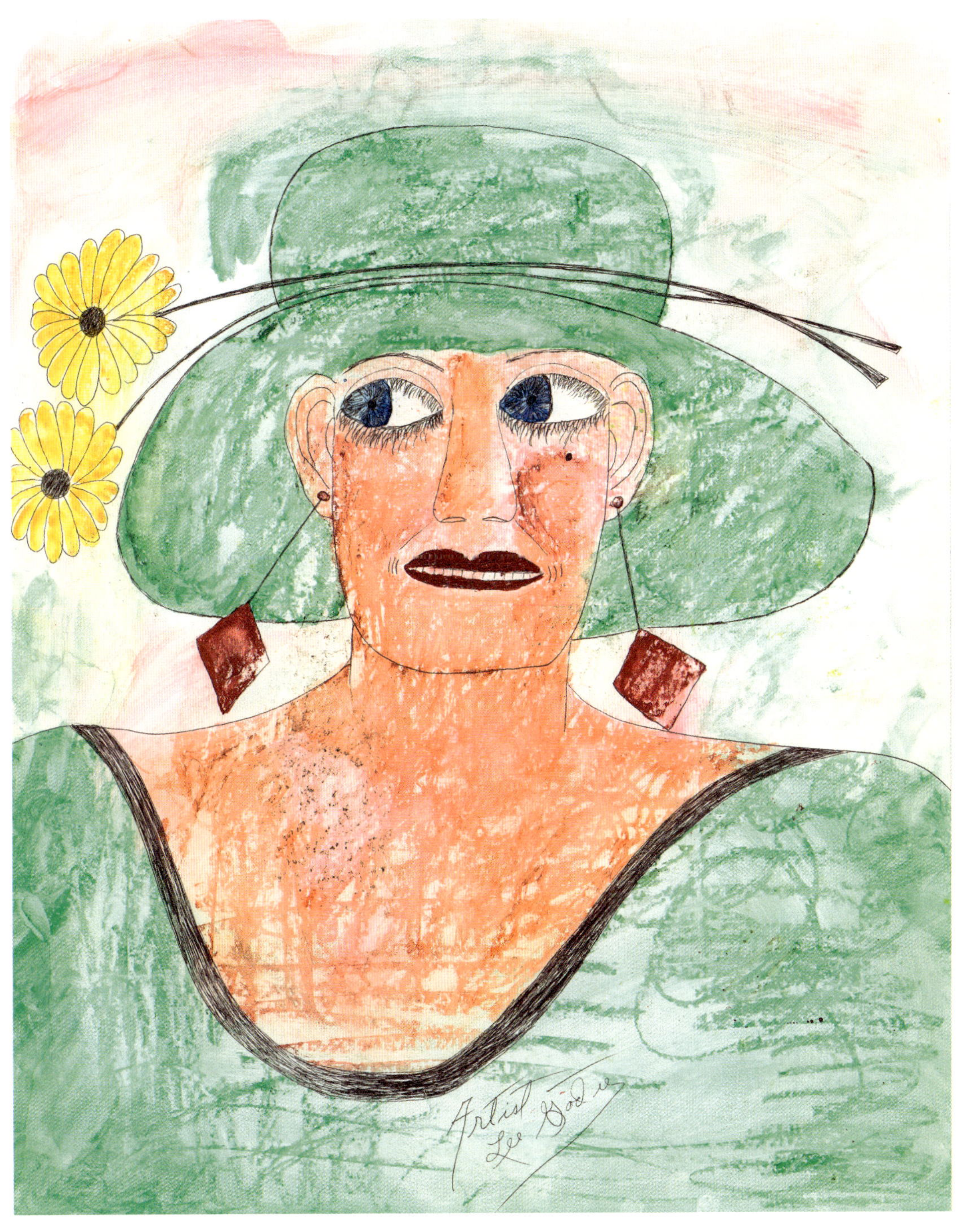

Lee Godie, *Untitled* , n.d. Crayon, watercolor, and ink on paper, 26 × 22 in. (66 × 55.9 cm)

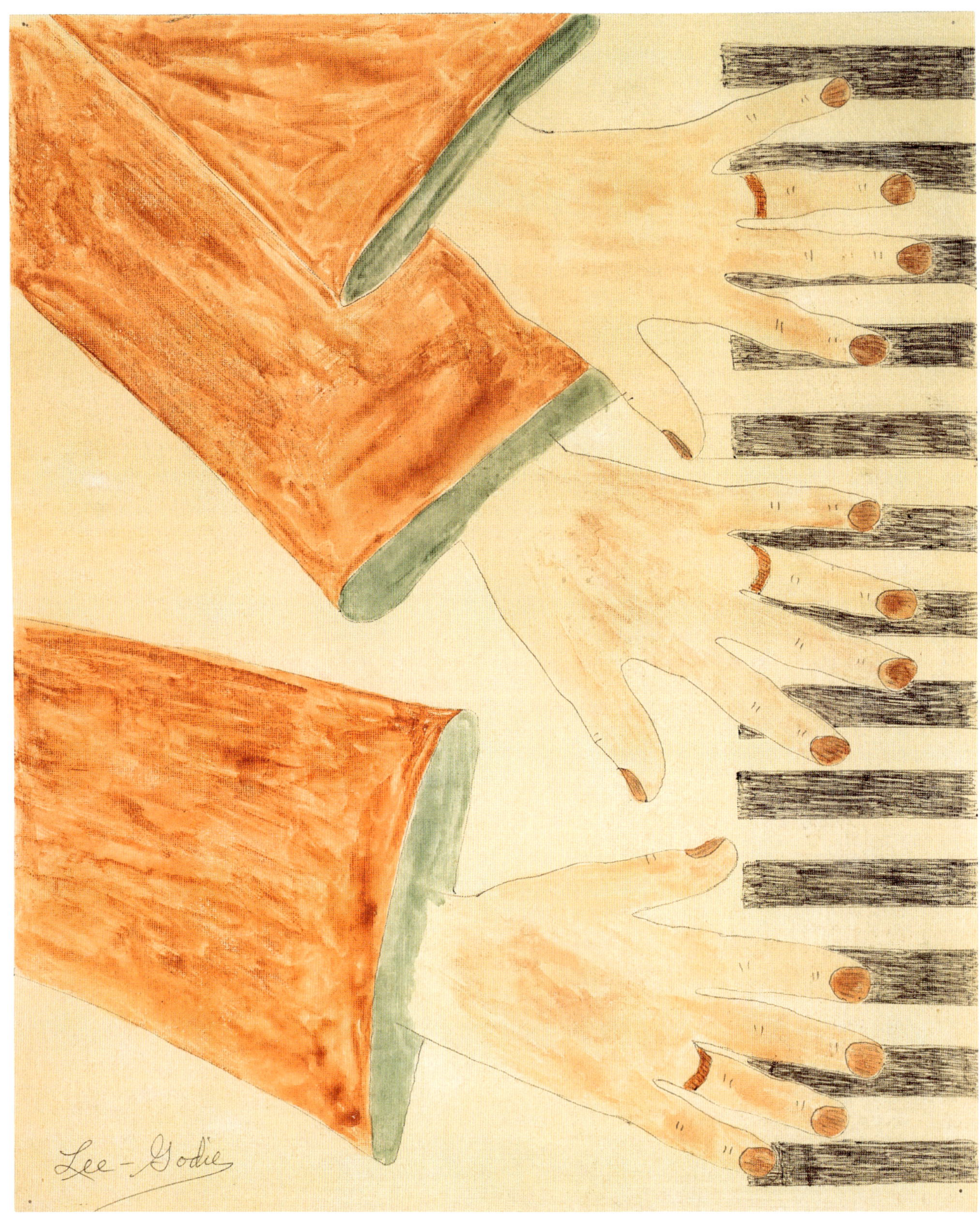

Lee Godie, *Three Hands on a Piano*, n.d. Watercolor and ink on paper, 20 × 16 in. (50.8 × 40.6 cm)

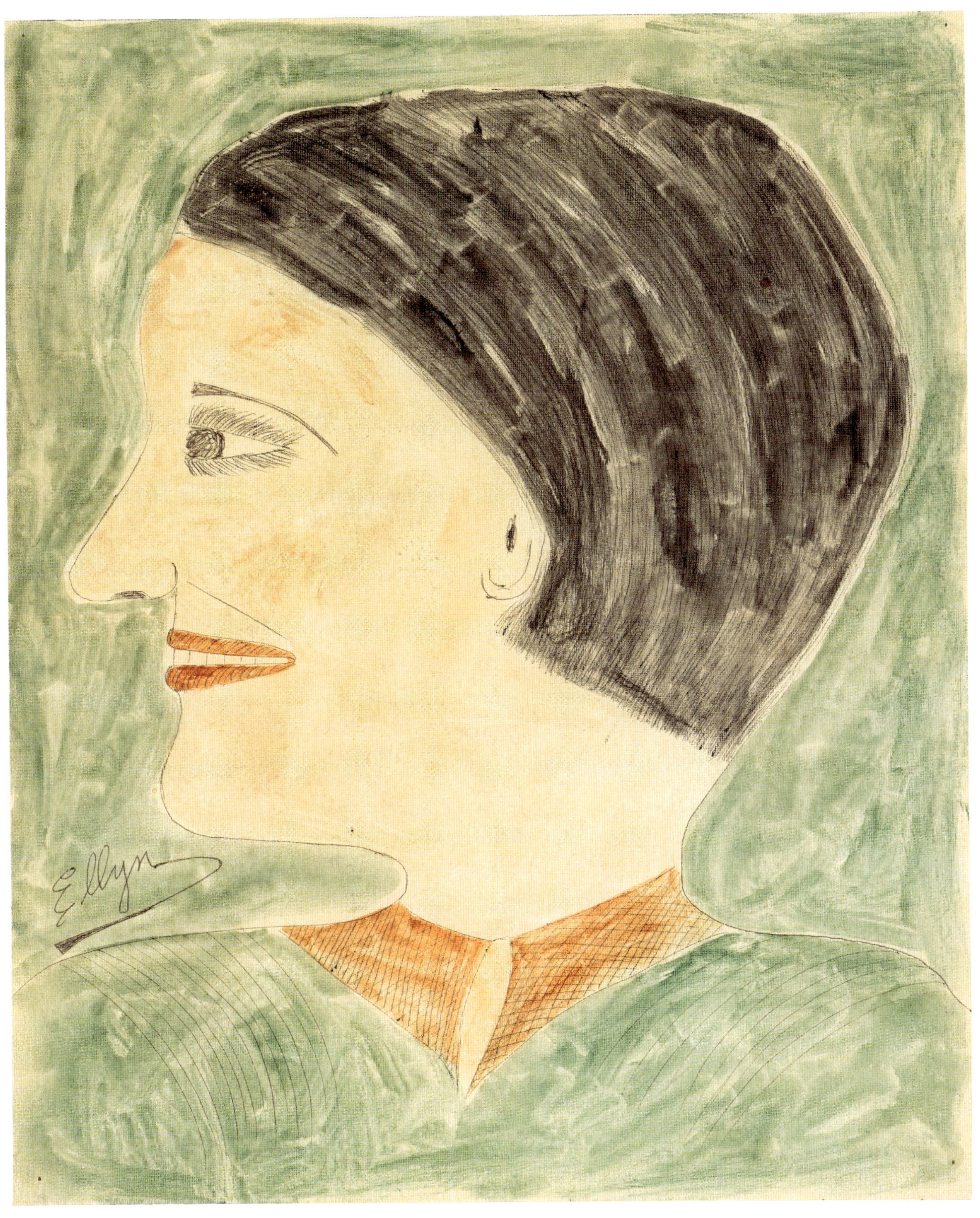

Lee Godie, *Ellyn in Profile*, n.d. Watercolor and ink on paper, 20 × 16 in. (50.8 × 40.6 cm)

KEN GRIMES OF CHESHIRE ENG CALLED 7 STRAIGHT SOCCER TIES AND WON THE LARGEST SOCCER POOL IN HISTORY $1,332,988 KEN GRIMES OF CHESHIRE CONN TRIED TO PSYCHE OUT A WIN AT THE CONN STATE LOTTERY DRAWING HELD AT CHESHIRE INDOOR TENNIS CENTER WITH THE GRAND PRIZE OF $75.000 THE WEEK BEFORE · 11\71

POOL DIAGRAM

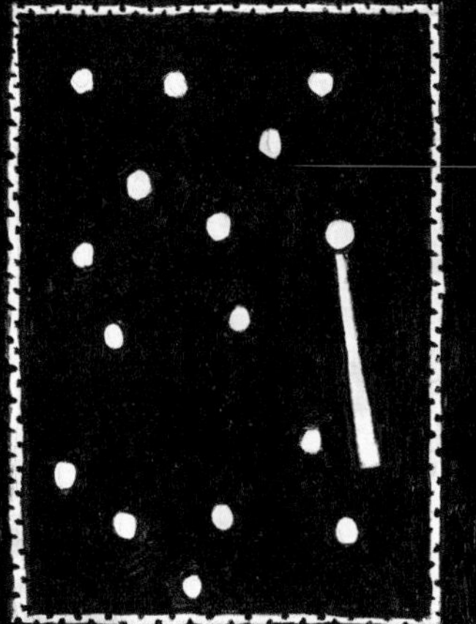

SOMETIMES I WONDER IF THIS STRANGE CO-INCIDENT HAS E.T. OVERTONES BECAUSE IT INVOLVED 2 PLACES WITH THE SAME NAME

KG 03

TENNIS AND SOCCER BALLS

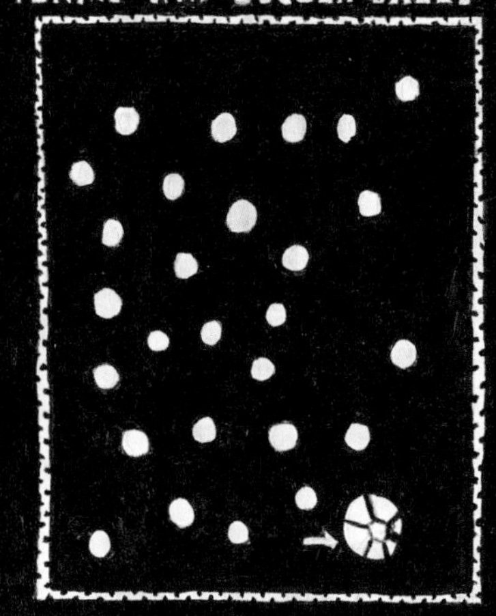

+ HIGH ODDS OF WINNING. I ALSO FEEL THAT MY COUSIN BETTY HILL WHO HAS THE SAME NAME AS THE MOST WIDELY KNOWN ALIEN

BETTY HILL STAR MAP

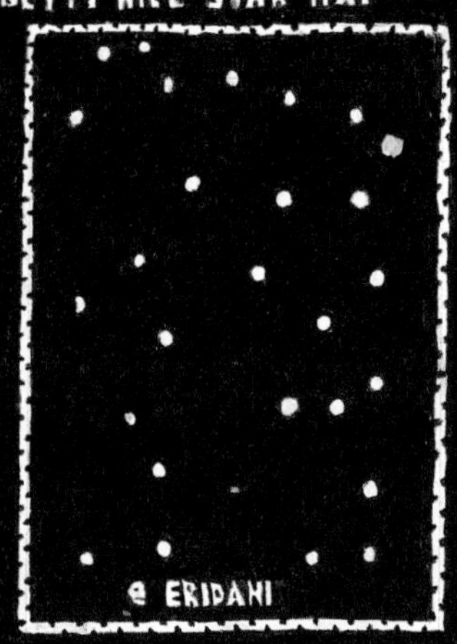

ABDUCTEE PLAYED A PART. BETTY DREW A STAR MAP UNDER HYPNOSIS. AN ASTRONOMER MATCHED ALL 28 STARS

KEN GRIMES

b. 1947

Ken Grimes was born in New York City and grew up in Cheshire, Connecticut. In his early twenties he was diagnosed with paranoid schizophrenia, which forced him to withdraw from college during his sophomore year. Between 1971 and 1978 he was hospitalized five times. Toward the end of the Vietnam War, Grimes's father sold his business, which manufactured parts for rifles, trigger guards, grenade launchers, and other weapons, and built a four-court tennis center, partly to give his son something fun and stress-free to do. "I think my father felt kind of responsible for my illness, so in a way he wanted to get involved," Grimes explained.

The Cheshire tennis center would eventually become one of the main motifs in Grimes's art. One day after a hospital release in 1971, Grimes helped out at a public state lottery drawing that his father hosted at the center to attract business. Following an impulse that he has never been able to explain, Grimes walked among the people gathered, trying to influence the outcome in his favor by envisioning stacks of bills and bags of money. A week after the lottery drawing, Grimes received a letter from a high school friend with a newspaper clipping tucked inside. The news story was about a sixty-two-year-old man named Ken Grimes in Cheshire, England, who won a large soccer pool by calling seven straight ties at 1.5 million-to-one odds. Grimes still keeps the timeworn flyer that was handed out to promote the public drawing and another short newspaper article about the incident, which opens, "What's in a name? A new house, car, an early retirement and a $1,332,988 payoff on a soccer pool, perhaps, if your name happens to be Ken Grimes of Cheshire. Cheshire, England, that is." Since then, Grimes has observed a string of "synchronicities" in books involving his name and Cheshire as a word or a location, which he has always suspected were clues to an alien signal.

Grimes has painted in only black and white for more than thirty years. This constraint is meant to give the message of his paintings the force of truth against deceit. His paintings oscillate between whimsical and stern but are often both. Never-ending variations on the conceptual theme of extraterrestrial intelligence, they are a window to a world where aliens, flying saucers, UFOs, crop circles, radio telescopes, and interstellar signals are an essential part of reality. Grimes's personal mythology, the substance of his artwork, is a pastiche of his autobiography, outer space imagery, and references handpicked from pop culture, science fiction, and astronomy. Text always appears in his paintings—an allusion to the explanatory graphic format of science books. In some of his works all figuration has been dropped in favor of text messages. Through his art, Grimes hopes to prompt others to think about the existence of aliens and the importance of contacting them. In his most recent works on paper, originally conceived as preliminary works for larger compositions but subsequently refined as finished, independent works, Grimes interlaces excerpts from his favorite writers, Carl Sagan and Frank Drake, with his own narrative voice, giving a sense of the continual thought process happening inside his mind.

Ken Grimes, *Untitled (Psyche Out a Win)*, 2003. Acrylic on board, 48 × 72 in. (121.9 × 182.9 cm)

In the 1998 traveling exhibition *Self-Taught Artists of the 20th Century* organized by the American Folk Art Museum Grimes was one of the four extant artists among the thirty-one included. His work is in the permanent collections of the Milwaukee Art Museum, the Philadelphia Museum of Art, the Museum of Contemporary Art in Chicago, and the American Folk Art Museum. In 2018 Grimes's work was selected as one of the exhibitions in a six-part yearly series titled "Field Station" at Michigan State University's Eli and Edythe Broad Art Museum.

Text excerpted and adapted from Alejandra Russi, "Alienated: A Creative Life on the Margins" (master's thesis).

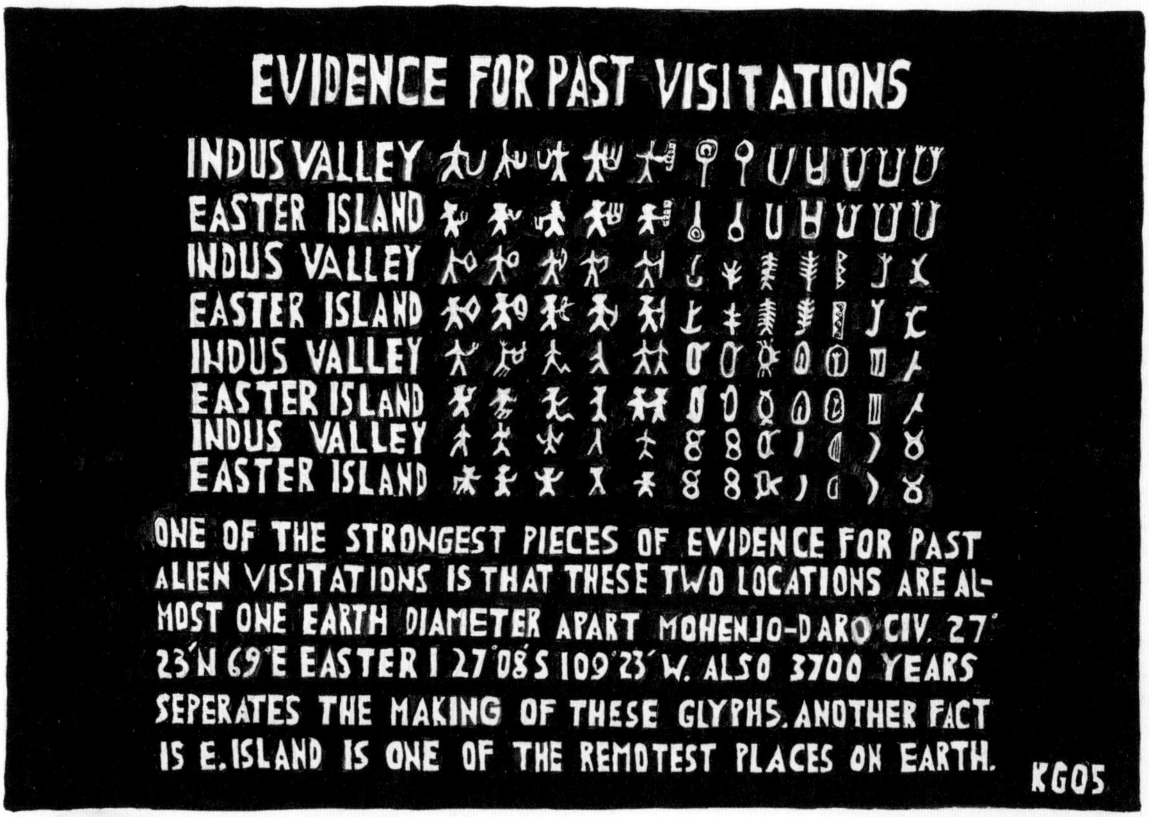

ABOVE: Ken Grimes, *Evidence for Past Visitation*, n.d. Acrylic on canvas, 22 × 30 in. (55.9 × 76.2 cm)

OPPOSITE: Ken Grimes, *Untitled* (four of twelve panels), 2013–2015. Acrylic on canvas, 28 × 20 in. (71.1 × 50.8 cm) each

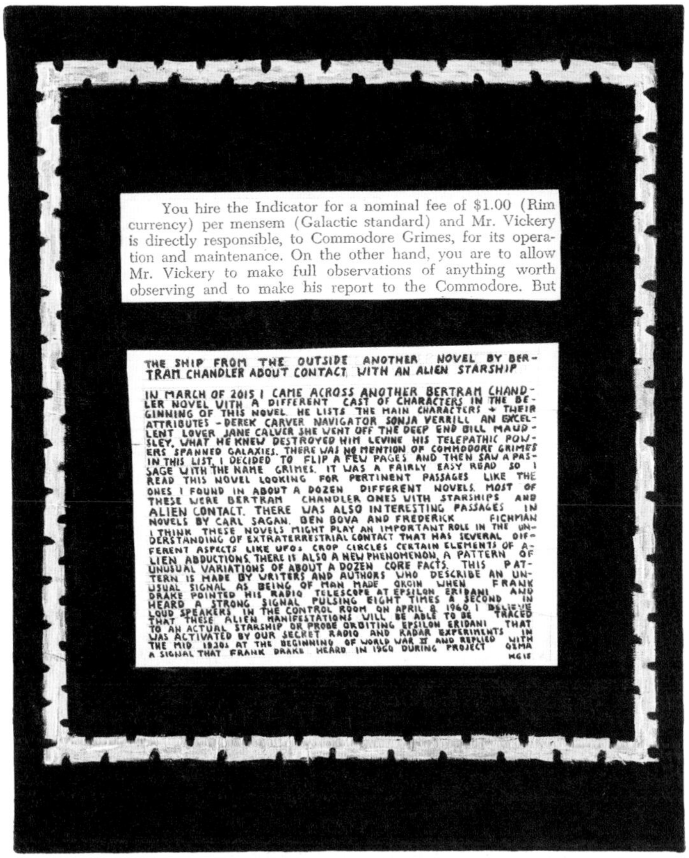

You hire the Indicator for a nominal fee of $1.00 (Rim currency) per mensem (Galactic standard) and Mr. Vickery is directly responsible, to Commodore Grimes, for its operation and maintenance. On the other hand, you are to allow Mr. Vickery to make full observations of anything worth observing and to make his report to the Commodore. But

THE SHIP FROM THE OUTSIDE ANOTHER NOVEL BY BERTRAM CHANDLER ABOUT CONTACT WITH AN ALIEN STARSHIP

IN MARCH OF 2015 I CAME ACROSS ANOTHER BERTRAM CHANDLER NOVEL VITH A DIFFERENT CAST OF CHARACTERS IN THE BEGINNING OF THIS NOVEL. HE LISTS THE MAIN CHARACTERS + THEIR ATTRIBUTES - DEREK CARVER NAVIGATOR SONJA VERRILL AN EXCELLENT LOVER JANE CALVER SHE WENT OFF THE DEEP END BILL MAUDSLEY, WHAT HE KNEW DESTROYED HIM LEVINE HIS TELEPATHIC POWERS SPANNED GALAXIES. THERE WAS NO MENTION OF COMMODORE GRIMES IN THIS LIST. I DECIDED TO FLIP A FEW PAGES AND THEN SAW A PASSAGE WITH THE NAME GRIMES. IT WAS A FAIRLY EASY READ SO I READ THIS NOVEL LOOKING FOR PERTINENT PASSAGES LIKE THE ONES I FOUND IN ABOUT A DOZEN DIFFERENT NOVELS. MOST OF THESE WERE BERTRAM CHANDLER ONES VITH STARSHIPS AND ALIEN CONTACT. THERE WAS ALSO INTERESTING PASSAGES IN NOVELS BY CARL SAGAN. BEN BOVA AND FREDERICK FICHMAN I THINK THESE NOVELS MIGHT PLAY AN IMPORTANT ROLE IN THE UNDERSTANDING OF EXTRATERRESTRIAL CONTACT THAT HAS SEVERAL DIFFERENT ASPECTS LIKE UFOs CROP CIRCLES CERTAIN ELEMENTS OF ALIEN ABDUCTIONS. THERE IS ALSO A NEW PHENOMENON, A PATTERN OF UNUSUAL VARIATIONS OF ABOUT A DOZEN CORE FACTS. THIS PATTERN IS MADE BY WRITERS AND AUTHORS WHO DESCRIBE AN UNUSUAL SIGNAL AS BEING OF MAN MADE ORGIN WHEN FRANK DRAKE POINTED HIS RADIO TELESCOPE AT EPSILON ERIDANI AND HEARD A STRONG SIGNAL PULSING EIGHT TIMES A SECOND IN LOUD SPEAKERS IN THE CONTROL ROOM ON APRIL 8 1960. I BELIEVE THAT THESE ALIEN MANIFESTATIONS WILL BE ABLE TO BE TRACED TO AN ACTUAL STARSHIP OR PROBE ORBITING EPSILON ERIDANI THAT WAS ACTIVATED BY OUR SECRET RADIO AND RADAR EXPERIMENTS IN THE MID 1930s AT THE BEGINNING OF WORLD WAR II AND REPLIED WITH A SIGNAL THAT FRANK DRAKE HEARD IN 1960 DURING PROJECT OZMA

KG15

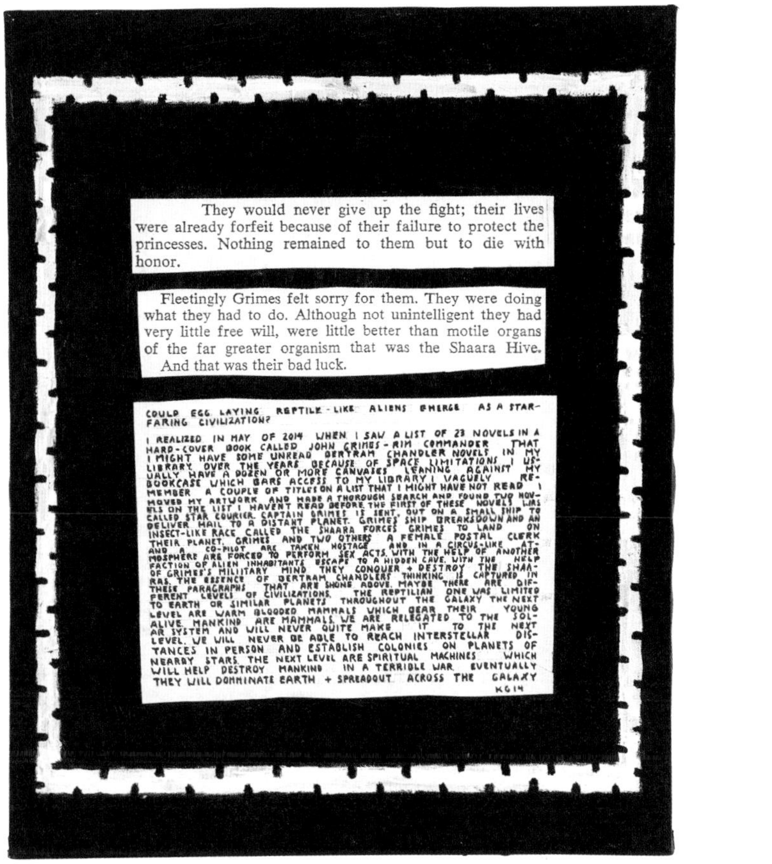

They would never give up the fight; their lives were already forfeit because of their failure to protect the princesses. Nothing remained to them but to die with honor.

Fleetingly Grimes felt sorry for them. They were doing what they had to do. Although not unintelligent they had very little free will, were little better than motile organs of the far greater organism that was the Shaara Hive.

And that was their bad luck.

COULD EGG LAYING REPTILE-LIKE ALIENS EMERGE AS A STARFARING CIVILIZATION?

I REALIZED IN MAY OF 2014 WHEN I SAW A LIST OF 23 NOVELS IN A HARD-COVER BOOK CALLED JOHN GRIMES - RIM COMMANDER THAT I MIGHT HAVE SOME UNREAD BERTRAM CHANDLER NOVELS IN MY LIBRARY. OVER THE YEARS BECAUSE OF SPACE LIMITATIONS I USUALLY HAVE A DOZEN OR MORE CANVASES LEANING AGAINST MY BOOKCASE WHICH BARS ACCESS TO MY LIBRARY I VAGUELY REMEMBER A COUPLE OF TITLES ON A LIST THAT I MIGHT HAVE NOT READ I MOVED MY ARTWORK AND MADE A THOROUGH SEARCH AND FOUND TWO NOVELS ON THE LIST I HAVENT READ BEFORE. THE FIRST OF THESE NOVELS WAS CALLED STAR COURIER. CAPTAIN GRIMES IS SENT, OUT ON A SMALL SHIP TO DELIVER MAIL TO A DISTANT PLANET. GRIMES' SHIP BREAKSDOWN AND AN INSECT-LIKE RACE CALLED THE SHAARA FORCES GRIMES TO LAND ON THEIR PLANET. GRIMES AND TWO OTHERS A FEMALE POSTAL CLERK AND A CO-PILOT ARE TAKEN HOSTAGE AND IN A CIRCUS-LIKE ATMOSPHERE ARE FORCED TO PERFORM SEX ACTS. WITH THE HELP OF ANOTHER FACTION OF ALIEN INHABITANTS ESCAPE TO A HIDDEN CAVE. WITH THE HELP OF GRIMES'S MILIITARY MIND THEY CONQUER + DESTROY THE SHAARAS. THE ESSENCE OF BERTRAM CHANDLERS THINKING IS CAPTURED IN THESE PARAGRAPHS THAT ARE SHONE ABOVE. MAYBE THERE ARE DIFFERENT LEVELS OF CIVILIZATIONS. THE REPTILIAN ONE WAS LIMITED TO EARTH OR SIMILAR PLANETS THROUGHOUT THE GALAXY THE NEXT LEVEL ARE WARM BLOODED MAMMALS WHICH BEAR THEIR YOUNG ALIVE. MANKIND ARE MAMMALS. WE ARE RELEGATED TO THE SOLAR SYSTEM AND WILL NEVER QUITE MAKE IT TO THE NEXT LEVEL. WE WILL NEVER BE ABLE TO REACH INTERSTELLAR DISTANCES IN PERSON AND ESTABLISH COLONIES ON PLANETS OF NEARBY STARS. THE NEXT LEVEL ARE SPIRITUAL MACHINES WHICH WILL HELP DESTROY MANKIND IN A TERRIBLE WAR. EVENTUALLY THEY WILL DOMMINATE EARTH + SPREADOUT ACROSS THE GALAXY

KG14

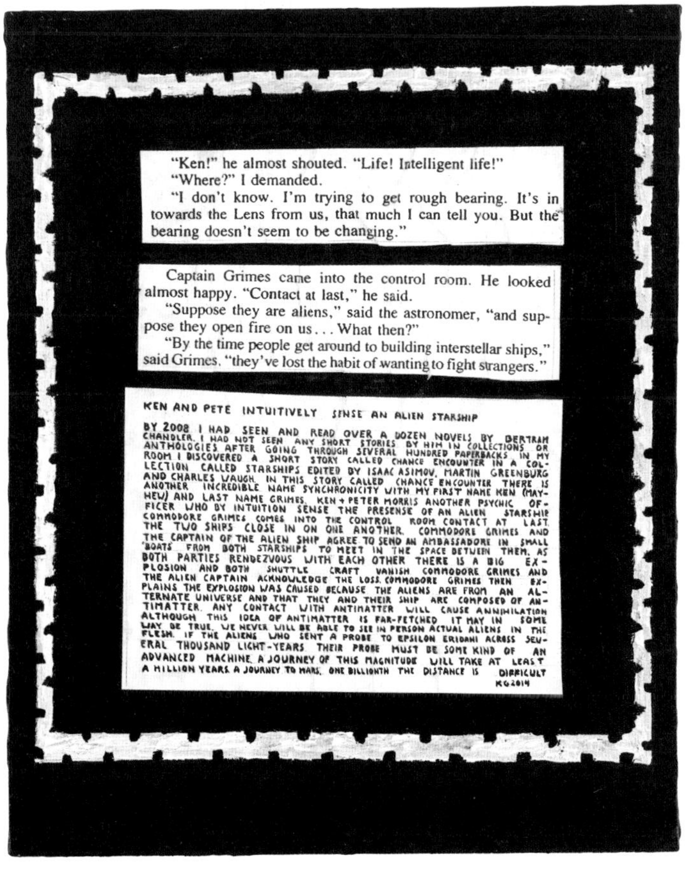

"Ken!" he almost shouted. "Life! Intelligent life!"

"Where?" I demanded.

"I don't know. I'm trying to get rough bearing. It's in towards the Lens from us, that much I can tell you. But the bearing doesn't seem to be changing."

Captain Grimes came into the control room. He looked almost happy. "Contact at last," he said.

"Suppose they are aliens," said the astronomer, "and suppose they open fire on us... What then?"

"By the time people get around to building interstellar ships," said Grimes, "they've lost the habit of wanting to fight strangers."

KEN AND PETE INTUITIVELY SENSE AN ALIEN STARSHIP

BY 2008 I HAD SEEN AND READ OVER A DOZEN NOVELS BY BERTRAM CHANDLER. I HAD NOT SEEN ANY SHORT STORIES BY HIM IN COLLECTIONS OR ANTHOLOGIES AFTER GOING THROUGH SEVERAL HUNDRED PAPERBACKS IN MY ROOM I DISCOVERED A SHORT STORY CALLED CHANCE ENCOUNTER IN A COLLECTION CALLED STARSHIPS EDITED BY ISAAC ASIMOV, MARTIN GREENBURG AND CHARLES WAUGH. IN THIS STORY CALLED CHANCE ENCOUNTER THERE IS ANOTHER INCREDIBLE NAME SYNCHRONICITY WITH MY FIRST NAME KEN (MAYHEW) AND LAST NAME GRIMES. KEN + PETER MORRIS ANOTHER PSYCHIC OFFICER WHO BY INTUITION SENSE THE PRESENSE OF AN ALIEN STARSHIP COMMODORE GRIMES COMES INTO THE CONTROL ROOM CONTACT AT LAST. THE TWO SHIPS CLOSE IN ON ONE ANOTHER. COMMODORE GRIMES AND THE CAPTAIN OF THE ALIEN SHIP AGREE TO SEND AN AMBASSADORE IN SMALL 'BOATS' FROM BOTH STARSHIPS TO MEET IN THE SPACE BETWEEN THEM. AS BOTH PARTIES RENDEZVOUS WITH EACH OTHER THERE IS A BIG EXPLOSION AND BOTH SHUTTLE CRAFT VANISH COMMODORE GRIMES AND THE ALIEN CAPTAIN ACKNOWLEDGE THE LOSS. COMMODORE GRIMES THEN EXPLAINS THE EXPLOSION WAS CAUSED BECAUSE THE ALIENS ARE FROM AN ALTERNATE UNIVERSE AND THAT THEY AND THEIR SHIP ARE COMPOSED OF ANTIMATTER. ANY CONTACT WITH ANTIMATTER WILL CAUSE ANNIHILATION ALTHOUGH THIS IDEA OF ANTIMATTER IS FAR-FETCHED IT MAY IN SOME WAY BE TRUE. WE NEVER WILL BE ABLE TO SEE IN PERSON ACTUAL ALIENS IN THE FLESH. IF THE ALIENS WHO SENT A PROBE TO EPSILON ERIDANI ACROSS SEVERAL THOUSAND LIGHT-YEARS THEIR PROBE MUST BE SOME KIND OF AN ADVANCED MACHINE. A JOURNEY OF THIS MAGNITUDE WILL TAKE AT LEAST A MILLION YEARS. A JOURNEY TO MARS, ONE BILLIONTH THE DISTANCE IS DIFFICULT

KG2014

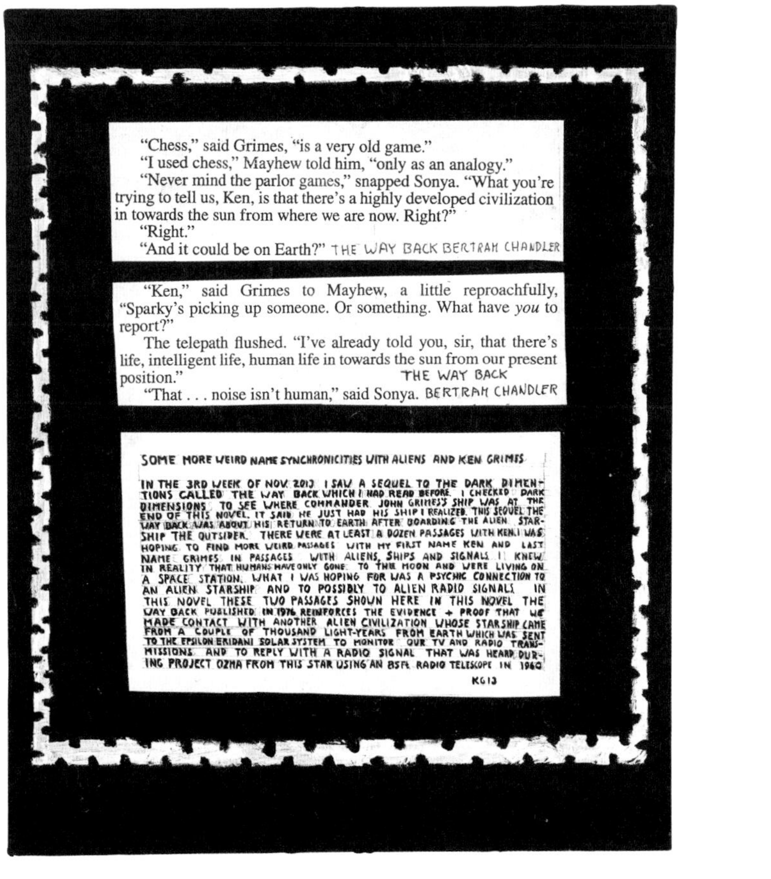

"Chess," said Grimes, "is a very old game."

"I used chess," Mayhew told him, "only as an analogy."

"Never mind the parlor games," snapped Sonya. "What you're trying to tell us, Ken, is that there's a highly developed civilization in towards the sun from where we are now. Right?"

"Right."

"And it could be on Earth?" THE WAY BACK BERTRAM CHANDLER

"Ken," said Grimes to Mayhew, a little reproachfully, "Sparky's picking up someone. Or something. What have *you* to report?"

The telepath flushed. "I've already told you, sir, that there's life, intelligent life, human life in towards the sun from our present position." THE WAY BACK

"That . . . noise isn't human," said Sonya. BERTRAM CHANDLER

SOME MORE WEIRD NAME SYNCHRONICITIES WITH ALIENS AND KEN GRIMES

IN THE 3RD WEEK OF NOV 2013 I SAW A SEQUEL TO THE DARK DIMENTIONS CALLED THE WAY BACK WHICH I HAD READ BEFORE. I CHECKED DARK DIMENSIONS TO SEE WHERE COMMANDER JOHN GRIMES'S SHIP WAS AT THE END OF THIS NOVEL. IT SAID HE JUST HAD HIS SHIP I REALIZED. THIS SEQUEL THE WAY BACK WAS ABOUT HIS RETURN TO EARTH AFTER BOARDING THE ALIEN STARSHIP THE OUTSIDER. THERE WERE AT LEAST A DOZEN PASSAGES WITH KEN. I WAS HOPING TO FIND MORE WEIRD PASSAGES WITH MY FIRST NAME KEN AND LAST NAME GRIMES IN PASSAGES WITH ALIENS, SHIPS AND SIGNALS I KNEW IN REALITY THAT HUMANS HAVE ONLY GONE TO THE MOON AND WERE LIVING ON A SPACE STATION. WHAT I WAS HOPING FOR WAS A PSYCHIC CONNECTION TO AN ALIEN STARSHIP AND TO POSSIBLY TO ALIEN RADIO SIGNALS IN THIS NOVEL THESE TWO PASSAGES SHOWN HERE IN THIS NOVEL THE WAY BACK PUBLISHED IN 1976 REINFORCES THE EVIDENCE + PROOF THAT WE MADE CONTACT WITH ANOTHER ALIEN CIVILIZATION WHOSE STARSHIP CAME FROM A COUPLE OF THOUSAND LIGHT-YEARS FROM EARTH WHICH WAS SENT TO THE EPSILON ERIDANI SOLAR SYSTEM TO MONITOR OUR TV AND RADIO TRANSMISSIONS AND TO REPLY WITH A RADIO SIGNAL THAT WAS HEARD DURING PROJECT OZMA FROM THIS STAR USING AN 85Ft RADIO TELESCOPE IN 1960

KG13

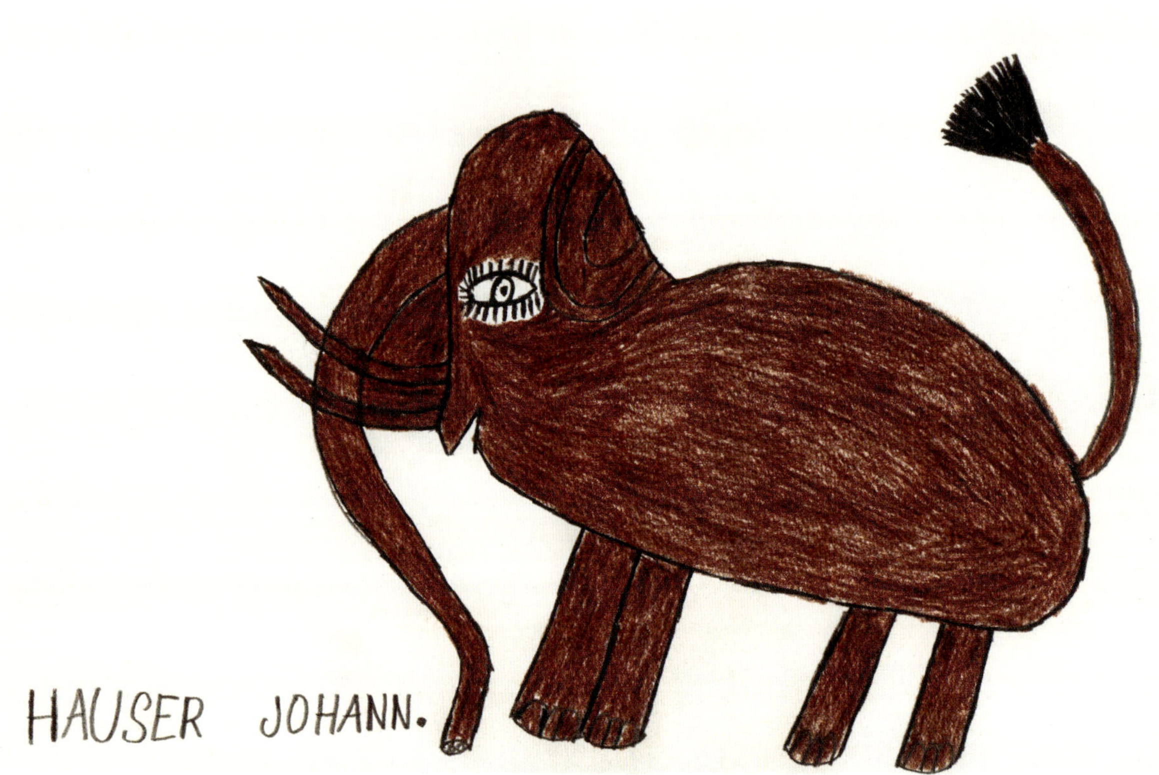
HAUSER JOHANN.

JOHANN HAUSER

1926–1996

Johann Hauser showed signs of mental disability and social dissociation from a young age and attended a school for feeble-minded children through the second grade. He remained illiterate and never learned to write or understand the logic of numbers. Hauser was born in Bratislava, Slovakia, but his family spoke German. In 1943, when he was seventeen, as the end of World War II was near, he moved with his mother to Lower Austria and was immediately committed to the Mauer-Öhling state psychiatric hospital. From there, sometime before 1950, he was transferred to the Maria Gugging State Psychiatric Clinic on the outskirts of Vienna, where he was diagnosed as schizophrenic, and where he produced his first drawings with the encouragement of Dr. Leo Navratil, who had fostered a creative environment for his patients. Hauser was one of the original residents of the Gugging House of Artists (see p. 143), where he lived from 1981 until his death—and remains its most celebrated artist to this day.

Despite being a mental patient for most of his life, Hauser achieved international recognition as an artist during his lifetime. In bold color palettes created with colored pencils, graphite, and crayons, he created intensely gestural drawings and minimalist compositions representing single subjects. This technical fluctuation, according to Dr. Navratil, was owing to Hauser's mental state: manic episodes yielded larger, vibrant works (with a painterly and almost aggressive application of color) and depressive episodes smaller, abstracted, or geometric works. Hauser's personal iconography ranged from animals, everyday objects, aircraft, and machinery, to human subjects (mostly empowered women) depicted with distinctly eroticized physiognomies and flourishes. He drew inspiration and imagery from popular culture and printed media, which he reimagined with his unique style and in disregard of perspective and proportion.

Hauser influenced Dr. Navratil's development of a nonpsychiatric approach to treating creatively inclined asylum patients and his work was shown widely across Europe in the 1970s. His first major solo exhibition took place in 1979 at the municipal gallery in Munich's Lenbachhaus; in the same year his work was included in Victor Musgrave's groundbreaking show *Outsiders* at the Hayward Gallery in London, where he met Roger Cardinal. In later years, his work was exhibited worldwide, including exhibitions at the Museum of Modern Art in Vienna, the Los Angeles County Museum of Art, the Setagaya Art Museum in Tokyo, and the Weserburg Museum in Bremen. Hauser's work can be found in the Collection de l'Art Brut (Lausanne, Switzerland), the Lille Métropole Museum of Modern, Contemporary and Outsider Art (Villeneuve-d'Ascq, France), the abcd Collection (Paris), the Arnulf Rainer Collection (Vienna), the Treger Saint Silvestre Collection (São João da Madeira, Portugal), Intuit: The Center for Intuitive and Outsider Art (Chicago), the Philadelphia Museum of Art, and the Museum of Modern Art (New York).

Johann Hauser, *Elephant*, n.d. Mixed media on drawing paper, 8.25 in. × 11.75 in. (21 × 29.8 cm)

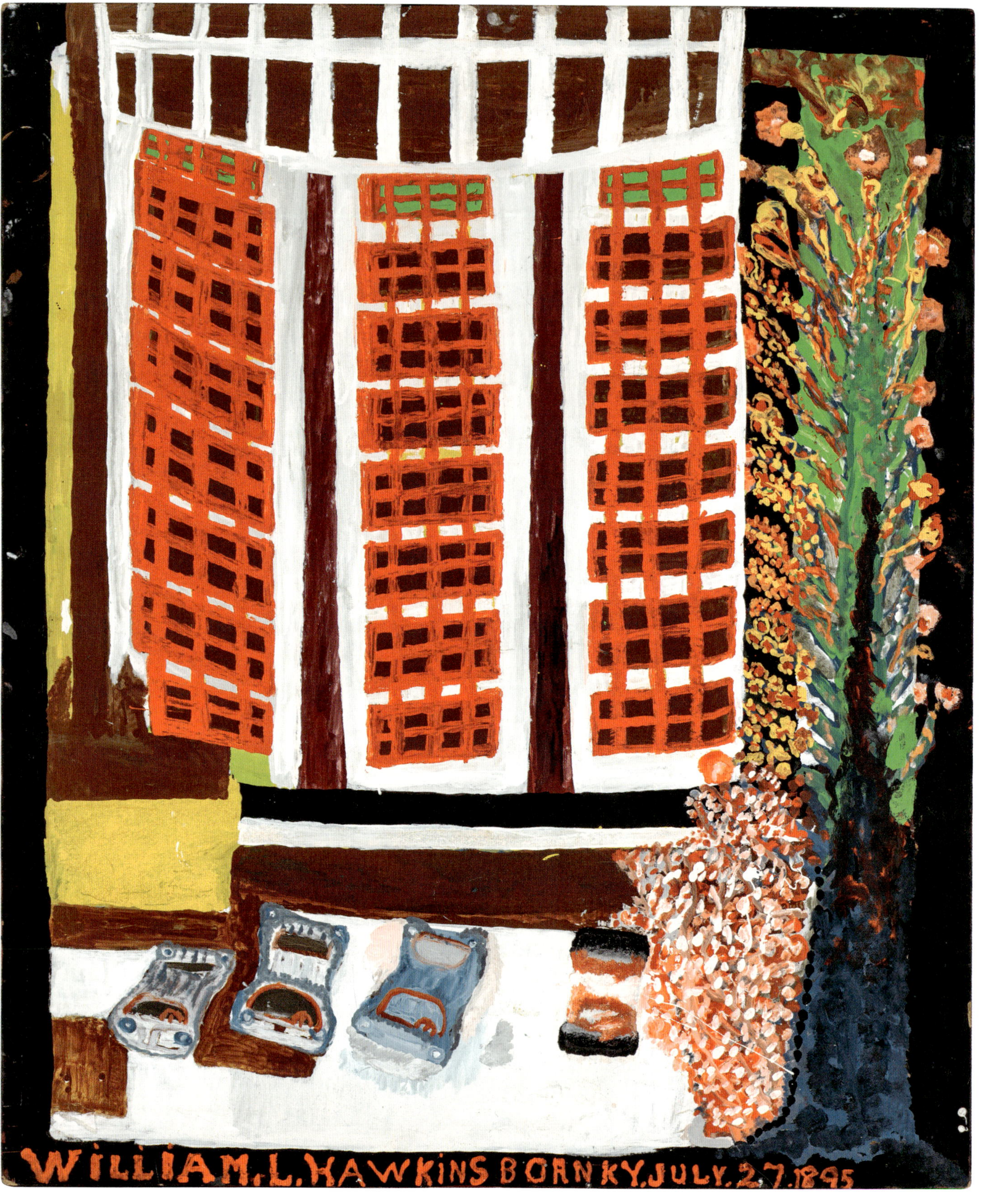
WILLIAM.L.HAWKINS BORN KY.JULY.27.1895

WILLIAM HAWKINS

1895–1990

William Hawkins lived most of his life in Columbus, Ohio, after fleeing his Kentucky home state in his twenties to avoid a shotgun wedding. In his youth on a rural farm in Kentucky he developed a knowledge and love of animals, which he later expressed in many of his paintings. In Columbus he worked a variety of jobs, many of which took him across the country as a traveling salesman. He took black-and-white photographs as he drove through, and many of these served as inspiration for his paintings. He was drawing and selling his work as early as the 1930s, but it was not until the mid-1970s that he began painting in the style for which he is best known, creating many works from then on in spite of illness and advancing age.

The main source of Hawkins's inspiration were the print media of his time. As Lyle Rexer has described it, "The pictures in magazines and newspapers, which he hoarded in a suitcase and carefully sorted through . . . opened up the world and acted as a catalyst. . . He felt that these photographs could be made more interesting, pretty, exotic by painting, and only by painting. He also knew they could save him a lot of trouble, substituting for labor-intensive elements he had trouble rendering—faces, for example."

At first, Hawkins painted in primary color enamels on plywood; later he worked on Masonite, which he preferred because it did not "suck up the paint." He liked using a single threadbare brush and pouring and dripping paint, often directly from the can, and tilting the surface to let the paint flow across it so that he could, as he put it, "watch the painting make itself." Hawkins's primary subject matter includes common, exotic, extinct, and semi-fantastical animals; cityscapes, landmarks, and prominent buildings; and religious and popular culture iconography. Along with collaging photos into his work, Hawkins also added wood, gravel, sand, cornmeal, and found objects, and he often painted decorative borders around his works, very frequently including his name and birth date and place in large handwriting—a poignant feature, as Hawkins could scarcely read or write.

It was not until his friend Lee Garrett entered one of his paintings at the Ohio State Fair in 1982, where it won first prize, that Hawkins received recognition for his work. In his late eighties by then, Hawkins continued to work immensely prolifically. By 1983 Ricco/Maresca Gallery represented him, launching his career nationally and internationally. In 1989 Hawkins suffered a stroke from which he only partly recovered and a few months later he died. Hawkins's work is in the permanent collections of, among others, the Milwaukee Art Museum, the Brooklyn Museum, the American Folk Art Museum (New York), the Philadelphia Museum of Art, the High Museum of Art (Atlanta), the Columbus Museum of Art, and the Smithsonian American Art Museum (Washington, D.C.). In 2018 *William L. Hawkins: An Imaginative Geography*, an exhibition including sixty of Hawkins's most important works and an accompanying catalogue, opened at the Columbus Museum of Art and traveled to the Mingei International Museum (San Diego), the Figge Art Museum (Davenport, Iowa), and the Columbus Museum in Georgia.

William Hawkins, *Tower Motor Inn*, 1984. Enamel on Masonite, 60 × 48 in. (152.4 × 121.9 cm)

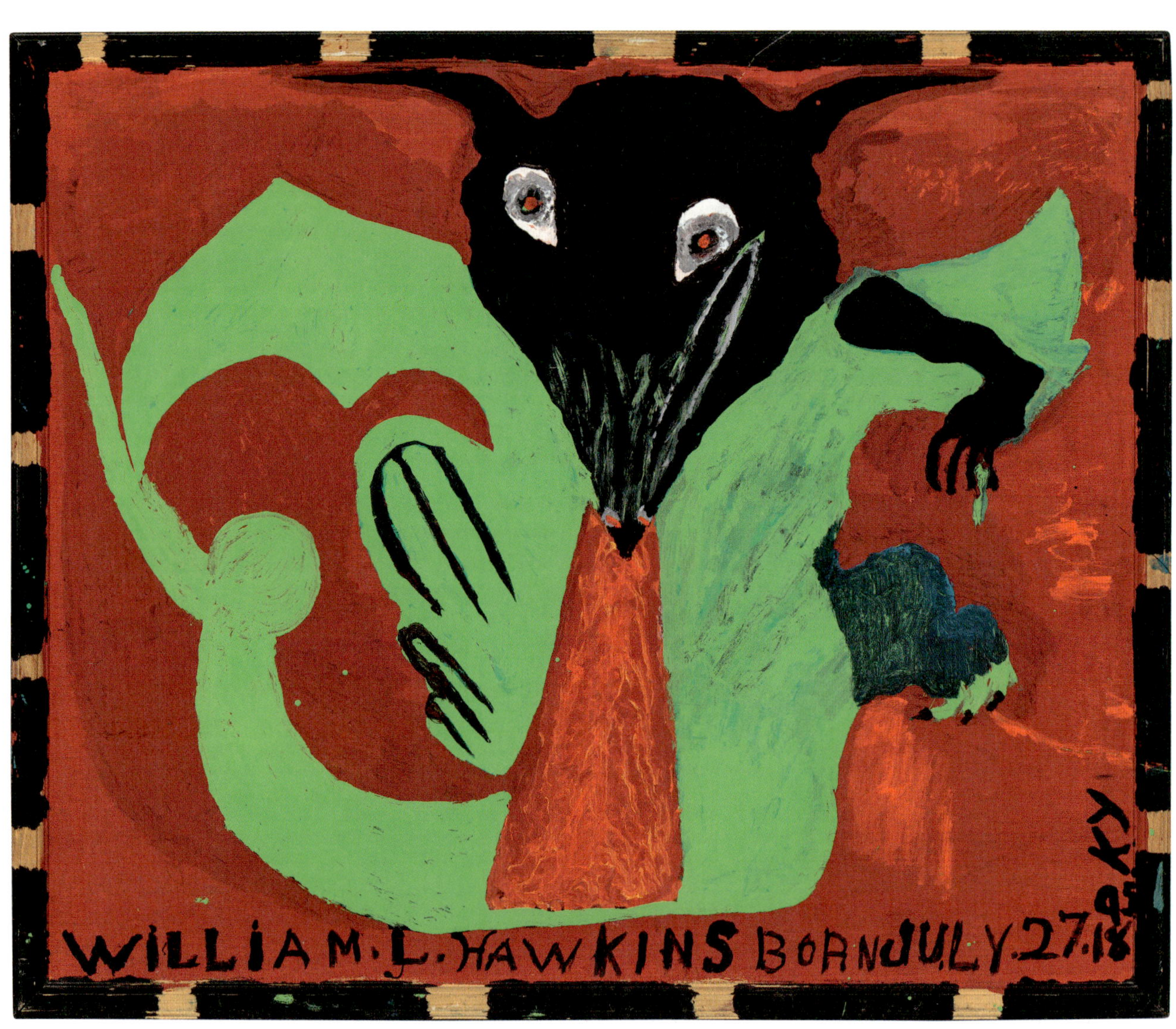

William Hawkins, *Bat Man*, 1984. Enamel on Masonite, 34 × 39 in. (86.4 × 99.1 cm)

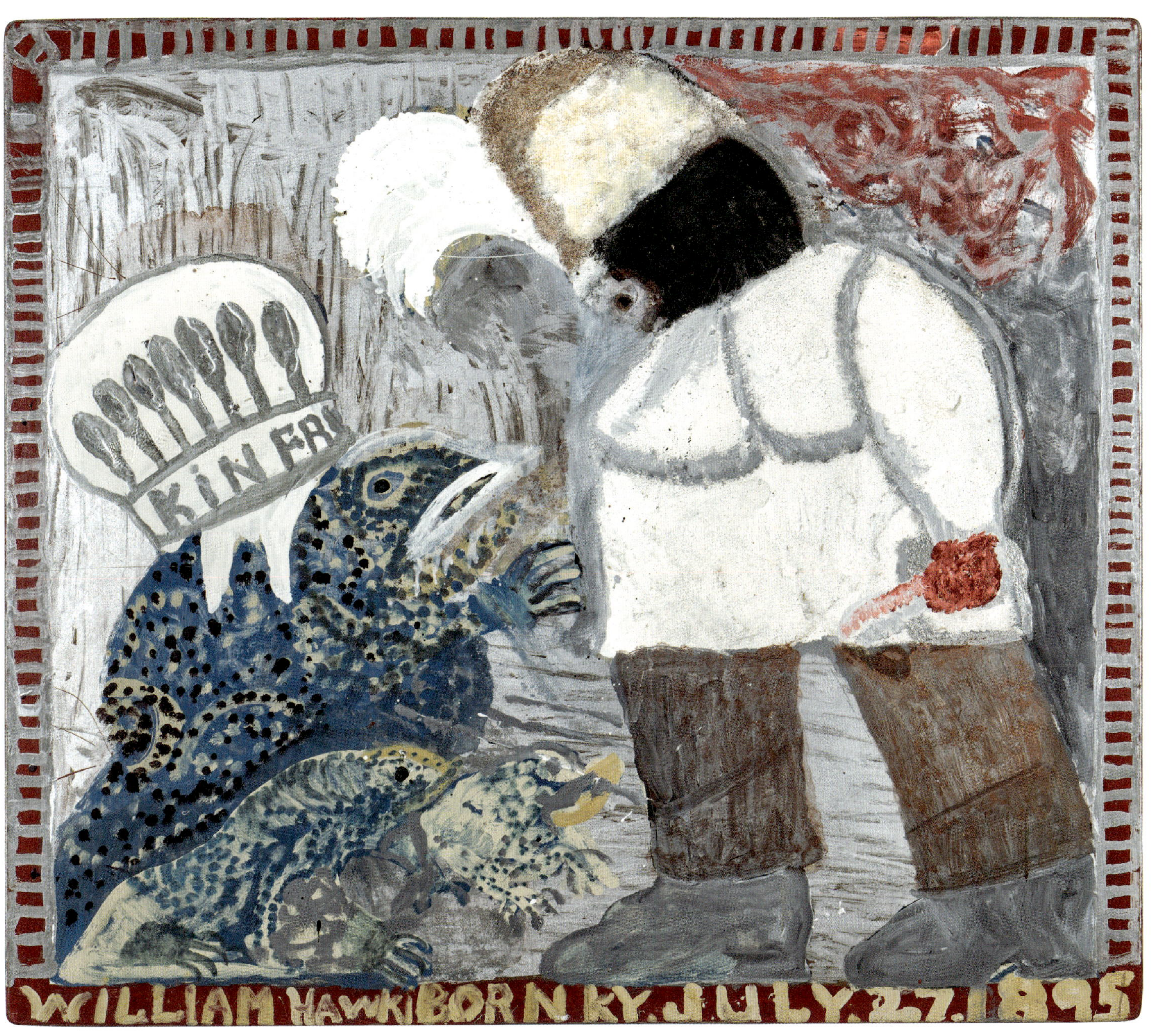

William Hawkins, *Magical Toad (Kin Frog)*, 1987. Oil, enamel on Masonite, 43 × 48 in. (109.2 × 121.9 cm)

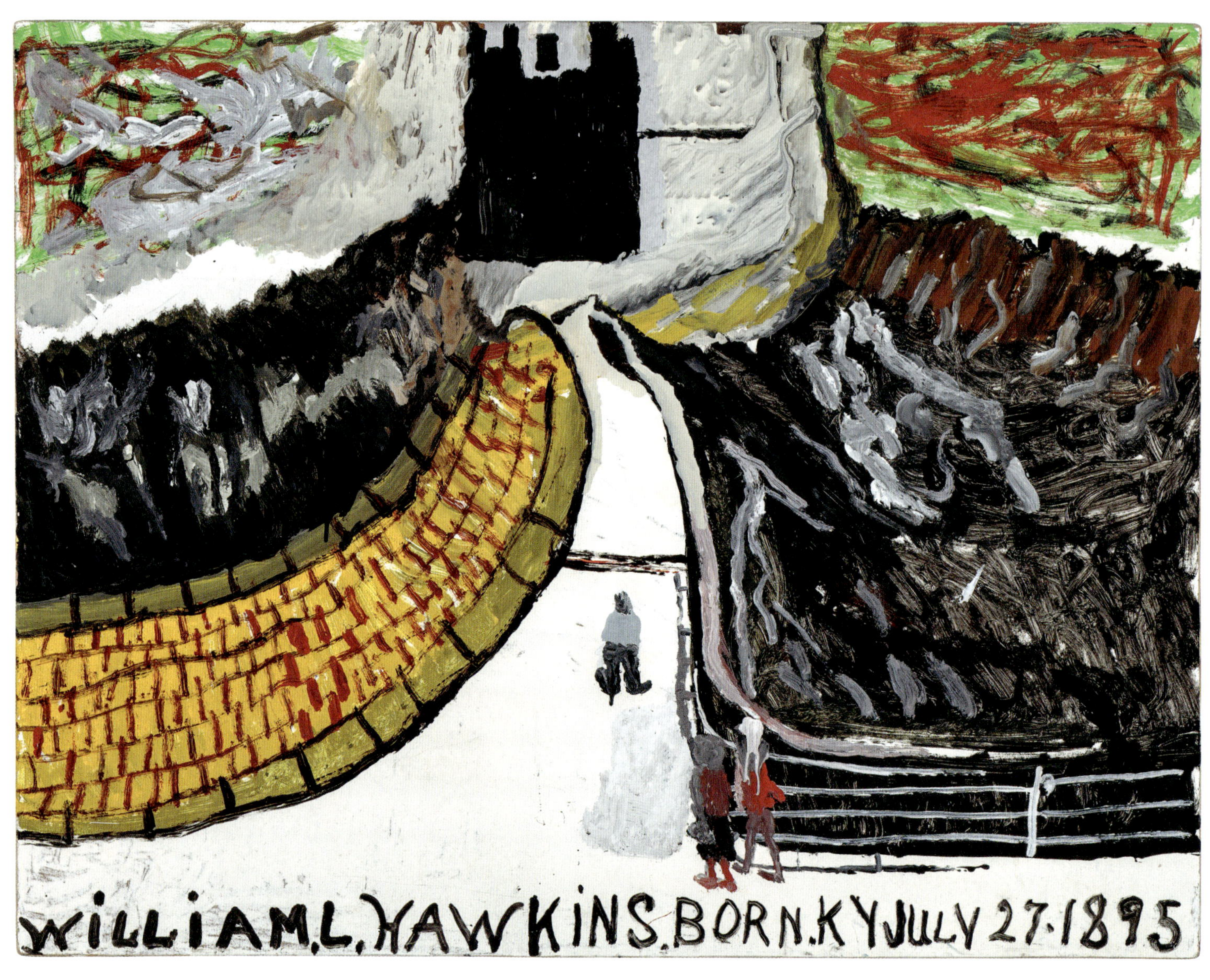

William Hawkins, *Great Wall of China*, 1985. Enamel on Masonite, 43 × 54 in. (109.2 × 137.2 cm)

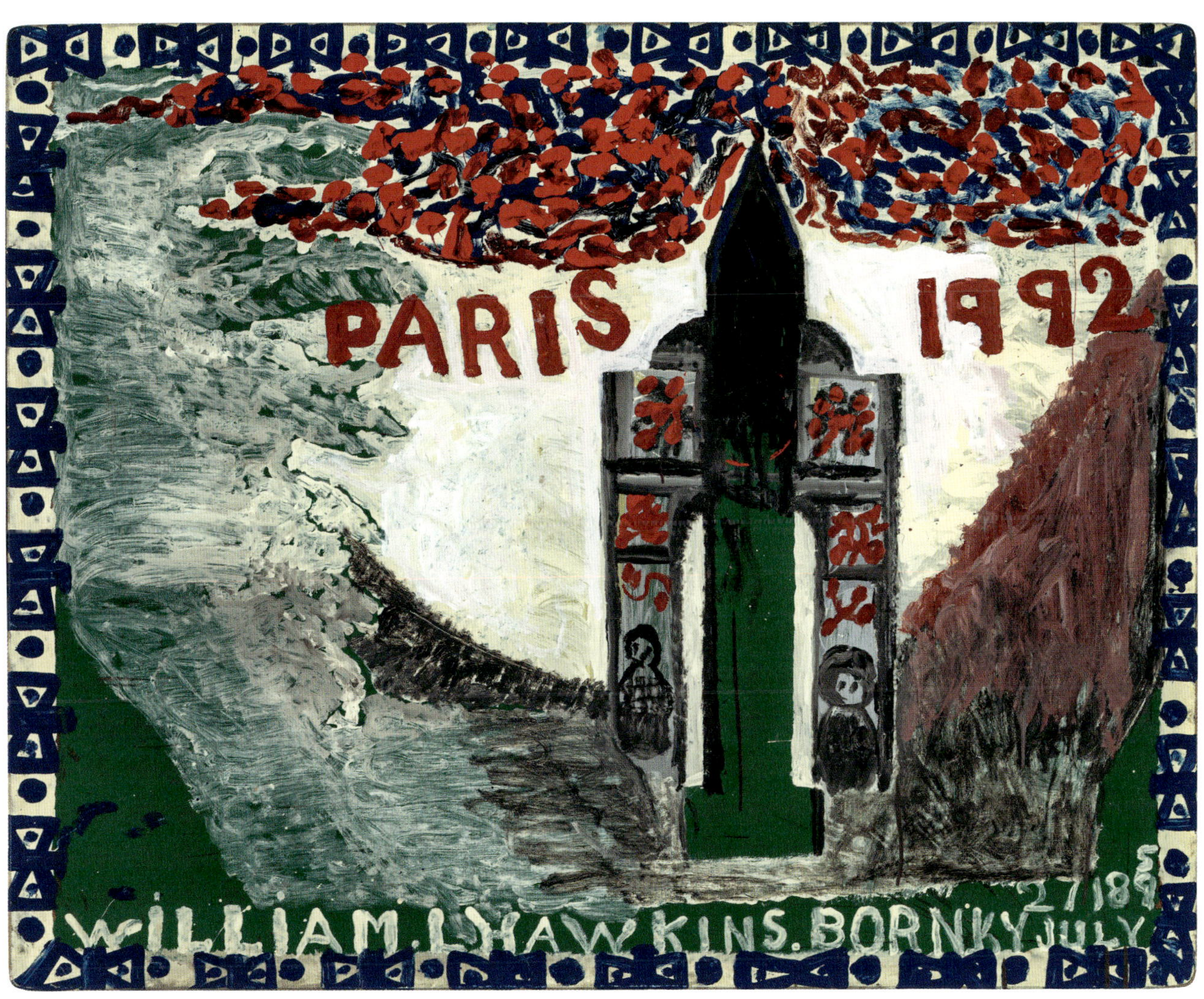

William Hawkins, *Paris*, 1992. Enamel on Masonite, 39¼ × 48 in. (99.7 × 121.9 cm)

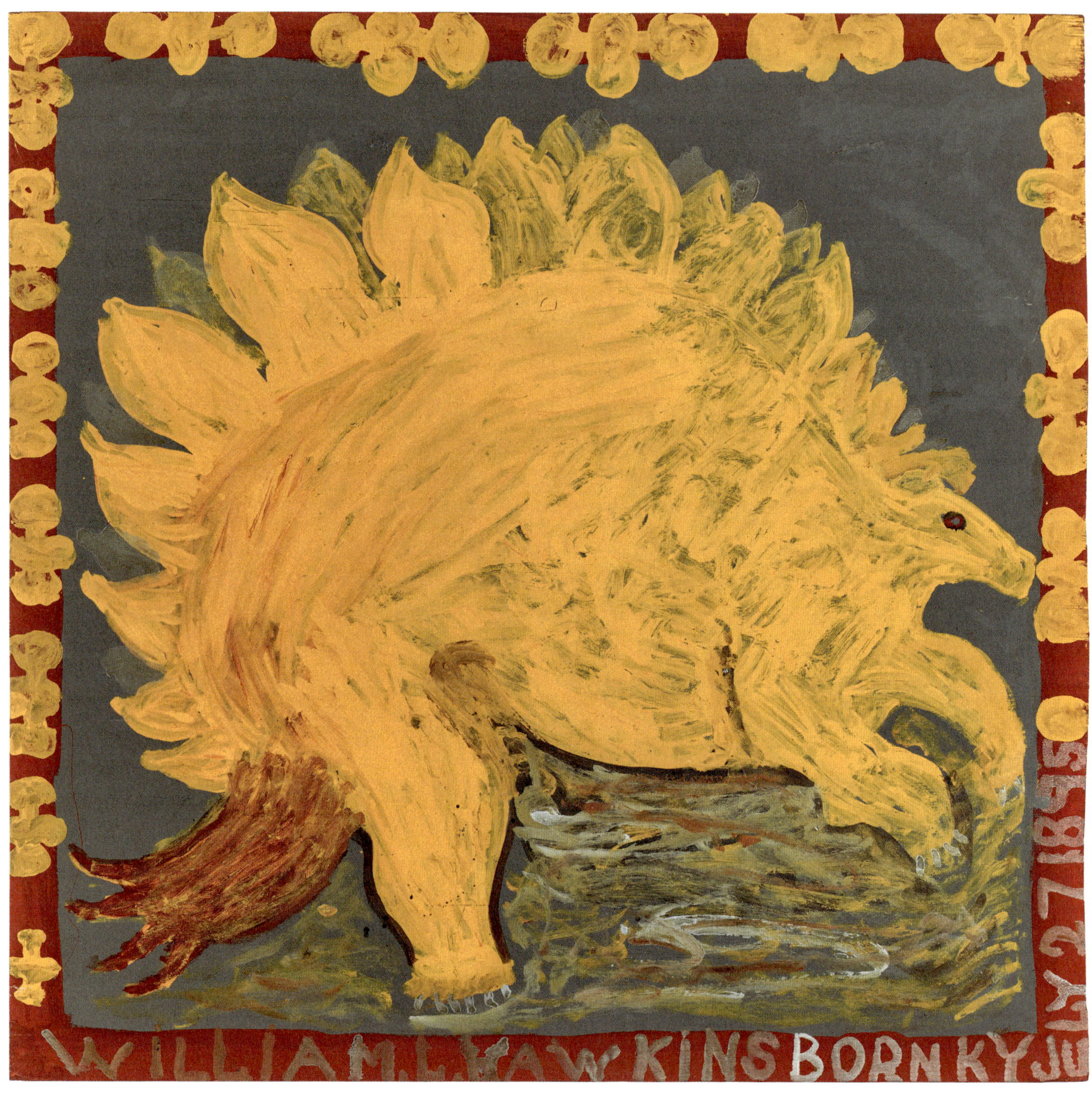

William Hawkins, *Yellow Stegosaurus*, c.1985–87. Enamel on Masonite, 48 × 48 in. (121.9 × 121.9 cm)

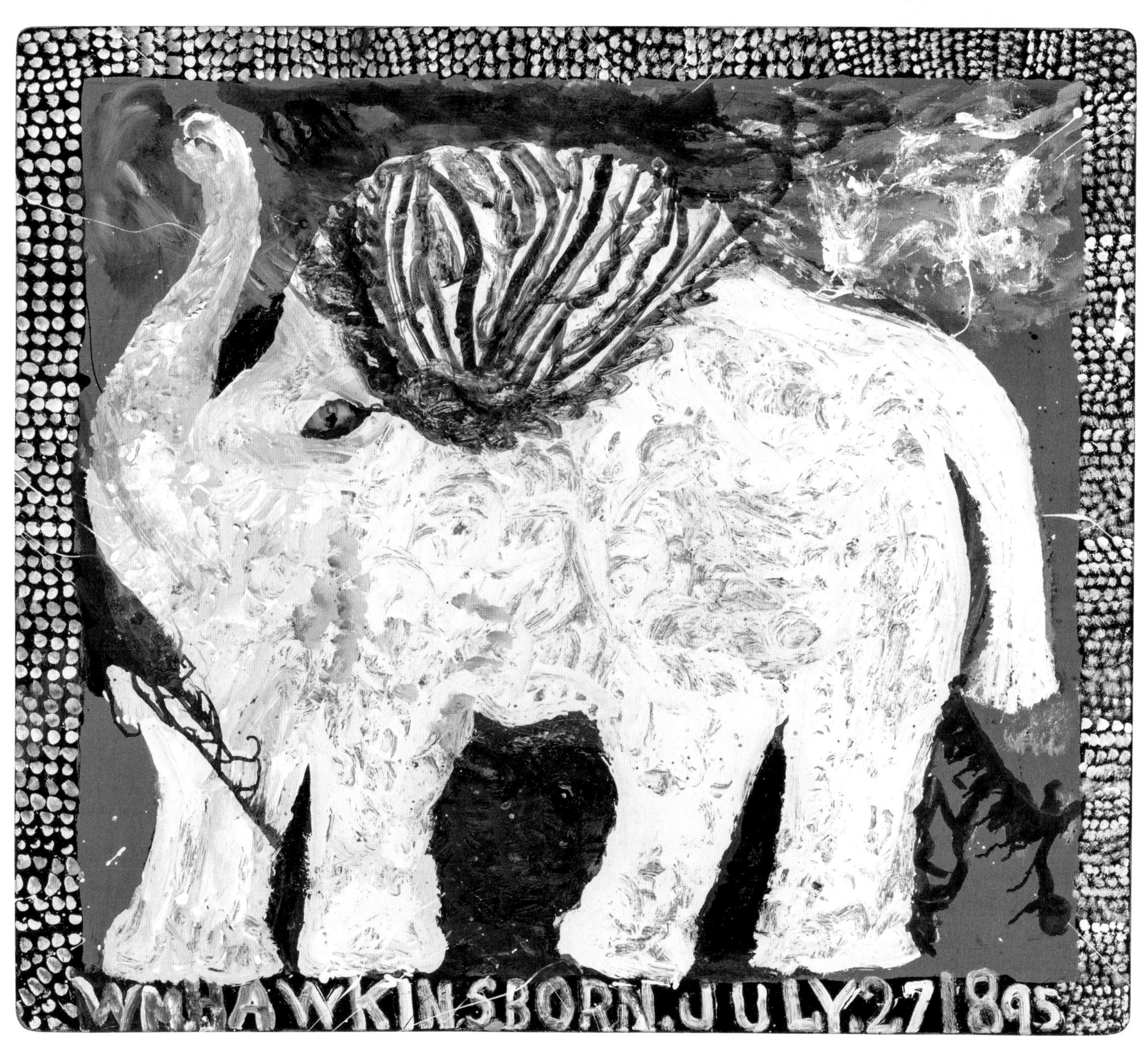

William Hawkins, *White Elephant*, 1989. Enamel on Masonite, 42½ × 46½ in. (108 × 118.1 cm

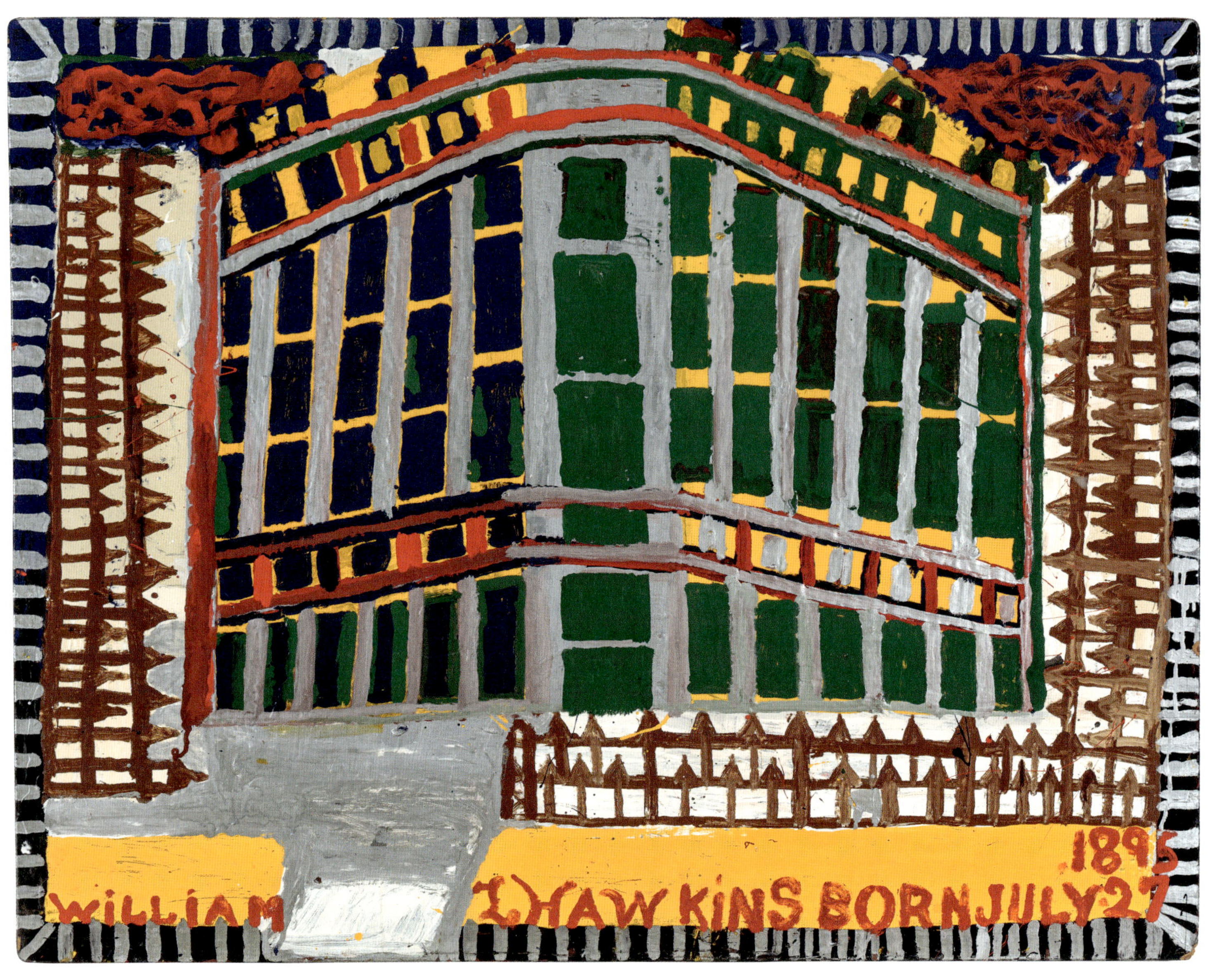

William Hawkins, *Willard Hotel*, 1987. Enamel on Masonite, 48 × 60 in. (121.9 × 152.4 cm)

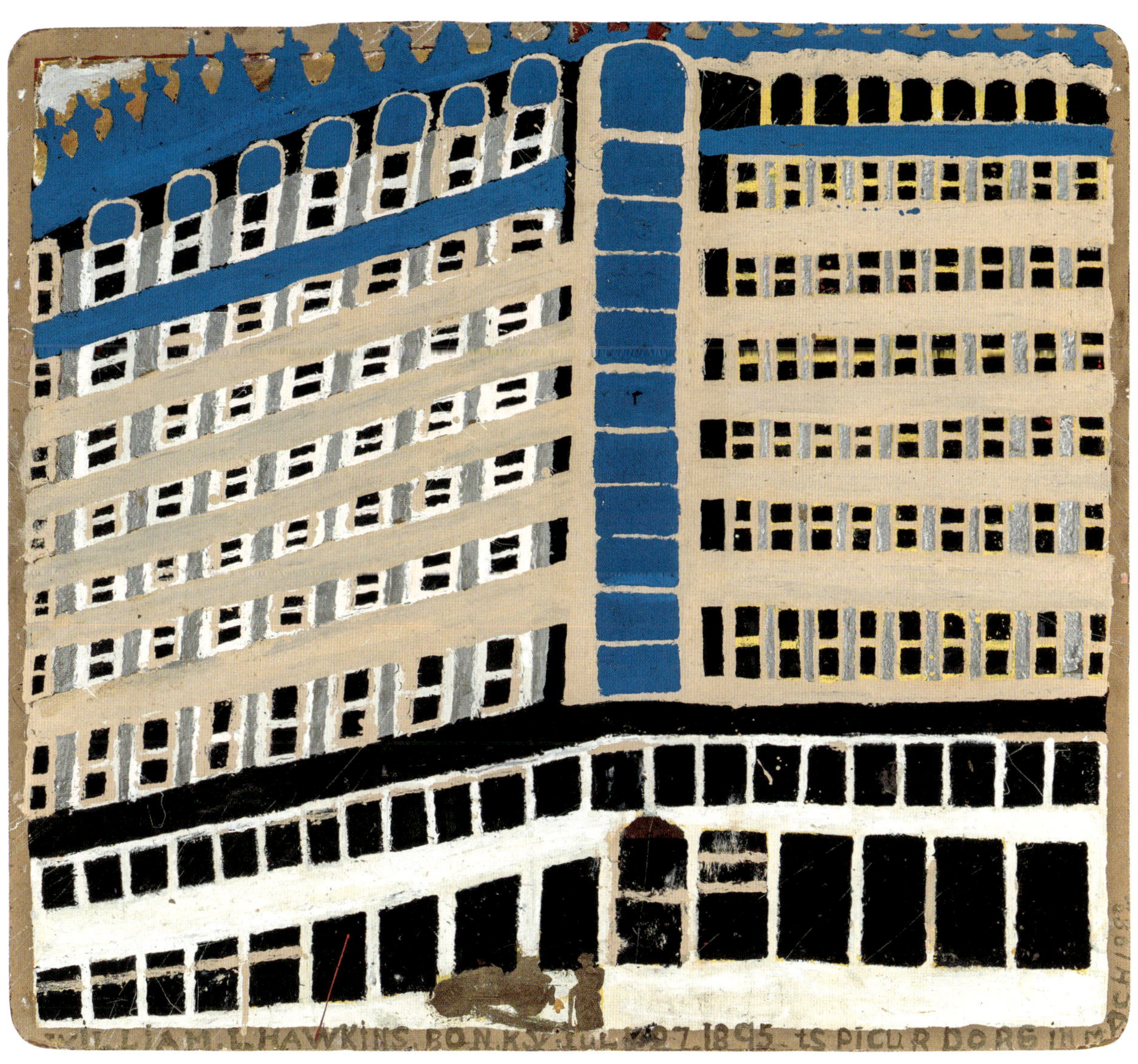

William Hawkins, *Deshler Hotel #3*, 1985. Enamel on Masonite, 43¾ × 47½ in. (111.1 × 120.7 cm)

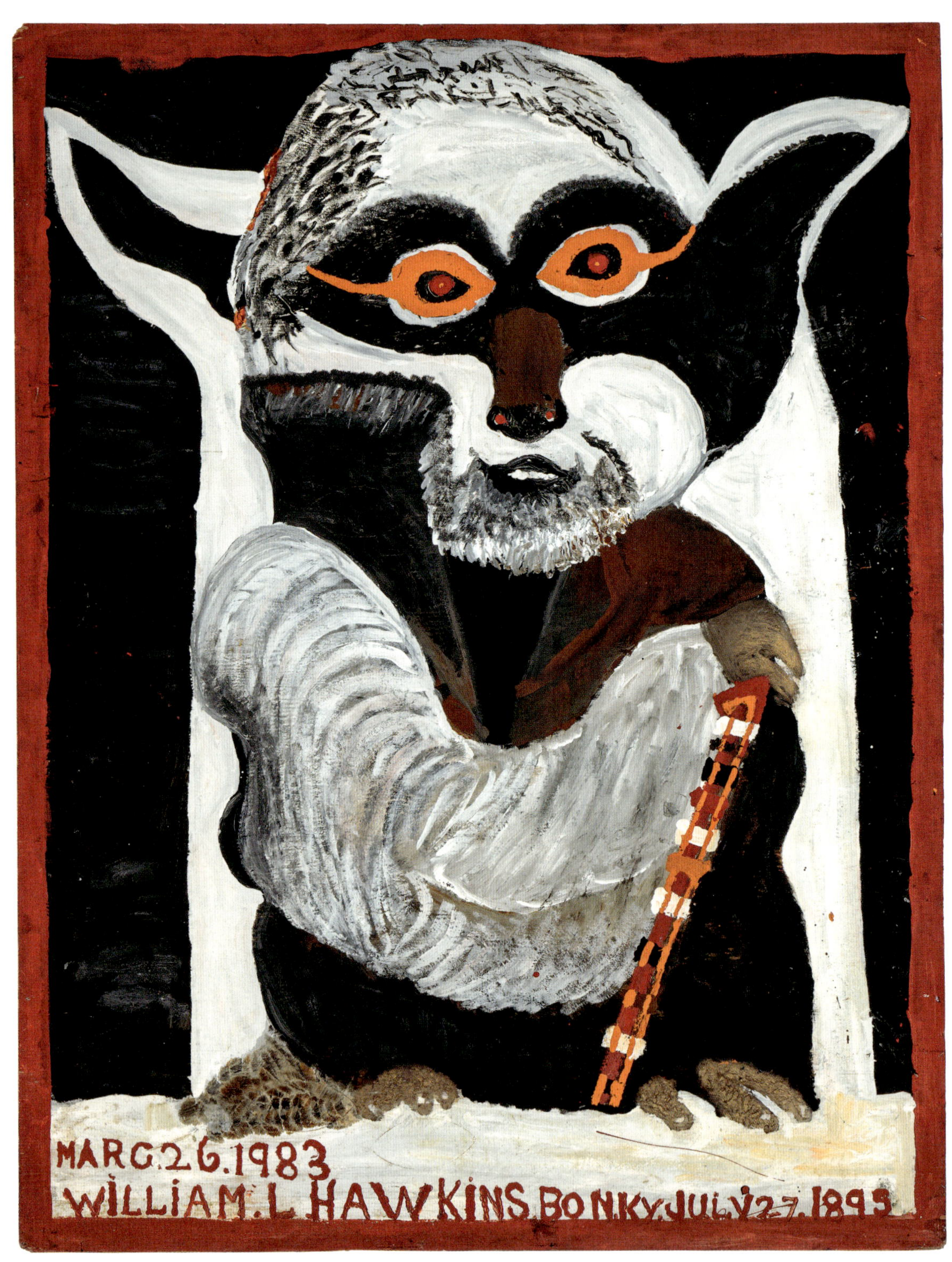

William Hawkins, *Untitled (Yoda)*, 1983. Enamel on Masonite, 48 × 36 in. (121.9 × 91.4 cm)

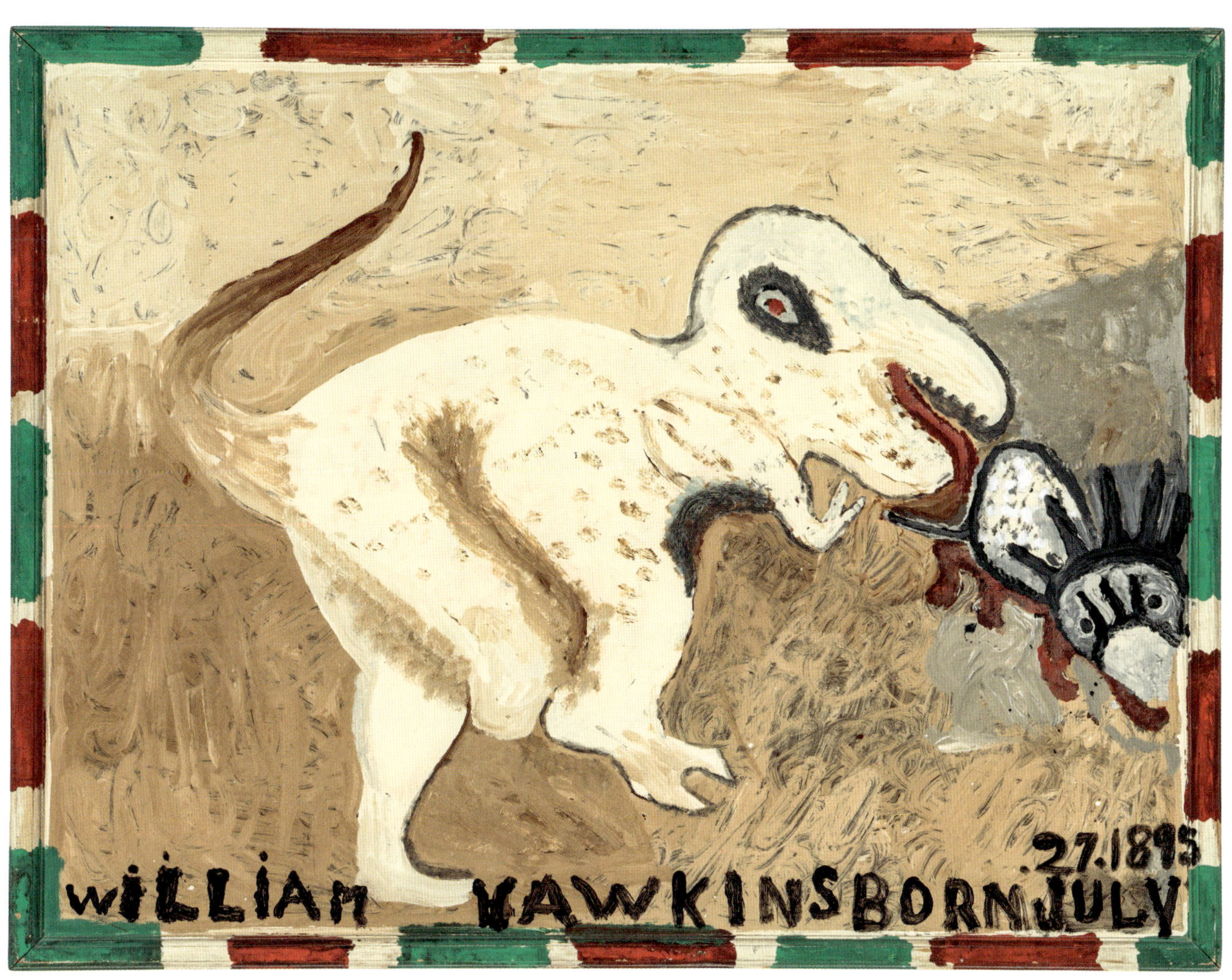

William Hawkins, *Dinosaurs*, n.d. Enamel on Masonite, 34½ × 44 in. (87.6 × 111.8 cm)

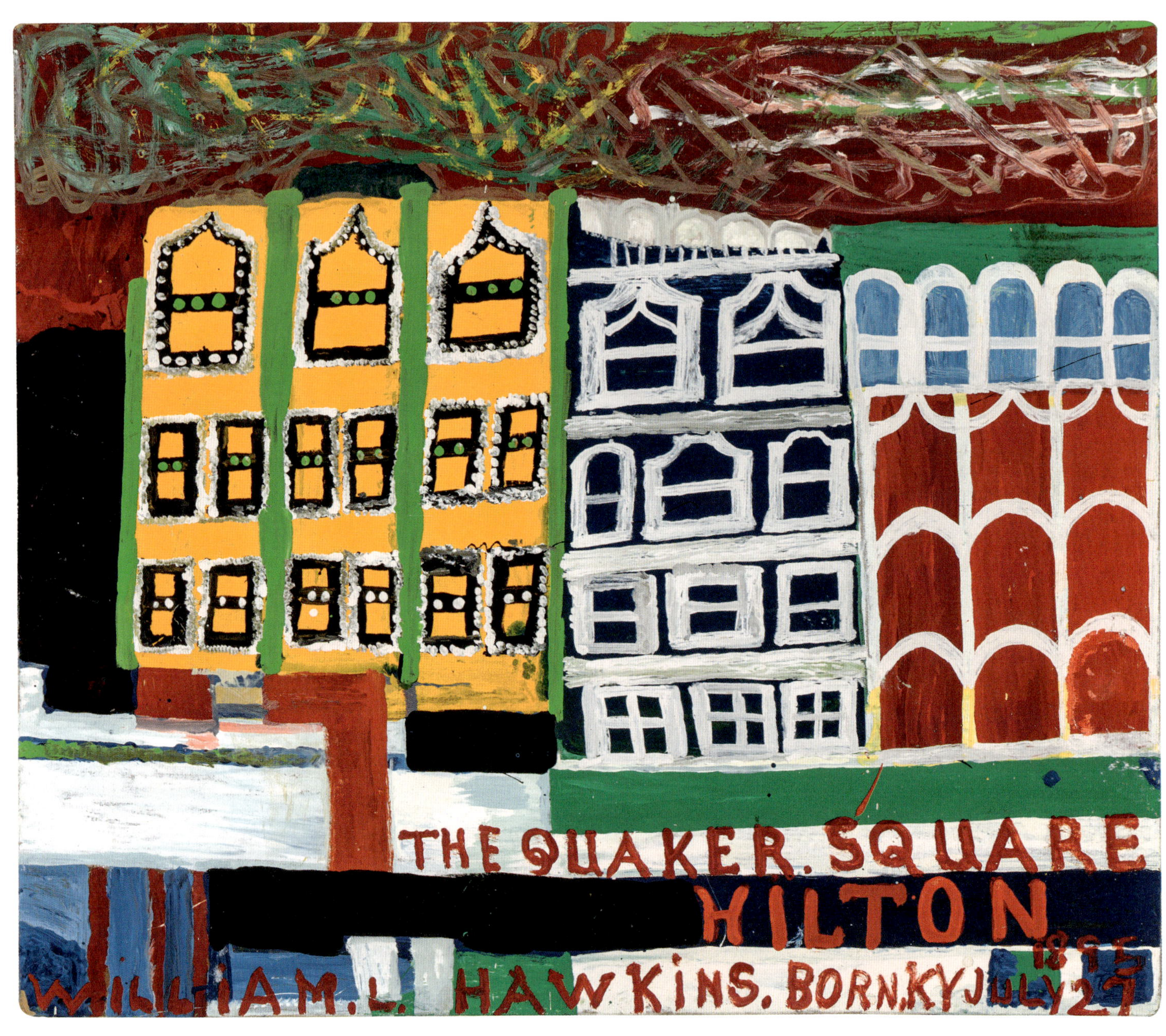

William Hawkins, *Quaker Square Hilton*, 1985. Enamel on Masonite, 42 × 48 in. (106.7 × 121.9 cm)

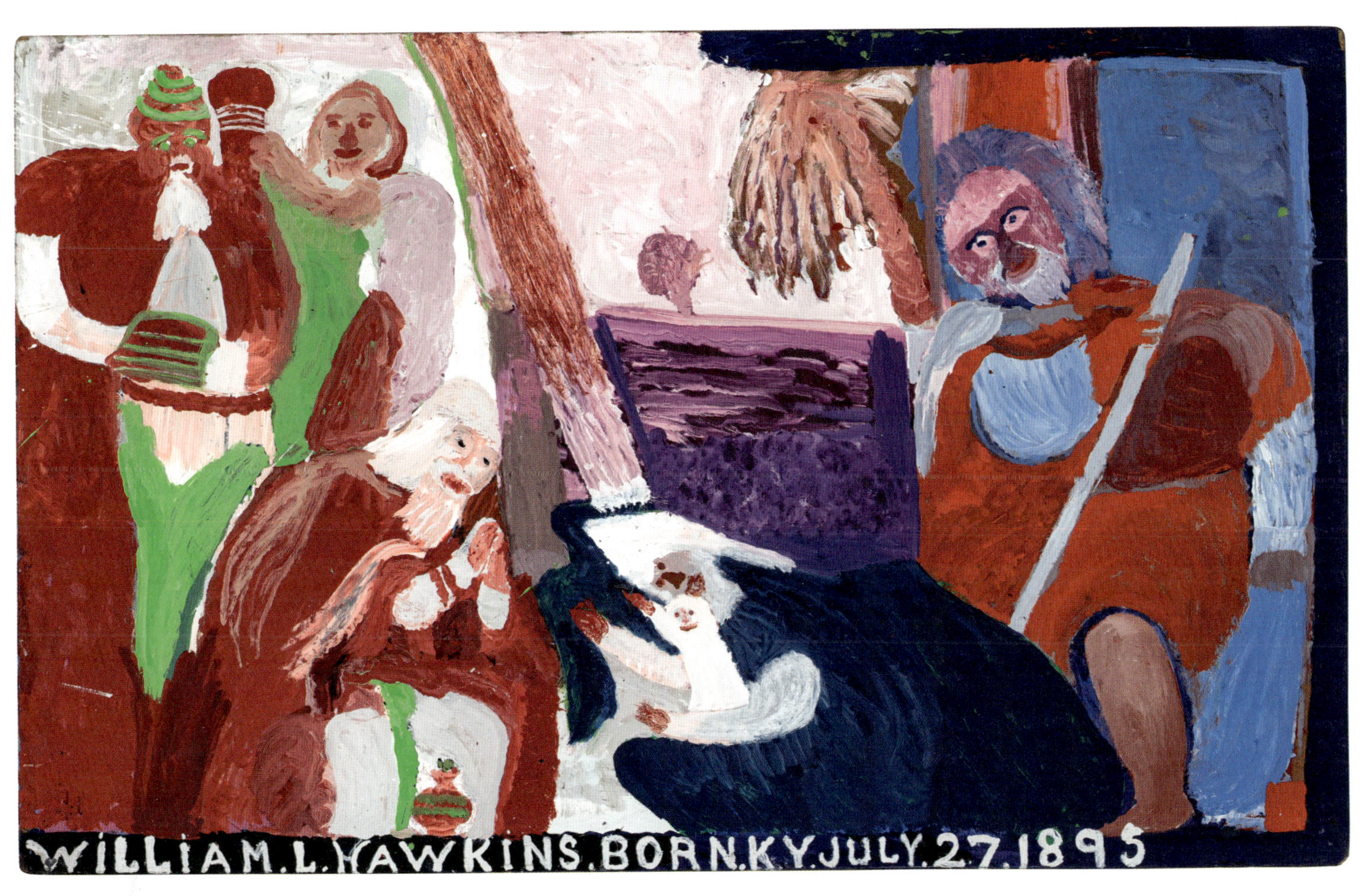

William Hawkins, *Adoration of the Wise Men*, 1985. Enamel on Masonite, 36 × 56 in. (91.4 × 142.2 cm)

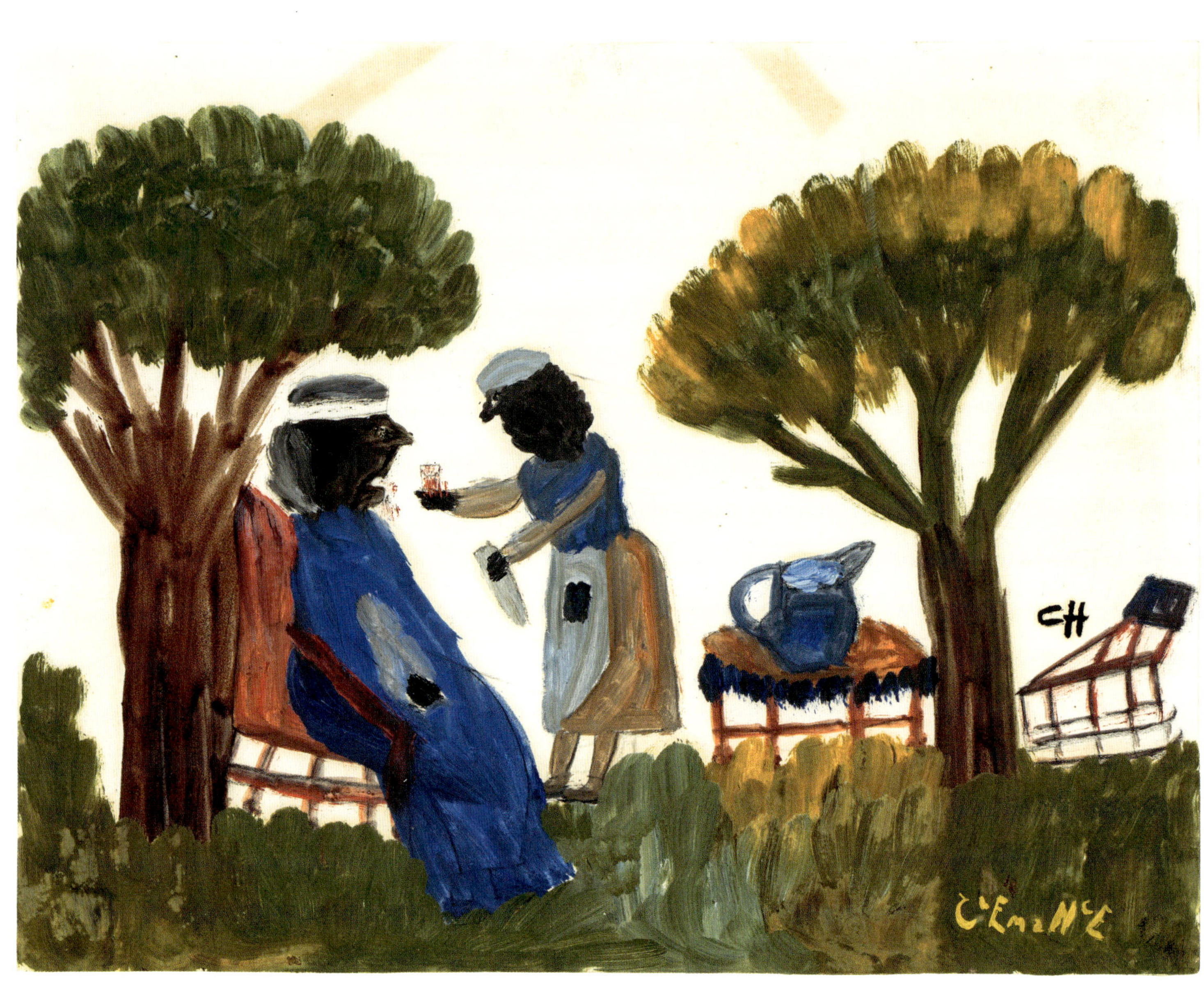
CH

CLEMENTINE HUNTER

ca. 1886–1988

A Creole descendant of slaves, Clementine Hunter worked as a field hand, cotton picker, and housemaid, and she produced a vast opus—several thousand paintings—re-creating life as she knew it as an African American woman in the Deep South. Hunter was born into a family of sharecroppers at the Hidden Hill Plantation in northwestern Louisiana and lived to age 101. She briefly attended a local Catholic school but never learned to read or write. As a teenager, she moved with her family to the Melrose Plantation near Natchitoches in the same county, one of the largest plantations in the United States.

She had two children with Charles Dupree, who died in 1914, and ten years later married Emmanuel Hunter, a woodchopper, with whom she had five children (two stillborn). She worked in the crop field until her thirties when, shortly after her marriage, Carmelite Henry, the owner of Melrose, brought her into the big house to do domestic work. When Mrs. Henry's husband, John, died in 1917, "Miss Cammie," as she was affectionately called, opened her home to writers and artists, hosting them for extended stays to live and work, turning Melrose into an artist colony. At some point in the late 1930s, inspired by this new environment, Hunter, who had already begun to explore her creativity with sewing, quilting, and doll making, picked up a brush and began painting.

Legend has it that Hunter gathered some discarded tubes of paint left by Alberta Kinsey, a visiting artist to Melrose, and used them to paint the scene of a baptism in Cane River on a discarded window shade. Melrose Plantation's curator, François Mignon, and University of Oklahoma faculty member James Register encouraged Hunter and are largely responsible for setting her on the path to recognition. Through Register's efforts, in 1944 Hunter received a Julius Rosenwald Foundation grant for African American visual artists, and in 1953 she was featured in a *Look* magazine article, "Innocence Regained" (June 16, 1953), which included a photograph of the artist in her cabin surrounded by her paintings, and brought her national attention. Hunter remained in Melrose Plantation's employ until 1970, painting every night after completing her chores. At first, she used readily available materials such as house paint on cardboard, paper bags, scrap wood, snuff boxes, cutting boards, wine bottles, and milk jugs, but she moved on to the more conventional materials of oil and watercolors on canvas. She did not typically title her paintings, but when asked for a title she would provide descriptive or narrative lines.

In the thousands of works that she painted (said to be between five and ten thousand), Hunter left behind a visual history of life in the confines of a plantation. With simplified figures, usually in profile, and a lack of scale and perspective, her compositions are imaginative and effective. Aside from a number of Christian religious works, still lifes, and landscapes, the predominant subject of her work is ordinary and anonymous folk working the land, cooking, washing, resting, going to church, participating in dances, celebrating weddings and baptisms, and attending funerals. This theocentric,

Clementine Hunter, *Bringing Mother a Cool Drink*, c. 1945. Paint on paper, 11½ × 14½ in. (29.2 × 36.8 cm)

orderly world, uncomplicated for those inside it, is rich with insight for those with the benefit of historical hindsight. Hunter also painted murals, the best known being the *African House Murals* that she painted in 1955 on the walls of a plantation food storehouse building at Melrose. When she completed the mural, a local newspaper ran a story headlined "A 20th Century Woman of Color Finishes a Story Begun 200 Years Ago by an 18th Century Congo-Born Slave Girl, Marie-Therese, the original grantee of Melrose Plantation."

Even though Hunter's work was exhibited as early as 1949, she did not receive widespread recognition until the 1970s, when the American Folk Art Museum (New York) and the Los Angeles County Museum of Art showed her paintings. In the years that followed, she became the first African American given a solo exhibition at the Delgado Museum (now the New Orleans Museum of Art). When the wife of a former Louisiana senator arranged a trip for her to the White House to meet President Jimmy Carter, she declined the opportunity, saying, "If Jimmy Carter wants to see me, he knows where I am," typical of her personal lack of interest in fame. When Northwestern State University of Louisiana awarded her an honorary Doctor of Fine Arts degree in 1985, it was only the fourth degree of this kind issued by the hundred-year-old institution, and the first to an African American. Hunter's works have been included in many exhibitions and they can be found in the permanent collections of the American Folk Art Museum (New York), the High Museum of Art (Atlanta), the Los Angeles County Museum of Art, the Milwaukee Art Museum, the New Orleans Museum of Art, the Ogden Museum of Southern Art (New Orleans), the Philadelphia Museum of Art, and the Smithsonian American Art Museum (Washington, D.C.).

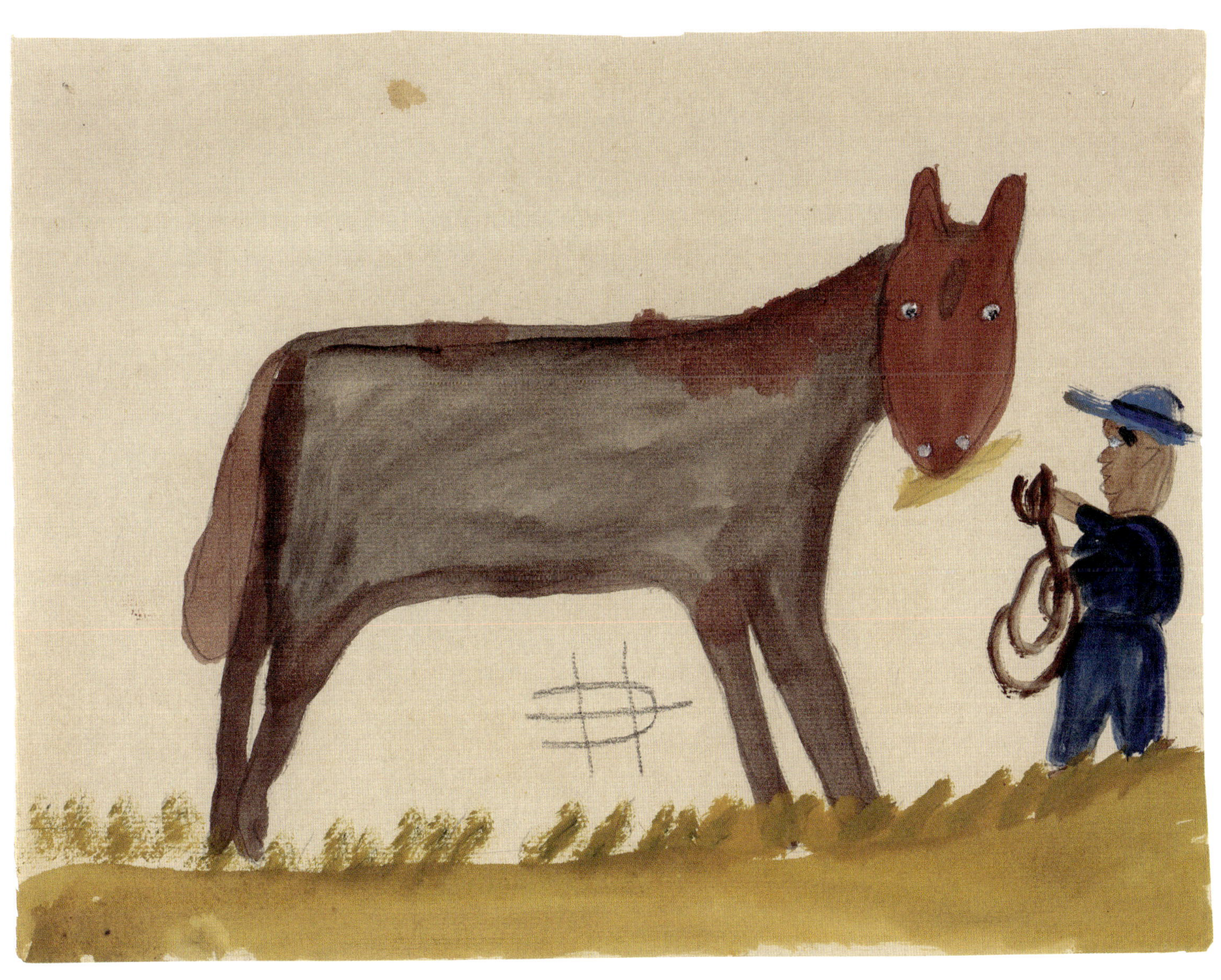

Clementine Hunter, *Boy with Horse*, n.d. Paint on paper, 10 × 12¾ in. (25.4 × 32.4 cm)

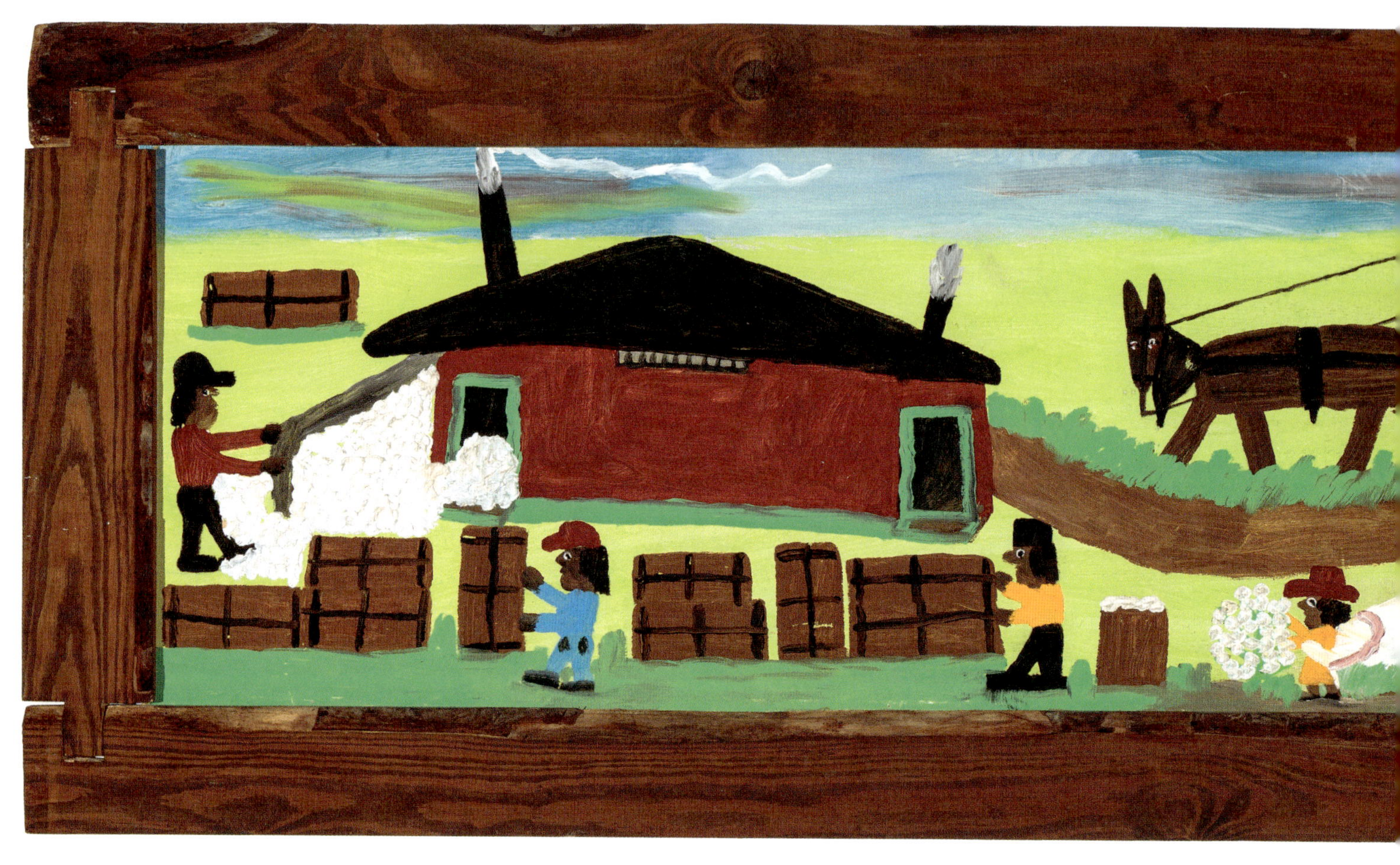

Clementine Hunter, *Plantation Life*, c. 1970–80. Oil on paper board, 22 × 78 in. (55.9 × 198.1 cm)

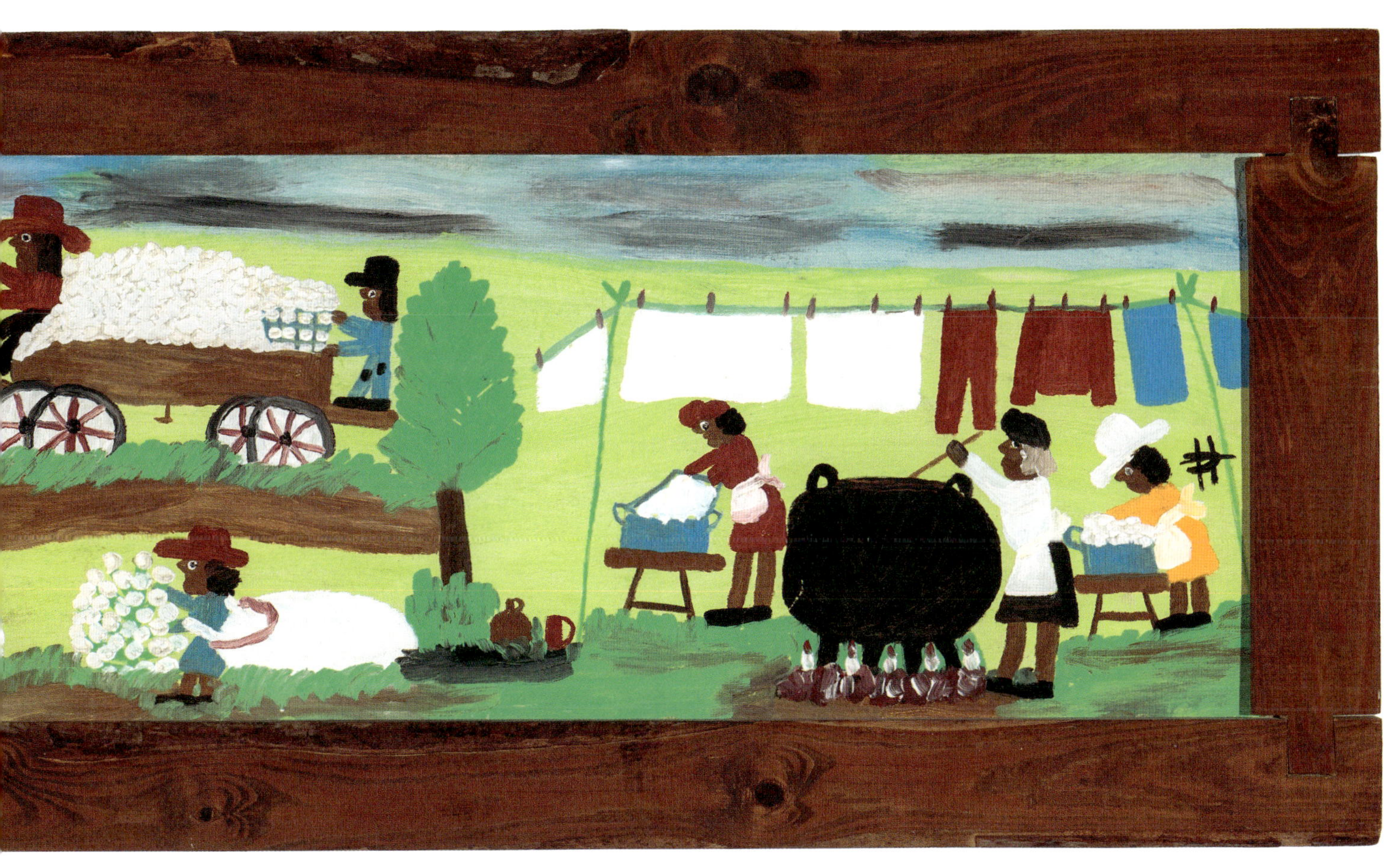

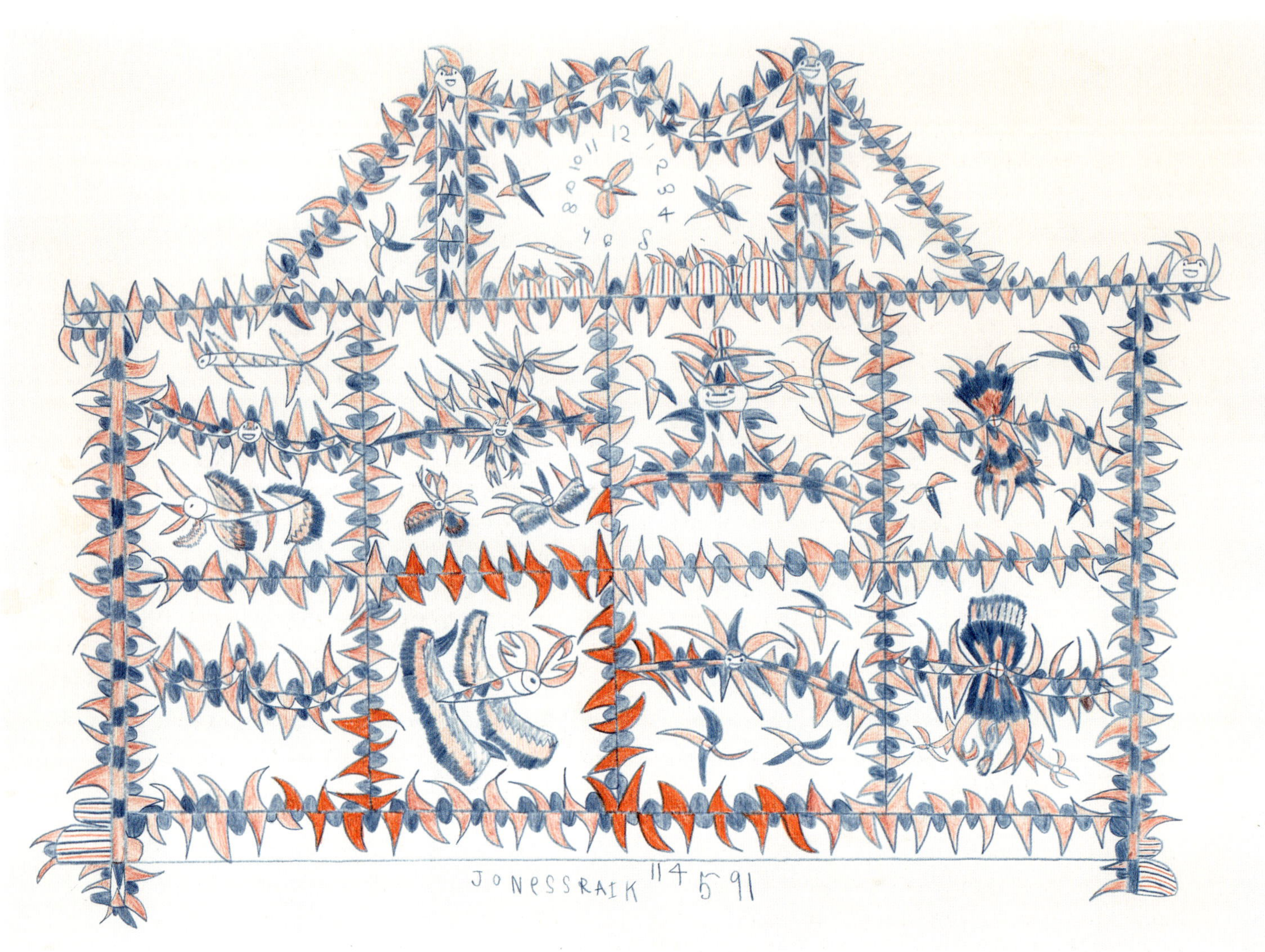
JONESSRAIK 11 4 5 91

FRANK JONES

ca. 1900–1969

An elusive figure with a poignant if obscure biography, Frank Jones was born near Clarksville, Texas, a city very much segregated in Jones's lifetime. After his father deserted the family when Jones was three or four, his mother too abandoned him when he was five or six. An elderly woman took him in and raised him in a religious, profoundly superstitious household still under the specter of slavery; he never received formal education, and he remained illiterate.

Jones recounted that his mother had told him that a veil, also known as a caul, covered his left eye when he was born, a singularity interpreted in African American lore as a sign of supernatural sight into the spirit world. He claimed to have seen ghosts (or "haints") and haunted forms inanimate and animate since his youth.

Between 1941 and 1964 he was incarcerated three times, in each case for crimes (rape, robbery, and homicide) he may not have committed. At each sentencing he claimed innocence. After infringing parole, he spent the rest of his life incarcerated at Huntsville State Prison, where he began to draw and in 1964 won first prize in the inaugural Texas Department of Corrections Art Show, the same event at which Henry Ray Clark (p. 67) was discovered in 1989. Murray Smither of Atelier Chapman Kelley Gallery in Dallas attended the prison exhibition, discovered Jones, and introduced his work into the art world while Jones was still incarcerated.

Initially Jones made his pictures with foraged materials: scrap paper from wastebaskets and prison staff blue and red pencils, keeping his palette limited to the colors, as he described them, of fire and smoke. When the Dallas gallery supplied him with a variety of colored pencils, he still seldom branched out to shades of green and orange. "Devil houses" were his sole subject: tiered, compartmentalized structures into which he trapped the spirits that spooked him.

Jones's devils create a hide-and-seek game for the viewer; often only a single primitive monster with many appendages appears. The occupants of Jones's houses morph into shapes suggestive of birds, bats, fish, dragonflies, crustaceans, cacti, air plants, and mysterious life-forms from deep within the forest or sea. Most have horns atop their head, usually with several more horns poking out elsewhere, and those with a face always grin broadly. Some mimic architectural elements, like gargoyles or whirligigs.

Jones often signed his work with his prison ID number, 114591, and sometimes his name, or many variations thereof. Although in early February 1969 Jones was granted the new parole he had long sought, just two weeks later, still behind bars, he died after a sudden downturn in his cirrhosis.

Jones's work is in the collections of the American Folk Art Museum (New York), the High Museum of Art (Atlanta), the Menil Collection (Houston), the American Visionary Art Museum (Baltimore), the Asheville Art Museum, the Philadelphia Museum of Art, the New Orleans Museum of Art, and the Smithsonian American Art Museum (Washington, D.C.).

Text excerpted and adapted from Alejandra Russi, "Insiders: Henry Ray Clark and Frank Jones," www.riccomaresca.com.

Frank Jones, *Untitled*, 1960. Colored pencil on paper, 18¾ × 25 in. (47.6 × 63.5 cm)

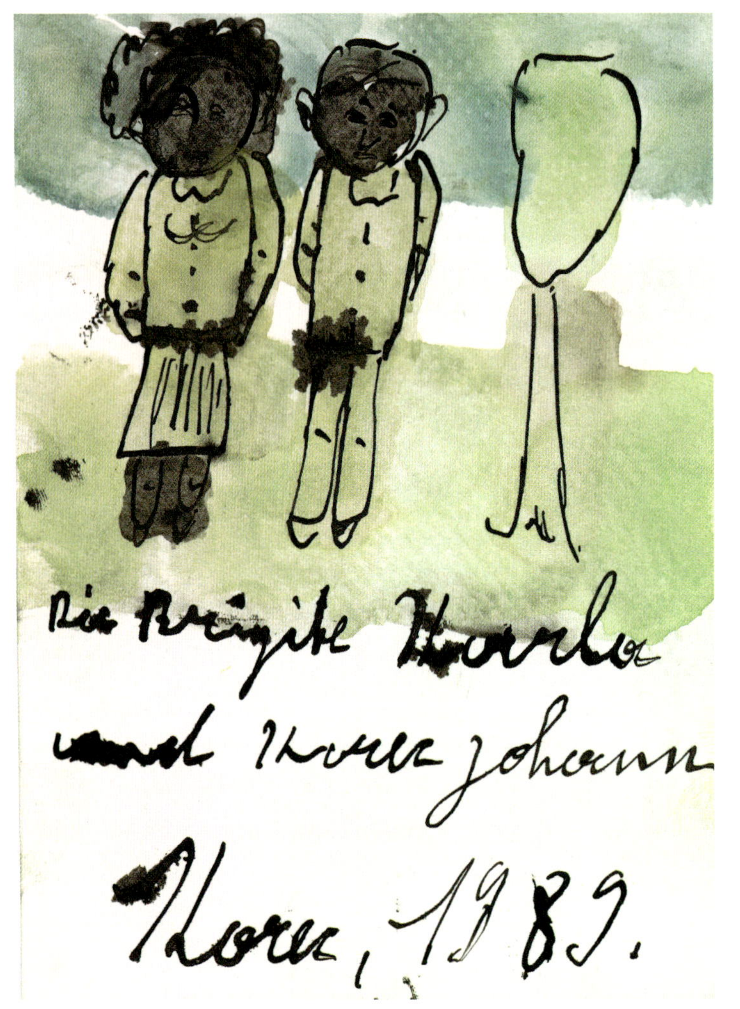
Die Brigite Karla
und Korec Johann
Korec, 1989.

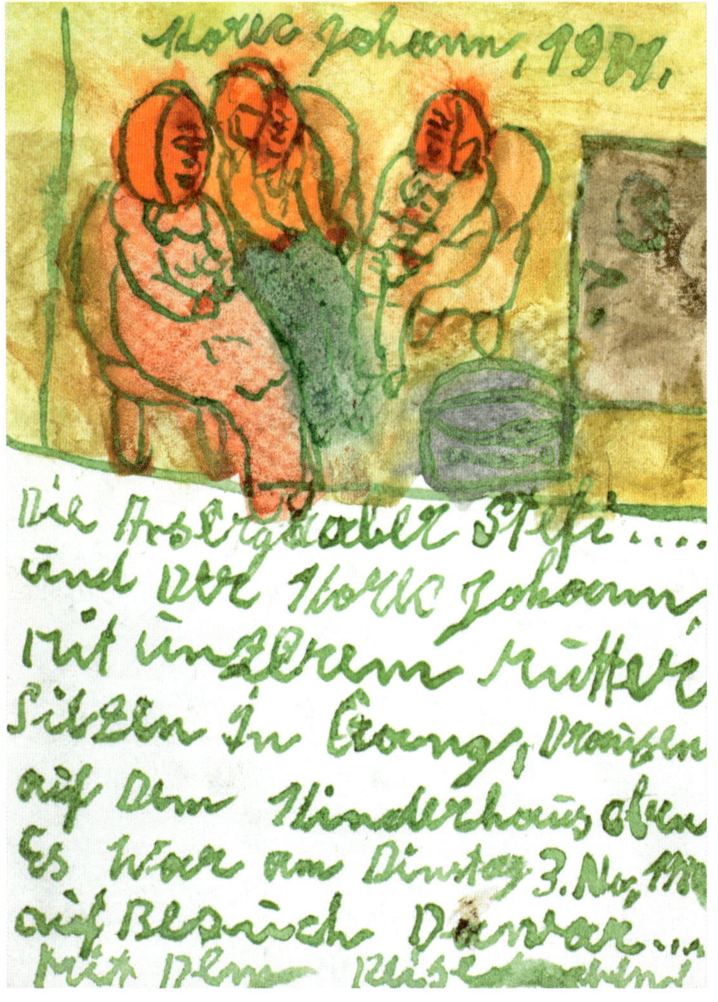
Korec Johann, 1994.
Die Stefi...
und der Korec Johann,
mit unzerem Mutter
Sitzen in Gang, draußen
auf dem Kinderhaus oben
Es war am Dinstag 3. No,
auf Besuch Da war...

JOHANN KOREC

1937–2008

Johann Korec grew up in orphanages in Vienna and from age thirteen worked as a farm laborer and shepherd. His dream was to care for animals in a circus, but manic depression and hypomania led to his commitment to the Maria Gugging Psychiatric Clinic just north of Vienna in 1958. Only four years earlier, psychiatrist Leo Navratil had administered diagnostic drawing tests to his patients at the clinic, discovering that several of them had artistic talent. Navratil's first book, *Schizophrenie und Kunst* (Schizophrenia and Art), was published in 1965. In 1970 the Gugging artists had their first exhibition in the Viennese Galerie nächst St. Stephan. By 1981 all artistically talented patients at Gugging (including Korec) were housed under one roof—the Center for Art-Psychotherapy—and exhibitions featuring their work began to appear throughout Europe. Eventually, the center's name was changed to House of Artists and psychological analysis of the residents' art was no longer the focus, as care shifted to providing a protected community to pursue their individual talents and develop skills despite mental illness. Navratil's successor, Johann Feilacher, has sought to promote the artists' work widely in the international art market and, to this day, the Gugging artists have been part of more than 250 exhibitions in galleries and museums worldwide.

Johann Korec's interest in art emerged in the 1960s, when he started collecting images from print media and tracing the figures that appealed to him. At one point, he began to combine the tracings with his own compositions—retracing all contours with India ink and filling them with watercolors. A favorite motif soon developed: lovers locked in intimacy, which he depicts in multiple variations and describes within his pictures with a large text section that identifies each figure, the male invariably being himself and the various women his real or fictional girlfriends. The narrative is an essential graphic component of each work, a pictorial diary documenting an erotic story unfolding in Korec's mind. Korec's work is in the abcd Collection (Paris), the Arnulf Rainer Collection (Vienna), the Charlotte Zander Museum (Bönnigheim, Germany), the Collection de l'Art Brut (Lausanne, Switzerland), the Stadshof Collection (Netherlands), the Lille Métropole Museum of Modern, Contemporary and Outsider Art (Villeneuve-d'Ascq, France), the Musée de la Creation Franche (Bègles, France), the Setagaya Museum (Tokyo), and the Museum of Outsider Art (Moscow). Korec's work was included in the exhibition *Known/Unknown: Private Obsession and Hidden Desire in Outsider Art* in 2017 at the Museum of Sex (New York).

Johann Korec, *The Brigite Karia . . .*, 1989. Ink and watercolor on paper, 5¾ × 4 in. (14.6 × 10.2 cm)

Johann Korec, *Untitled*, 1981. Ink and watercolor on paper, 5¾ × 4 in. (14.6 × 10.2 cm)

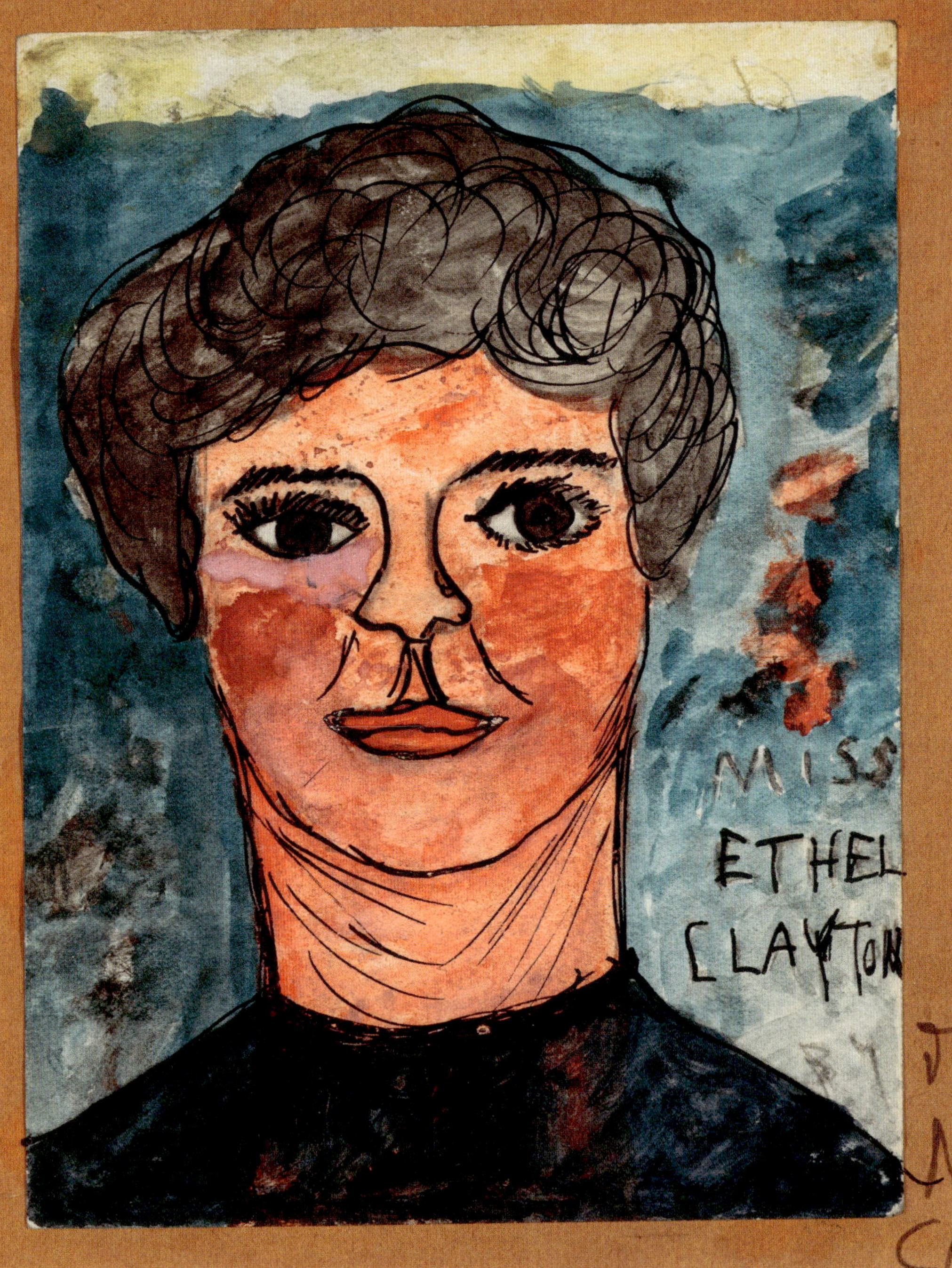
ETHEL CLAYTON
MISS
ETHEL
CLAYTON
BY
JOS
Mc
CARTH

JUSTIN McCARTHY

1892–1977

The eldest son of John McCarthy, the very affluent publisher of the *Hazleton Sentinel* newspaper, Justin McCarthy lived most of his life in Weatherly, Pennsylvania. After his younger brother died of pneumonia in 1907, the family traveled to Paris, where McCarthy frequently visited the Louvre. Soon after their return home John McCarthy died in 1908, and the McCarthys lost their family fortune. McCarthy attended the University of Pennsylvania Law School but failed final exams in his second year and suffered a serious nervous breakdown. He spent five years in the Rittersville State Home for the Insane in Pennsylvania, where he began drawing and painting, signing his early works with pseudonyms such as "Gaston Deauville" and "Prince Dashing." After treatment he returned to the family mansion and lived with his mother, and he continued to make art while he grew and sold vegetables and fruits on the mansion grounds to support himself. His mother died in 1940, leaving him alone in the tumbledown mansion, which he filled with unsold paintings.

McCarthy's range of subjects was wide; he painted and drew nature (landscapes and still lifes), historical or biblical events, and portraits of sports celebrities, movie stars, and fashion models. He had a special penchant for stylish women, Marilyn Monroe, Marie Prevost, and Linda Darnell among them. His fascination with mass media iconography makes him a precursor of Pop Art, although his style varied greatly, ranging from detailed cartoon-like drawings to abstracted and expressionistic compositions emphasizing texture, vibrant color combinations, and subjective perception. Versatile in his choice of materials, he worked in watercolor, crayon, graphite, ink, oil (his principal medium in the 1950s and 1960s), and acrylic (which he started using in the early 1970s) on cardboard, Masonite, canvas, and found paper.

McCarthy was unrecognized for most of his life and held an assortment of menial jobs, working for Penn Dixie Cement, Just Born Candy Company, Bethlehem Steel, and Allentown State Memorial Hospital. He lived a secluded life in Weatherly but enjoyed going to the movies, watching sports, and the Ice Capades, which he depicted in several works. He occasionally sold his work from his home and at regional outdoor art fairs. In 1960 Dorothy and Sterling Strauser—collectors and important supporters of folk art—discovered him at an outdoor show in Stroudsburg, Pennsylvania, and included him in the "Strauser Circle," a group of artists that the couple discovered and sponsored. The Strausers were pivotal in McCarthy's inclusion in *Seventeen Naïve Painters*, a 1966–67 traveling exhibition organized by the Museum of Modern Art in New York. Shortly after, as his health began to deteriorate, McCarthy moved to Tucson, Arizona, where he died in 1977.

McCarthy's work is in the Akron Art Museum (Ohio), the American Folk Art Museum (New York), the Birmingham Museum of Art, Intuit: The Center for Intuitive and Outsider Art (Chicago), the Milwaukee Art Museum, the Lille Métropole Museum of Modern, Contemporary and Outsider Art (Villeneuve-d'Ascq, France), the New Orleans Museum of Art, and the Smithsonian American Art Museum (Washington, D.C.).

Justin McCarthy, *Ethel Clayton*, n.d. Mixed media on paper, 6½ × 5 in. (16.5 × 12.7 cm)

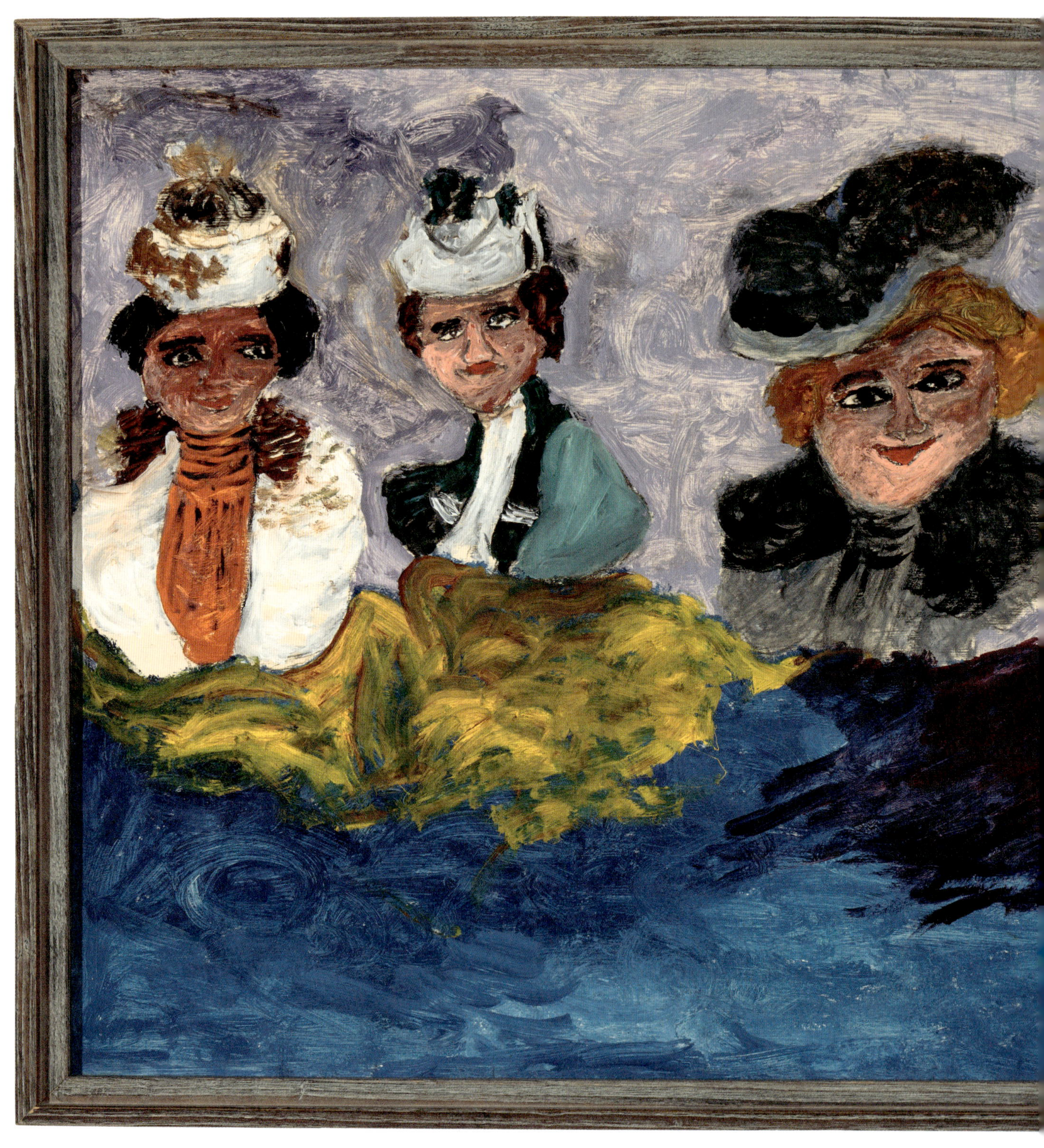

Justin McCarthy, *Six Ladies with Fancy Hats*, 1968. Oil on Masonite, 24 × 48 in. (61 × 121.9 cm)

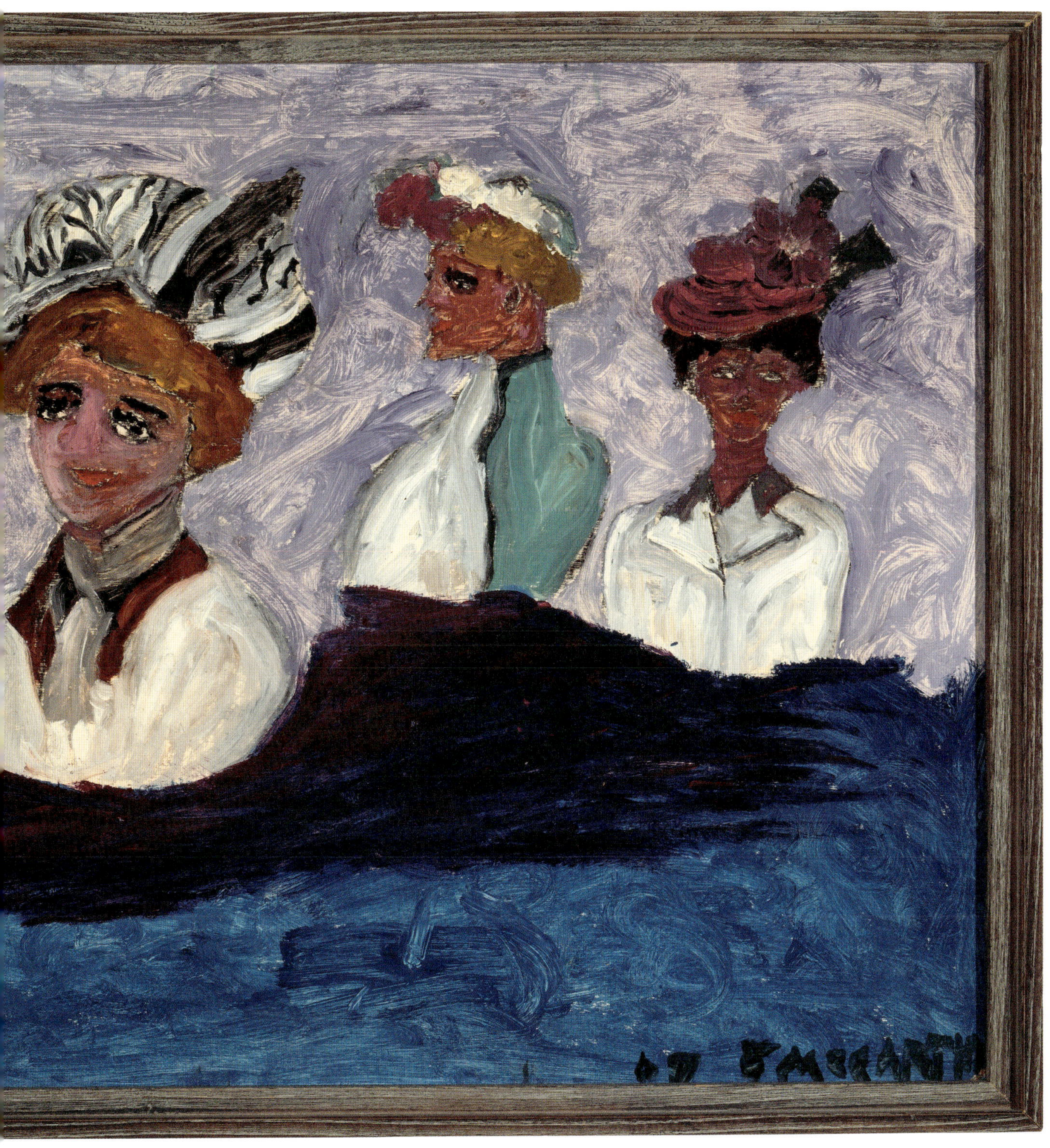

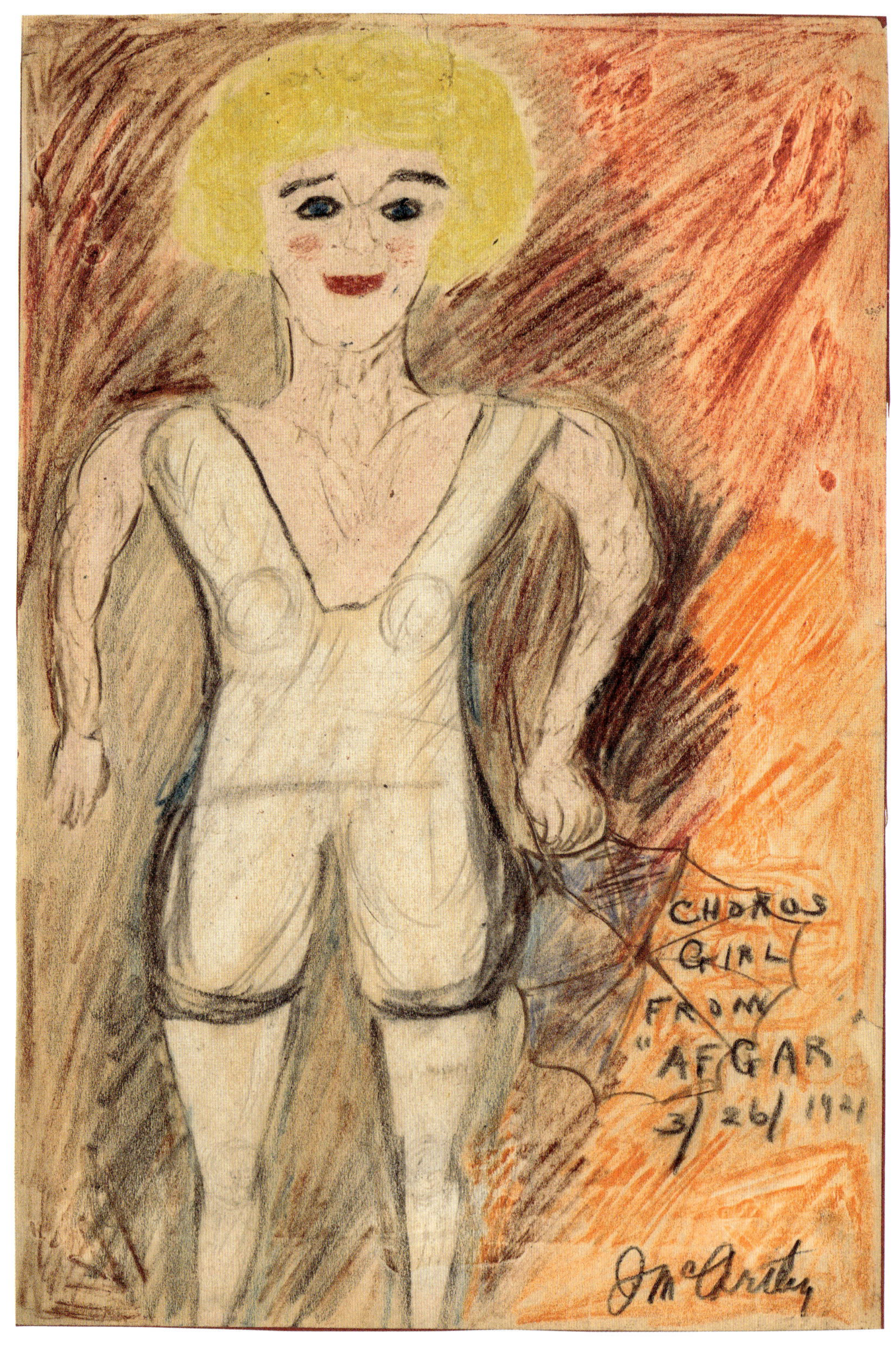

Justin McCarthy, *Chorus Girl from "Afgar,"* 1921. Mixed media on paper, 13 × 8½ in. (33 × 21.6 cm)

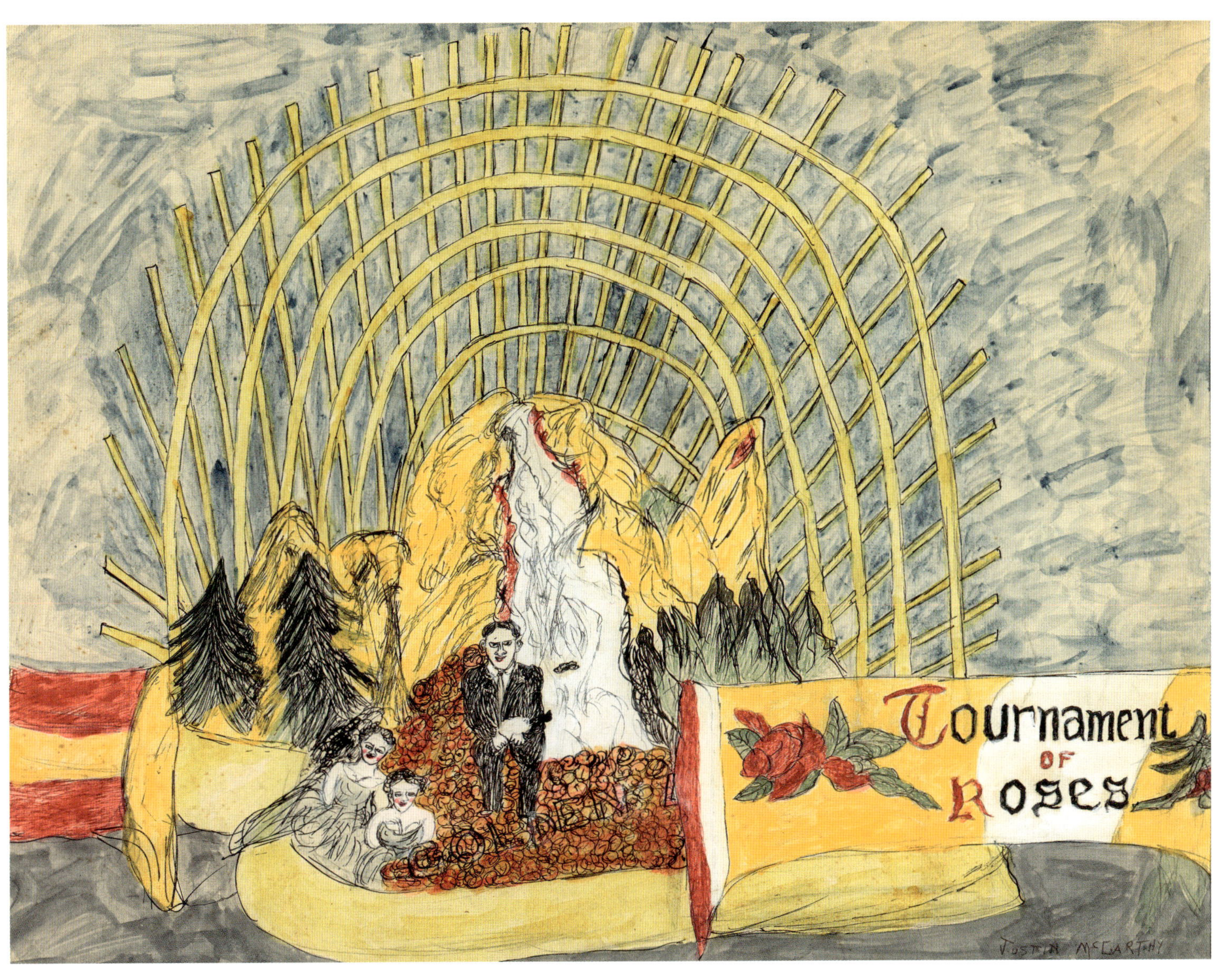

Justin McCarthy, *Tournament of Roses*, c. 1965. Watercolor, graphite, and ink on cardboard, 22 × 28 in. (55.9 × 71.1 cm)

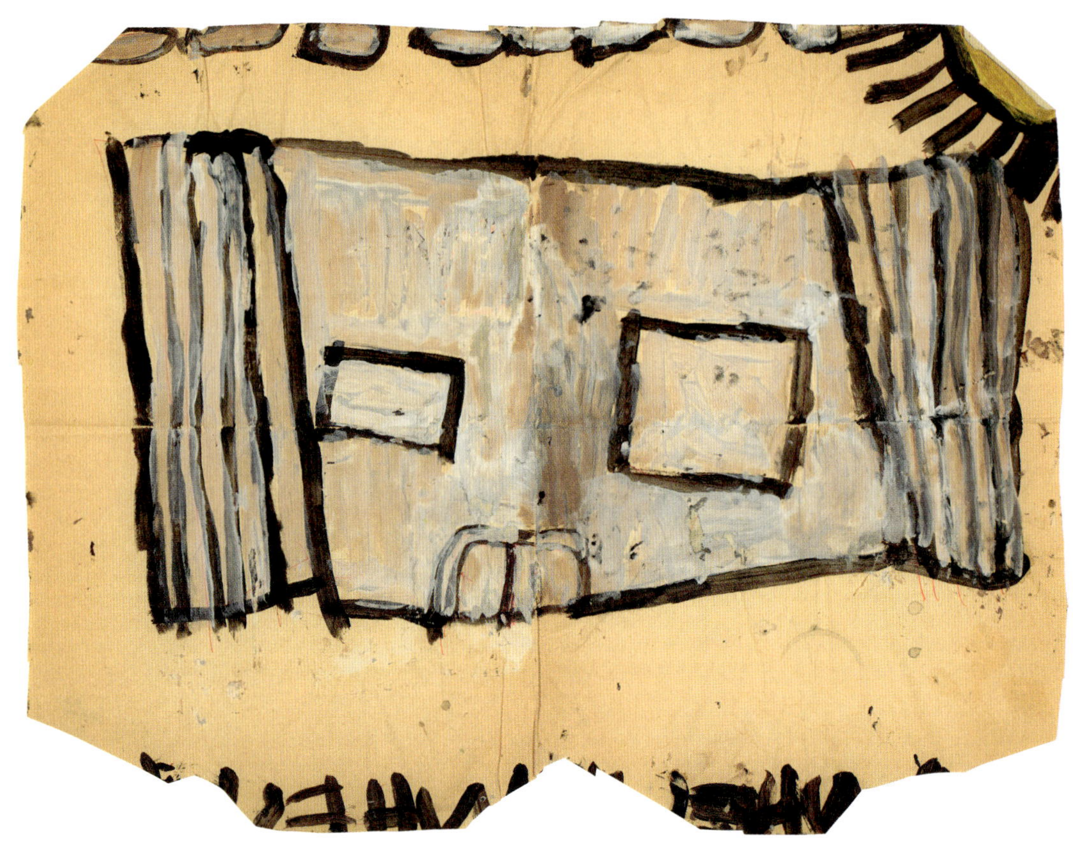

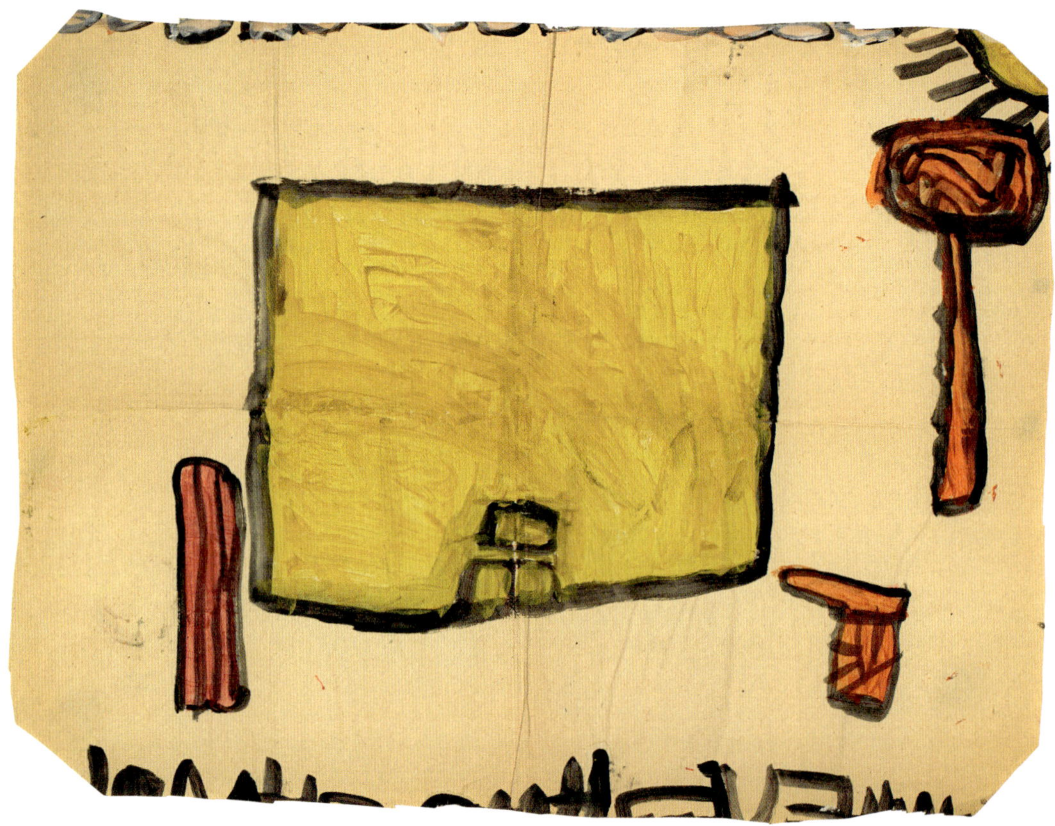

LAURA CRAIG McNELLIS

b. 1957

The youngest child and fourth sister in a close-knit family that always encouraged her artistic gift, Laura McNellis was born in Nashville, Tennessee. From an early age she was prolific in creating art, habitually painting late into the night. Although developmentally disabled and autistic, she was never institutionalized. With abiding commitment her family raised her and provided her a variety of social stimuli in the large house her parents bought when she was an infant. She lived with them until they both passed away in the late 1980s. Until then most of her work remained there, stuffed in drawers and bags or stored in the attic.

McNellis's work depicts a range of treasured objects and buildings. She prefers painting on blank newsprint paper that her late father, who worked as a post office sorter, would bring home folded in stacks. McNellis usually draws before painting—either from memory or going back and forth between object and sketch until she is satisfied. Her works are fundamentally two-dimensional, yet they regularly present three-dimensional subjects. As she applies paint (typically tempera) to create a picture, it often takes on a life of its own, covering a lot of the drawn minutiae and giving her works the character of improvisation.

McNellis's architectural works depict existing buildings rendered in a way that could be considered archetypal but that she makes her own through her fluency with color mixing and her play between symmetries and asymmetries. Seen through McNellis's depictions, these structures suggest the familiar tenderness of old friends and a sense of sanctuary and security, physical and spiritual.

While McNellis does not engage in creating backdrops, she has often painted a sun, its rays poking out, perched on the upper right-hand corner of her paintings, fronted by a row of small, lumpy clouds. This visual rubric, often unrelated to the scene or other elements portrayed in the work, seems a symbolic anchor to the world that McNellis strives to comprehend and portray. Likewise, her recurrent inclusion of a jumbled succession of letters at the bottom edge of the composition, which vary from work to work, form a spellbinding but unknowable statement, and seem an expression of a desire for verbal communication. Finally, when she has finished a work, swiftly and with great deliberation McNellis often cuts the corners and trims the edges of her paintings. Over the years McNellis has acquired a spoken vocabulary (generally understood, however, only by those close to her), but McNellis is on the whole nonliterate, unable to make connections between sound and written language. Her inclusion of letters is evidence of the earnestness of her pursuit of communication despite her limited access to language.

McNellis's work is in private collections in both the United States and Europe and is in the permanent collection of the Collection de l'Art Brut in Lausanne, Switzerland.

Text excerpted and adapted from Alejandra Russi, "Laura Craig McNellis: Structures," www.riccomaresca.com.

Laura Craig McNellis, *Untitled (Light Gray House)*, c. 1972–80. Tempera on paper, 21 × 28 in. (53.3 × 71.1 cm)

Laura Craig McNellis, *Untitled (No. 2)*, c. 1972–80. Tempera on paper, 21 × 27 in. (53.3 × 68.6 cm)

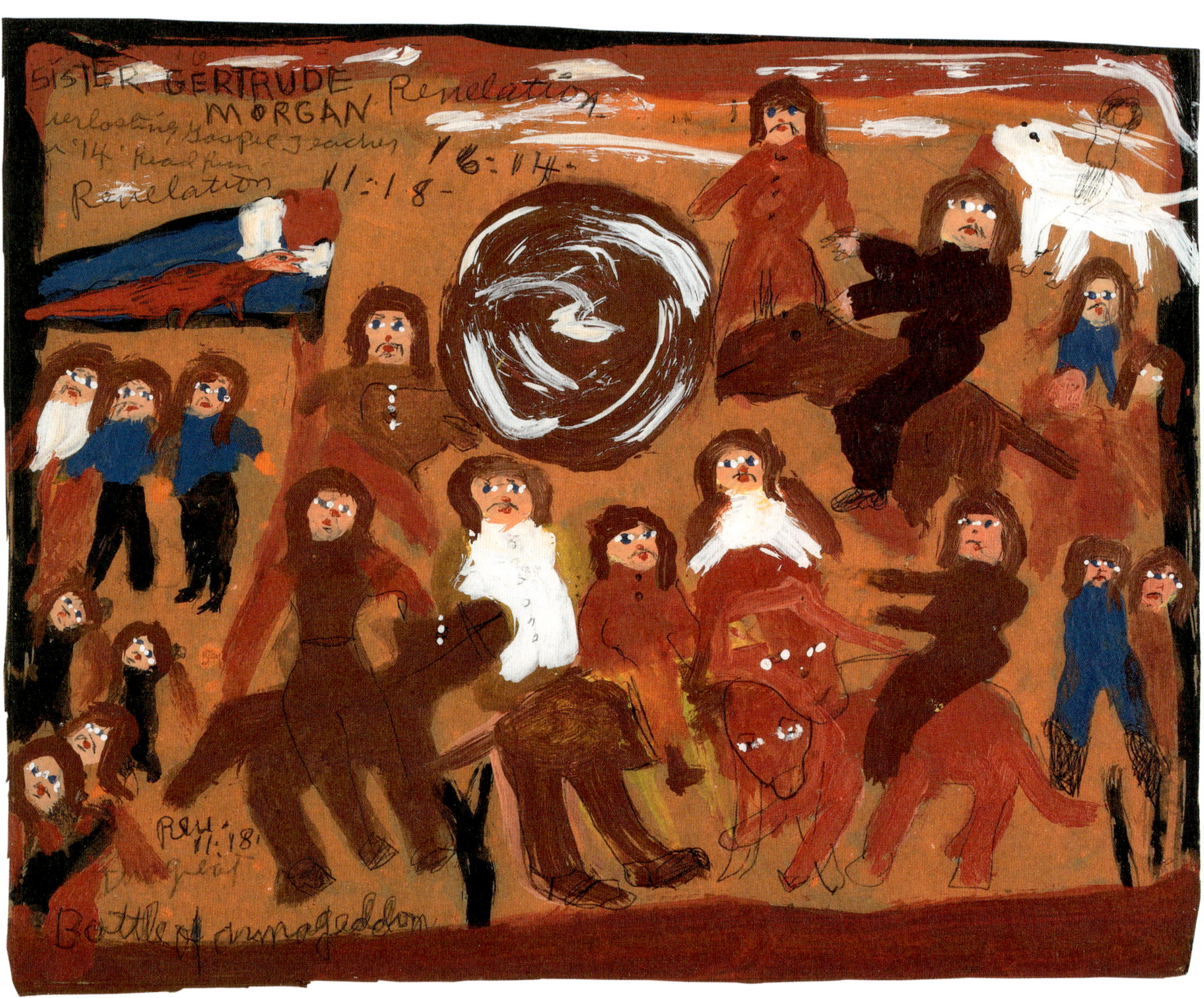
SISTER GERTRUDE MORGAN
Revelation 16:14
Gospel Teacher
Revelation 11:18
Rev. 11:18
Battle of armageddon

SISTER GERTRUDE MORGAN

1900–1980

Weaving biblical tradition and her own written interpretations of the Bible, Sister Gertrude Morgan—a preacher who became an artist and poet—created art that illuminated and expanded the gospel. She believed herself to be first and foremost God's instrument—a missionary before an artist—and her dynamic, boldly original compositions mirror her religious enthusiasm as well as her personal quirks. Born in Lafayette, Alabama, she moved to New Orleans in the late 1930s after the end of her first marriage. In New Orleans, she associated with religious groups and street missionaries who spread God's teachings through song and dance, and she adopted the title "Sister" in the early 1940s.

Using money collected through street preaching, Morgan, Mother Margaret Parker, and Sister Cora Williams bought a plot of land in the Gentilly section of New Orleans where they built a chapel and opened a childcare facility. They offered food and shelter to orphans and children in need until a hurricane destroyed the facility in 1965. Around this time, Morgan had a vision that the Holy Ghost designated her as God's bride. From this time on, she wore only white to honor and symbolize her unworldly matrimony.

Morgan began to concentrate on making art in the mid-1950s and worked with a variety of found and easily obtainable materials: ink, crayons, poster paint, acrylics, and watercolors on cardboard, wood and Styrofoam surfaces, window or lamp shades, and found signs, among many others. The main distinguishing stylistic feature throughout her work is her elaborate juxtaposition of pictures and handwriting working in tandem to convey a forceful message. Morgan's work is in the collections of the New Orleans Museum of Art, the Milwaukee Art Museum, the Museum of Fine Arts (Houston), the Philadelphia Museum of Art, Intuit: The Center for Intuitive and Outsider Art (Chicago), the American Folk Art Museum (New York), the National Gallery of Art, and the Smithsonian American Art Museum (Washington, D.C.).

Sister Gertrude Morgan, *Battle of Armageddon*, n.d. Paint and ink on found cardstock, 16 × 18 in. (40.6 × 45.7 cm)

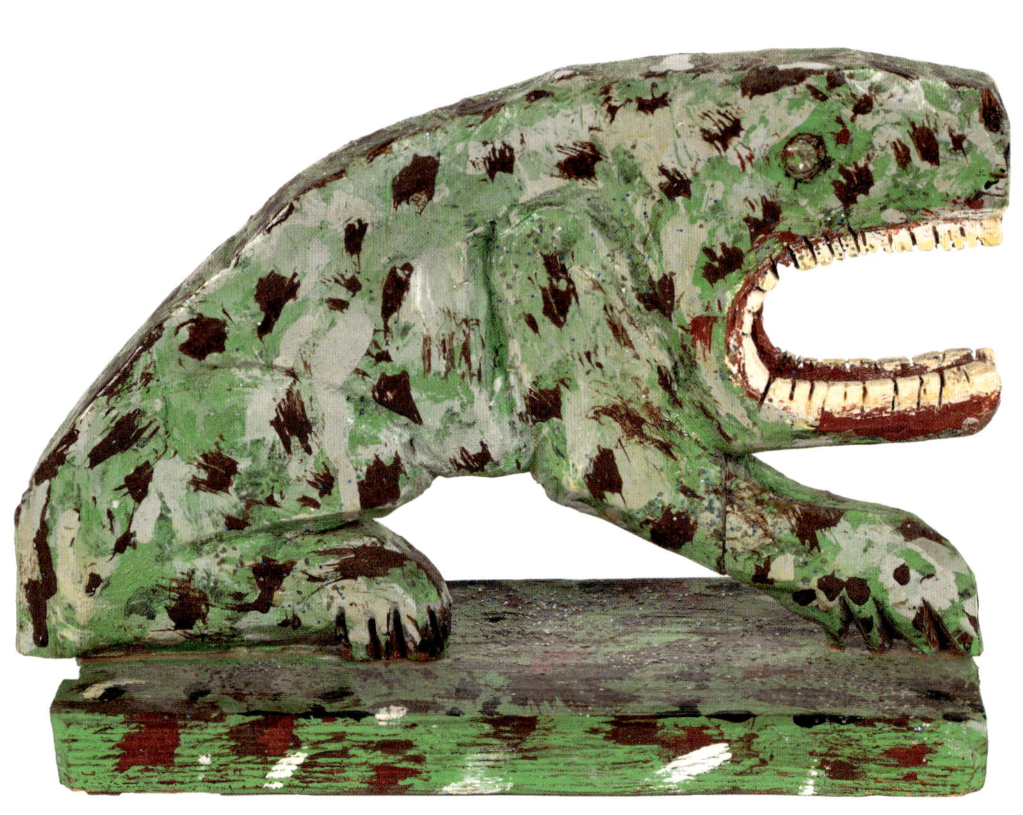

ELIJAH PIERCE

1892–1984

A reflective child, Elijah Pierce loved to walk in the woods with his dog, fish by the creek, play with animals that he would capture and release unharmed, and when his father gave him a pocketknife he enjoyed carving into trees and whittling scraps of wood. His uncle taught him about different wood types and how to work with them, and by age seven Pierce was carving small figures and giving them away to classmates and friends. Born and raised in Baldwyn, Mississippi, he was the youngest son of a farming family, and his father was a former slave. He did not enjoy farmwork, but as a teenager he became interested in barbering, a skill he learned from hanging around a Baldwyn barbershop, where he eventually learned everything about the trade. In his early twenties, Pierce married Zetta Palm, who died in 1915 shortly after the birth of their son, Willie. After drifting around for a few years as an itinerant railroad worker, he was encouraged by his mother to follow his religious calling and in 1920 received his preacher's license from the Mount Zion Baptist Church in Baldwyn.

Pierce eventually joined the Great Migration to the North and met Cornelia Houeston, in Illinois, and followed her to her hometown of Columbus, Ohio, where they were married in 1923. In Columbus, Pierce continued to preach, found work as a barber, and pursued his carving more seriously; some of his painted carvings became narrative embodiments of his sermons. In the late 1920s Pierce carved a small elephant for Cornelia's birthday, and she was so pleased with it that he vowed to make her an entire zoo and went on to carve every animal he could think of.

By the early 1930s, Pierce had matured into his signature style, creating wooden bas-reliefs featuring a range of subjects, from biblical tableaux to historical events, and from national heroes (particularly African Americans) to popular culture such as sports, films, and comics. In 1932 he completed the *Book of Wood*, thirty-three reliefs, each depicting a year in the earthly life of Jesus. A superb example of Pierce's gift, the *Book of Wood* is today in the Columbus Museum of Art, which, at more than three hundred pieces, owns the largest collection of Pierce's work. In 1993 the museum mounted the retrospective exhibition *Elijah Pierce, Woodcarver*, which included more than 170 pieces and traveled to several other venues.

Cornelia died of cancer in 1948 and Pierce was married a third time, to Estelle Greene, a year after opening his own barbershop in 1951 on Long Street. He continued to preach and hung his works along the walls of his shop. When he retired from barbering in 1978, he carved full time and changed the name of the shop to E. Pierce Art Gallery.

Before the early 1970s, Pierce was unknown outside of his community, but when Boris Gruenwald, a sculptor and graduate student at Ohio State University, discovered Pierce's work in a Columbus YMCA exhibition, he made it his mission to promote Pierce's work. In a matter of a few years, Pierce was shown in exhibitions at the Krannert Art Museum at the University of Illinois at Urbana-Champaign, the Phyllis Kind Gallery (New York), and the Smithsonian American Art Museum (Washington, D.C.). In 1973 Pierce won

Elijah Pierce, *Untitled (Frog Sculpture)*, 1979. Carved and painted wood, 6¼ × 8 × 3¼ in. (15.9 × 20.3 × 8.3 cm)

first prize in the International Meeting of Naive Art in Zagreb (former Yugoslavia). In 1982 the National Endowment for the Arts awarded him a National Heritage Fellowship as one of a select group of master folk and traditional artists. After his death the Martin Luther King Jr. Performing and Cultural Arts Complex (Columbus, Ohio) recognized his work by naming the Elijah Pierce Gallery in his honor. Today, Pierce's work is in the permanent collections of the Akron Art Museum (Ohio), the American Folk Art Museum (New York), the High Museum of Art (Atlanta), the Montgomery Museum of Fine Arts, and the New Orleans Museum of Art.

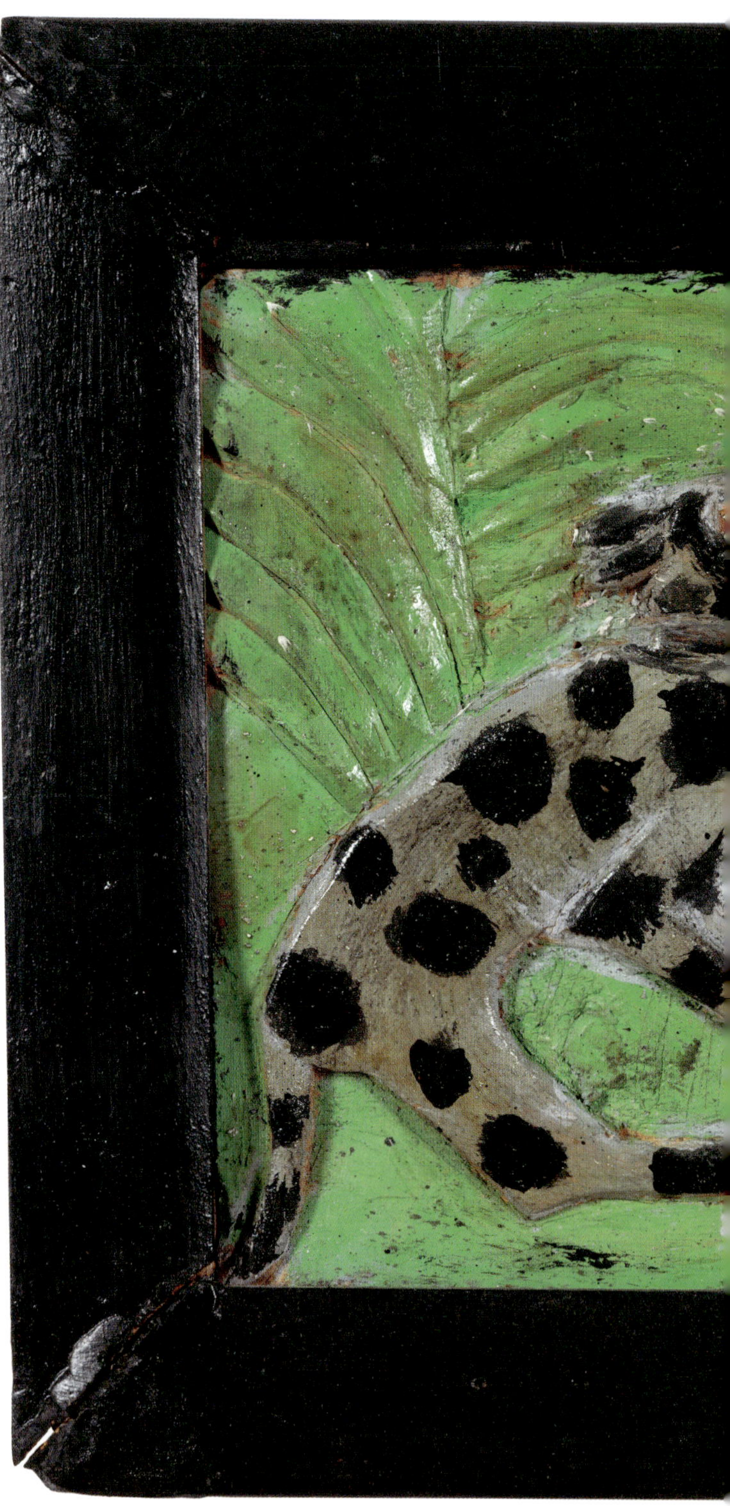

Elijah Pierce, *Couple with Stubborn Mules*, 1978. Carved wood, paint, glitter, and plastic gems, 16 × 25 in. (40.6 × 63.5 cm)

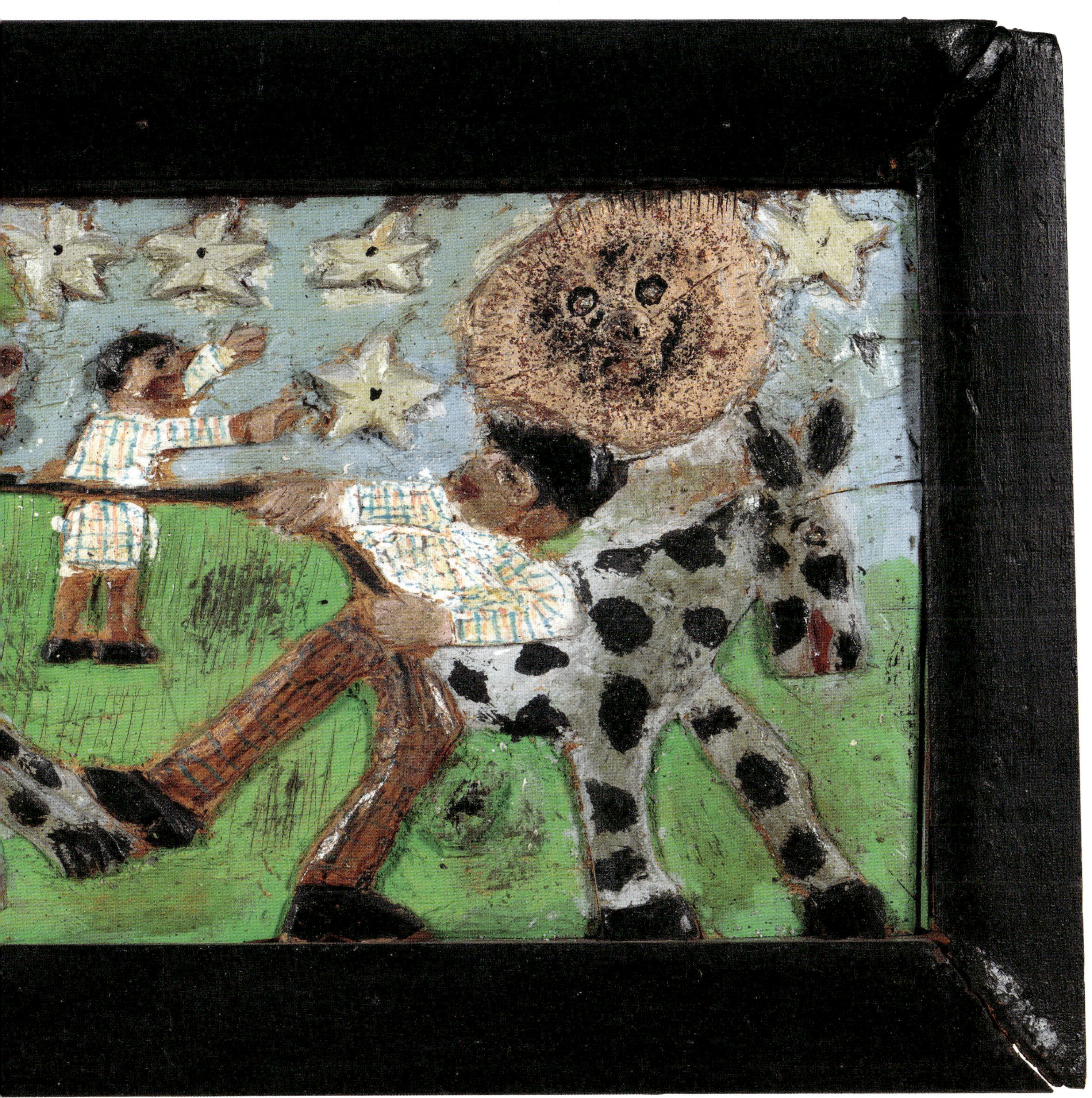

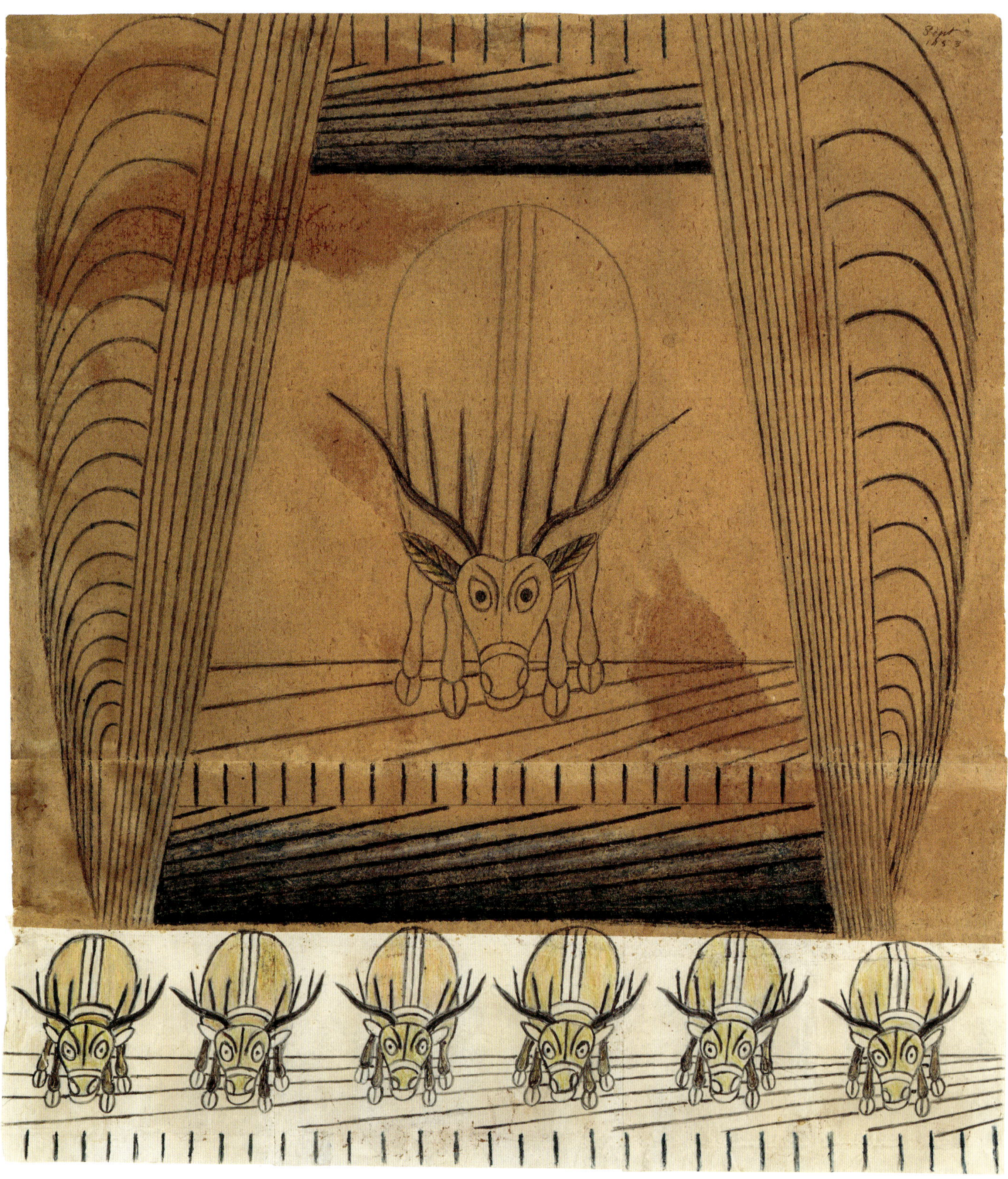
Sept
1953

MARTÍN RAMÍREZ

1895–1963

At age thirty Martín Ramírez, a faithful Catholic and a practiced horseback rider, left his native Jalisco, Mexico, to look for work in California. As Ramírez's biographer the sociologist Víctor M. Espinosa recounted, Ramírez left behind a wife and four children while Mexico was immersed in the aftermath of the revolution, and he effectively walked into a maze never to find his way out. Before the Great Depression he worked in mines and on the railroads in northern California and began drawing on the margins of his letters home.

In 1931 he was institutionalized for presumed manic depression and later diagnosed a catatonic schizophrenic. In clinical examinations he repeatedly said that he could not speak English and that he was not insane. Thereafter, he expressed himself through art and spent the rest of his life in psychiatric facilities—first Stockton State Hospital, from which he attempted escape, and some years later he was placed in the DeWitt State Hospital in Auburn. The drawings he made at DeWitt were preserved by Tarmo Pasto, a painter and professor of art and psychology who gave him materials (apart from those he salvaged himself), and by Max Dunievitz, the physician at the ward where Ramírez lived out his last years.

Ramírez's work shows a compulsion to encapsulate and a concern with boundaries, and he often merges alienating landscapes with Mexican iconography. His assemblages and graphic mise-en-scènes, Madonnas and caballeros, animals and trains framed within visually reverberating lineal shapes are like missives from an alternate world, familiar yet eerie. Profound isolation reaches a point where representation fails to meet life and becomes something else altogether. Ramírez is indisputably among the great self-taught masters of the past century, and the formidable artistic will expressed in his opus is evidence of the tragic personal wreckage of confinement and psychological and cultural segregation.

In his lifetime Ramírez was the subject of four solo exhibitions, at the Crocker Art Museum in Sacramento (1952), the Stephens Union at the University of Berkeley (1952), the Mills College of Art Museum in Oakland (1954), and the Joe and Emily Lowe Art Center at Syracuse University (1961)—all of which excluded his name because of policies aimed to protect the privacy of psychiatric patients. A decade after Ramírez died at age sixty-eight the art dealer Phyllis Kind and artist Jim Nutt introduced his work into the art market. There have since been five retrospectives of Ramírez's work, at the Moore College of Art (Philadelphia, 1985), the Centro Cultural/Arte Contemporáneo (Mexico City, 1989), the American Folk Art Museum (New York, 2007), the Museo Nacional Centro de Arte Reina Sofía (Madrid, 2010), and the Institute of Contemporary Art (Los Angeles, 2017). His work is in the permanent collections of the Milwaukee Art Museum, the High Museum of Art (Atlanta), the Philadelphia Museum of Art, the Museum of Modern Art (New York), and the Solomon R. Guggenheim Museum (New York). In 2015 the United States Postal Service issued a set of five "forever" stamps featuring Ramírez's work and honoring his life.

Text excerpted and adapted from Alejandra Russi, "Martín Ramírez: Forever," www.riccomaresca.com.

Martín Ramírez, *Untitled (Seven Stags)*, 1953. Graphite and crayon on pieced paper, 28 × 24 in. (71.1 × 61 cm)

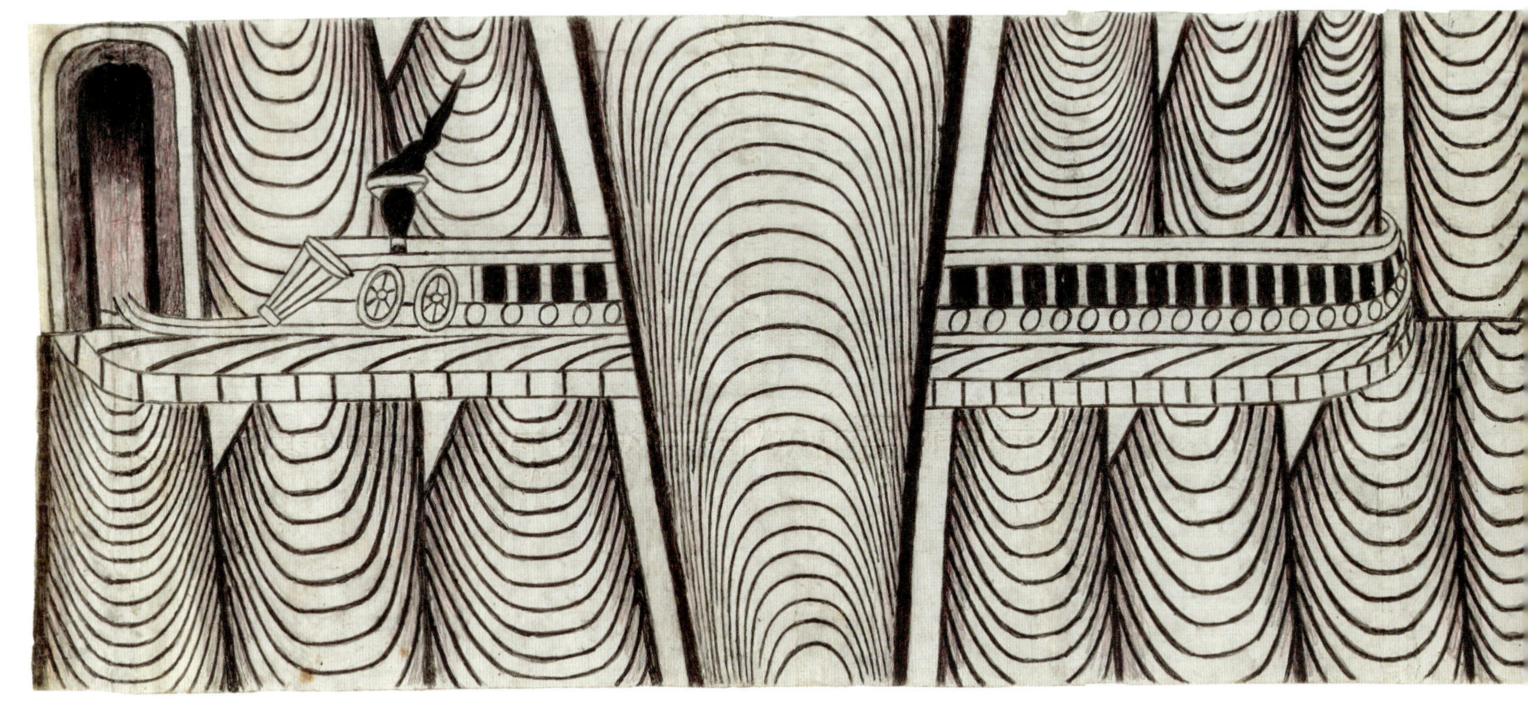

Martín Ramírez, *Untitled (Trains and Tunnels) A, B*, c. 1960–63. Graphite, gouache, crayon, and colored pencil on pieced paper, 17 × 78 in. (43.2 × 198.1 cm)

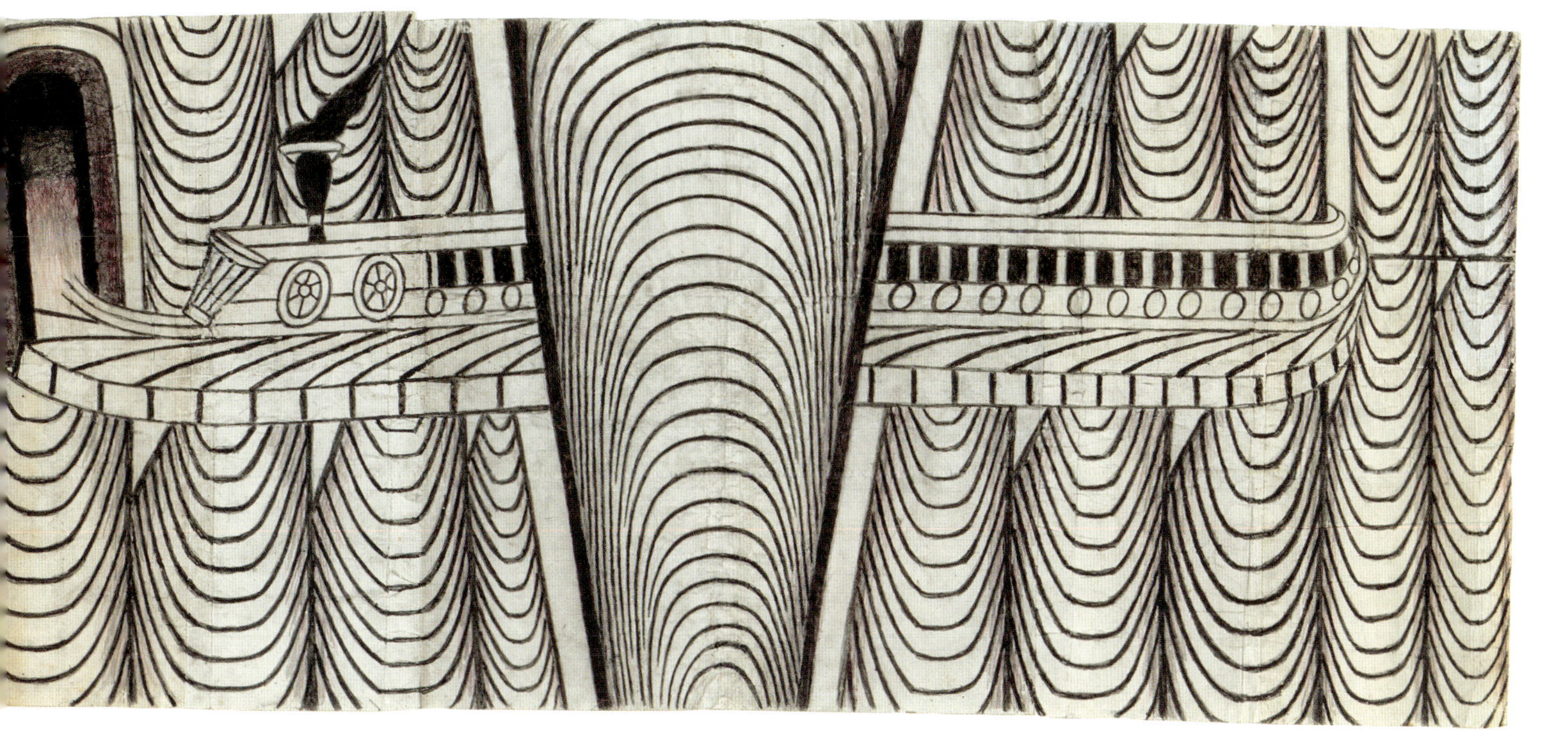

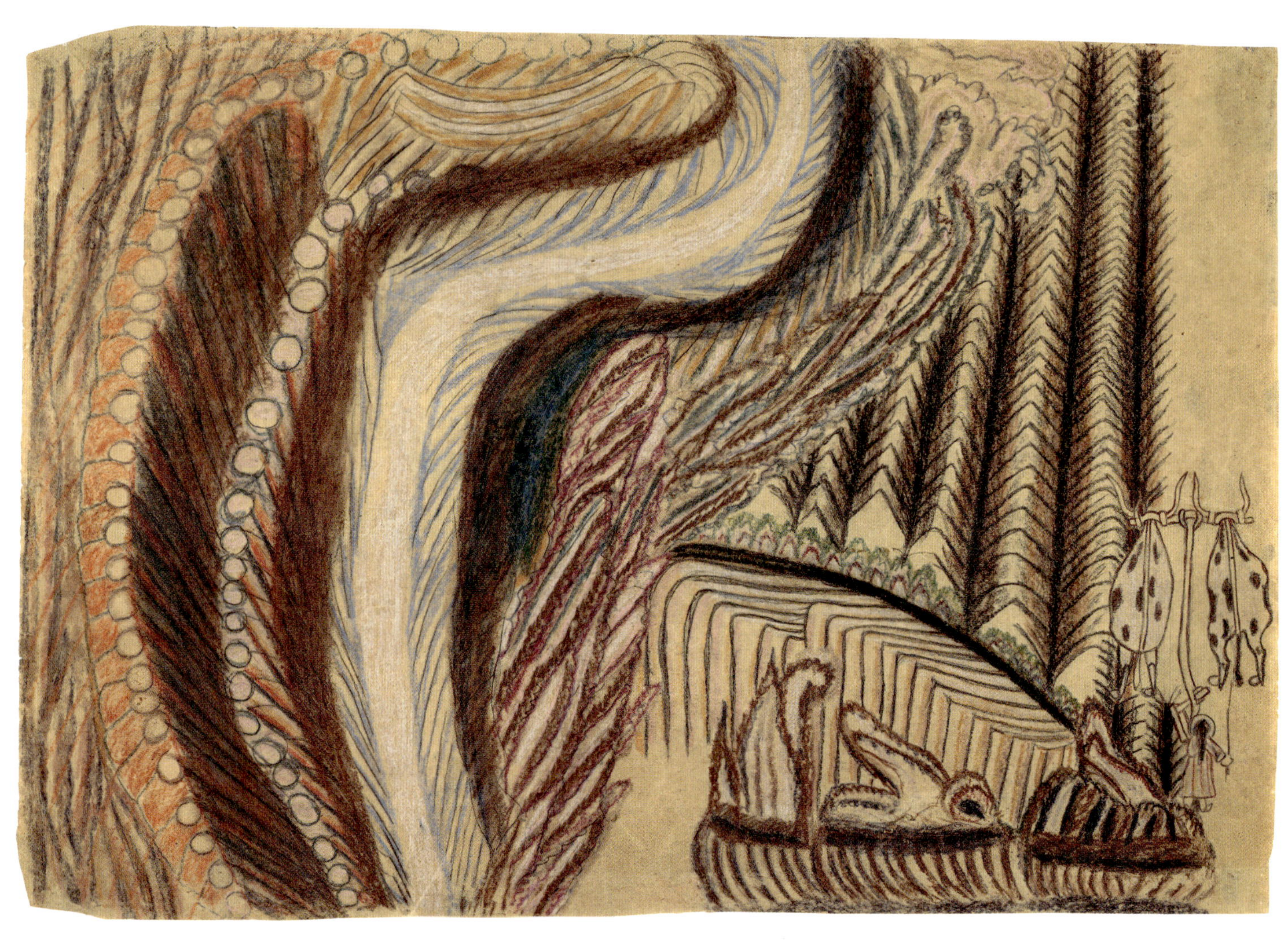

Martín Ramírez, *Untitled (Landscape with Oxen and Woman)*, n.d. Graphite and crayon on pieced paper, 23 × 32⅝ in. (58.4 × 82.9 cm)

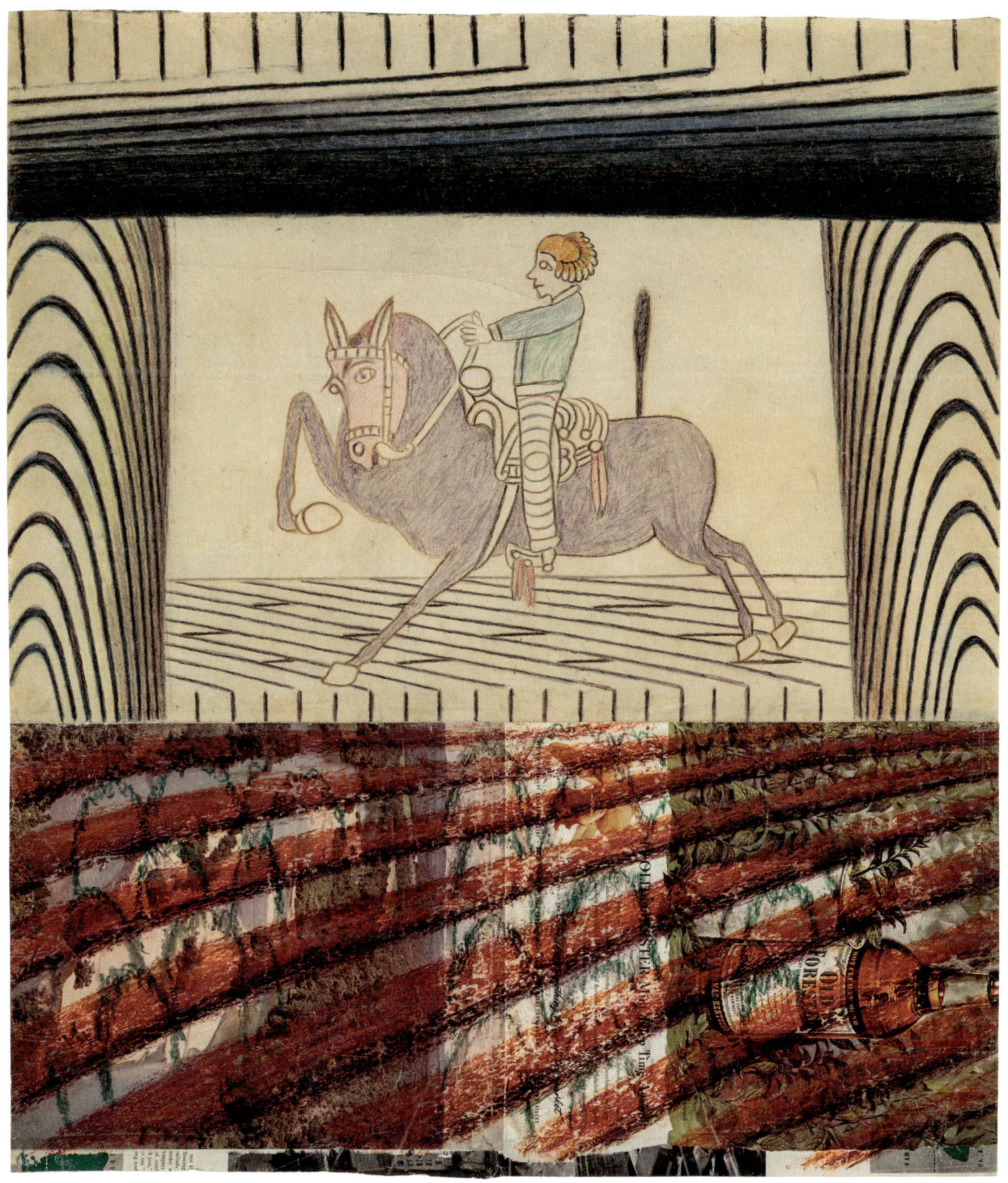

Martín Ramírez, *Untitled (Caballero)*, n.d. Crayon on paper, 30¾ × 24 in. (78.1 × 61 cm)

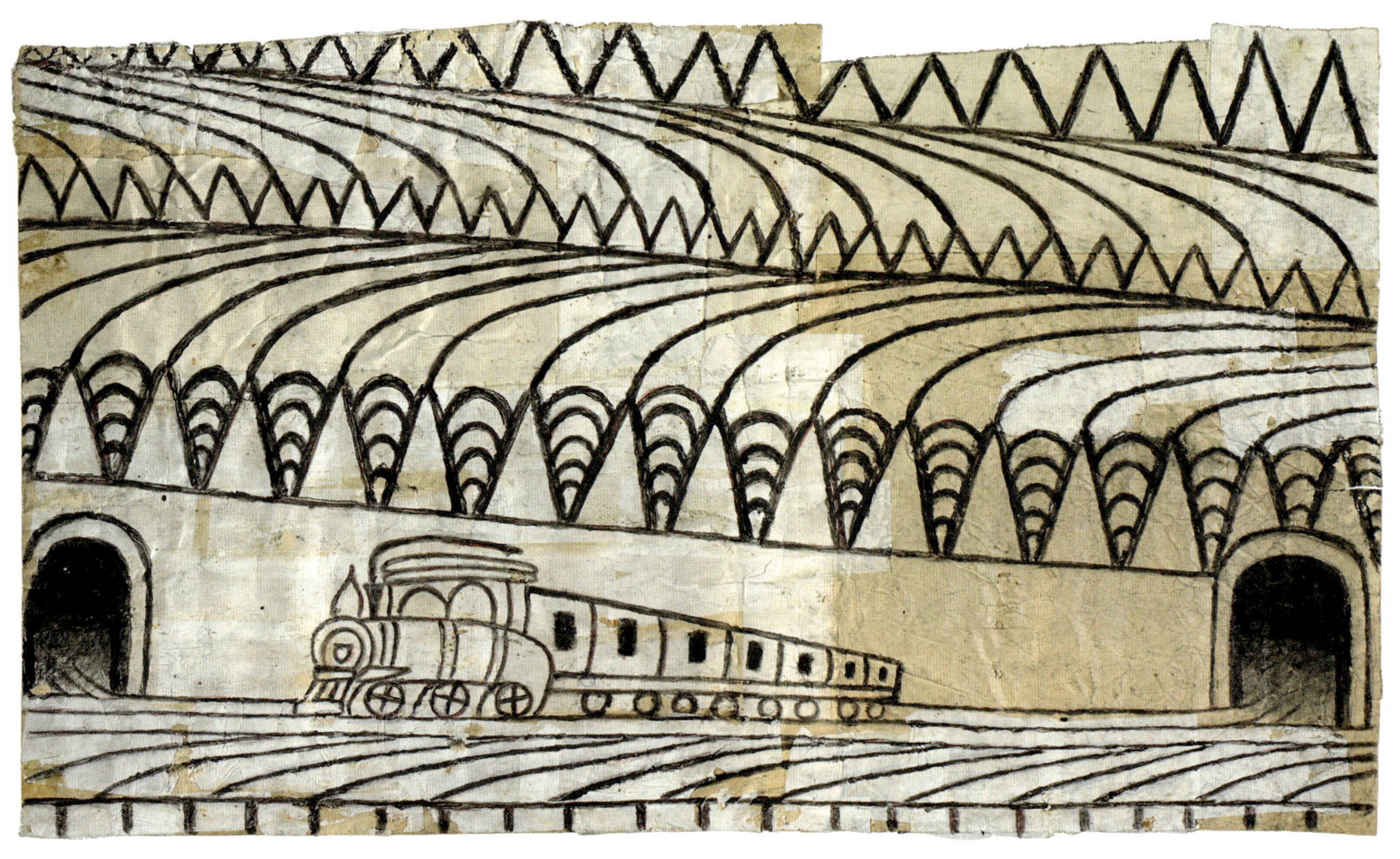

Martín Ramírez, *Untitled 811*, c. 1952–53. Graphite, gouache, and colored pencil on pieced paper, 28 × 24 in. (71.1 × 61 cm)

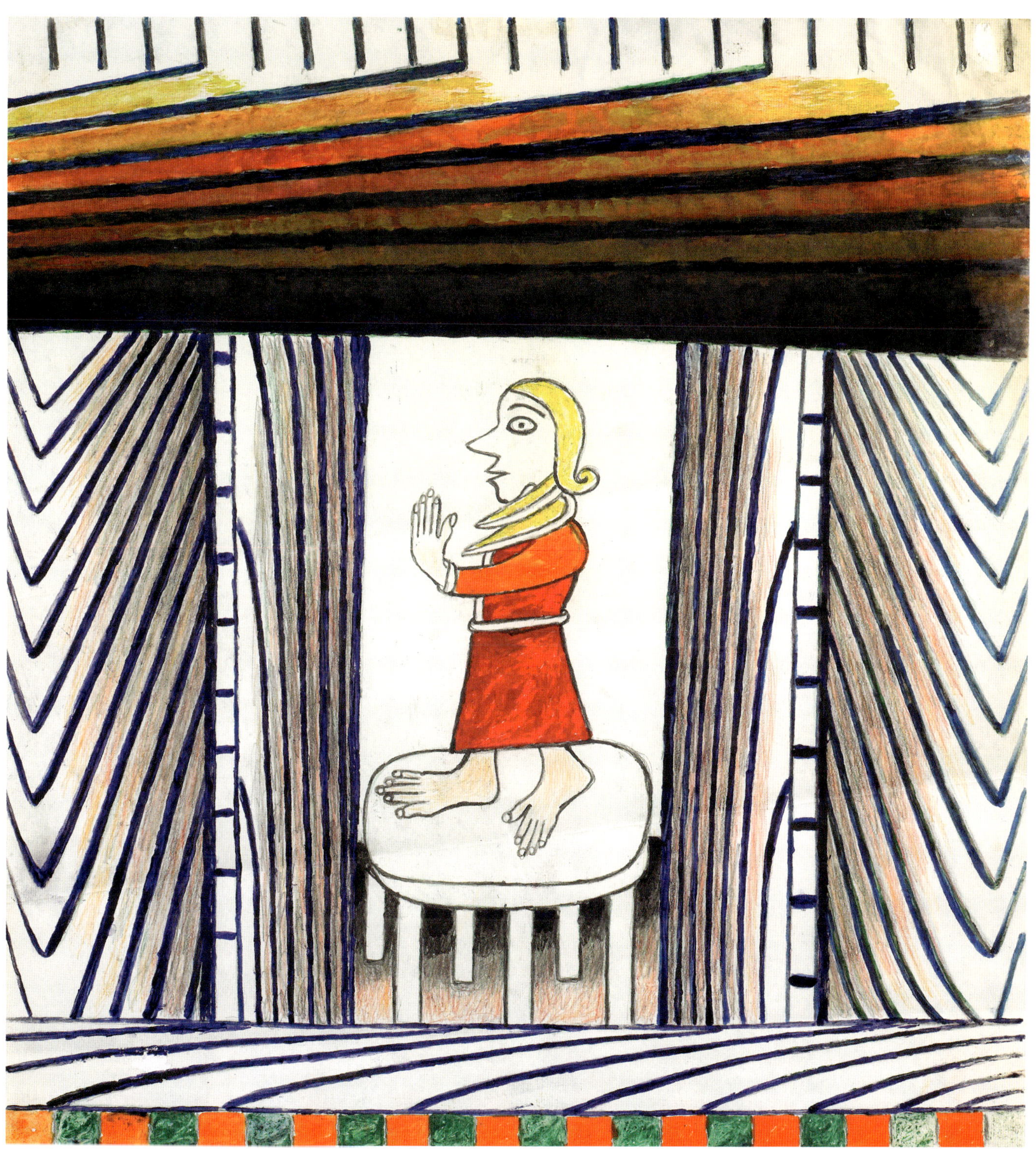

Martín Ramírez, *Untitled (Woman in a Red Dress)*, c. 1960–63. Mixed media on paper, 22⅝ × 20 in. (57.5 × 50.8 cm)

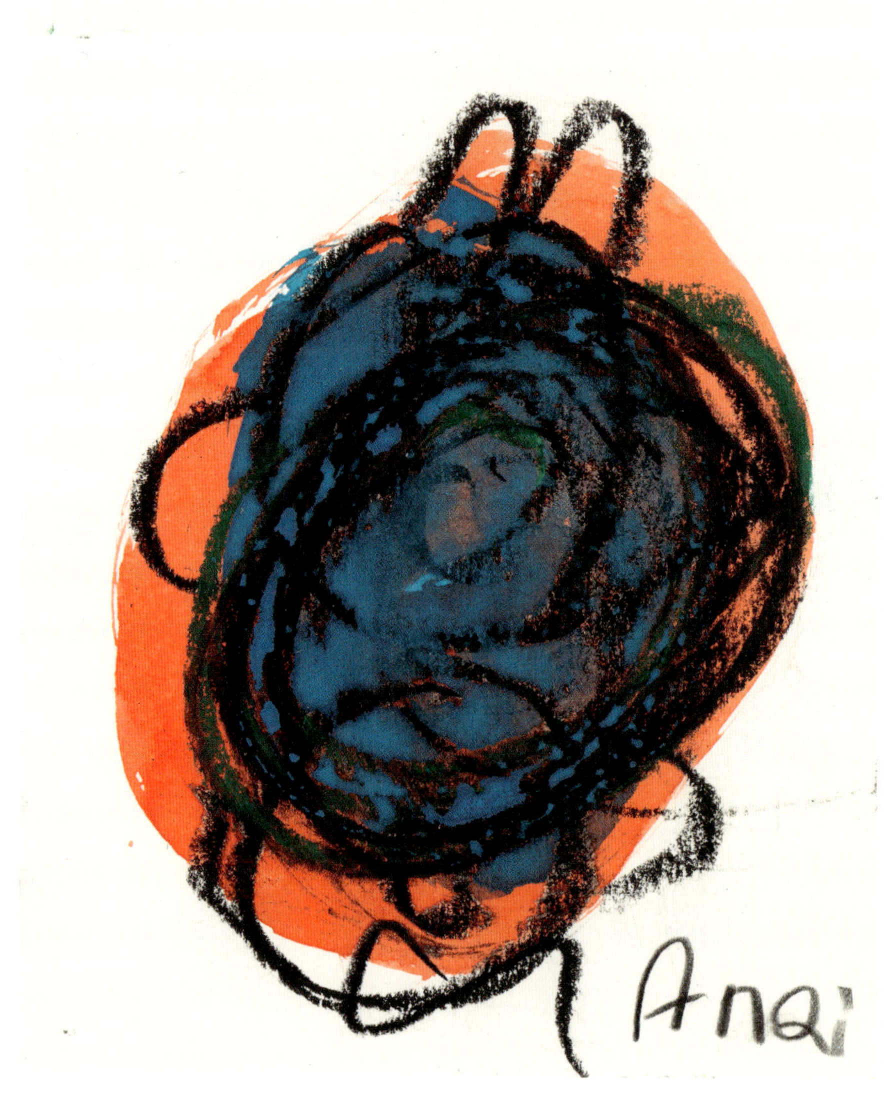
Anai

ARNOLD SCHMIDT

b. 1959

Arnold Schmidt's works are swift, spontaneous, and intuitive. In acrylic, oil crayons, graphite, colored pencils, and watercolors on paper and canvas he depicts human shapes, airplanes, bicycles, and birds through quick, loose lines, often circular, and signs his work "Andi." His compositions are centralized and suspended within white space; his figures fluctuate between abstraction and figuration and echo the archetypical power of the Venus of Willendorf merged with the liveliness of Cy Twombly's abstract expressionism.

Schmidt was born in Wiener Neustadt in Lower Austria and has received psychiatric treatment since he was a boy. He has lived and worked at the Gugging House of Artists in Vienna (see p. 143) since 1986, where he is one of the younger residents. His work has been exhibited in Austria, Germany, Switzerland, and the United States and can be found in private and public collections, including the Peter Infeld Private Foundation, the Lower Austria Regional Collection, the former Essl Collection (now part of the Albertina in Vienna), and the Milwaukee Art Museum.

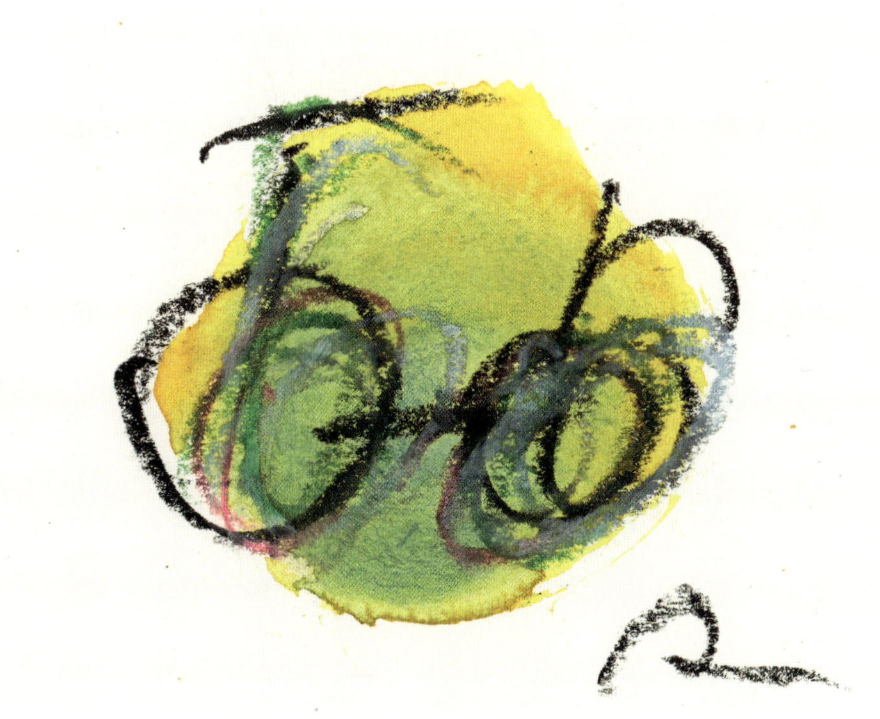

OPPOSITE: Arnold Schmidt, *Human*, 2016. Charcoal, watercolor, and crayon on paper, 5¾ × 4 in. (14.6 × 10.2 cm)

ABOVE: Arnold Schmidt, *Bicycle*, 2010. Charcoal, watercolor, and crayon on paper, 4 × 5¾ in. (10.2 × 14.6 cm)

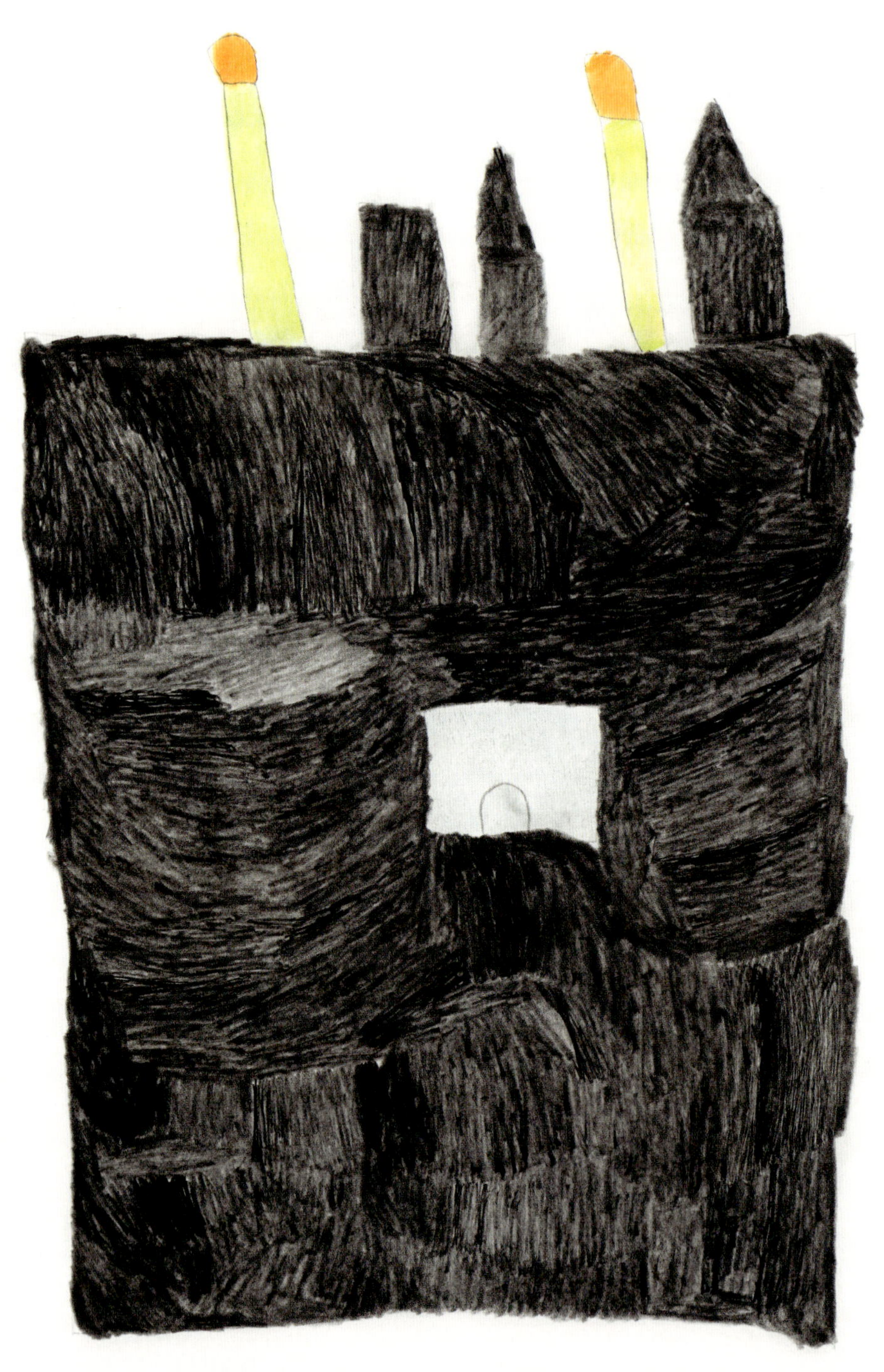

SCHÜTZENHÖFER 2012

GÜNTHER SCHÜTZENHÖFER

b. 1965

Günther Schützenhöfer is one of the twelve creative residents in the House of Artists on the outskirts of Vienna (see p. 143). Born in Mödling, Austria, he lived in various other care facilities before arriving at age thirty-four at Gugging in 1999. His daily routine includes at least one visit to his spot at a massive table covered with art supplies in the office of Nina Katschnig, the director of the Galerie Gugging, where he draws undisturbed, producing at least one work per day.

"During the first years," writes Katschnig,

> he worked very cautiously, and mostly in small formats; over time, the formats grew larger, and his very fine lines gave way to strong, determined strokes. . . . [He] works in pencil and colored pencils on paper and cardboard. Before putting his pencil to paper, he rolls it back and forth between his thumb and forefinger until he gets a really good grip. He sketches out his theme in a few lines, then uses strong strokes to bring it to life. He likes to fill large areas in pencil, giving them a fascinating life of their own. Sometimes he applies so much pressure that the lead of his pencil cracks and breaks; for this reason he keeps at least 5 sharpened pencils next to him, and once he has used them all, grabs any other pencils lying around on the table. This constant change in pencils with different hardness grades and the varying amount of pressure he applies while drawing result in idiosyncratic shadings, which make his works exciting and alive. Sparingly and skillfully he places additional accents in colored pencil.
>
> Schützenhöfer chooses his themes spontaneously, often related to the current season or situation. Lately, he repeatedly asks for a printout of his motif—be it a TV set, a radio, a lawn mower or the Eiffel Tower—to serve him as a template. But then he only glances briefly at the image, says, "Yes, I know," and commences his work. His approach is particular and entirely focused on the essence, the gist of his theme. Limiting himself to the vital elements, he produces abstract drawings that are unique in their overall elegance.
>
> Over the past 15 years . . . [he] has developed his unique, unmistakable style, which never ceases to amaze the onlooker. With his view of things around him, portrayed stylized and devoid of perspective, he creates enigmatic drawings, pervaded by [his] subtle humor. He is a great illustrator and interpreter of his surroundings, a world he very much enjoys living in, he says.

Schützenhöfer's works have been exhibited worldwide since 2001 and are part of the Lower Austria Regional Collection, the Museum of Everything (London), and the Peter Infeld Private Foundation and the Arnulf Rainer Collection (Vienna).

Günther Schützenhöfer, *Castle "Neuschwanstein,"* 2012. Graphite and colored pencil on paper, 26½ × 19½ in. (67.3 × 49.5 cm)

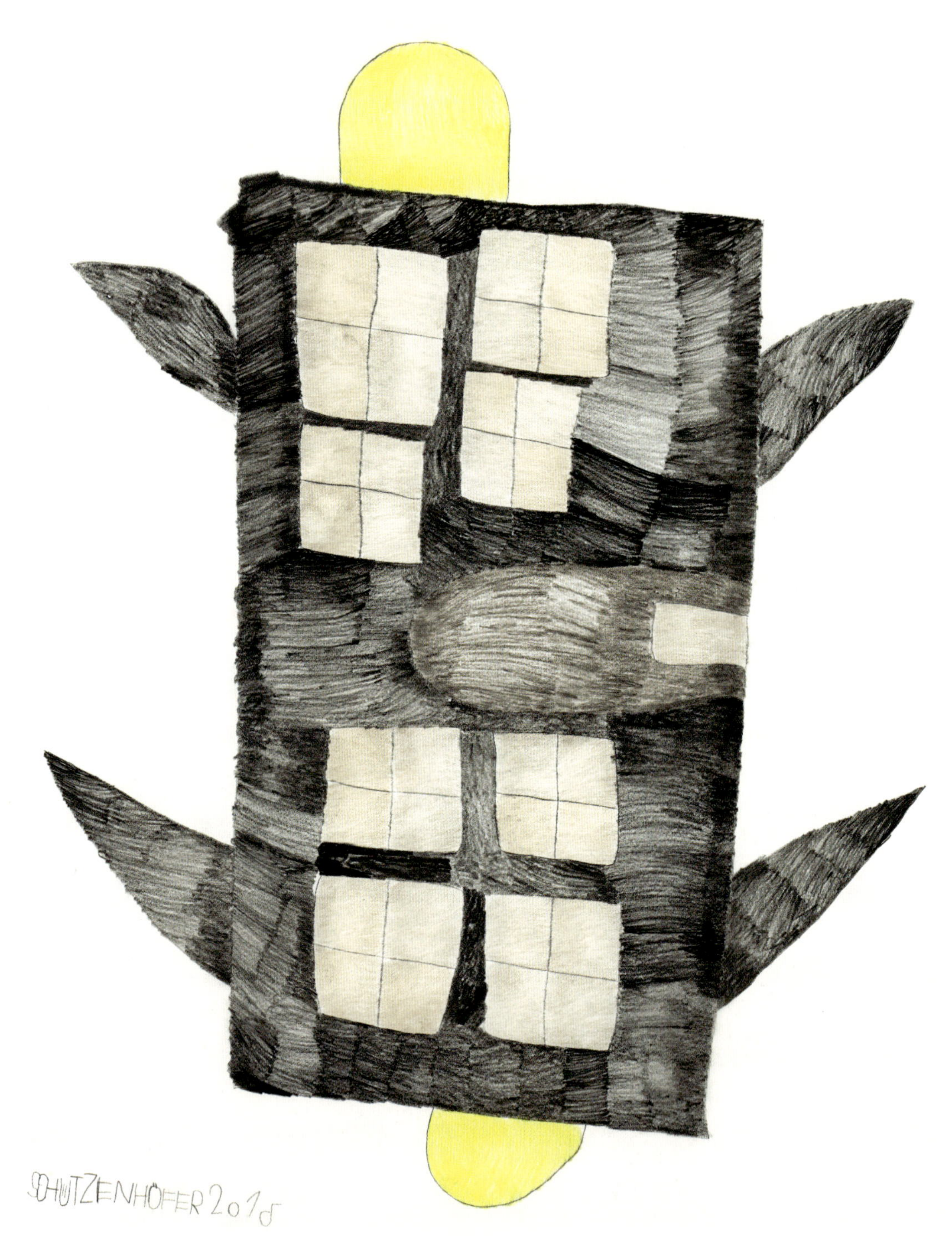

Günther Schützenhöfer, *Aeroplane*, 2015. Graphite and colored pencil on paper, 34¾ × 24¾ in. (88.3 × 62.9 cm)

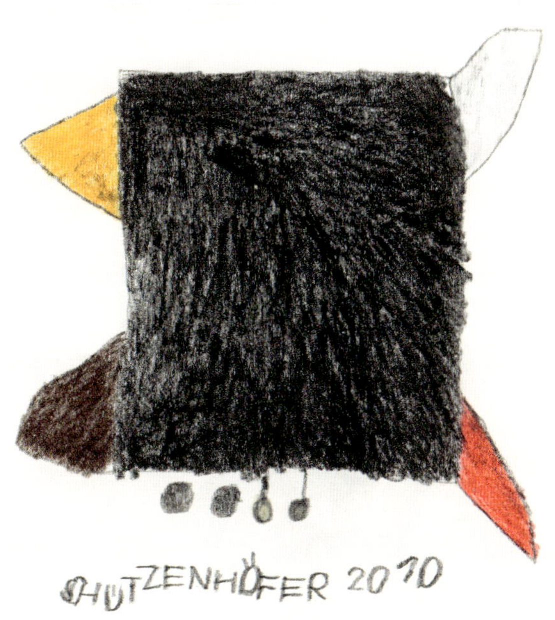

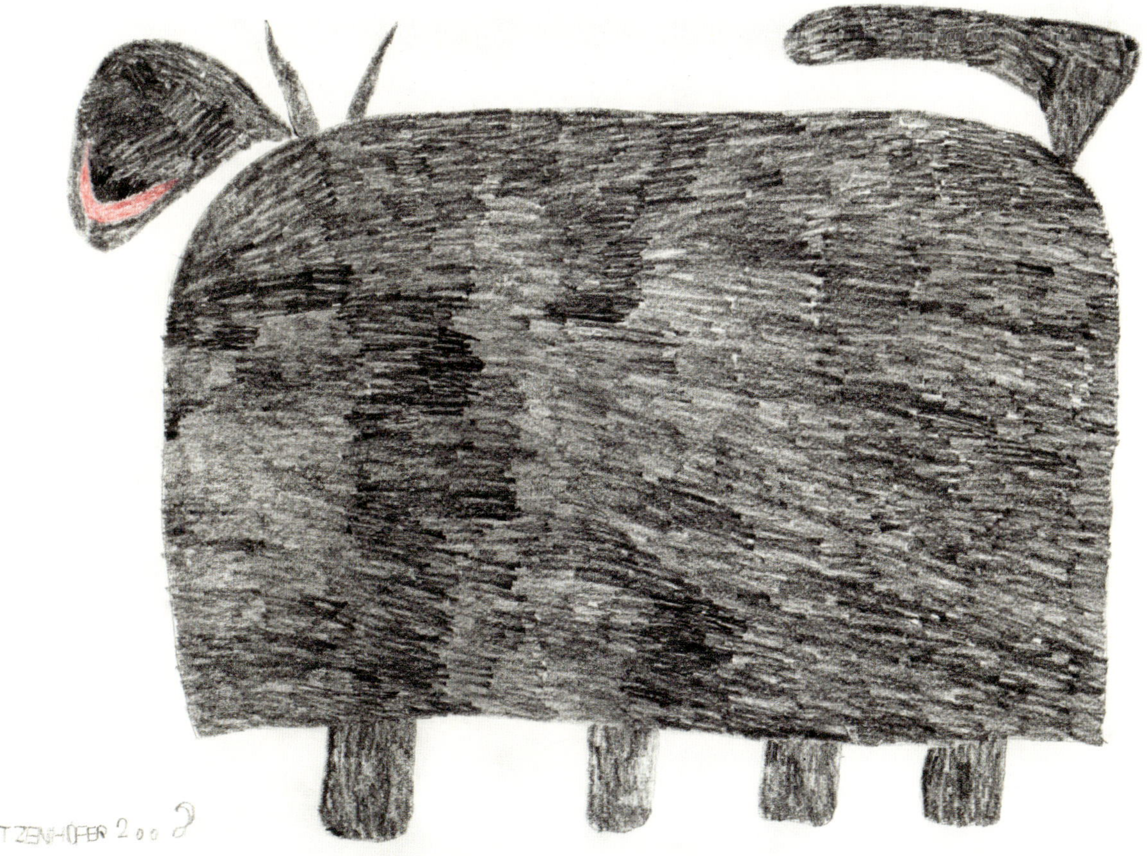

Günther Schützenhöfer, *Untitled*, 2010. Graphite and colored pencil on paper, $6\frac{7}{8} \times 5\frac{15}{16}$ in. (17.5 × 15 cm)

Günther Schützenhöfer, *Cow*, 2008. Graphite and colored pencil on paper, $11\frac{3}{4} \times 16\frac{1}{2}$ in. (29.8 × 41.9 cm)

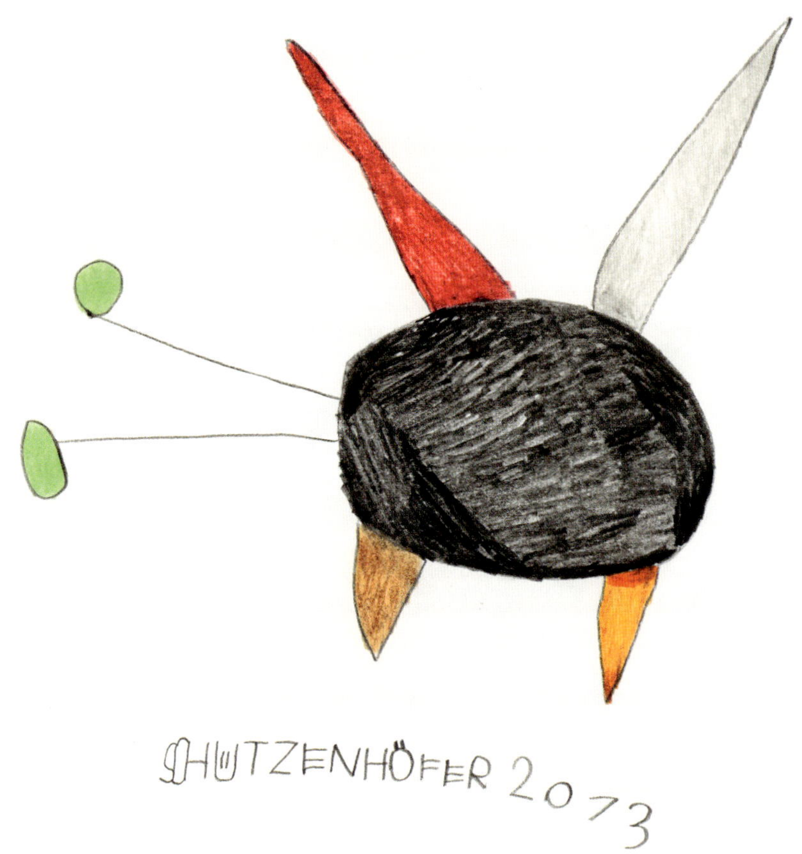

Günther Schützenhöfer, *Butterfly*, 2013. Graphite and colored pencil on paper, 11¾ × 16½ in. (29.8 × 41.9 cm)

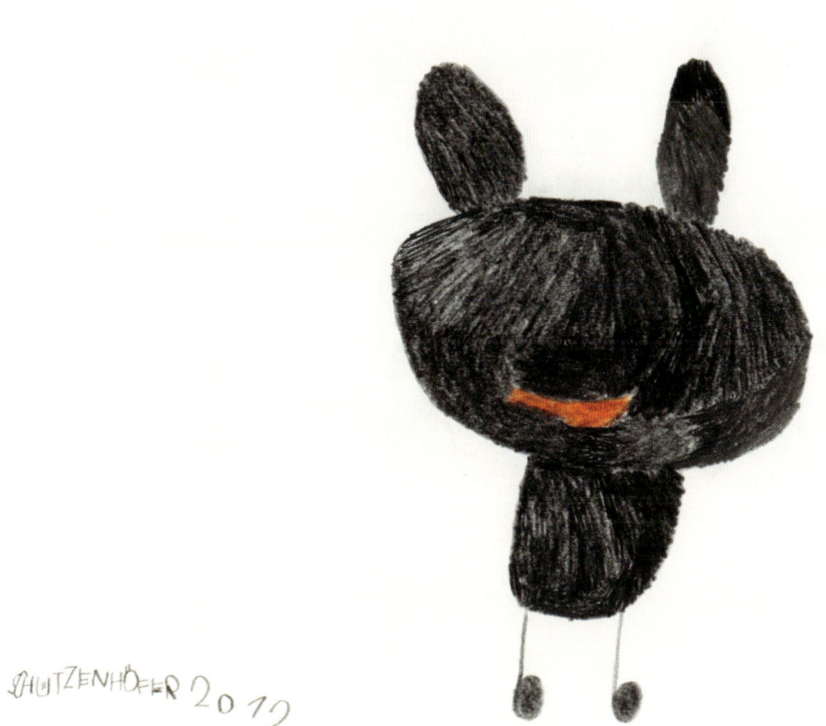

Günther Schützenhöfer, *Rabbit*, 2012. Graphite and colored pencil on paper, 11¾ × 16½ in. (29.8 × 41.9 cm)

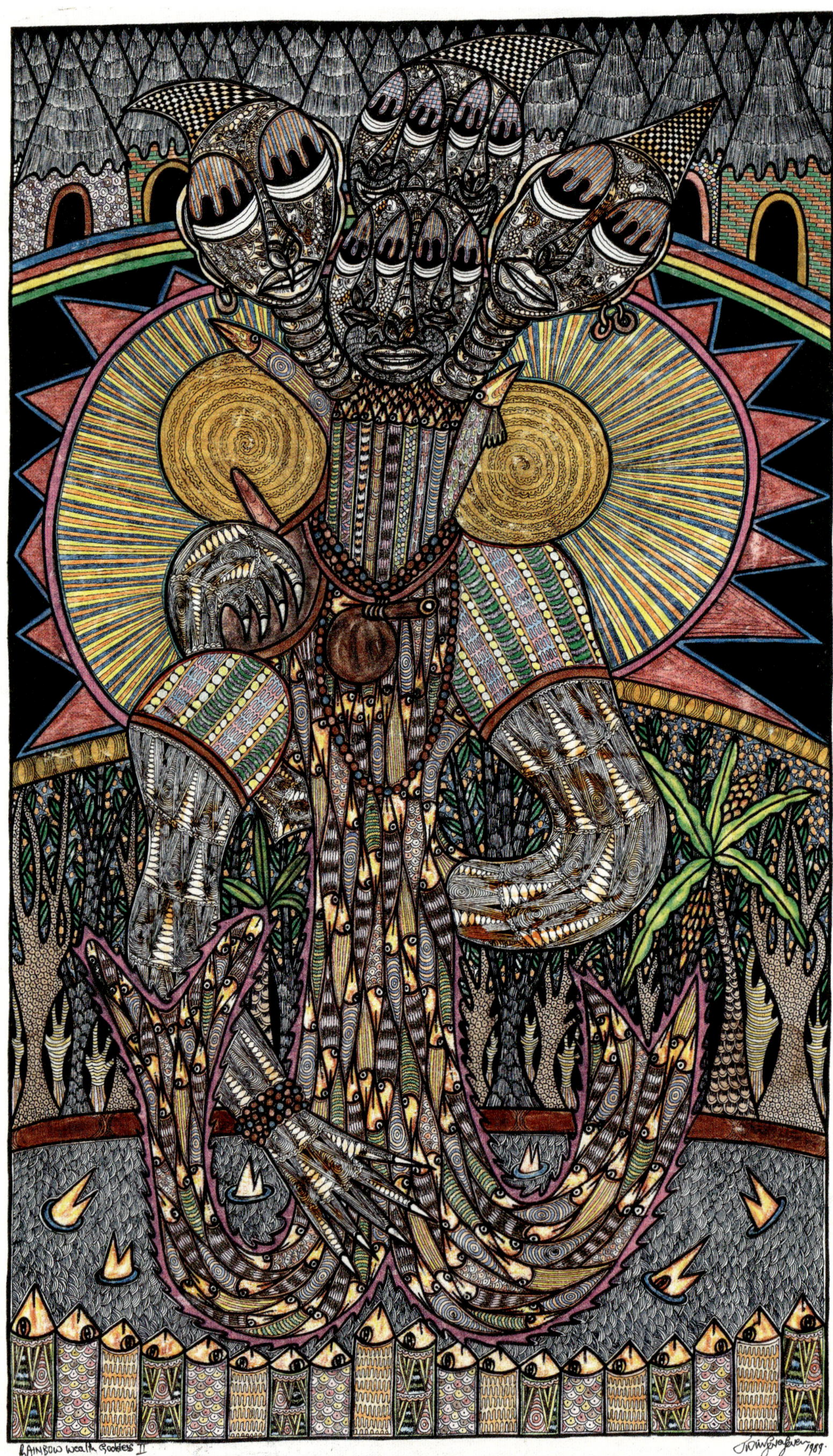
RAINBOW Wealth Goddess II
1989.

PRINCE TWINS SEVEN-SEVEN

1944–2011

Taiwo Bamidele Olaniyi Oyewale Oyekale Aitoyeje Osuntoki changed his birth name to Prince Twins Seven-Seven in recognition of his standing as the sole survivor of his seven sets of twins born to his parents. He was born in Ijara in northern Nigeria and came from the royal clan of Osuntoki. He believed himself to be an "abiku"—a person predestined to die young, possessed by a spirit who returns to the same mother to be reborn and die many times—and thus endowed with a singular connection to the spirit world. Twins Seven-Seven began his career as an itinerant dancer and singer, but he started making art in the 1960s when he joined a workshop in the city of Osogbo led by Ulli Beier, a German linguist and promoter of African culture, and his wife, Georgina, founders of the Mbari Club, an important center for cultural activity in Africa's post-independence era.

With imagery that pays homage to the folklore and the mythology in the Yoruba culture, Twins Seven-Seven worked with ink, pastel, and oil on paper, canvas, and carved plywood. Using the oral tradition and literary sources of his people, he depicted village scenes, animals, exotic deities, and anthropomorphic spirits in dense, graphically powerful compositions packed with symbolism. Although Twins Seven-Seven's works are stylistically reminiscent of complex traditional textile weaving, he often broke through the limits of figuration with his instinctive, improvisational technique, filling the surface with lines and intricately detailed rhythmic patterns. In his 2010 biography and art catalogue *Prince Twins Seven-Seven: His Art, His Life in Nigeria, His Exile in America* the folklorist and scholar Henry Glassie wrote, "Twins was the great modernist of the Yoruba tradition . . . He turned back to tradition, just as Kandinsky or Klee did, but in his context drew on Yoruban sources to figure out an escape from tradition into modernity."

After a promising inclusion in the exhibition *Magiciens de la Terre* (Magicians of the Earth) at the Centre Georges Pompidou in Paris in 1989, Twins Seven-Seven began traveling frequently and finally settled in Philadelphia. This marked the start of a period in his life dominated by gambling, drinking, and financial difficulties. It was during this time, when he worked as a parking lot attendant for a housewares store, that the store owner found out he was an artist, had him embellish the store's wrapping paper, and later gave him a small space to use as a studio. Twins Seven-Seven's career revived in 2000, when the Indianapolis Museum of Art (now Newfields) opened a wing devoted to contemporary African art with an exhibition of his work. In 2005 Twins Seven-Seven was named a UNESCO "Artist for Peace," a title that brought him international visibility six years before he died at age sixty-seven from complications of a stroke. His work has been shown in museums throughout the world, including the Musée de L'Homme (Paris), the Houston Contemporary Arts Museum, the Fowler Museum (Los Angeles), the Museum of Modern Art (New York), the National Museum of African Art (Washington, D.C.), and the National Gallery of Modern Art (Lagos).

Prince Twins Seven-Seven, *Rainbow Wealth Goddess*, 1989. Ink, pastel, and oil on canvas, 55 × 33 in. (139.7 × 83.8 cm)

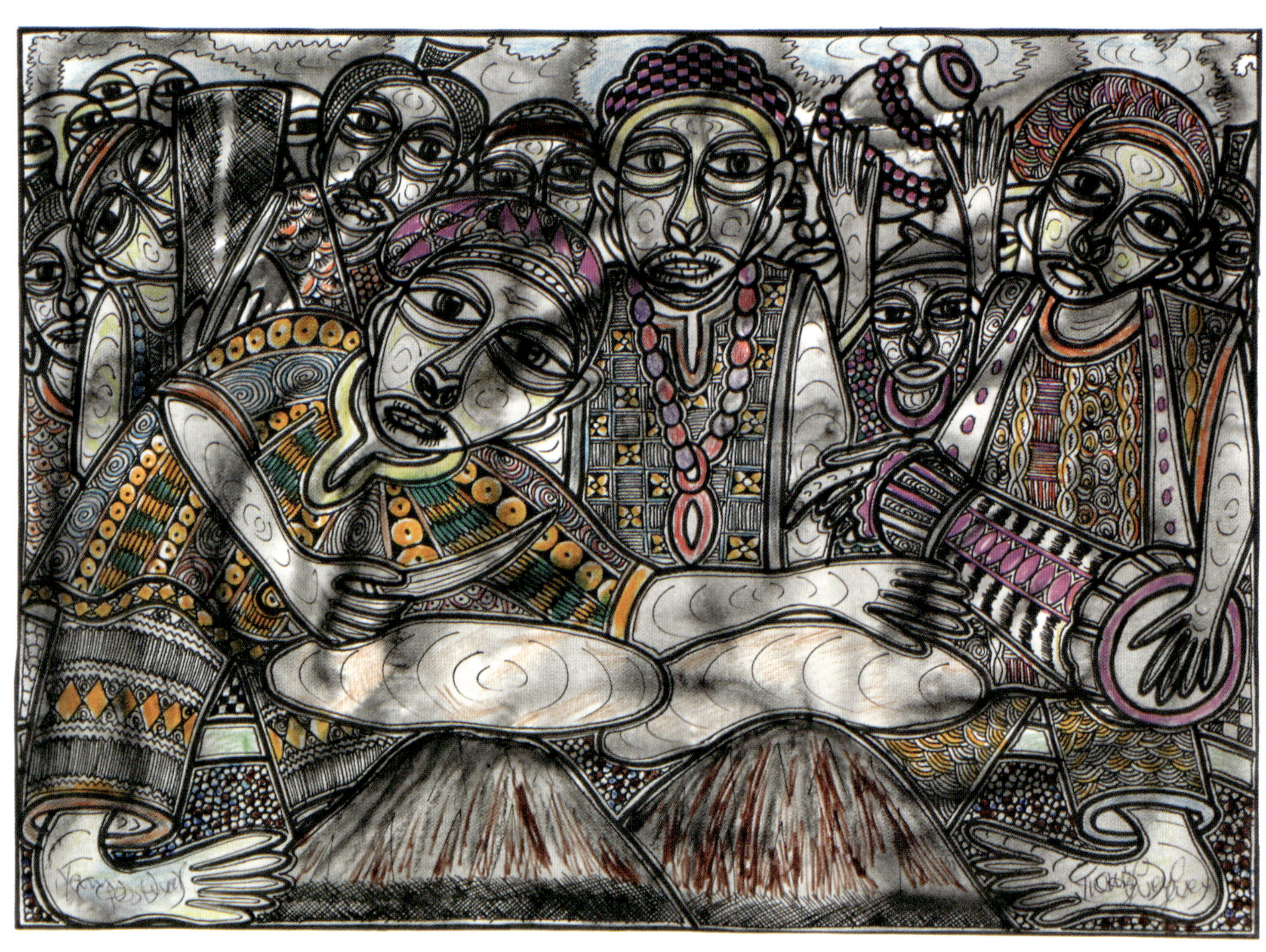

Prince Twins Seven-Seven, *Yam Festival*, n.d. Mixed media on paper, 12½ × 17 in. (31.8 × 43.2 cm)

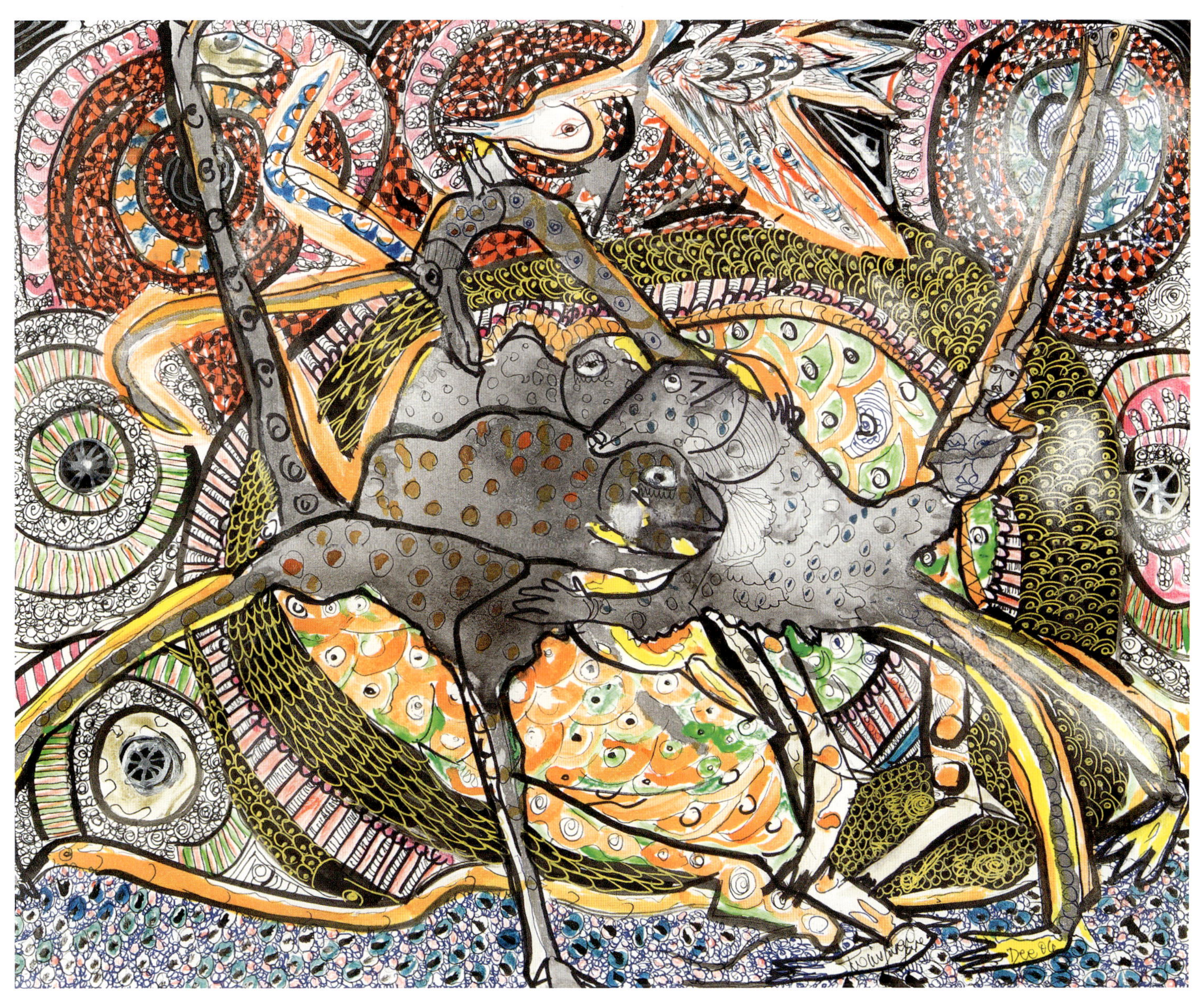

Prince Twins Seven-Seven, *Untitled*, 2009. Ink, watercolor, and acrylic on paper, 14 × 17 in. (35.6 × 43.2 cm)

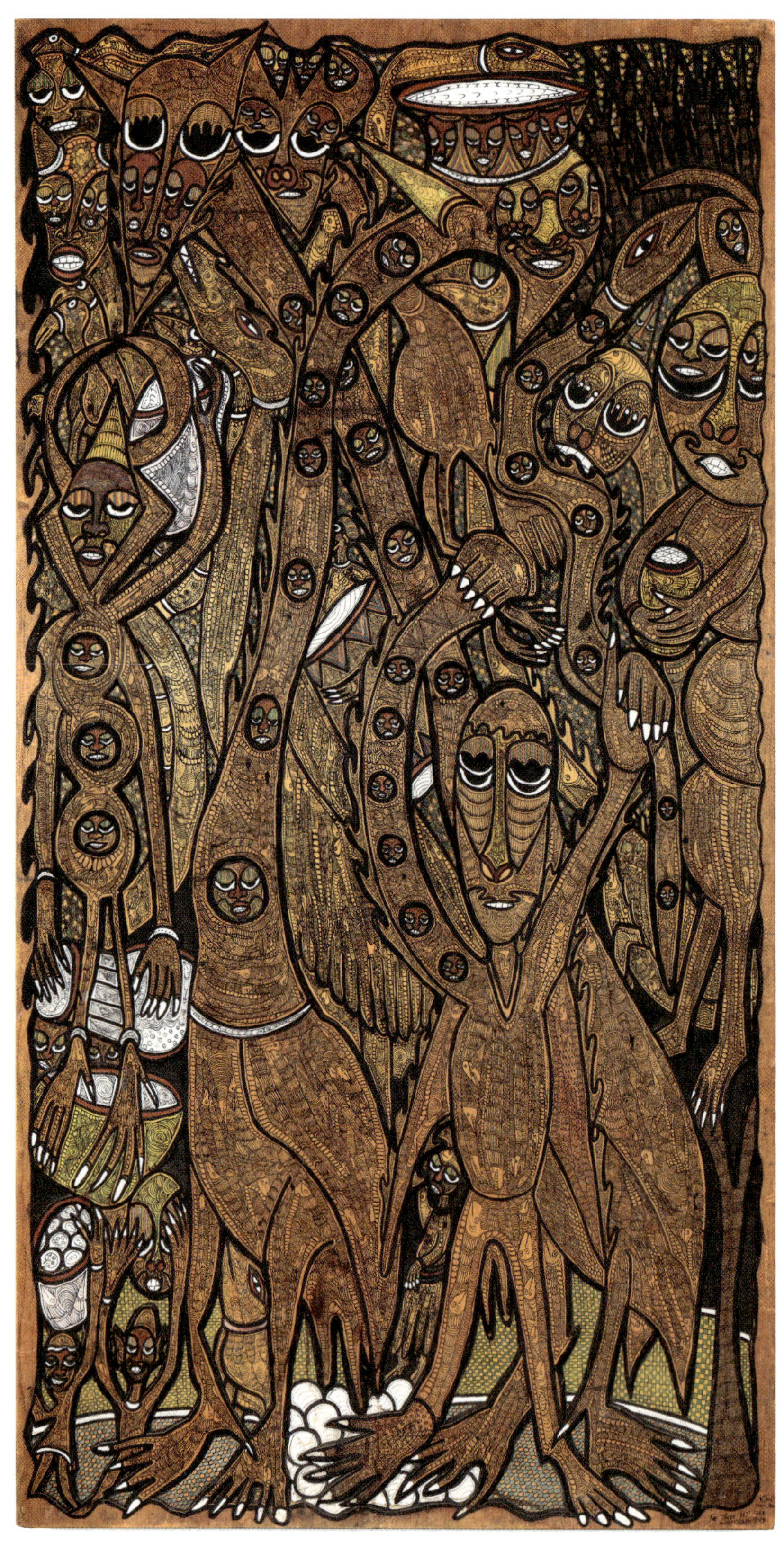

Prince Twins Seven-Seven, *Conference of Noisy Birds*, 1979. Ink, watercolor, and oil on carved wood, 96 × 48 in. (243.8 × 121.9 cm) (detail opposite)

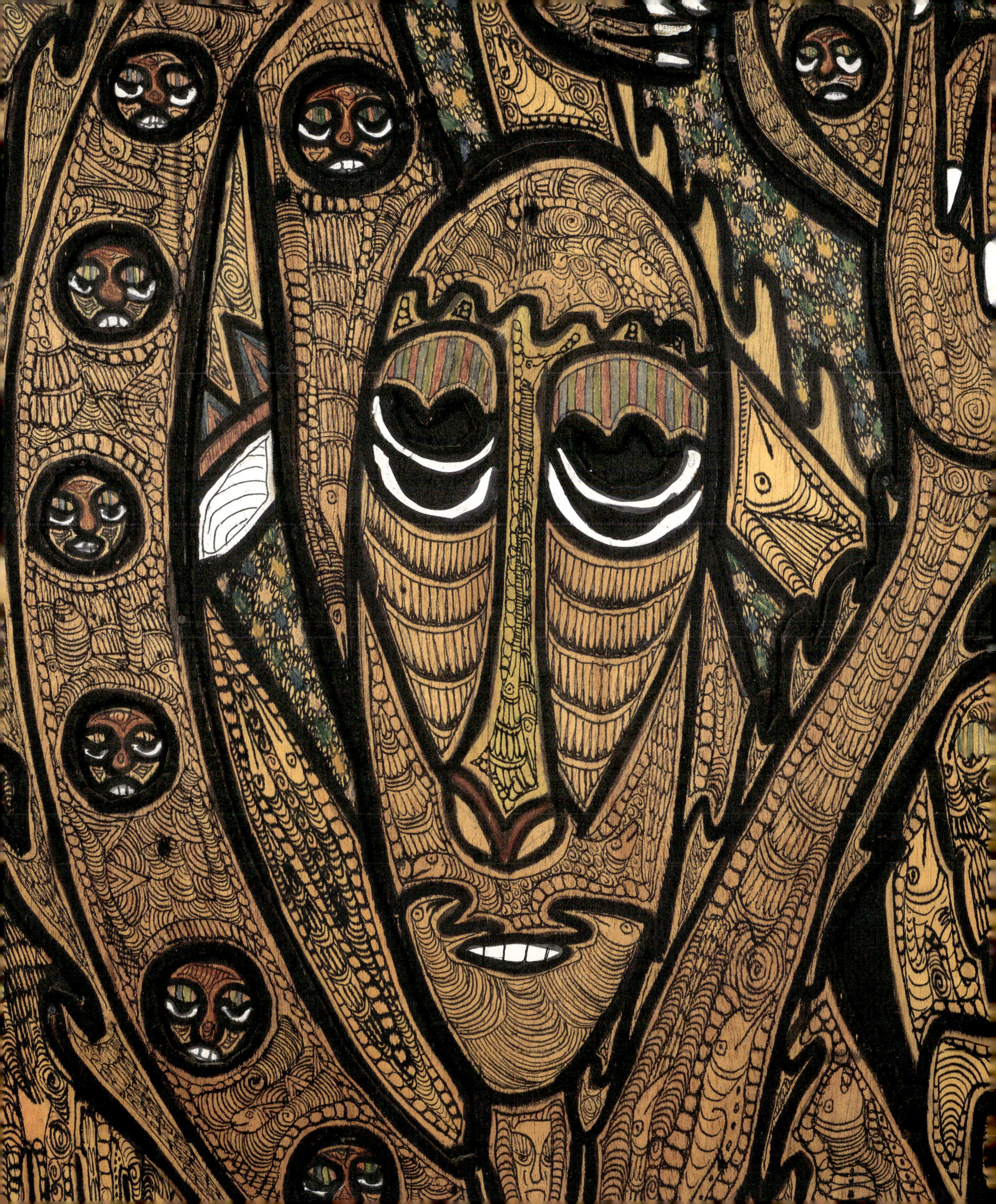

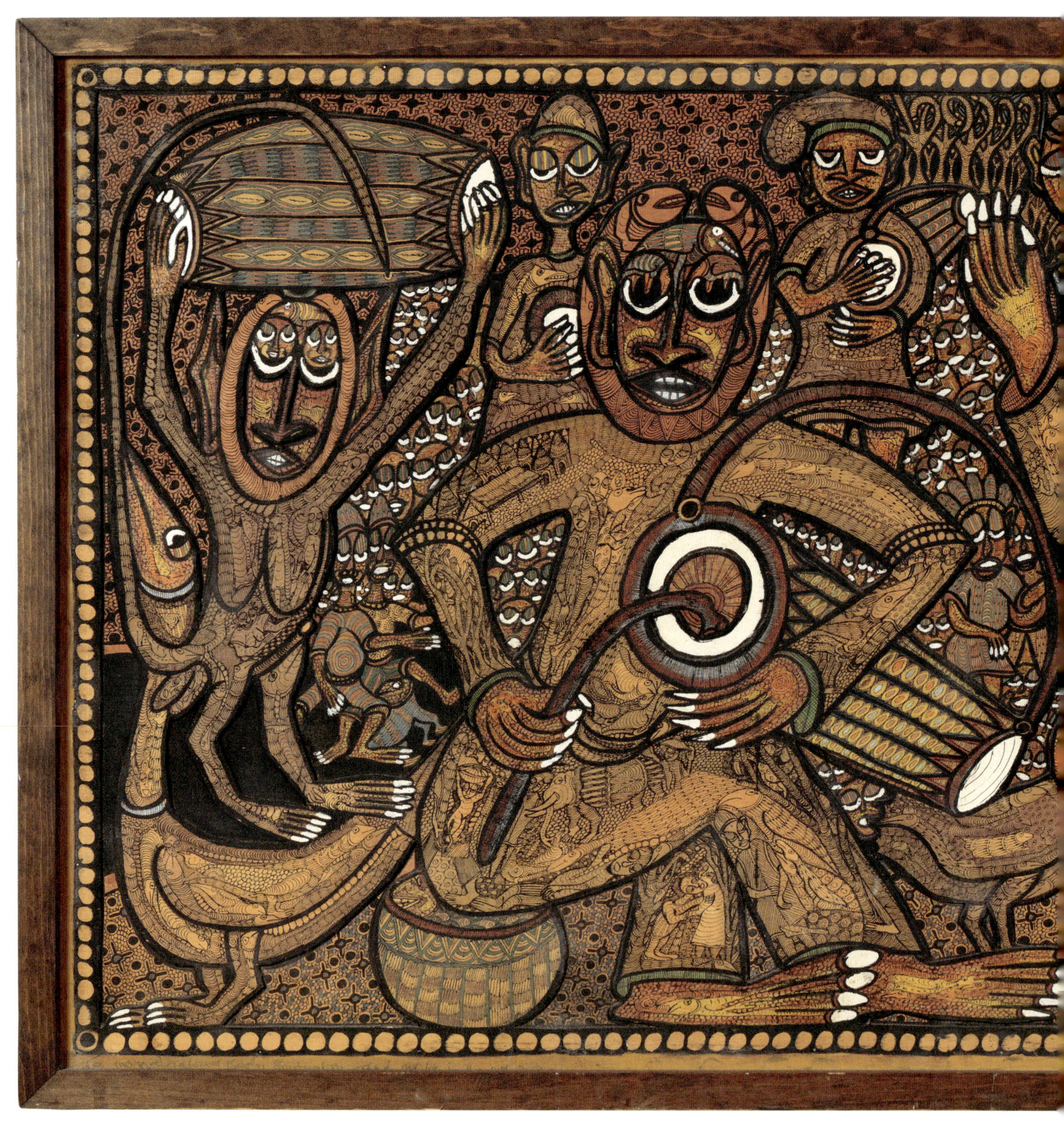

Prince Twins Seven-Seven, *The Mother and Tattooed Body* . . . , 1980. Ink, watercolor, and oil on carved wood, 48 × 96 in. (121.9 × 243.8 cm)

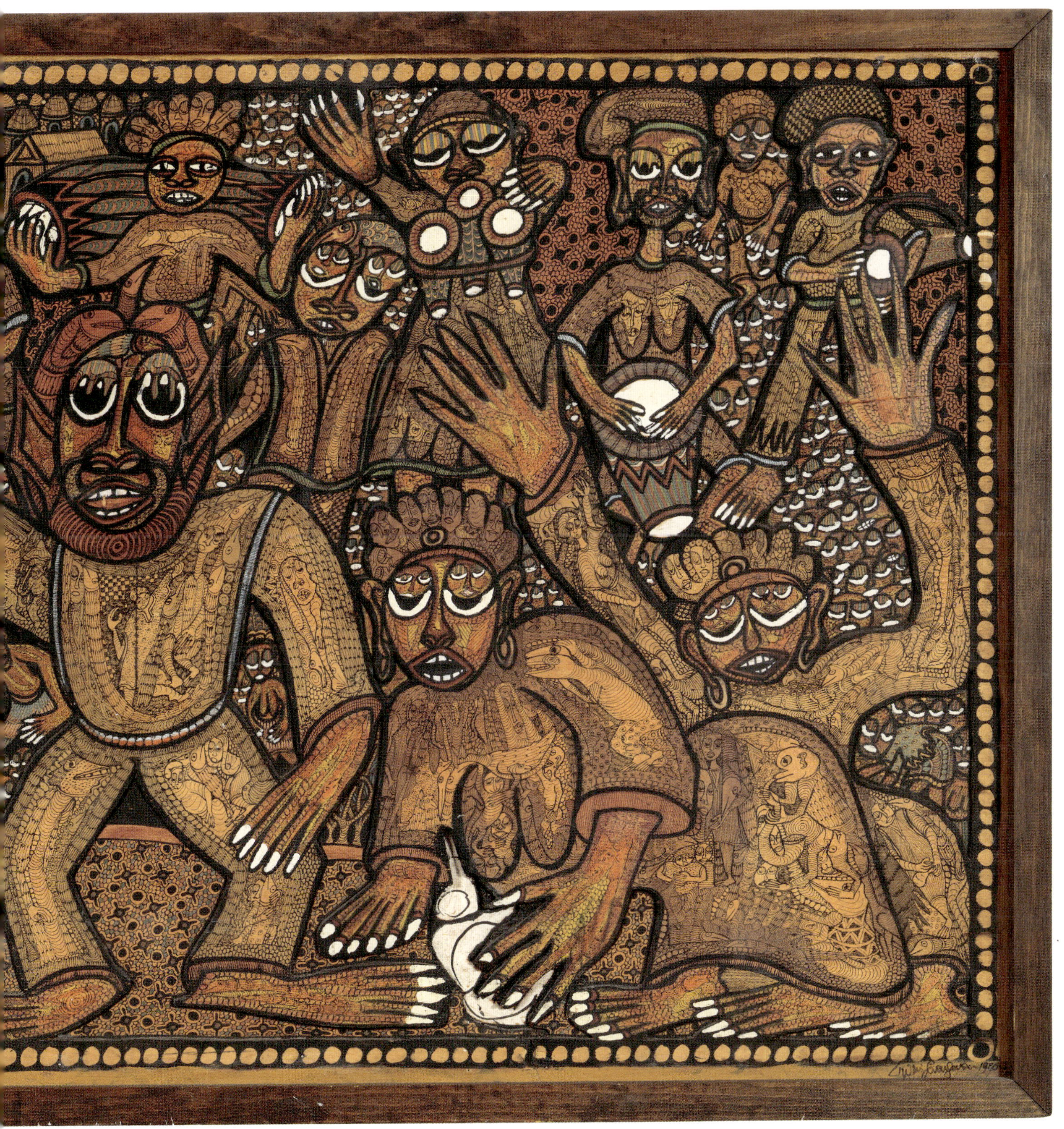

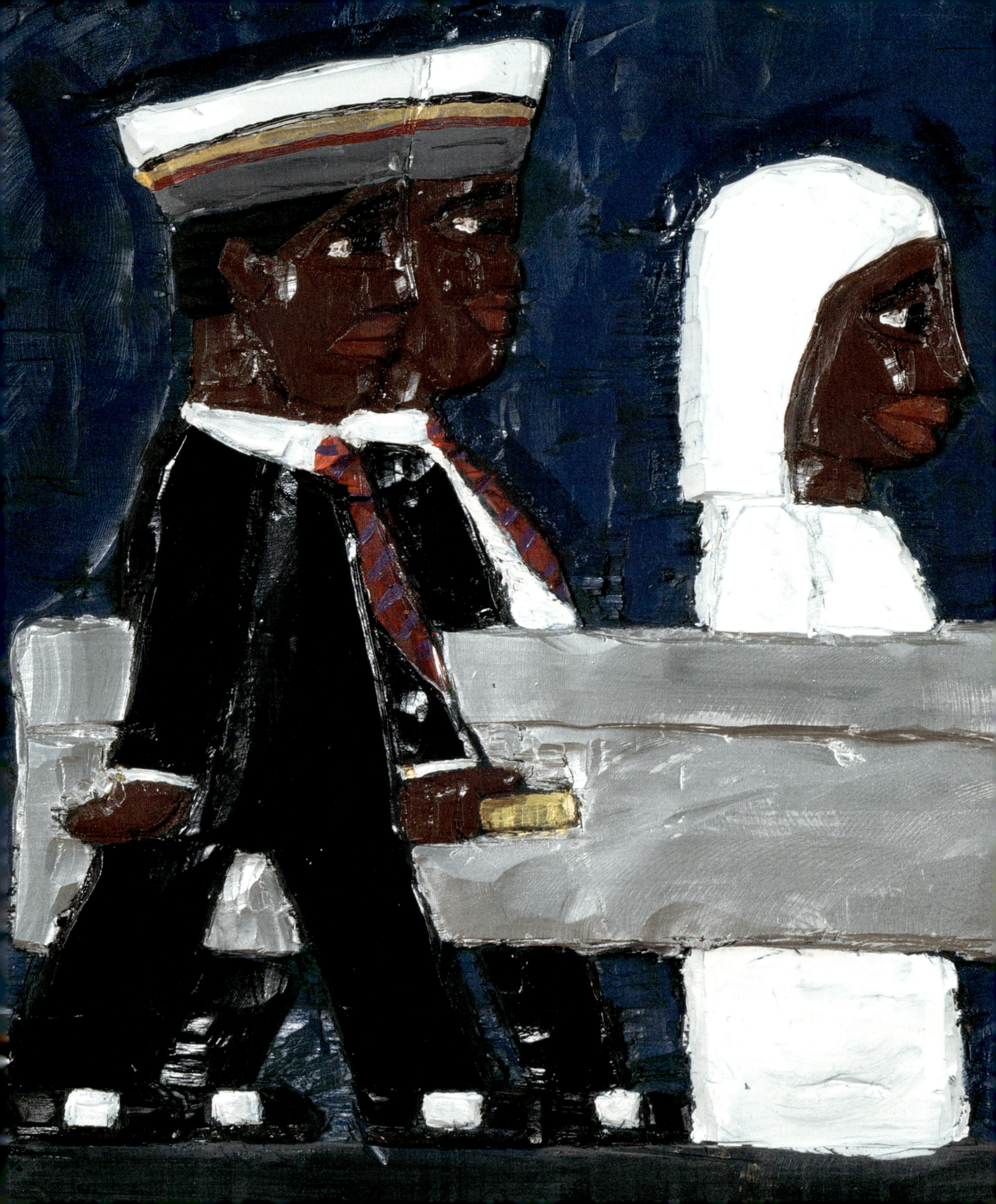

HERBERT SINGLETON

1945–2007

Herbert Singleton's painted wood bas-reliefs present a painfully honest chronicle of his life and of the self-destruction he witnessed in the New Orleans African American community. Social injustice, faith, vice, violence, and death are constant themes in his depictions of brutal scenarios from life and of biblical stories. The oldest of eight children, Singleton was born in the New Orleans district of Algiers, Louisiana. His father abandoned the family when he was around ten years old and he dropped out of school after the seventh grade and spent most of his time on the streets amid gangs, prostitutes, and pimps, and he experimented with drugs. Singleton worked a number of odd jobs but eventually found a steady position as a carpenter. He was involved in many violent encounters with the nefarious lot out on the streets and with the police, which left him with several knife and bullet scars. In 1984 a New Orleans Police Department squad broke into a house in an unwarranted raid and killed three people, Singleton's sister among them. Singleton was picked up and interrogated and beaten. After the American Civil Liberties Union sued on his behalf, Singleton was eventually awarded $47,500 from the city. Singleton was twice imprisoned for drug-related offenses and he spent nearly fourteen years at the Louisiana State Penitentiary in Angola, where he learned how to carve.

Singleton's work evolved from totemic sculptures, walking sticks, and "voodoo protection" stumps that he began making in the 1970s to narrative bas-reliefs carved into panels of salvaged wood and painted with household enamels. Some of his best-known works depict funeral processions with stylized, blocky figures that call to mind similar scenes in Egyptian art, but Singleton's art is imbued with jazz and a gritty urban sensibility, and a comics-like commentary text.

The New Orleans art dealer Andy Antippas has written of Singleton, " It seems that everything Singleton does . . . is associated with the theme of confusion—its exposure and its avoidance."

> Singleton sees the destructive effects of confusion all around him: the Deacon of the nearby church preying on his female parishioners; the ten-year-old boy selling crack; the funeral director trying to seduce the grieving widow at the funeral; the AIDS-riddled mother carrying her infected child in her arms while offering herself to a passerby; the teenager killed by another teenager for his Buffalo Bills warm-up jacket or his gold plated medallion of Malcolm. Drunks, pimps, hustlers, gangsters, transvestites, all spreading confusion everywhere. These malignant creatures are the subjects of Singleton's most provocative painted wood relief carvings and sculptures—he calls these his "struggle pieces." Each is an entry in a catalog that inventories the self-destruction of the African American community.
>
> The other principal subject matter Singleton carves comes from the Old and New Testaments and the Apocrypha.

Herbert Singleton, *Going Home Brother* (detail), c. 1980s. Carved and painted wood, 20 × 60 in. (50.8 × 152.4 cm)

Although the sources of imagery are different for both, the biblical scenes, like the "struggle pieces," take up the theme of confusion. Both subject matter—the secular and the sacred—relate to each other in an anagogic or metaphoric way along the lines of St. Augustine's axiom that the Old Testament is revealed in the New, and the New concealed in the Old.

Singleton's work is in the collections of the High Museum of Art (Atlanta), the Los Angeles County Museum of Art, the Mississippi Museum of Art (Jackson), the New Orleans Museum of Art, the Ogden Museum of Southern Art (New Orleans), the Philadelphia Museum of Art, the Smithsonian American Art Museum (Washington, D.C.), and the Collection de l'Art Brut (Lausanne, Switzerland).

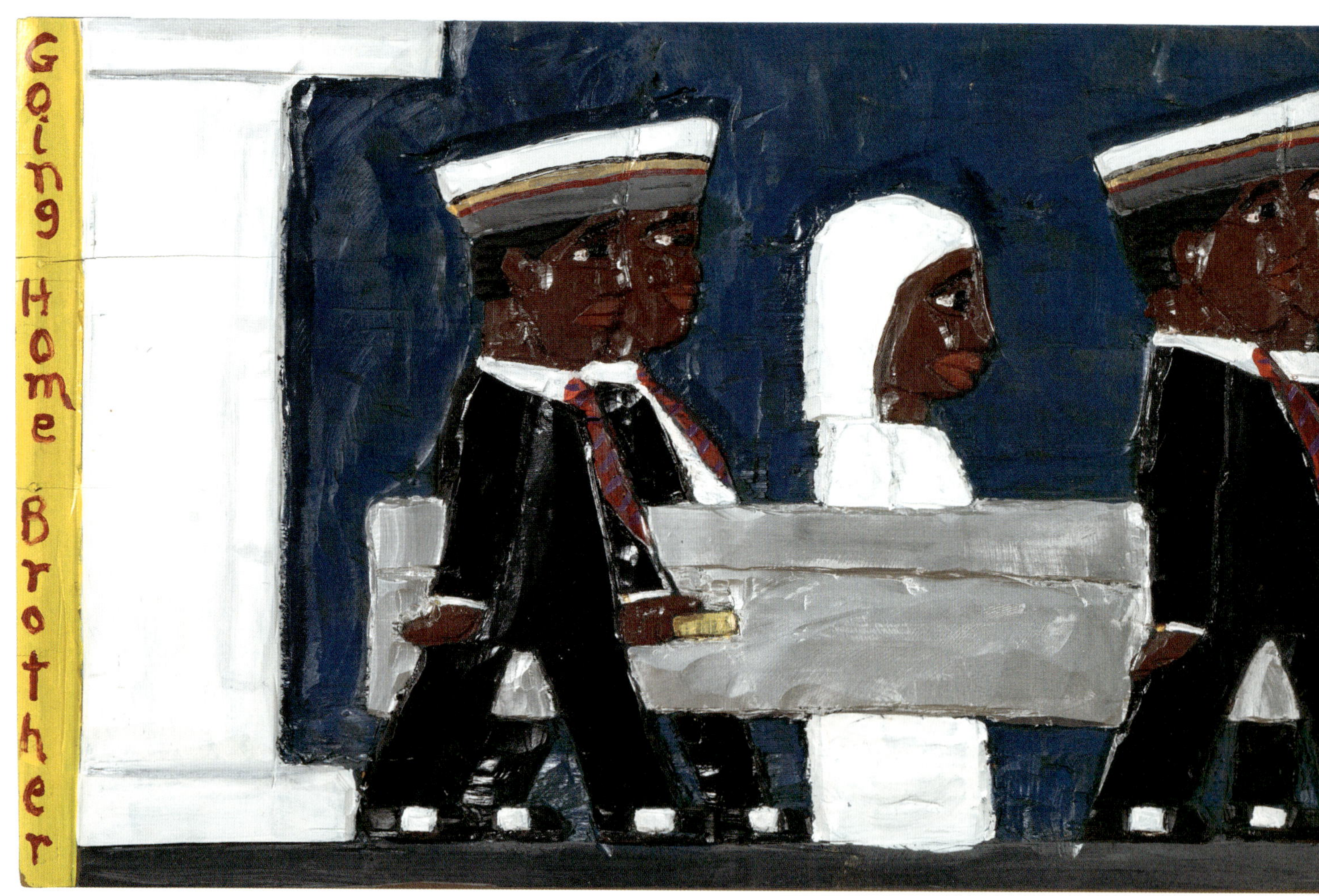

Herbert Singleton, *Going Home Brother*, c. 1980s. Carved and painted wood, 20 × 60 in. (50.8 × 152.4 cm)

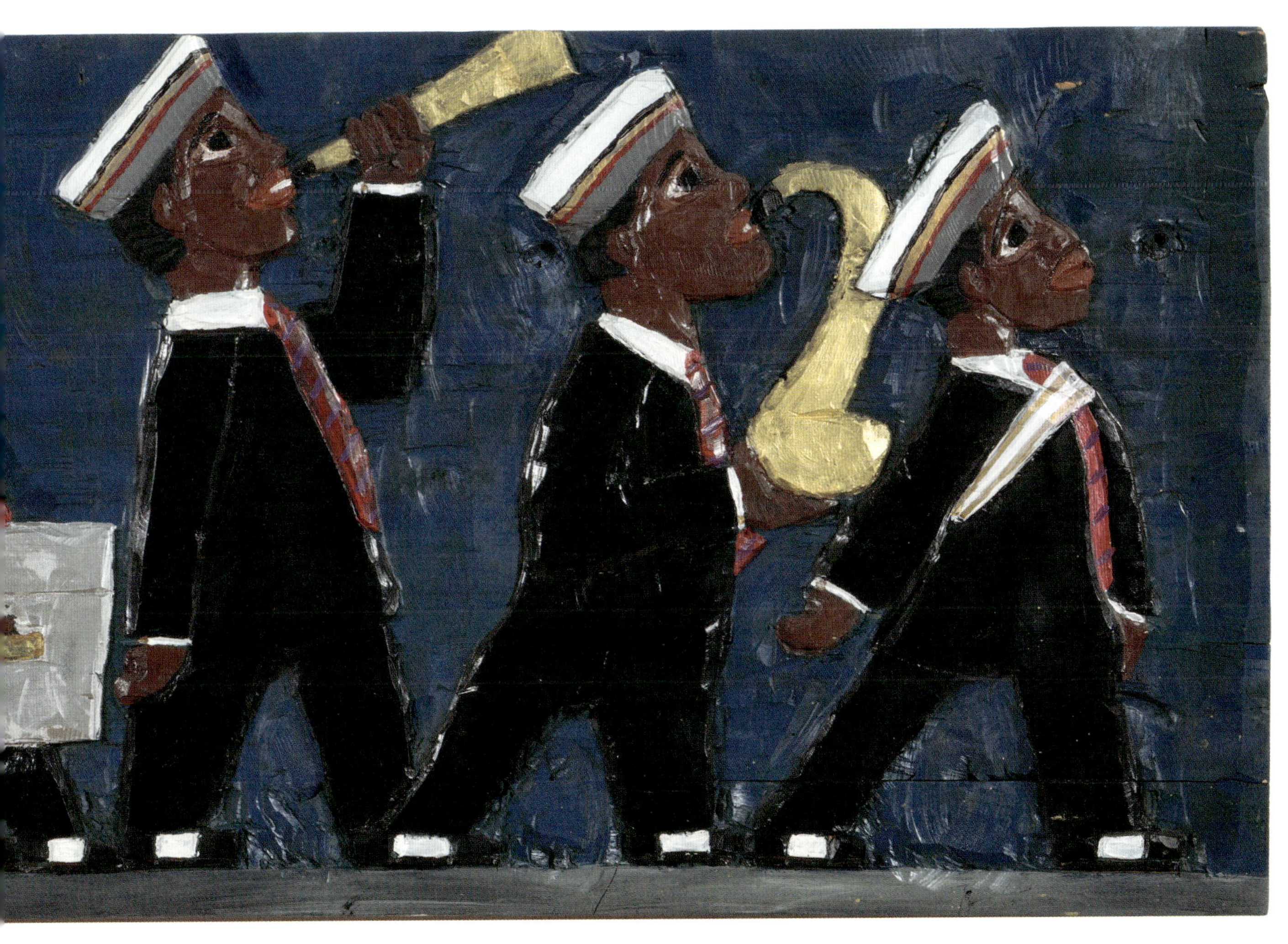

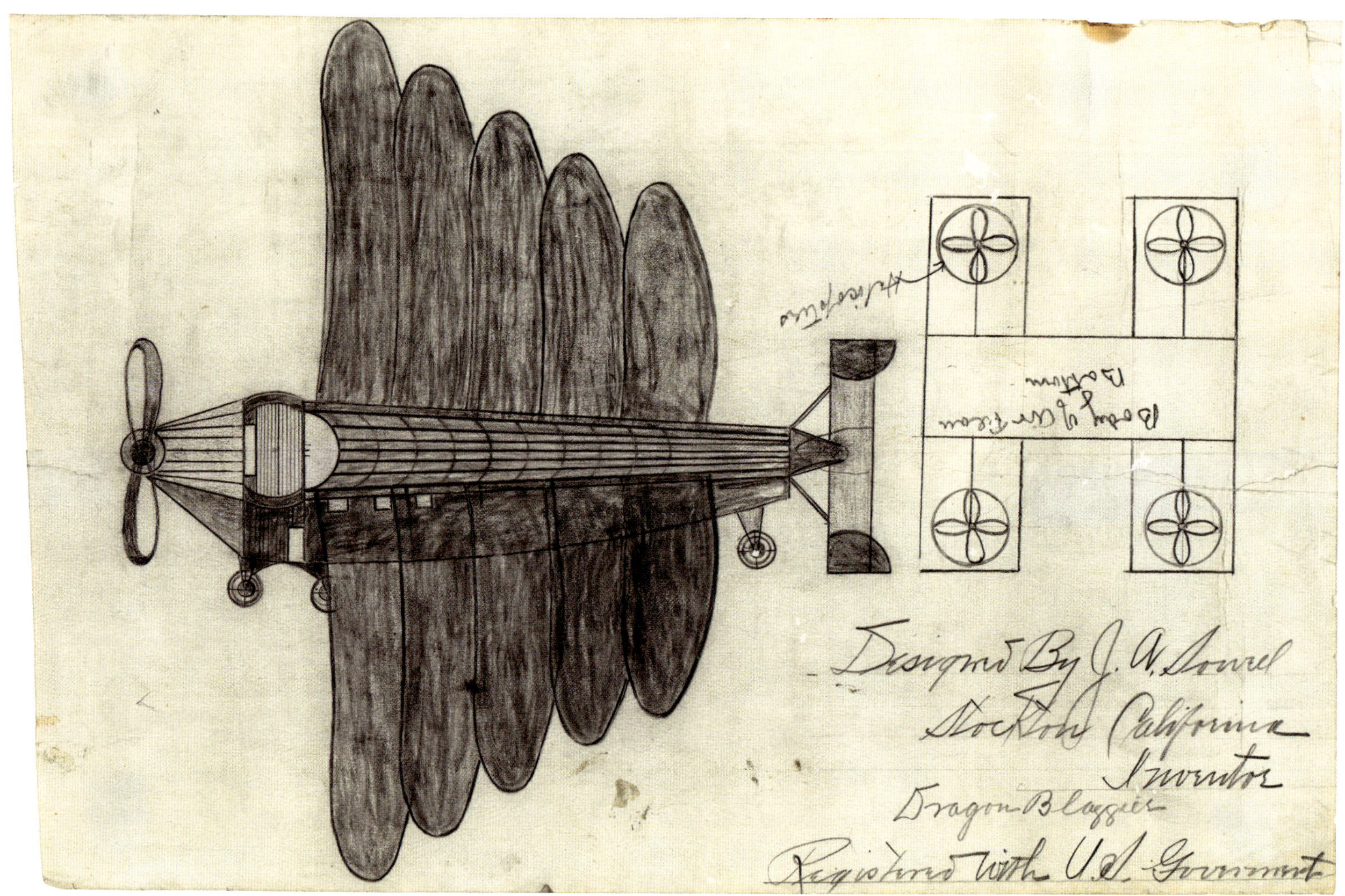
Designed By J. A. Sowell
Stockton California
Inventor
Dragon Blagger
Registered with U.S. Government

JOHN A. SOWELL

1864–1951

Very little is known about the long life and artistic aspirations of John Sowell, but the drawings he left behind (many of which are on file at the United States Patent and Trademark Office) are evidence of an ingenious mind and novel futuristic visions. Sowell was born in Grass Valley, California, and from a young age built mechanical contraptions. During World War I he worked at a machine shop in Stockton and in his free time created patent drawings and models (sometimes in partnership with an Ernest E. Sowell). He was particularly interested in aeronautical theory and engineering, with one patent application (filed in 1918 and granted in 1920) reading, "This invention relates to improvements in aeroplanes, the principal object being to produce an aeroplane which will control the air instead of the machine being controlled by the air; by means of construction, I am able to shut off the driving power and remain stationary in the air or ascend and descend at will thereby, and in a vertical plane."

Sowell was neither a scientist nor a formally educated artist but an inventor in the broadest sense; his imagination seems to have been the main drive behind his creations and it is unclear whether he pursued any practical application of his ideas. The works in Victor Keen's collection demonstrate Sowell's earnest desire to advance the mechanics of aviation as they also demonstrate the creative possibilities within the rigid requirements of mechanical representation. Sowell's illustrations surpass mere patent drawings; a surreal undercurrent suggests the connection between science fiction and technology. Sowell's work was shown in the group show *Visions from the Left Coast: California Self-Taught Artists* at the Santa Barbara Contemporary Arts Forum in 1995.

John Sowell, *Drawing of Dragon Blazzer*, n.d. Graphite on paper, 12 × 18 in. (30.5 × 45.7 cm)

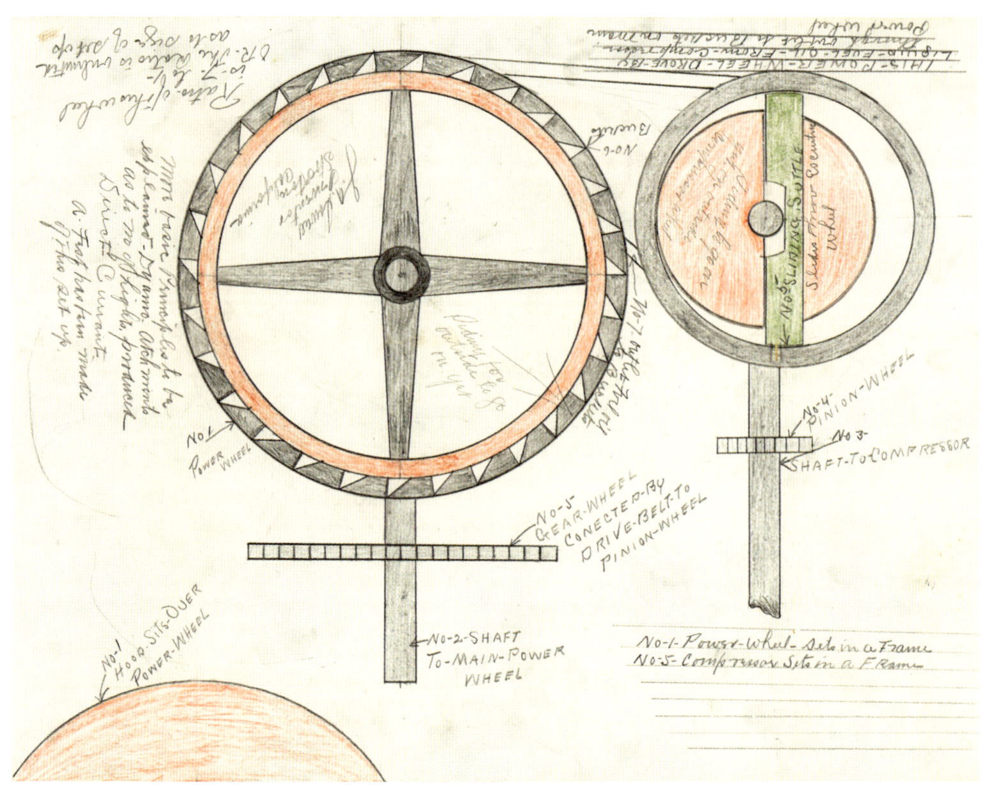

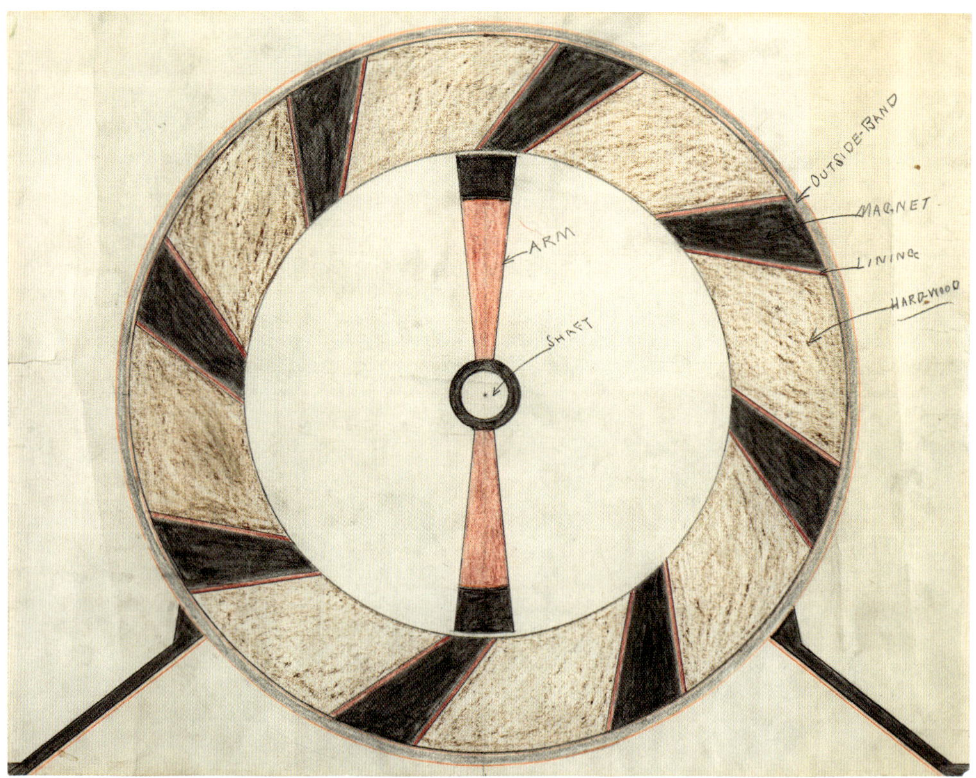

John Sowell, *Power Wheels*, n.d. Graphite and crayon on paper, 19 × 24 in. (48.3 × 61 cm)

John Sowell, *Rotary Power Setups*, c. 1940s. Graphite and crayon on paper, 19 × 24 in. (48.3 × 61 cm)

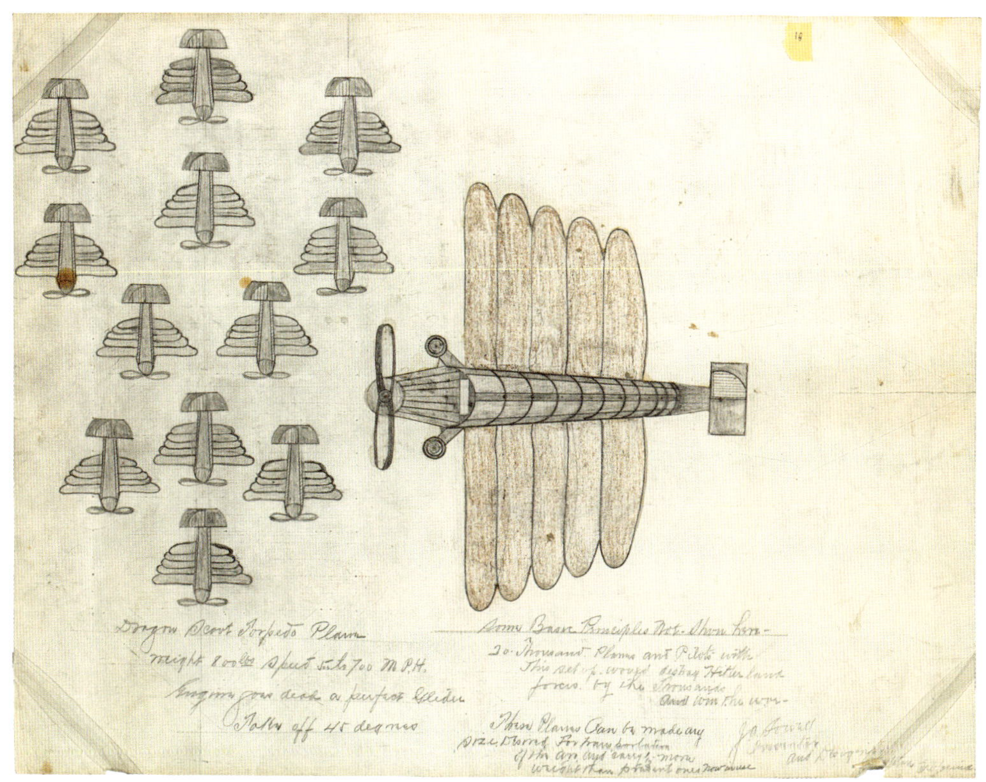

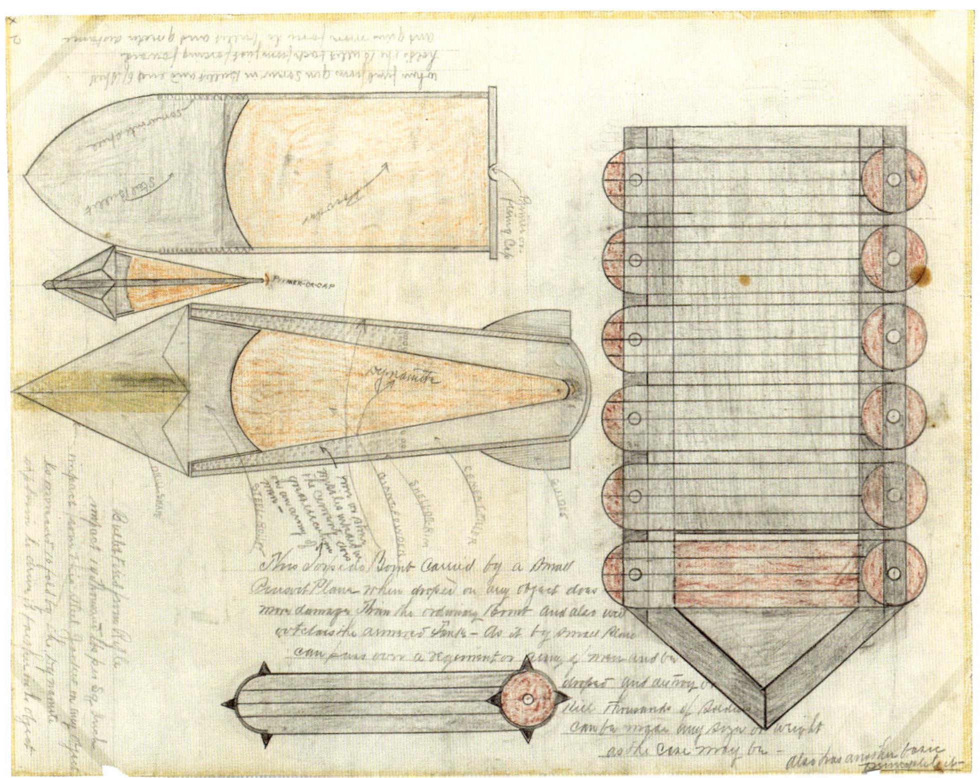

John Sowell, *Dragon Scout Torpedo Plane* (two-sided drawing), n.d. Graphite and crayon on paper, 19 × 24 in. (48.3 × 61 cm)

John Sowell, *Untitled* (two-sided drawing), n.d. Graphite, crayon, and collage on paper, 19 × 24 in. (48.3 × 61 cm)

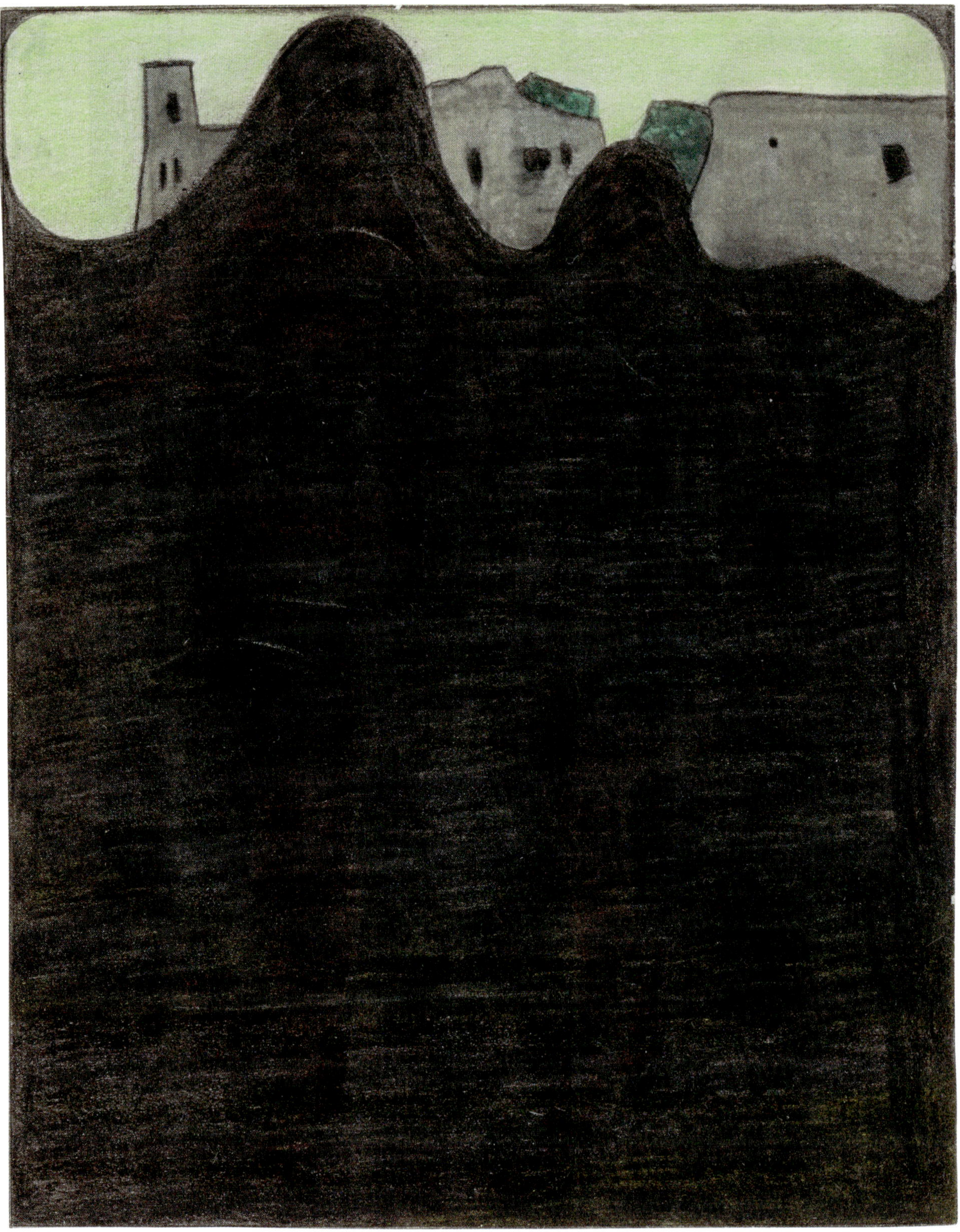

LEOPOLD STROBL

b. 1960

Leopold Strobl's intimately scaled drawings (many of his works measure approximately 4½ × 4 inches) lead the viewer into landscapes of haunting beauty. In every work he presents a deliberately partial view, covering portions he does not wish to show. Reposing forms suggest hills or crests or prehistoric rocks; nervy trees and melancholy shrubs may fill the visible part of the picture plane; segments of quiet roads, castles, fortresses, clock towers, or precise schematic houses and constructions may partially appear, with windows peeking back at the viewer like multiple all-black eyes. Strobl's worlds are steeped in shades of ochre yellow, raw umber, sage, pine, olive, and moss greens, with touches of bone white, graphite, and gunpowder grays. Skies are minty, dawns are not roseate, and yet the contours of this realm express an almost meditative state, an intense quietude or perhaps an extreme suspense. Strobl was born in Mistelbach, Lower Austria, and has devoted himself exclusively to art for more than thirty-five years. Since 2004 he has been a guest of the Open Studio program at the Gugging House of Artists in Vienna (see p. 143), where he draws in the morning and finishes a new piece per session.

Strobl renders his drawings on newspaper clippings he selects and adheres to clean drawing paper. The undergirding of published media furnishes his works with pictorial facets and meaning. With an intuitive grasp of solid color and transparency Strobl allows a portion of the printed image to appear while obscuring other parts. In some compositions, he heightens natural elements with a flush of color for visual texture or three-dimensionality in his abstractions. In other drawings, the newsprint becomes a palimpsest with a faint trace of words or letters barely visible under the pigment.

The signature feature of Strobl's work is his incorporation of bold, dark masses that create overpowering negative spaces, which become the primary subject of the work. These dark areas, which he outlines and colors in before anything else, may form an integral part of a landscape or appear to be mercurial matter as amorphous as dough. They can almost completely swallow a scene, create an extreme vignette, or form a deckle-edged border around the composition. In the unpopulated scenes of Strobl's vision, these abstract volumes occasionally suggest humanoid forms. Strobl's virtuosic sense of perspective and framing permits the viewer to see only what he allows. The negation of being able to know the full picture is a reminder that every story has its limits of knowability. Strobl's debut in the United States occurred in 2016 with the solo exhibition *Smallscapes* at Ricco/Maresca Gallery in New York, and two years later the Museum of Modern Art (New York) acquired five of his works. Strobl's works are also in the Treger Saint Silvestre Collection (São João da Madeira, Portugal), and the abcd Collection (Paris).

Text excerpted and adapted from Alejandra Russi, "Leopold Strobl: Smallscapes," www.riccomaresca.com.

Leopold Strobl, *Untitled (2015-171)*, 2015. Graphite and colored pencil on newsprint mounted on paper, 5 × 3⅞ in. (12.7 × 9.8 cm)

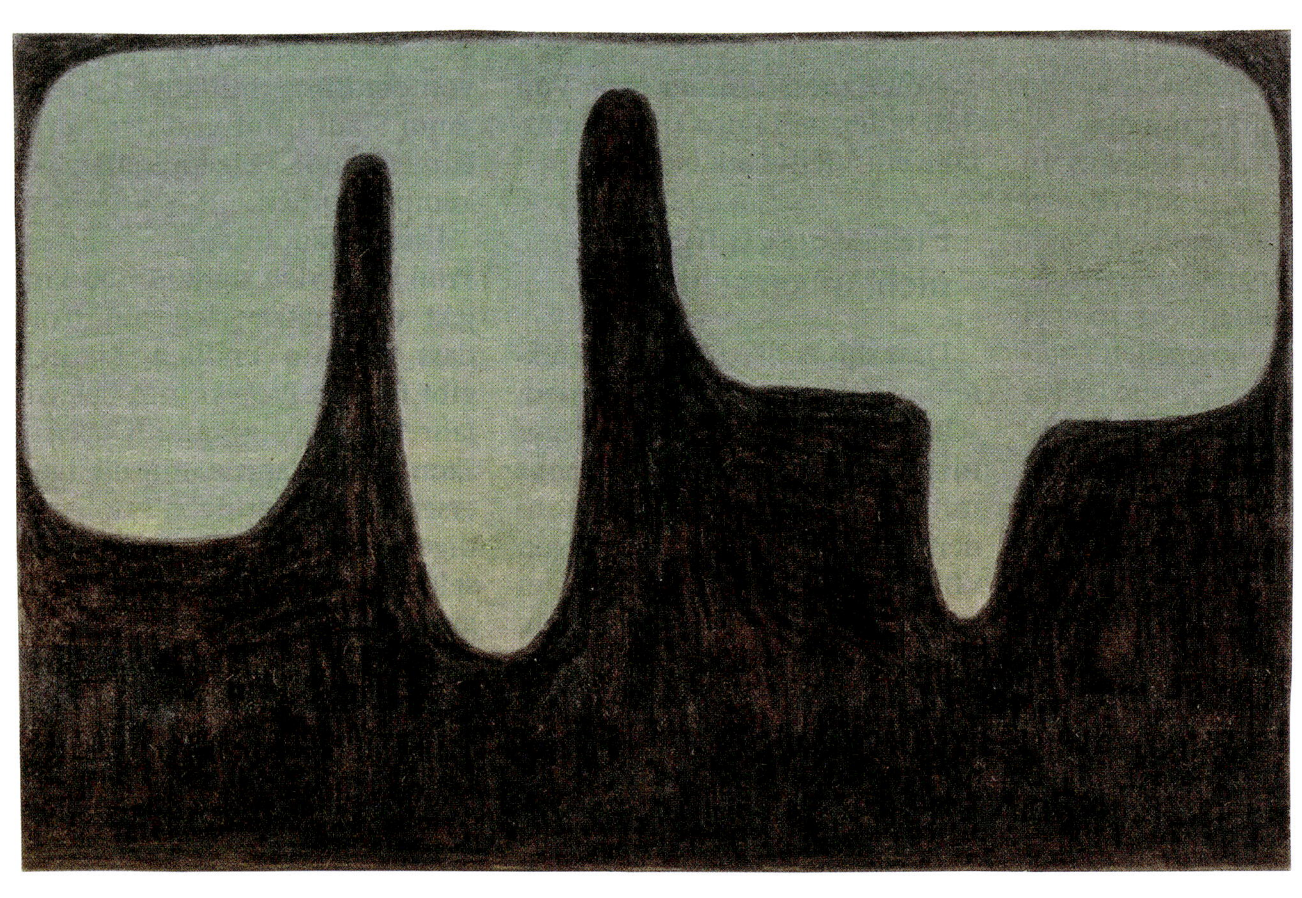

Leopold Strobl, *Untitled (2014-075)*, 2014. Graphite and colored pencil on newsprint mounted on paper, 3⅜ × 5 in. (8.6 × 12.7 cm)

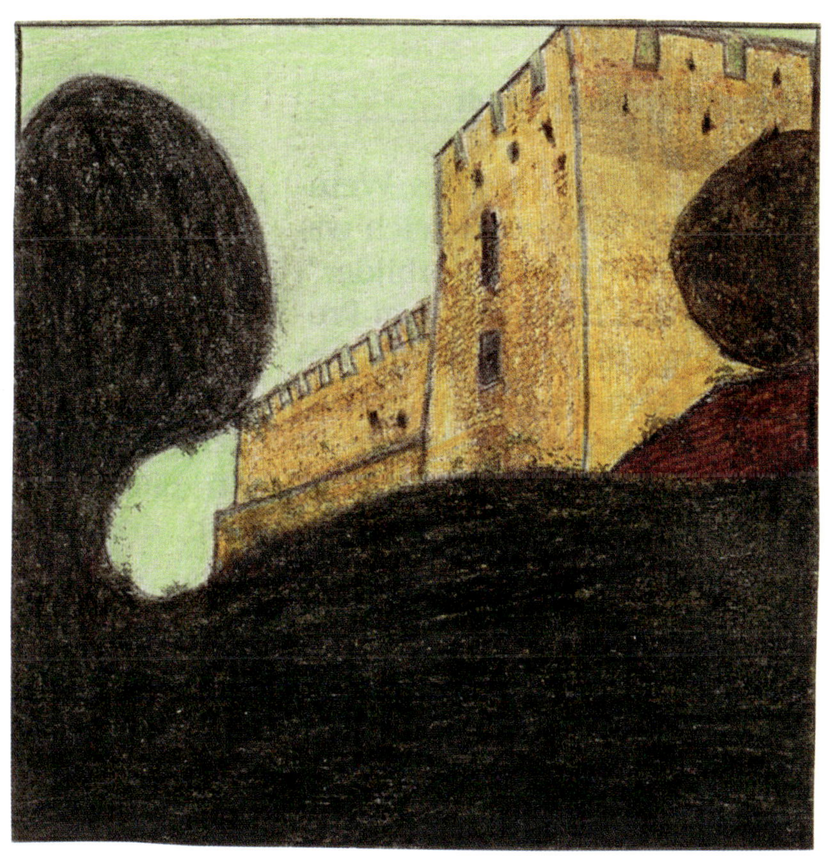

Leopold Strobl, *Untitled (2014-152)*, 2014. Graphite and colored pencil on newsprint mounted on paper, 3 × 2⅞ in. (7.6 × 7.3 cm)

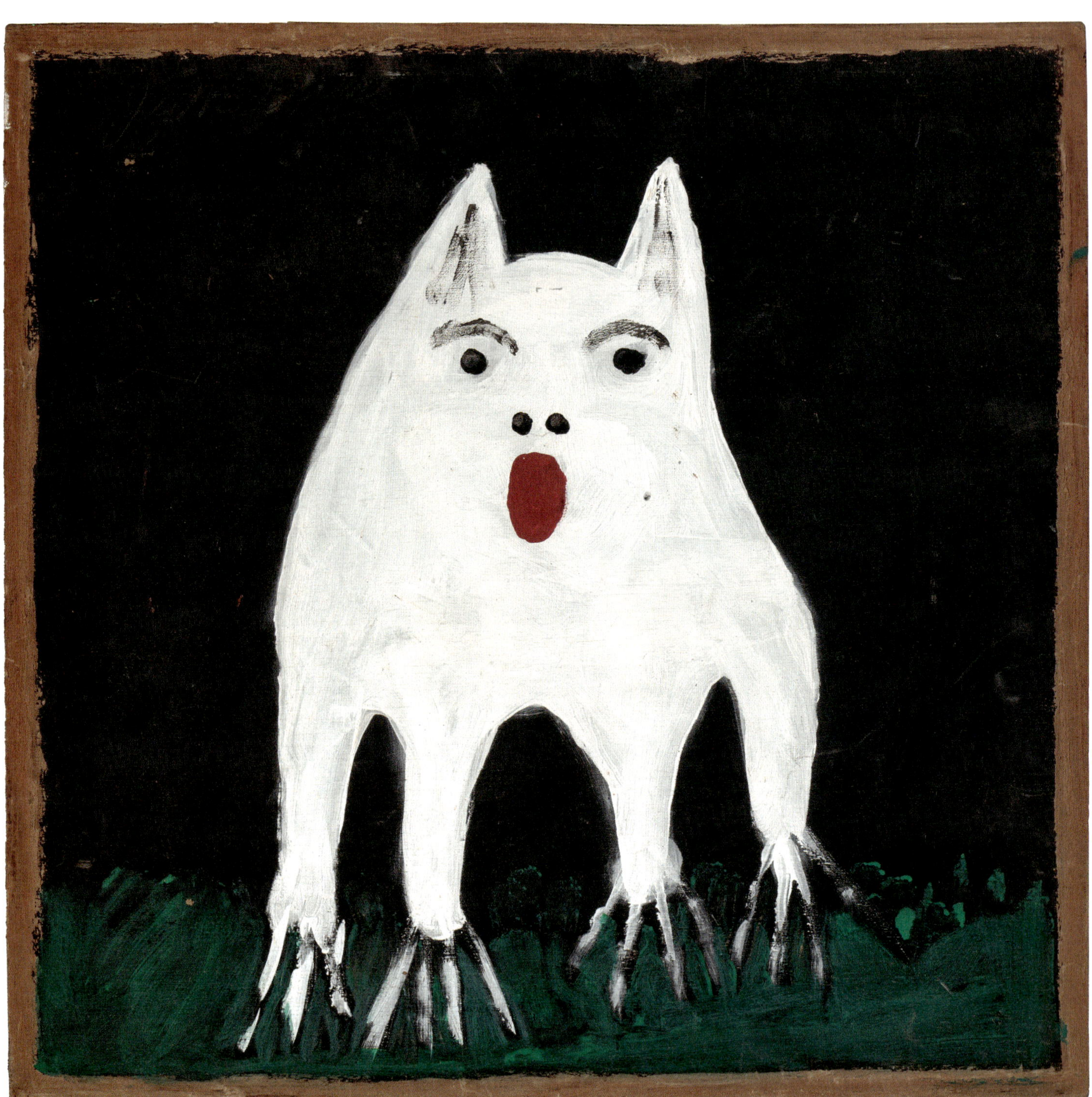

JIMMY LEE SUDDUTH

1910–2007

Jimmy Lee Sudduth extracted many of his pigments from nature and preferred to paint with his fingers rather than brushes. In his art he celebrated and re-created the world around him, representing the local architecture of his hometown of Fayette, Alabama, iconic American landscapes and symbols such as the New York City skyline and the Statue of Liberty, people he knew, self-portraits as a musician (he was an accomplished harmonica and banjo player), and animals, including his beloved dog Toto (of which there was a succession after the first Toto died). Sudduth grew up on a farm in Cains Ridge (near Fayette) with his adoptive parents, itinerant farm laborers. His mother was part Native American and a practitioner of herbal medicine, and she would bring him along from a very early age on excursions into the woods in search of medicinal flora. Sudduth's earliest memories included painting with mud on a tree when he was three years old, and he credits those sojourns in the woods as the catalyst for his impulse to use natural tinctures.

Sudduth spent most of his life working on farms, at a grist mill, and at a lumber mill. In the 1950s he also worked as a gardener and handyman. After the death of his first wife in 1941, with whom he had a daughter, he remarried. He and his second wife adopted a son and were together more than thirty years until her death in 1992. Sudduth lived in a small house near a railroad track, where he painted and played the blues on his harmonica. As a mature artist he started working with house paint and acrylic but kept exploring the expressive potential of mud and its ochre gradations. First tracing a composition on a scavenged wooden surface with a soft stone that he referred to as a "dye rock," he would apply a layer of mud and add more colors from organic matter (wild berries, grass, coffee, and soot) mixed with binders (syrup, sugar, soft drinks, and caulk). Sudduth never learned to read or write but he could "draw" his name on his finished works.

Although he became diabetic and suffered bouts of pneumonia in the last years of his life, it was not until he was placed in a nursing home that he stopped painting and died some months later at the age of ninety-seven. Sudduth's first exhibition was held in 1968 at Stillman College in Tuscaloosa. A 1971 exhibition of his work at the museum in Fayette's City Hall Auditorium was organized by Jack Black, a Fayette businessman and local newspaper publisher, who became Sudduth's longtime friend and an early supporter. Sudduth was selected to represent Alabama in the Smithsonian Institution's Bicentennial Festival of American Folk Life in 1976. The Birmingham Museum of Art exhibited his paintings in 1978 and he appeared on *The Today Show* and *60 Minutes* in 1980. In 2005 a solo show of his work was organized at the Montgomery Museum of Fine Arts, with a catalogue, *The Life and Art of Jimmy Lee Sudduth*.

Sudduth's work is in the collections of the African American Museum (Dallas), the American Folk Art Museum (New York), the Birmingham Museum of Art, the Fayette Art Museum and the Montgomery Museum of Fine Arts (Alabama), the Milwaukee Art Museum, the Mississippi Museum of Art (Jackson), the Smithsonian American Art Museum (Washington, D.C.), and the New Orleans Museum of Art.

Jimmy Lee Sudduth, *Large Toto*, n.d. Paint on plywood, 24 × 24 in. (61 × 61 cm)

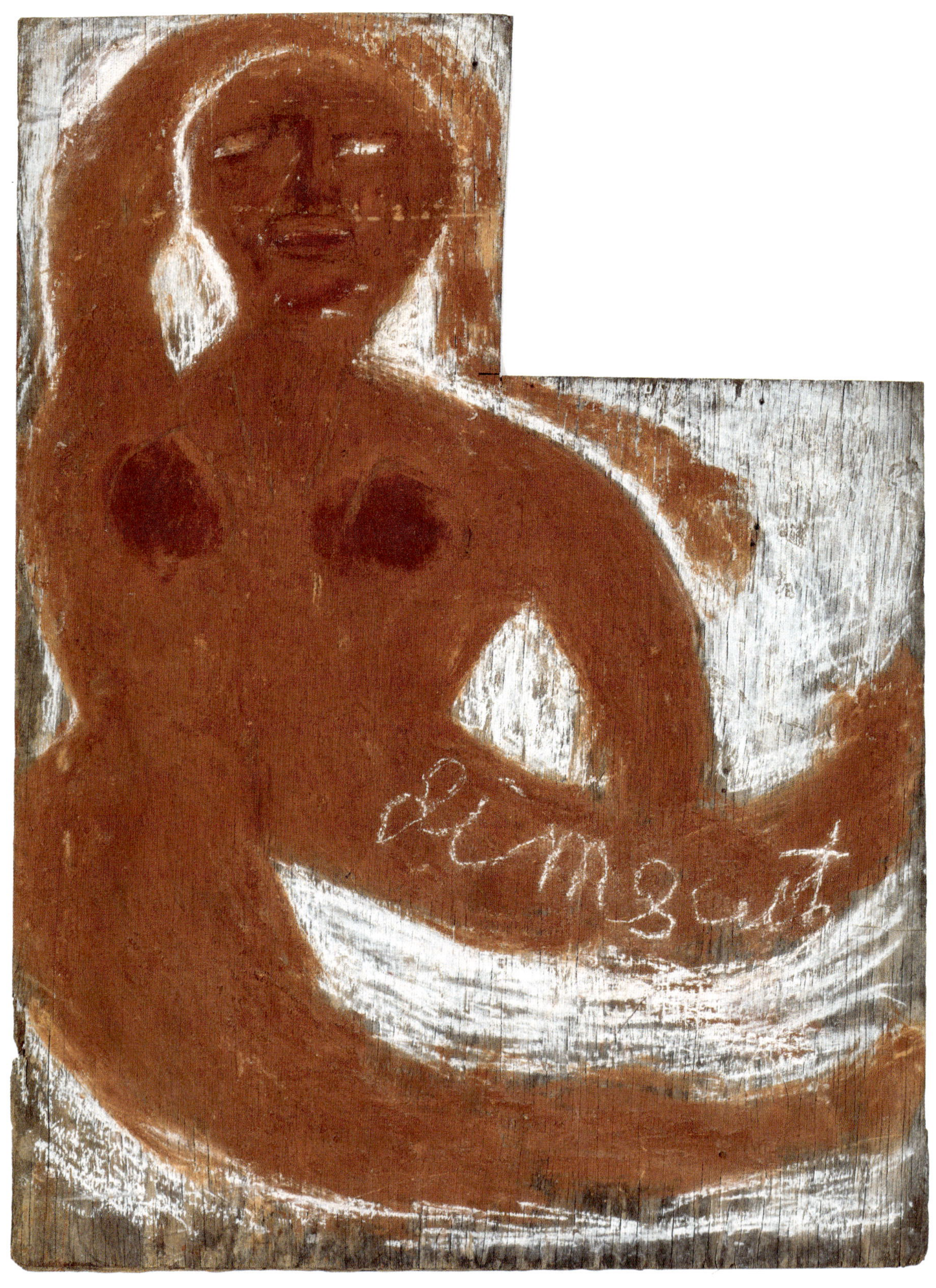

Jimmy Lee Sudduth, *Nude Woman*, n.d. Paint on plywood, 49½ × 36¼ in. (125.7 × 92.1 cm)

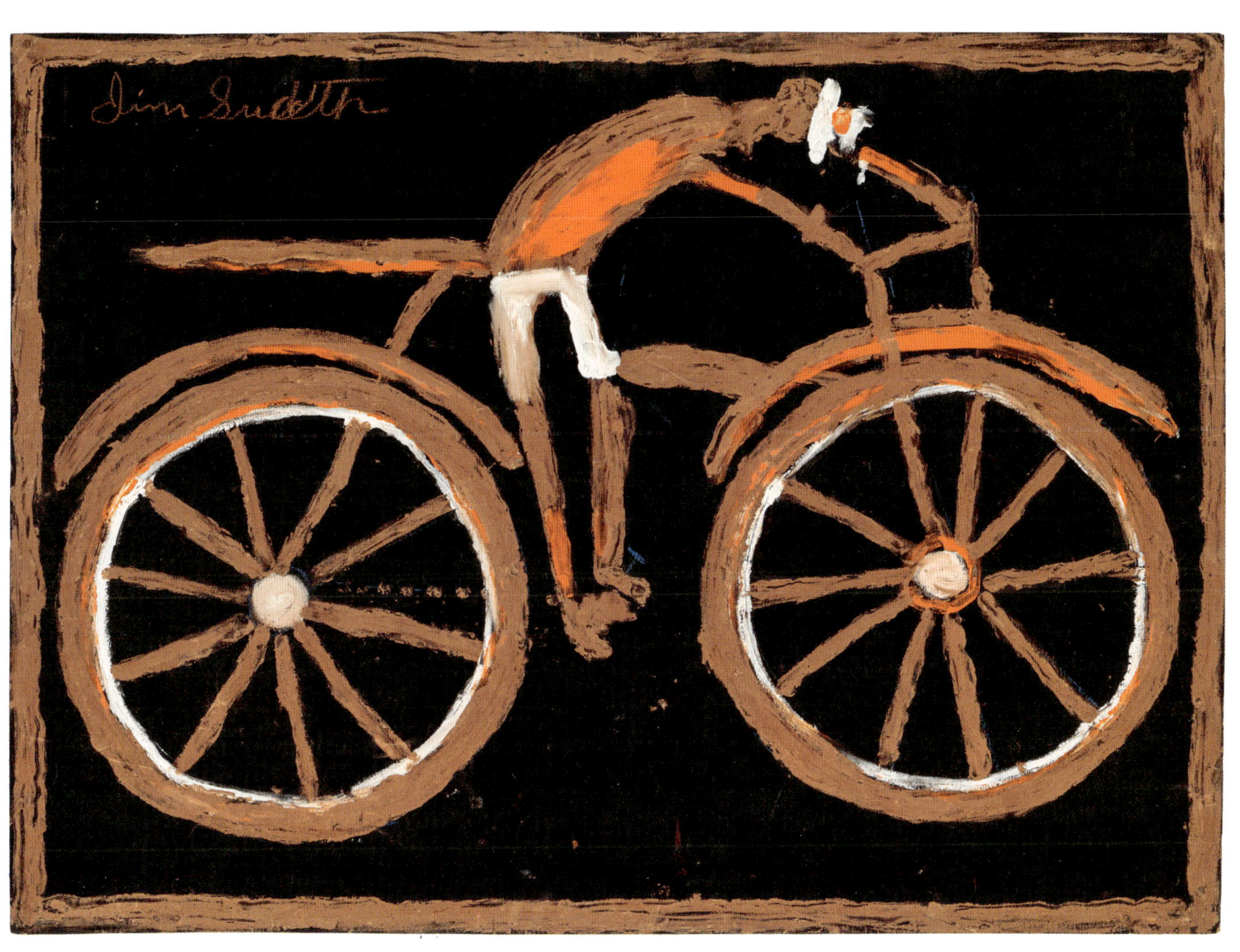

Jimmy Lee Sudduth, *Untitled (Orange Bicycle Man)*, n.d. Paint on plywood, 36 × 48 in. (91.4 × 121.9 cm)

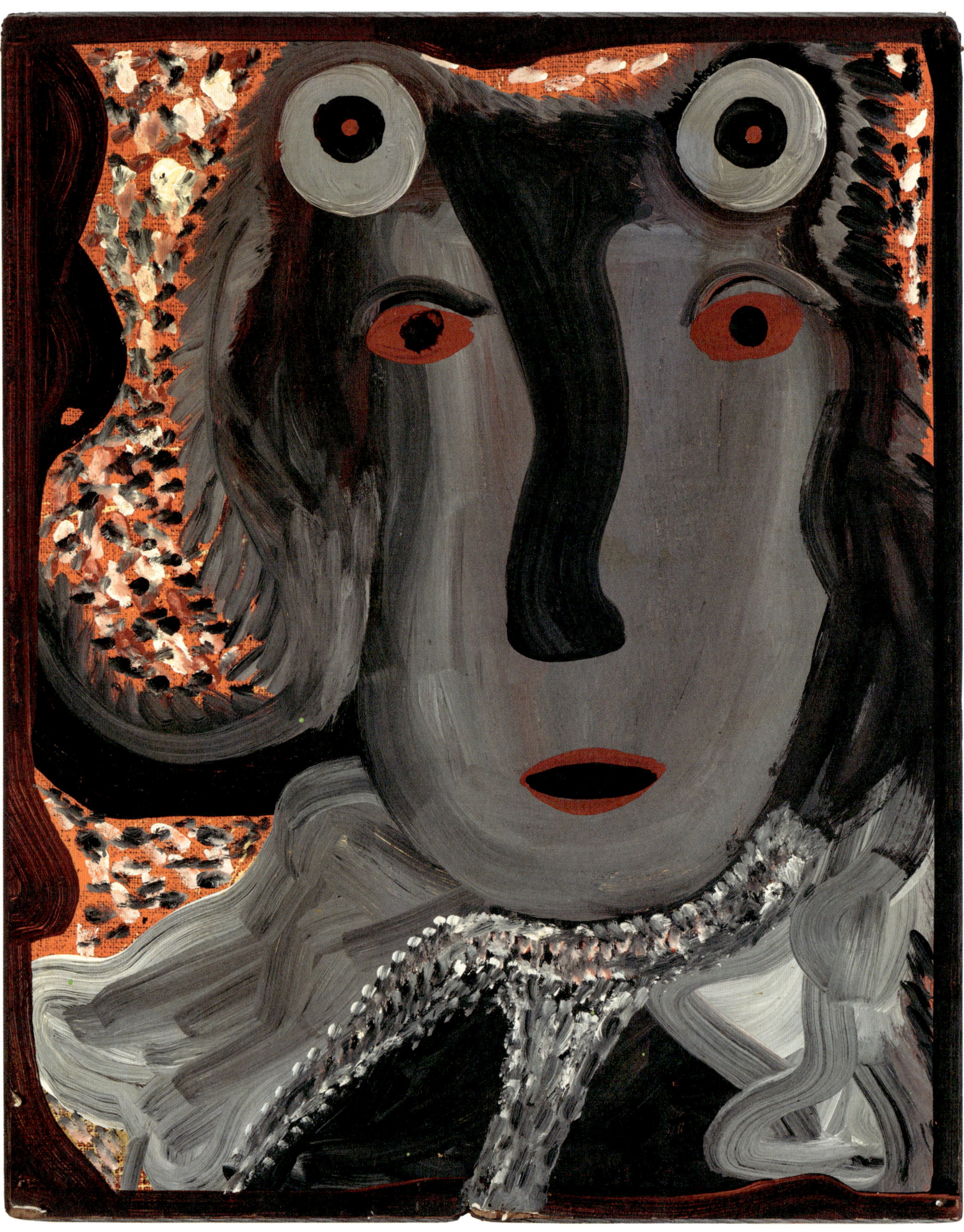

MOSE TOLLIVER

1919–2006

Mose Tolliver was the youngest of seven sons in a family with twelve children. His father was a sharecropper and farm laborer in the Pike Road rural community, near Montgomery in the state of Alabama, where Tolliver lived his entire life. He attended school through the third grade and as a teenager worked gathering and selling produce for a truck farmer. He also worked as a house painter, a carpenter, and a plumber, and off and on cleaning up the shipping area at the McLendon Furniture Company, where in the late 1960s a crate full of marble fell from a forklift and crushed Tolliver's left ankle, leaving him permanently unable to walk unassisted. After a period of drinking and depression he started to paint in earnest and developed his characteristic style.

Tolliver began painting on any available surface (scraps from packing crates, Masonite, tabletops, and metal trays) and later on sheets of plywood with house paint. His color palettes, like his compositions, are clean and refined. Tolliver worked quickly and was extremely prolific, creating hundreds of pictures of birds, plant life, anthropomorphic figures, and people—including self-portraits with crutches and portraits of his wife. Many of his images are sexually suggestive (or "nasty paintings" as he would call them), particularly his "moose ladies," or women hovering spread-legged over rounded objects that he called "scooters" or "exercising bicycles." Tolliver's visual vocabulary is whimsical and instantly recognizable: his brushstrokes are thick, rhythmic, and expressionistic; his figures flat and abstracted with exaggerated round heads, seen from a full-frontal perspective and generally dominating the entire picture plane. He often added a painted frame around his subjects and always signed them with the inscription "MOSET," with an inverted "S," a possible indication of dyslexia.

Tolliver began displaying his paintings on his front porch, where they got the attention of Mitchell Kahan, then curator of the Montgomery Museum of Fine Arts, which mounted a solo show of his work in 1981. In the exhibition catalog Kahan wrote, "The naiveté of the improbable and bizarrely constructed animals is comical in a charming way. The humor . . . results from the unintentional discrepancy between the painted image and the real-life source. . . . Often the humor is linked to elements of fantasy and eroticism." In an article published in the *Montgomery Advertiser* in 1981, Robert Bishop, then director of the American Folk Art Museum, wrote, "You can hang him beside a Picasso, and you have the same kind of creativity and deep personal vision." A year later, Tolliver's work was included in the groundbreaking exhibition *Black Folk Art in America 1930–1980* at the Corcoran Gallery of Art (Washington, D.C.). Tolliver's work is in the collections of the African American Museum (Dallas), the American Folk Art Museum (New York), the Birmingham Museum of Art, the High Museum of Art (Atlanta), Intuit: The Center for Intuitive and Outsider Art (Chicago), the Milwaukee Art Museum, the Montgomery Museum of Fine Arts, the New Orleans Museum of Art, and the Smithsonian American Art Museum (Washington, D.C.).

Mose Tolliver, *Something Like a Wild Man*, n.d. Paint on found board, 28¼ × 19½ in. (71.8 × 49.5 cm)

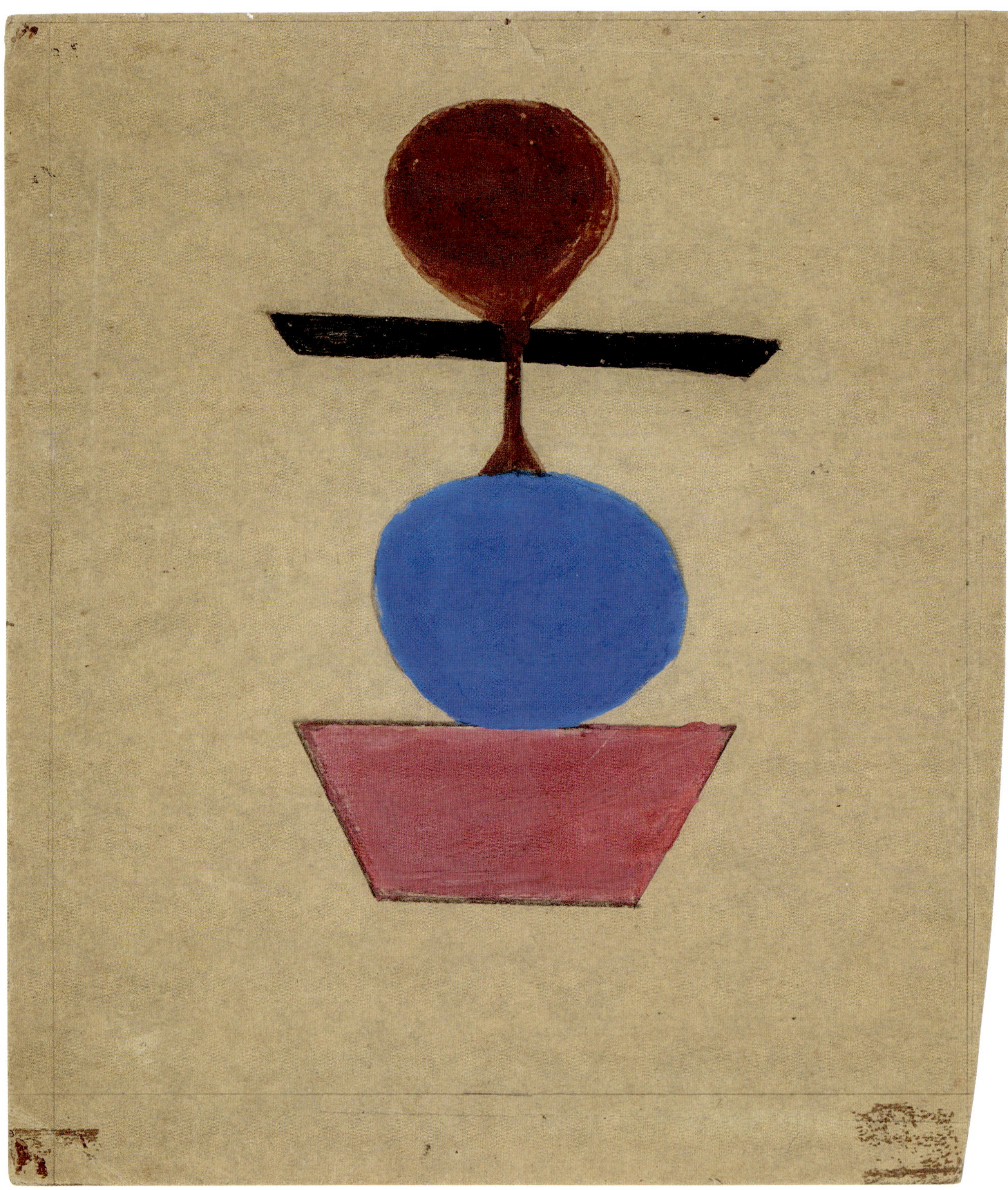

BILL TRAYLOR

ca. 1853–1949

Although emancipated as a boy, Bill Traylor continued to labor until around 1908 on a neighboring plantation to the cotton plantation near Benton, Alabama, where he was born into slavery. By 1910 he was a tenant farmer near Montgomery.

It was only when he was in his eighties and no longer able to do physical work that he started making art with materials that lay to hand, learning to write his name so he could sign his work. From 1939 to 1942, Traylor produced more than 1,200 drawings that are of crucial significance in American art and social history. Visitors to the black neighborhood of Montgomery, where Traylor had moved in 1928, according to a 1930 U.S. Census, after spending most of his life on plantations, could have encountered Traylor, a bearded old man sitting on a sidewalk on Monroe Street next to a Coca-Cola cooler, a drawing board across his lap—he drew all day and slept for free in the back of a funeral parlor. In 1939 Traylor caught the attention of a passerby named Charles Shannon—a young artist who led the New South cultural center with a group of progressive white artists in Montgomery. Shannon became Traylor's friend and patron, safeguarding finished works and offering additional art supplies (though Traylor tended to prefer salvaged materials such as found cardboard, graphite, and poster paint).

Traylor's imagery consists of laborers with hammers, drinkers with flasks, hunters with shotguns, dandies in hats, seniors with canes, rural pedestrians, and some anthropomorphic figures often overlooked. People quarrel and point, live poultry flap wings, and frightening dogs go on the attack; characters hide beneath or stand atop and stumble off structures; there is a lot of apparent pursuit and escape. Many things may be inferred from this dynamic, but Traylor's message is not necessarily knowable. His simplified, modern figures, especially in works he referred to as "exciting events," seem not to be straightforward depictions of what he may have seen but, rather, projections from the heart of his experience, distilled by memory. The abstract, minimalist figures and shapes in his work exemplify Traylor's wildly original, true naïveté.

In 1942 Traylor interrupted his artwork when he traveled to several northern cities through 1945 to stay with a few of his children (all told, numbering some twenty-odd, according to Traylor). After he lost a leg to gangrene, the social agency that delivered his welfare check discovered a daughter living in Montgomery and suggested that he live with her, and he returned to Montgomery in 1946. Discouraged, Traylor lost all motivation to make art. He died at Oak Street Hospital in Montgomery a few days after summoning Shannon for a final visit.

Although Shannon had mounted an exhibition, *Bill Traylor: People's Artist*, in 1940, the public at large did not know Traylor's work until it was included in the 1982 exhibition *Black Folk Art in America 1930–1980* at the Corcoran Gallery of Art, in Washington, D.C. His posthumous recognition has expanded steadily ever since, and today his work is in important private and museum collections, including the Metropolitan

Bill Traylor, *Untitled (Red, Blue, Black and Brown Construction)*, c. 1939–42. Tempera and graphite on cardboard, 14⅞ × 12½ in. (37.8 × 31.8 cm)

Museum of Art and The Whitney Museum of American Art (New York), the Montgomery Museum of Fine Arts, and the High Museum of Art (Atlanta). A wide-ranging retrospective, *Between Worlds: The Art of Bill Traylor*, organized by Leslie Umberger and shown from September 28, 2018, to March 17, 2019, at the Smithsonian American Art Museum in Washington, D.C., included several works from the Victor Keen collection and was accompanied by an extensive monograph that constitutes the most comprehensive study to date of Traylor's life and art.

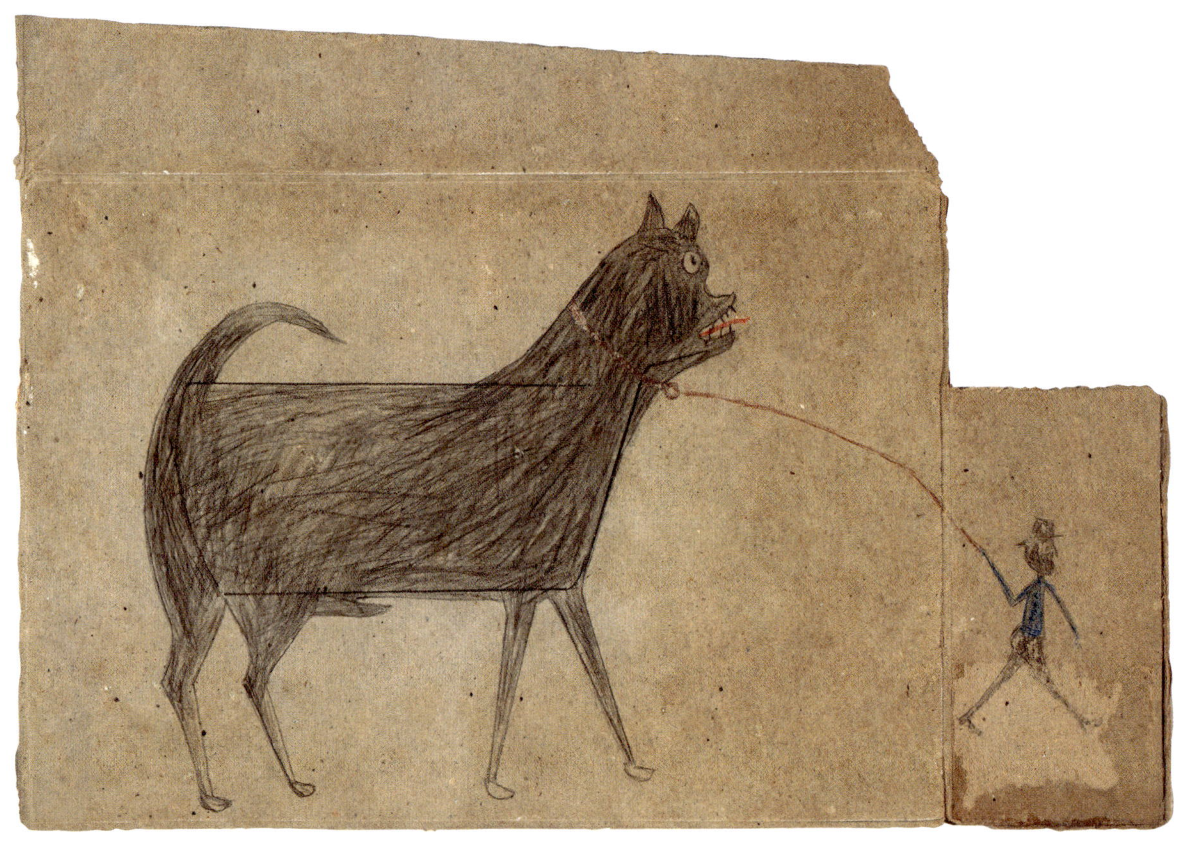

Bill Traylor, *Untitled (Man Walking Dog)*, c. 1939. Graphite on found cardboard (Chipso dish soap box), 8 × 11 in. (20.3 × 27.9 cm)

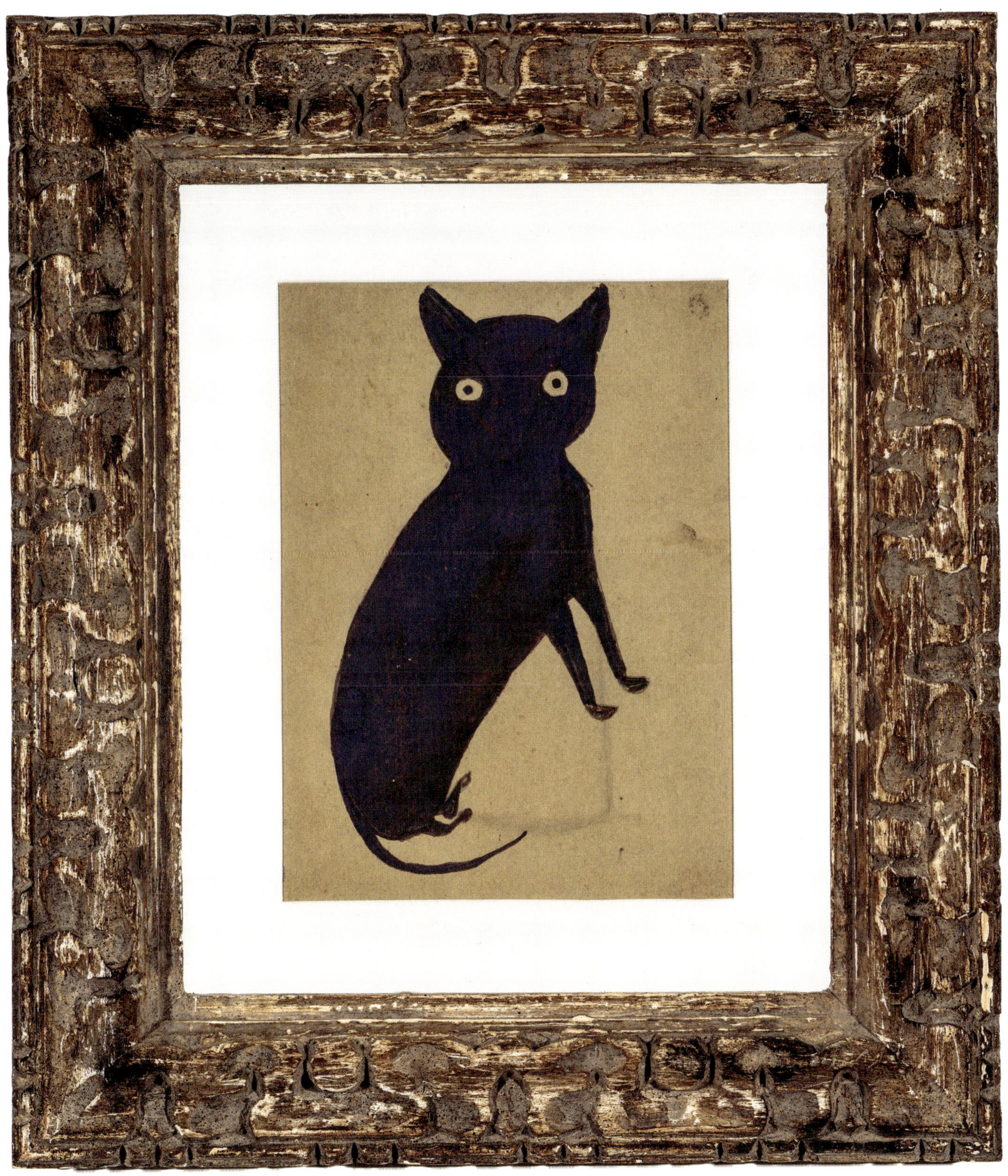

Bill Traylor, *Blue Cat*, c. 1939–42. Paint on found cardboard (Curtis Candy Co. box), 11 × 8 in. (27.9 × 20.3 cm)

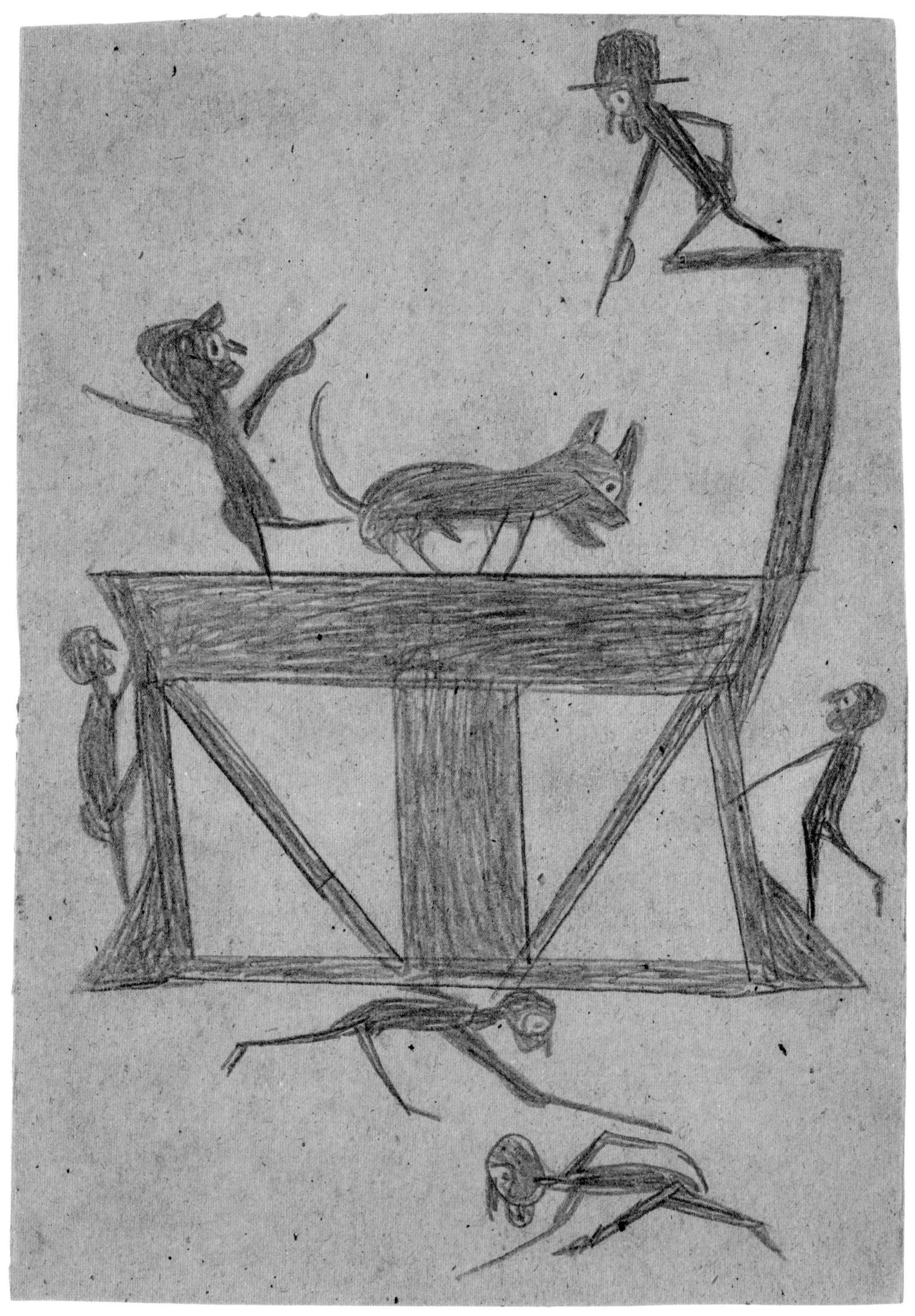

Bill Traylor, *Untitled (Construction with Six Figures and a Dog)*, c.1939–42. Crayon on cardboard (reverse marked "Charles Shannon No. 2"), 11½ × 7⅞ in. (29.2 × 20 cm)

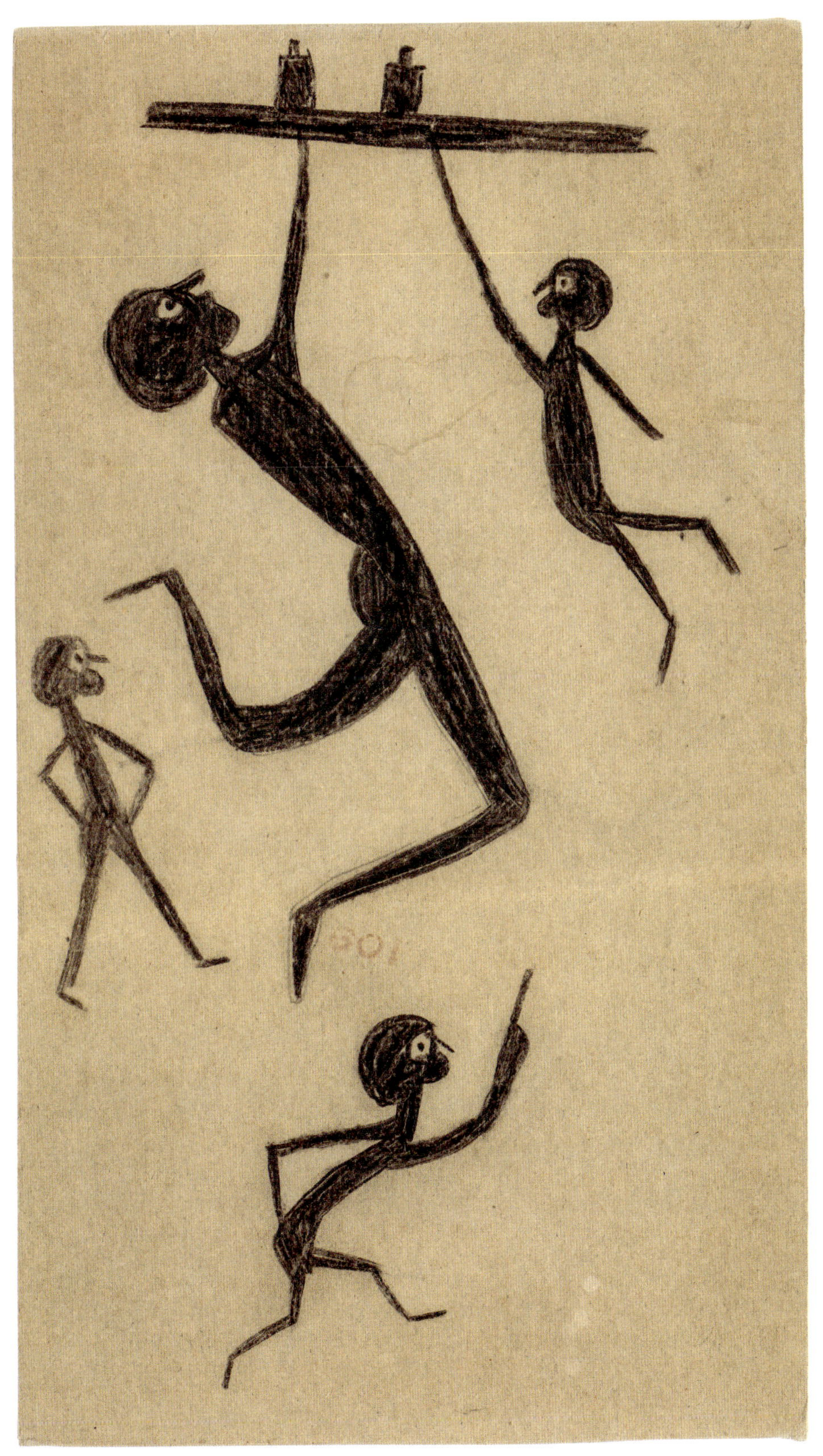

Bill Traylor, *Four Men, Bottles on a Shelf*, c. 1939–42. Crayon on cardboard, 13½ × 7½ in. (34.3 × 19.1 cm)

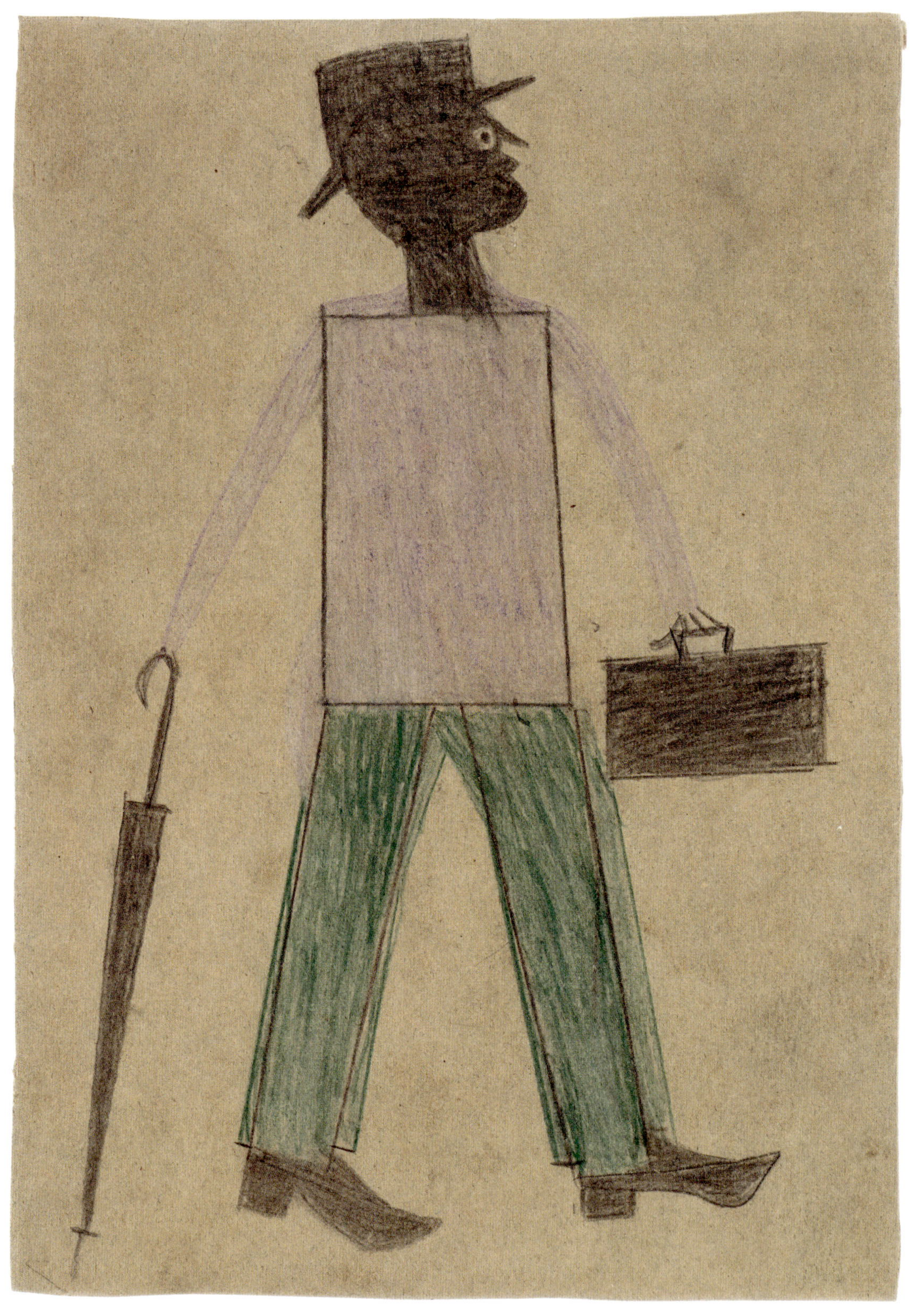

Bill Traylor, *Untitled (Purple and Green Man with Umbrella)*, c. 1939–42. Crayon and graphite on cardboard (candy bar advertisement on verso), 11½ × 8 in. (29.2 × 20.3 cm)

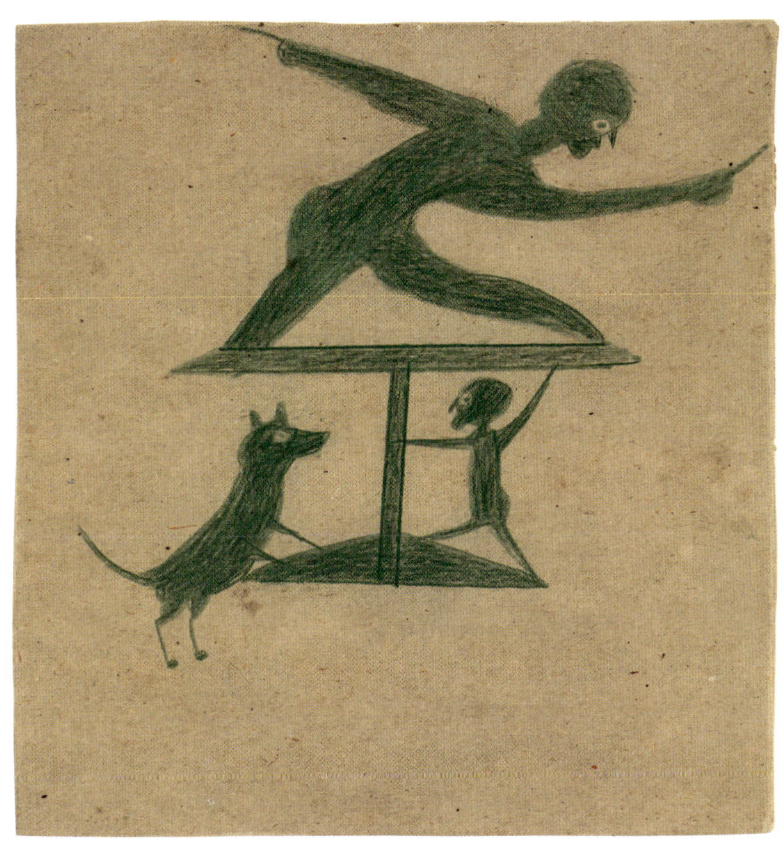

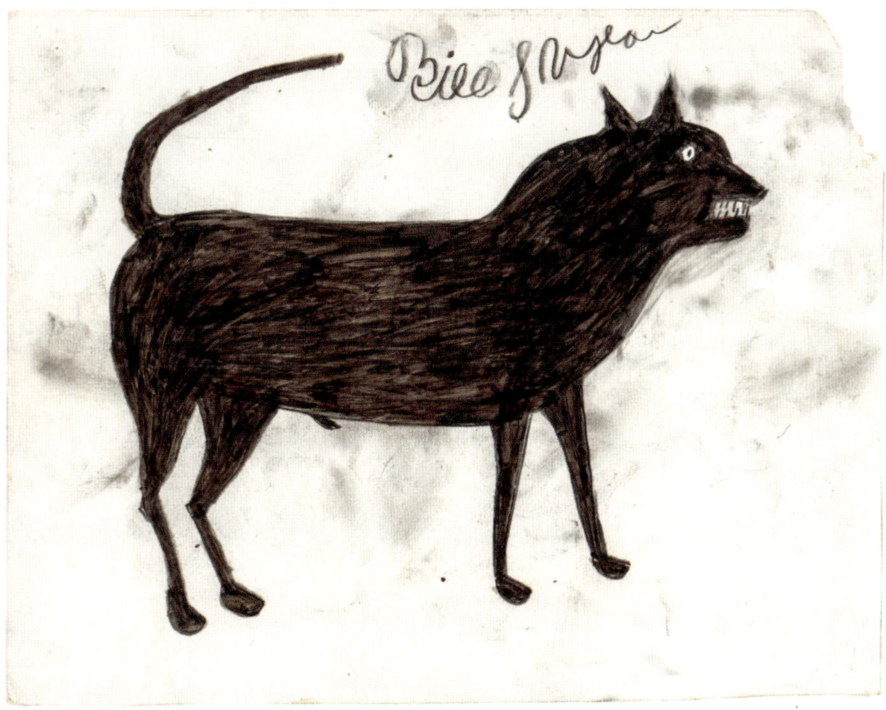

Bill Traylor, *Untitled (Green Construction with Two Men and a Dog)*, c. 1939–42. Crayon on cardboard, $10\frac{3}{8} \times 9\frac{5}{8}$ in. (26.4 × 24.4 cm)

Bill Traylor, *Black Dog*, c. 1939–42. Graphite on cardboard, $11\frac{1}{4} \times 14$ in. (28.6 × 35.6 cm)

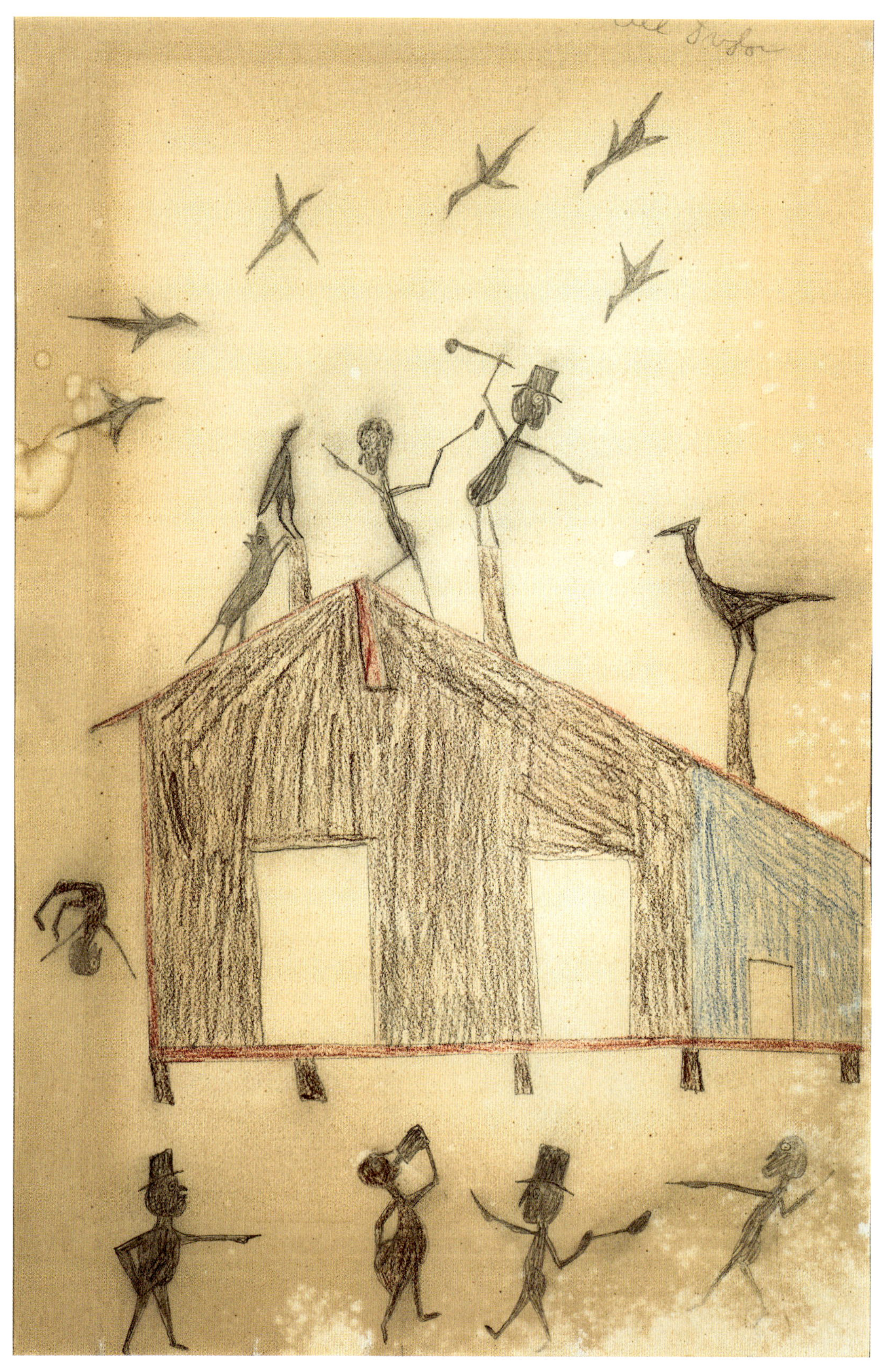

Bill Traylor, *Men on Roof (Crazy House with Figures)*, c. 1939–42. Graphite and crayon on paper, 24¼ × 15½ in. (61.6 × 39.4 cm)

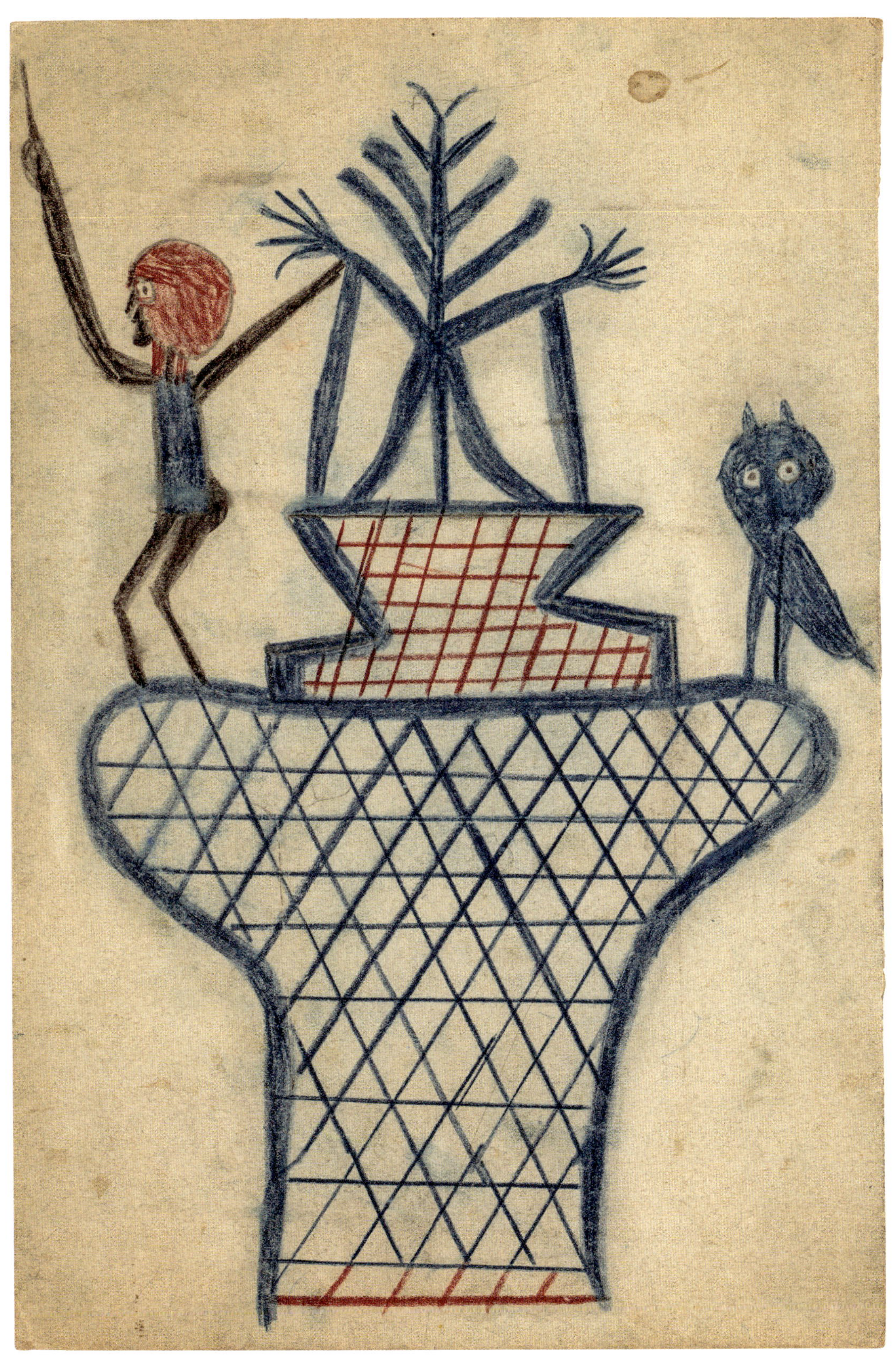

Bill Traylor, *Man and Bird on Woven Form*, c. 1939. Colored pencil on cardboard, 14 × 9 in. (35.6 × 22.9 cm)

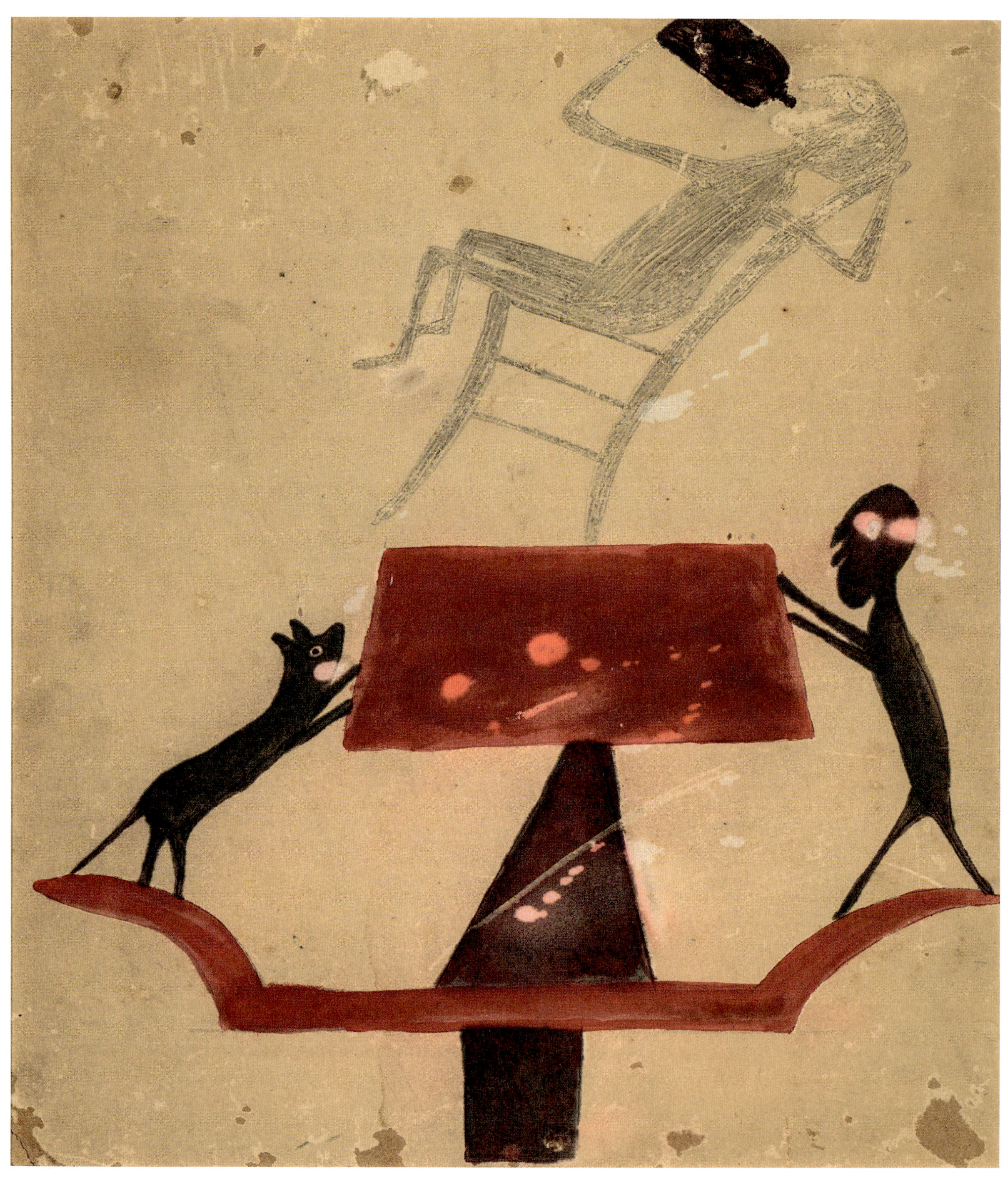

Bill Traylor, *Dog, Man and Drunk*, c. 1939–42. Ink and graphite on cardboard, 13¼ × 11¼ in. (33.7 × 28.6 cm)

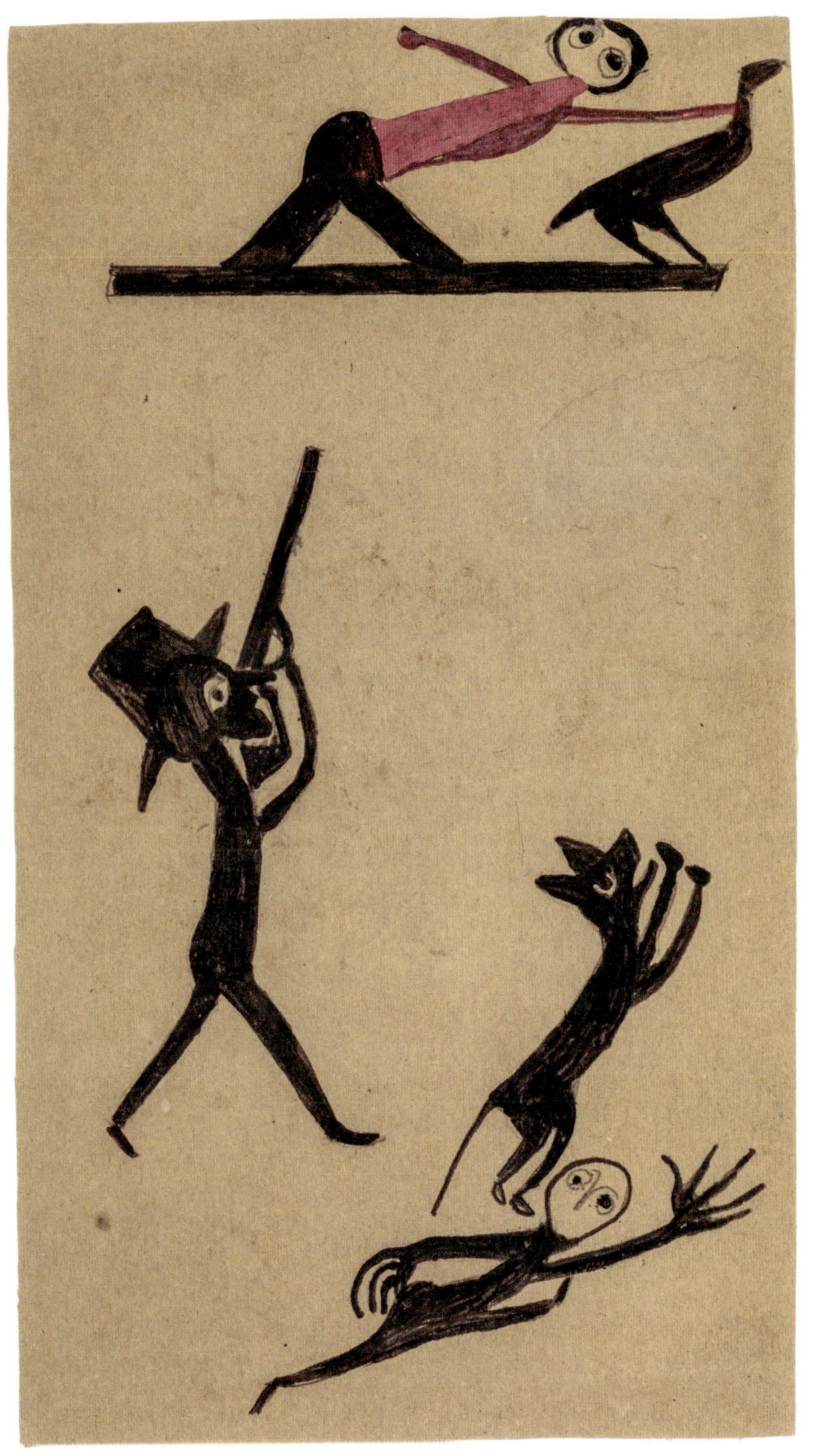

Bill Traylor, *Chicken Stealing*, c. 1939–42. Poster paint on cardboard, 13¼ × 7 in. (33.7 × 17.8 cm)

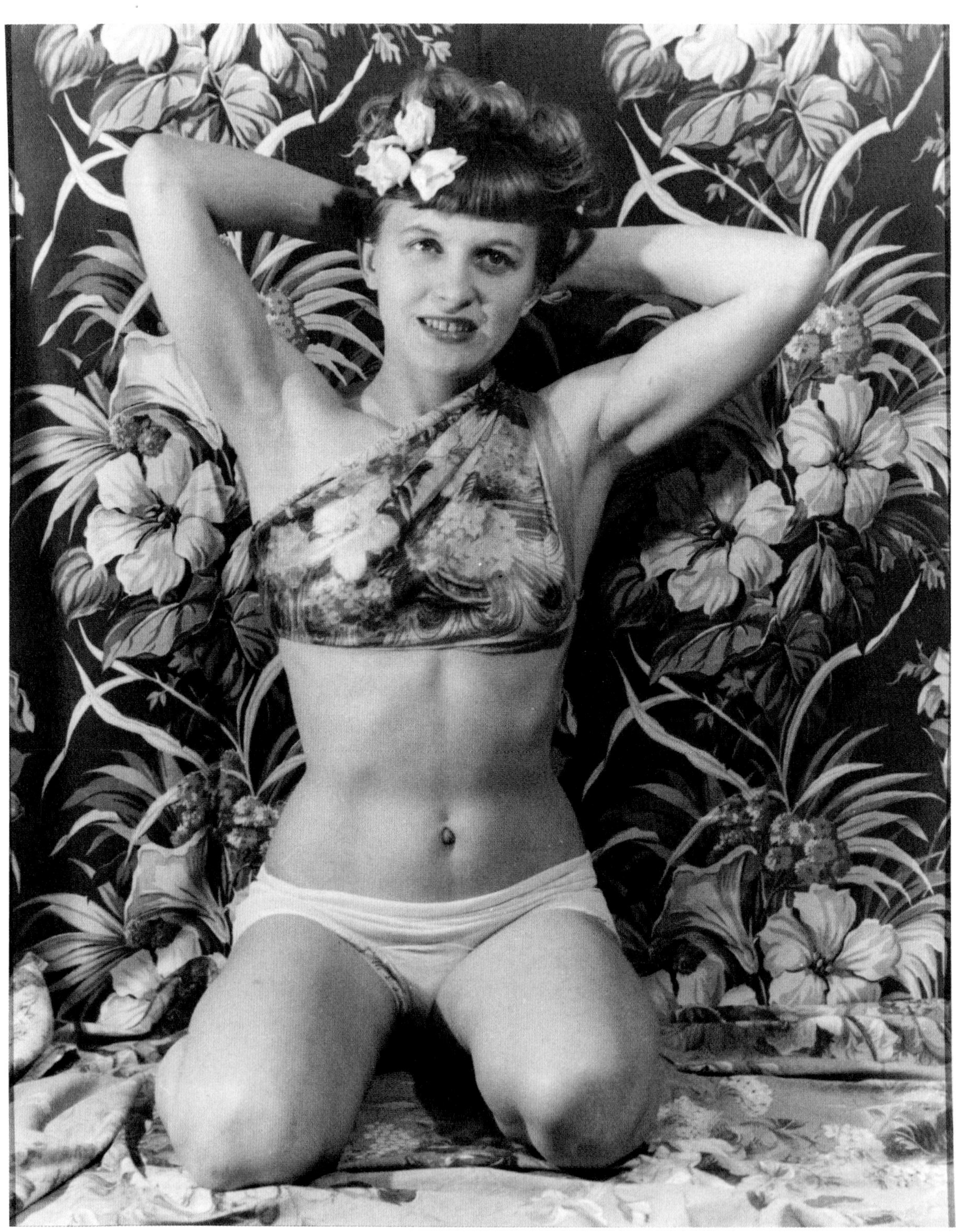

EUGENE VON BRUENCHENHEIN

1910–1983

A bakery worker by day, Eugene Von Bruenchenhein was a photographer, painter, sculptor, and poet by night. Although he had full confidence in his talent (calling himself a "Freelance Artist—Poet and Sculptor—Inovator [*sic*]—Arrow maker and Plant man—Bone artifacts constructor—Photographer and Architect—Philosopher"), his oeuvre was known only to his wife and a few others in his lifetime. He was born in Marinette, Wisconsin, and lived most of his life in Milwaukee, where he met his wife, Evelyn Kalka (ten years his junior), in 1939. They lived modestly in a small house that his father, a sign painter, had built, but their everyday life was rich with imagination. Von Bruenchenhein shot countless erotic photographs of Evelyn, whom he nicknamed "Marie," his muse and queen of the kingdom of their bungalow.

In the portraits, Marie poses in every stage of dress and undress, in ordinary attire or luscious fabrics, with tin crowns, flowers, or Christmas ornaments. Von Bruenchenhein staged and styled the photographs with materials and props at hand, such as densely patterned drapes and quilts for backdrops, and he printed the images in his home darkroom. While some portraits of Marie are dramatic and seductive, others are quotidian and evoke an innocent sensuality. Most are black-and-white, and some are hand-tinted with capricious hues. Although Von Bruenchenhein was influenced by the pinup culture of the 1940s and 1950s, his photographic work—all revolving around Marie—offers something subtler, a convergence of imagination and domesticity, a shared intimacy between wife and husband, both of whom have real presence in the final images.

Von Bruenchenhein never finished high school and was completely self-taught in art. After his mother died when he was seven, his father remarried, and Von Bruenchenhein's stepmother, a former schoolteacher, writer, and painter of floral still lifes, became his mentor. Enormously prolific, he left behind several thousand works, including sculptures made from poultry bones, concrete masks, musical instruments, poetry, prose, and paintings. The latter—which he rendered with his bare fingers, edges of corrugated cardboard, or brushes made from Marie's hair—depict otherworldly landscapes with mysterious plantlike forms and apocalyptic visions evincing his fear and fascination with the Cold War and the nuclear bomb. When Von Bruenchenhein died in January 1983, his home was crammed full with his unseen oeuvre. That same year, Daniel Nycz, a close friend, stirred the interest of the Milwaukee Art Museum in the work, and by September the John Michael Kohler Arts Center in Wisconsin began cataloguing the entire collection. Since then, Von Bruenchenhein's work has been exhibited widely and accessioned into the collections of the Kohler Arts Center (Sheboygan, Wisconsin), the Milwaukee Art Museum, the High Museum of Art (Atlanta), Intuit: The Center for Intuitive and Outsider Art (Chicago), the Los Angeles County Museum of Art, the Smithsonian American Art Museum (Washington, D.C.), the Nelson-Atkins Museum of Art (Kansas City, Missouri), the Philadelphia Museum of Art, the New Orleans Museum of Art, the American Folk Art Museum (New York), and the Collection de l'Art Brut (Lausanne, Switzerland).

Eugene Von Bruenchenhein, *Untitled (Marie with Floral Halter Top, Flower in Hair, Hibiscus Background 1)*, c. 1940s. Gelatin silver print, 3½ × 2½ in. (8.9 × 6.4 cm)

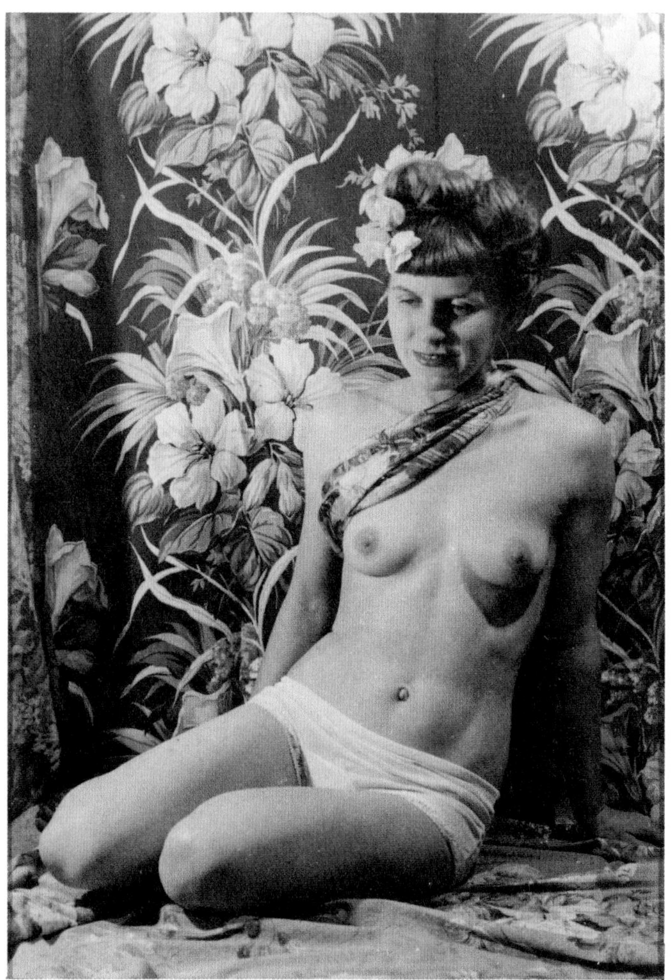

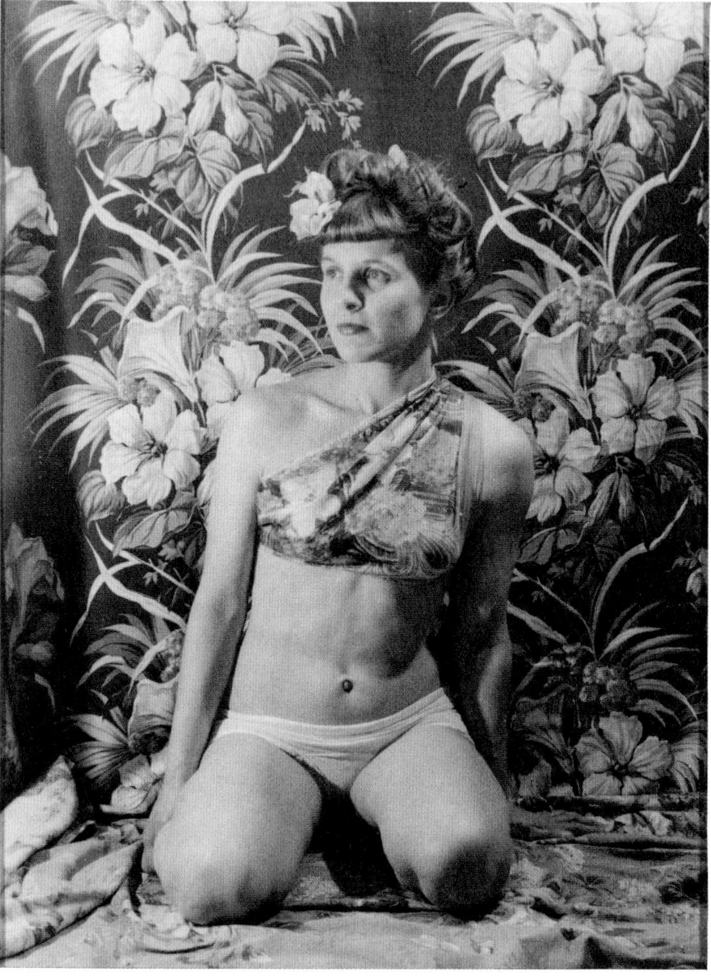

Eugene Von Bruenchenhein, *Untitled (Marie with Floral Halter Top, Flower in Hair, Hibiscus Background 2* and *3)*, c. 1940s. Gelatin silver prints, 3½ × 2½ in. (8.9 × 6.4 cm) each

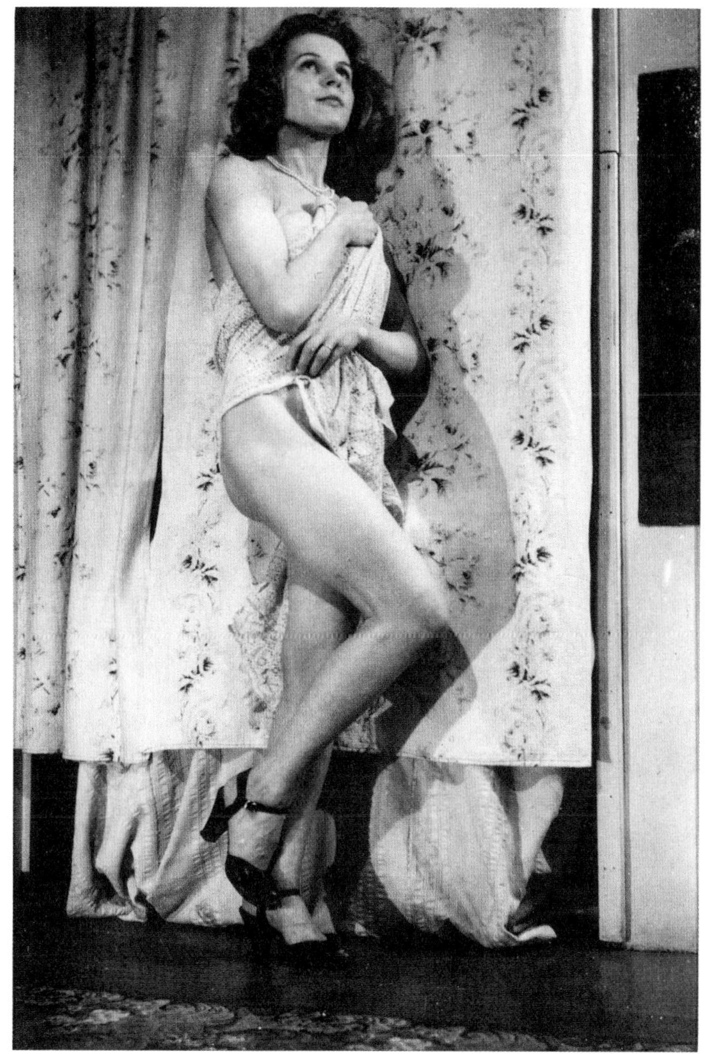

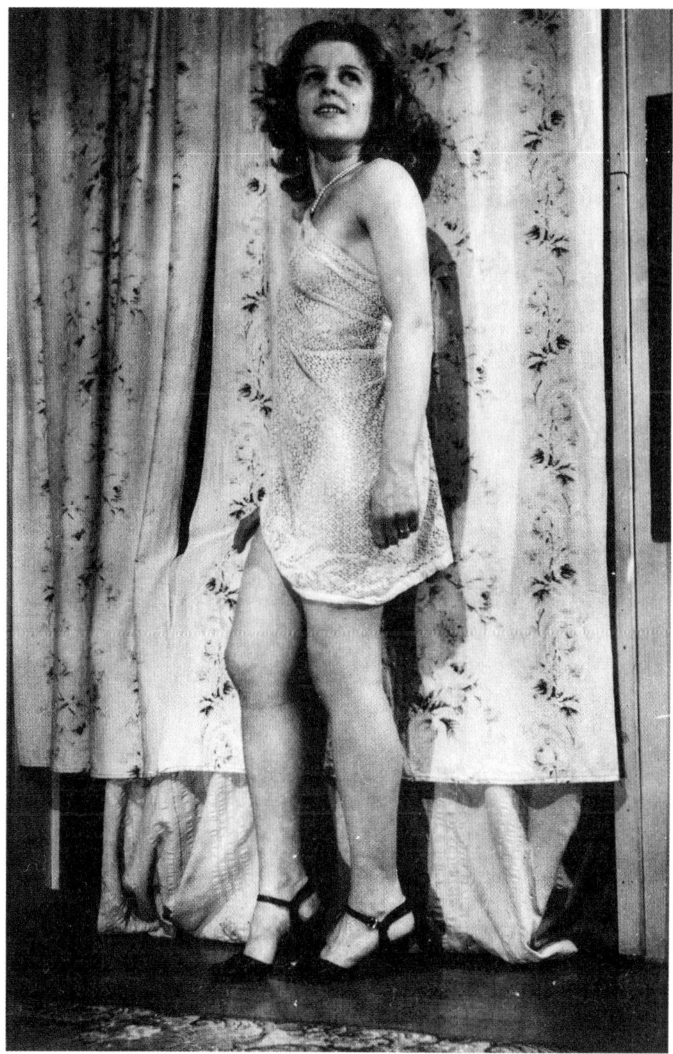

Eugene Von Bruenchenhein, *Untitled (Marie Wearing Lace Tablecloth 1* and *2)*, c. 1940s. Gelatin silver prints, 4 × 2¾ in. (10.2 × 7 cm) each

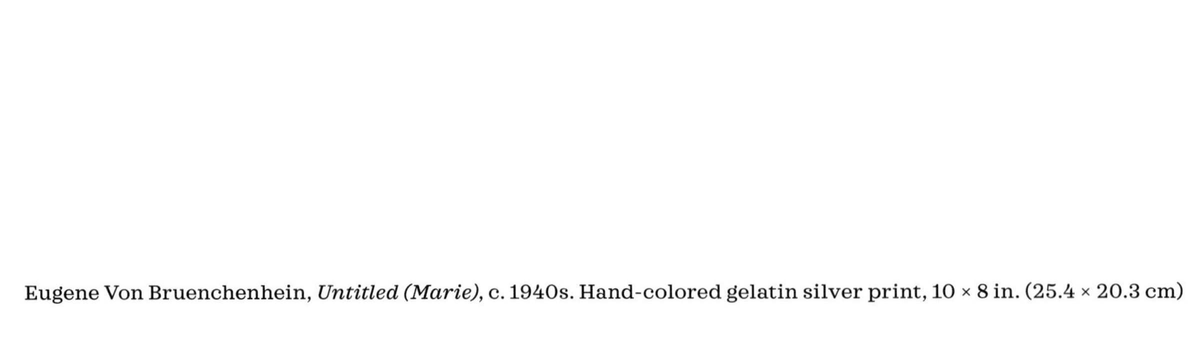

Eugene Von Bruenchenhein, *Untitled (Marie)*, c. 1940s. Hand-colored gelatin silver print, 10 × 8 in. (25.4 × 20.3 cm)

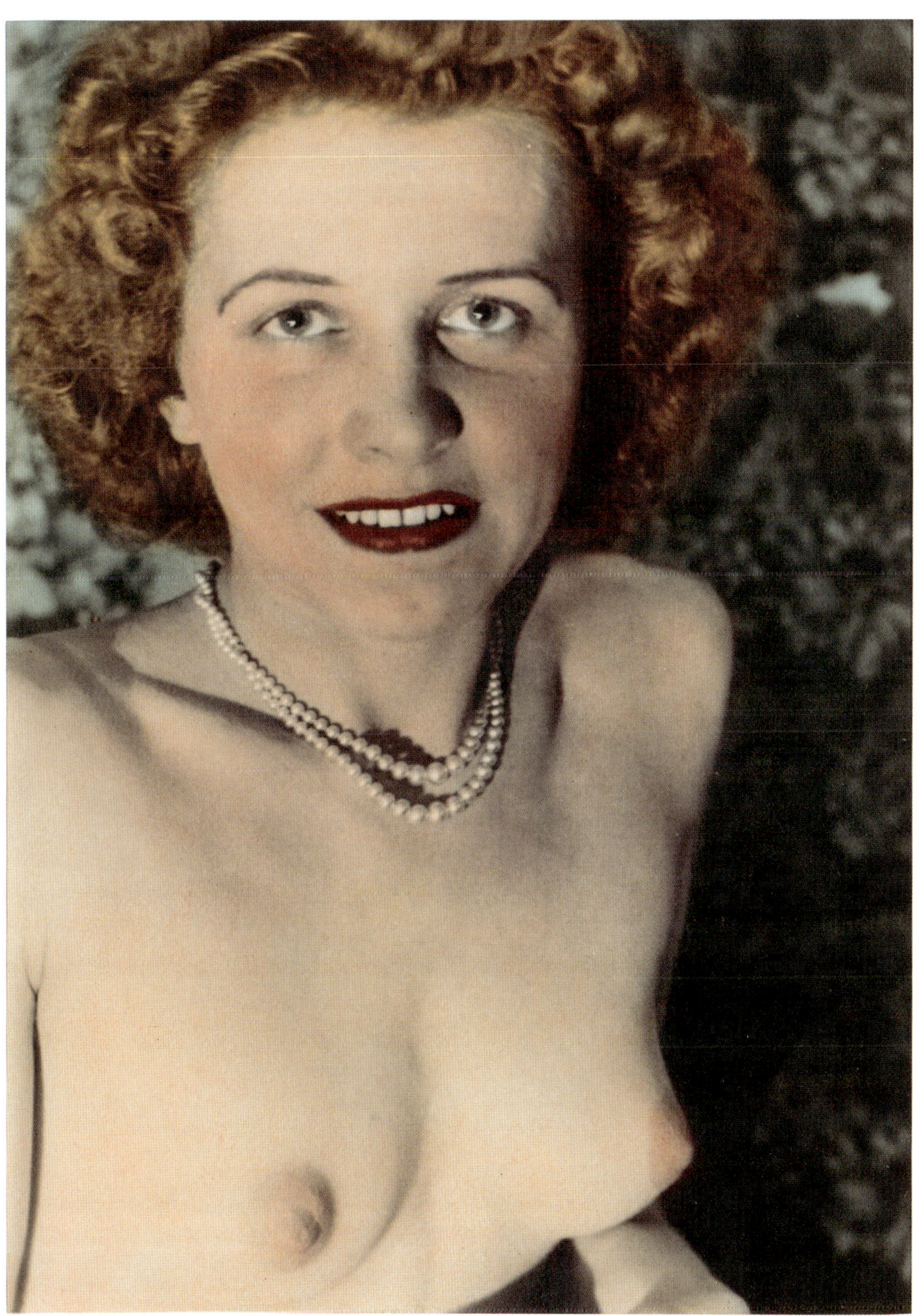

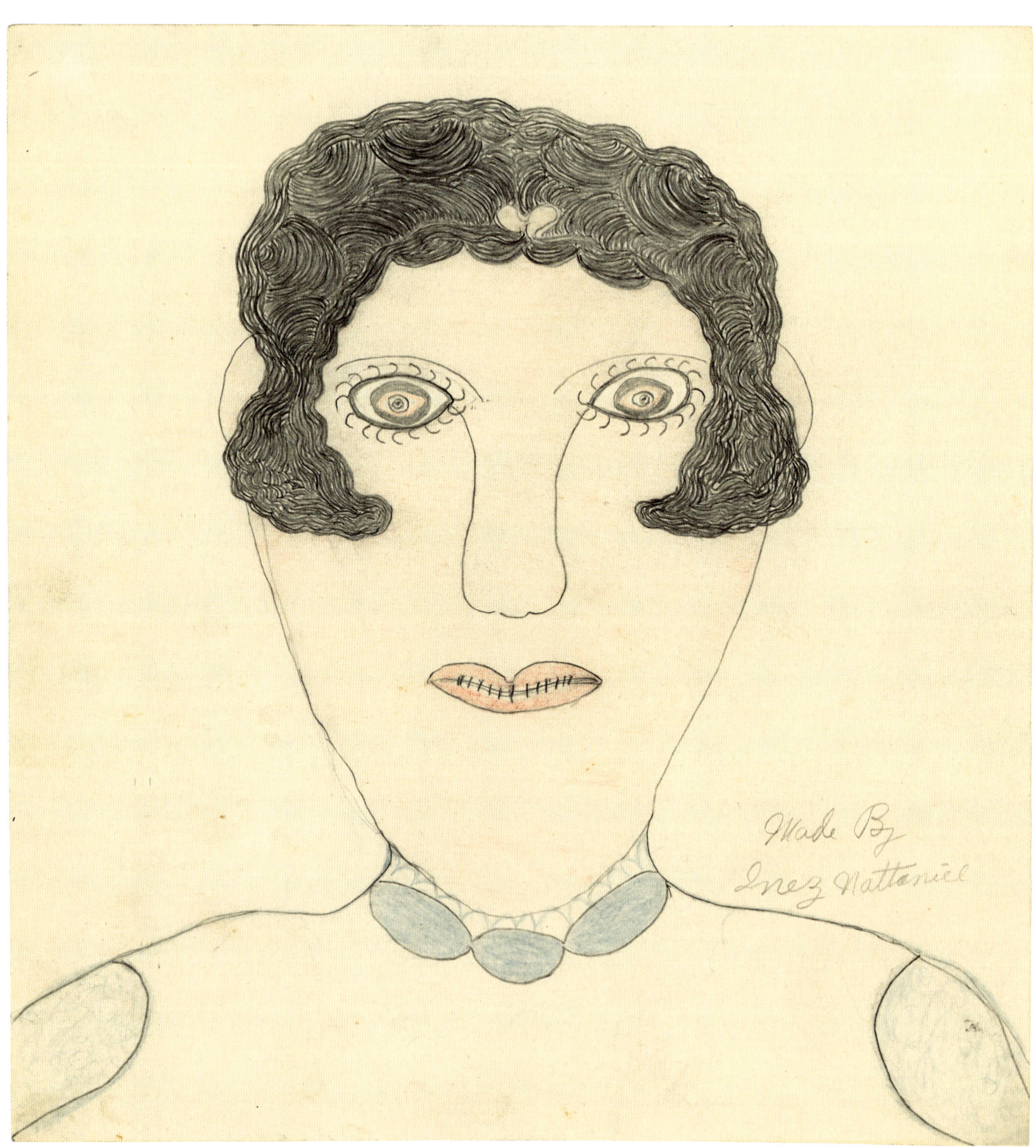
Made By
Inez Nathaniel

INEZ NATHANIEL WALKER

1911–1990

Born into poverty in Sumter, South Carolina, Inez Nathaniel Walker (née Stedman) had been orphaned as a young child. At sixteen she married and had four children. To escape the harsh world of farm labor, in the 1930s she joined the Great Migration and moved to Philadelphia and then in the 1940s to New York state, where she lived in a number of different towns over the years, working menial jobs.

In 1971 Inez Nathaniel (Walker, after she remarried in 1975) began making art at the Bedford Hills Correctional Facility in Westchester County, New York, where she was incarcerated for two years for killing a man who had abused her. When a remedial English teacher in the penitentiary, Elizabeth Bayley, found a stack of nearly eighty unsigned drawings left in her classroom, she discovered they were made by her student Inez Nathaniel. Bayley asked to buy the drawings, encouraged her to continue drawing, and soon the art teacher of the prison gave her paper and drawing supplies. By the time Walker was released from prison in 1972, she had become enormously prolific and had caught the attention of a local folk art dealer, Pat Parsons, who began to bring her better art supplies and organized her first exhibition that same year.

Her early drawings were made on the back of prison newsletters, evaluation forms, and the like, using graphite, pens, and crayons; her later works are made with watercolor, ink, and felt-tip pens on high-quality paper. Her drawings are mostly portraits of women and self-portraits. Her subjects' heads, with detailed hair and sometimes hats, are always the most detailed part of her work, along with distinctively large eyes framed with curly lashes, which always face the viewer, even in profile portraits. Even if creating a true likeness eluded her, Walker was gifted at conveying a person's essence.

After she remarried, Walker lived in New York's Finger Lakes region and devoted herself to making art, welcoming visitors to see her work. Almost every significant anthology and catalogue documenting the work of African American folk and self-taught artists in the United States includes her work, among them: *Museum of American Folk Art Encyclopedia of Twentieth-Century Folk Art and Artists* and *Contemporary American Folk Art: A Collectors Guide* (both by Chuck Rosenak and Jan Rosenak), *Black Folk Art in America 1930–1980* (Jane Livingston, John Beardsley, and Regenia Perry), and *American Folk Art of the Twentieth Century* (Jay Johnson and William Ketchum). Her work is in the collections of the American Folk Art Museum (New York), the Museum of International Folk Art (Santa Fe, New Mexico), the Smithsonian American Art Museum (Washington, D.C.), and the Collection de l'Art Brut (Lausanne, Switzerland).

Inez Nathaniel Walker, *Untitled (Portrait of a Woman)*, n.d. Graphite and colored pencil on paper, 12 × 11 in. (30.5 × 27.9 cm)

Inez Nathaniel Walker, *Man with Goatee*, 1977. Ink and colored pencil on paper, 18 × 12 in. (45.7 × 30.5 cm)

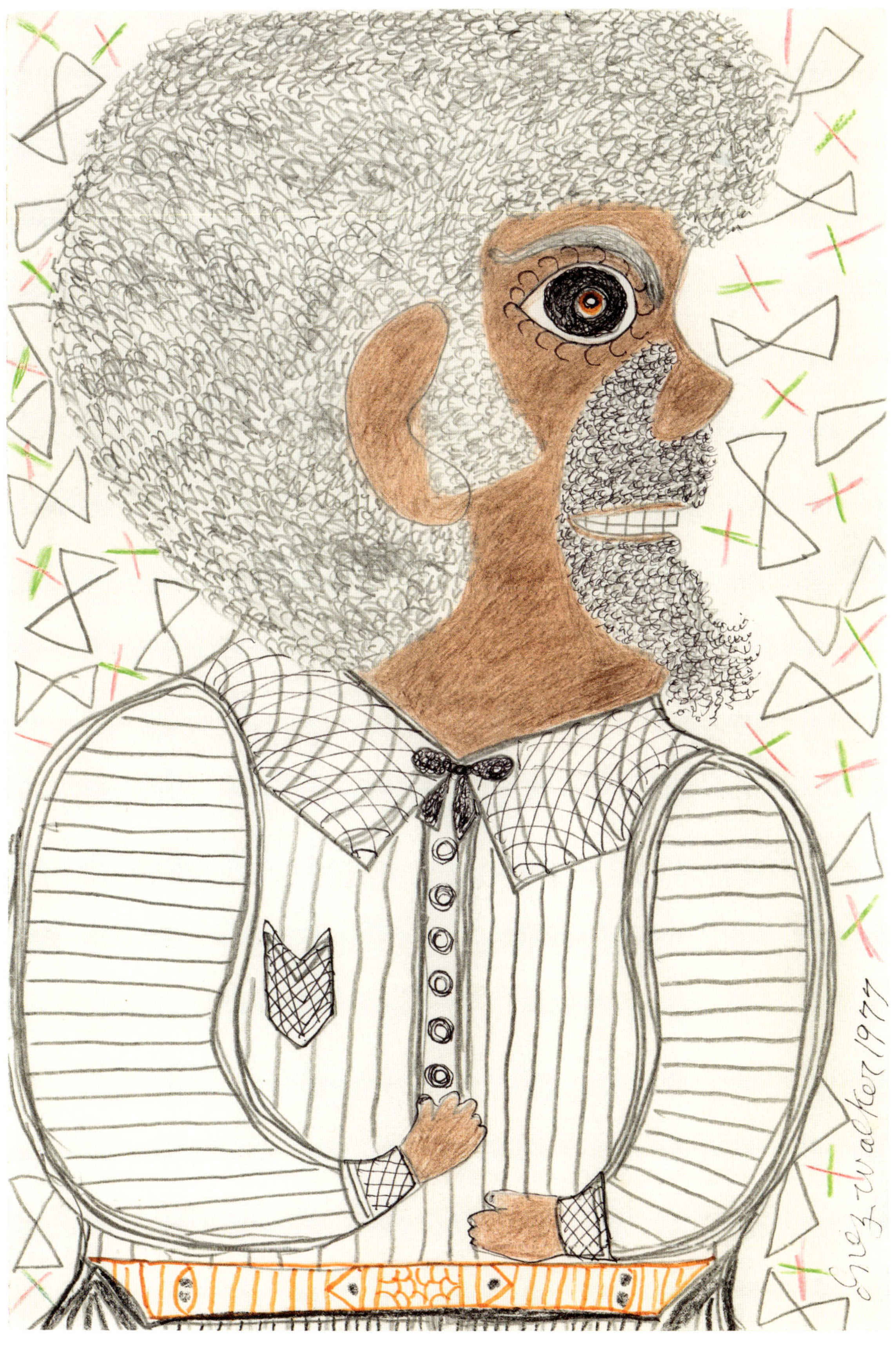
Grez-walker 1977

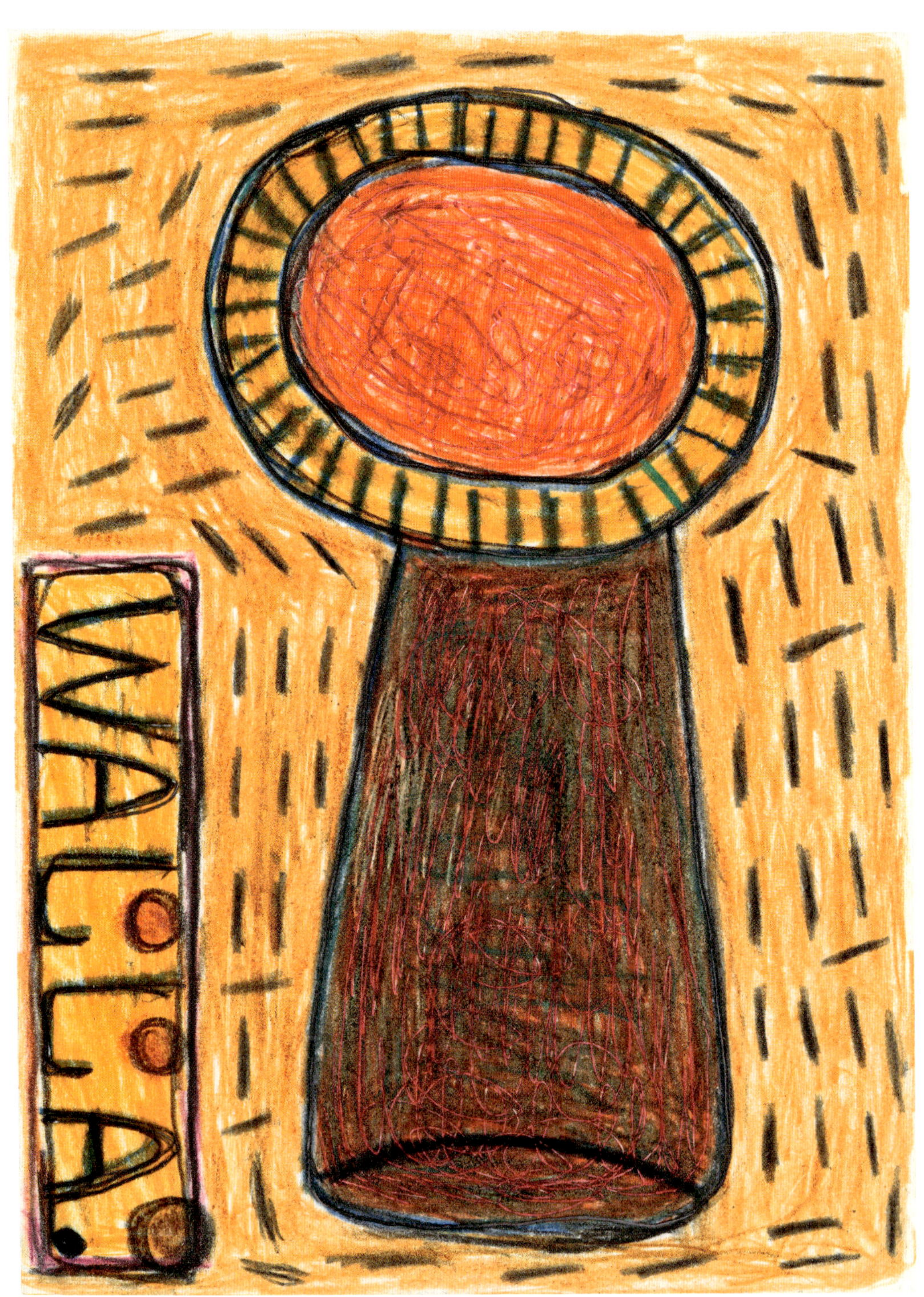

AUGUST WALLA

1936–2001

August Walla is one of the most well known artists to have resided at the Gugging House of Artists' (see p. 143). His artistic compulsion extended beyond customary pictorial surfaces, and he drew and painted on everything his world had to offer: walls, ceilings, furniture, trees, among many other objects.

Walla was born in Klosterneuburg, near Vienna, Austria. His father died when Walla was young and his unwed mother left him for a time under the care of her mother. He was creative at an early age, playing alone for hours and constructing figures of people and animals out of paper. Walla was diagnosed with schizophrenia and committed to a mental institution at age sixteen after threatening suicide and trying to set the house afire.

From 1941 to 1945 he was in various institutions, including Am Spiegelgrund Clinic in Vienna; in 1945, he came to live again with his mother. They lived in a small apartment and spent summers in a cottage by the Danube, which he decorated with paintings and murals combining emblems and words. Walla first went to the Maria Gugging Psychiatric Clinic in 1970 and was treated by Dr. Leo Navratil, who visited the cottage and was captivated by his talent. By 1983, when the Wallas had lost their apartment, Navratil and Johann Feilacher offered a room at Gugging for Walla and his mother to share. Later, Walla was moved to the House of Artists, where he remained until his death.

Walla constructed objects from found materials and painted on canvas and paper, as well as bottles, ceramics, cans, wooden planks, and even public roadways. His densely packed compositions are filled with abstract figurative imagery, symbols, emblems, and words (sometimes of his own invention, from using many foreign language dictionaries) drawn in bold calligraphy. Walla did not speak much but kept a written and photographic log that documented his relentless creative activity. The walls and ceiling of his former room at the House of Artists, left uninhabited as a tribute to his legacy, remain covered by layers of his paintings.

Walla is considered to be a classic example of art brut and his work can be found in the abcd Collection (Paris), the Arnulf Rainer Collection (Vienna), the Collection de l'Art Brut (Lausanne, Switzerland), the Art/Brut Center at Gugging (Vienna), the Irish Museum of Modern Art (Dublin), the Lille Métropole Museum of Modern, Contemporary and Outsider Art (Villeneuve d'Ascq, France), the Musée de la Création Franche (Bègles, France), Intuit: The Center for Intuitive and Outsider Art (Chicago), and the Milwaukee Art Museum.

August Walla, *1 Red Brittlegill*, 2000. Colored pencil on paper, 5⅞ × 4 in. (14.9 × 10.1 cm)

August Walla, *(Salz.?)* *(Salt.?)*, 2001. Colored pencil on paper, 5⅞ × 4 in. (14.9 × 10.1 cm)

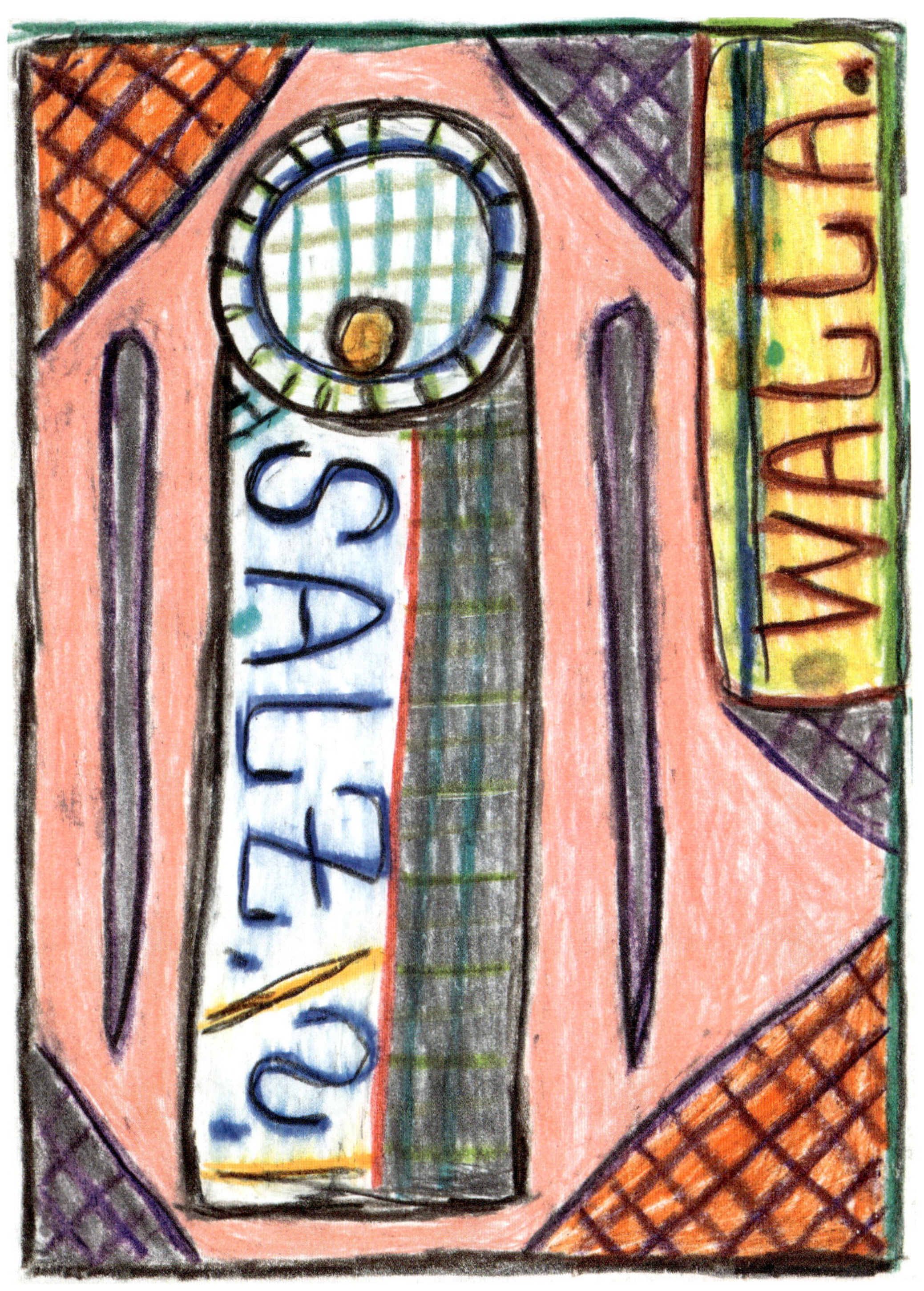
SALZ,?
WALLA

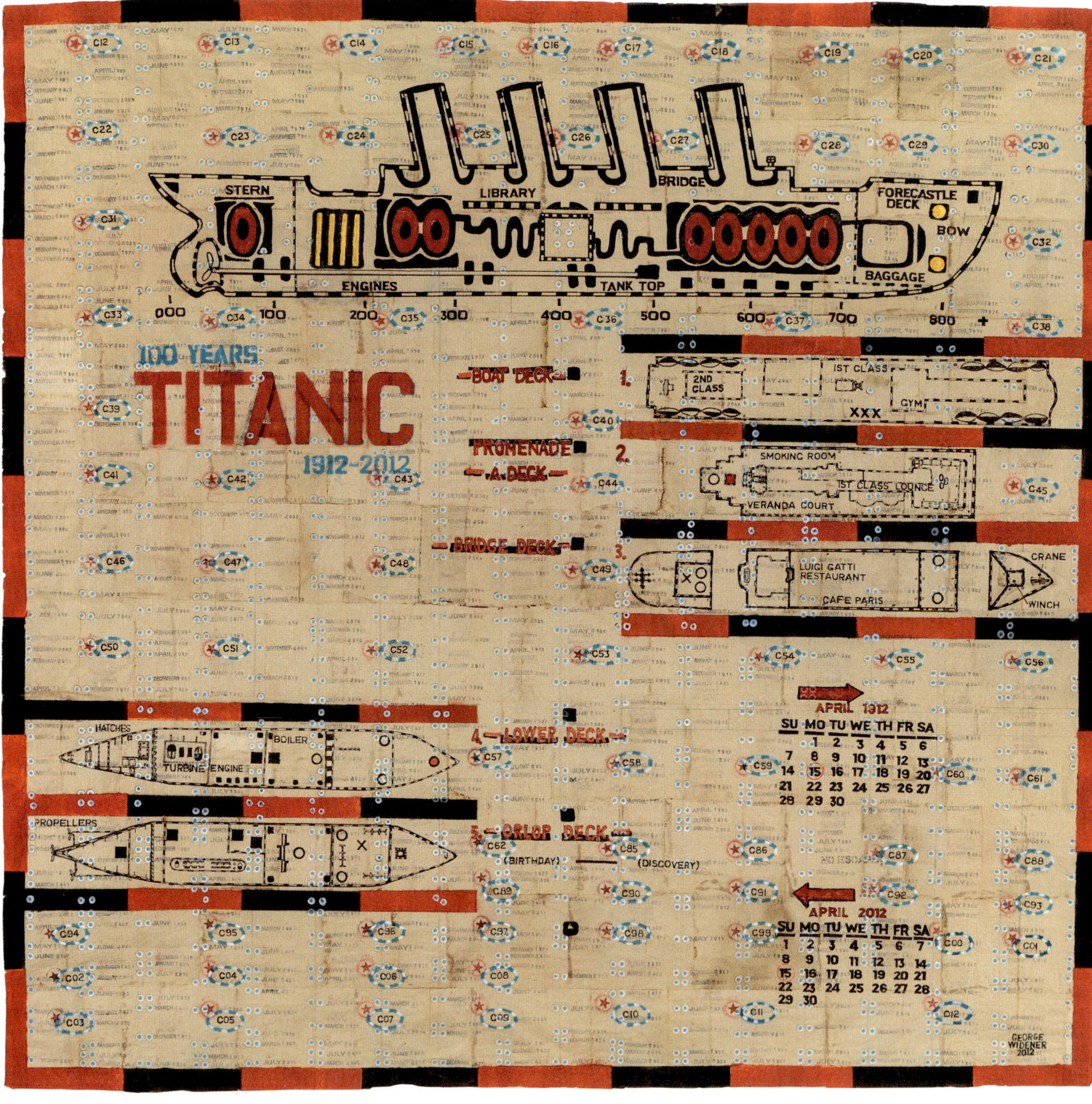

STERN
LIBRARY
BRIDGE
FORECASTLE DECK
BOW
BAGGAGE
ENGINES
TANK TOP
000 100 200 300 400 500 600 700 800
100 YEARS
TITANIC
1912–2012
BOAT DECK
1.
2ND CLASS
1ST CLASS
GYM
XXX
PROMENADE
A DECK
2.
SMOKING ROOM
1ST CLASS LOUNGE
VERANDA COURT
BRIDGE DECK
3.
LUIGI GATTI RESTAURANT
CAFE PARIS
CRANE
WINCH
HATCHES
BOILER
TURBINE ENGINE
4. LOWER DECK
PROPELLERS
5. ORLOP DECK
(BIRTHDAY)
(DISCOVERY)
APRIL 1912
SU MO TU WE TH FR SA
1 2 3 4 5 6
7 8 9 10 11 12 13
14 15 16 17 18 19 20
21 22 23 24 25 26 27
28 29 30
APRIL 2012
SU MO TU WE TH FR SA
1 2 3 4 5 6 7
8 9 10 11 12 13 14
15 16 17 18 19 20 21
22 23 24 25 26 27 28
29 30
GEORGE WIDENER 2012

GEORGE WIDENER

b. 1962

"Functional MRI have shown that my brain is wired slightly differently; it seems to have unusual activity that results in some innate math, memory, and drawing skills. I've calculated dates and specific number systems since I was a child. I'd see common numbers around me (a license plate, a house number) and immediately transform them into dates," remembers George Widener about his early experience as an odd and gifted child. Widener was born in Cincinnati, Ohio, and although he had an outstanding ability with numbers, his childhood was marked by awkward social behavior. At eighteen he enlisted in the U.S. Air Force, where he worked as a technician for four years and then did some college coursework in mechanical engineering until mental breakdowns and financial difficulties caused him to drop out. Around this time, he became obsessed with historical dates and automatic memory drawing and focused solely on creating a counting system that he documented in notebooks, making drawings for more than a decade before anyone saw them. For a time he slept in shelters and worked in the library on his project during the day, and then decided to travel the world on a very limited budget, visiting more than seventy countries. In the late 1990s Widener was diagnosed with Asperger's syndrome and enrolled in a Tennessee State vocational rehabilitation program, where he was discovered and introduced to the art world.

Widener uses found and pieced paper or a support composed of layers of tea-stained paper napkins to create mixed-media works with bold color palettes and intricate patterning. His innate ability in drawing materializes in conjunction with his preoccupation with the space/time continuum, possible numerical systems, and mind games based on historical events and dates. The sinking of the *Titanic* has been a fixation since he discovered that a George D. Widener from Philadelphia and his son died on the ship. "The subject of my work is that of time and, more precisely, the shifting and symmetry of time—which I believe occupy every individual's subconscious," says the artist, adding: "I believe that truths are often revealed in unexpected divergent events, the past and the future are joined in subtle ways. I've been interested in disasters as an anthropology project of sorts." Lately, Widener has been exploring the concept of magic squares (grids of integers in which all rows and columns add up to an identical sum) to create "magic time squares" where integers are replaced with dates that not only add up to an identical sum but reflect a common theme. "For example, I might fit natural disasters to the above magic square and find hurricanes that not only fit the integers but also occurred on Fridays," says Widener. The resulting "Magic Circles" series reflects Widener's interest in the future development of artificial intelligence, looking forward to a future when machines will become a new species with higher creative intelligence and humans will be enhanced with skills that seem improbable today. The magic circles would thus be a form of recreation, allowing the user to "program" them by choosing a specific theme and then fitting the provided days of the week

George Widener, *Titanic, 100 Years, 1912–2012*, 2012. Paint and ink on joined paper, 60 × 60 in. (152.4 × 152.4 cm)

with appropriate dates, creating “crossdate” or “crosstime” puzzles.

Widener is today highly visible in the contemporary art arena and has had significant film and media exposure: he was a subject in the documentary film *My Brilliant Brain: Accidental Genius* (2007) and was profiled in the last episode of *Ingenious Minds*, a six-part series of films focusing on savants and geniuses, which aired on the Discovery Science Channel (2011). His work has been exhibited extensively worldwide, including *Hiding Places: Memory in the Arts* (John Michael Kohler Arts Center, 2011), *The Alternative Guide to the Universe* (Hayward Gallery, London 2012), and *Secret Universe* (Hamburger Bahnhof, Berlin 2013). His work is in the collections of the Smithsonian American Art Museum (Washington, D.C.), the Philadelphia Museum of Art, the High Museum of Art (Atlanta), the American Folk Art Museum (New York), the Collection de l’Art Brut (Lausanne, Switzerland), the Kröller-Müller Museum (Otterlo, Netherlands), the Treger Saint Silvestre Collection (São João da Madeira, Portugal), the abcd Collection (Paris), and the Hamburger Bahnhof National Museum (Berlin).

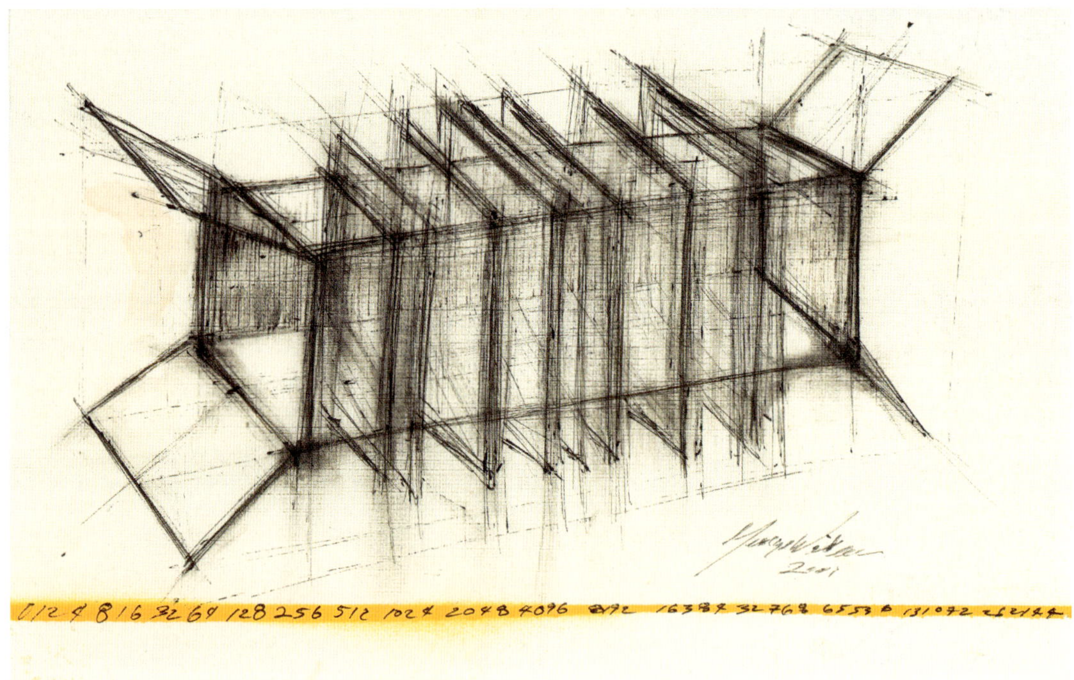

George Widener, *Untitled*, 2001. Ink on paper, 3¾ × 9 in. (9.5 × 22.9 cm)

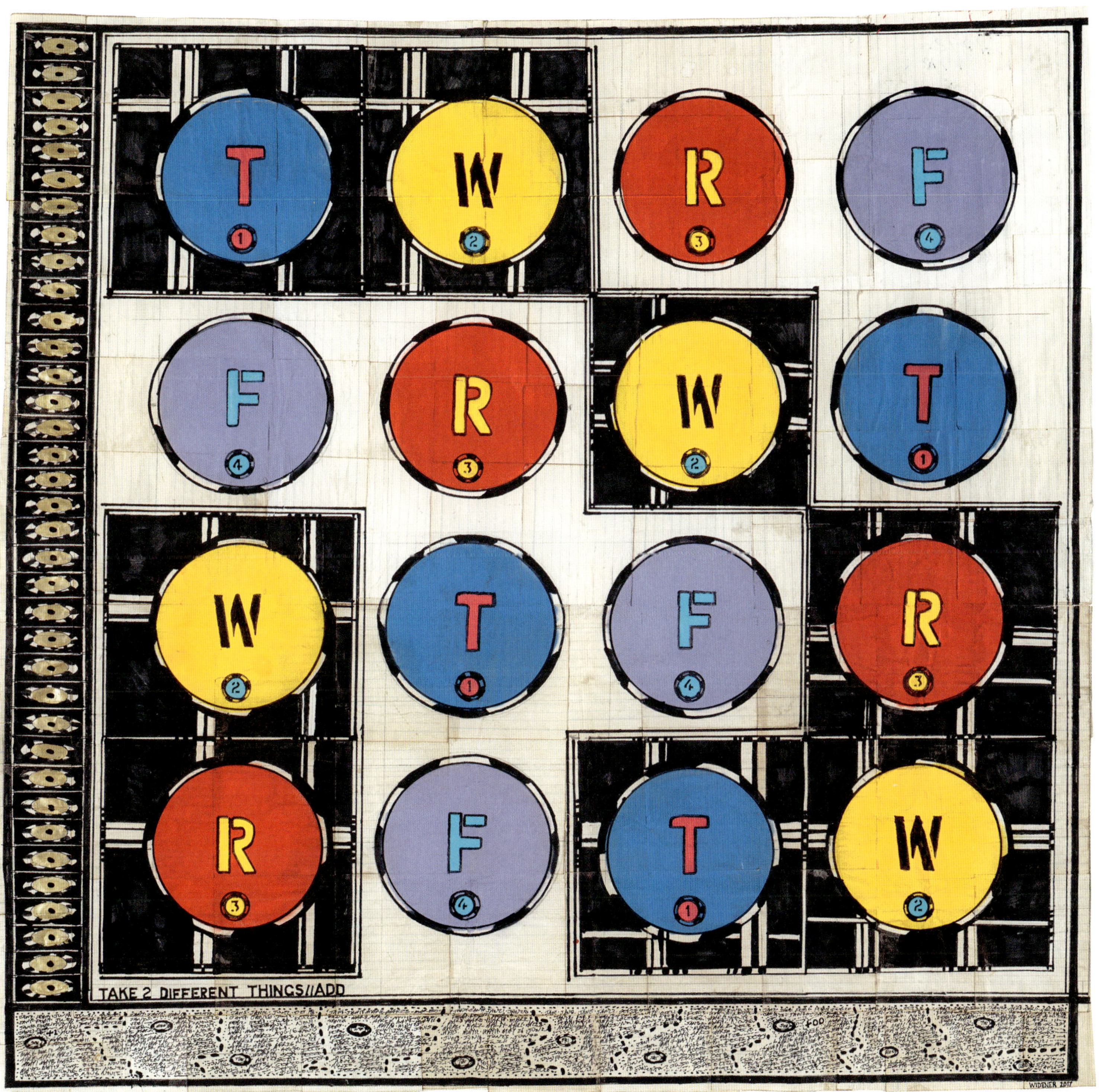

George Widener, *Magic Circles*, 2017. Mixed media on joined paper, 39 × 39 in. (99.1 × 99.1 cm)

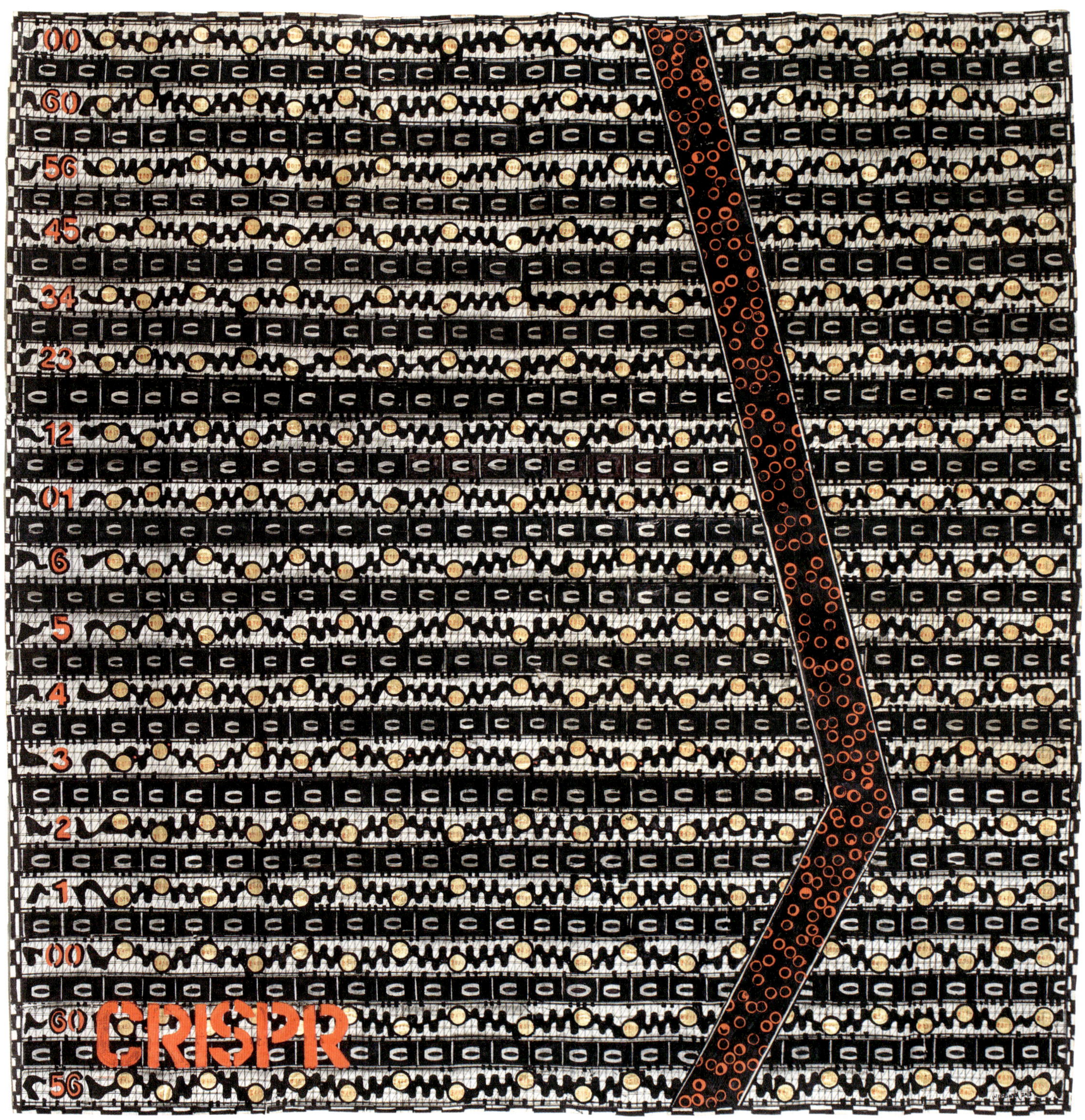

George Widener, *CRISPR No. 2*, 2015. Ink and paint on joined paper, 50 × 48 in. (127 × 121.9 cm)

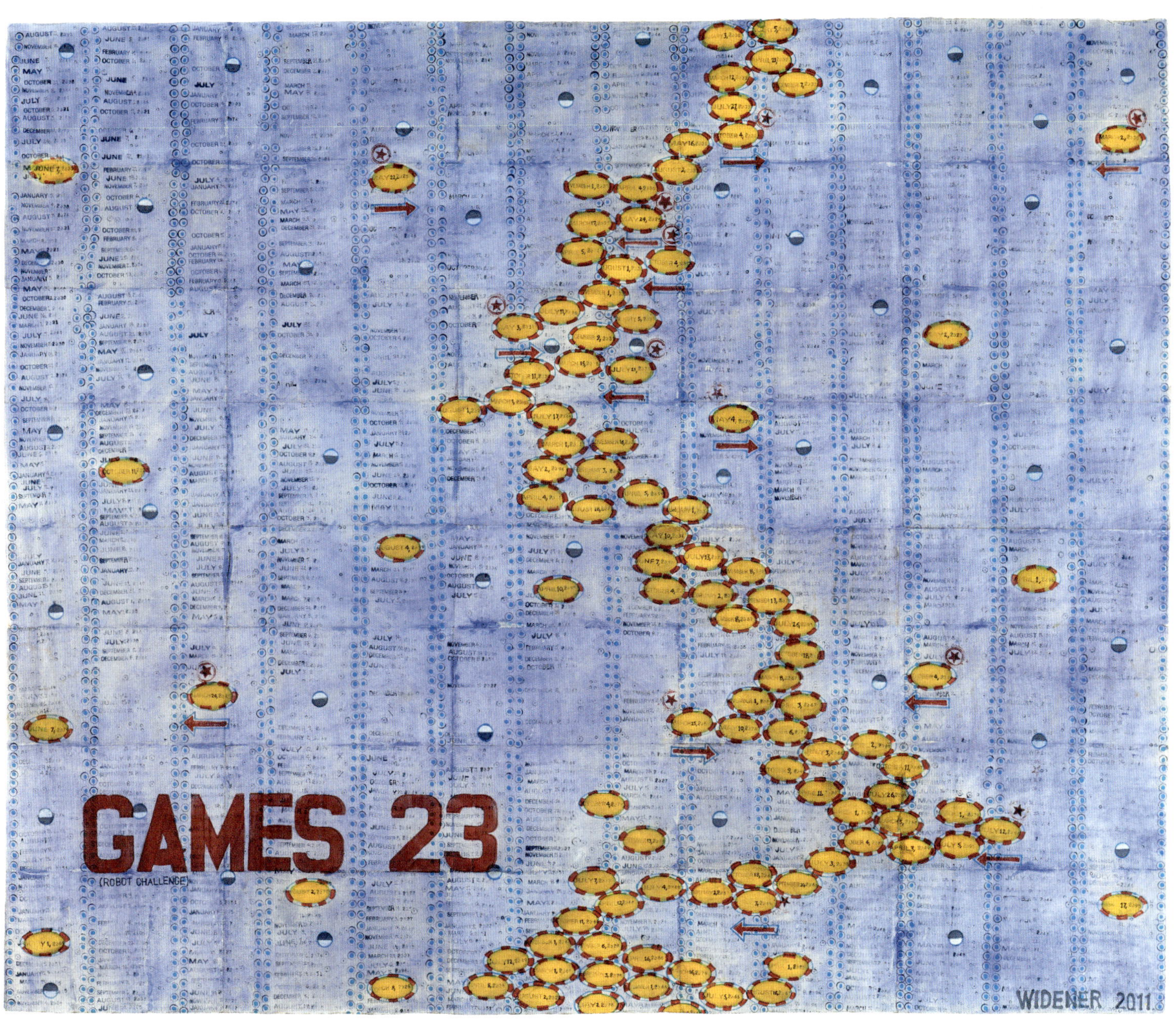

George Widener, *Games 23*, 2011. Ink and paint on joined paper, 49 × 56½ in. (124.5 × 143.5 cm)

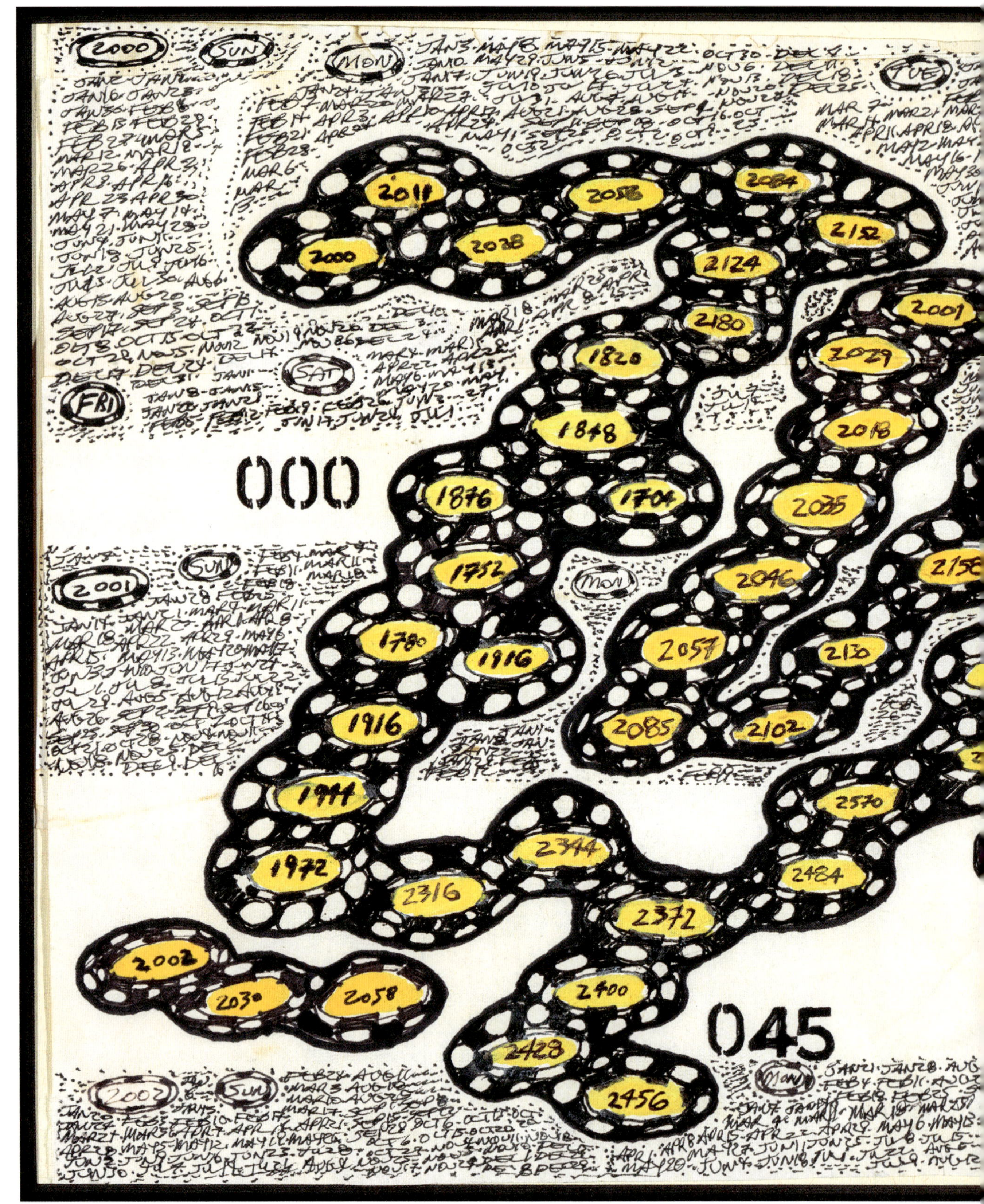

George Widener, *Untitled*, 2012. Ink and paint on joined paper, 8½ × 14½ in. (21.6 × 36.8 cm)

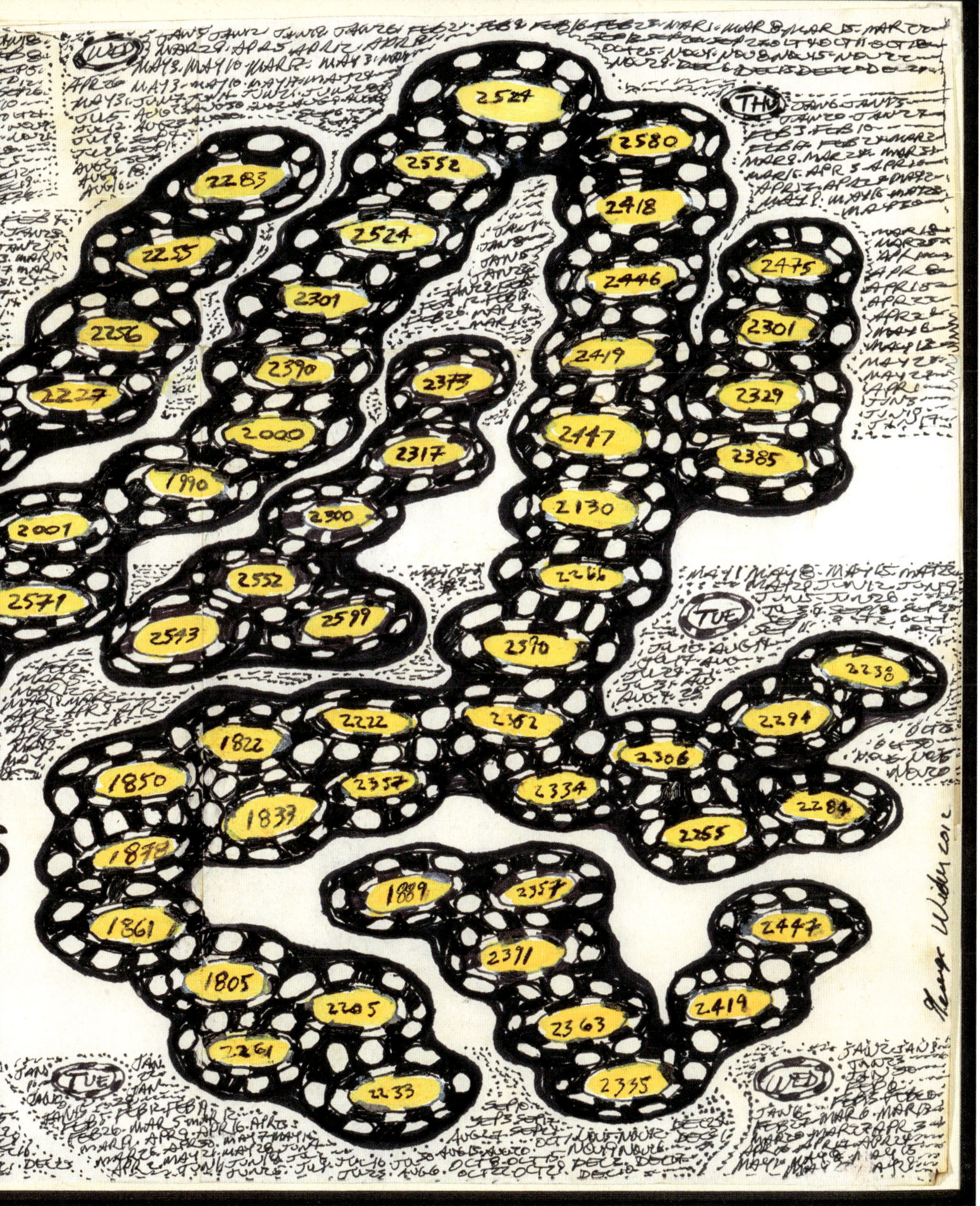
WED
THU
TUE
TUE
WED
2524
2580
2552
2283
2418
2524
2255
2446
2475
2301
2301
2256
2419
2390
2373
2329
2227
2447
2000
2317
2385
1990
2130
2300
2001
2552
2571
2599
2543
2370
2238
2222
2382
2294
1822
2306
1850
2357
2334
1833
2284
2255
1889
2357
1861
2447
2391
1805
2205
2419
2363
2261
2335
2233

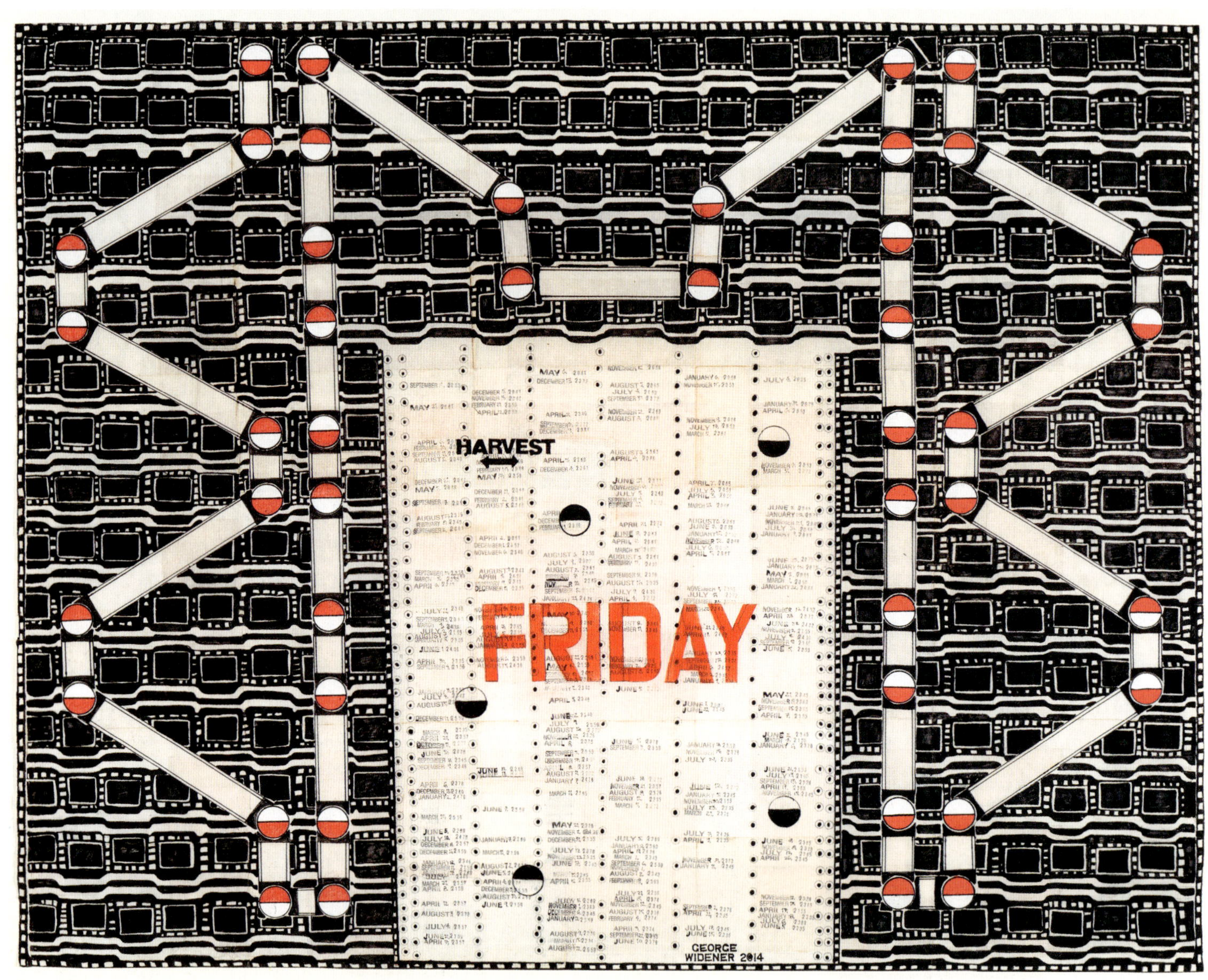

George Widener, *Harvest*, 2014. Mixed media on joined paper, 47½ × 59½ in. (120.7 × 151.1 cm)

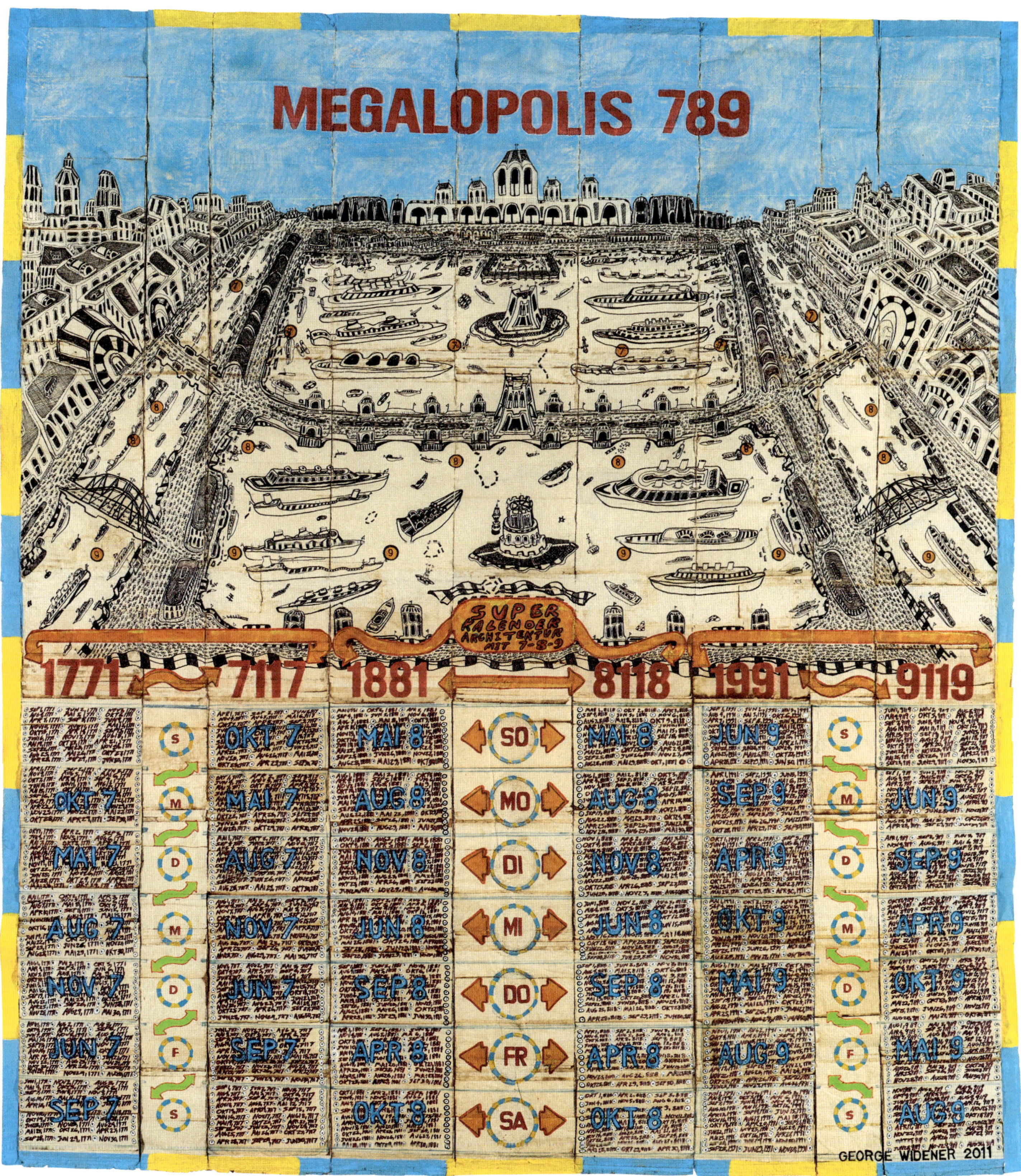

George Widener, *Megalopolis 789*, 2011. Mixed media on joined paper, 66 × 55 in. (167.6 × 139.7 cm)

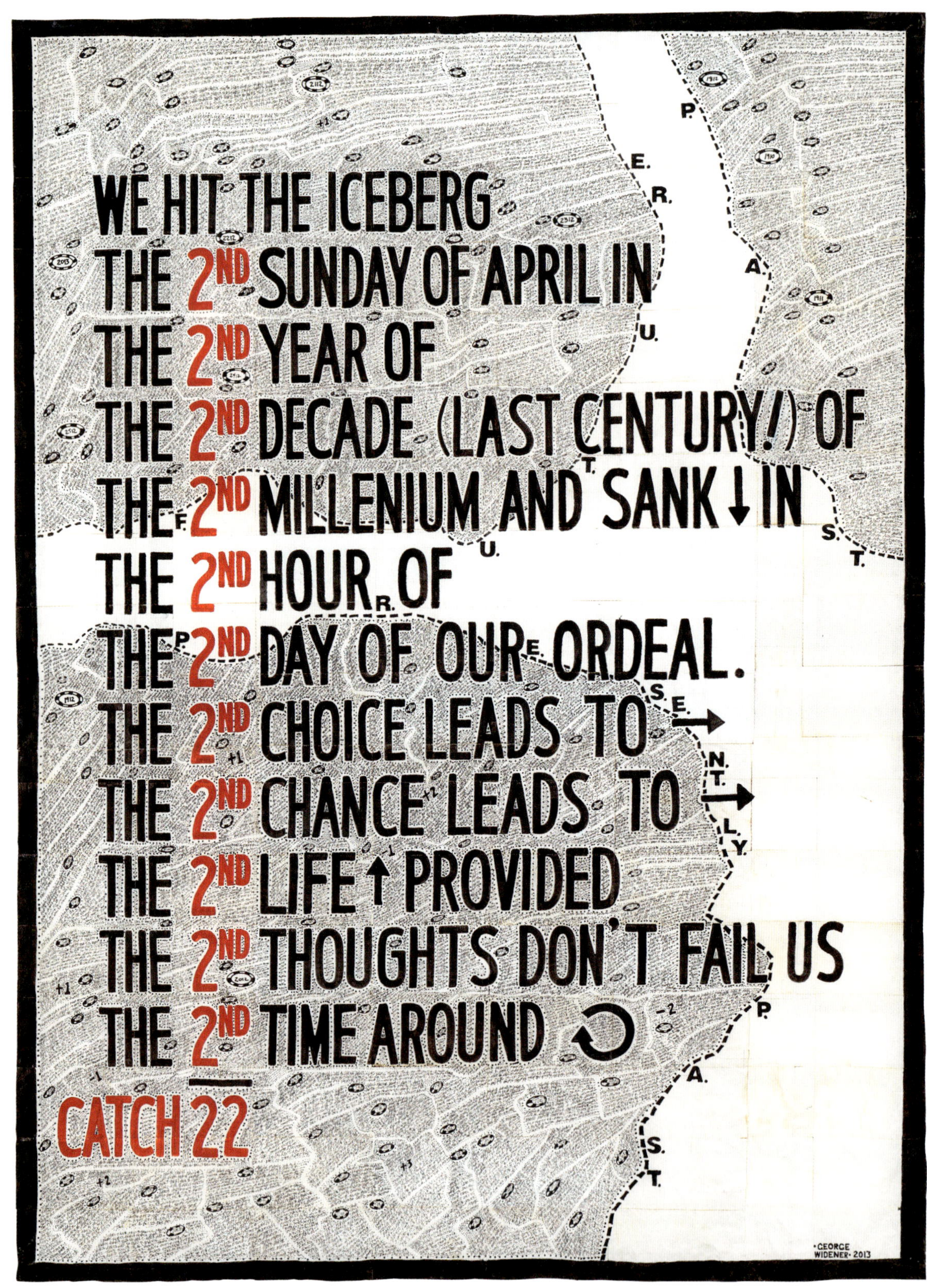

George Widener, *CATCH 22*, 2013. Mixed media on joined paper, 83½ × 59 in. (212.1 × 149.9 cm)

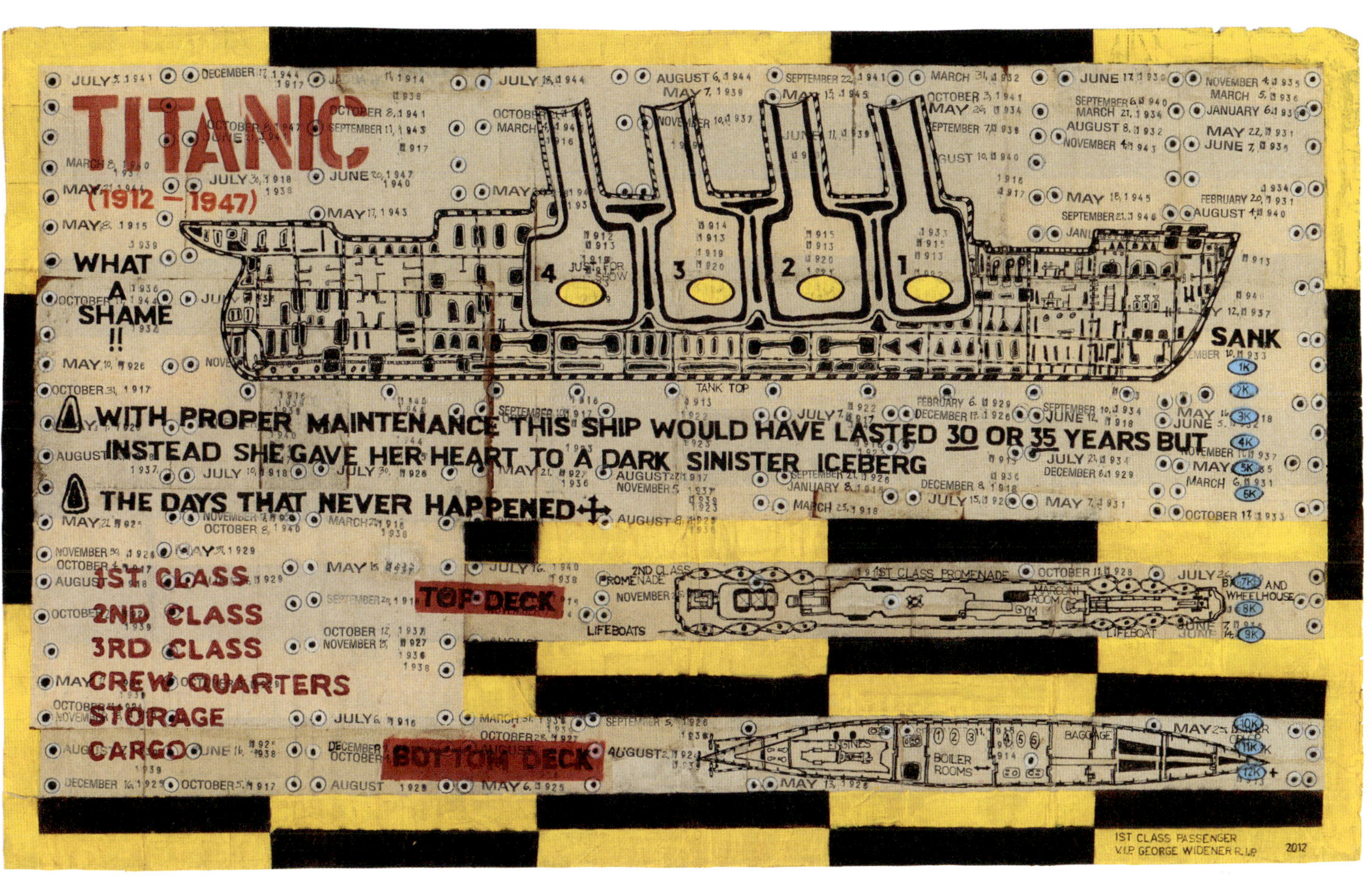

George Widener, *TITANIC (1912–1947)*, 2012. Ink and acrylic on joined paper (napkins), 22½ × 36 in. (57.2 × 91.4 cm)

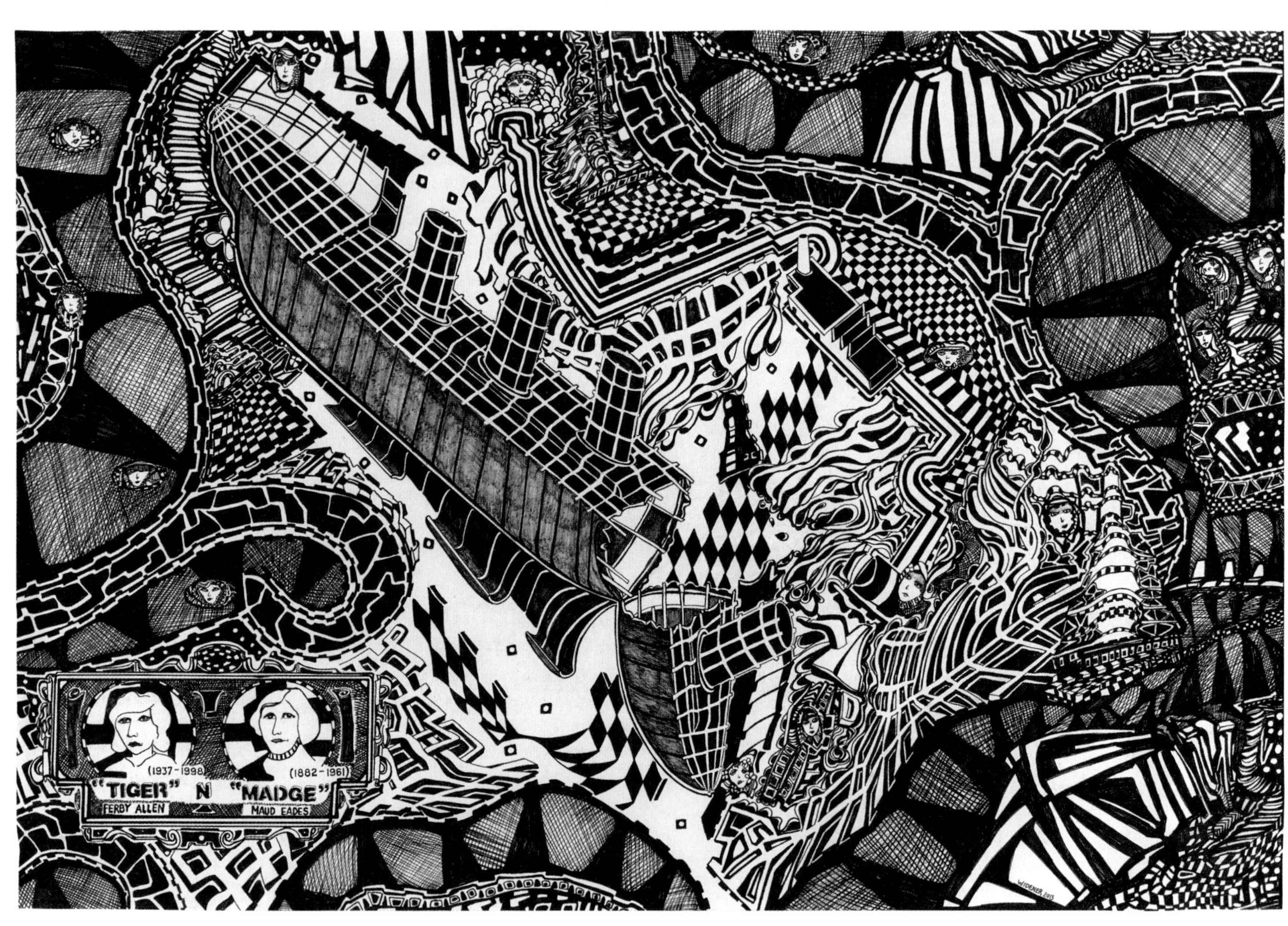

George Widener, *“TIGER” N “MADGE,”* 2013. Ink on paper, 48 × 68 in. (121.9 × 172.7 cm)

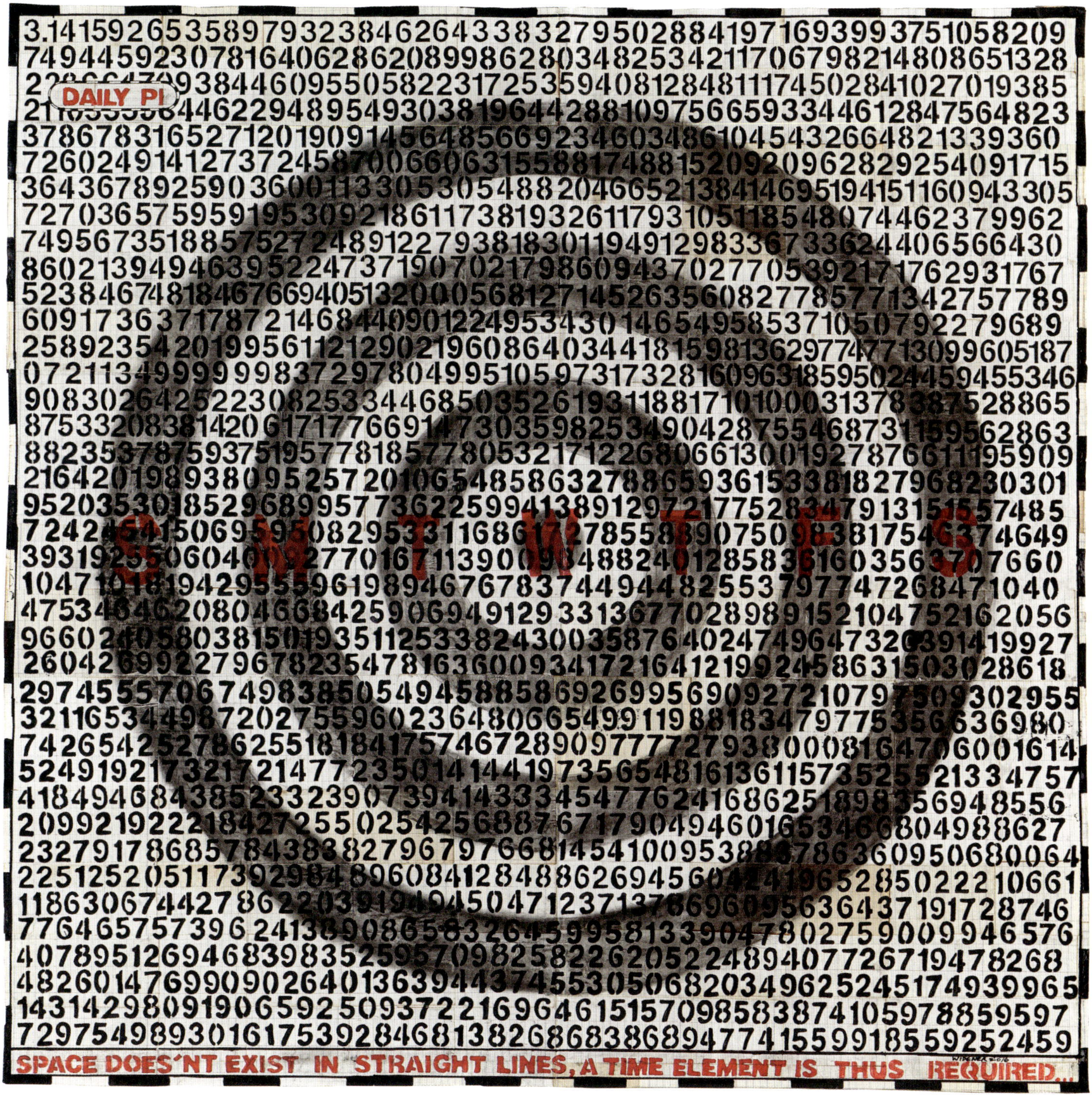

George Widener, *PI Target*, 2016. Ink on paper, 41¼ × 41 in. (104.8 × 104 cm)

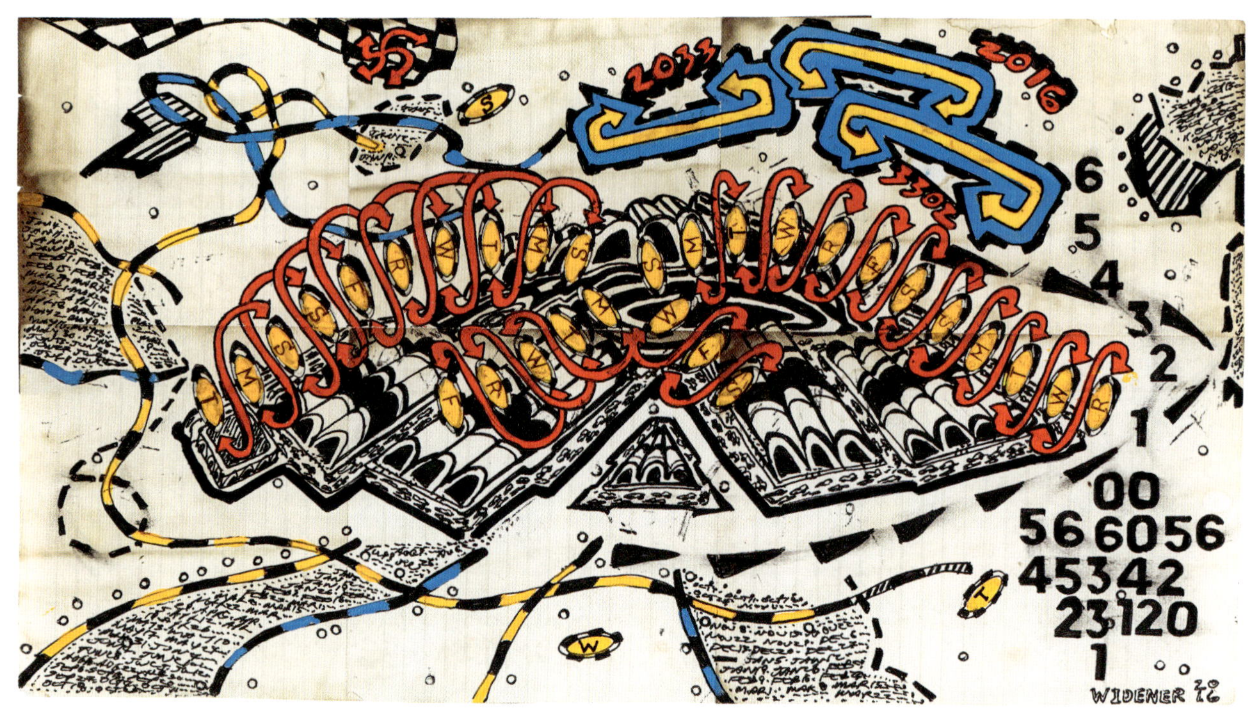

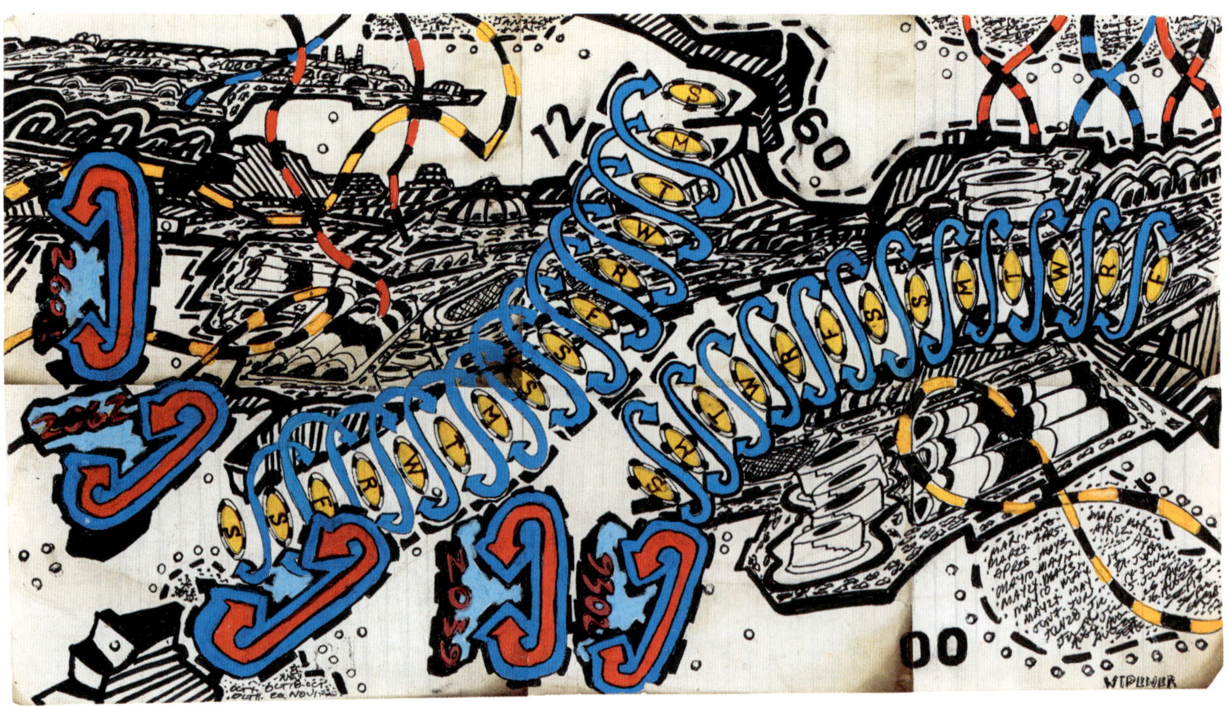

ABOVE AND OPPOSITE: George Widener, *Work in 8 Parts* (four of eight), 2016. Ink on paper, 9 × 16⅛ in. (22.8 × 40.9 cm) each

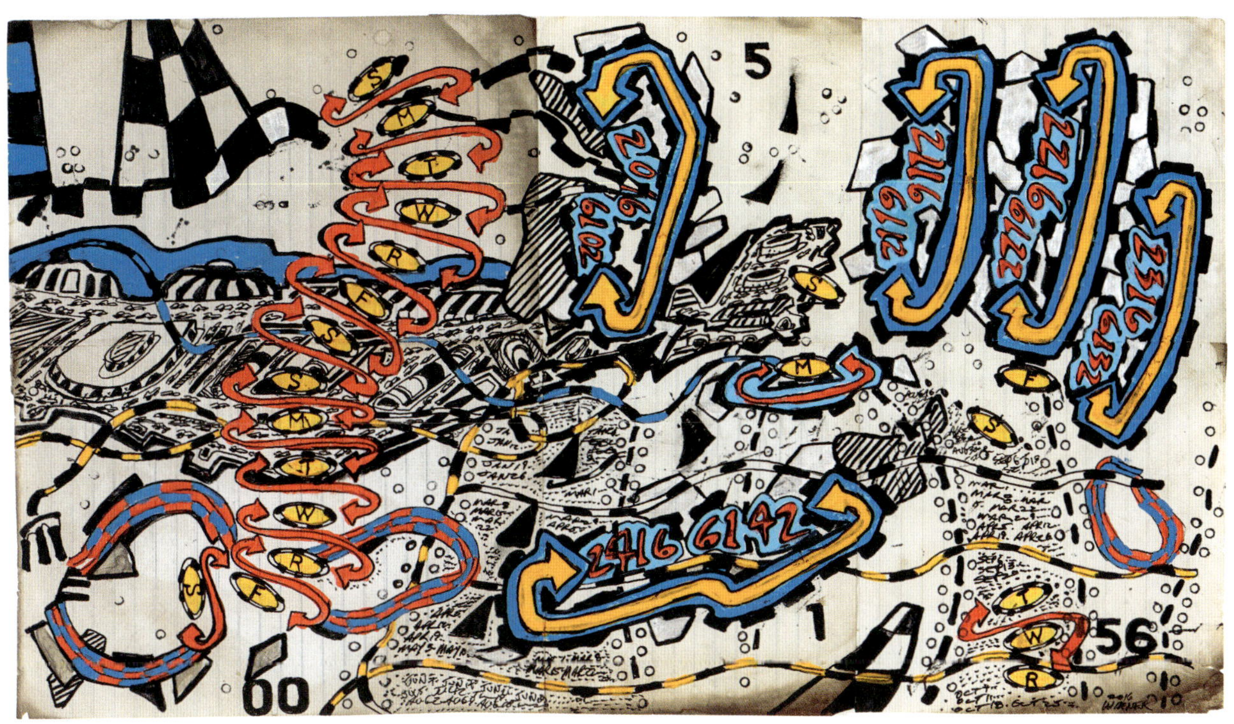
5
2416 6142
56
00

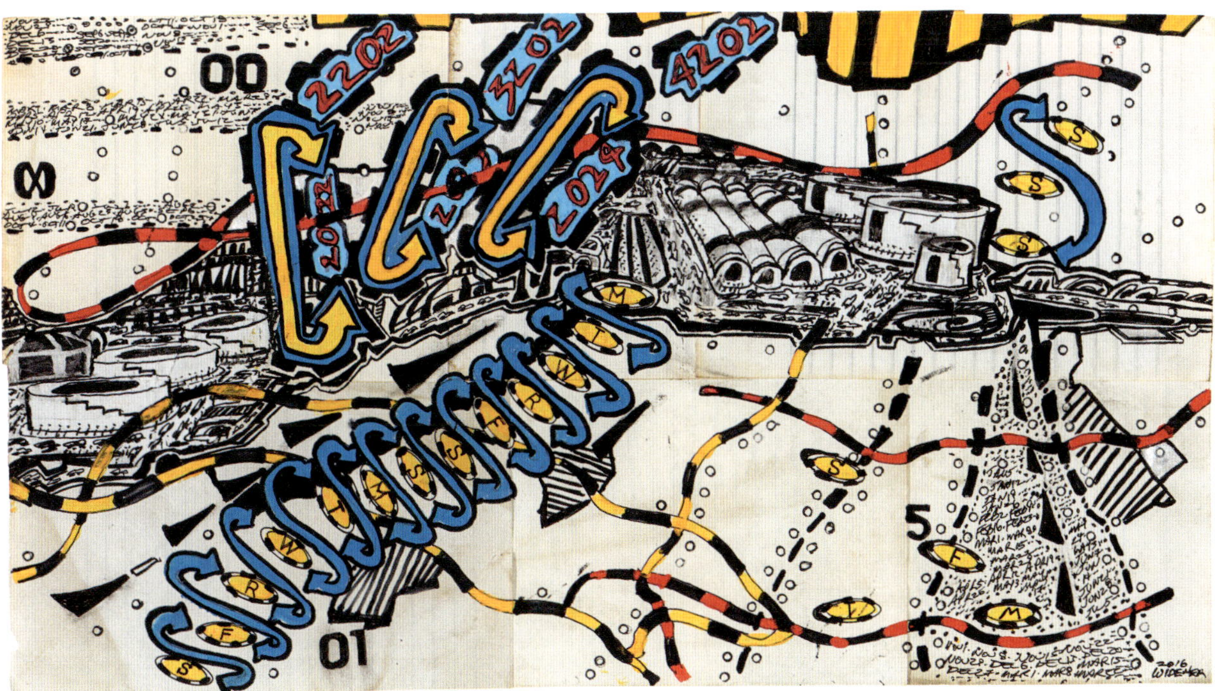
00
2202
3202
4202
5
01

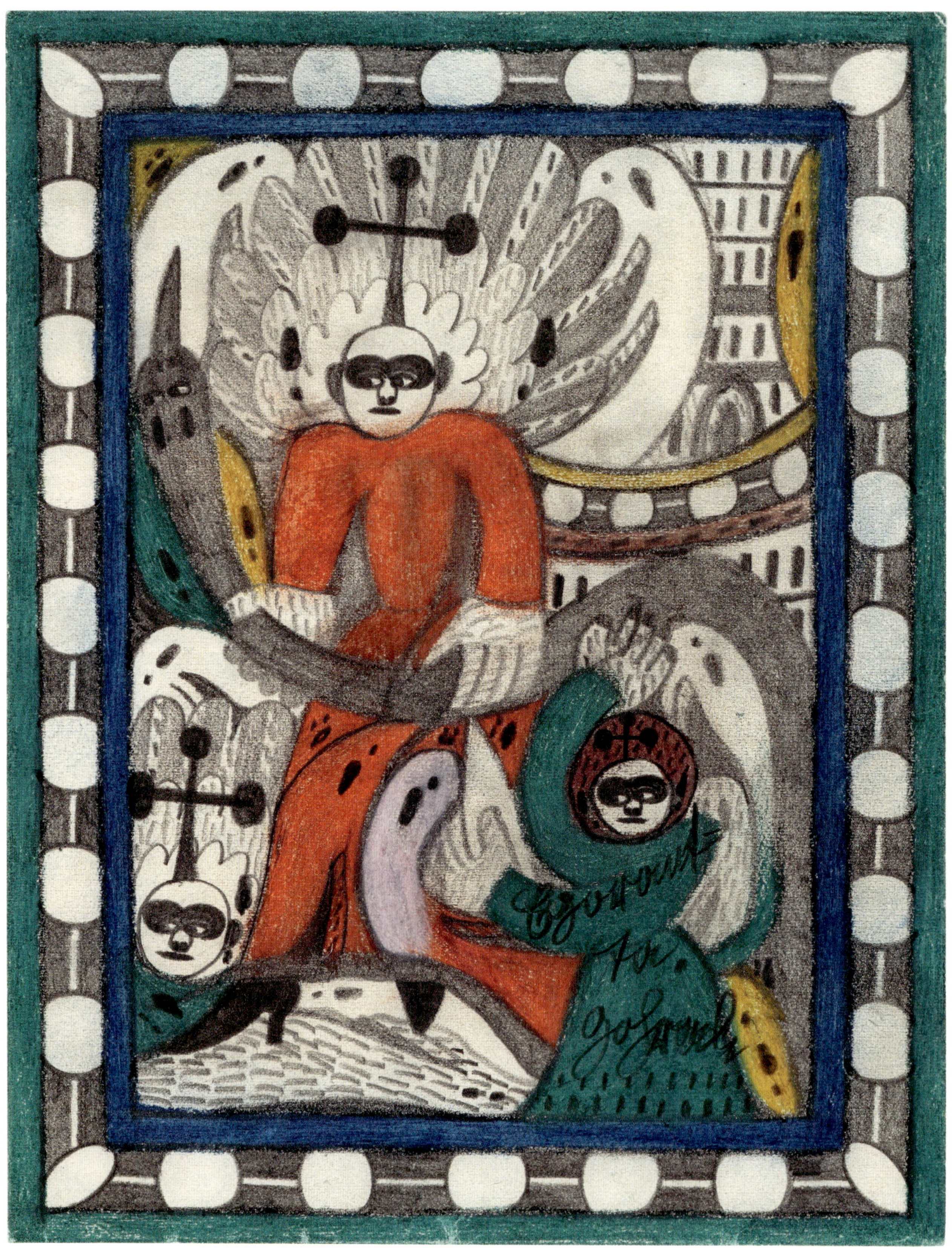

ADOLF WÖLFLI

1864–1930

Adolf Wölfli spent much of his life in the Waldau Clinic, outside of Bern, Switzerland. Before being institutionalized and diagnosed with schizophrenia, he was a farmworker and handyman. Wölfli's early life was marked with physical and sexual abuse; his alcoholic father left the family when Wölfli was still a boy, and he attended school only intermittently until age nine. Shortly after, he became a *Verdingbub*—an indentured child laborer. *Verdingkinder* were children in Switzerland who were taken from their parents, generally owing to poverty, and sent to live with new families—often farmers in need of cheap labor. Wölfli's mother died when he was just ten years old, leaving him at the mercy of state-run foster homes. When he was old enough, he joined the army for a short time. Later he was convicted of attempted child molestation and served time in prison. After being released, he was again arrested for a related offense and eventually admitted to the Waldau Clinic, where he spent the rest of his life.

As a psychiatric patient, Wölfli exhibited violent impulses and had hallucinations that were appeased only through art making. His earliest surviving works, a series of fifty graphite drawings, are dated between 1904 and 1906. He produced a vast oeuvre of condensed and meticulous compositions that wove together abstracted human figures, religious iconography, animals, architecture, symbols, text, intricate patterning, and musical notation—which he played on a rolled-cardboard "trumpet." Wölfli's works are a classic example of horror vacui: he was compelled to fill or contain every bit of a pictorial plane and often turned negative spaces between picture elements into bird outlines. In 1908 Wölfli began a narrative work that, at forty-five volumes of twenty-five hundred pages and sixteen hundred illustrations, would be his chef d'oeuvre. An epic narrative, this fusion of fact and fiction was Wölfli's means to orchestrate his rebirth as the more powerful and free alter ego "St. Adolf II."

From 1907 to 1919 a young resident psychiatrist, Walter Morgenthaler, worked intermittently and in various capacities at Waldau. Morgenthaler took interest in Wölfli's art, provided him with materials and encouragement, and in 1921 published a book about him, *Ein Geisteskranker als Künstler* (A Mental Patient as Artist, published in English in 1992 as *Madness & Art: The Life and Works of Adolf Wölfli*). This landmark publication was the first to present a study of a mental patient as an artist. In time, Wölfli became recognized as a foundational figure in art brut, a nomenclature he predated. A year after the publication of Morgenthaler's book, Hans Prinzhorn, a German psychiatrist with art history training, published *Das Bildernei des Geisteskrankers* (The Artistry of the Mentally Ill), a study about the art made by his patients in a Heidelberg psychiatric hospital. More than twenty years later, Prinzhorn's book inspired the French artist Jean Dubuffet to coin the term *art brut*—meaning art that was crude, raw, uninfluenced, and not ego driven. Dubuffet believed that art brut was the antidote to the corruptive power of mainstream culture in art.

Adolf Wölfli, *Untitled (Christ Figure with Serpent)*, c. 1915–16. Colored pencil and graphite on paper, 11 × 8½ in. (27.9 × 21.6 cm)

After Wölfli died at Waldau in 1930, the Adolf Wölfli Foundation was created for the preservation of his oeuvre, and the foundation's collection is now exhibited at the Museum of Fine Arts in Bern. Wölfli's works are in the collections of the Charlotte Zander Museum (Bönnigheim, Germany), the Lille Métropole Museum of Modern, Contemporary and Outsider Art (Villeneuve-d'Ascq, France), the Collection de l'Art Brut (Lausanne, Switzerland), the American Folk Art Museum (New York), the Milwaukee Art Museum, and the Smithsonian American Art Museum (Washington, D.C.).

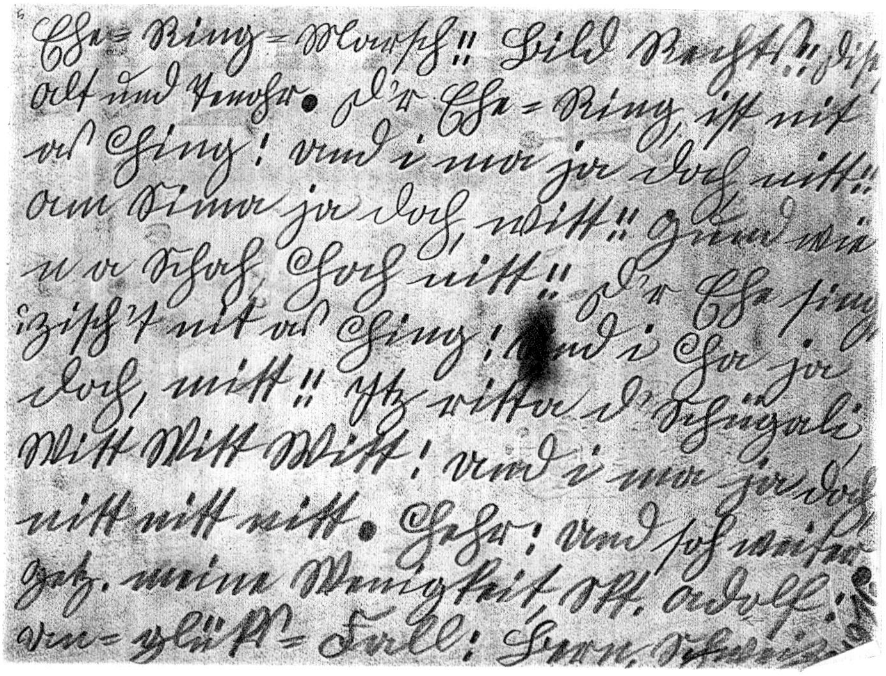

Adolf Wölfli, verso of *Untitled (Christ Figure with Serpent)* (p. 242)

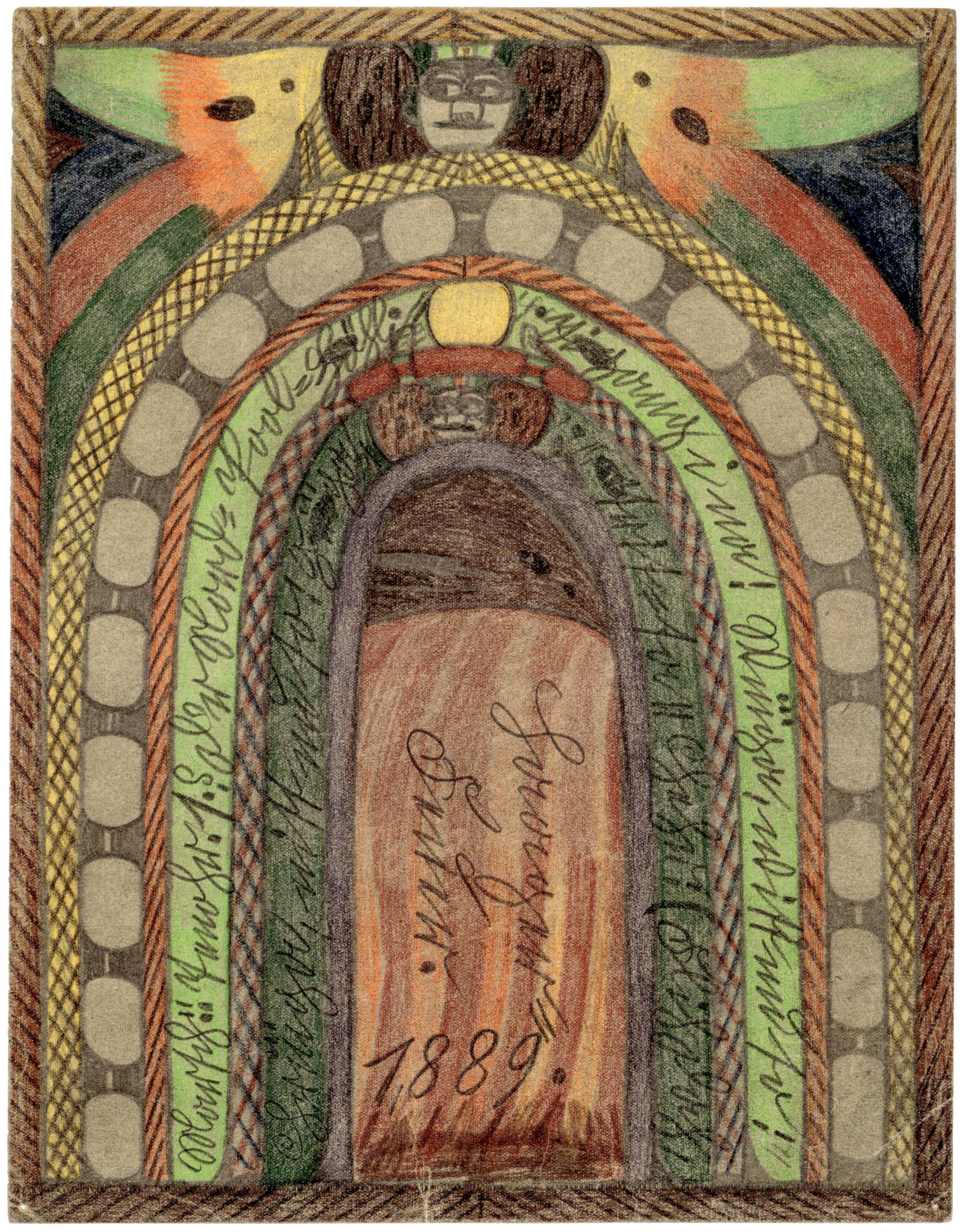

Adolf Wölfli, *Lagerfeuer*, c. 1915–16. Colored pencil and graphite on paper, 12¾ × 9¾ in. (32.4 × 24.8 cm)

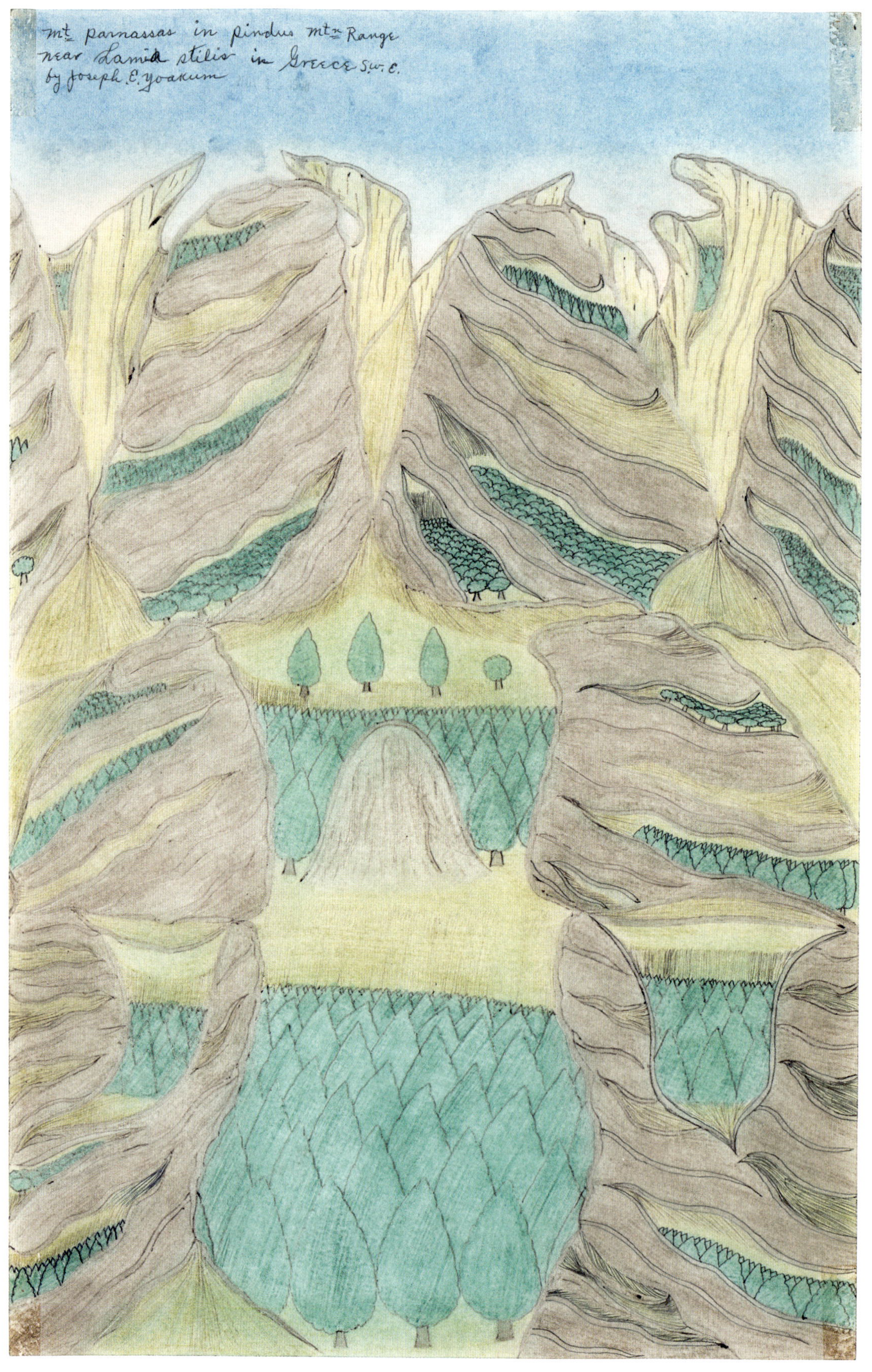
Mt parnassas in pindus Mtn Range
near Lamia stilis in Greece S.W. E.
by Joseph E. Yoakum

JOSEPH YOAKUM

ca. 1890–1972

Official records indicate that Joseph Yoakum's birthplace was Ash Grove, Missouri, but he liked to say that he was born on an Indian reservation in Window Rock, Arizona. His mother, born into slavery in the 1850s, was of African, French American, and Native American descent, and his father was a farmer of Cherokee and Creek descent. Yoakum was one of many children and received very little formal education. He grew up on a farm near Walnut Grove, Missouri, from which (according to his own account) he escaped at age nine to join the Great Wallace Circus. For the next decade he led a nomadic life, traveling across the United States and abroad with other itinerant shows—Buffalo Bill Cody's Wild West and the Ringling Brothers, among others—for which he worked tending to horses and posting bills.

In 1908 he returned to Missouri, where he met his first wife. The couple married and had five children, and Yoakum settled down for the next ten years, working as a coal miner to support his family. In 1918, however, he was drafted to serve in World War I as part of the all-African American 805th Pioneer Infantry repairing roads, bridges, and railroads, and he was later stationed in France. After the war he returned to his nomadic lifestyle rather than his family, working as a railroad porter, a sailor, and an apple picker, among other jobs. He traveled extensively and claimed to have visited every continent except for Antarctica. At one point in the 1920s he moved to Chicago, where he remarried in 1929 and remained for the rest of his life. In the mid-1940s Yoakum began to experience symptoms of dementia and lived for a time in a psychiatric ward. A few years later he was widowed and residing in a housing project for the elderly until he moved in 1966 to a storefront on Chicago's South Side. Sometime between the early or mid-1950s and early 1960s, no longer able to work a regular job, Yoakum started making art.

His early drawings were primarily monochrome pen-and-graphite works on small sheets of white or manila paper, but he soon started working in larger formats and experimenting with color. Yoakum made more than two thousand drawings, most of them landscapes of mountains and water. A unique fusion of reality and imagination, these compositions are dreamscapes where Yoakum's memories and visions merge. He used a variety of encyclopedias, atlases, and travel books as reference material, but he described his process as a "spiritual enfoldment." With a ballpoint pen he sketched his winding outlines freehand, delicately tinted the negative spaces with colored pencils, pastels, watercolors, or chalk, and then buffed the surface with a bit of toilet paper to give his drawings an ethereal finish. He signed and dated most of his works and often wrote small indicators of the locations depicted although the scenes were generally not identifiable.

Yoakum was quiet and introverted, his religious and artistic ethos grounded in the belief that God and nature were one and the same. At some point after moving to the South Side, he decided to hang some of his drawings by a string along his window, and they caught the attention of a neighbor named John Hobgood,

Joseph Yoakum, *Mt. Parnassas in Pindus Mountain Range*, c. 1960s. Pastel, ink, and colored pencil on paper, 19 × 12 in. (48.3 × 30.5 cm)

an anthropologist and professor at Chicago State College (now Chicago State University). Hobgood's purchase of several drawings led to a small exhibition in the basement of St. Bartholomew's Lutheran Church, whose pastor sent a letter to the *Chicago Daily News*, which ran a profile on the artist—after which fascination with Yoakum's artwork snowballed.

In 1969 Yoakum's work was included in an exhibition at Chicago's Museum of Contemporary Art, and in 1971 his drawings were shown at the Museum of Modern Art in New York. Shortly before he died, the Whitney Museum of American Art mounted a solo exhibition of his work. His drawings are in the Museum of Modern Art, the American Folk Art Museum (New York), the Milwaukee Art Museum, Intuit: The Center for Intuitive and Outsider Art (Chicago), the New Orleans Museum of Art, the Smithsonian American Art Museum (Washington, D.C.), the Philadelphia Museum of Art, and the abcd Collection (Paris).

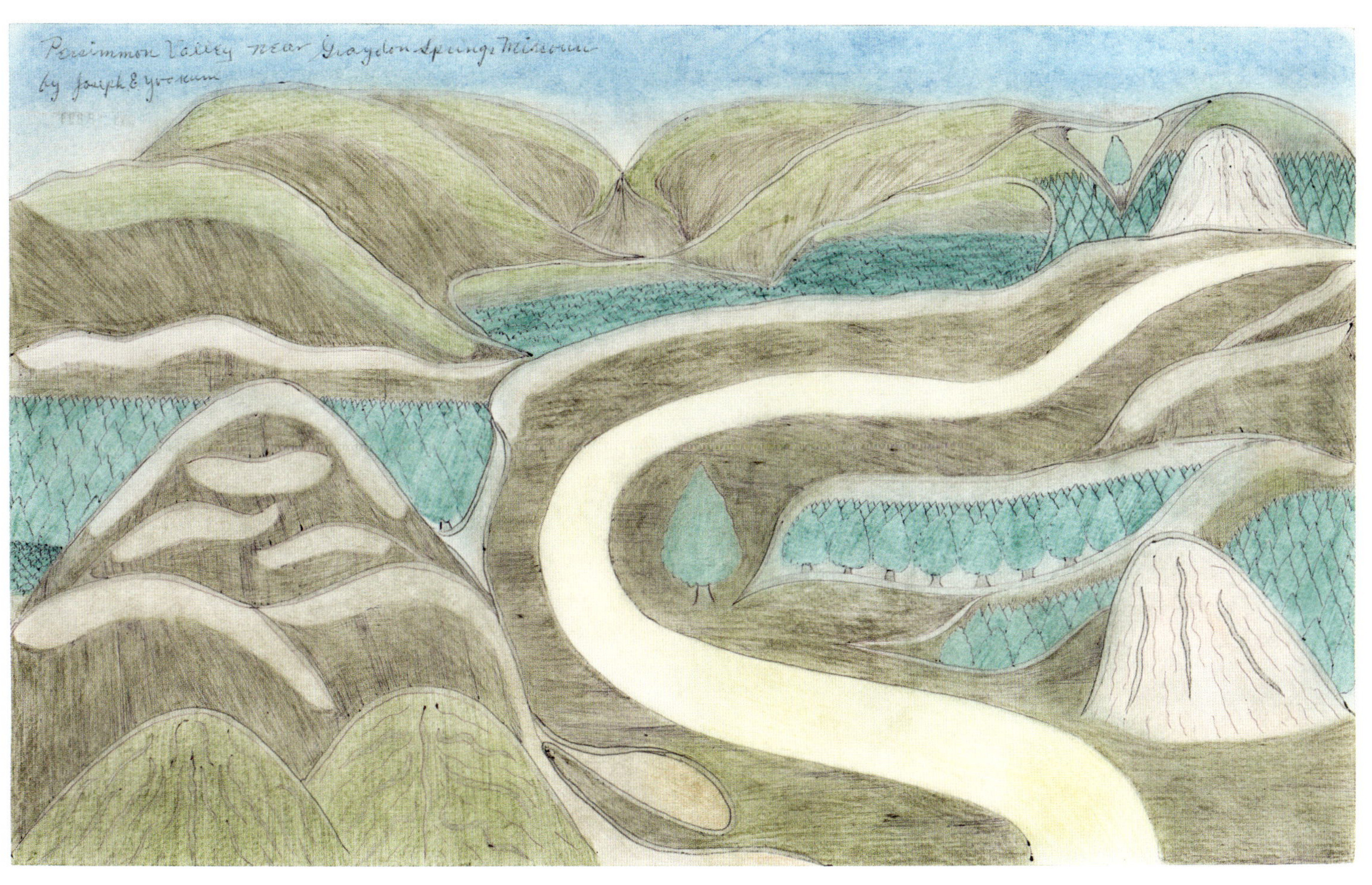

Joseph Yoakum, *Persimmon Valley near Graydon Springs Missouri*, 1968. Colored pencil and graphite on paper, 12 × 19 in. (30.5 × 48.3 cm)

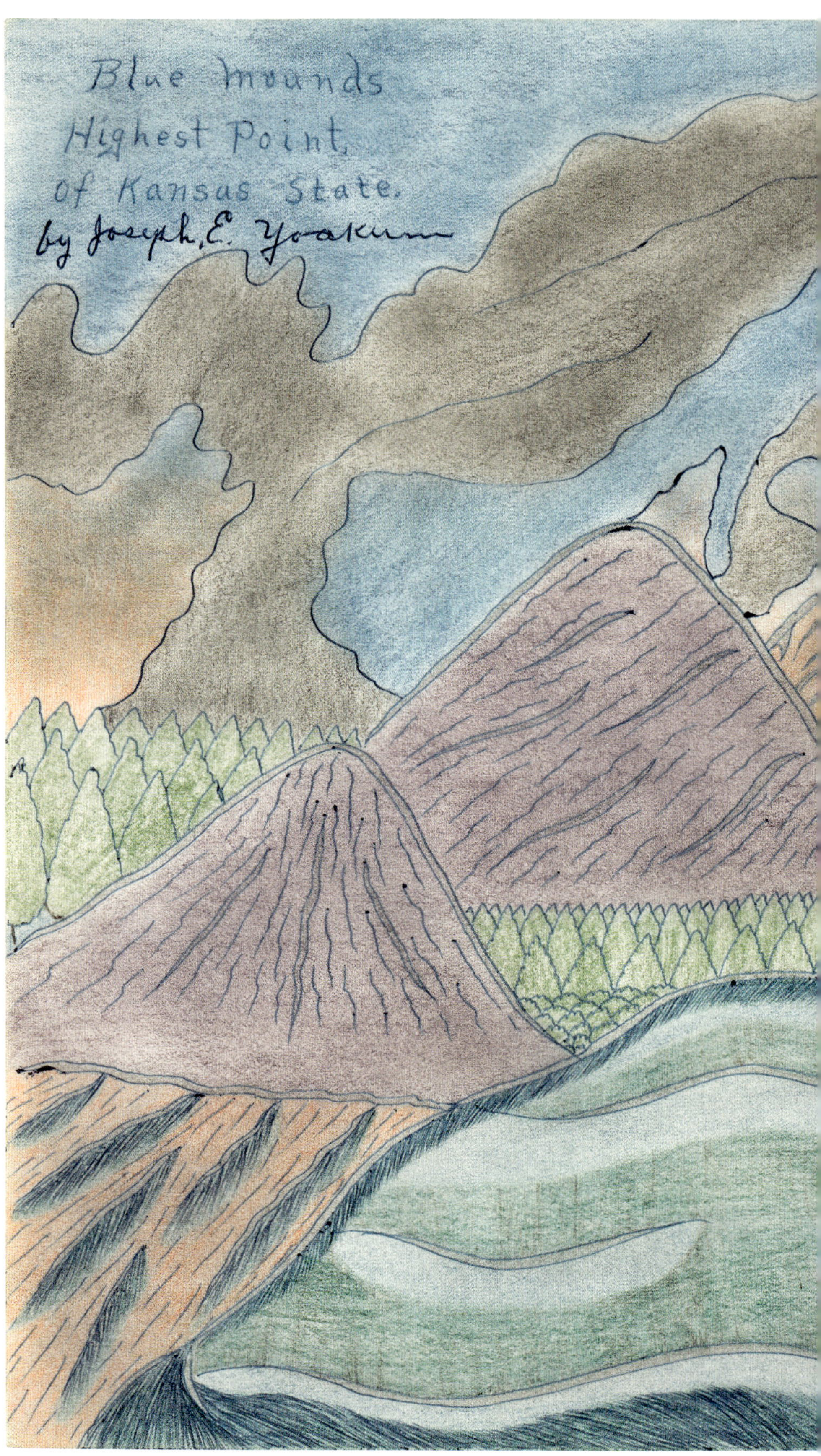

Joseph Yoakum, *Blue Mounds Highest Point of Kansas State*, c. 1960s. Colored pencil and pen on paper, 12 × 18 in. (30.5 × 45.7 cm)

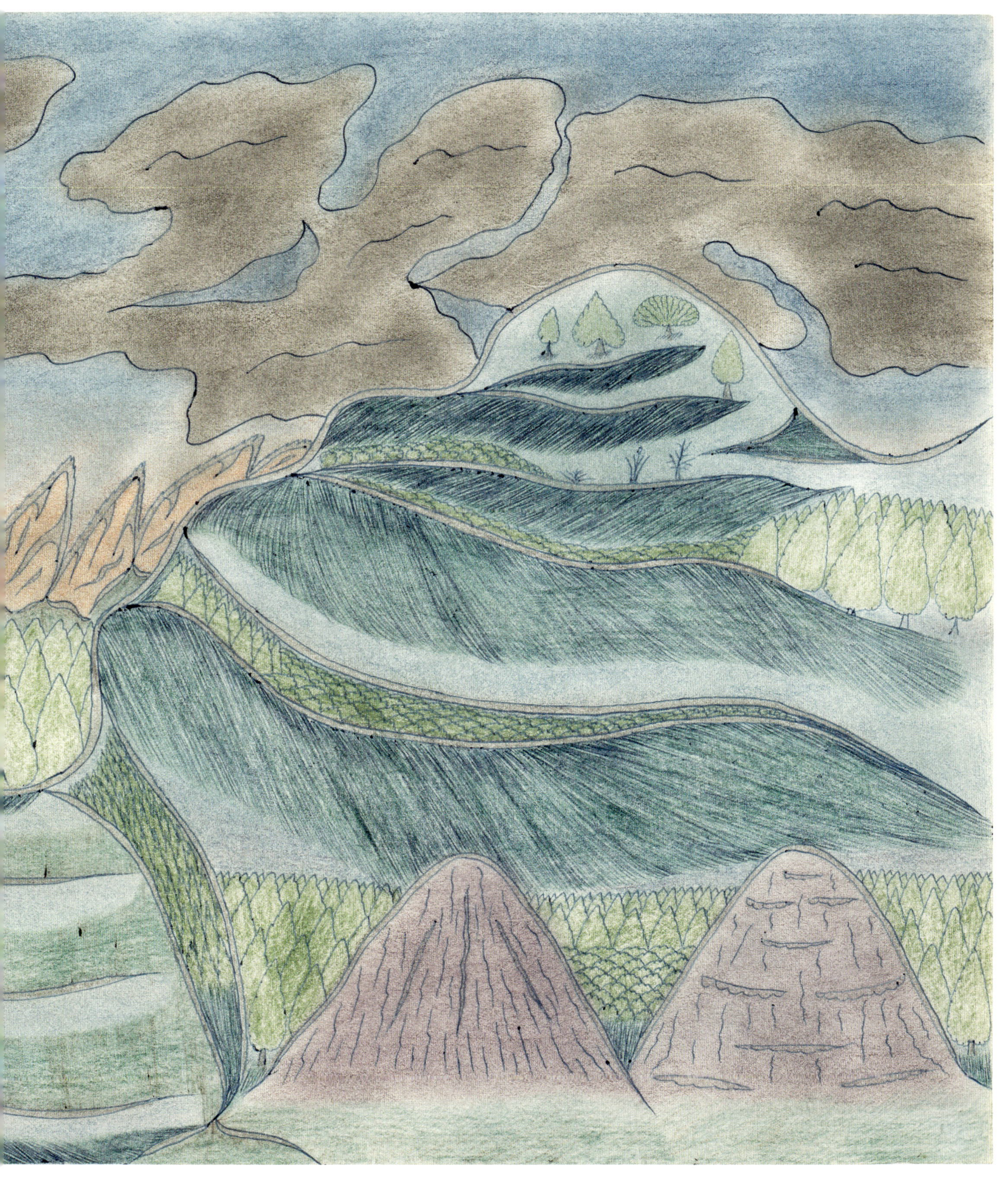

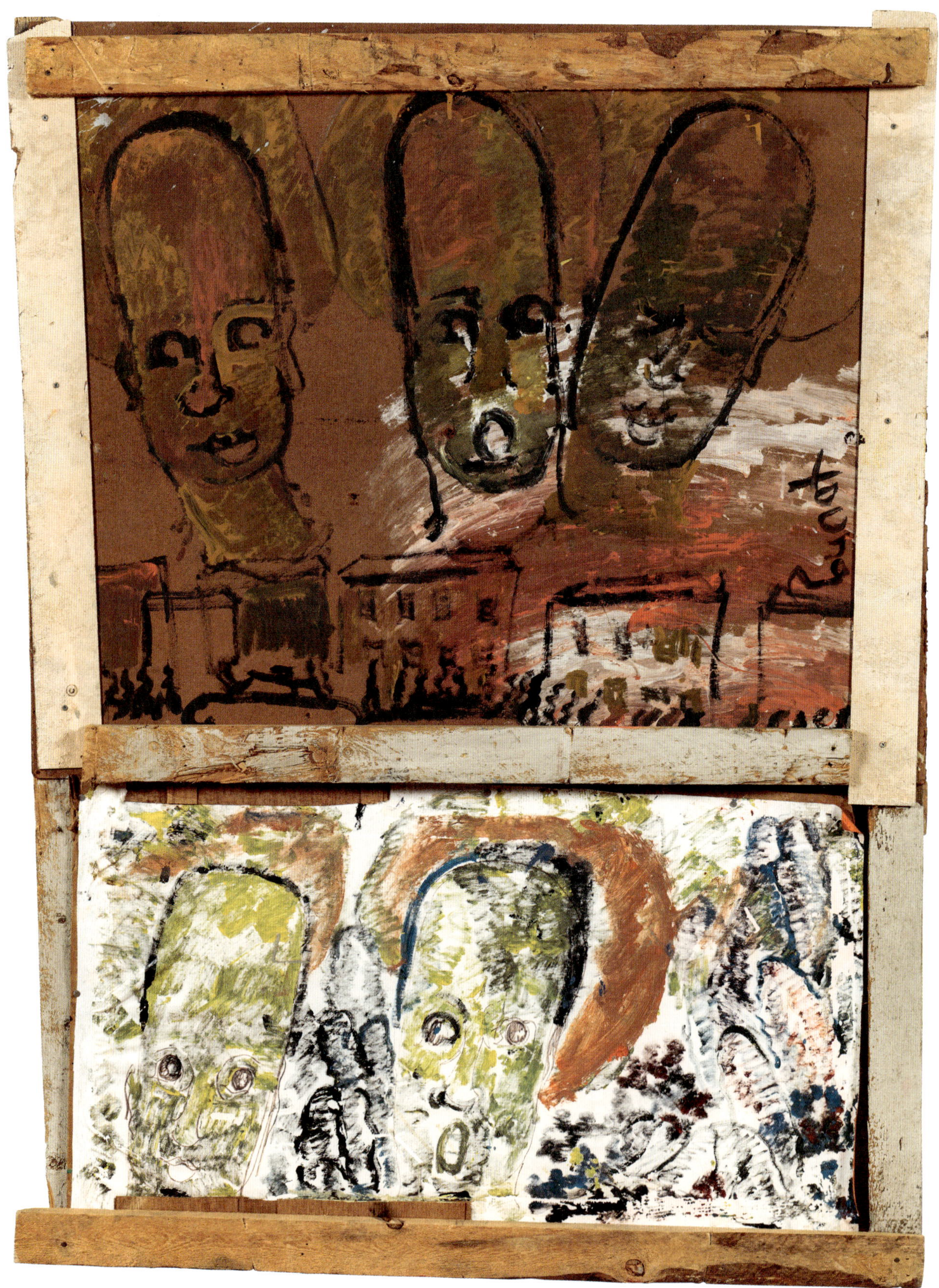

PURVIS YOUNG

1943–2010

The neighborhood of Overtown in downtown Miami, designated a "colored" area after the incorporation of Miami in 1896, was home to Purvis Young for most of his life. Overtown had been an entertainment hot spot in post–World War II years, but after an economic downturn in the 1950s, the construction in the 1960s of Interstate 95 cut through the neighborhood, decimated its population, and turned it into a ghetto.

Young received little education and worked various menial jobs in his teens, barely making a living. At eighteen, he was convicted of breaking and entering and served three years (1961–64) in Raiford State Penitentiary. As noted in Young's obituary in the *New York Times*, he emerged from prison as a young man and "by dint of his striking, expressionist vision of urban life and mammoth output over more than three decades transformed a forgotten Miami neighborhood into a destination for contemporary art aficionados." From his release, Young focused all his energy on making art—his form of social and political awareness.

In 1972, after Young learned about protest art and the "Walls of Freedom" made by artists in Chicago and Detroit, he decided to make his first public art project, the mural *Good Bread Alley*. Nailed onto boarded-up buildings on a deserted stretch of Goodbread Alley in Overtown, Young's mural consisted of hundreds of colorfully painted neoexpressionistic panels depicting political and religious themes and African American history. The mural's visibility from the new Interstate 95 attracted the attention of Miami's mainstream art community, including Bernard Davis (then director of the Miami Museum of Modern Art, now the Pérez Art Museum), who bought several works from Young and eventually introduced him to a broader audience.

Young continued to paint with house paint, colored pens and pencils, and crayons on discarded and scavenged materials such as wooden boards and Formica plates. With a gritty combination of urban black culture and classical references, Rembrandt, El Greco, van Gogh, and Delacroix, among them, Young captured the chaos and mayhem of the streets, the noise as much as the music, the confusion and poetry of a moment in time and its symbolic undercurrents. Young's creative drive was inexhaustible, and over time he produced thousands of works. His main theme was the African American experience in all its facets; his scenes and cityscapes depicted human figures interacting with each other and their environment, synching and clashing in a kind of collective rhythm. His technique was free-flowing and improvisational, a natural projection of his background and persona.

In 2006 Shaun Conrad and David Raccuglia released the documentary film *Purvis of Overtown*, which portrayed the artist as a national icon of black history and culture. Young's work is in the permanent collections of the Metropolitan Museum of Art (New York), the American Folk Art Museum (New York), the High Museum of Art (Atlanta), the Los Angeles County Museum of Art, the Philadelphia Museum of Art, the Milwaukee Art Museum, the New Orleans Museum of Art, and the Smithsonian American Art Museum (Washington, D.C.).

Purvis Young, *Untitled*, n.d. Mixed media assemblage (enamel on fabric, coated particle board), 63 × 47 in. (160 × 119.4 cm)

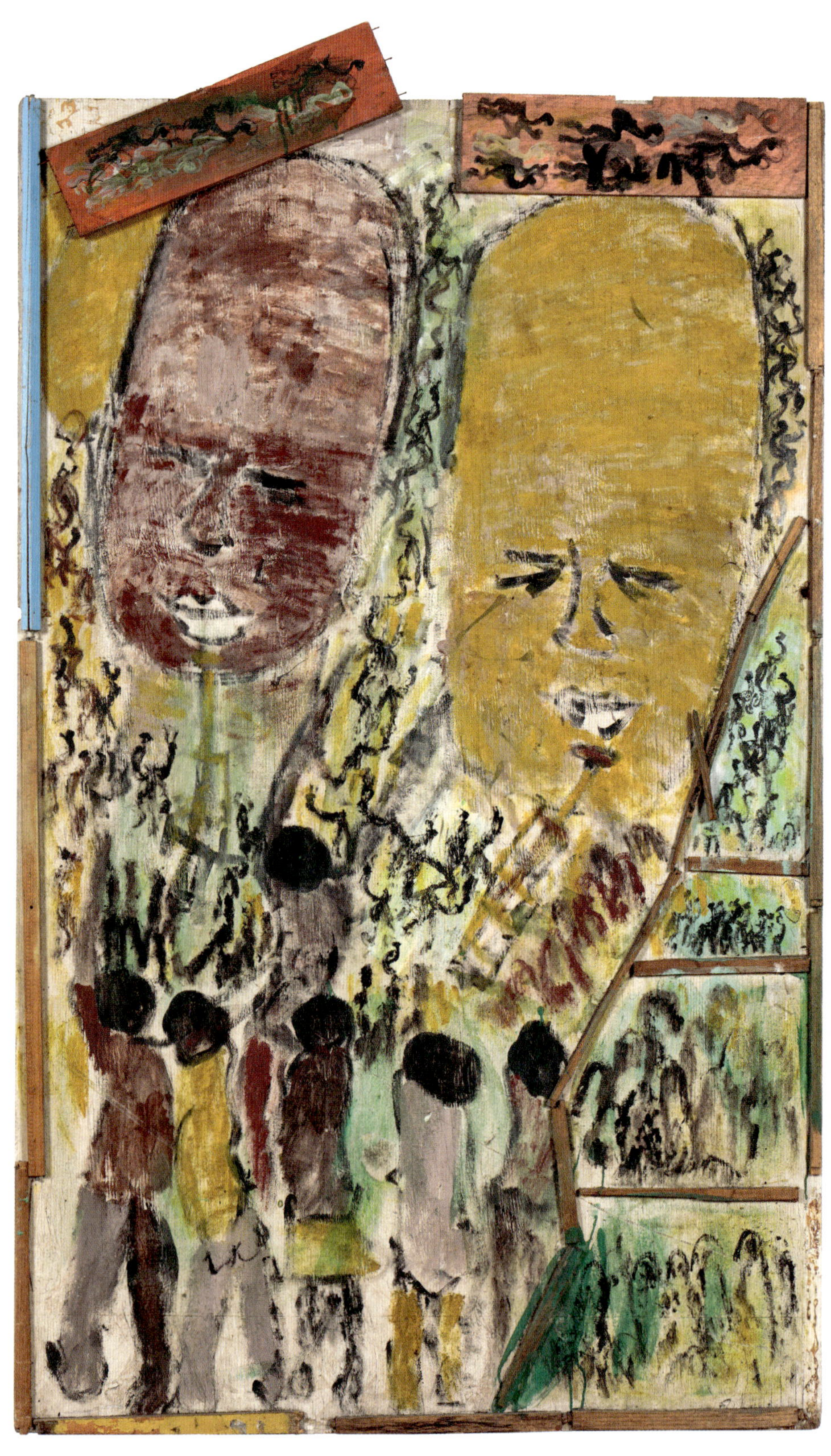

Purvis Young, *Untitled (Colorful Figures)*, n.d. Paint on plywood with attached found wood, 84 × 48 in. (213.4 × 121.9 cm)

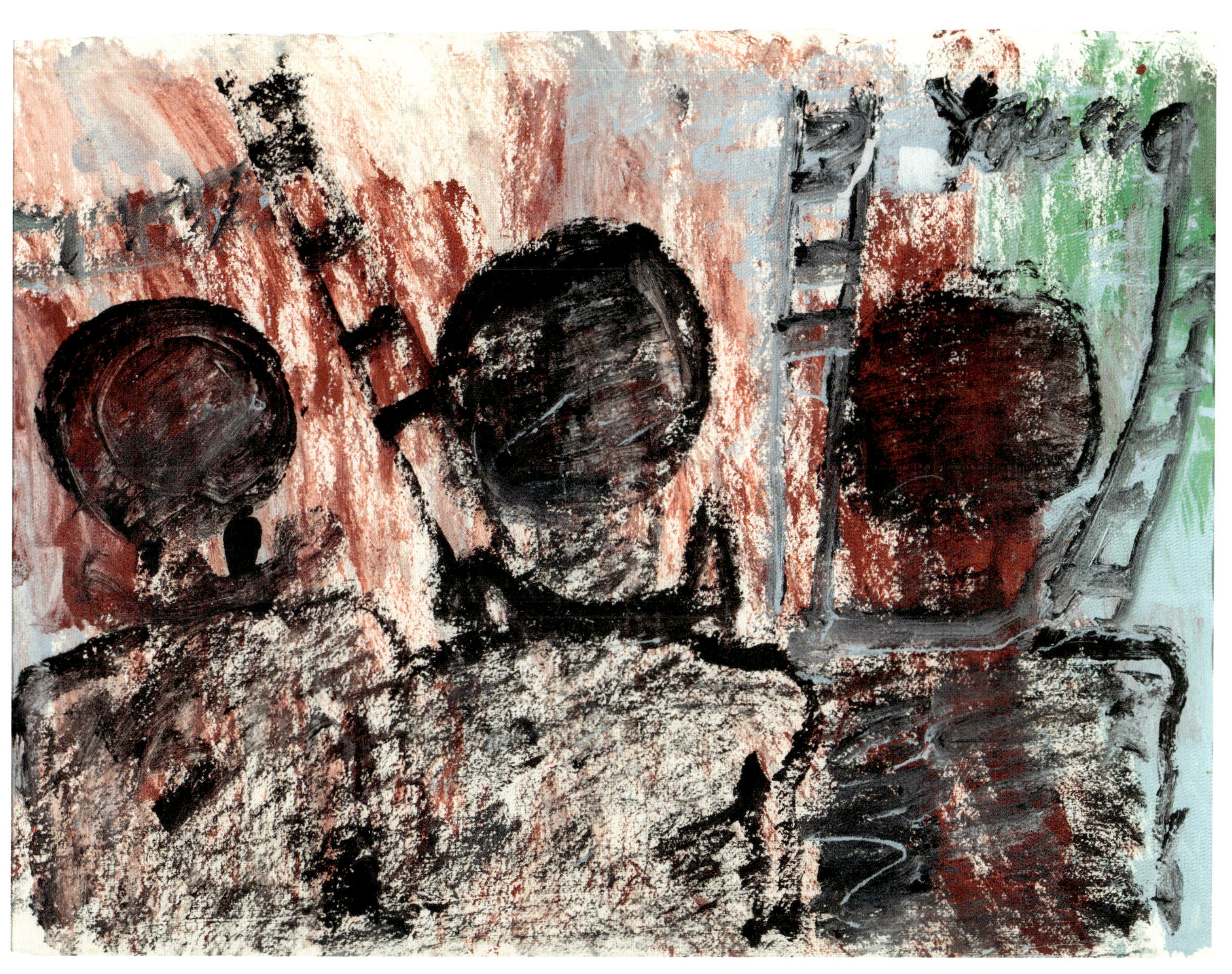

Purvis Young, *Untitled (Narrative Scene)*, 1975. Mixed media collage on found paper, 10¼ × 9¾ in. (26 × 24.8 cm)

VERNACULAR AND FOLK ART

In addition to its extensive holdings of outsider art, the Keen collection includes a lively collection of vernacular and folk art, including dozens of toys and banks, milk glass objects of every description, Victorian ceramic jars with decorated lids, bread toasters of an astonishing variety, and, notably, delightfully colorful Catalin radios manufactured from 1928 to the 1940s.

In 1927 the American Catalin Corporation took over patents for the Bakelite resin casting process and in 1928 secured importing rights to a German resin dye formula. Catalin began to manufacture plastics by pouring resin into molds, a process that created a plastic that was stronger, thicker, and brighter in color than Bakelite, and with a smooth polished surface.

The period in which Catalin plastics development occurred was a forward-looking era that saw technological marvels such as the automobile and airplane. As the radio became a popular household item during this time, manufacturers such as Catalin recognized that style—largely art deco in its day—dictated purchase. Catalin's production peaked in the decade and a half before World War II, slowed greatly during the war effort, and resumed but at a reduced pace after the war. In their heyday, Catalin radios came in all sizes, shapes, styles, and colors.

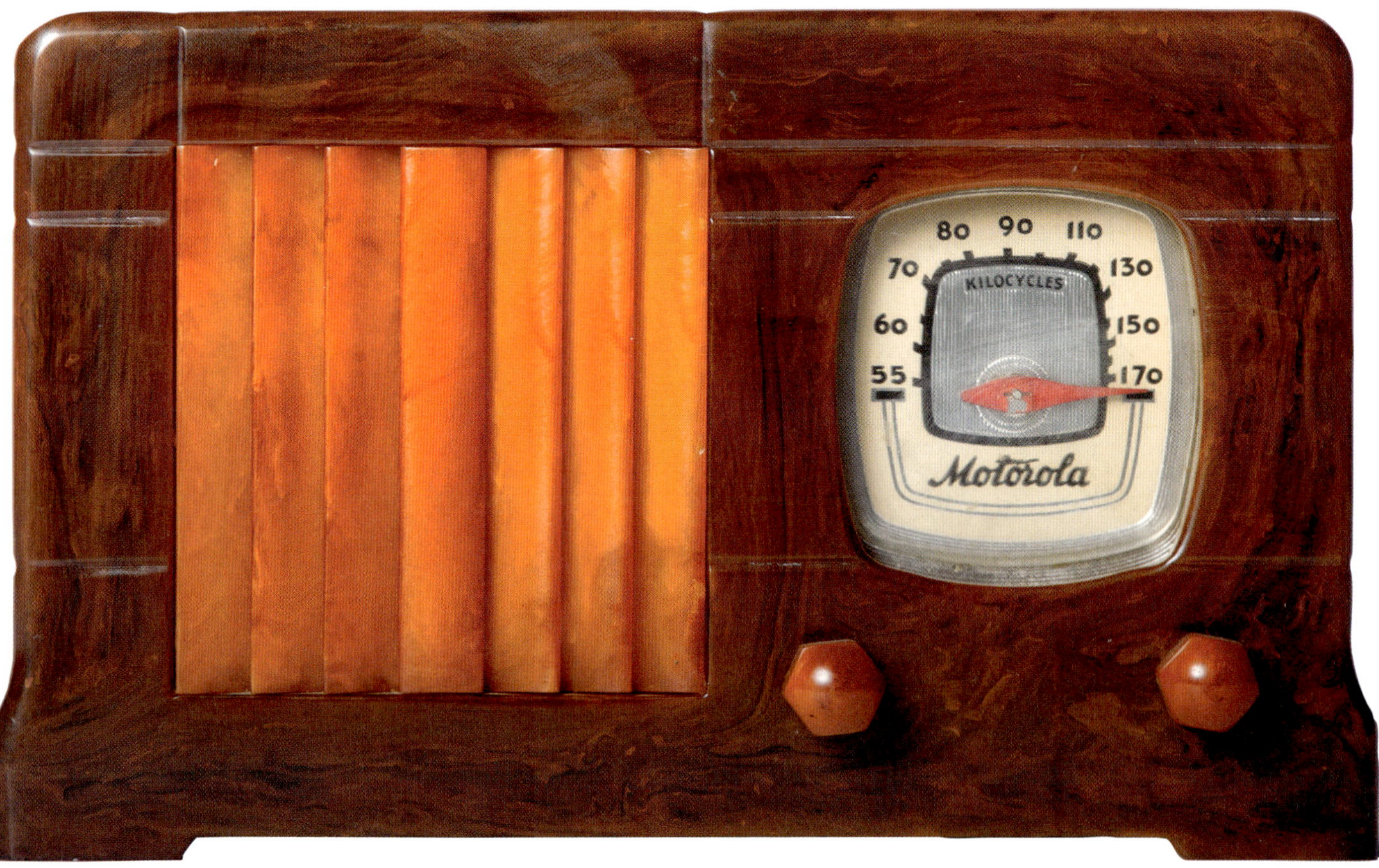

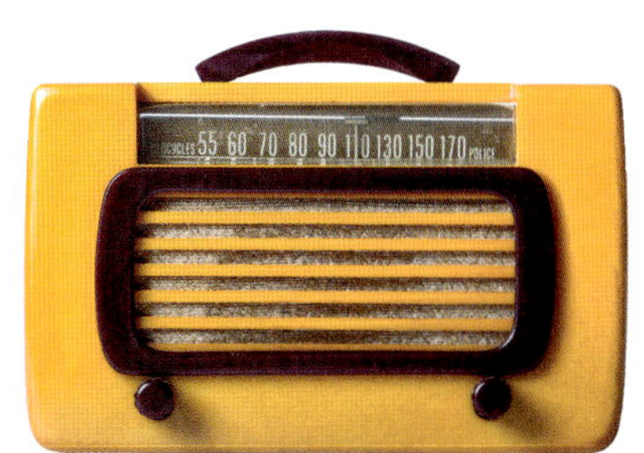
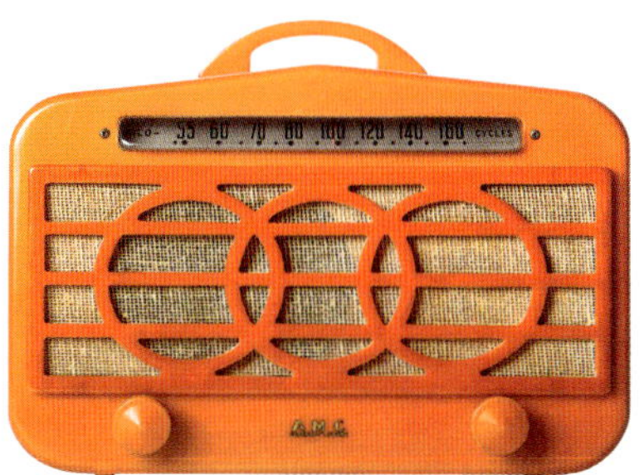
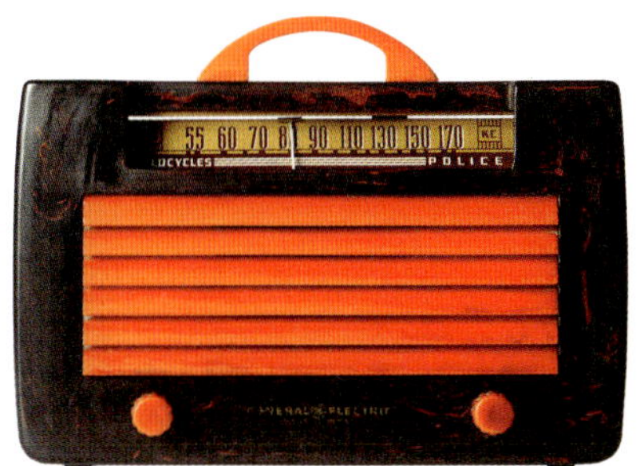
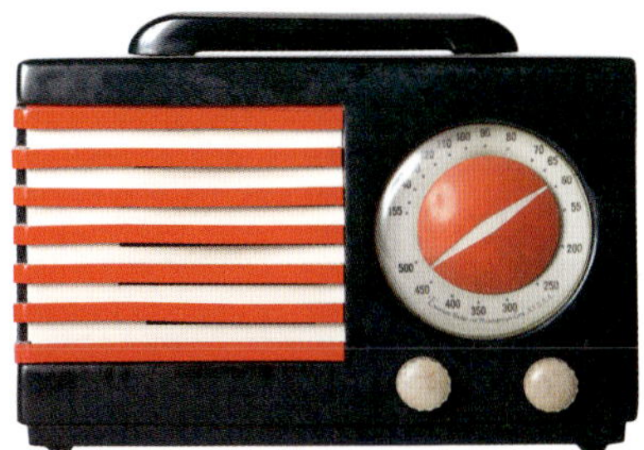
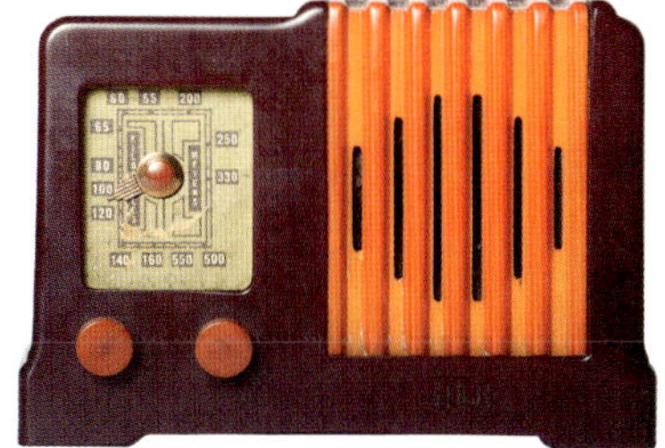
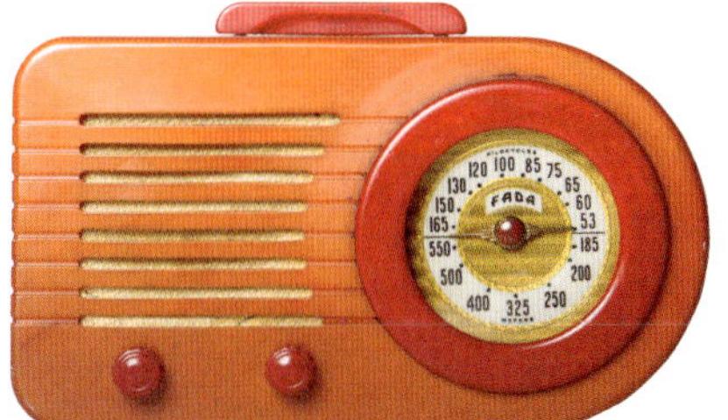
FADA
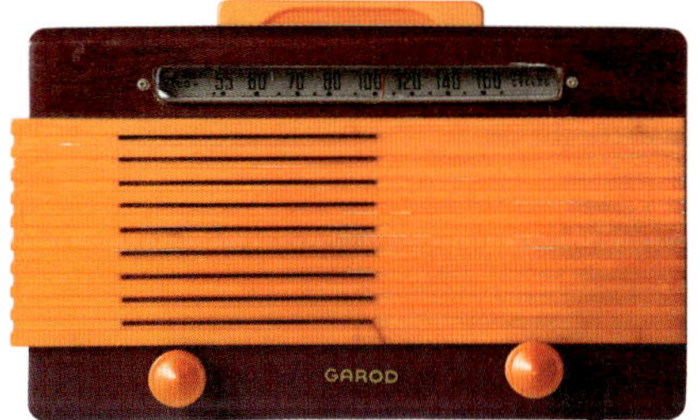
GAROD
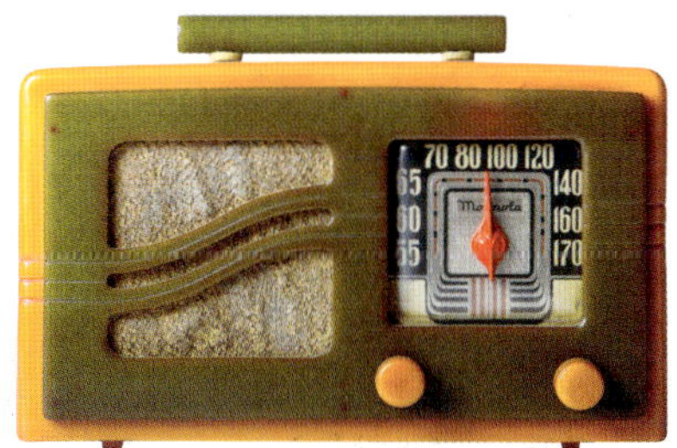
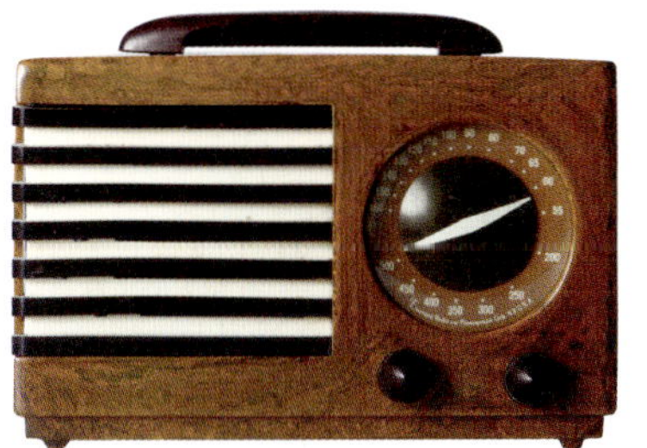
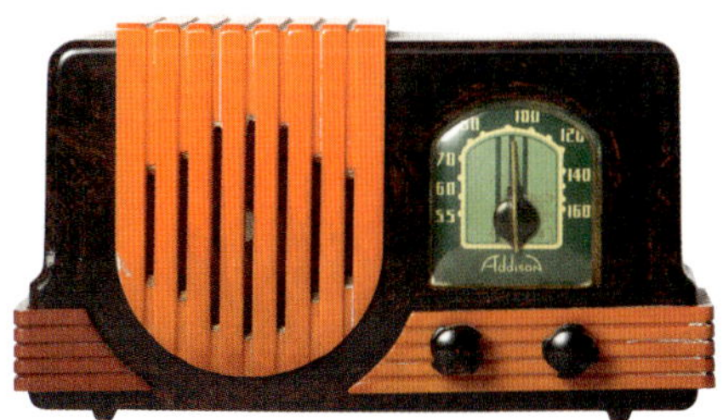
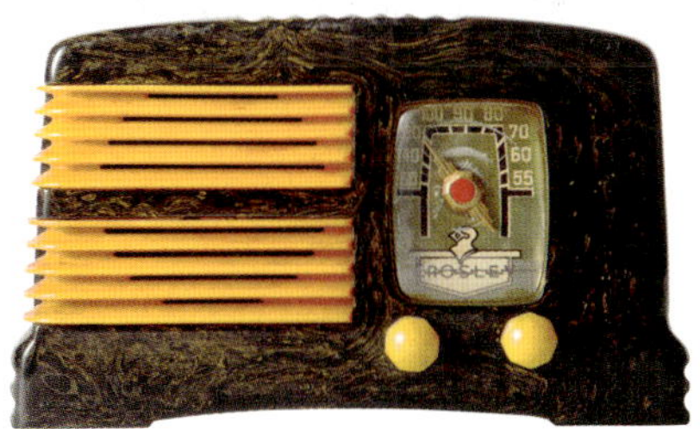
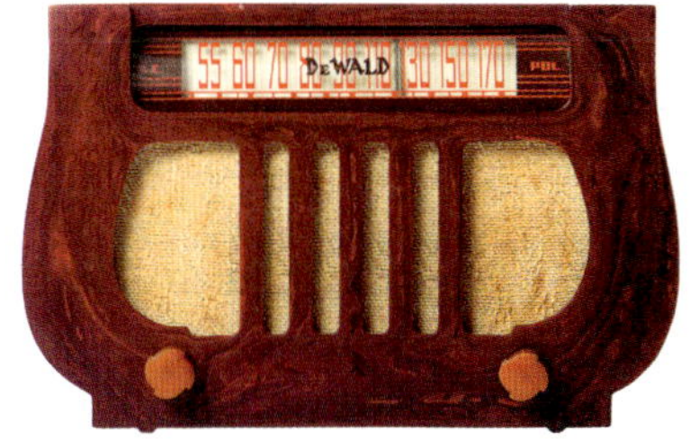
DeWALD
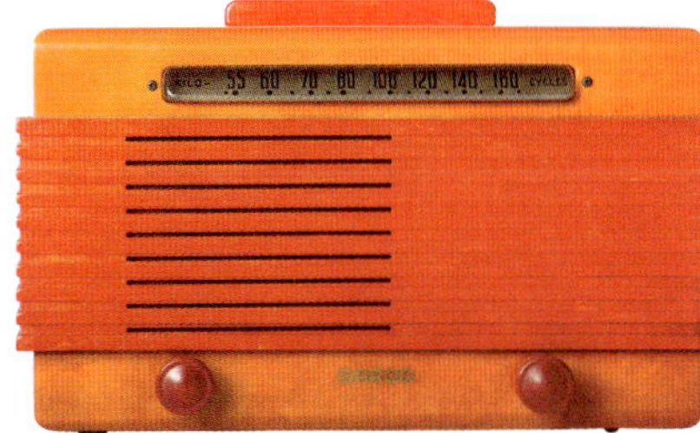
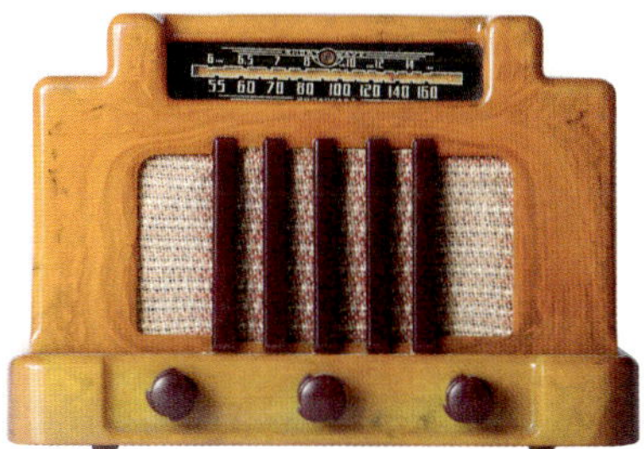
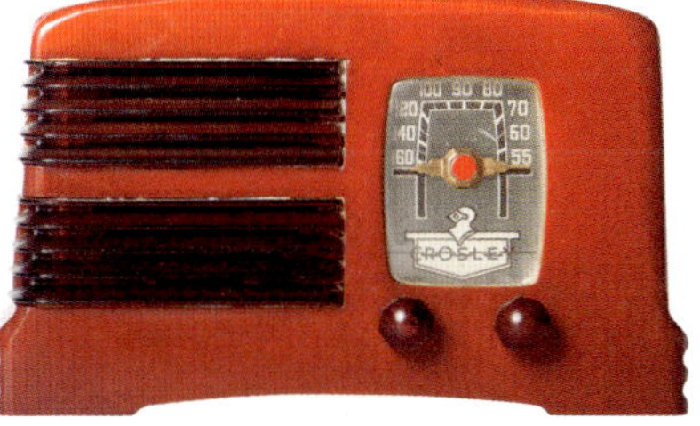
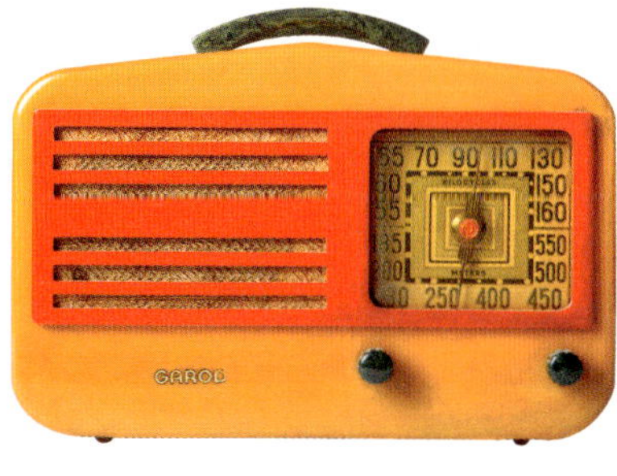
GAROD
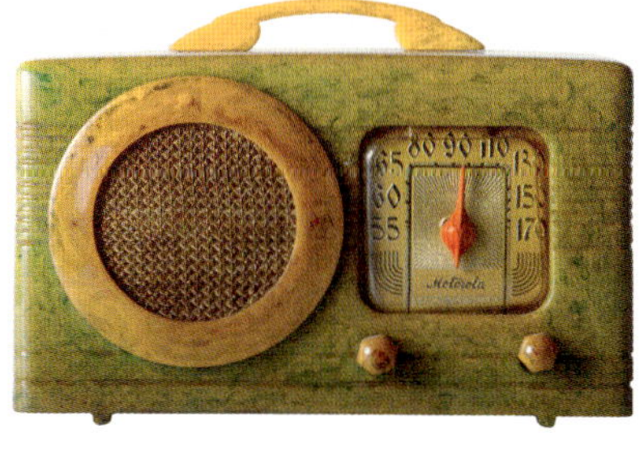
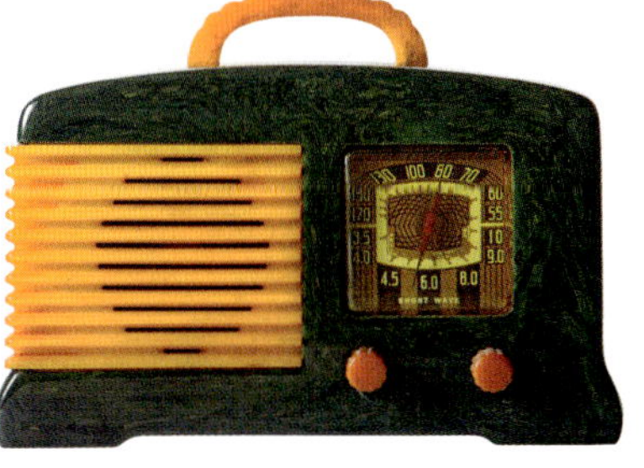

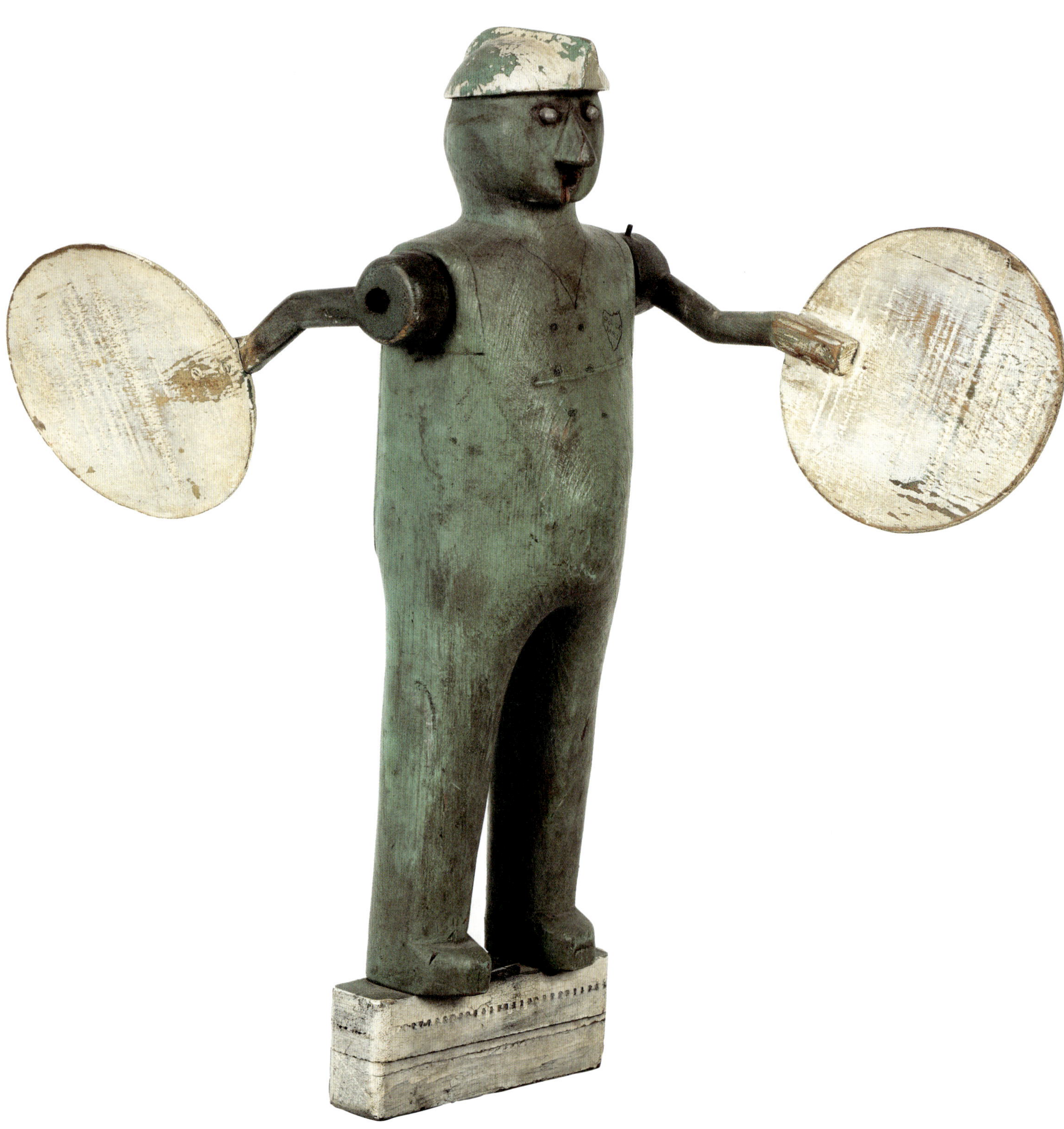

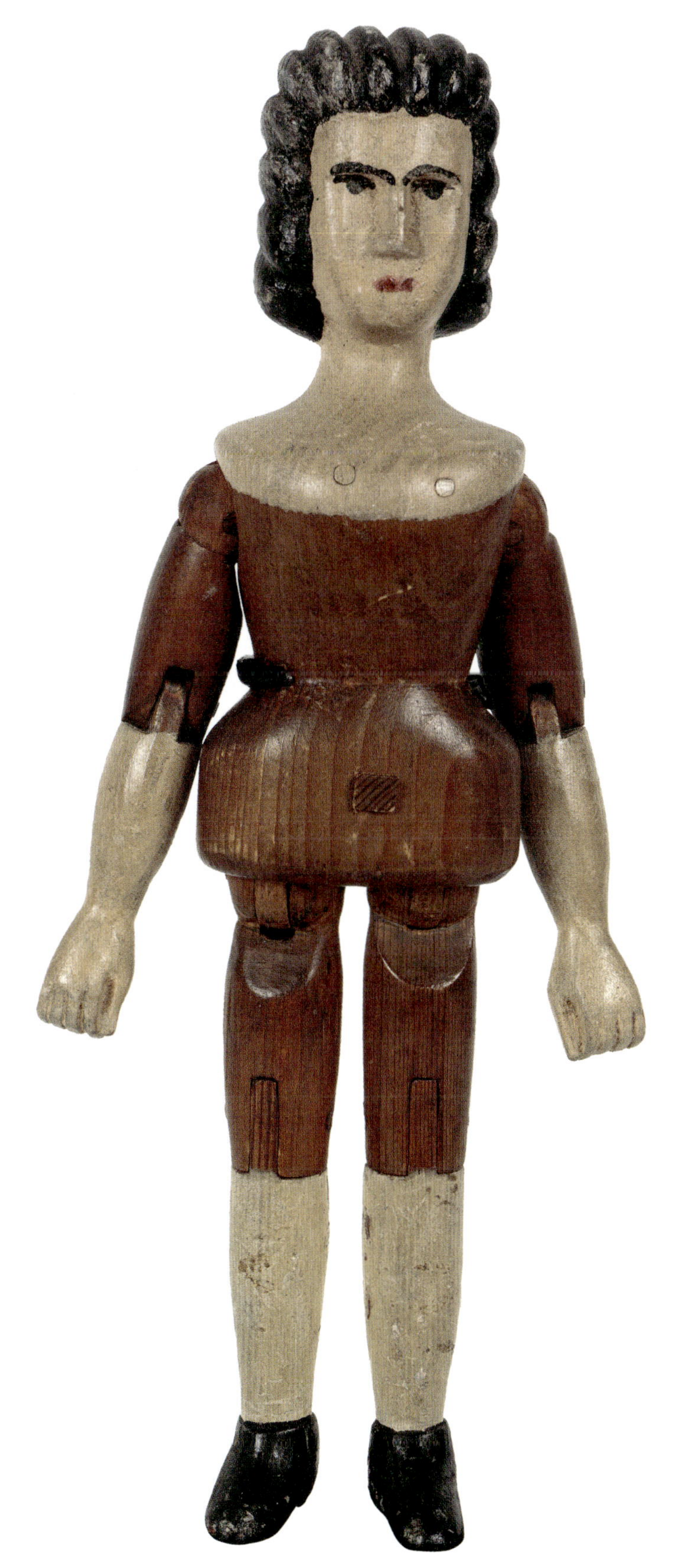

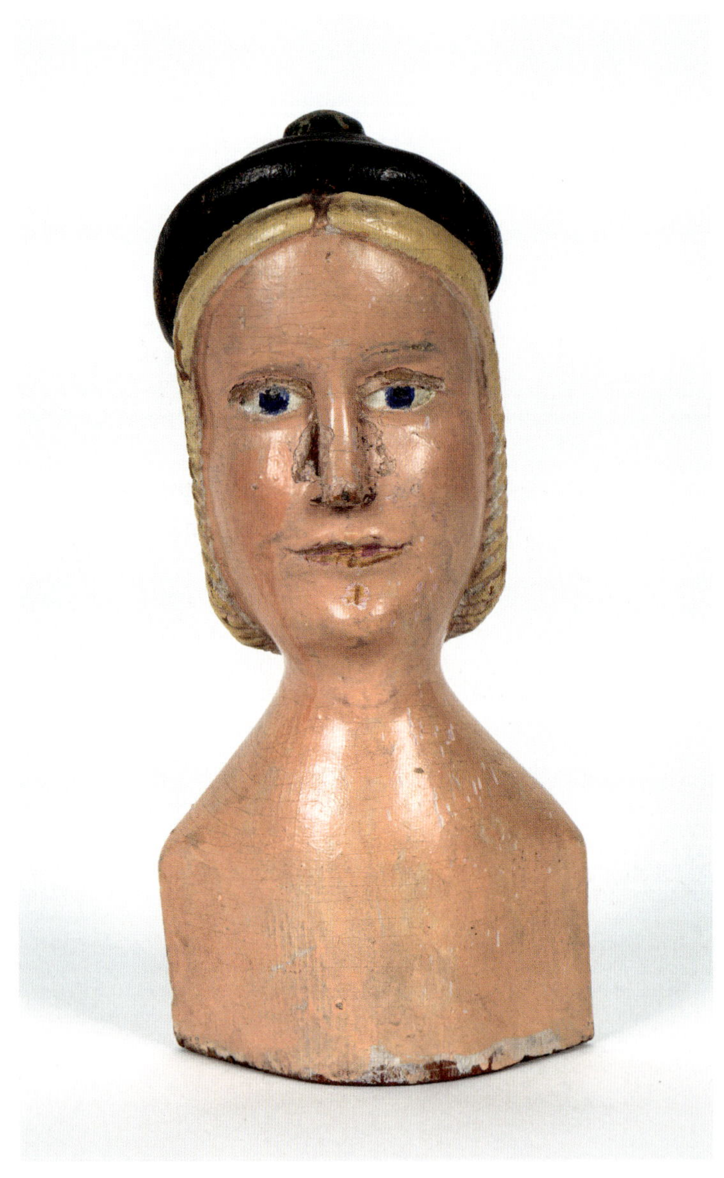

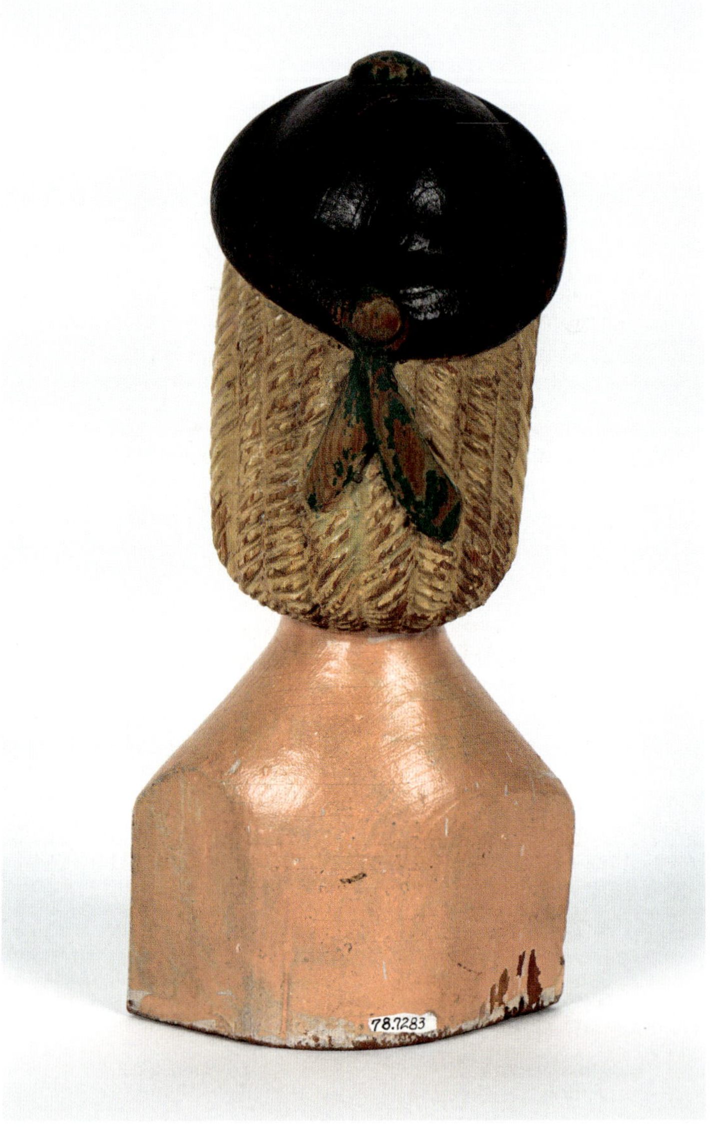
78.7283

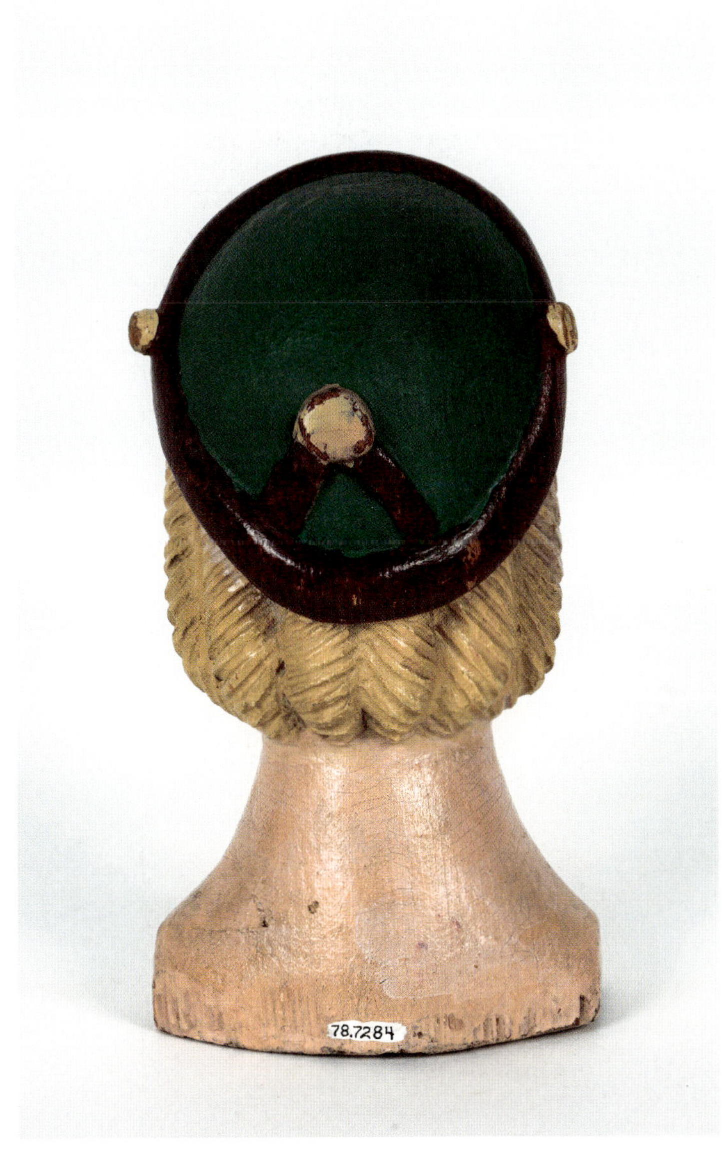
78.7284

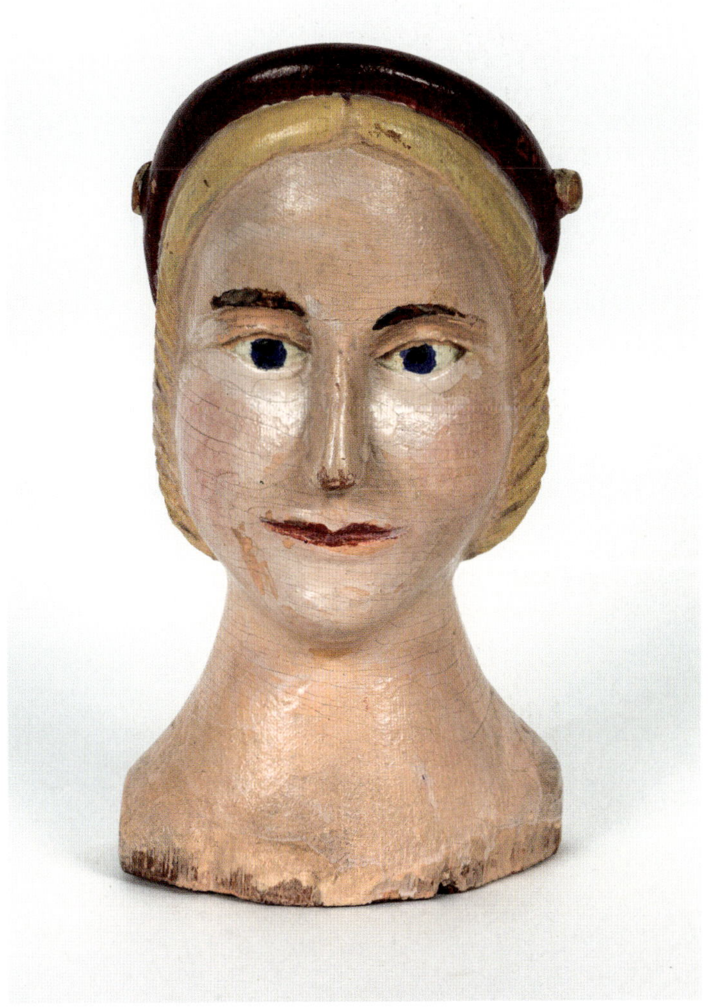

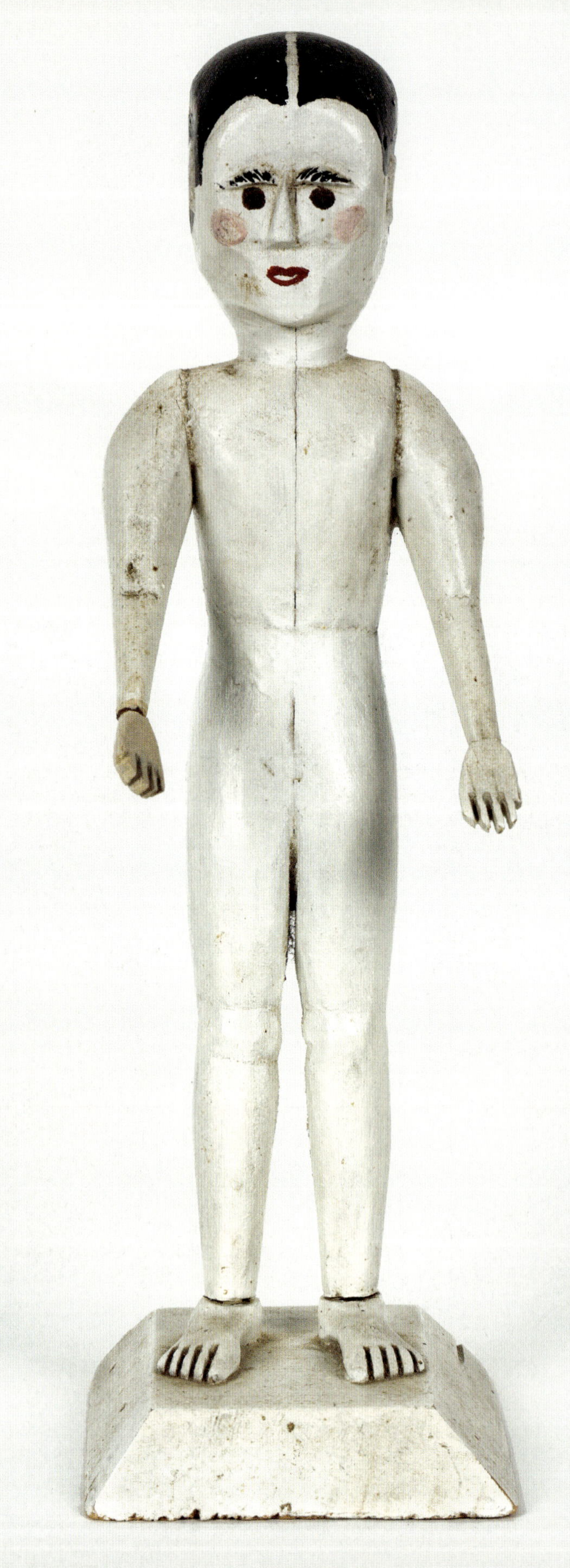

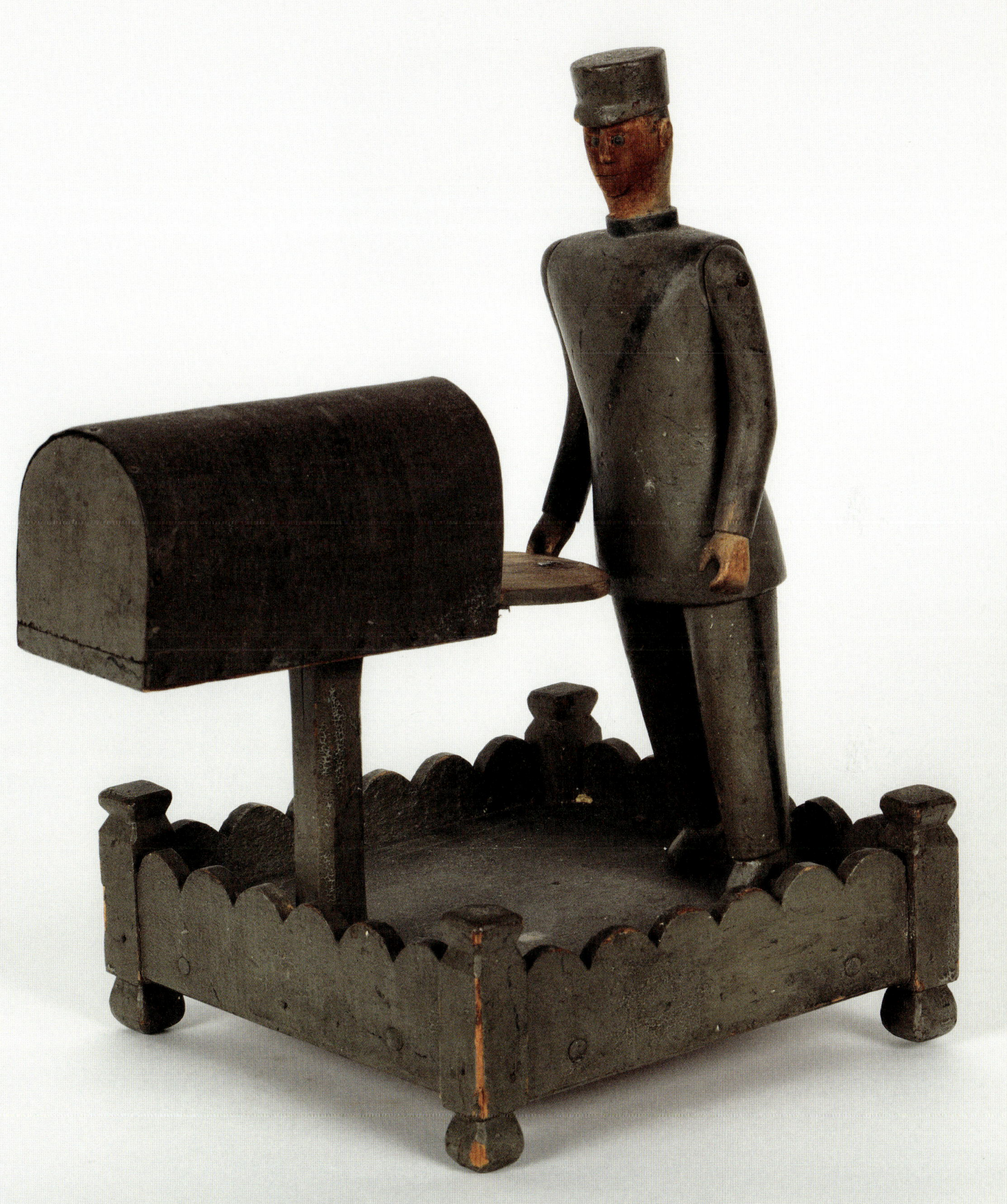

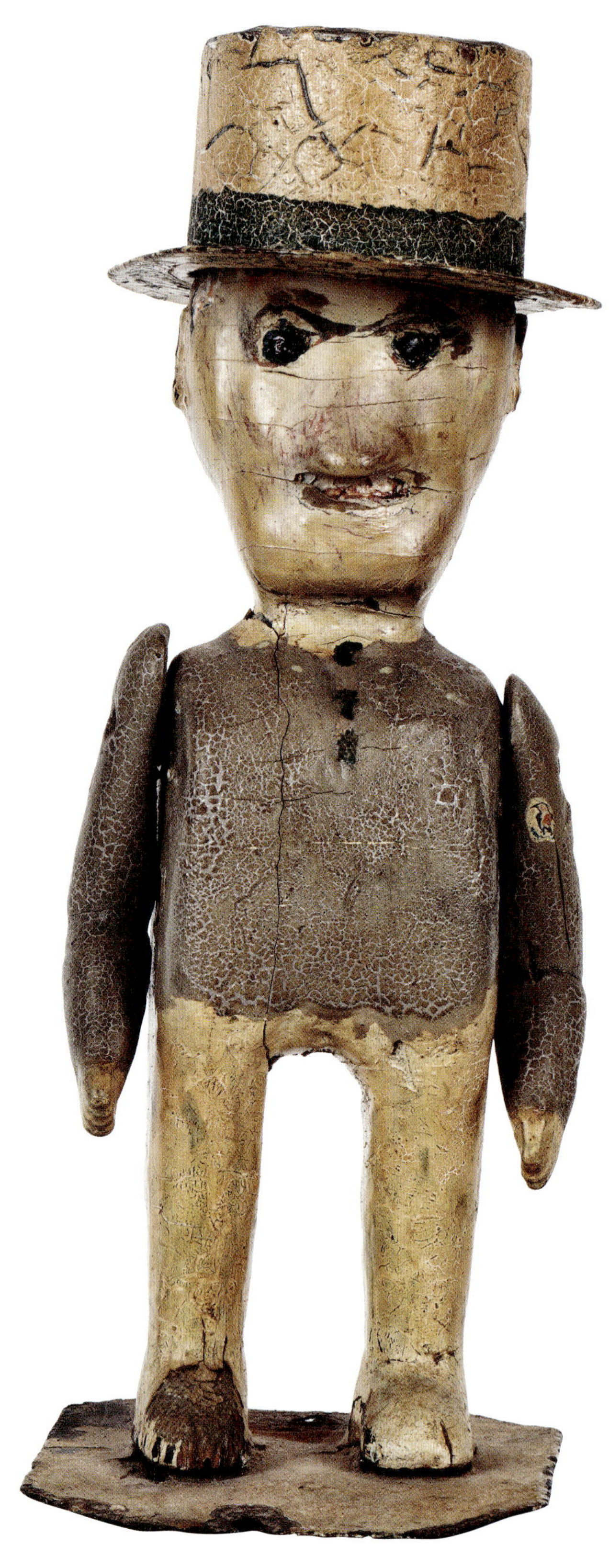

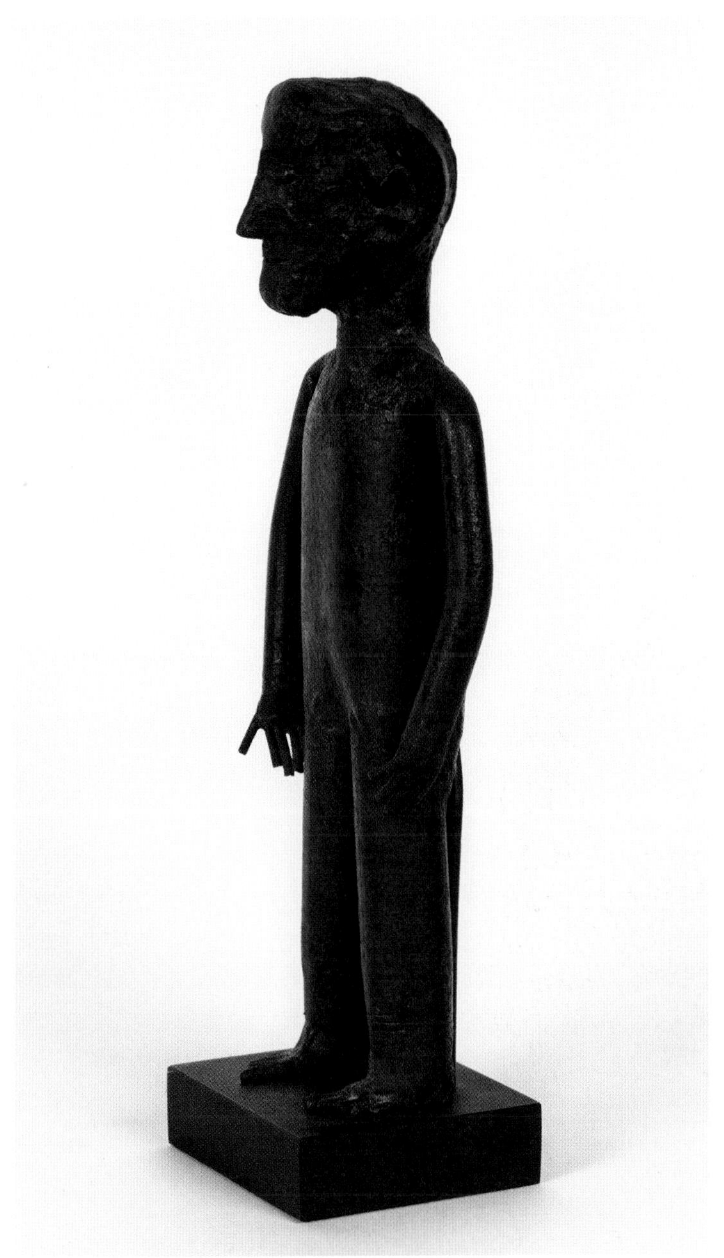

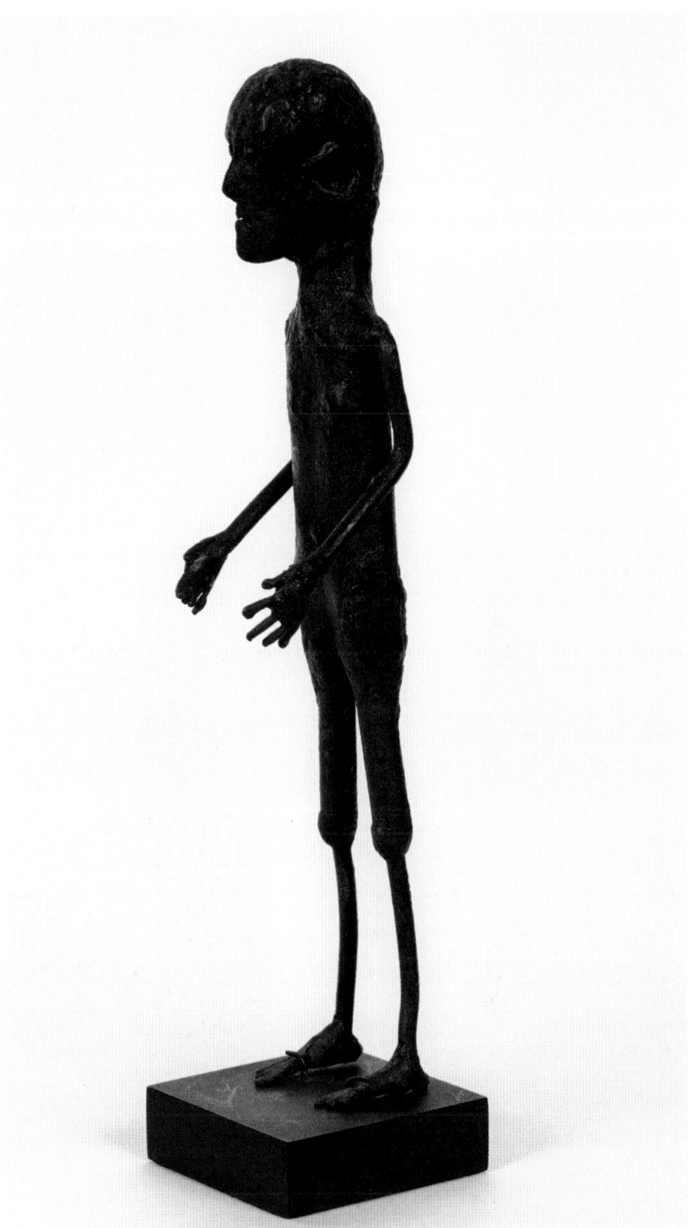

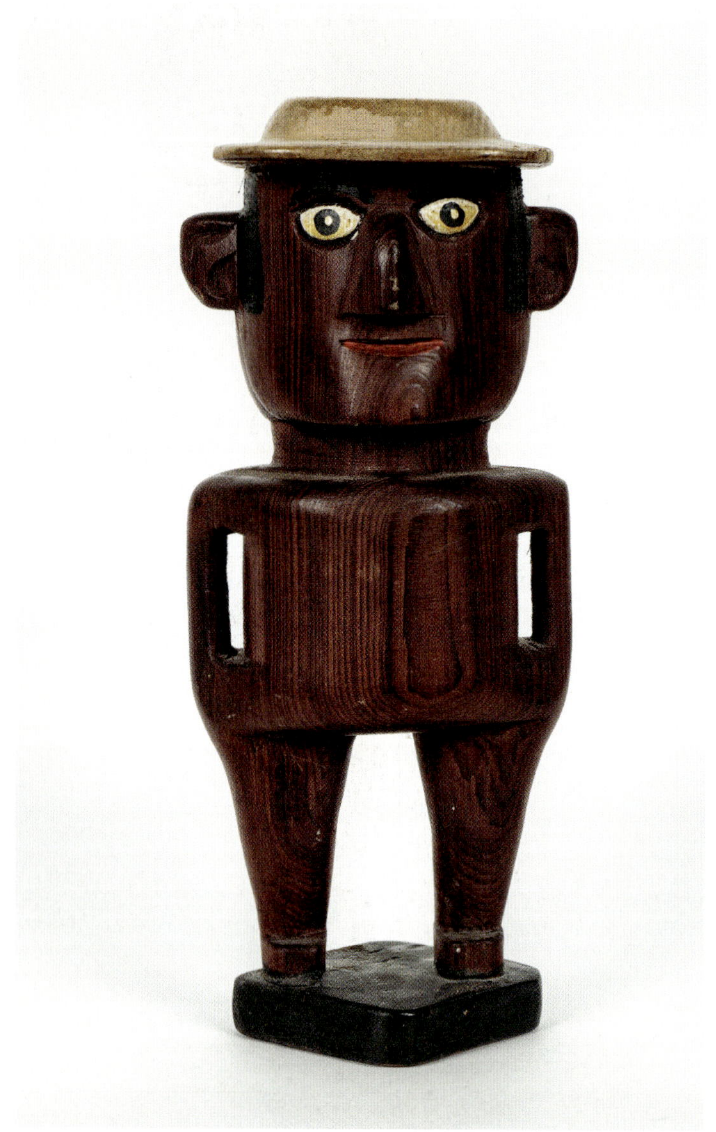

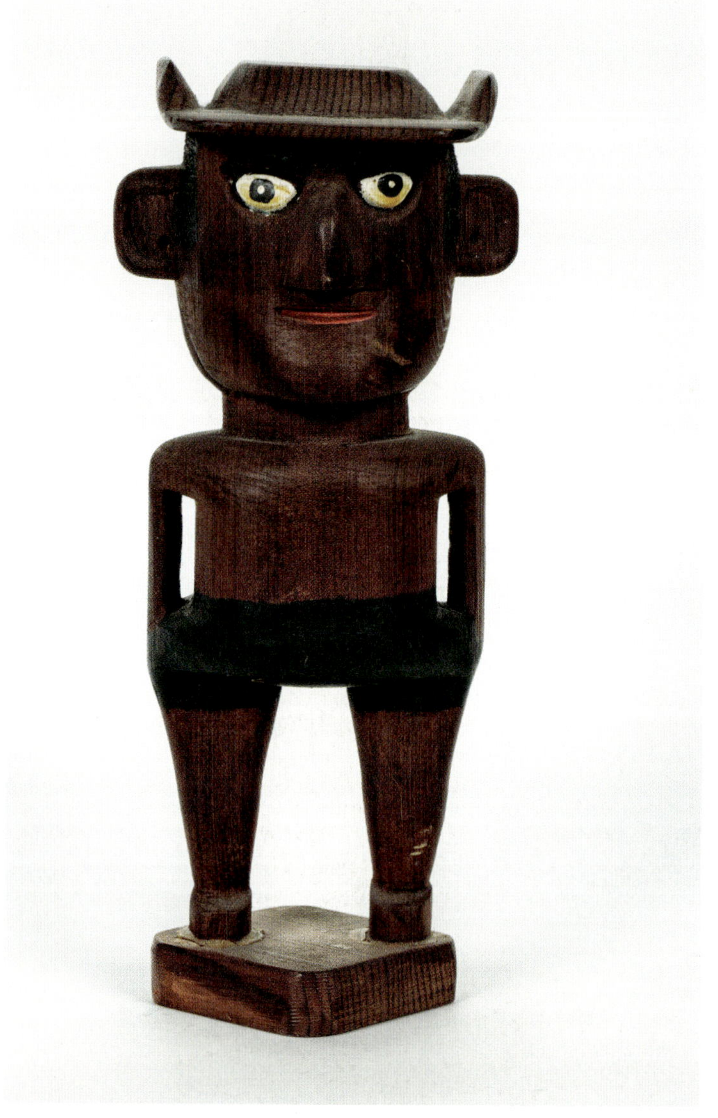

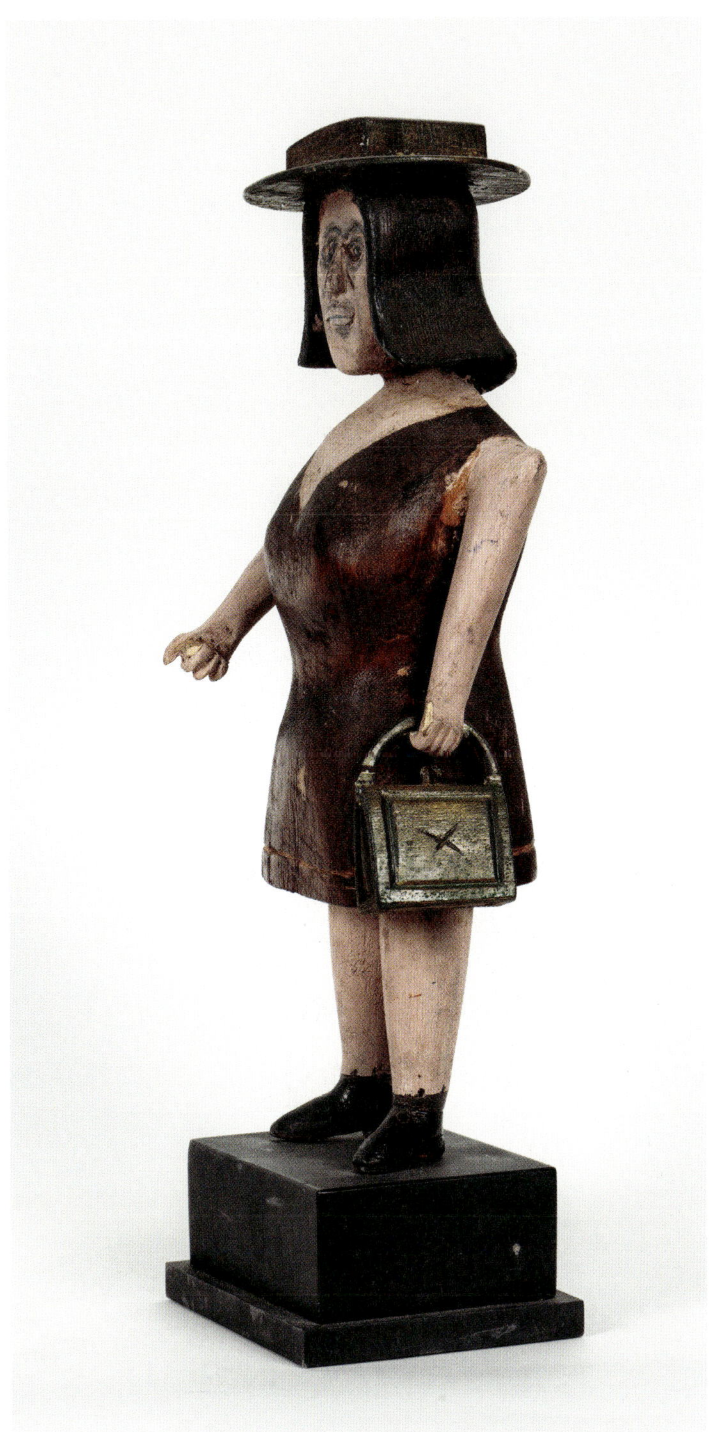

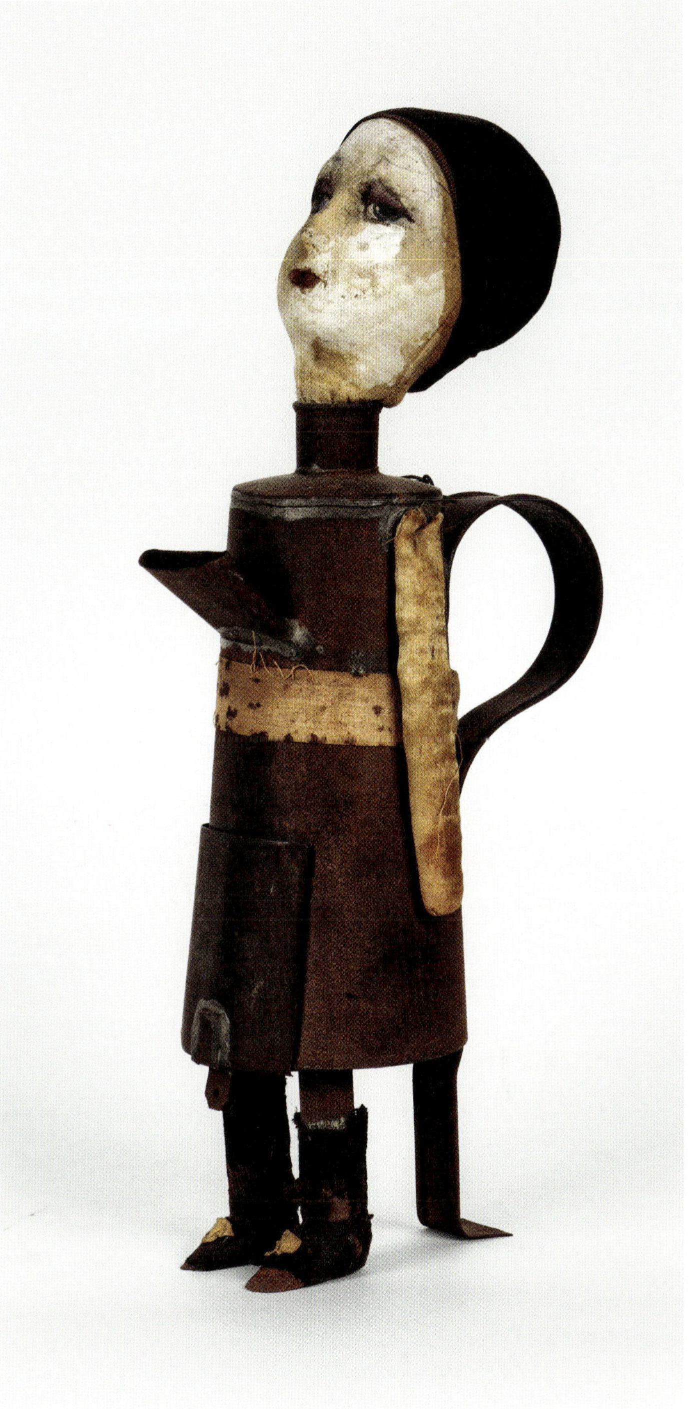

SELECTED BIBLIOGRAPHY

ARNING

Holstein, Jonathan. "Eddie Arning (1898–1993): Under the Influence." Accessed September 28, 2018. https://www.riccomaresca.com/portfolio-items/eddie-arning-under-the-influence/?portfolioCats=32.

Maizels, John, ed. *Outsider Art Sourcebook: International Guide to Art Brut and Outsider Art*. 3rd ed. s.v. "Eddie Arning." London: Raw Vision, 2016.

Maresca, Frank, and Roger Ricco. "Eddie Arning." In *American Self-Taught: Paintings and Drawings by Outsider Artists*, 9–13. New York: Knopf, 1993.

BLACK

Kohler Foundation Inc. "Calvin Black (Possum Trot)." Accessed September 28, 2018. http://www.kohlerfoundation.org/preservation/other-artists/calvin-black-possum-trot/.

Possum Trot. Directed by Allie Light and Irving Saraf. San Francisco: Possum Trot Productions, 1977.

Rosen, Seymour, and Jo Farb Hernández. "Calvin & Ruby Black, Possum Trot." Accessed September 28, 2018. http://www.spacesarchives.org/explore/collection/environment/possum-trot/.

BLOOM

Schira, Ron. "Jim Bloom: Stories of Wit and Irony." *Raw Vision* no. 75 (2012).

BOLDEN

Arnett, William. "Hawkins Bolden." Souls Grown Deep. Accessed October 3, 2018. http://www.soulsgrowndeep.org/artist/hawkins-bolden.

Intuitive Eye. "Scarecrow by Hawkins Bolden." Accessed October 3, 2018. http://intuitiveeye.org/SCARECROW-by-Hawkins-Bolden.

Maizels, John, ed. *Outsider Art Sourcebook: International Guide to Art Brut and Outsider Art*. 3rd ed. s.v. "Hawkins Bolden." London: Raw Vision, 2016.

BONTEMPO

Carl Hammer Gallery. "Marcos Bontempo." Accessed April 3, 2019. http://www.carlhammergallery.com/artists/marcos-bontempo

CASTLE

Cooke, Lynne. "James Castle." In *The Hidden Art: 20th- & 21st-Century Self-Taught Artists from the Audrey B. Heckler Collection*, 144–49. New York: Skira Rizzoli, 2017.

James Castle Collection and Archive. "Biography." Accessed October 3, 2018. http://jamescastle.com/james-castle-biography/.

Trusky, Tom. "James Castle and the Burden of Art." *Raw Vision* no. 23 (1998).

HENRY RAY CLARK

Intuitive Eye. "I Am the Day Star by Henry Ray Clark." Accessed April 3, 2019. http://intuitiveeye.org/I-AM-THE-DAY-STAR-by-Henry-Ray-Clark.

Wehnert, Jay. *Outsider Art in Texas*. College Station: Texas A&M University Press, 2018.

DEEDS

Bruney, Gabrielle. "The Incredible Story of 'Drawings from Inside State Hospital No. 3.'" *Vice*, May 13, 2016. Accessed October 8, 2018. https://creators.vice.com/en_uk/article/9anvey/lost-artist-drawings-state-hospital-no-3.

Deeds, James Edward, Jr. *The Electric Pencil: Drawings from Inside State Hospital No. 3*. New York: Princeton Architectural Press. 2016.

Meier, Allison. "Quiet Drawings from a Life Lost in Mental Institutions." *Hyperallergic*, February 9, 2016. Accessed October 8, 2018. https://hyperallergic.com/274054/quiet-drawings-from-a-life-lost-in-mental-institutions/.

DIAL

Maresca, Frank, and Roger Ricco. "Thornton Dial, Sr." In *American Self-Taught: Paintings and Drawings by Outsider Artists*, 53–56. New York: Knopf, 1993.

Metcalf, Gene. "Bill Arnett, Thornton Dial and the Myth of America." *Raw Vision* no. 55 (2006).

Souls Grown Deep. "Thornton Dial." Accessed September 29, 2018. http://www.soulsgrowndeep.org/artist/thornton-dial.

DOYLE

Maresca, Frank, and Roger Ricco. "Sam Doyle." In *American Self-Taught: Paintings and Drawings by Outsider Artists*, 57–62. New York: Knopf, 1993.

Perry, Regenia A. "Sam Doyle, St. Helena Island's Native Son." *Raw Vision* no. 23 (1998).

William Arnett. "Sam Doyle," Souls Grown Deep. Accessed September 29, 2018. http://www.soulsgrowndeep.org/artist/sam-doyle.

DÛ-GLASS

Cascone, Sarah. "Unexpected Artworks Dominate This Year's Outsider Art Fair." *Artnet News*, January 22, 2016. Accessed October 8, 2018. https://news.artnet.com/market/unexpected-unsettling-artworks-dominate-years-outsider-art-fair-412016.

EVANS

Maresca, Frank, and Roger Ricco. "Minnie Evans." In *American Self-Taught: Paintings and Drawings by Outsider Artists*, 69–71. New York: Knopf, 1993.

Perry, Regenia A. "Minnie Evans." Accessed January 31, 2019. https://americanart.si.edu/artist/minnie-evans-1466.

That Angel Stands by Me. Directed by Allie Light and Irving Saraf. San Francisco: Possum Light-Saraf Films, 1983.

FINSTER

Kirwin, Liza. "Howard Finster." Accessed September 29, 2018. https://americanart.si.edu/artist/howard-finster-1543.

Maresca, Frank, and Roger Ricco. "Howard Finster." In *American Self-Taught: Paintings and Drawings by Outsider Artists*, 72–77. New York: Knopf, 1993.

Paradise Garden Foundation. "A Man of Vision." Accessed September 29, 2018. http://paradisegardenfoundation.org/history/the-man-of-vision/.

Patton, Phil. "Howard Finster and the Art of the Coke Bottle." Accessed September 29, 2018. https://www.coca-colacompany.com/stories/howard-finster-and-the-art-of-the-coke-bottle.

Smith, Roberta. "Howard Finster, Folk Artist and Preacher, Dies at 84." *New York Times*. October 23, 2001. Accessed September 29, 2018. https://www.nytimes.com/2001/10/23/arts/howard-finster-folk-artist-and-preacher-dies-at-84.html.

GODIE

Maresca, Frank, and Roger Ricco. "Lee Godie." In *American Self-Taught: Paintings and Drawings by Outsider Artists*, 80–81. New York: Knopf, 1993.

Saunders, Anna. "Lee Godie: The Artist not in Residence." *The Telegraph* (London), June 10, 2013. Accessed October 3, 2018. https://www.telegraph.co.uk/culture/art/art-news/10073752/Lee-Godie-The-artist-not-in-residence.html.

GRIMES

Ewing, Caroline. "Ken Grimes: Elusive Messages." Accessed April 3, 2019. http://fnewsmagazine.com/2007-mar/ken-grimes.php.

Charles Russell "Ken Grimes: Truth in Black and White." *Raw Vision* 50 (2005).

HAUSER

Galerie Gugging. "Johann Hauser." Accessed January 31, 2019. https://galeriegugging.com/en/kuenstler/hauser-johann-2/.

Navratil, Leo. "In Memoriam: Johann Hauser (1926–1996)." *Raw Vision* no. 14 (1996).

HAWKINS

Maresca, Frank, and Roger Ricco. "William L. Hawkins." In *American Self-Taught: Paintings and Drawings by Outsider Artists*, 89–95. New York: Knopf, 1993.

Rexer, Lyle. "William Hawkins." *Raw Vision* no. 45 (2003).

Schwindler, Gary. Foreword to *William Hawkins Paintings*. v–xiii. New York: Knopf, 1997.

HUNTER

Catlin, Roger. "Self-Taught Artist Clemetine Hunter Painted the Bold Hues of Souther Life." October 18, 2018. Accessed April 2, 2019. https://www.smithsonianmag.com/smithsonian-institution/self-taught-artist-clementine-hunter-painted-bold-hues-southern-life-180970572/.

"Clementine Hunter." January 27, 2015. Accessed October 8, 2018. http://www.melroseplantation.org/blog/2015/1/27/clementine-hunter.

Shiver, Art, and Tom Whitehead. *Clementine Hunter: Her Life and Art*. Baton Rouge: Louisiana State University Press, 2012.

Wilson, James L. *Clementine Hunter, American Folk Artist*. Louisiana: Pelican Publishing, 1990.

JONES

Maresca, Frank, and Roger Ricco. "Frank Jones." In *American Self-Taught: Paintings and Drawings by Outsider Artists*, 109–10. New York: Knopf, 1993.

Perry, Regenia A. "Frank Jones." Accessed April 3, 2019. https://americanart.si.edu/artist/frank-jones-2495.

Wehnert, Jay. *Outsider Art in Texas*. College Station: Texas A&M University Press, 2018.

KOREC

Galerie Gugging. "Johann Korec." Accessed October 3, 2018. https://galeriegugging.com/en/kuenstler/korec-johann-2/.

Maizels, John, ed. *Outsider Art Sourcebook: International Guide to Art Brut and Outsider Art*. 3rd ed. s.v. "Johann Korec." London: Raw Vision, 2016.

McCARTHY

Maizels, John, ed. *Outsider Art Sourcebook: International Guide to Art Brut and Outsider Art*. 3rd ed. s.v. "Justin McCarthy." London: Raw Vision, 2016.

Maresca, Frank, and Roger Ricco. "Justin McCarthy." In *American Self-Taught: Paintings and Drawings by Outsider Artists*, 142–45. New York: Knopf, 1993.

McNELLIS

Romero, Rachael, and Roger Ricco. *Laura Craig McNellis: Different Lens*. Accessed April 3, 2019. https://www.youtube.com/watch?v=AafjlcKVj1I.

Wynn Newhouse Awards. "Laura Craig McNellis." Accessed April 3, 2019. https://www.wnewhouseawards.com/lauramcnellis.html.

MORGAN

Maresca, Frank, and Roger Ricco. "Sister Gertrude Morgan." In *American Self-Taught: Paintings and Drawings by Outsider Artists*, 155–58. New York: Knopf, 1993.

Perry, Regenia A. "Sister Gertude Morgan." Accessed January 31, 2019. https://americanart.si.edu/artist/sister-gertrude-morgan-3413.

PIERCE

Columbus State Library. "Elijah Pierce." Accessed October 9, 2018. http://library.cscc.edu/libraryartcollection/ElijahPierce.

Elijah Pierce: Sermons in Wood. Directed by Carolyn Allport. Columbus: The Ohio Arts Council, 1980.

Maresca, Frank, and Roger Ricco. "Elijah Pierce." In *American Self-Taught: Paintings and Drawings by Outsider Artists*, 175–78. New York: Knopf, 1993.

Rosenak, Chuck, and Jan Rosenak. *Contemporary American Folk Art: A Collector's Guide*. New York: Abbeville, 1996.

RAMÍREZ

Espinosa, Víctor M. *Martín Ramírez: Framing His Life and Art*. Austin: University of Texas Press, 2015.

SCHMIDT

Galerie Gugging. "Arnold Schmidt." Accessed October 8, 2018. https://galeriegugging.com/en/kuenstler/schmidt-arnold-2/.

SCHÜTZENHÖFER

Katschnig, Nina. *Günther Schützenhöfer "As I See It."* Accessed October 3, 2018. http://www.riccomaresca.com/portfolio-items/gunther-schutzenhofer-as-i-see-it/.

SEVEN-SEVEN

Grimes, William. "Prince Twins Seven-Seven, Nigerian Artist, Dies at 67." *New York Times*, July 3, 2011. Accessed October 8, 2018. https://www.nytimes.com/2011/07/04/arts/design/prince-twins-seven-seven-nigerian-artist-dies-at-67.html.

Magnin, André, and Jacques Soulillou, eds. *Contemporary Art of Africa*. New York: Abrams, 1996.

SINGLETON

Antippas, Andy P. "Herbert Singleton: Secular and Sacred." Souls Grown Deep. Accessed October 9, 2018. http://www.soulsgrowndeep.org/artist/herbert-singleton.

Maizels, John, ed. *Outsider Art Sourcebook: International Guide to Art Brut and Outsider Art*. 3rd ed. s.v. "Herbert Singleton." London: Raw Vision, 2016.

Sasser, Bill. "Herbert Singleton." *Raw Vision* no. 40 (2002).

SOWELL

askArt. "John A. Sowell." Accessed October 11, 2018. http://www.askart.com/artist/John_A_Sowell/11309065/John_A_Sowell.aspx.

Google Patents. "Ball-bearing Lock-Nut." Accessed October 11, 2018. https://patents.google.com/patent/US1267927A/en.

Issuu. "Slotin Folk Art Auction Nov. 11–12, 2017 Catalog." October 3, 2017. Accessed October 11, 2018. https://issuu.com/slotinfolkart/docs/slotinfolkartauctionnov2017catalog.

STROBL

Galerie Gugging. "Leopold Strobl." Accessed April 3, 2019. https://galeriegugging.com/en/kuenstler/strobl-leopold-2/.

Rieger, Hannah. "Leopold Strobl." Accessed April 3, 2019. https://livinginartbrut.com/index.php/en/artists/artists-r-z/leopold-strobl.

SUDDUTH

Encyclopedia of Alabama. "Jimmy Lee Sudduth." http://www.encyclopediaofalabama.org/article/h-2048

Maizels, John, ed. *Outsider Art Sourcebook: International Guide to Art Brut and Outsider Art*. 3rd ed. s.v. "Jimmy Lee Sudduth." London: Raw Vision, 2016.

Maresca, Frank, and Roger Ricco. "Jimmy Lee Sudduth." In *American Self-Taught: Paintings and Drawings by Outsider Artists*, 233–37. New York: Knopf, 1993.

TOLLIVER

Maizels, John, and Colin Rhodes. *Raw Erotica: Sex, Lust and Desire in Outsider Art*. London: Raw Vision, 2013.

Maizels, John, ed. *Outsider Art Sourcebook: International Guide to Art Brut and Outsider Art*. 3rd ed. s.v. "Mose Tolliver." London: Raw Vision, 2016.

Marcia Weber Art Objects. "Mose Tolliver." Accessed April 3, 2019. https://marciaweberartobjects.com/tolliverm.html.

Maresca, Frank, and Roger Ricco. "Mose Tolliver." In *American Self-Taught: Paintings and Drawings by Outsider Artists*, 240–44. New York: Knopf, 1993.

Souls Grown Deep. "Mose Tolliver." Accessed October 11, 2018. http://www.soulsgrowndeep.org/artist/mose-tolliver.

TRAYLOR

Anthony Petullo Collection of Self-Taught and Outsider Art. "Bill Traylor." Accessed October 10, 2018. http://www.petulloartcollection.org/the_collection/about_the_artists/artist.cfm?a_id=56.

DC Moore Gallery. "Bill Traylor." Accessed October 10, 2018. http://www.dcmooregallery.com/artists/bill-traylor.

Maresca, Frank, and Roger Ricco. *Bill Traylor: His Art, His Life*. New York: Knopf, 1991.

Schjeldahl, Peter. "The Utterly Original Bill Traylor." *The New Yorker*. October 8, 2018. Accessed October 10, 2018. https://www.newyorker.com/magazine/2018/10/08/the-utterly-original-bill-traylor.

VON BRUENCHENHEIN

Gardner, James. "Eugene Von Bruenchenhein." *The Magazine Antiques*, November 16, 2010. Accessed October 3, 2018. http://www.themagazineantiques.com/article/eugene-von-bruenchenhein/.

Gómez, Edward M. "An Artist Couple's Domestic Gesamtkunstwerk." *Hyperallergic*. July 8, 2017. Accessed October 3, 2018. https://hyperallergic.com/389404/mythologies-eugene-von-bruenchenhein-john-michael-kohler-arts-center/.

Maizels, John, and Colin Rhodes. *Raw Erotica: Sex, Lust and Desire in Outsider Art*. London: Raw Vision, 2013.

Maresca, Frank, and Roger Ricco. "Eugene Von Bruenchenhein." In *American Self-Taught: Paintings and Drawings by Outsider Artists*, 256–58. New York: Knopf, 1993.

Smith, Roberta. "Meager Means, Rich Imagination." *New York Times*, November 4, 2010. Accessed September 29, 2018. https://www.nytimes.com/2010/11/05/arts/design/05eugene.html.

WALKER

Inez Nathaniel Walker. "Inez Nathaniel Walker." Accessed October 11, 2018. http://www.inezwalker.com.

Maresca, Frank, and Roger Ricco. "Inez Nathaniel Walker." In *American Self-Taught: Paintings and Drawings by Outsider Artists*, 259–60. New York: Knopf, 1993.

WALLA

Feilacher, Johann. "Walla: Artist of the Universe." *Cambridge Core*, August 8, 2016. Accessed October 11, 2018. https://www.cambridge.org/core/services/aop-cambridge-core/content/view/AD10E17D2A66F74AADC4C3308E3CF911/S2045796016000639a.pdf/div-class-title-walla-artist-of-the-universe-div.pdf.

Living in Art Brut. "August Walla." Accessed October 11, 2018. https://livinginartbrut.com/index.php/en/artists/artists-r-z/august-walla.

Tuchman, Maurice, and Carol S. Eliel. "August Walla." In *Parallel Visions: Modern Artists and Outsider Art*. Los Angeles: Princeton University Press, 1992.

WIDENER

Patterson, Tom. "George Widener." In *The Alternative Guide to the Universe: Mavericks, Outsiders, Visionaries*. London: Hayward Gallery Publishing, 2013.

Ricco/Maresca Gallery. "George Widener: Magic Circles." Accessed October 3, 2018. https://www.riccomaresca.com/portfolio-items/george-widener-magic-circles/?portfolioCats=32.

Widener, George. "Post-Dubuffet: Self-Taught Art in the Twenty-First Century" (Speech at the American Folk Art Museum). Accessed October 3, 2018. https://www.riccomaresca.com/post-dubuffet-self-taught-art-twenty-first-century-speech-afam/.

WÖLFLI

Maizels, John, ed. *Outsider Art Sourcebook: International Guide to Art Brut and Outsider Art*. 3rd ed. s.v. "Adolf Wölfli." London: Raw Vision, 2016.

Morgenthaler, Walter. *Madness & Art: The Life and Works of Adolf Wölfli*. Translated by Aaron H. Esman. Lincoln: University of Nebraska Press, 1992.

Tuchman, Maurice, and Carol S. Eliel. "Adolf Wölfli." In *Parallel Visions: Modern Artists and Outsider Art*. Los Angeles: Princeton University Press, 1992.

YOAKUM

Encyclopaedia Britannica. "Joseph Yoakum." Accessed October 11, 2018. https://www.britannica.com/biography/Joseph-Yoakum.

Maresca, Frank, and Roger Ricco. "Joseph Elmer Yoakum." In *American Self-Taught: Paintings and Drawings by Outsider Artists*, 266–72. New York: Knopf, 1993.

Perry, Regenia A. "Joseph E. Yoakum." Accessed October 11, 2018. https://americanart.si.edu/artist/joseph-e-yoakum-5515.

YOUNG

Bailey, Gordon W. "Purvis Young." In *The Hidden Art: 20th- & 21st-Century Self-Taught Artists from the Audrey B. Heckler Collection*, 216–19. New York: Skira Rizzoli, 2017.

Maresca, Frank, and Roger Ricco. "Purvis Young." In *American Self-Taught: Paintings and Drawings by Outsider Artists*, 273–76. New York: Knopf, 1993.

Moreno, Gean. "Purvis Young's Predicament." *Raw Vision* no. 36 (2001).

Weber, Bruce. "Purvis Young, Folk Artist Who Peppered Miami with Images, Dies at 67." *New York Times*. April 24, 2010. Accessed October 11, 2018. https://www.nytimes.com/2010/04/24/arts/24young.html.

Wikipedia. "Purvis Young." Accessed October 11, 2018. https://en.wikipedia.org/wiki/Purvis_Young.

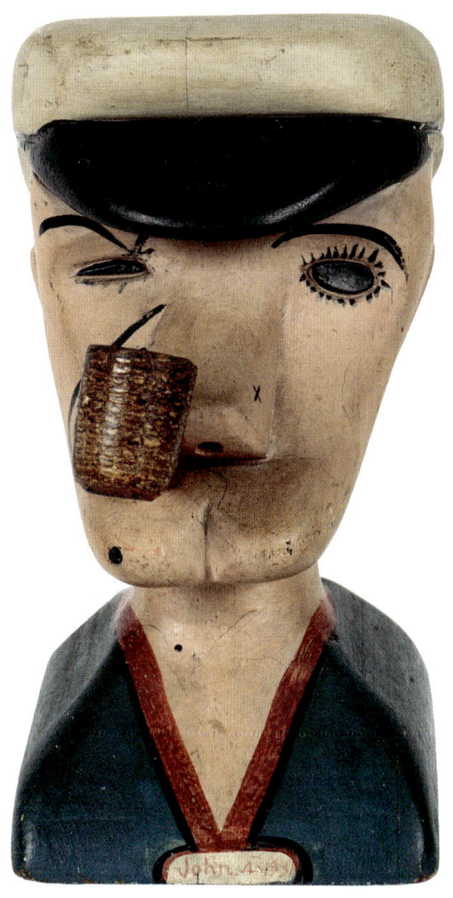

Published in conjunction with the exhibition
Outsider & Vernacular Art: The Victor F. Keen Collection, which was organized by Jim Richerson and Elizabeth Szabo at the Sangre de Cristo Arts and Conference Center, Pueblo, Colorado.

Sangre de Cristo Arts and Conference Center
October 5, 2019–January 12, 2020

Intuit: The Center for Intuitive and Outsider Art, Chicago
February 6–May 3, 2020

Published by
The Bethany Mission Gallery
1527 Brandywine Street
Philadelphia, PA 19130
http://bethanymissiongallery.org

and

Hirmer Publishers
Bayerstraße 57–59
80335 Munich
Germany
www.hirmerpublishers.com

Texts excerpted and adapted from essays by Alejandra Russi: p. 45: "Marcos Bontempo: Light and Dark," www.riccomaresca.com/portfolio-items/marcos-bontempo-light-dark/?portfolioCats=32; p. 67: "Insiders: Henry Ray Clark and Frank Jones," www.riccomaresca.com/portfolio-items/henry-ray-clark-frank-jonesinsiders/?portfolioCats=32; p. 115: "Alienated: A Creative Life on the Margins" (master's thesis, Columbia University, 2013); p. 141: "Insiders: Henry Ray Clark and Frank Jones," www.riccomaresca.com/portfolio-items/henry-ray-clark-frank-jonesinsiders/?portfolioCats=32; p. 151: "Laura Craig McNellis: Structures," www.riccomaresca.com/portfolio-items/laura-craig-mcnellis-structures/?portfolioCats=32; p. 159: "Martín Ramírez: Forever," www.riccomaresca.com/martin-ramirez-forever/; p. 191: "Leopold Strobl: Smallscapes," www.riccomaresca.com/portfolio-items/leopold-strobl-smallscapes/

Editor, designer, and project manager: Laura Lindgren
Proofreader: Donald Kennison
Hirmer project manager: Rainer Arnold
Prepress: Reproline mediateam, Munich
Printing and binding: Printer Trento

Set in Sagona and Noyh

Printed and bound in Italy on Garda Ultramatt 150 g/sqm

Cover: Detail, Bill Traylor, *Chicken Stealing*, c. 1939–42, p. 211
Front endpaper: Detail, Leopold Strobl, *Untitled (2014-075)*, 2014, p. 192
Page 1: Detail, Martín Ramírez, *Untitled (Seven Stags)*, c. 1953, p. 158
Page 2: Detail, Lee Godie, *Three Hands on a Piano*, n.d., p. 112
Page 4: Detail, George Widener, *"TIGER" N "MADGE,"* 2013. p. 238
Pages 28–29: Detail, Joseph Yoakum, *Persimmon Valley near Graydon Springs Missouri*, 1968, p. 249
Back endpaper: Detail, Martín Ramírez, *Untitled (Trains and Tunnels) A, B*, c. 1960–63, pp. 160–61
Back cover: Detail, Martín Ramírez, *Untitled (Caballero)*, n.d., p. 163

PHOTOGRAPHY CREDITS
All photographs by Stan Narten except: p. 8: Courtesy of Haverford College Libraries archives; pp. 11, 177, 197 bottom, 256–257: Ryan Brandenberg; p. 100, 152: Courtesy of Slotin Folk Art; p. 176: Courtesy of Material Art

ISBN 978-3-7774-3318-9

First Edition 2019

5 4 3 2 1

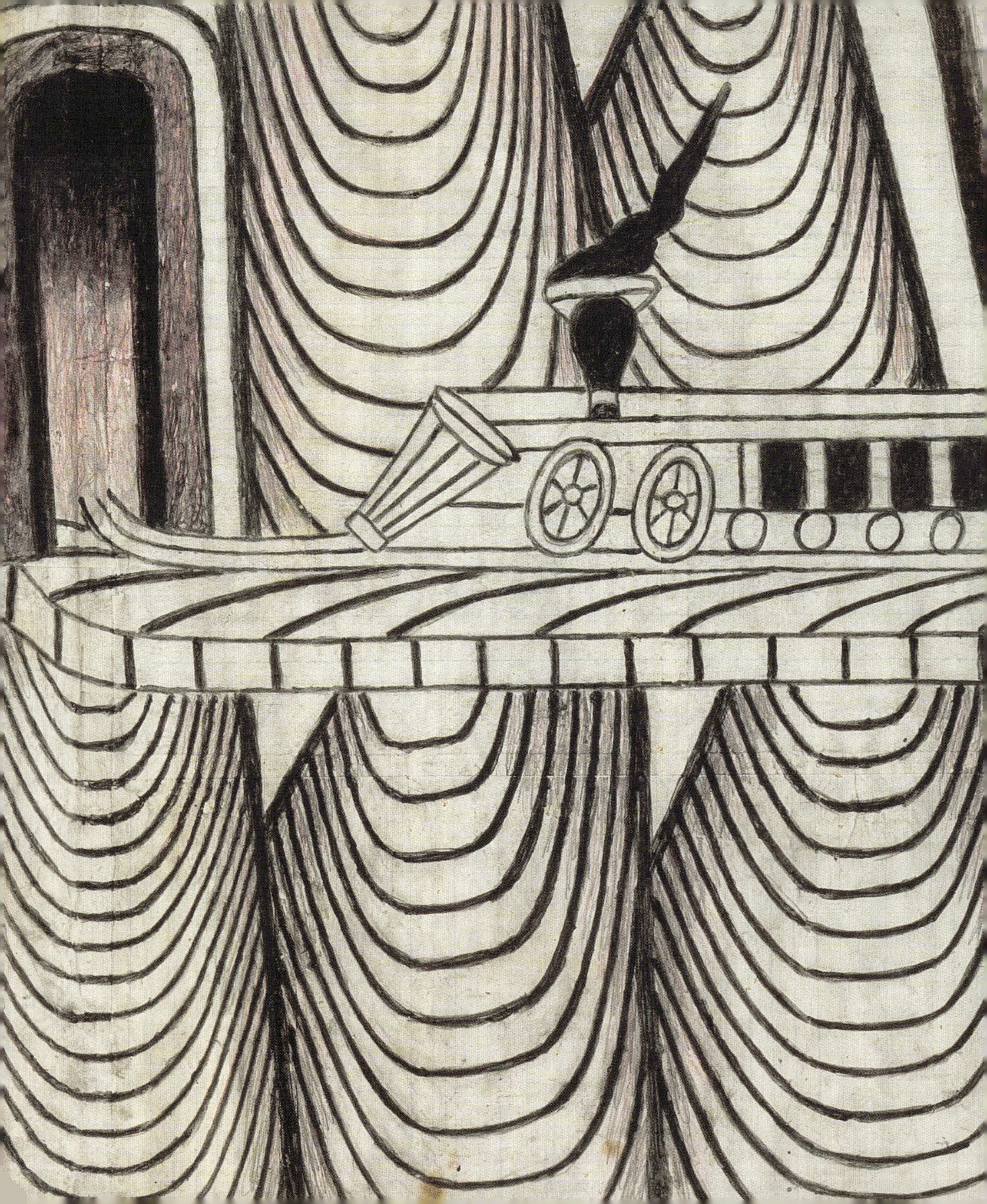